THE PAPERS OF

Thomas Jefferson

Volume 13

March to 7 October 1788

JULIAN P. BOYD, EDITOR

MINA R. BRYAN, ASSOCIATE EDITOR

PRINCETON, NEW JERSEY

PRINCETON UNIVERSITY PRESS

1956

L.C.CARD 50-7486

Printed in the United States of America by
Princeton University Press, Princeton, New Jersey

THE PAPERS OF
THOMAS JEFFERSON

DEDICATED TO THE MEMORY OF

ADOLPH S. OCHS

PUBLISHER OF THE NEW YORK TIMES

1896-1935

WHO BY THE EXAMPLE OF A RESPONSIBLE

PRESS ENLARGED AND FORTIFIED

THE JEFFERSONIAN CONCEPT

OF A FREE PRESS

ADVISORY COMMITTEE

DAVID K. E. BRUCE, *CHAIRMAN*
FRANCIS L. BERKELEY, JR.
SOLON J. BUCK
L. H. BUTTERFIELD
GILBERT CHINARD
HENRY STEELE COMMAGER
HAROLD W. DODDS
LUTHER H. EVANS
A. WHITNEY GRISWOLD
BRECKINRIDGE LONG
ARCHIBALD MAC LEISH
DUMAS MALONE
BERNARD MAYO
RICARDO A. MESTRES
SAMUEL E. MORISON
HOWARD W. SMITH
DATUS C. SMITH, JR.
IPHIGENE OCHS SULZBERGER
WILLIAM J. VAN SCHREEVEN
LAWRENCE C. WROTH
JOHN C. WYLLIE

CONSULTANTS

PROFESSOR ARCHIBALD T. MAC ALLISTER, *Consultant in Italian*
PROFESSOR RAYMOND S. WILLIS, *Consultant in Spanish*
FRANCE C. RICE, *Consultant in French*
HOWARD C. RICE, JR., *Consultant*, Princeton University Library
DOROTHY S. EATON, *Consultant*, The Library of Congress

FOREWORD

THE table of contents in each of the preceding volumes in this series has been arranged in chronological order. Since this parallels the arrangement of the matter and since our editorial plan does not provide for indexes to individual volumes, the Editors, though regretting for the sake of users that they did not anticipate at the outset the advantages and conveniences of a different form, have decided to substitute an alphabetical for a chronological order. It should be emphasized that this does not in any respect alter the policy concerning the Index: that policy provides for the publication periodically of preliminary indexes for groups of volumes (one of which, covering Volumes 1-6, has already been published) and for the issuance at the conclusion of the series of a final, comprehensive index of persons, places, subjects, &c., arranged in a single consolidated sequence. The present departure affects only the table of contents, and while the alphabetical arrangement has some of the appearance and advantages of an index, it should nevertheless be made clear that the matter indexed under this arrangement is only that which appears in the customary table of contents—that is, the names of writers and recipients of letters. To be sure, there are occasional cross-references appearing under such headings as *American trade*, *beef*, *plants*, *tobacco*, *whale-oil*, &c., and there is even one addressee who seems describable only as *unidentified recipient*; but these index-like entries are made necessary by the character of the captions, beyond which they do not go.

The new arrangement seems not only to have brevity and utility, but also to be revealing. It shows at a glance which correspondents occupied Jefferson most, and which—in numbers of communications at least—had a debit or a credit balance in the correspondence. It tells us something about Jefferson as a diplomat to know that he received far more letters from the always-scribbling Dumas and the intrigue-loving Carmichael than he wrote to them; that he dispatched many more communications to the Secretary for Foreign Affairs and to the Commissioners of the Treasury than he received from them; and that his correspondence with Madison—the most extended, the most elevated, and the most significant exchange of letters between any two men in the whole sweep of American history—was, like the writers themselves in their reciprocal influence upon each other, in a perfect state of equilibrium. It also exhibits, in regrettable brevity, the fact that Jefferson's most intimate and effective collaborator during the Paris years—the Marquis de Lafayette—appears to have written only one letter and to have received none during the months covered by the present volume. We know that, as Lafayette expressed it, Jefferson, Paine, and himself debated the proposed Federal Constitution early in 1788 as if they were themselves a convention having the responsibility of deciding whether to adopt. But the fact that they were able to do so in conversation makes this table of contents, this volume, and ourselves all the poorer.

GUIDE TO EDITORIAL APPARATUS

1. *TEXTUAL DEVICES*

The following devices are employed throughout the work to clarify the presentation of the text.

[. . .], [. . . .]	One or two words missing and not conjecturable.
[. . .][1], [. . . .][1]	More than two words missing and not conjecturable; subjoined footnote estimates number of words missing.
[ ]	Number or part of a number missing or illegible.
[roman]	Conjectural reading for missing or illegible matter. A question mark follows when the reading is doubtful.
[*italic*]	Editorial comment inserted in the text.
⟨*italic*⟩	Matter deleted in the MS but restored in our text.
⟦ ⟧	Record entry for letters not found.

2. *DESCRIPTIVE SYMBOLS*

The following symbols are employed throughout the work to describe the various kinds of manuscript originals. When a series of versions is recorded, *the first to be recorded is the version used for the printed text.*

Dft	draft (usually a composition or rough draft; later drafts, when identifiable as such, are designated "2d Dft," &c.)
Dupl	duplicate
MS	manuscript (arbitrarily applied to most documents other than letters)
N	note, notes (memoranda, fragments, &c.)
PoC	polygraph copy
PrC	press copy
RC	recipient's copy
SC	stylograph copy
Tripl	triplicate

All manuscripts of the above types are assumed to be in the hand of the author of the document to which the descriptive symbol pertains. If not, that fact is stated. On the other hand, the following types of manuscripts are assumed *not* to be in the hand of the author, and exceptions will be noted:

FC file copy (applied to all forms of retained copies, such as letter-book copies, clerks' copies, &c.)

Tr transcript (applied to both contemporary and later copies; period of transcription, unless clear by implication, will be given when known)

3. *LOCATION SYMBOLS*

The locations of documents printed in this edition from originals in private hands, from originals held by institutions outside the United States, and from printed sources are recorded in self-explanatory form in the descriptive note following each document. The locations of documents printed from originals held by public institutions in the United States are recorded by means of the symbols used in the National Union Catalog in the Library of Congress; an explanation of how these symbols are formed is given above, Vol. 1: xl. The list of symbols appearing in each volume is limited to the institutions represented by documents printed or referred to in that and previous volumes.

CLU William Andrews Clark Memorial Library, University of California at Los Angeles

CSmH Henry E. Huntington Library, San Marino, California

Ct Connecticut State Library, Hartford, Connecticut

CtY Yale University Library

DLC Library of Congress

DNA The National Archives

G-Ar Georgia Department of Archives and History, Atlanta

ICHi Chicago Historical Society, Chicago

IHi Illinois State Historical Library, Springfield

MB Boston Public Library, Boston

MH Harvard University Library

MHi Massachusetts Historical Society, Boston

MHi:AMT Adams Family Papers, deposited by the Adams Manuscript Trust in Massachusetts Historical Society

MdAA Maryland Hall of Records, Annapolis

MdAN U.S. Naval Academy Library

MeHi	Maine Historical Society, Portland
MiU-C	William L. Clements Library, University of Michigan
MoSHi	Missouri Historical Society, St. Louis
MWA	American Antiquarian Society, Worcester
NBu	Buffalo Public Library, Buffalo, New York
NcD	Duke University Library
NcU	University of North Carolina Library
NHi	New-York Historical Society, New York City
NK-Iselin	Letters to and from John Jay bearing this symbol are used by permission of the Estate of Eleanor Jay Iselin.
NN	New York Public Library, New York City
NNC	Columbia University Libraries
NNP	Pierpont Morgan Library, New York City
NNS	New York Society Library, New York City
NjP	Princeton University Library
NjMoW	Washington Headquarters Library, Morristown, N.J.
PBL	Lehigh University Library
PHC	Haverford College Library
PHi	Historical Society of Pennsylvania, Philadelphia
PPAP	American Philosophical Society, Philadelphia
PPL-R	Library Company of Philadelphia, Ridgway Branch
PU	University of Pennsylvania Library
RPA	Rhode Island Department of State, Providence
RPB	Brown University Library
Vi	Virginia State Library, Richmond
ViHi	Virginia Historical Society, Richmond
ViRVal	Valentine Museum Library, Richmond
ViU	University of Virginia Library
ViW	College of William and Mary Library
ViWC	Colonial Williamsburg, Inc.
WHi	State Historical Society of Wisconsin, Madison

4. OTHER SYMBOLS AND ABBREVIATIONS

The following symbols and abbreviations are commonly employed in the annotation throughout the work.

Second Series The topical series to be published at the end of this edition, comprising those materials which are best suited to a classified rather than a chronological arrangement (see Vol. 1: xv-xvi)

TJ Thomas Jefferson

TJ Editorial Files Photoduplicates and other editorial materials in the office of *The Papers of Thomas Jefferson*, Princeton University Library

TJ Papers Jefferson Papers (applied to a collection of manuscripts when the precise location of a given document must be furnished, and always preceded by the symbol for the institutional repository; thus "DLC: TJ Papers, 4:628-9" represents a document in the Library of Congress, Jefferson Papers, volume 4, pages 628 and 629)

PCC Papers of the Continental Congress, in the National Archives

RG Record Group (used in designating the location of documents in the National Archives)

SJL Jefferson's "Summary Journal of letters" written and received (in DLC: TJ Papers)

SJPL "Summary Journal of Public Letters," an incomplete list of letters written by TJ from 16 Apr. 1784 to 31 Dec. 1793, with brief summaries, in an amanuensis' hand (in DLC: TJ Papers, at end of SJL)

V Ecu

f Florin

£ Pound sterling or livre, depending upon context (in doubtful cases, a clarifying note will be given)

s Shilling or sou

d Penny or denier

tt Livre Tournois

℔ Per (occasionally used for pro, pre)

5. *SHORT TITLES*

The following list includes only those short titles of works cited with great frequency, and therefore in very abbreviated form, throughout this edition. Their expanded forms are given here only in the degree of fullness needed for unmistakable identification. Since it is impossible to anticipate all the works to be cited in such very abbreviated form, the list is appropriately revised from volume to volume.

Atlas of Amer. Hist., Scribner, 1943 James Truslow Adams and R. V. Coleman, *Atlas of American History*, N.Y., 1943

Barbary Wars Dudley W. Knox, ed., *Naval Documents Related to the United States Wars with the Barbary Powers*

Betts, *Farm Book* Edwin M. Betts, ed., *Thomas Jefferson's Farm Book*

Betts, *Garden Book* Edwin M. Betts, ed., *Thomas Jefferson's Garden Book*

Biog. Dir. Cong. *Biographical Directory of Congress, 1774-1927*

B.M. Cat. British Museum, *General Catalogue of Printed Books*, London, 1931—. Also, *The British Museum Catalogue of Printed Books 1881-1900*, Ann Arbor, 1946

B.N. Cat. *Catalogue général des livres imprimés de la Bibliothèque Nationale. Auteurs.*

Burnett, *Letters of Members* Edmund C. Burnett, ed., *Letters of Members of the Continental Congress*

Cal. Franklin Papers *Calendar of the Papers of Benjamin Franklin in the Library of the American Philosophical Society*, ed. I. Minis Hays

CVSP *Calendar of Virginia State Papers . . . Preserved in the Capitol at Richmond*

DAB *Dictionary of American Biography*

DAE *Dictionary of American English*

DAH *Dictionary of American History*

DNB *Dictionary of National Biography*

Dipl. Corr., 1783-89 *The Diplomatic Correspondence of the United States of America, from the Signing of the Definitive Treaty of Peace . . . to the Adoption of the Constitution*, Washington, Blair & Rives, 1837, 3 vol.

Elliot's *Debates* *The Debates of the Several State Conventions on the Adoption of the Federal Constitution . . . together with the Journal of the Federal Convention . . . Collected and Revised from Contemporary Publications by Jonathan Elliot.* 2d. ed., Philadelphia, 1901

Evans Charles Evans, *American Bibliography*

Ford Paul Leicester Ford, ed., *The Writings of Thomas Jefferson*, "Letterpress Edition," N.Y., 1892-1899

Freeman, *Washington* Douglas Southall Freeman, *George Washington*

Fry-Jefferson Map *The Fry & Jefferson Map of Virginia and Maryland: A Facsimile of the First Edition*, Princeton, 1950

Gottschalk, *Lafayette, 1783-89* Louis Gottschalk, *Lafayette between the American Revolution and the French Revolution (1783-1789)*, Chicago, 1950

Gournay *Tableau général du commerce des marchands négocians, armateurs, &c., . . . années 1789 & 1790*, Paris, n.d.

HAW Henry A. Washington, ed., *The Writings of Thomas Jefferson*, Washington, 1853-1854

Hening William W. Hening, *The Statutes at Large; Being a Collection of All the Laws of Virginia*

Henry, *Henry* William Wirt Henry, *Patrick Henry, Life, Correspondence and Speeches*

JCC *Journals of the Continental Congress, 1774-1789*, ed. W. C. Ford and others, Washington, 1904-1937

JHD *Journal of the House of Delegates of the Commonwealth of Virginia* (cited by session and date of publication)

Jefferson Correspondence, Bixby *Thomas Jefferson Correspondence Printed from the Originals in the Collections of William K. Bixby*, ed. W. C. Ford, Boston, 1916

Johnston, "Jefferson Bibliography" Richard H. Johnston, "A Contribution to a Bibliography of Thomas Jefferson," *Writings of Thomas Jefferson*, ed. Lipscomb and Bergh, XX, separately paged following the Index.

L & B Andrew A. Lipscomb and Albert E. Bergh, eds., *The Writings of Thomas Jefferson*, "Memorial Edition," Washington, 1903-1904

L.C. Cat. *A Catalogue of Books Represented by Library of Congress Printed Cards*, Ann Arbor, 1942-1946; also *Supplement*, 1948-

Library Catalogue, 1783 Jefferson's MS list of books owned and wanted in 1783 (original in Massachusetts Historical Society)

Library Catalogue, 1815 *Catalogue of the Library of the United States*, Washington, 1815

Library Catalogue, 1829 *Catalogue. President Jefferson's Library*, Washington, 1829

MVHR *Mississippi Valley Historical Review*

OED *A New English Dictionary on Historical Principles*, Oxford, 1888-1933

PMHB *The Pennsylvania Magazine of History and Biography*

Randall, *Life* Henry S. Randall, *The Life of Thomas Jefferson*

Randolph, *Domestic Life* Sarah N. Randolph, *The Domestic Life of Thomas Jefferson*

Sabin Joseph Sabin and others, *Bibliotheca Americana. A Dictionary of Books Relating to America*

Sowerby *Catalogue of the Library of Thomas Jefferson*, compiled with annotations by E. Millicent Sowerby, Washington, 1952-55

Swem, *Index* E. G. Swem, *Virginia Historical Index*

Swem, "Va. Bibliog." Earl G. Swem, "A Bibliography of Virginia," Virginia State Library, *Bulletin*, VIII, X, XII (1915-1919)

TJR Thomas Jefferson Randolph, ed., *Memoir, Correspondence, and Miscellanies, from the Papers of Thomas Jefferson*, Charlottesville, 1829

Tucker, *Life* George Tucker, *The Life of Thomas Jefferson*, Philadelphia, 1837

Tyler, *Va. Biog.* Lyon G. Tyler, *Encyclopedia of Virginia Biography*

Tyler's Quart. *Tyler's Quarterly Historical and Genealogical Magazine*

VMHB *Virginia Magazine of History and Biography*

Wharton, *Dipl. Corr. Am. Rev.* *The Revolutionary Diplomatic Correspondence of the United States*, ed. Francis Wharton

WMQ *William and Mary Quarterly*

CONTENTS

continued

CONTENTS

ILLUSTRATIONS

FACING PAGE

This bit of musical annotation was evidently made by Jefferson when he was in Amsterdam in March 1788, but was set down on a separate slip of paper instead of being incorporated into his draft of notes on other observations he made while he was in that city (Notes of a Tour, &c., p. 8-12). The *Westerkerk*, built between 1620 and 1631, is situated between the Keizersgracht and the Prinsengracht and between Leliegracht and Reestraat, facing on Keizersgracht. The chimes are located in the tower, which was described in 1793 as "surpassing all the others of the city in height and in beauty" (*Le guide d'Amsterdam*, Amsterdam, 1793, p. 182-4). The manuscript is in DLC: TJ Papers, 233:41789. (Courtesy of the Library of Congress.)

This price list, in DLC: TJ Papers, 234:42007-9, is the one to which Jefferson refers in his Notes of a Tour as "the annexed bill of prices current" (p. 21, 34). Jefferson there describes John Adam Dick as "keeper of the Rothen-house tavern at Francfort, a great wine merchant, who has between 3. and 400. tons of wine in his cellars" (p. 20); see also his comments in Hints to Americans Travelling in Europe, p. 266. (Courtesy of the Library of Congress.)

It is possible to date with precision these exploratory sketches which represent the very beginning of Jefferson's life-long effort to achieve an improved method of constructing an efficient moldboard for this elemental instrument of agriculture. On 19 Apr. 1788, on his journey from Strasbourg to Meaux, Jefferson observed: "The awkward figure of their mould board leads one to consider what should be it's form" (p. 27, 34-5). Under 23 Apr. 1788 he entered the following in his Account Book: "Espagnol's expenses 44.tt by a note he now gives in." The "note" contained a list of miscellaneous expenses made by Jefferson's servant, Espagnol, between Strasbourg and Meaux, and it is on the verso of this memorandum that Jefferson made these exploratory sketches. This observing traveller, who also had time under the slow means of travel in the 18th century to contemplate a technological improvement that would develop into one of his major contributions to the welfare of mankind, thus afforded the evidence by which we can be fairly certain that these preliminary sketches were set down sometime during the day of 23 Apr. 1788. For that evening Jefferson arrived in Paris to face a great accumulation of business and, as he expressed it to Maria Cosway, "a bushel of letters presented . . . by way of reception" (TJ to Maria Cosway, 24 Apr. 1788). The observing traveller changed abruptly to the busy diplomat with little time for technological speculation; but the seed that had been planted in Champagne would continue to germinate and would flower in Albemarle. See Jefferson's diagrams and description of his proposed method, p. 27; see also, Betts, *Farm Book*, p. 47-64. As indicated in the notes to Jefferson's Notes of a Tour through Holland, the draft or basic text was actually composed en route and then altered and rearranged later. In that draft the description and diagrams of Jefferson's proposed method of making a moldboard are set down under date of 19 Apr.—and are in finished form. This concluding part of Jefferson's Notes could not, of course, have been put down in such finished form a week before Jefferson made his first tentative calculations on the verso of Espagnol's memorandum of expenses. That memorandum therefore, in addition to its value in dating Jefferson's calculations, proves that the final two pages of the draft of the Notes were revised and made into a fair copy of some now missing rough notes. This revision may have taken place around mid-June when Jefferson utilized his Notes of a Tour for the travel hints that he sent to Rutledge and Shippen. (Courtesy of the Massachusetts Historical Society.)

"HET WAPEN VAN AMSTERDAM," JEFFERSON'S HOTEL IN AMSTERDAM 16

This lithograph by Desguerrois after a drawing by Arton was executed ca. 1830, but represents nevertheless "The Amsterdam Arms" (right) much as the hostelry appeared when Jefferson stayed there from 10 March to 30 March 1788. In his Account Book, 29 March 1788, he recorded a payment of 187 florins for "entertainment at the Waping van Amsterdam"; in the travel memorandum subsequently prepared for Rutledge and Shippen, 19 June 1788, he noted: "At Amsterdam I lodged at the Wapping van Amsterdam. I liked the Valet de place they furnished me. He spoke French, and was sensible and well informed, his name was Guillaume or William" (p. 264). The building, although no longer used as a hotel and considerably modi-

FACING PAGE

fied, is still standing at the corner of Rusland and the Kloveniersburgwal. (Courtesy of the Prentenkabinet, Rijksmuseum, Amsterdam, through Howard C. Rice, Jr.)

HOPE'S HOUSE, HAARLEM 16

This view of "Welgelegen" in the Wood of Haarlem, a country house belonging to the Amsterdam banker, Henry Hope, was engraved by Chr. Haldenwang (1792) after a drawing made by H. P. Schouten in 1791. The house, completed in 1788, was built by Jean-Baptiste Dubois (b. 1762), a Flemish architect, from plans drawn by Friquetti, Sardinian consul. In 1808 Hope's "Paviljoen" was sold to Louis Napoleon, King of Holland, who signed his act of abdication there on 1 July 1810. The estate later became national property; the house, located in the Frederiks Park facing the Haarlem Wood, is now the seat of the North Holland provincial government. Jefferson, who visited Hope's House on 20 March 1788, included a description and sketch of it in his travel memoranda (p. 11-12). The "separation between the middle building and wings in the upper story has a capricious appearance, yet a pleasing one," Jefferson thought; this appearance was subsequently altered by the complete removal of the "wings in the upper story." Hope's House—a cousin to the houses by Chalgrin, Clérisseau, Ledoux, and others that Jefferson admired in France—is a characteristic example of the contemporary neo-classic style that he later fostered and practiced in the United States. (Courtesy of the Prentenkabinet, Rijksmuseum, Amsterdam, through Howard C. Rice, Jr.)

JEFFERSON'S HOTEL IN STRASBOURG, AND HIS BILL FOR LODGINGS THERE 17

The hotel where Jefferson stayed during his brief sojourn in Strasbourg, 16-18 April 1788 (p. 25-6; 267)—depicted in an engraving executed about 1790 by Benjamin Zix (1772-1811)—was situated on the embankment of the river Ill, facing the Pont Saint-Nicolas, not far from the Douane or Kaufhaus (extreme right of the picture), the center of river trade. It was one of the city's oldest hostelries, known in the Middle Ages as the "Hospitium zu dem Heiligen Geist" and celebrated by later generations as the place where Herder and Goethe met in 1770, which continued to receive travellers until the 1830's. Although the Pont Saint-Nicolas now occupies a site slightly to the right of the one shown in Zix's engraving, and although certain of the houses were destroyed in the 1930's to make way for a new thoroughfare (the Rue de la Division

FACING PAGE

Leclerc), the characteristic silhouettes of many of the buildings along the Ill, with the cathedral looming in the background, can still be identified. A narrow street leading away from the embankment—the Ruelle de l'Esprit—preserves the name of the former hotel. (View of the hotel: courtesy of the Cabinet des Estampes, Musées de la Ville de Strasbourg, through Howard C. Rice, Jr. Bill for lodgings: courtesy of the Massachusetts Historical Society.)

AMAND KOENIG'S BOOKSHOP IN STRASBOURG 17

This "true delineation" was painted in gouache in a "Stammbuch," or friendship album, about 1762, by Jean-Georges Treuttel, who has represented himself seated in the center, with his two close friends: Jean-Daniel Lorentz, a theological student, at the left; and Georges-Jacques Eissen, recently promoted Master of Arts, at the right. Treuttel, a brother-in-law of Amand Koenig and then an apprentice-clerk in the shop, later founded the publishing and bookselling firm of Treuttel & Würtz. Although Koenig himself is not shown, his initials appear on the bundle of books in the foreground, and a Latin pun on his name is included in the inscription at the top of the page. According to Jefferson, who made purchases in Koenig's shop during his brief visit to Strasbourg in April 1788—and subsequently by correspondence—"Koenig . . . has the best shop of classical books I ever saw" (p. 267). When Treuttel's sketch was drawn and when TJ visited it, Koenig's bookshop was situated in the Rue des Grandes Arcades at the corner of the Rue des Hallebardes; the building, which was destroyed by aerial bombardment in 1944, has now been replaced by a modern structure occupied (1956) by a department store, La Belle Jardinière. (Courtesy of the Cabinet des Estampes, Musées de la Ville de Strasbourg, through Howard C. Rice, Jr.)

JOHN TRUMBULL'S SKETCHES OF THE RHINE IN THE VICINITY OF MAINZ 448

The sketches which John Trumbull made when he descended the Rhine in 1786 are reproduced here from his *Autobiography* (N.Y., London, and New Haven, 1841). Of the electoral palace, Trumbull wrote: "on the bank of the Rhine, stands the electoral palace, externally an old, irregular Gothic building; the interior is said to be decent, not magnificent; I did not enter it, but made a slight drawing of the river front" (*Autobiography*, p. 17). On 23 Sep. 1786 he embarked at Mainz for Cologne in a "batteau with oars and an awning," from which he made the second

sketch of "Elvent" (Eltville?). He described the morning as "fine, the sky and the river clear and undisturbed," and "the country surrounding us rich, various, and bright; the banks of the river covered with villages, and boats and barges crossing and recrossing" (same, p. 130; see also Trumbull to TJ, 9 Oct. 1786, 10: 438-41). Undoubtedly Trumbull's journey influenced Jefferson, not only in determining his own course along the Rhine, but also in shaping his advice on an itinerary for Shippen and Rutledge. For Jefferson's observations on this region, see p. 18-22; 265-6.

PORTRAIT OF MARIA COSWAY BY RICHARD COSWAY 449

Of the number of portraits of Maria Cosway painted by her husband, Richard Cosway, this miniature portrait, or a variation of it, may have been executed while the Cosways were in Paris, for Jefferson must have seen it before he wrote to Mrs. Cosway on 27 July 1788: "with none do I converse more fondly than with my good Maria: not her under the poplar, with the dog and string at her girdle . . ." (p. 423-4). (Courtesy of The Henry E. Huntington Library and Art Gallery.)

"THE HOURS," BY BARTOLOZZI AFTER A PAINTING BY MARIA COSWAY 449

In his letter to Mrs. Cosway, quoted above, Jefferson continued: ". . . but the Maria who makes the Hours her own, who teaches them to dance for us in so charming a round, and lets us think of nothing but her who renders them *si gracieuses.* Your Hours, my dear friend, are no longer your own. Every body now demands them; and were it possible for me to want a memorandum of you, it is presented to me in every street of Paris" (p. 423-4). In 1783 Maria Cosway exhibited a painting of "The Hours" in the Royal Academy in London, No. 261 in the catalogue (Algernon Graves, *The Royal Academy of Arts. A Complete Dictionary of Contributors and Their Work*, London, 1905-06, II, 174). Francesco Bartolozzi apparently used this painting for his engraving of "The Hours" which appeared as Plate No. 1, dated 4 Apr. 1788, in a portfolio published by Thomas Macklin in London in 1788, entitled *British Poets* (A. W. Tuer, *Bartolozzi and His Works*, London, [1881], II, 106-7). It is not certain whether the print that Jefferson saw "suspended against the walls of the Quai des Augustins, the Boulevards, the Palais royale &c. &c. with a 'Maria Cosway delint.' at the bottom," was that by Bartolozzi or was another by some other engraver. (Courtesy of the New York Public Library.)

This plan of the De Tessés' country estate at Chaville, on the road to Versailles, and the view of one of the garden ornaments there are both taken from G. L. Lerouge's *Jardins Anglo-Chinois* (Cahiers XI, III), a series of plates issued periodically in parts beginning in 1777. The fashionable "English gardens" depicted in Lerouge's compilation, many of which Jefferson saw and admired when he was in Europe, were inspired in part by Thomas Whately's *Observations on Modern Gardening*, a volume which Jefferson acquired early in life, which inspired his early dreams for the grounds at Monticello, and which he used on his tour through the gardens of England (Marie Kimball, *Jefferson: the Road to Glory*, p. 160-5; Vol. 9: 369-75). "Modern gardens" required exotic trees and shrubs and Jefferson was tireless in his efforts to procure plants from America for his friends in France, including Mme. de La Rochefoucauld, Boutin, Malesherbes, but especially for Mme. de Tessé (see p. 108, 110, 187, 476, 484).

This contemporary engraving is not sufficiently inclusive to convey an accurate impression of the audience which Jefferson reported to John Jay as an occasion of "unusual pomp," and the "presence so numerous that little could be caught of what they said to the king, and he answered to them" (p. 497). Jefferson was accurate in his surmise that "nothing more passed than mutual assurances of good will," although there had been speculation about the purpose of the event and much preparation at court for it (p. 464, 467, 479, 492). Perhaps if Madame de Bréhan had been present, as Jefferson wrote to Moustier (p. 494), to paint what he called "this jeu d'enfants" she might have done justice to the pomp and color. Tipoo Sahib (Tipú Sultán, 1753-1799) was the son of Haidar Ali and succeeded his father as the sultan of Mysore in 1782. "On the conclusion of the treaty with the Madras Government at Mangalore in 1784, Tipú, inflated with notions of his own prowess, and inspired with hostile feelings against the English, was most anxious to unite himself closely with the French, by whose assistance he hoped to subvert the power he both feared and hated. With this object he sent an embassy, which was instructed, after sounding the views of the Sublime Porte, to repair to France to secure the co-operation of that Government. But the reception

FACING PAGE

which his envoys met with at Constantinople, where Tipú's name had probably never been heard of, was so unfavourable, that they returned in a rage. In 1787 a second embassy, headed by Muhammad Darvesh Khán, was despatched direct to Paris, where the delegates were received most graciously by Louis XVI and hospitably entertained. Louis was himself, however, environed by domestic difficulties, and the cataclysm which shortly afterwards overwhelmed his country was rapidly approaching. He therefore contented himself with profuse promises of future support, and the ambassadors returned to India, discredited, to meet the wrath of their master" (L. B. Bowring, *Haidar Ali and Tipú Sultán* [Oxford, 1899, *Rulers of India*, W. W. Hunter, ed., xi], p. 137-8). (Courtesy of the Cabinet des Estampes, Bibliothèque Nationale, through Howard C. Rice, Jr.)

MADAME DE BREHAN'S SKETCH OF NEW YORK HARBOR 481

Jefferson expressed a high regard for Mme. de Bréhan's ability as an artist and, at various times, mentioned her interest in painting. In his first letter to her after her arrival in America early in 1788, he wrote: "The season is now approaching when you will be able to go and visit the magnificent scenes which nature has formed upon the Hudson, and to make them known to Europe by your pencil" (p. 150). The "Vue de Paulus hook prise de l'apartement de Mde. la Mquise. de Brehan à Newyork," here reproduced, is a water-color drawing. It has generally been dated ca. 12 Oct. 1789 on the assumption that the ship in the foreground is probably the French frigate *l'Active* which was in New York on 11 and 12 Oct. 1789. However, since George Washington sent letters, dated 13 and 14 Oct. 1789, to persons in France, by Moustier, indicating that he and Mme. de Bréhan were on the point of departure for France at that time, it is possible that the sketch was made sometime in 1788 or earlier in 1789 and that it was made from one of the upper windows of her residence on Broadway, near the Bowling Green. See I. N. Phelps Stokes, *The Iconography of Manhattan Island*, N.Y., 1928, v, 1255; vi, Pl. 90; I. N. Phelps Stokes and Daniel C. Haskell, *American Historical Prints*, N.Y., 1933, p. 35; Washington, *Writings*, ed. Fitzpatrick, xxx, 437, 439, 448. (Courtesy of the New York Public Library.)

Volume 13

March to 7 October 1788

JEFFERSON CHRONOLOGY

1743 · 1826

1743.	Born at Shadwell.
1772.	Married Martha Wayles Skelton.
1775-76.	In Continental Congress.
1776.	Drafted Declaration of Independence.
1776-79.	In Virginia House of Delegates.
1779.	Submitted Bill for Establishing Religious Freedom.
1779-81.	Governor of Virginia.
1782.	His wife died.
1783-84.	In Continental Congress.
1784-89.	In France as commissioner and minister.
1790-93.	U.S. Secretary of State.
1797-1801.	Vice President of the United States.
1801-09.	President of the United States.
1814-26.	Established the University of Virginia.
1826.	Died at Monticello.

VOLUME 13

March to 7 October 1788

31	Mch.	Left Amsterdam for Utrecht and Nimeguen.
2	Apr.	At Essen, Duisburg, and Düsseldorf.
4	Apr.	Left Cologne for Coblenz.
7-9	Apr.	At Frankfurt.
11-12	Apr.	At Mainz.
14	Apr.	At Mannheim and Heidelberg.
16	Apr.	Left Karlsruhe for Strasbourg.
19	Apr.	Arrived at Nancy.
22	Apr.	At Epernay.
23	Apr.	Arrived in Paris.
19	June	Sent suggestions on travel to Shippen and Rutledge.
21	June	The ninth state (New Hampshire) ratified the Federal Constitution.
25	June	Virginia ratified.
13	Sep.	Congress provided for setting new government in motion on 4 Mch. 1789.

THE PAPERS OF THOMAS JEFFERSON

[William Coxe, Jr. to John Brown Cutting]

Our Ship Canton is just arriv'd from China with a cargo of 100000 dollars, 19/35 of her belong'd to us. Mr. D—— and myself had the entire direction and management of the property. From these circumstances I have had the best opportunities of getting to the bottom of that business. I have made every use of them in my power. I will venture to pronounce that it contains an increasing and profitable branch of our commerce. We have realized a neat profit of 126 per cent. A larger capital is subscribed and the ship returns immediately. I mention this to you as a national object. You probably have intercourse with the American Ministers at the Courts of Versailles and St. James's. The nature of our government requires the employment of every channel through which a public character can receive information or have useful truths reiterated and confirm'd. I do not flatter you when I say, were the case otherwise our Ambassadours abroad wou'd lend you their ear with complacency. I wish to make an observation to them through you. The british nation possess an immoderate share of the trade of India and China. The Dutch also have a great deal of the former and some of the latter. It appears to me that it wou'd be sound policy in those nations who have very little of that trade to permit the Americans to enjoy the privilege of their ports. France for instance by permitting us to use Pondicherry wou'd give us an opportunity of acting with them in gaining ground upon the British. The Chinese shewed a weakness if I may so call it, in favour of our people from their resemblance to the british. The Nations on the coast of whose feelings that nation have got hold wou'd be more or less partial to us in the same way. The french united with us, or rather acting in concert wou'd gain upon the british in that quarter of the world, and it wou'd have a good effect in regard to the french by contributing to wean those people from their prejudice and exclusive predilection in favour of Britain. The commerce with the East shou'd if it were possible be made common by all the powers of inconsiderable influence in that country. To our ministers you may also mention confidentially that the principal american sales of fine teas are made for smuggling to Ireland and the british Islands—of Nankeens to the same—and likewise to the french and spanish colonies but more largely to the latter. Foreigners have bought in this port double the quantity brought in the Canton.

Tr of Extract (DLC: TJ Papers, 42:7231); in Cutting's hand, but erroneously catalogued as a postscript to Cutting to TJ, 30 Aug. 1788; unsigned, undated, and endorsed by TJ: "Cutting." The Editors are indebted to Eugene S. Ferguson, Ames, Iowa, for the almost certain attribution of authorship to William Coxe, Jr. (1762-1831), brother of Tench Coxe; for the conjectural date of composition as the summer of 1787; and for the information given in the notes below. There is less certainty about the time and manner of transmittal from Cutting to TJ. During his conversations with TJ in Paris in the autumn of 1787 Cutting had advanced the idea of challenging British supremacy in the Oriental trade (Cutting to TJ, 4 Nov. 1787) and he may have handed the present extract to TJ at that time; he may possibly have enclosed it in a (missing) letter to TJ during the winter of 1787-1788; or he may have sent it in an undated (and missing) letter recorded in SJL Index as having been written between Cutting's letters of 11 July and 3 Aug. 1788.

There can be no doubt, however, that this letter was as much intended for TJ (and for John Adams) as if the author had addressed it to them formally instead of phrasing it as AN OBSERVATION TO THEM THROUGH YOU. Nor can there be any doubt that its main argument—that of forming commercial links with France—was one calculated to enlist TJ's sympathy. The *Canton*, Thomas Truxtun, cleared Philadelphia on her outward voyage on 30 Dec. 1785, and her owners were then listed as "John Donnaldson, Wm. Coxe, Tench Coxe, Nalbro Frazier, John Pringle, Thos. Truxtun, all of Phila." She had been built in 1785 by Joshua Humphreys for Donnaldson & Coxe, and on her first voyage that year had brought back Benjamin Franklin from Cowes. She ARRIV'D FROM CHINA on 20 May 1787 and departed on her second voyage in Dec. 1787. MR. D—— was clearly John Donnaldson, and the firm of Donnaldson & Coxe was probably owner of the share that BELONG'D TO US; the goods were advertised for sale by Coxe & Frazier and Donnaldson & Coxe as agents (communication from Eugene S. Ferguson to the Editors, 14 June 1956, citing Customs House Records, PHi, and *Penna. Packet*, 31 Dec. 1785, 21 May 1787). THIS PORT was Philadelphia.

From Thomas Paine

After I got home, being alone and wanting amusement I sat down to explain to myself (for there is such a thing) my Ideas of natural and civil rights and the distinction between them. I send them to you to see how nearly we agree.

Suppose 20 persons, strangers to each other, to meet in a Country not before inhabited. Each would be a sovereign in his own natural right. His will would be his Law, but his power, in many cases, inadequate to his right, and the consequence would be that each might be exposed, not only to each other, but to the other nineteen.

It would then occur to them that their condition would be much improved, if a way could be devised to exchange that quantity of danger into so much protection, so that each individual should possess the strength of the whole number.

As all their rights, in the first case, are[1] natural rights, and the exercise of those rights supported only by their own natural individual power, they would begin by distinguishing between these rights they could individually exercise fully and perfectly and those they could not.

Of the first kind are the rights of thinking, speaking, forming and giving opinions, and perhaps all those which can be fully exercised by the individual without the aid of exterior assistance, or in other words, rights of personal competency. Of the second kind are those of personal protection of acquiring and possessing property, in the exercise of which the individual natural power is less than the natural right.

Having drawn this line they agree to retain individually the first Class of Rights or those of personal Competency; and to detach from their personal possession the second Class, or those of defective power and to accept in lieu thereof a right to the whole power produced by a condensation of all the parts. These I conceive to be civil rights or rights of Compact, and are distinguishable from Natural rights, because in the one we act wholly in our own person, in the other we agree not to do so, but act under the guarantee of society.

It therefore follows that the more of those imperfect natural rights, or rights of imperfect power we give up and thus exchange the more security we possess, and as the word liberty is often mistakenly put for security Mr. Wilson has confused his Argument by confounding the terms.

But it does not follow that the more natural rights of *every kind* we resign the more security we possess, because if we resign those of the first class we may suffer much by the exchange, for where the right and the power are equal with each other in the individual naturally they ought to rest there.

Mr. Wilson must have some allusion to this distinction or his position would be subject to the inference you draw from it.

I consider the individual sovereignty of the states retained under the Act of Confederation to be of the second class of rights. It becomes dangerous because it is defective in the power necessary to support it. It answers the pride and purpose of a few Men in each State, but the State collectively is injured by it.

RC (DLC); unsigned and undated. This famous letter has been variously dated and has even been attributed to TJ. There can be no question of Paine's authorship, but the matter of date cannot be precisely determined. Copeland made the first careful examination of the vexed problem of dating various items in the Paine-Jefferson correspondence of 1788-1789 and concluded on the basis of physical characteristics that the evidence "argues for the spring of 1788" as the period to which the letter belongs: the paper is a "pale-green, over-sized sheet" on which Paine also wrote two other undated memoranda to TJ and one letter that is definitely dated "May 1788" (Thomas W. Copeland, *Our Eminent Friend, Edmund Burke*, New Haven, 1949, p. 184; see also the note to Paine to TJ, at end of May 1788). Koch, rejecting with Copeland the former attribution to 1789 and basing her estimate on substance and chronology, concluded that the probable date was "February or May 1788," since it clearly could not have been written during March or April while TJ was in Holland (Adrienne Koch, *Jefferson and Madison: The Great Collaboration*, New York, 1950, p. 83). The Editors agree with this conclusion, but incline to believe that the earlier date is more nearly correct and that late January or early February may be the best approximation. The letter had to be written after the arrival in Paris of a text of James Wilson's speech in the Pennsylvania ratifying convention of 24 Nov. 1787, which was issued as a pamphlet, *The Substance of a Speech delivered by James Wilson, Esq. Explanatory of the general Principles of the proposed Fœderal Constitution*, Philadelphia, Thomas Bradford, 1787; a certificate on the final page shows that Bradford recorded publication of the pamphlet "this 26th day of November, 1787" at the prothonotary's office for Philadelphia county. TJ's copy is in DLC (Sowerby, No. 3013). By 2 Feb. 1788 TJ had received Madison's letter of 20 Dec. 1787 and within the week following he wrote three letters in which his disapproval of the lack of a bill of rights in the proposed Constitution was strongly emphasized. In one of these letters he went so far as to say that he regarded this as evidence of "a degeneracy in the principles of liberty to which I had given four centuries instead of four years" (TJ to Smith, 2 Feb. 1788; TJ to Madison, 6 Feb. 1788; TJ to Donald, 7 Feb. 1788). It was precisely in the middle of the week covered by these letters that Lafayette wrote Henry Knox that "Mr. Jefferson, Common Sense," and himself were debating the Constitution "in a convention of our own as earnestly as if we were to decide upon it" (Lafayette to Knox, 4 Feb. 1788, quoted in Gottschalk, *Lafayette, 1783-89*, p. 374). The evidence seems to point to this as the period when TJ and Paine carried on their discussion of natural and civil rights, and in a context which involved the very first reported debates to reach Europe. There is no letter from any of TJ's friends in America that shows how he received Wilson's pamphlet, or when, but a remarkable coincidence of dates suggests a plausible conjecture on these points. We know that Thomas Lee Shippen was much interested in the great constitutional debate in America, and that he was kept informed upon its progress by his uncles Arthur and Richard Henry Lee (see William Lewis to Thomas Lee Shippen, printed above, 11 Oct. 1787). Indeed, in letters to his son written in Nov. and Dec. 1787, Dr. Shippen sent a packet containing "all the papers Against and for the New Constitution" and added: "Lloyd will publish the whole debates as soon as possible and they will be a treat to you and Mr. Jefferson" (see notes, Vol. 12: 231). There can scarcely be any doubt that young Shippen brought to Paris a variety of printed materials on the Constitution and that these almost certainly included the pamphlet version of Wilson's speech. We do not know precisely what day he arrived in Paris. His father, in Philadelphia, wrote TJ a letter of introduction on 5 Dec. 1787, and Smith, in London, wrote another on 9 Jan. 1788, though it is very unlikely that Shippen, already in London, could have received by the latter date his father's letter of 12 Dec. or the packet of pamphlets and newspapers mentioned therein. However, on 16 Jan. 1788 Smith forwarded to TJ "2 Letters received within the ½ hour from New York addressed to you," and asked, if they contained public intelligence, to be informed of it. Neither Smith nor TJ in his reply of 2 Feb. 1788 mentioned the writer of either of the enclosures, but one of these was obviously that from Madison of 20 Dec. 1787. It may be noted that, in his reply to Smith, TJ said: "Mr. Payne happened to be present when I received your favour of January 16." From these facts it is clear that Shippen had had time, by 2 Feb., to receive his father's communications, with the accompanying packet—probably did receive them in London on 16 Jan.—and to have arrived in Paris in late January. His first letter from Paris to his father, dated 14 Feb. 1788, indicates that he had been enjoying for some time the hospitality at the Hôtel de Langeac and the circles of Parisian society to which TJ had introduced him (see note to Smith to TJ, 9 Jan. 1788). There can scarcely be any doubt that Wilson's speech was before Paine and TJ by 2 Feb. and probably a few days earlier.

Thoughtful and informed European opinion, whether in the banking houses of Amsterdam, the cabinets of London and Paris, or the intellectual and diplomatic groups in which TJ circulated, was keenly aware in the spring of 1788 of the importance of the great debate on government that was taking place in America. The latest letters, newspapers, and pamphlets arriving at London or Le Havre were received with tense eagerness, and passed back and forth among correspondents as the procession of ratifying conventions during the early part of 1788 met, debated, and cast their fateful decisions. But in all Europe, perhaps, no one watched these events with deeper interest than the three remarkable champions of republican principles whom Lafayette likened to a small ratifying convention of their own—Jefferson, Paine, and himself. To these three was added a fourth who was also devoted to such principles—Dr. Gem, who, in attending Martha and Mary Jefferson in their illness, gained TJ's lasting affection and respect, and who must have lingered on in the evenings to join in the long discussions which, like the best of those being carried on publicly in America, went straight to the fundamental objects of government. The present letter emerged from one of these stimulating explorations of the question of man's relation to society. As Adrienne Koch has shown in a cogent chapter of her *Jefferson and Madison: The Great Collaboration*, p. 62-96, Paine's letter should be considered in relation to the political theory that TJ advanced in his famous letter to Madison of 6 Sep. 1789—that is, whether "the earth belongs always to the living generation" and whether one generation has a right to bind another. For, as she points out, this great theme, to which TJ gave unwavering allegiance throughout life and which profoundly affected his view of constitutions and bills of rights, is also set forth in a strikingly parallel development by Paine in *The Rights of Man.* The long talks of Paine, Jefferson, and Lafayette, with the interesting but obscure figure of Dr. Gem hovering in the background, not only had some influence on the later discussions of the French Declaration of Rights but, in America, through Paine's and Jefferson's devotion to the "rational hope that man is at length destined to be happy and free," profoundly affected the course of modern political thought (TJ to Dr. Gem, 4 Apr. 1790; TJ to Madison, 6 Sep. 1789; TJ to Dr. Gem, 9 Sep. 1789; TJ to Madison, 9 Jan. 1790; Madison to TJ, 4 Feb. 1790).

In making his distinction between the two classes of natural rights and in charging Wilson with having CONFUSED HIS ARGUMENT BY CONFOUNDING HIS TERMS, Paine referred specifically to the following part of Wilson's speech of 24 Nov. 1787: "Our wants, imperfections, and weakness, Mr. President, naturally incline us to society; but it is certain, society cannot exist without some restraints. In a state of nature each individual has a right, uncontrolled, to act as his pleasure or his interest may prevail, but it must be observed that this license extends to every individual, and hence the state of nature is rendered insupportable, by the interfering claims and the consequent animosities of men, who are independent of every power and influence but their passions and their will. On the other hand, in entering into the social compact, though the individual parts with a portion of his natural rights, yet it is evident that he gains more by the limitation of the liberty of others, than he loses by the limitation of his own,—so that in truth, the aggregate of liberty is more in society, than it is in a state of nature." Wilson called this "a fundamental principle of society" and went on, in a telling passage, to draw the conclusion that "the situation and circumstances of states may make it as necessary for them as for individuals to associate" (*Substance of a Speech Delivered by James Wilson*, p. 7).

[1] Paine first wrote, then deleted, "would be."

Notes of a Tour through Holland and the Rhine Valley

MEMORANDUMS ON A TOUR FROM PARIS TO AMSTERDAM, STRASBURG AND BACK TO PARIS. 1788. March. 3.

Post[1]	Face of country	Soil	Produce	Animals	Inclosures	Wood
Bourget						
Louvres } Chapelle }	broad low hills	reddish loam, some sand	corn	none	none	none
Senlis	do.	barren	nothing	none	none	scraggy trees

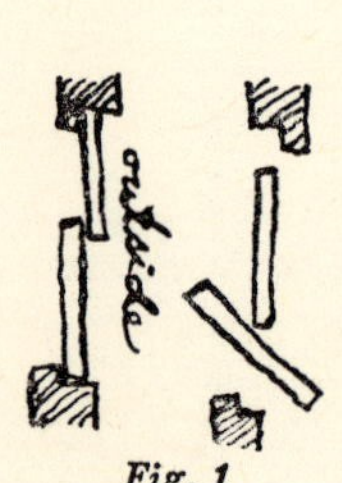

Fig. 1

Amsterdam. Joists of houses placed, not with their sides horizontally and perpendicular[ly] but diamond-wise thus ◇ first for greater strength, 2. to arch between with brick thus . Windows opening so that they admit air, and not rain. The upper sash opens on [a hori]zontal axis, or pins in the center of the sides thus [*see Fig. 1*]. The lower sash slides up.

Manner of fixing a flag staff, or the mast of a vessel [*see Fig. 2*]. a. is the bolt on which it turns. b. a bolt which is taken in and out to fasten it or to let it down. When taken out, the lower end of the staff is shoved out of it's case, and the upper end being heaviest brings itself down. A rope must have been previously fastened to the butt end, to pull it down again when you want to raise the flag end.

Fig. 2

Dining tables letting down with single or double leaves so as to take the room of their thickness only with a single leaf when open, thus or thus double leaves open when shut, thus or thus shut,

Peat costs about 1. doit each, or 12½ stivers the 100. 100.

makes 7. cubic feet, and to keep a tolerably comfortable fire for a study or chamber takes about 6. every hour and a half.

A machine for drawing light *empty* boats over a dam at Amsterdam. It is an Axis in peritrochio fixed on the dam. From the dam each way is a sloping stage. The boat is presented to this, the rope of the axis made fast to it, and it is drawn up. The water [on one] side of the dam is about 4.f. higher than on the other.

The Camels used for lightering ships over the Pampus will raise the ship 8. fe[et.] There are beams passing through the ship's sides, projecting to the off side of the Came[l] and resting on it. Of course that alone would keep the Camel close to the ship. Besides this there are a great number of windlasses on the Camels, the ropes of which are made fast to the gunwale of the ship. The Camel is shaped to the ship on the near side, and straight on the off one. When placed alongside, water is let into it, so as nearly to sink it. In this state it receives the beams &c. of the ship: and then the water is pumped out.

Wind saw mills. See the plans detailed in the Moolen book which I bought. A circular foundation of brick is raised about 3. or 4. feet high, and covered with a curb or [sill] of wood, and has little rollers under it's sill which make it turn easily on the cu[rb. A] hanging bridge projects at each end about 15. or 20. feet beyond the circular area thus [*see Fig. 3*] horizontally, and thus [*see Fig. 4*] in the profile to increase the play of the timbers on the frame. The wings are at one side, as at a. There is a shelter over the hanging bridges, [b]ut of plank, with scarce any frame, very light.

Fig. 3

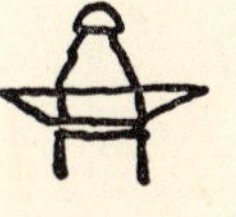

Fig. 4

A bridge across a canal formed by two scows which open each to the opposite shore, and let boats pass.

A lanthern over the street door which gives light equally into the antichamber and the street. It is a hexagon, and occupies the place of the middle pane of [gla]ss in the circular top of the street door.

[A] bridge on a canal, turning on a swivel, by which means it is arranged along the [side] of the canal, so as not to be in the way of boats when not in use. When used it is turned across the canal. It is of course a little more than double the width of the canal.

Hedges of beach, which not losing the old leaf till the new bud pushes it off, has the effect of an evergreen, as to cover.

Mr. Ameshoff merchant at Amsterdam. The distribution of his aviary worthy notice. Each kind of the large birds has it's coop

8.f. wide and 4.f. deep. The middle of the front is occupied by a broad glass window, on one side of which is a door for the keeper to enter at, and on the other a little trap door for the birds to pass in and out. The floor strowed with clean hay. Before each coop is a court of 8. by 16.f. with wire in front, and netting above if the fowls be able to fly. For such as require it there are bushes of evergreen growing in their court for them to lay their eggs under. The coops are frequently divided into two stories, the upper for those birds which perch, such as pigeons &c. the lower for those which feed on the ground, as pheasants, partridges &c. The court is in common for both stories, because the birds do no injury to each other. For the waterfowl there is a pond of water passing thro' the courts, with a moveable separation. While they are breeding they must be separate. Afterwards they may come together. The small birds [are some] of them in a common aviary, and some in cages.

The Dutch wheel-barrow is in this form [*see Fig. 5*] which is very convenient for loading and unloading.

Fig. 5

Mr. Hermen Hend Damen, merchant-broker of Amsterdam tells me that the emigrants to America come from the Palatinate down the Rhine and take shipping from Amsterdam. Their passage is 10. guineas if paid here, and 11. if paid in America. He says they might be had in any number to go to America and settle lands as tenants on half stocks or metairies. Perhaps they would serve their employer one year as an indemnification for the passage, and then be bound to remain on his lands 7. years. They would come to Amsterdam at their own expence. He thinks they would employ more than 50. acres each. But qu? especially if they have 50. acres for their wife also?

Hodson the best house. Stadhouderian. His son in the government. Friendly, but old and very infirm.

Hope. The first house in Amsterdam. His first object England: but it is supposed he would like to have the American business also. Yet he would probably make our affairs subordinate to those of England.

Vollenhoven. An excellent old house, connected with no party.

Sapportus. A broker. Very honest and ingenuous. Well disposed. Acts for Hope; but will say with truth what he can do for us. The best person to consult with as to the best house to undertake a piece of business. He has brothers in London in business.

Jacob Van Staphorst tells me there are about 14. millions of florins, new money, placed in loans in Holland every year, being the savings of individuals out of their annual revenue &c. Besides this there are every year reimbursements of old loans from some quarter or other, to be replaced at interest in some new loan.

1788. March 16. Baron Steuben has been generally suspected of having suggested the first idea of the self-styled order of Cincinnati. But Mr. Adams tells me that in the year 1776. he had called at a tavern in the state of N. York to dine, just at the moment when the British army was landing at Frog's neck. Genls. Washington, Lee, Knox, and Parsons came to the same tavern. He got into conversation with Knox. They talked of antient history, of Fabius who used to raise the Romans from the dust, of the present contest &c. and Genl. Knox, in the course of the conversation, said he should wish for some ribbon to wear in his hat, or in his button hole, to be transmitted to his descendants as a badge and a proof that he had fought in defence of their liberties.'[2] He spoke of it in such precise terms as shewed he had revolved it in his mind before. Mr. Adams says he and Knox were standing together in the door of the tavern, and does not recollect whether Genl. Washington and the others were near enough to hear the conversation, or were even in the room at that moment. Baron Steuben did not arrive in America till above a year after that. Mr. Adams is now 53. years old; i.e. 9. more than I am.

HOPE'S HOUSE NEAR HARLAEM.

It is said this house will cost 4 tons of silver, [or] 40,000. £ sterl. The separation between the middle building and wings in the upper story has a capricious appearance, yet a pleasing one. The right wing of the house (which is the left in the plan) extends back to a great length so as to make the ground plan in the form of an L. The parapet has a pannel of wall, and a pannel of wall, and a pannel of ballusters alternately, which lighten it. There is no portico, the columns being backed against the wall of the front.[3]

Mar. 30. 31. AMSTERDAM, UTRECHT, NIMEGUEN. The lower parts of the low countries seem partly to have been gained from the sea, and partly to be made up of the plains of the Yssel, the Rhine, the Maese and the Schelde united. To Utrecht nothing but plain is seen, a rich black mould, wet, lower than the level of the waters which intersect it; almost entirely in grass; few or no farm houses, as the business of grazing requires few labourers. The canal is lined with country houses which bespeak the wealth and cleanliness of the country; but generally in an uncouth state[4] and exhibiting no regular architecture. After passing Utrecht the hills N.E. of the Rhine come into view, and gather in towards the river till, at Wyck Dursted they are within 3. or 4. miles and at Amelengen they join the river. The plains, after passing Utrecht become more sandy; the hills are very poor and sandy, generally waste in broom, sometimes a little corn. The plains are in corn, grass and willow. The plantations of the latter are immense, and give it the air of an uncultivated country. There are now few chateaux. Farm houses abound, built generally of brick, and covered with tile or thatch. There are some apple trees, but no forest. A few inclosures of willow wattling. In the gardens are hedges of beach[5] 1. foot apart, which, not losing it's old leaves till they are pushed off in the spring by the young ones, gives the shelter of evergreens. The Rhine is here about 300. yards wide, and the road to Nimeguen passing it a little below Wattelingen leaves Hetern in sight on the left. On this side, the plains of the Rhine, the Ling, and the Waal unite. The Rhine and Waal are crossed on vibrating boats, the rope supported by a line of 7. little barks. The platform by which you go on to the ferry boat is supported by boats. The view from the hill at Gress [Grebbe] is sublime. It commands the Waal, and extends far up the Rhine. That also up and down the Waal from the Bellevue of Nimeguen is very fine. The chateau here is pretended to have lodged Julius Caesar. This is giving it an antiquity of at least 18. centuries, which must be apocryphal. Some few sheep to-day, which were feeding in turnep-patches.

Apr. 1. CRANENBURG. CLEVES. SANTEN. REYNBERG. HOOGSTRAAT. The transition from ease and opulence to extreme poverty is remarkeable on crossing the line between the Dutch and Prussian territory. The soil and climate are the same. The governments alone differ. With the poverty, the fear also of slaves is visible in the faces of the Prussian subjects. There is an improvement however in the physiognomy, especially could it be a little brightened up. The road leads generally over the hills, but sometimes thro' skirts of the plains of the Rhine. These are always extensive and good. They want manure, being visibly worn down. The hills are almost always sandy, barren, uncultivated, and insusceptible of culture, covered with broom and moss. Here and there a little indifferent forest, which is sometimes of beach. The plains are principally in corn, some grass and willow. There are no chateaux, nor houses that bespeak the existence even of a middle class. Universal and equal poverty overspreads the whole. In the villages too, which seem to be falling down, the overproportion of women is evident. The cultivators seem to live on their farms. The farmhouses are of mud, the better sort of brick, all covered with thatch. Cleves is little more than a village. If there are shops or magazines of merchandize in it, they shew little. Here and there at a window some small articles are hung up within the glass. The gooseberry beginning to leaf.

Apr. 2. Passed the Rhine at ESSENBERG. It is there about ¼ of a mile wide, or 500 yds. It is crossed in a scow with sails. The wind being on the quarter we were 8. or 10′ only in the passage. Duysberg is but a village, in fact, walled in; the buildings mostly of brick. No new ones which indicate a thriving state. I had understood that near that were remains of the encampment of Varus, in which he and his legions fell by the arms of Arminius (in the time of Tiberius I think it was) but there was not a person to be found in Duysberg who could understand either English, French, Italian or Latin. So I could make no enquiry.

From DUYSBERG to DUSSELDORP the road leads sometimes over the hills, sometimes thro' the plains of the Rhine, the quality of which are as before described. On the hills however are considerable groves of oak, of spontaneous growth, which seems to be of more than a century: but the soil being barren, the trees, tho' high, are crooked and knotty. The undergrowth is broom and moss. In the plains is corn entirely, as they are become rather sandy for grass. There are no inclosures on the Rhine at all. The houses are poor and ruinous, mostly of brick and scantling mixed, a good deal of rape cultivated.

DUSSELDORP. The gallery of paintings is sublime, particularly the room of Vander Werff. The plains from Dusseldorp to Cologne are much more extensive, and go off in barren downs at some distance from the river. These downs extend far, according to appearance. They are manuring the plains with lime. A gate at the elector's chateau on this road in this form [*see Fig. 6*] [which would be better thus perhaps] [*see Fig 7*].[6] We cross at Cologne on a pendulum boat. I observe the hog of this country (Westphalia) of which the celebrated ham is made, is tall, gaunt, and with heavy lop ears. Fatted at a year old, would weigh 100. or 120 ℔. at 2 years old 200 ℔. Their principal food is acorns. The pork fresh sells @ 2½d sterl. the ℔. The ham ready made @ 5½d sterl. the ℔. 106. ℔ of this country is equal to 100. ℔ of Holland. About 4. ℔ of fine Holland salt is put on 100. ℔ of pork. It is smoked in a room which has no chimney. Well informed people here tell me there is no other part of the world where the bacon is smoked. They do not know that we do it. Cologne is the principal market of exportation. They find that the small hog makes the sweetest meat.

Fig. 6

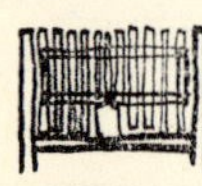

Fig. 7

COLOGNE is a sovereign city, having no territory out of it's walls. It contains about 60.000. inhabitants; appears to have much commerce, and to abound with poor. It's commerce is principally in the hands of protestants, of whom there are about 60. houses in the city. They are extremely restricted in their operations, and otherwise oppressed in every form by the government which is catholic, and excessively intolerant. Their Senate some time ago, by a majority of 22. to 18. allowed them to have a church: but it is believed this privilege will be revoked. There are about 250. catholic churches in the city. The Rhine is here about 400. yds. wide. This city is in 50.° Lat. wanting about 6.′ Here the vines begin, and it is the most Northern spot on the earth on which wine is made. Their first grapes came from Orleans, since that from Alsace, Champagne &c.[7] It is 32. years only since the first vines were sent from Cassel, near Mayence, to the Cape of good hope, of which the Cape wine is now made. Afterwards new supplies[8] were sent from the same quarter. That I suppose is the most Southern spot on the globe where wine is made and it is singular that the same vine should have furnished two wines as much opposed to each other in quality, as in situation. Note I was addressed here by Mr. Damen of Amsterdam to Mr. Jean Jaques Peuchen of this place merchant.[9]

Apr. 4. COLOGNE. BONNE. ANDERNACH. COBLENTZ. I see many walnut trees to-day in the open fields. It would seem as if this tree and wine required the same climate. The soil begins now to be reddish, both on the hills and in the plains. These from Cologne to Bonne extend about 3. miles from the river on each side: but, a little above Bonne, they become contracted, and continue from thence to be from 1. mile to nothing, comprehending both sides of the river. They are in corn, some clover, and rape, and many vines. These are planted in rows 3. feet apart both ways. The vine is left about 6. or 8.f. high, and stuck with poles 10. or 12.f. high. To these poles they are tied in two places, at the height of about 2. and 4.f. They are now performing this operation. The hills are generally excessively steep, a great proportion of them barren, the rest in vines principally, sometimes small patches of corn. In the plains, tho' rich, I observe they dung their vines plentifully; and it is observed here, as elsewhere, that the plains yield much wine, but bad. The good is furnished from the hills. The walnut, willow, and appletree beginning to leaf.

ANDERNACH is the port on the Rhine to which the famous millstones of Cologne are brought, the quarry, as some say, being at Mendich, 3. or 4. leagues from thence. I suppose they have been called Cologne millstones because the merchants of that place having the most extensive correspondence, have usually sent them to all parts of the world. I observed great collections of them at Cologne. This is one account.

Apr. 5. COBLENTZ, NASSAU. Another account is that these stones are cut at Triers, and brought down the Moselle. I could not learn the price of them at the quarry; but I was shewn a grindstone, of the same stone, 5.f. diam. which cost at Triers 6. florins. It was but of half the thickness of a millstone. I suppose therefore that two millstones would cost about as much as 3. of these grindstones, i.e. about a guinea and a half. This country abounds with slate.

The best Moselle wines are made about 15. leagues from hence, in an excessively mountainous country. The 1st. quality (without any comparison) is that made on the mountain of Brownberg, adjoining to the village of Dusmond, and the best crop is that of the Baron Breidbach Burrhesheim grand chambellan et grand Baillif de Coblentz. His Receveur, of the name of Mayer, lives at Dusmond. The last fine year was 1783. which sells now at 50. Louis the foudre, which contains 6 aumes of 170 bottles each = about 1100. bottles. This is about 22. sous Tournois the bottle. In general the Baron Burresheim's crop will sell as soon as made, say at the vintage, for 130. 140. 150. ecus the foudre (the ecu is 1½ florin of Holland) say 200*f*. 2. Vialen is the 2d. quality, and sells new at 120. ecus the futre. 3. Crach, Bisport are the 3d. and sell for about 105. ecus. I compared Crach of 1783. with Baron Burrhesheim's of the same year. The latter is quite clear of acid, stronger, and very sensibly the best. 4. Selting, which sells at 100. ecus. 5. Kous, Berncastle the 5th. quality sells at 80. or 90. After this there is a gradation of qualities down to 30. ecus.

These wines must be 5. or 6. years old before they are quite ripe for drinking. 1000. plants yeild a foudre of wine a year in the most plentiful vineyards. In other vineyards it will take 2000. or 2500. plants to yield a foudre. The culture of 1000. plants costs about 1. Louis a year. A day's labour of a man is paid in Winter 20 kreitzers (i.e. ⅓ of a florin) in Summer 26. A woman's is half that. The red wines of this country are very indifferent and will not keep. The Moselle is here from 100. to 200. yds. wide, the Rhine 300. to 400. A jessamine in the Ct. de Moustier's garden in leaf.

In the Elector of Treves' palace at Coblentz, are large rooms very well warmed by warm air conveyed from an oven below through tubes which open into the rooms. An oil and vinegar cruet in this form [*see Fig. 8*]. At Coblentz we pass the river on a pendulum boat, and the road to Nassau is over tremendous hills, on which is here and there a little corn, more vines, but mostly barren. In some of these barrens are forests of beach and oak, tolerably large, but crooked and knotty, the undergrowth beach brush, broom and moss. The soil of the plains, and of the hills where they are cultivable, is reddish. Nassau is a village the whole rents of which should not amount to more than a hundred or two guineas, yet it gives the title of Prince to the house of Orange to which it belongs.

Fig. 8

Apr. 6. NASSAU, SCHWELBACH, WISBADEN, HOCHHEIM, FRANKFORT. The road from Nassau to Schwelbach is over hills, or rather mountains, both high and steep; always poor, and above half of them barren in beach and oak. At Schwelbach there is some chesnut. The other parts are either in winter grain, or preparing for that of the Spring. Between Schwelbach and Wisbaden we come in sight of the plains of the Rhine, which are very extensive.

"The chime of Amsterdam West church." (See p. xxv.)

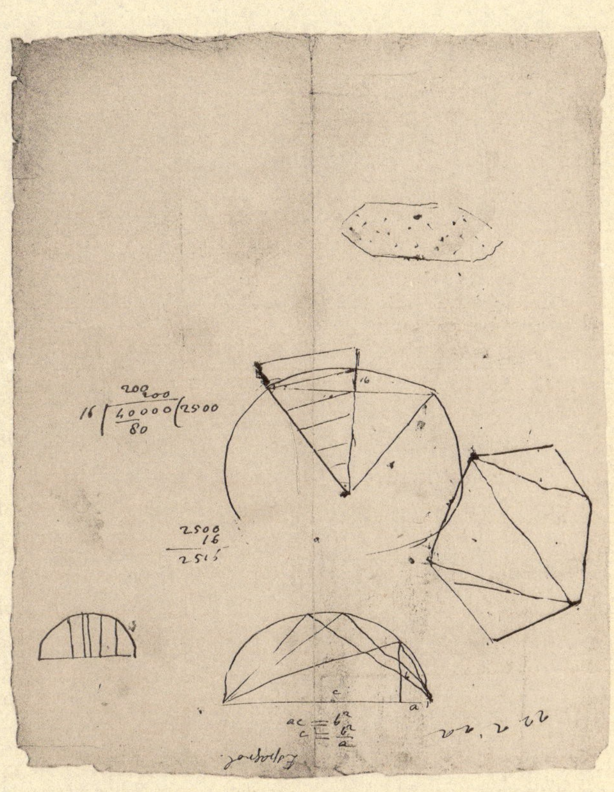

Preliminary sketches for the moldboard plow. (See p. xxv.)

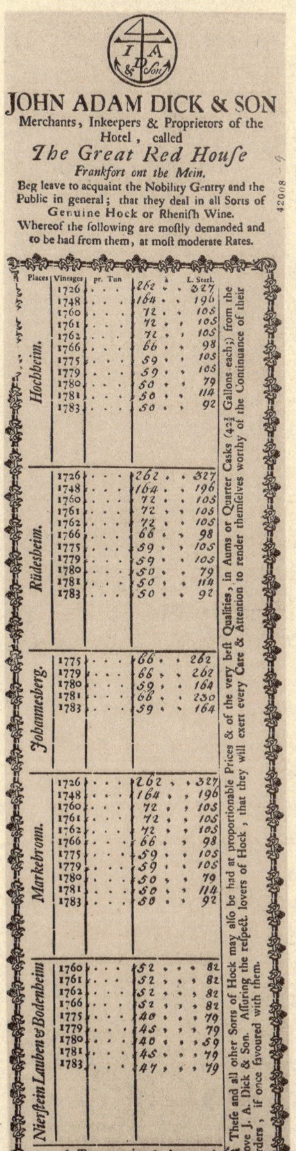

JOHN ADAM DICK & SON

Merchants, Inkeepers & Proprietors of the Hotel, called

The Great Red House

Frankfort ont the Mein.

Beg leave to acquaint the Nobility Gentry and the Public in general; that they deal in all Sorts of Genuine Hock or Rhenish Wine.

Whereof the following are mostly demanded and to be had from them, at most moderate Rates.

Places	Vintages	pr. Tun	à L. Sterl.
Hochheim.	1726	262	327
	1748	164	196
	1760	72	105
	1761	72	105
	1762	72	105
	1766	66	98
	1775	59	105
	1779	59	105
	1780	50	79
	1781	50	114
	1783	50	92
Rüdesheim.	1726	262	327
	1748	164	196
	1760	72	105
	1761	72	105
	1762	72	105
	1766	66	98
	1775	59	105
	1779	59	105
	1780	50	79
	1781	50	114
	1783	50	92
Johannesberg.	1775	66	262
	1779	66	262
	1780	59	164
	1781	66	230
	1783	59	164
Markebronn.	1726	262	327
	1748	164	196
	1760	72	105
	1761	72	105
	1762	72	105
	1766	66	98
	1775	59	105
	1779	59	105
	1780	50	79
	1781	50	114
	1783	50	92
Nierstein Lauben & Bodenheim	1760	52	82
	1761	52	82
	1762	52	82
	1766	52	82
	1775	40	79
	1779	45	79
	1780	40	59
	1781	45	79
	1783	47	79

A Tun contains 8. Aums. 1360 bottles
An Aum contains $42\frac{1}{2}$ Gallons. 170 bottles

These and all other Sorts of Hock may also be had at proportionable Prices & of the very best Qualities, in Aums or Quarter Casks ($42\frac{1}{2}$ Gallons each;) from the above J. A. Dick & Son. Assuring the respect. lovers of Hock, that they will exert every Care & Attention to render themselves worthy of the Continuance of their Orders, if once favoured with them.

42008

Wine list of John Adam Dick & Son. (See p. xxv.)

Gezigt van het Amsterdamsche Wapen Logement.

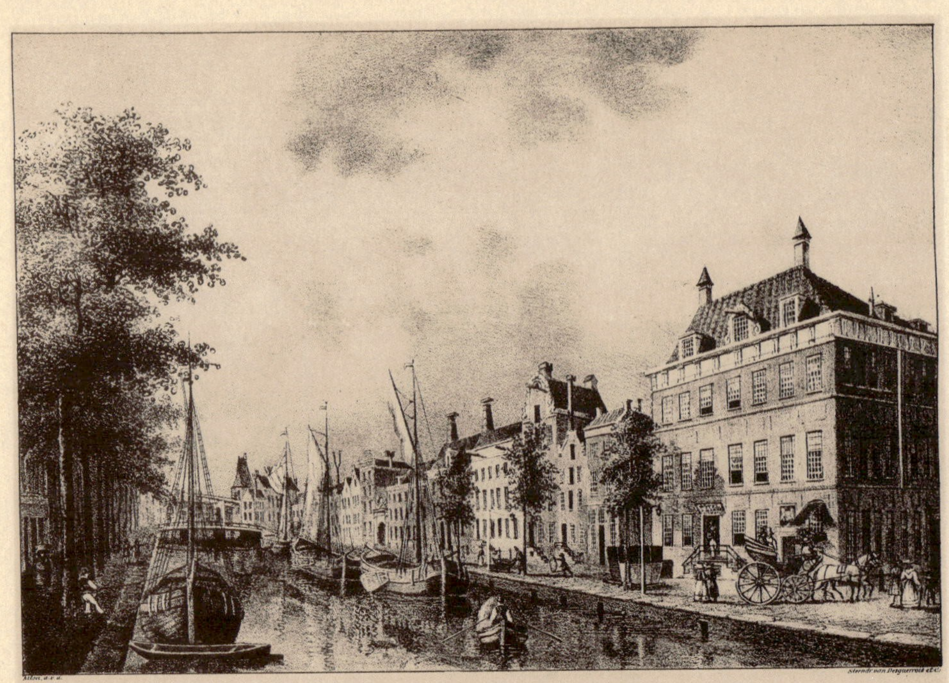

"Het Wapen van Amsterdam," Jefferson's hotel in Amsterdam. (See p. xxvi.)

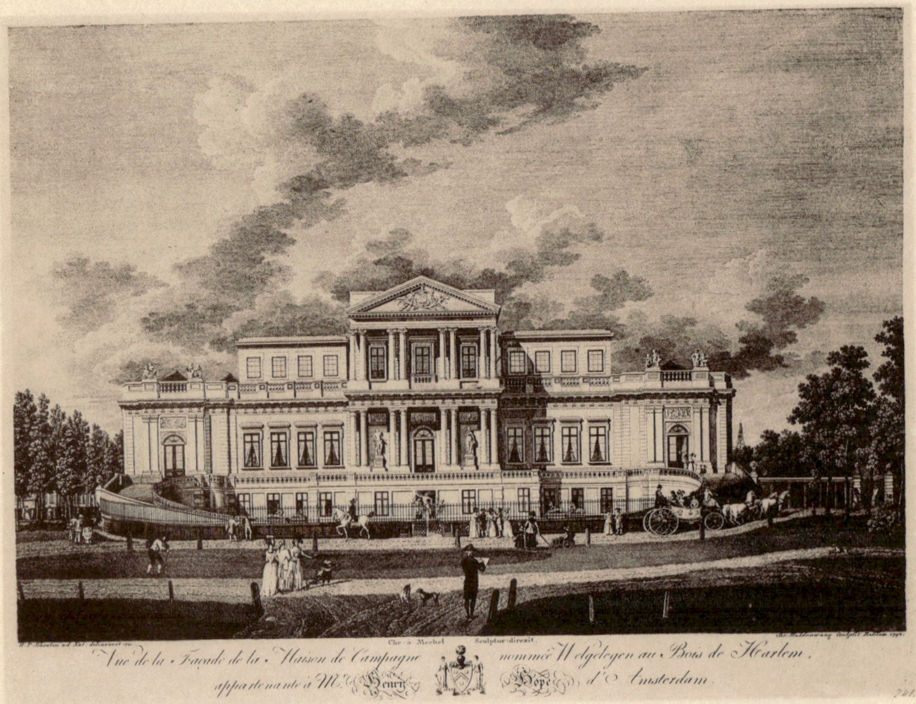

Vue de la Façade de la Maison de Campagne nommée Welgelegen au Bois de Harlem,
appartenante à Mr. Henry Hope d'Amsterdam

Hope's house, Haarlem. (See p. xxvii.)

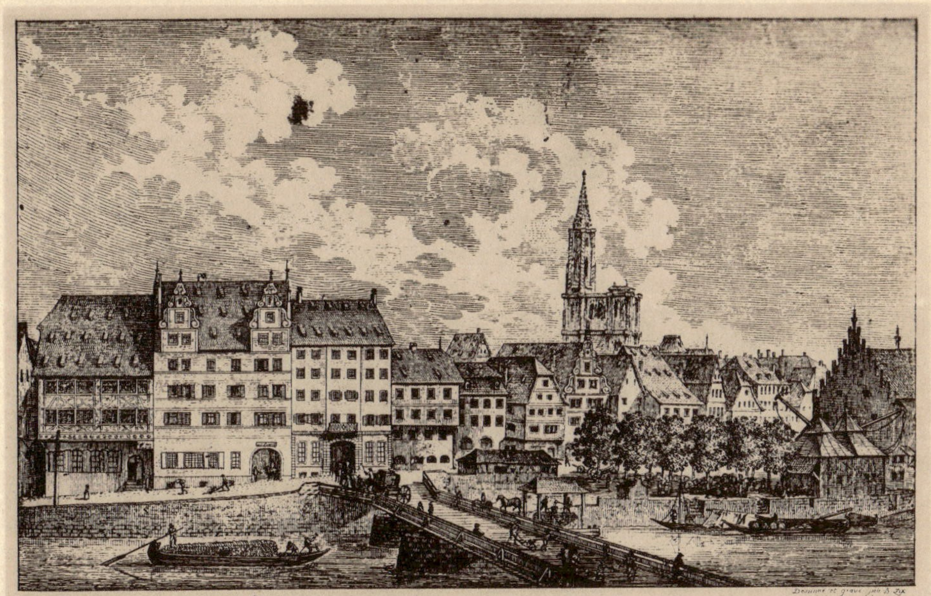

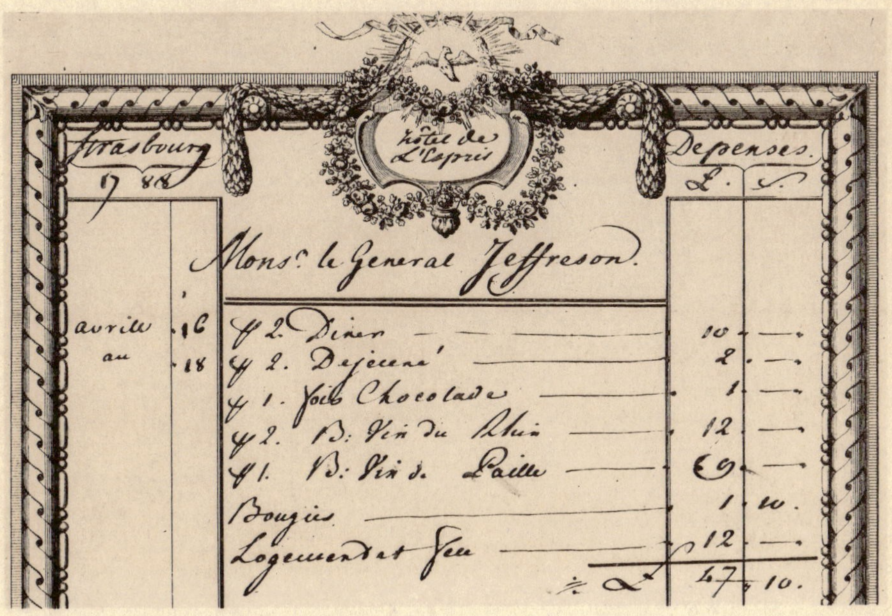
Strasbourg 1788

hotel de L'Esprit

Mons.r le General Jeffreson.

			Depenses L.	s.
avril	16	p.r 2. Diner	10	—
au	18	p.r 2. Dejeuné	2	—
		p.r 1. fois Chocolade	1	—
		p.r 2. B: Vin du Rhin	12	—
		p.r 1. B: Vin de Paille	9	—
		Bougies	1	10
		Logement et feu	12	—
		L	47	10

Jefferson's hotel in Strasbourg, and his bill for lodging. (See p. xxvii.)

Amand Koenig's bookshop in Strasbourg. (See p. xxviii.)

From hence the lands, both high and low are very fine, in corn, vines, and fruit trees. The country has the appearance of wealth, especially in the approach to Frankfort.

Apr. 7. FRANCFORT. Among the poultry, I have seen no turkies in Germany till I arrive at this place. The Stork, or Crane, is very commonly tame here. It is a miserable, dirty, ill-looking bird. The Lutheran is the reigning religion here and is equally intolerant to the Catholic and Calvinist, excluding them from the free corps.

Apr. 8. FRANCFORT, HANAU. The road goes thro' the plains of the Maine, which are mulatto and very fine. They are well cultivated till you pass the line between the republic and the Landgraviate of Hesse, when you immediately see the effect of the difference of government, notwithstanding the tendency which the neighborhood of such a commercial town as Francfort has to counteract the effects of tyranny in it's vicinities, and to animate them in spite of oppression. In Francfort all is life, bustle and motion. In Hanau the silence and quiet of the mansions of the dead. Nobody is seen moving in the streets; every door is shut; no sound of the saw, the hammer, or other utensil of industry. The drum and fife is all that is heard. The streets are cleaner than a German floor, because nobody passes them. At Williamsbath, near Hanau, is a country seat of the Landgrave. There is a ruin which is clever. It presents the remains of an old castle. The ground plan is in this form [*see Fig. 9*]. The upper story in this [*see Fig. 10*], a circular room of 31½f. diameter within. The 4. little square towers, at the corners, finish at the floor of the upper story, so as to be only platforms to walk out on. Over the circular room is platform also, which is covered by the broken parapet which once crowned the top, but is now fallen off in some parts, whilst the other parts remain. I like better however the form of the ruin at Hagley in England which was thus [*see Fig. 11*].[10] A centry box here[11] covered over with bark, so as to look exactly like the trunk of an old tree. This is a good[12] idea, and may be of much avail in a garden.[13] There is a hermitage in which is a good figure of a hermit in plaister, coloured to the life, with a table and book before him, in the attitude of reading and contemplation. In a little cell is his bed, in another his books, some tools &c., in another his little provision of fire wood &c. There is a monument erected to the son of the present landgrave in the form of a pyramid, the base of which is 18½f. The side declines from the perpendicular about 22½.° An arch is carried through it both ways so as to present a door in each side. In the middle of this, at the crossing

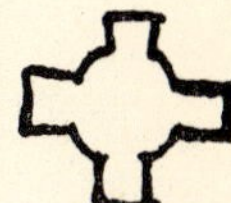

Fig. 9

Fig. 10

Fig. 11

of the two arches, is a marble monument with this inscription 'ante tempus.' He died at 12. years of age. Between Hanau and Frankfort, in sight of the road, is the village of Bergen, where was fought the battle of Bergen in the war before last.—Things worth noting here are 1. a folding ladder, 2. manner of packing china cups and saucers, the former in a circle within the latter.[14] 3. the marks of different manufactures of china, to wit. Dresden with two swords, Hecks with a wheel, with a W.[15] Frankendaal with (for Charles Theodore) and a over it. Berlin with 4. the top rail of the waggon supported by the washers on the ends of the axle-trees.

Apr. 10. FRANKFORT, HOCHEIM. MAYENCE. The little tyrants round about having disarmed their people, and made it very criminal to kill game, one knows when they quit the territory of Frankfort by the quantity of game which is seen. In the Republic, every body being allowed to be armed, and to hunt on their own lands, there is very little game left in it's territory. The hog hereabouts resembles extremely the little hog of Virginia, round like that, a small head, and short upright ears. This makes the ham of Mayence, so much esteemed at Paris.[16]

We cross the Rhine at Mayence on a bridge 1840. feet long, supported by 47. boats. It is not in a direct line, but curved up against the stream, which may strengthen it, if the difference between the upper and lower curve be sensible, if the planks of the floor be thick, well jointed together, and forming sectors of circles, so as to act on the whole as the stones of an arch. But it has by no means this appearance. Near one end, one of the boats has an Axis in peritrochio, and a chain, by which it may be let drop down stream some distance, with the portion of the floor belonging to it, so as to let a vessel through. Then it is wound up again into place, and to consolidate it the more with the adjoining parts, the loose section is a little higher, and has at each end a folding stage, which folds back on it when it moves down, and when brought up again into place, these stages are folded over on the bridge. This whole operation takes but 4. or 5. minutes. In the winter the bridge is taken away entirely, on account of the ice, and then every thing passes on the ice, thro' the whole winter.

Apr. 11. MAYENCE. RUDESHEIM. JOHANSBERG. MARKEBRONN.[17] The women do everything here. They dig the earth, plough, saw, cut, and split wood, row, tow the batteaux &c. In a small but dull kind of batteau, with two hands rowing with a kind of large paddle, and a square sail but scarcely a breath of wind we went down the river at the rate of 5. miles an hour, making it 3½ hours to Rudesheim. The floats of wood which go with the current only, go 1½ mile an hour. They go night and day. There are 5. boatmills abreast here. Their floats seem to be about 8.f. broad. The Rhine yields salmon, carp, pike, and perch, and the little rivers running into it yield speckled trout. The plains from Maintz to Rudesheim are good and in corn: the hills mostly in vines. The banks of the river are so low that, standing up in the batteau, I could generally see what was in the plains, yet they are seldom overflowed.

Though they begin to make wine, as has been said, at Cologne, and continue it up the river indefinitely, yet it is only from Rudesheim to Hocheim, that wines of the very first quality are made. The river happens there to run due East and West, so as to give to it's hills on that side a Southern aspect, and even in this canton, it is only Hocheim, Johansberg, and Rudesheim that are considered as of the very first quality. Johansberg is a little mountain (berg signifies mountain) wherein is a religious house, about 15. miles below Mayence, and near the village of Vingel. It has a Southern aspect, the soil a barren mulatto clay, mixed with a good deal of stone, and some slate. This wine used to be but on a par with Hocheim and Rudesheim; but the place having come to the Bp. of Fulda, he improved it's culture so as to render it stronger, and since the year 1775. it sells at double the price of the other two. It has none of the acid of the Hocheim and other Rhenish wines. There are about 60. tons made in a good year, which sell, as soon as of a drinkable age, at 1000.*f*. each. The ton here contains 7½ aumes of 170. bottles each. Rudesheim is a village about 18. or 20. miles below Mayence. It's fine wines are made on the hills about a mile below the village, which look to the South, and on the middle and lower parts of them. They are terrassed. The soil is grey, about one half of slate and rotten stone, the other half of barren clay, excessively steep. Just behind the village also is a little spot, called hinder house, belonging to the Counts of Sicken and Oschstein, wherein each makes about a ton of wine of the first quality. This spot extends from the bottom to the top of the hill. The vignerons of Rudesheim dung their vines about[18] once in 5. or 6. years putting a one-horse tumbrel load of dung on every 12.f. square. 1000 plants yield about 4. aumes in a good year.

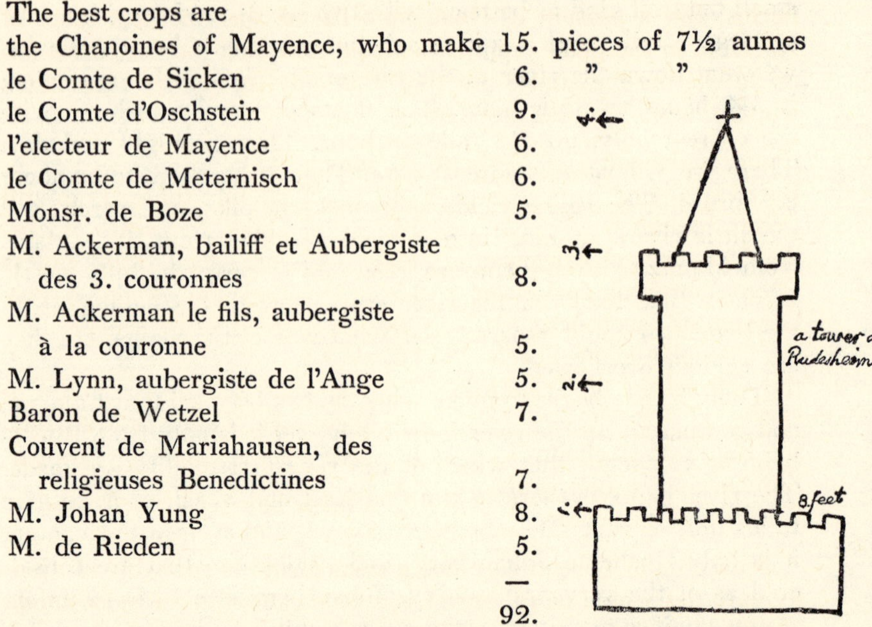

The best crops are

the Chanoines of Mayence, who make	15.	pieces of 7½ aumes
le Comte de Sicken	6.	" "
le Comte d'Oschstein	9.	
l'electeur de Mayence	6.	
le Comte de Meternisch	6.	
Monsr. de Boze	5.	
M. Ackerman, bailiff et Aubergiste des 3. couronnes	8.	
M. Ackerman le fils, aubergiste à la couronne	5.	
M. Lynn, aubergiste de l'Ange	5.	
Baron de Wetzel	7.	
Couvent de Mariahausen, des religieuses Benedictines	7.	
M. Johan Yung	8.	
M. de Rieden	5.	
	92.	

These wines begin to be drinkable at about 5. years old. The proprietors sell them old or young, according to the price offered, and according to their own want of money. There is always a little difference between different casks, and therefore when you chuse and buy a single cask, you pay 3, 4, 5, or 600. florins for it. They are not at all acid, and to my taste much preferable to Hocheim, tho' but of the same price. Hocheim is a village about 3. miles above Mayence, on the Maine where it empties into the Rhine. The spot whereon the good wine is made is the hill side from the church down to the plain, a gentle slope of about ¼ of a mile wide and extending half a mile towards Mayence. It is of South Western aspect, very poor, sometimes grey, sometimes mulatto, with a moderate mixture of small broken stone. The vines are planted 3.f. apart, and stuck with sticks about 6.f. high. The vine too is cut at that height. They are dunged once in 3. or 4. years. 1000 plants yield from 1. to 2. aumes a year. They begin to yield a little at 3. years old, and continue to 100. years, unless sooner killed by a cold winter. Dick, keeper of the Rothen-house tavern at Francfort, a great wine merchant, who has between 3. and 400. tons of wine in his cellars, tells me that Hocheim of the year 1783. sold, as soon as it was made, at 90. florins the aume, Rudesheim of the same year, as soon as made at 115. florins, and Markebronn 70.

florins. But a peasant of Hocheim tells me that the best crops of Hocheim in the good years, when sold new, sell but for about 32. or 33. florins the aume: but that it is only the poorer proprietors who sell new. The fine crops are

Count Ingleheim	about 10. tons	all of these keep till about 15. years old before they sell, unless they are offered a very good price sooner.
Baron d'Alberg	8.	
Count Schimbon	14.	
the Chanoines of Mayence	18.	
Counsellor Schik de Vetsler	15.	
Convent of Jacobsberg	8.	
the Chanoine of Fechbach	10.	
the Carmelites of Frankfort	8.	who only sell by the bottle in their own tavern in Francfort.
the Bailiff of Hocheim	11.	who sells at 3. or 4. years old
Zimmerman, a bourgeois	4.	these being poor sell new.
Feldman, a carpenter	2.	

Markebronn (bronn signifies a spring, and is probably of affinity with the Scotch word, burn) is a little canton in the same range of hills, adjoining to the village of Hagenheim, about 3. miles above Johansberg, subject to the elector of Mayence. It is a sloping hill side of Southern aspect, mulatto, poor, and mixed with some stone. This yields wine of the 2d. quality.

Apr. 12. MAYENCE. OPPENHEIM. WORMS. MANHEIM. On the road between Mayence and Oppenheim are three cantons which are also esteemed as yielding wines of the 2d. quality. These are Laudenheim, Bodenheim, and Nierstein. Laudenheim is a village about 4. or 5. miles from Mayence. It's wines are made on a steep hill side, the soil of which is grey, poor and mixed with some stone. The river happens there to make a short turn to the S.W. so as to present it's hills to the S.E. Bodenheim is a village 9. miles, and Nierstein another about 10. or 11. miles from Mayence. Here too the river is N.E. and S.W. so as to give to the hills between these villages a S.E. aspect; and at Nierstein a valley making off, brings the face of the hill round to the South. The hills between these villages are almost perpendicular, of a vermillion red, very poor, and having as much rotten stone as earth. It is to be observed that these are the only cantons on the South side of the river which yield good wine, the hills on this side being generally exposed to the cold winds, and turned from the sun. The annexed bill of prices current will give an idea of the estimation of these wines respectively.

With respect to the grapes in this country, there are three kinds in use for making white wine (for I take no notice of the red wines as being absolutely worthless.) 1. The Klemperien, of which the inferior qualities of Rhenish wines are made, and is cultivated because of it's hardness. The wines of this grape descend as low as 100. florins the ton of 8. aumes. 2. The Rhysslin grape which grows only from Hocheim down to Rudesheim. This is small and delicate, and therefore succeeds only in this chosen spot. Even at Rudesheim, it yields a fine wine only in the little spot called Hinder-house before mentioned: the mass of good wines made at Rudesheim below the village being of the 3d. kind of grape, which is called the Orleans grape.

To Oppenheim the plains of the Rhine and Maine are united. From that place we see the commencement of the Berg-strasse, or mountains which separate at first the plains of the Rhine and Maine, then cross the Neckar at Heidelberg, and from thence forms the separation between the plains of the Neckar and Rhine, leaving those of the Rhine about 10. and 12. miles wide. These plains are sometimes black, sometimes mulatto, always rich. They are in corn, potatoes, and some willow. On the other side again, that is, on the West side, the hills keep at first close to the river. They are 150. or 200.f. high, sloping, red, good, and mostly in vines. Above Oppenheim, they begin to go off till they join the mountains of Lorraine and Alsace, which separate the waters of the Moselle and Rhine, leaving to the whole valley of the Rhine about 20. or 25. miles breadth. About Worms these plains are sandy, poor, and often covered only with small pine.

April 13. MANHEIM. There is a bridge over the Rhine here supported on 39. boats, and one over the Neckar on 11. boats. The bridge over the Rhine is 21½f. wide from rail to rail. The boats are 4.f. deep, 52.f. long, and 9f. 8I. broad. The space between boat and boat is 18f. 10I. From these data the length of the bridge should be 9f.−8I+18f−10I×40=1140. feet. In order to let vessels pass through, two boats well framed together, with their flooring are made to fall down stream together.—Here too they make good ham. It is fattened on round potatoes and Indian corn. The farmers smoke what is for their own use in their chimnies. When it is made for sale, and in greater quantities than the chimney will hold, they make the smoke of the chimney pass into an adjoining loft or apartment from which it has no issue; and here they hang their hams.

An economical curtain bedstead. The bedstead is 7.f. by 4.f.2 I.

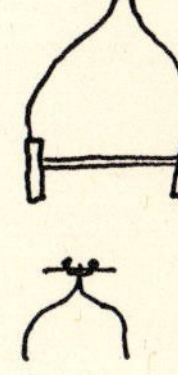

From each leg there goes up an iron rod ⅜I. diam. Those from the legs at the foot of the bed meeting at top as in the margin, and those from the head meeting in like manner, so that the two at the foot form one point, and the two at the head another. On these points lays an oval iron rod, whose long diameter is 5.f. and short one 3f. 1.I. There is a hole through this rod at each end, by which it goes on firm on the point of the upright rods. Then a nut screws it down firmly. 10. breadths of stuff 2.f. 10I. wide and 8.f. 6.I. long form the curtains. There is no top nor vallons. The rings are fastened within 2½ or 3.I. of the top on the inside, which 2½I. or 3.I. stand up and are an ornament somewhat like a ruffle.[19]

I have observed all along the Rhine that they make the oxen draw by the horns. A pair of very handsome chariot horses, large, bay, and 7. years old sell for 50. Louis. 1 ℔ of beef sells for 8 kreitzers (i.e. 8/60 of a florin) 1 ℔ of mutton or veal 6. kreitzers, 1 ℔ of pork 7½ kr., of ham 12. kr., of fine wheat bread 2. kr., of butter 20. kr. 160 ℔ wheat 6 *f.* 160 ℔ maize 5.*f.* 160 ℔ potatoes 1 *f.* 100. ℔ hay 1 *f.* a cord of wood (which is 4. 4. and 6.f.) 7 *f.* A labourer by the day recieves 24. kr. and feeds himself. A journee or arpent of land (which is 8. by 200. steps) such as the middling plains of the Rhine will sell for 200. *f.* There are more souldiers here than other inhabitants, to wit, 6000. souldiers and 4000. males of full age of the citizens, the whole number of whom is reckoned at 20,000.

Apr. 14. MANHEIM. DOSSENHEIM. HEIDELBERG. SCHWETZINGEN. MANHEIM. The elector placed in 1768. 2. male and 5. females of the Angora goat at Dossenheim, which is at the foot of the Bergstrasse mountains. He sold 25. last year, and has now 70. They are removed into the mountains 4. leagues beyond Dossenheim. Heidelberg is on the Neckar just where it issues from the Bergstrasse mountains, occupying the first skirt of a plain which it forms. The Chateau is up the hill a considerable height. The gardens lie above the Chateau, climbing up the mountain in terrasses. This chateau is the most noble ruin I have ever seen, having been reduced to that state by the French in the time of Louis XIV. 1693. Nothing remains under cover but the chapel. The situation is romantic and pleasing beyond expression. It is on a great scale much like the situation of Petrarch's chateau at Vaucluse on a small one. The climate too is like that of Italy. The apple, the pear, cherry, peach, apricot and almond are all in bloom. There is a station in the garden to which the chateau reechoes distinctly 4. syllables. The famous ton of Heidelberg was new built in 1751. and made to contain 30. foudres more than the antient one. It is said to contain 236. foudres of 1200. bottles each. I measured it, and found it's length external to be 28.f. 10.I. it's diameter at the end 20.f. 3.I. the thickness of the staves 7½I. thickness of the hoops 7½I. besides a great deal of external framing. There is no wine in it now. The gardens at Schwetzingen shew how much money may be laid out to make an ugly thing. What is called the English quarter however relieves the eye from the strait rows of trees, round and square basons which constitute the great mass of the garden. There are some tolerable morsels of Graecian architecture, and a good ruin. The Aviary too is clever. It consists of cells of about 8.f. wide, arranged round, and looking into, a circular area of about 40. or 50.f. diameter. The cells have doors both of wire and glass, and have small shrubs in them. The plains of the Rhine on this side are 12. miles wide, bounded by the Bergstrasse mountains. These appear to be 800. or 1000.f. high; the lower part in vines, from which is made what is called the vin de Nichar; the upper in chesnut. There are some cultivated spots however quite to the top. The plains are generally mulatto,[20] in corn principally; they are planting potatoes in some parts, and leaving others open for Maize and tobacco. Many peach and other fruit trees on the lower part of the mountain. The paths on some parts of these mountains are somewhat in the style represented in

the margin.[21]

MANHEIM. KAEFERTHAL. MANHEIM. Just beyond Kaerferthal is an extensive sandy waste planted in pine, in which the elector has about 200 sangliers, tamed. I saw about 50. The heaviest I am told would weigh about 300 ℔. They are fed on round potatoes and range in an extensive forest of small pines. At the village of Kaeferthal is a plantation of Rhubarb begun in 1769 by a private company. It contains 20 arpens or journees, and it's culture costs about 4. or 500*f*. a year. It sometimes employs 40 to 50 labourers at a time. The best age to sell the Rhubarb at is the 5th. or 6th. year; but the sale being dull they keep it sometimes to the 10th. year. They find it best to let it remain in the earth, because when taken out it is liable to the worm. At about 10. years old however it begins to rot in the ground. They sell about 200 quintals a year at 2 or 3*f*. a ℔. and could sell double that quantity from this ground if they could find a market. The apothecaries of Frankfort and of England are the principal buyers. It is in beds resembling lettuce beds, the plants 4. 5 or 6I. apart. When dug, a thread is passed thro' every peice of root and it is hung separate in a kind of rack. When dry it is rasped. What comes off is given to the cattle.

Apr. 15. MANHEIM. SPIRE. CARLSRUH. The valley preserves it's width, extending on each side of the river about 10. or 12. miles.[22] But the soil loses much in it's quality, becoming sandy and lean, often barren and overgrown with pine thicket. At Spire is nothing remarkeable. Between that and Carlsruh we pass the Rhine in a common Skow with oars where it is between 3. and 400. yards wide. Carlsruh is the residence of the Margrave of Baden, a sovereign prince. His chateau is built in the midst of a natural forest of several leagues diameter, and of the best trees I have seen in these countries. They are mostly oak, and would be deemed but indifferent in America. A great deal of money has been spent to do more harm than good to the ground, cutting a number of straight allies through the forest. He has a pheasantry of the gold and silver kind, the latter very tame, but the former excessively shy. A little inclosure of stone 2½f. high and 30.f. diameter in which are two tamed beavers. There is a pond of 15.f. diameter in the center and at each end a little cell for them to retire into, which is stowed with boughs and twigs with leaves on them which are their principal food. They eat bread also. Twice a week the water is changed. They cannot get over this wall.—Some cerfs of a peculiar kind, spotted like fawns. The horns remarkeably long, small and sharp, with few points. I am not sure there were more than two to each main beam, and I saw distinctly there came out a separate and subordinate beam from the root of each. 8 Ancora goats, beautiful animals, all white. This town is only an appendage of the Chateau, and but a moderate one. It is a league from Durlach, halfway between that and the river.—I observe they twist the funnels[23] of their stoves about in any form, for ornament merely, without fearing their smoking, as thus e.g. [*see Fig. 12*].

Fig. 12

Apr. 16. CARLSRUH. RASTADT. SCHOLHOVEN. BISCHOFHEIM. KEHL. STRASBOURG. The valley of the Rhine still preserves it's width,[24] but varies in quality, sometimes a rich mulatto loam, sometimes a poor sand, covered with small pine. The culture is generally corn. It is to be noted that thro the whole of my route through the Netherlds. and the valley of the Rhine there is a little red clover every here and there, and a great deal of rape cultivated. The seed of this is sold to be made into oil. The rape is now in blossom. No inclosures. The fruit trees are generally blossoming thro' the whole valley. The high mountains of the Bergstrasse as also of Alsace are[25] crowned with snow within this day or two. The every day dress of the country women here is black.

Rastadt is a seat also of the Margrave of Baden. Scholhoven and Kehl are in his territory but not Bischofheim. I see no beggars since I enter his government nor is the traveller obliged to ransom himself every moment by a chaussée gold. The roads are excellent, and made so I presume out of the coffers of the prince. From Cleves till I enter the Margravate of Baden the roads have been strung with beggars, in Hesse the most, and the road tax very heavy. We pay it chearfully however through the territory of Frankfort and thence up the Rhine, because fine gravelled roads are kept up. But through the Prussian and other parts of the road below Frankfort the roads are only as made by the carriages, there not appearing to have been ever a day's work employed on them.—At Strasburg we pass the Rhine on a wooden bridge.

At Brussell and Antwerp the fuel is pit-coal, dug in Brabant. Thro' all Holland it is turf. From Cleves to Cologne it is pit coal brought from Engld. They burn it in open stoves. From thence it is wood burnt in close stoves, till you get to Strasbourg, where the open chimney comes again into use.

April 16. 17. 18. STRASBOURG. The Vin de paille is made in the neighborhood of Colmar in Alsace about from this place. It takes it's name from the circumstance of spreading the grapes on straw where they are preserved till spring, and then made into wine. The little juice then remaining in them makes a rich sweet wine, but the dearest in the world without being the best by any means. They charge 9^{tt} the bottle for it in the taverns of Strasbourg. It is the caprice of wealth alone which continues so losing an operation. This wine is sought because dear, while the better wine of Frontignan is rarely seen at a good table because it is cheap.

STRASBOURG. SAVERNE. PHALSBOURG. As far as Saverne, the country is in waving hills and hollows, red, rich enough, mostly in small grain, but some vines. A little stone. From Saverne to Phalsbourg we cross a considerable mountain which takes an hour to rise it.

April 19. PHALSBOURG. FENESTRANGE. MOYENVIC. NANCY. Asparagus to-day at Moyenvic. The country is always either mountainous or hilly, red, tolerably good, and in small grain. On the hills about Fenestrange, Moyenvic and Nancy are some small vineyards where a bad wine is made. No inclosures. Some good sheep, indifferent cattle and small horses. The most forest I have seen in France, principally of beech, pretty large. The houses, as in Germany are of scantling, filled in with wicker and morter, and covered either with thatch or tiles. The people too here, as there, gathered in villages. Oxen plough here with collars and hames. The awkward figure of their mould board leads one to consider what should be it's form. The offices of the mouldboard are to receive the sod after the share has cut under it, to raise it gradually and reverse it. The fore end of it then should be horizontal to enter under the sod, and the hind end perpendicular to throw it over, the intermediate surface changing gradually from the horizontal to the perpendicular. It should be as wide as the furrow, and of a length suited to the construction of the plough. The following would seem a good method of making it. Take a block whose length, breadth and thickness is that of your intended mouldboard, suppose 2½f. long and 8I. broad and thick. Draw the lines a. d. and c. d. Fig. 1. [*see Fig. 13*]. With a saw, the toothed edge of which is straight, enter at, a, and cut on, guiding the hind part of the saw on the line a. b. and the fore part on the line a. d. till the saw reaches the points b. and d. Then enter it at, c. and cut on, guiding it by the lines c. b. and c. d. till it reaches the points b. and d. The quarter a. b. c. d. will then be completely cut out, and the diagonal from d. to b. laid bare. The peice may now be represented as in fig. 2 [*see Fig. 13*]. Then saw in transversly, at every 2. inches, till the saw reaches the line c. e. and the diagonal b. d. and cut out the peices with a chissel.[26] The upper surface will thus be formed. With a gage opened to 8.I. and guided by the line c. e. scribe the upper edge of the board from d. to b. Cut that edge perpendicular to the face of the board and scribe it of the proper thickness. Then form the under side by the upper, by cutting transversely with the saw, and taking out the peices with a chissel.[26] As the upper edge of the share fin[27] rises a little, the fore end of the board b. c. will rise as much from a strict horizontal position, and will throw the hind end a. d. exactly as much beyond the perpendicular so as to ensure[28] the reversing of the sod.—The women here, as in Germany do all sorts of work. While one considers them as useful and rational companions, one cannot forget that they are also objects of our pleasures. Nor can they ever forget it. While employed in dirt and drudgery some tag of a ribbon, some ring or bit of bracelet, earbob or necklace, or something of that kind will shew that the desire of pleasing is never suspended in them.[29] How valuable is that state of society which allots to them internal emploiments only, and external to the men. They are formed by nature for attentions and not for hard labour. A woman

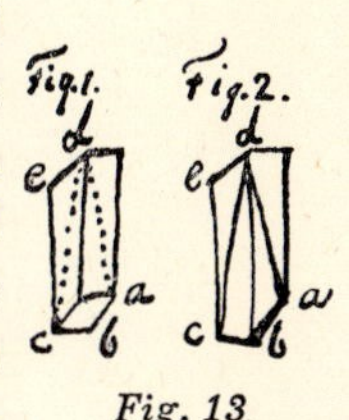

Fig. 13

never forgets one of the numerous train of little offices which belong to her; a man forgets often.

Apr. 20. NANCY. TOULE. VOID. LIGNY EN BARROIS. BAR LE DUC. ST. DIZIER. Nancy itself is a neat little town, and it's environs very agreeable. The valley of the little branch of the Moselle on which it is, is about a mile wide. The road then crossing the head waters of the Moselle, the Maes, and the Marne, the country is very hilly, and perhaps a third of it poor and in forests of beach. The other two thirds from poor up to midling, red, and stony, almost entirely in corn, now and then only some vines on the hills. The Moselle at Toul is 30 or 40 yds. wide, the Maese near Void about half that, the Marne at St. Dizier about 40. yds. They all make good plains of from a quarter of a mile to a mile wide. The hills of the Maese abound with chalk.[30] The rocks coming down from the tops of the hills on all the road of this day at regular intervals like the ribs of an animal, have a very singular[31] appearance. Considerable flocks of sheep and asses, and in the approach to St. Dizier great plantations of apple and cherry trees. Here and there a peach tree, all in general bloom. The roads thro' Lorraine are strung with beggars.

Apr. 21. ST. DIZIER. VITRY LE FRANÇAIS. CHALONS SUR MARNE. EPERNAY. The plains of the Marne and the Sault uniting, appear boundless to the eye till we approach their confluence at Vitry where the hills come in on the right. After that the plains are generally about a mile, mulatto, of middling quality sometimes stony. Sometimes the ground goes off from the river so sloping, that one does not know whether to call it high or low land. The hills are mulatto also but whitish, occasioned by the quantity of chalk[30] which seems to constitute their universal base. They are poor and principally in vines. The streams of water are of the colour of milk, occasioned by the chalk[30] also. No inclosures. Some flocks of sheep. Children gathering dung in the roads. Here and there a chateau, but none considerable.

Apr. 22. EPERNAY. The hills abound with chalk. Of this they make lime, not so strong as stone lime, and therefore to be used in greater proportion. They cut the blocks into regular forms also like stone and build houses of it. The common earth too, well impregnated with this, is made into mortar, moulded in the form of brick, dried in the sun, and houses built of them which last 100 or 200 years. The plains here are a mile wide, red, good, in corn, clover, Luzerne, St. foin. The hills are in vines, and this being precisely the canton where the most celebrated wines of Champagne are made details must be entered into. Remember however that they will relate always to the white wines unless where the red are expressly mentioned. The reason is that their red wines, tho much esteemed on the spot, are by no means esteemed elsewhere equally with their white, nor do they merit it.

A Topographical sketch of the position of the wine villages, the course of the hills, and consequently the aspect of the vine-yards.[32]

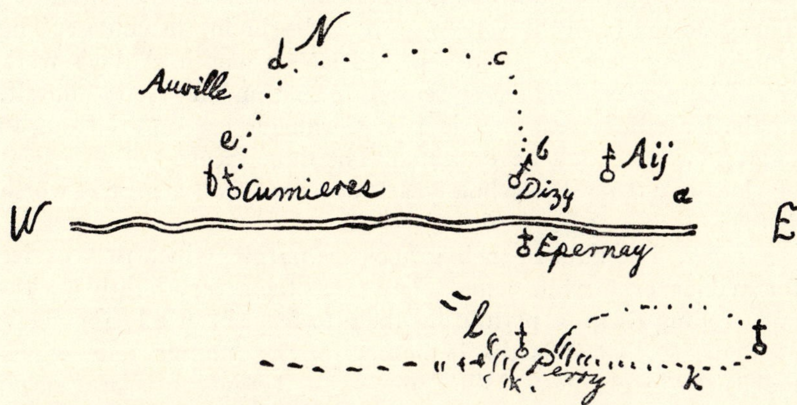

Soil. Meagre mulatto clay mixt with small broken stones, and a little hue of chalk. Very dry.

Aspect. May be better seen by the annexed diagram, observing that the wine of Aij is made from a. to b. Dizy b. to c. Auvillij d. to e. Cumieres e. to f. Epernay g. to h. Perry l. to k. The hills from Aij to Cumieres[33] are generally about 250f. high. The good wine is made only in the middle region. The lower region however is better than the upper because this last is exposed to cold winds and a colder atmosphere.

Culture. The vines are planted 2f. apart. Afterwards they are multiplied (provignés) when a stock puts out two shoots they lay them down, spread them open and cover them with earth so as to have in the end about a plant for every square foot. This operation is performed with the aid of a hook formed thus ϒ and 9.I. long which being stuck in the ground holds down the main stock while the labourer separates and covers the new shoots. They leave two buds above the ground. When the vine has shot up high enough, they stick it with oak sticks[34] of the size and length of our tobacco sticks and tie the vine to them with straw. These sticks cost 2^{tt} the hundred and will last 40. years. An arpent, one year with another in the fine vineyards gives 12. peices and in the inferior vineyards 25. pieces. Each piece is of 200. bottles. An arpent of the first quality sells for 3000^{tt} and there have been instances of 7200^{tt} (the arpent contains 100 verges of 22 pieds square). The arpent of inferior quality sells at 1000.^{tt} They plant the vines in a hole about a foot deep, and fill that hole with good mould to make the plant take. Otherwise it would perish. Afterwards if ever they put dung it is very little. During wheat harvest there is a month or 6. weeks that nothing is done in the vineyards. That is to say from the 1st. Aug. to the beginning of vintage. The vintage commences early in Sep. and lasts a month. A day's work of a labourer in the busiest season is 20s. and he feeds himself. In the least busy season it is 15s. Cornlands are rented from 4^{tt} to 24,^{tt} but vinelands never rented. The three façons[35] of an arpent of vines cost 15.^{tt} The whole year's expence of an arpent is worth 100.^{tt}

Grapes. The bulk of their grapes are purple, which they prefer for making even white wine. They press them very lightly (without treading them or permitting them to ferment at all) for about an hour, so that it is the beginning of the running only which makes the bright wine. What follows the beginning is of a straw colour and therefore not placed on a level with the first; the last part of the juice produced by strong pressure is red and ordinary. They chuse the bunches with as much care to make wine of the very 1st. quality as if to eat. Not above one eighth of the whole grapes will do for this purpose. The white grape, tho not so fine for wine as the red, when the red can be produced, and more liable to rot in a moist season, yet grows better if the soil be excessively poor, and therefore in such a soil it is preferred:[36] because there indeed the red would not grow at all.

Wines. The white wines are either 1. mousseux (sparkling)[37] or 2. non mousseux (still). The sparkling[37] are little drank in France but are alone[38] known and drank in foreign countries. This makes so great a demand and so certain a one that it is the dearest by about an eigth and therefore they endeavour to make all sparkling[37] if they can. This is done by bottling in the spring from the beginning of March to June. If it succeeds they lose abundance of bottles from 1/10 to 1/3. This is another cause encreasing the price. To make the still wine they bottle in September. This is only done when they know from some circumstance that the wine will not be brisk.[39] So if the spring bottling fails to make a brisk[39] wine, they decant it into other bottles in the fall and it then makes the very best still wine. In this operation it[40] loses from 1/10 to 1/20 by sediment. They let it stand in the bottles in this case 48. hours with only a napkin spread over their mouths, but no cork. The best sparkling[41] wine decanted in this manner makes the best still wine and which will keep much longer than that originally made still by being bottled in September. The brisk[39] wines lose their briskness the older they are, but they gain in quality with age to a certain length. These wines are in perfection from 2. to 10. years old, and will even be very good to 15. 1766 was the best year ever known. 1775. and 1776 next to that. 1783 is the last good year, and that not to be compared with those. These wines stand icing very well.

Aij. M. Dorsay makes 1100 peices which sell as soon as made at 300.ᵗᵗ and in good years 400 in the cask. I paid in his cellar to M. Louis his homme d'affaires for the remains of the year 1783. 3ᵗᵗ-10 the bottle. Brisk champaigne of the same merit would have cost 4.ᵗᵗ[42] (The piece and demiqueue are the same. The feuillette is 100. bouteilles.) M. le Duc 400 to 500 pieces. M. de Villermont 300. pieces. Mr. Janson 250. pieces. All of the 1st. quality, red and white in equal quantities.

Auvillij. Les moines Benedictins, 1000 peices red and white but three fourths[43] red. Both of the first quality. The king's table is supplied by them. This enables them to sell at 550ᵗᵗ the piece tho' their white is hardly as good as Dorsay's, and their red is the best. L'Abbatiale belonging to the bishop of the place 1000 to 1200 pieces red and white, three fourths red at 400.ᵗᵗ to 550.ᵗᵗ because neighbors to the monks.

Cumieres is all of a 2d quality. Both red and white 150ᵗᵗ to 200ᵗᵗ the piece.

Epernay. Mde. Jermont 200 pieces @ 300.ᵗᵗ—M. Patelaine 150 pieces. M. Marc 200 peices. M. Chertems 60 pieces. M. Lauchay 50 peices. M. Cousin 100 pieces (Aubergiste de l'hotel de Rohan á Epernay.) M. Pierrot 100 pieces. Les Chanoines regulieres d'Epernay 200. pieces. Mesdames les Urselines religieuses 100. pieces. M. Gilette 200.p. All of the 1st. quality red and white in equal quantities.

Pierrij. M. Casotte 500 pieces. M. de la Motte 300 pieces. M. de Failli 300 pieces. I tasted his wine of 1779 which was really very good,[44] tho not equal to that of M. Dorsay of 1783. He sells it at 2—10 to merchants and 3.ᵗᵗ to individuals. Les Semnaristes 150.p. M. Hoquart 200.p. all of 1st. quality, white and red in equal quantities. At Cramont also there are some wines of 1st.

quality made. At Avize also, and Aucy, Le Meni, Mareuil, Verzy-Verzenni. This last place (Verzy Verzenni)[45] belongs to the M. de Sillery, the wines are carried to Sillery and there stored, whence they are called Vins de Sillery, tho not made there.

All these wines of Epernay and Pierrij sell almost as dear as M. Dorsay's, their quality being nearly the same.[46] There are many small proprietors who might make all wines of the 1st. quality if they would cull their grapes: but they are too poor for this. Therefore the proprietors beforenamed, whose names are established buy of the poorer ones the right to cull their vineyards, by which means they increase their quantity, as they find about ⅓ of the grapes fit to make wine of the 1st. quality.

The lowest priced wines of all are 30ᵗᵗ the peice, red or white. They make brandy of the pumice. In very bad years when their wines become vinegar they are sold for 6ᵗᵗ the peice and made into brandy. They yield ⅒ brandy.

White Champaigne is good[47] in proportion as it is silky and still. Many circumstances derange the scale of wines. The proprietor of the best vineyard, in the best year, having bad weather come upon while he is gathering his grapes, makes a bad wine, while his neighbor holding a more indifferent vineyard, which happens to be ingathering while the weather is good, makes a better. The M. de Casotte at Pierrij formerly was the first house. His successors by some imperceptible change of culture have degraded the quality of their wines. Their cellars are admirably made, being about 6. 8. or 10f. wide vaulted and extending into the ground in a kind of labyrinth to a prodigious distance, with an air hole of 2.f. diameter every 50. feet. From the top of the vault to the surface of the earth is from 15. to 30f. I have no where seen cellars comparable to these. In packing their bottles they lay a row on their side, then across them at each end they lay laths, and on these another row of bottles, heads and points on the others. By this means they can take out a bottle from the bottom or where they will.

Apr. 23. Epernay. Chateau Thieray. St. Jean. Meaux. Vergalant. Paris. From Epernay to St. Jean the road leads over hills which in the beginning are indifferent, but get better towards the last. The plains wherever seen are inconsiderable. After passing St. Jean the hills become good and the plains increase. The country about Vert-galant is pretty. A skirt of a low ridge which runs in on the extensive plains of the Marne and Seine is very picturesque. The general bloom of fruit trees proves there are more of them than I had imagined from travelling in other seasons when they are less distinguishable at a distance from the Forest trees.

MS (ViWC); entirely in TJ's hand; portions of MS have been marked or crossed out by H. A. Washington, who used the original for printer's copy and indicated on it his directions to the compositor, a fact which may explain why a part of the MS is missing (see note 21). It is clear that this MS is a fair copy of two different rough drafts: one, which is missing, being devoted to the notes jotted down while TJ was in Amsterdam (and perhaps at The Hague), and the other to the return journey. Dft (MHi); bears the following caption on its otherwise blank page [1]: "Notes & notions on a journey from Paris to Amsterdam, thence up the Rhine to Strasburg & thence to Paris"—a caption evidently inscribed after his return to Paris. This Dft has on the verso of page [1] a series of vertical lines running the whole length of the page, and begins with the matter indicated in note 1, or that part covering the journey from Paris as far as Senlis, where TJ, in his haste to reach Amsterdam before Adams left, suspended his notes, resuming them on this page only when he departed from Amsterdam on the return journey on 30 Mch. 1788. When he resumed them in Dft, TJ found—as he had found on the journey to the south of France in 1787—that the tabular form was too inflexible for his needs, and also too wasteful of space for exact description; in consequence, the notes for the return journey, which begin in Dft immediately below the reference to Senlis, are in running form and go across the vertical lines. The manuscript of this return journey—referred to here as Dft because TJ obviously composed it en route—is, especially in its pages covering the vineyards of the Moselle, the Rhine, and the Marne, exceedingly crowded, rearranged, and written in TJ's most minuscule hand. While Dft agrees with MS in substance, the former is more highly abbreviated, varies somewhat in spelling, is less carefully punctuated, has portions of its text crossed out and rewritten for greater clarity, and the sequence of subject-matter altered by complicated deletions, insertions, and enclosed passages keyed by alphabetical references to other parts of the text. Some of these variants are indicated in the notes below, the most interesting of which reveals the fact that TJ observed wooded paths along the Bergstrasse mountains that he thought might be adapted for use at Monticello. The missing rough draft of the "notions," jotted down in Holland and copied in MS between the reference to Senlis and the notes of the return journey, clearly anticipates in substance the nature of the loose memoranda that TJ kept more or less systematically after his return to America and ultimately called "Anas," for it includes not only observations about things of a mechanical or architectural interest, but also records of conversations, such as that with Adams about the origin of the Society of the Cincinnati, or of comment on individuals, such as that (possibly provided by Dumas but more likely by Jacob van Staphorst) concerning the attitudes of Amsterdam bankers.

TJ's travel journals of 1787 and 1788, like *Notes on Virginia*, continued to grow and to serve different purposes long after the first object had been met—memoranda on Parmesan cheese, canals, wines, rice, mechanical arts, and agriculture continued to be culled from these repositories of useful information and adapted to new ends. Both journals were drawn upon for the memoranda that TJ wrote from time to time advising friends in America about their purchases of European wines. Both also furnished the basis for the hurried but remarkably cogent hints that TJ forwarded, somewhat apologetically, to young Shippen and Rutledge for their guidance in travels through northern and southern Europe. Indeed, those hints need to be taken as an additional dimension of the journals of 1787 and 1788, for they incorporate much that was still fresh in TJ's memory but not actually recorded in the journals themselves (see TJ to Shippen, 19 June 1788, where these notes are printed as an enclosure)—for example, the reference to the steeple at Strasbourg. The present journal records, too, the stimulus provided by THE AWKWARD FIGURE OF

THEIR MOULD-BOARD which prompted TJ to consider what its form should be and how to devise a method for making it—a subject that continued to challenge him over a period of many years (Betts, *Farm Book*, p. 47-64). An illustration in this volume reproduces for the first time TJ's preliminary sketches for an improved mouldboard, jotted down on the back of a memorandum of expenses between Strasbourg and Meaux—the region in which TJ observed the awkward form of the peasants' plows. The fact that AXIS IN PERITROCHIO was a somewhat pedantic expression is proved not only by TJ's lapsing into the familiar usage in the same context, but also by the fact that a contemporary, Maria Edgeworth, though admitting that the expression was used in writings on mechanics, stated that "the word windlass or capstan would convey a more distinct idea to our pupils" (*Practical Education*, London, 1822, II, 121). The PLANS DETAILED IN THE MOOLEN BOOK I BOUGHT evidently were those found in Johannis van Zyl's *Theatrum Machinarum Universale; of Groot Algemeen Moolen-Boek* (Amsterdam, 1761), a copy of which was owned by TJ (Sowerby, No. 1179). A modern version of the VIBRATING ferry on which TJ crossed the Rhine near Essenberg, or PENDULUM boat as he expressed it elsewhere, is still employed in that vicinity: the rather imperfect analogy of its principle to that of the pendulum may be seen when it is noted that the ferry itself represents the bob, and that the cable, supported by a string of boats on the upstream side of the ferry with the one farthest away being securely anchored in midstream, corresponds to the rod of the pendulum; the oscillation from bank to bank, is caused by the force of the current operating against the side of the ferry, the movement of which is determined by manipulation of cables so that either end of the ferry can be presented at an oblique angle to the direction of the current. TJ's reference, under date of 5 Apr. when he was in the neighborhood of Coblentz, to A JESSAMINE IN CT. DE MOUSTIER'S GARDEN being in leaf is puzzling; it refers, of course, to Moustier's garden in Paris, not to one on the Rhine or Moselle, but, while it is understandable that he would wish to record the fact under the date of leafing, it is not clear why he inserted the fact in both the Dft and MS of his travel journal, even if, as presumably was the case, he learned of it through a letter received when he arrived at Strasbourg (such a letter is not known, though it may have been in one of the letters that Martha promised to write—no letters survive to show that she did so—or in Short's missing letter of 8 Apr. 1788). For the ANNEXED BILL OF PRICES CURRENT for wines produced on the left bank of the Rhine (DLC), see illustration in this volume.

There is a miscellany of documents in MHi that pertain to the journey to Holland and that, like TJ's letters and his notes of advice to Shippen and Rutledge, amplify and add much of interest to the journal itself. These consist of some 54 pages of documents bearing this endorsement in TJ's hand: "Tavern bills, memorandums, addresses &c on a journey through the Low countries Germany and eastern parts of France March and April 1788." The most informative of these items is a rough state of travel expenses, copied later by TJ into his Account Book and to be printed in Second Series, showing, among other things, his exact route and whereabouts from the time of leaving Paris on 4 Mch. to the time of arrival back there on 23 Apr. Supplementing this record and forming about half of the miscellany are bills for lodging, meals, coach hire, and various purchases made in the following places (texts in French, Dutch, English, and German): Moerdyk, Rotterdam, The Hague, Amsterdam Düsseldorf, Cologne, Coblentz, Mainz, Frankfort, Karlsruhe, and Strasbourg. Another group consists of printed trade cards of inns at Brussels (Hôtel d'Hollande, printed in French and English), Mainz (The Three Crowns, printed in German, French, and English), Meaux (Grand Hôtel Royal), and Epernay (Hôtel du Palais Royal); of Gerard Walter, merchant at Strasbourg and dealer in fine furniture, objets d'art, &c.; and of La Libraire Academique of Strasbourg, specializing in French and German books. A final group in this miscellany consists of itineraries, estimates, &c.: one, probably furnished by Jacob van Staphorst before TJ left Paris, advised about the route from Paris to Amsterdam by way of Antwerp, Rotterdam, and The Hague; another (in TJ's hand) listed alternate routes and the time required; and the last, also probably furnished by Staphorst, suggesting routes, distances, costs, and inns from Amsterdam by way of the Rhine valley to Strasbourg (with notes made by TJ along the route, much of which is incorporated in TJ's journal, or Account Book, or his advice to Shippen and Rutledge).

See also, Marie Kimball, *Jefferson: The Scene of Europe*, p. 218-41; Edward Dumbauld, *Thomas Jefferson: American Tourist*, p. 110-22.

[1] Dft has one additional column, headed, "people," and one entry under this heading, "villages." At the upper righthand corner of Dft, TJ wrote, "Miscellanea."

[2] No beginning quote in MS.

[3] Dft resumes at this point.

[4] Dft reads: "taste."

[5] Dft reads: "planted 1 foot apart."

[6] The drawing in Fig. 7 and the words in brackets (supplied) are not in MS and are taken from Dft. Evidently TJ decided that his suggested improvement, which certainly provided better lateral bracing, was not of sufficient interest to be recopied in MS.

[7] The following is deleted in Dft at this point: "The wine on the North side the Rhine is best, because less exposed to cold winds than that on the South. Their good wines can not be drank till 15. or 20. years old. They are kept to that age by the rich seigneurs and then sold. A peice of 1200 French bottles sells at that age for 1000 florins (of Holld.) but if found exquisite, for double that price. The monasteries also keep it to be old for sale. Hocheim is the strongest but not the most delicate. Rudelsheim is the most delicate. The very best of that quality belongs to the monks of Erbach." It is possible that TJ made these notes in Dft on the basis of conversations he had in Cologne and deleted them, substituting more detailed information, after he made his own observations in the Rheingau (see text under 11 Apr. where some of this deleted matter is incorporated).

[8] Dft reads: "reinforcements."

[9] The passage "Cologne is a sovereign city . . . in 51.° Lat." is at this point in Dft, but keyed by a footnote to the place it occupies above.

[10] In Dft at this point TJ drew merely the outline of the floor plan of the ruin in Hagley Park. In the margin of Dft he drew two other floor plans with indications of interior partitions, doors, and stairs in one of the turrets. These are the drawings represented in Fig. 11, the upper one of which is the only one that was copied in margin of MS. From this it is plain that when TJ and Adams climbed the long hill at Hagley, they went all the way to the "ruinated castle" at the summit, entered its ground floor, and took the stairs to the top of one of the turrets.

[11] Dft reads: "There is a centry box covered," &c.

[12] Dft reads: "fine."

[13] Last three words not in Dft.

[14] Preceding eight words not in Dft.

[15] Both in MS and in Dft TJ left a blank for the name of the town preceding this symbol and a blank for the symbol following Berlin, as if two separate places and two separate symbols were involved. If this was, in fact, what he supposed, he was in error, for this mark is that of Wilhelm Caspar Wegeli of Berlin (Eberlein and Ramsdell, *The Practical Book of Chinaware*, New York, 1925, p. 187-90).

[16] At this point in Dft TJ began setting down the information he had assembled on Rhenish viticulture; he later deleted and rearranged these passages, incorporating the information in his notes under 11 Apr.; the rewritten text agrees with MS as printed here.

[17] Following this Dft has: "Mantz."

[18] Dft reads: "at least."

[19] Following this Dft reads: "as we sometimes practice in Virginia."

[20] Dft reads: "mulatto, rich, in corn," &c.

[21] The following interesting sentence is interlined in TJ's most minuscule hand: "The paths on some parts of these mountains give me the idea of making paths on Monticello and Mont Alto as represented in the margin." MS ends at this point and the remainder of the text is printed from Dft. An extensive search has failed to locate these pages of MS, although it was complete at the time that H. A. Washington printed the full text in his edition of TJ's writings (HAW, IX, 373-403). The portion of MS extant in ViWC has Washington's instructions to the printer written at the head of the first page and in the margins of other pages. It is possible, therefore, that the rest of the MS was lost by the printer. From this point on the text of Dft has been compared with Washington's text (re-

ferred to as HAW) and some of the variations have been noted.

22 The following is deleted in Dft at this point: "to the mountains of Lorrain and Alsace which separate the waters of the Rhine and Moselle."

23 HAW reads: "flues."

24 HAW reads: "breadth."

25 TJ deleted "now" in Dft.

26 HAW reads: "adze."

27 HAW reads: "wing of the share."

28 HAW reads: "promote."

29 In HAW the rest of this paragraph reads as follows: "It is an honorable circumstance for a man, that the first moment he is at his ease, he allots the internal employments to his female partner, and takes the external on himself. And this circumstance, or its reverse, is a pretty good indication that a people are, or are not at their ease. Among the Indians, this indication fails from a particular cause: every Indian man is a soldier or warrior, and the whole body of warriors constitute a standing army, always employed in war or hunting. To support that army, there remain no laborers but the women. There, then, is so heavy a military establishment, that the civil part of the nation is reduced to women only. But this is a barbarous perversion of the natural destination of the two sexes. Women are formed by nature for attentions, not for hard labor. A woman never forgets one of the numerous train of little offices which belong to her. A man forgets often."

30 This word interlined in substitution for "gypsum," deleted.

31 HAW reads: "irregular"; this is certainly an error of transcription on the part of the editor.

32 This caption is not in Dft, but is taken from HAW, IX, 398, which in turn derived it from the missing latter part of the fair copy. In Dft at this point TJ wrote: "[here insert them.]," referring to a separate leaf on which the details concerning the wines of Champagne are set forth on its two pages, at the top of the first of which occurs the diagram, followed by the notes as here presented, which are inserted (as TJ intended and as the missing part of the fair copy must have had them) between this point and the final paragraph beginning "Apr. 23. EPERNAY," &c.

33 The phrase "from Aij to Cumieres" is not in HAW.

34 HAW reads: "with split sticks of oak, from an inch to an inch and a half square, and four feet long, and tie the vine to its stick with straw."

35 HAW reads, following this: "(or workings)."

36 HAW reads: "preferred, or rather, is used of necessity, because."

37 TJ first wrote "frothy," substituted "brisk," and then finally chose "sparkling."

38 HAW reads: "almost alone."

39 HAW reads: "sparkling."

40 This word not in Dft; supplied from HAW.

41 This word written in substitution for "brisk," deleted.

42 HAW reads: "Sparkling Champagne, of the same degree of excellence, would have cost four florins."

43 TJ first wrote, and then deleted, "the greater part," substituting "three fourths."

44 HAW reads: "one of the good years. It was fine, though not equal," &c.

45 Closing parenthesis supplied.

46 Preceding four words are drawn from HAW; Dft, owing perhaps to TJ's need to crowd every word into an exceedingly limited space, making this one of the most microscopic passages in all his writings, seems to leave the sentence incomplete with this reading: "their quality the same if nt."

47 HAW reads: "is deemed good."

From Benjamin Vaughan

DEAR SIR Jeffries Square London, April 5, 1788.

I have the honor to inclose a letter written at the time of its date, but which I have since had transcribed on account of an alteration I have since made in my sentiments. The letter was delayed to allow me time to make experiments, which I have not been able to accomplish.

I send the hygrometer I describe in it, somewhat doubtful however of its success. I have the pleasure to add another, invented by Mr. De Saussure, and executed by Messrs. Nairne and Blunt. The outer rim of the circular brass plate turns round and serves as a standard index.

I am doubtful whether I sent or you received one of the thermometers I take the liberty to allude to within. If you have not, I shall beg to be allowed the honor of sending you one.— In thermometers it is of advantage to see the thread with quickness and at a distance, and these two advantages seem obtained by the little artifice I describe.

With the above hygrometers, I take the liberty to send Dr. Crawford's book on Animal Heat and Combustion; and seven numbers of a new work to which you are, unknown to yourself, a contributor.

Lord Wycombe has been returned to us some time. It gives me extreme pleasure to find that both himself and Lord Lansdown Speak with respect and even considerable sensibility of your attentions to him, which will not easily be forgotten I hope on either side.

I have the honor to be, With great respect & esteem, Dear sir, Your most obedt. & most humble servt.,

Benjn. Vaughan

I have marked on the wooden hygrometer its position in a north room in London without a fire, and up one pair of stairs, on the 5th. of April, 1788. It has been made about 15 or 16 months.

The little slider to the magnet box I had the pleasure to forward, was too *long* by a trifle for its place; owing I suppose to the *sides* of the case having shrunk after making.

RC (DLC); endorsed. Enclosure: Vaughan to TJ, 26 Jan. 1787, which, with its covering letter, the two hygrometers, the book, and the periodical, arrived while TJ was in Germany (TJ to Vaughan, 23 July 1788).

The SEVEN NUMBERS OF A NEW WORK were Nos. i-vii of *The Repository* (1 Jan.–1 Apr. 1788), issued in London by Vaughan himself "or under his auspices" (Sir Samuel Romilly, *Memoirs*, London, 1890, I, 97); No. v, p. 336-7, contained what purported to be an extract of TJ's letter to Stiles, 1 Sep. 1786, but what was actually a full reprinting of the text, save for the opening sentence. Issue No. vii contained a comment on the "new Method of copying or multiplying Writings and Drawings, lately discovered in Paris, as mentioned in Mr. Jefferson's Letter"; the writer of this comment concluded that "those who know it, justly think it not a very extraordinary improvement" (p. 387), but, since it might be thought "of singular use in particular cases," he proceeded to describe Hoffman's invention of polytype printing—"or at least a process capable of performing" what TJ had described. The process set forth was a form of offset printing produced by putting reverse images, freshly struck from an intaglio plate, under pressure and in contact with wet paper—but this was not Hoffman's method (see Vol. 10: 321). Stiles had permitted TJ's letter to get into print (see note to Stiles to TJ, 30 Apr. 1788).

CRAWFORD'S BOOK: *Experiments and Observations on Animal Heat, and the Inflammation of Combustible Bodies; being an Attempt to resolve these Phenomena into a General Law of Nature*, by Adair Crawford (1748-1795). This work was first published in 1779; TJ's copy of the second edition (London, 1788), sent to him by Vaughan, is in DLC (Sowerby, No. 842). John Henry Petty, second marquis of Lansdowne, was LORD WYCOMBE; he was the eldest son of the first marquis of Lansdowne, better known as Lord Shelburne (DNB). "During 1789 and 1790 he [Shelburne] was kept carefully informed of everything that passed in Paris, not only by his old correspondent, Morellet, but by his eldest son Lord Wycombe, by Benjamin Vaughan, who made more than one journey at this period to the French capital, and by Dumont, who had gone thither to be by the side of his friend Mirabeau, and to assist him with his own invaluable political knowledge, during the crisis of French liberty" (Lord Edmond Fitzmaurice, *Life of William, Earl of Shelburne, afterwards first Marquess of Lansdowne*, London, 1876, III, 484). See also TJ to Wycombe, 25 July 1789. TJ also received information from Wycombe, as the following MS memorandum in DLC: TJ Papers, 36: 6195 testifies:

"An account of the nett produce of all the taxes of Great Britain, received from Lord Wycombe

	1786. July 5—Oct. 10			1787. July 5—Oct. 10		
Stamps	£306,095	4s.	5d¼	£340,593	10	8
Customs	1,337,005	9	9 ½	1,361,473	7	7¼
Excise	1,500,463	7	11 ¼	1,708,358		
Incidents	309,779	0	11 ¾	353,509	0	3
	3,453,343	3	1 ¾	3,763,933	18	6¼

Another state from the Cour. de l'Europe Dec. 18. 1787			
Douane	4,172,341	7	11½
Accise	6,156,797	4	9½
Timbre	1,168,236	16	7
Casuels	1,892,879	11	8½
Terres & malts	2,614,000	0	0
	16,004,255	1	0½
Total expences from May 10. 1780 to May 10. 87	15,500,000	0	0
Surplus	504,255	1	0½."

From Francis Hopkinson

DEAR SIR Philada. April 6th. 1788

It is a very long Time indeed since I have had the Satisfaction of a Line from you. Mr. Rittenhouse had a Letter last Fall in which you mention some Books to have been forwarded for him in a Package address'd either to me or Dr. Franklin, but those Books have not come to hand. I have another Gathering of Magazines, Museums, and News Papers for you, waiting a suitable opportunity.—We are in a high political Fermentation about our new proposed federal Constitution. There are in every State People who have Debts to pay, Interests to support, or Fortunes to make. These wish for scrambling Times, paper Money Speculations or partial Commercial advantages. An effective general Government will not suit their Views, and of Course there are great oppositions made to the new Constitution, but this opposition chiefly arises from a few leading Party Men in the Towns and Cities who have been very industrious in holding it up as a political Monster to the multitude who know nothing of Government and have gained many Proselytes in the back Counties.—The Lees and Mr. Mason have so exerted themselves in Virginia as to make the Determination of that State doubtful. Maryland is infected with a Mr. Martin, but I am told the Constitution will be adopted there. We shall know in a few Weeks. The Convention met in New Hampshire and adjourned to sometime in June. The City of New York is federal, but the Country much opposed, under the Influence of Govr. Clinton. Altho' Pennsylvania has long since adopted the proposed System, yet in no State have the People behaved so scandalously as here. George Bryan and his Party (formerly called the Constitutional Party) have been moving Heaven and Earth against the Establishment of a federal Government. Our Papers teem with the most opprobrious Recitings against the System and against all who befriend it. These Scriblers begin with Arguments against the proposed Plan such Arguments as would stand with equal Force against every or any Government that can be devised. They were Arguments against Government in general as an Infringement upon natural Liberty. They then poured forth a torrent of abuse against the Members of the late general Convention personally and individually. You will be surprized when I tell you that our public News Papers have announced General Washington to be a Fool influenced and lead by that Knave Dr. Franklin who is a public Defaulter for Millions of Dollars, that Mr. Morris has defrauded the Public out of many Millions as you please and that they are to cover their frauds by this new Government. What think you of this. Some of the Authors of these inflamatory Publications have been traced, and found to be men of desperate Circumstances. I had the Luck to discover and bring forward into public View on sufficient Testimony the Writer of a Series of abominable abuse, under the Signature *Philadelphiensis*. He is an Irishman who came from Dublin about 3 Years ago and got admitted as a Tutor in Arithmetic in our University. I am now under the Lash for this Discovery, scarce a Day passes without my Appearance in the News Paper in every scandalous Garb that scribling Vengeance can furnish. I wrote also a Piece stiled *The new Roof* which had a great Run. I would send you a Copy but for the Postage. You will probably see it in some of the Papers as it was reprinted in I believe every state.

I am sorry to tell you that our friend Mr. Rittenhouse is antifederal. However we never touch upon Politics. Dr. Franklin is as well as usual.

My Mother desires her Love to your Daughter, to which add my affectionate Regards.

I have long had it in Contemplation to establish a Wax Chandlery here and if I can get some Gentleman to join me in the Scheme, as I believe I shall, I will make the Trial. My Circumstances require some Exertion. I know of nothing so promising. Let me have your Opinion. If I determine upon it I shall request you to send over a Master Workman to superintend the Factory. Be so good as to enquire and inform me, what Capital would be requisite for such a Project, in the large Way. I shall depend much on your Encouragement. Yours ever, F. HOPKINSON

RC (DLC); endorsed.

The author of the SERIES OF ABOMINABLE ABUSE—a violent attack on the "haughty lordlings of the convention" who had already proclaimed "the chains of despotism . . . firmly rivetted"—was one James Workman, who warned the people in the 19 Dec. 1787 issue of the *Independent Gazetteer* that the "days of a cruel Nero approach fast"; that "the language of a monster, of a Caligula, could not be more imperious" than that of the "*well-born and their parasites*" of the Convention; and that, worse than anything George III had done, "self-important nabobs" had carried on "diabolical plots, and secret machinations" ever since the revolution to destroy the people's liberties. This intemperate production of an instructor at the University of Pennsylvania was made the object of Hopkinson's allegorical satire called "The New Roof," which appeared in the *Penna. Packet* for 29 Dec. 1787 and was widely reprinted. At a dinner party in Williamsburg, George Wythe supposed Hopkinson to be the author and Gouverneur and Robert Morris, who were present, concurred; the last made the obvious comment in a letter of 21 Jan. 1788 to Hopkinson that "there always appear some Characteristic Marks in your writings that disclose the Fountain from whence they spring" (quoted in Hastings, *Hopkinson*, p. 400). Hopkinson's allegory, however, was more important as a defense of the constitution than as a satire of Workman, and in this respect probably influenced contemporaries as well as historians to exaggerate the defects of the Confederation. In "The New Roof" the Confederation was a great house in need of a new roof after only twelve years and, what was worse, as the consulting architects discovered, was weak in its whole structure: there were thirteen rafters, but these "were not connected by any braces or ties, so as to form a union of strength"; they were in part "thick and heavy" and in part "slight"; and, having been put together "whilst the timber was yet green," they had become badly warped—some outward, bearing an undue proportion of weight, and some inward, bearing no weight at all. More, "the shingling and lathing had not been secured with iron nails, but only wooden pegs [*paper money, as Hopkinson had to explain*], which swelling and shrinking by successions of wet and dry weather, had left the shingles so loose, that many of them had been blown away by the wind." The "cornice"—presumably the Continental Congress—was "so ill proportioned, and so badly put up, as to be neither an ornament nor of use." Finally, "the roof was so flat as to admit the most idle servants in the family, their playmates and acquaintances, to trample upon and abuse it" (same, p. 398). Hopkinson explained the last to mean a lack of dignity in government, but this really begged the question: this part of the allegory could scarcely mean anything else than an attack upon the levelling process and a defense of the aristocratic principle, an attitude that led Hopkinson and other contemporaries (even Moustier, the newly-arrived French minister) as well as historians to denigrate to an unjustifiable extent the calibre of members of the Continental Congress during the latter part of its existence—a period that certainly included non-entities but also included such men as James Madison, Alexander Hamilton, John Langdon, and others of genuine stature. But "The New Roof" was all the more effective as a weapon for the Federalists because of its graphic oversimplifications which reduced a great political concept to everyday terms.

From John Rutledge

DR. SIR Charleston April 6. 1788

Having considered the Idea which you suggested, of my Son's going (after visiting Paris, London, and Amsterdam) to Madrid, Lisbon and Italy, I have, this day, written to him, advising to adopt that Plan.

I thank you, most cordially, for the very great Attention and Friendship, with which (as he has repeatedly inform'd me) you have been pleased to honour him, and request a Continuance of your Goodness and Favour to him, which, I am persuaded, he will endeavour to merit. I have the Honour to be with great Esteem Dr. Sir yrs. Sincerely, J. RUTLEDGE

RC (DLC); endorsed.

From William Short

MY DEAR SIR Paris April 6th. 1788

Your letter of March 29. arrived here yesterday. I see that you have received all the letters I have written. I have not been so fortunate. Your first (from Leyden) never reached me. Yours from Amsterdam of the 13th was the first I received.

I have heard no complaints from the convent and consequently suppose your daughters are perfectly well. I know they were so some days ago.

Letters by the French Packet arrived here the latter end of last month. Papers came by her as late as the 20th. of Feb. Everything seems to be going on well. Massachusetts has accepted the constitution by a majority of 19. in a convention of 335. The acceptation was solemn and honorable. The leading members of the minority declared the matter had been fairly canvassed and that although they had hitherto opposed, they would in future support, the constitution and engage their constituents to do the same. The convention after accepting the constitution in the terms proposed, recommend certain alterations. At present six states have accepted the constitution, six others called conventions, and the thirteenth (R. Island) has its assembly I believe now sitting.

Boats have already passed from Westham to the navigation below the falls. This work has been accomplished much sooner than was expected. Mayo's bridge advances also, 150 feet have been laid down and answers perfectly as the newspapers say.

The Packet brought also the information of Count de Moustier's arrival at N. York. I saw Mr. Grand to-day and desired him to mention to Mr. Dupont the circumstance you speak of. I communicated to him at the same time the part of your letter respecting him. It seemed to give him great pleasure.

Cyrus Griffin is President of Congress! Hamilton, a member from N. York. Some think this a favorable symptom in so antifederal a State, as he is a federal man.

Genl. Washington writes to the Marquis de la f. that there no longer remains any doubt of the constitution being accepted by at least nine States.

A *Conseil de marine* is at length appointed here. They are for the most part obscure names, none I believe known to you, unless it be a M. du fresne, who was the Marechal de Castries' right hand.—I do not send this letter to Frankfort because it is too late. It will be directed consequently to Strasburg, where I hope you will find it; I received the bill of exchange of 2400[tt] and shall have it disposed of as you direct. No Plants have yet arrived from Virga. Poor Banister is in a great deal of distress. His father has lost his senses. Nobody knows why, supposed by many on account of his deranged affairs, and it is said that his son's expences in Europe increased their disorder. You may judge how miserable such an idea must render such a man. Adieu my dear Sir, I hope we shall soon have the pleasure of seeing you here. All your friends desire it but none more than your friend & servant, W SHORT

RC (DLC); endorsed, in part: "recd. at Strasbourg Apr. 16." PrC (DLC: Short Papers).

The letter from GENL. WASHINGTON to Lafayette was written on 10 Jan. 1788 when only Delaware, Pennsylvania, and New Jersey had ratified the Constitution: Washington thought New England would "cheerfully and fully accept it" (aside from Rhode Island, "which seems itself, politically speaking, to be an exception from all that is good"), and that the southern states would do the same. In Virginia and New York he considered "its fate . . . somewhat more questionable: though, in my private opinion, I have no hesitation to believe there will be a Clear majority in its favor, in the former." Washington concluded that "the highest probability exists that the proposed Constitution will be adopted by more than nine States, at some period early in the coming summer" (Washington, *Writings*, ed. Fitzpatrick, XXIX, 376-77).

To Jean Jacques Peuchen

à Francfort sur Maine ce 7me Avril 1788.

Les attentions, Monsieur, que vous eutes la bonté de me faire pendant les peu de moments que j'eus le bonheur de passer avec vous a Cologne, m'encouragent de vous demander encore une grace. Vous vous rapellerez peut-etre que, pendant notre promenade, nous sommes entrés dans le magazin d'un marchand de poëles en fer fondu, et qu'il y avoit, dans la piece qui donnoit [dehors ?] une poële, dont la forme me frappoit particulierement. C'étoit en piédestal surmonté d'une partie de colonne, et couronné d'une vase antique. Si cette poële n'est pas déjà vendue, je souhaiterois d'en faire l'acquisition. Pour vous la faire rapeller plus surement, j'observerai encore que c'étoit celle dont vous avez demandé le poids, et le marchand repondit que ce pourroit peser environ 300 livres, et qu'il les vendoit à quatre sous et demi la livre. A coté de celle-là il y avoit encore une autre, plus petite, en piedestal aussi, surmonté d'une piece de colonne, et couronné d'une buste d'homme. Si, au-lieu de cette buste d'homme, le marchand substitueroit une vase telle qu'il y a sur l'autre, je la prendrois volontier aussi.—Je les trouvai plus agreables, ces deux poëles-là, sans dorure, que celles qui étoient dans la chambre interieure et qui etoient dorées. La grace que je vous demande donc, Monsieur, c'est d'acheter pour moi ces deux poëles, et de les faire expedier à Amsterdam à l'adresse de Messrs. Nichs. & Jacob Van Staphorst, qui paieront à votre ordre le montant du prix &c. La lettre que j'ai l'honneur de vous remettre sous cette enveloppe vous assurera ça. Le Marchand les fera mettre sans doute dans des fortes caisses avant de les expedier. Je vous prie de me pardonner la peine dont j'ose vous charger et d'agréer le renouvellement des assurances de consideration et d'attachement avec lesquelles j'ai l'honneur d'etre Monsr. votre très humble & très obeisst. serviteur,

TH: JEFFERSON

PrC (MHi). Enclosure: TJ to N. & J. van Staphorst, same date.

To Nicolas & Jacob van Staphorst

GENTLEMEN Francfort sur Maine April 7 1788.

Having asked the favour of Mr. Peuchen, merchant at Cologne, to send me a couple of stoves which I saw there, and which I have described to him in a letter of this date, I have taken the liberty of assuring him you will pay for me his draught on you for the amount, and that you will be so good as to receive and forward them to me to the care of Mr. Limozin merchant at Havre de grace. This favour I have therefore to ask of you, and farther that when you shall have sent them off for Havre you will be so kind as to notify it both to Mr. Limozin and myself, by a short line addressed on that subject.

I have the honour to be Gentlemen Your most obedt. & most humble servant, TH: JEFFERSON

PrC (DLC).

From John Paul Jones

SIR Copenhagen April 8. 1788.

By my Letters to the Count de Bernstorff, and his Excellency's Answer, you see that my Business here is at an end.—If I have not finally concluded the Object of my Mission, it is neither your fault nor mine: The Powers I received are found insufficient, and you could not Act otherwise than was prescribed in your Instructions. Thus it frequently happens, that good Opportunities are lost, when the Supreme Power does not place a sufficient confidence, in the distant Operations of Public Officers, whether Civil or Military. I have, however, the melancholy satisfaction to reflect, that I have been received and treated here, with a distinction far above the pretentions of my Public Mission; and I felicitate myself sincerely on being, at my own Expence, and even at the peril of my Life, (for my sufferings, from the inclemency of the Weather, and my want of proper means to guard against it on the Journey, were inexpressible; and I beleive, from what I yet feel, will continue to affect my Constitution) the Instrument to renew the Negociation between this Country and the United-States: The more so, as the honor is now reserved for you, to display your great Abilities and Integrity, by the completion and Improvement of what Dr. Franklin had wisely begun. I have done then, what, perhaps, no other person would have undertaken, under the same circumstances; and while I have the consolation to hope, that the United-States will derive solid advantages, from my Journey and efforts here, I rest perfectly satisfyed, that the Interests of the Brave Men I commanded, will experience in you Parental attention, and that the American Flag can loose none of it's lustre, but the contrary, while it's Honor is confided to you. America being a Young Nation, with an increasing Commerce, which will naturally produce a Navy, I please myself with the Hope, that in the Treaty you are about to conclude with Denmark, you will find it easy, and highly advantageous to include certain Articles, for admitting America into the Armed Neuterallity. I persuade myself before hand, that this would afford pleasure to the Empress of Russia, who is at the Head of that noble and humane Combination; and as I shall now set out immediately for St. Petersburg, I will mention the Idea to her Imperial Majesty, and let you know her Answer.

If Congress should think I deserve the Promotion, that was proposed when I was last in America, and should condescend to confer on me the Grade of Rear Admiral, from the Day I took the Serapis (23 Sept. 1779) I am persuaded it would be very agreeable to the Empress; who now deigns to offer me an equal Rank in her Service, although I never yet had the honor to draw my Sword in her Cause, nor to do any other Act that could, directly, merit her Imperial benevolence. While I express, in the warm effusion of a grateful Heart, the deep sense I feel of my eternal obligation to you, as the Author of the honorable prospect that is now before me, I must rely on your Friendship to justify to the United-States, the important Step I now take, conformable to your Advice. You know I had no Idea of this new Fortune, when I found that you had put it in train, before my last return to Paris from America. I have not forsaken a Country, that has had many disinterested and difficult Proofs of my steady Affection; and I can never renounce the glorious Title of *a Citizen of the United States*!

It is true I have not the express permission of the Sovereignty, to accept the Offer of her Imperial Majesty: Yet America is Independent, is in perfect Peace, has no public employment for my Military talents, and yeilds me no emolument or profit whatever from the Commission I hold.[1]—But why should I excuse a conduct, which I should rather hope, would meet with general approbation? In the latter part of the Year 1782 Congress passed an Act for my Embarkation in the Fleet of his most Christian Majesty. And when, a few Months ago, I left America to return to Europe, I was made the bearer of a Letter to his most Christian Majesty, requesting me to be permitted to embark in the Fleets of Evolution. Why did Congress pass those Acts? To facillitate my improvement, in the Art of conducting Fleet and Military Operations. I am then, conforming myself to the views of Congress; but the Roll alloted me, is infinitly more high, and difficult than Congress intended. Instead of receiving Lessons, from able Masters, in the Theory of War, I am call'd to immediate Practice; where I must command in Chief, conduct the most difficult Operations, be my own Preceptor, and instruct others.—Congress will allow me some Merit in daring to encounter such multiplied difficulties. The Mark I mentioned, of the approbation of that honorable Body, would be extremely flattering to me in the Career I am now to pursue, and would stimulate all my Ambition, to acquire the necessary Talents, to merit that and even greater favors, at a future Day.—I pray you, Sir, to explain the circumstances of my situation, and be the interpreter of my Sentiments, to the United-States in Congress. I ask for nothing; and beg leave to be understood only as having hinted, what is natural to conceive, that the Mark of approbation I mentioned, could not fail to be infinitly Servicable, to my views and Success, in the Country where I am going.

The 4. The Prince Royal sent me a Messenger, requesting me to come to his Appartment. His Royal Highness said a great many civil things to me, told me the King thanked me, for my attention and civil beheaviour to the Danish Flag, while I commanded in the European Seas; and that his Majesty wished for occasions to testify to me his personal Esteem. I was alone with the Prince half an hour.

I am, with perfect Esteem and sincere Regard, Sir, Your most obedient and most humble Servant, J PAUL JONES

RC (DLC: Personal Papers Misc.); endorsed by TJ and docketed in a clerk's hand; the RC begins in the middle of the page and is preceded by the end of the Tr of Bernstorff's letter to Jones of 4 Apr. 1788 (see enclosure 4), certified by Jones, on 4 Apr. 1788, as a true copy; this indicates that the transcripts (missing) of all the letters forwarded by Jones to TJ were probably written on continuous sheets at the head of this RC. Enclosures: (1) Tr of Jones to Bernstorff, 24 Mch. 1788, asking for a prompt decision from the court on the purpose of his mission because it is necessary for him to return to Paris or proceed to Russia (Tr in DNA: PCC, No. 87, II, in the hand of William Short; PrC of the preceding in DLC). (2) Tr of same to same, 30 Mch. 1788, repeating his request for a prompt decision (Tr in DNA: PCC, No. 87, II, in the hand of William Short). (3) Tr of Jones to Bernstorff, 5 Apr. 1788, (written before the receipt of Bernstorff's letter of 4 Apr.) stating that Jones expects to leave Copenhagen as soon as he receives a formal letter from Bernstorff confirming the statement made by the latter—that is, that Jones's want of plenary powers to make an ultimate disposition of the matter had caused the Danish court to authorize Baron de Blome to negotiate concerning the three prizes with TJ at Paris and at the same time to conclude a treaty of commerce between Denmark and the United States (Tr in CSmH, Jones Papers, certified by Jones and containing the notation copied by Short, as indicated below; Tr in DNA: PCC, No. 87, II, in Short's hand; PrC of same in DLC: TJ Papers). Between enclosures 3 and 4 in Short's Tr there is the following notation taken from Jones's Tr of his letter of 5 Apr.: "The three foregoing letters of 24, and 30 March and 5 April are exact copies of what I had the honour to write to the Count de Bernstorff. (signed) J Paul Jones.—N.B. After the above letter had been delivered to the Minister, the subsequent answer was received from his Excellency." (4) Tr of Bernstorff to Jones, 4 Apr. 1788, stating that, in response to Jones's request for an answer to the letter he had delivered from TJ, he has been authorized to pledge the king's word that negotiations for a treaty of amity and commerce would be renewed, on the basis of the forms already agreed upon, as soon as the new Constitution should be adopted; that, as stated in conversation, Jones's want of full powers from Congress presented a natural and insuperable objection to a definitive discussion of this primary object or even of the secondary object concerning the prizes; and that, moreover, it would be improper and contrary to all received usage to change the place of a negotiation from Paris to Copenhagen, since that negotiation had not been broken but only suspended (Tr, in French, DLC: Jones Papers, certified by Jones as a true copy on 29 Aug. 1788; Tr in DNA: PCC, No. 87, II, in the hand of William Short, accompanied by a translation by John Pintard; PrC of Short's Tr in DLC: TJ Papers. All of the enclosures are printed in *Dipl. Corr., 1783-89*, II, 152-5, and, again, III, 718-21, where Bernstorff's letter appears in a different translation).

1 The preceding thirteen words have been deleted in MS; it is very doubtful whether this was done by Jones or by TJ; possibly it was done by John Henry Sherburne, to whom TJ lent his recipient's copies of Jones' letters and who printed the present letter in his *Life of John Paul Jones*, Washington, 1825, p. 297-9.

From William Short

[*Paris, 8 Apr. 1778.* Recorded in SJL Index. Not found.]

From André Limozin

Le Havre, 9 Apr. 1778. Acknowledges TJ's letters of 3 and 27 Mch.; the latter informs him that TJ is having the Van Staphorsts ship three boxes containing "Iron works" costing 13 guilders; "a Wooden Screw press for Letters" costing 18 guilders, both of which may be imported; and "China ware such as Cups for tea, Coffee and Chocolate" which cannot be imported. Suggests that the Van Staphorsts "require the Master to take all that China out of the box, and to get it in his Lockers, as for his Cabbins use," so means can be found "to get it ashore by Small parcells." Capt. Oldener, "a British Master Sailing under american colors altho his owners live in Scotland," brought "two large Cases of Seeds" and trees for TJ from Portsmouth, Va., Limozin endeavored to have the articles landed at Le Havre but, the ship's cargo being destined for Dunkerque, the seeds and trees were carried to that place.

RC (MHi); 4 p.; addressed to TJ at Amsterdam; endorsed.

To William Short

Dear Sir Frankfort on the Maine April 9. 1788.

I arrived here on the 6th. inst. having been overtaken at Cleves by the commencement of a storm of rain hail and snow which lasted to this place, with intermissions now and then. The roads however continued good to Bonne, where beginning to be clayey and to be penetrated with the wet they became worse than imagination can paint for about 100 miles which brought me to the neighborhood of this place where the chaussee began. My old friend the Baron de Geismar met me here, on a letter I had written him from Amsterdam, and has been my Cicerone. It happens to be the moment of the fair of Frankfort which is very great. Yesterday we made an excursion up the Maine to Hanau, passing the ground where the battle of Bergen was fought in the war before last. Tomorrow we shall go to the vineyards of Hocheim, and perhaps to Rudesheim and Johannesberg, where the most celebrated wines are made. Then I shall pass on to Mayence, Worms, Manheim, Heidelberg and Spires, and from this last place to Strasburg. Unless I find there any thing from you which may call me to Paris directly, I shall probably go a little circuitously, perhaps by the way of Reims in Champagne, so that I am unable to say exactly when I shall be at Paris. I guess about the 20th. I met at Hanau with many acquaintances, the officers who had been stationed in Albemarle while in captivity. I have seen much good country on the Rhine, and bad whenever I got a little off of it. But what I have met with the most wonderful in nature is a set of men absolutely incorruptible by money, by fair words or by foul: and that this should, of all others, be the class of postillions. This however is the real character of German postilions whom nothing on earth can induce to go out of a walk. This has retarded me not a little: so that I shall be glad to be delivered over to the great jack boots.

The neighborhood of this place is that which has been to us a second mother country. It is from the palatinate on this part of the Rhine that those swarms of Germans have gone, who, next to the descendants of the English, form the greatest body of our people. I have been continually amused by seeing here the origin of whatever is not English among us. I have fancied myself often in the upper parts of Maryland and Pennsylvania. I have taken some measures too for realizing a project which I have wished to execute for 20 years past without knowing how to go about it. I am not sure but that you will enter into similar views when I can have the pleasure of explaining them to you at Paris. Being too long for a letter, and having already given you a sufficiency of egoismes, for want of other subjects I shall conclude with assurances of the esteem & attachment with which I am Dear Sir your affectionate friend & servt., TH: JEFFERSON

RC (ViW); endorsed. PrC (DLC).

From James Monroe

DEAR SIR Richmond April 10. 1788.

I must depend on your kindness to pardon my omission in not writing you oftener, for I will not pretend to justify it. I should have wrote you as before, and can give no satisfactory reason even to myself why I have not, for that my communications will not be of much importance I do not urge as an excuse. I will however make amends in future. The real pleasure of my life, which consists in being at home with my family, has been interrupted by an attendance at the bar and service in the legislature since I left N.Yk. Altho' neither of these employments has many allur'ments in it, yet I think the latter rather a more uncomfortable one than the former. Perhaps however I obtain'd a seat in it, at a very unfortunate period, both as to publick affairs and my own temper of mind. I doubt whether I can enumerate to you the several acts which pass'd the last assembly at present; I mean those that are worthy of note: the most material however were those respecting the revenue, and the Judiciary department: of the general court after this term, nothing is left but the name, and in its stead 18. district courts are establish'd. Each district court bears the same relation to the county courts within it that the general court did to all the counties within the Commonwealth. Over these is organis'd the court of appeals, consisting of the Judges of all the courts (4. additional having been added to the general court, Prentis, Tucker, Parker and G. Jones the latter of whom having declin'd acceptance White has been appointed in his room) with similar powers over the district that they have over the county courts: 3. Judges form a district court. The plan is I believe unpopular with the former Judges, and is most probably highly defective. It is however not improbable the puting the matter in motion may produce some beneficial effects. Tis presumeable the Judges may examine the subject themselves, for I hear some of them doubt the practicability of its execution as the law now stands, and suggest such amendments as they think necessary. The reduction of the number of districts to ⅓. would perhaps be greatly for the better. The taxes are reduc'd, those on slaves under 12. and on white male tithables are repeal'd. The Convention of this State is to meet in June to take up the report from Phila. The people seem much agetated with this subject in every part of the State. The principal partizans on both sides are elected. Few men of any distinction have fail'd taking their part. Six States have adopted it, N. Hampshire the 7th. that took the subject up adjourned untill late in June with a view it is presum'd, to await the decision of those States who postpon'd their meeting to the latest day as Virga. N. Yk. and No. Carolina, and from that circumstance suppos'd least friendly to it. The event of this business is altogether incertain, as to its passage thro the Union. That it will no where be rejected admits of little doubt, and that it will ultimately, perhaps in 2. or three years, terminate, in some wise and happy establishment for our country, is what we have good reason to expect. I have it not in my power at present to commit to cypher any comments on this plan but will very soon, I mean concisely as to its organization and powers: nor to give you the arrangement of characters on either side, with us. I write by Colo. Carrington and he leaves this immediately. It will give me infinite pleasure to hear from you occasionally. My county has plac'd me among those who are to decide on this question; I shall be able to give you a view of its progress that may be interesting to you. Can you command my services in any instance? Are you in health, how happend the dislocation of your wrist and is it well? I think I mention'd to you in my last Mrs. M. had made us happy by giving us a daughter who is now 16. months old and begins to talk. I hope Miss Patsy and Polly are well. I shall write you again soon and am affectionately your friend & servt.,

JAS. MONROE

Present my respects to Mr. Short.

RC (DLC); endorsed.

From Jacob Vernes

hôtel de Dannemark rue Neuve St. Augustin

MONSIEUR Paris le 10 avril 1788.

J'ai obtenu de M. le Controleur General une conférence composée des mêmes personnes qui se trouvoient à celle d'Octobre dernier, dans laquelle on éxaminera et l'on décidera si la ferme a rempli fidèlement l'engagement de la décision de Bernis, d'après le mémoire imprimé pour le port de L'orient que j'ai eu l'honneur de vous remettre. Le Ministre avoit bien voulu m'accorder cette conférence pour le 16 de ce mois, mais M. le Marquis de La Fayette et Mr. Short m'ayant dit que vous devez être à Paris seulement le 20 de ce mois, comme il est très important, sous divers rapports, que Vôtre Excellence puisse se trouver à cette conférence, je suis convenu avec M. Short que je prendrois la liberté de vous écrire pour vous demander le jour précis auquel vous arriverez à Paris. J'ai prié M. de Lambert de vouloir bien prendre un jour qui soit plus éloigné que le 20, parce que c'est du 15 au 18 que Mr. de La Fayette croit que vous devez arriver.

Je vous aurai, Monsieur, beaucoup d'obligation, si vous voulez avoir la bonté de m'écrire un mot sur ce jour de votre arrivée. J'aurai l'honneur de voir sur le champ vôtre Excellence et de vous communiquer ce qui s'est passé pendant votre absence.

Je suis avec respect Monsieur Votre très humble & très obeïssant serviteur,

VERNES

RC (DLC); endorsed in part: "recd at Strasbourg Apr. 16."

The MÉMOIRE IMPRIMÉ that Vernes had sent to TJ was almost certainly enclosed in a letter he wrote on 18 Feb. 1788 which is recorded in SJL Index but has not been found; Vernes had sent a copy of it to Montmorin three days earlier (Vernes to Montmorin, 15 Feb. 1788; Arch. Aff. Etr., Paris, Corr. Pol., E.-U., Vol. XXXIII; transcripts in DLC). This *Mémoire*, a formidable document, was principally the product of Vernes' pen, as indicated in the editorial note to the documents on the American tobacco trade, printed above (Vol. 12: 76-93), but it was also a document drawn up in close consultation with TJ and Lafayette (see Vernes to TJ, 13 Nov. 1787). It represents a culmination of the discussions of the preceding autumn among Lambert, Lafayette, TJ, Vernes, and others. For this reason it is here summarized as Document III in the following group of closely-connected documents.

Further Documents Concerning American Trade

I. JEFFERSON'S SUPPRESSED ARTICLE IN HIS OBSERVATIONS ON CALONNE'S LETTER OF 22 OCT. 1786

II. RAPPORT SUR LE COMMERCE DES ETATS-UNIS DE L'AMERIQUE AVEC LA FRANCE, FAIT A MONSIEUR LE CONTROLEUR GENERAL LE 15 OCTOBRE 1787

III. MEMOIRE POUR DES NEGOCIANS DE L'ORIENT, INTERESSES AU COMMERCE DES ETATS-UNIS; CONTRE LA FERME GENERALE

EDITORIAL NOTE

The preceding letter and the following documents present further aspects of the thoroughgoing investigation of American trade in general and the tobacco trade in particular that Lambert insisted upon when he became controller-general. This was carried out by Lambert, as Jefferson was careful to indicate in his *Observations on the Whale-Fishery*, "with a patience and assiduity almost unexampled" and with a determination by the minister to investigate every detail necessary in order to "assure himself that the conclusions of the Committee [leading up to the decision of Berni] had been just." This was high praise from one whose industry in this matter, as in all others, was unflagging and far above the capacity or the aim of most men.

As indicated in the Editorial Note to the documents on the American tobacco trade printed above under 3 Sep. 1787 and in the note to the preceding letter of 10 Apr. 1788 from Vernes, Jefferson was intimately connected with developments in the tobacco situation, which Lafayette had described to Lambert in September as being "très urgent" and of which these documents are a product. Though his diplomatic position required him to avoid a conspicuously responsible part as author or compiler, Jefferson nevertheless exercised a direct and traceable influence upon these documents. So, of course, did Lafayette, who in September had suggested that Lambert call together such members of the Committee on American Commerce as La Boullaye, Le Noir, Boyetet, Dupont, and others (Lafayette to Lambert, 10 Sep. 1787, printed as enclosure to Lafayette to TJ, 18 Sep. 1787). Lafayette, Vernes, and Jefferson were certainly included among those present with Lambert in the fall of 1787 and, as Vernes' preceding letter makes clear, the same group was called together again in the spring of 1788 by the controller-general. By the time Jefferson returned from Holland, he was faced with further developments in the old struggle with the farmers-general over tobacco, and also with a new problem for the American whale fishery that had grown out of that struggle.

The first of the following documents bears a close resemblance to the argument in Vernes' *Mémoire* (Document III) concerning the trade with Irish and Scottish smugglers, in that Jefferson looked upon the African tobacco trade as another branch of commerce that might be used in the same way to augment American tobacco trade with French ports. This document never saw the light of day, however, for in his Observations on Calonne's letter, Jefferson suppressed it as the sixth point that, in his draft, he intended it to be. Montmorin saw only the text of the Observations as printed above (Vol. 11: 539-42), and at the time the MS was thus printed the Editors believed it to be the whole of Jefferson's comments; however, there has subsequently come to light the additional text presented here as Document I. This text exists in only one copy which, as the notes to it indicate, was separated from the leaf to which it belongs, perhaps by Jefferson himself, and has remained unidentified ever since. It is not clear why Jefferson suppressed it, though it was perfectly characteristic of him to confine the Observations to the briefest limits possible (cf. his letter to Vergennes of 15 Aug. 1785 and his *Observations on the Whale-Fishery*), and this may have been the sole or principal reason for its deletion.

Jefferson's Observations on Calonne's letter, accepting it as being "conclusive as to the articles on which satisfactory information had then been obtained," reopened in mid-summer the question of certain other articles "needing further inquiry." This brought under review by the ministry the general subject of American trade, which had been one of the instructions given to Moustier, the new French minister to the United States. While Moustier waited for a fresh wind at Brest in early October, Montmorin sent him his instructions and promised to forward the report on commerce the moment he received it from the controller-general: "vous savez," he added, "qu'elle doit renfermer le resultat d'un comité qui a eu pour objet de determiner les avantages que la france peut accorder au commerce Américain" (Montmorin to Moustier, 13 Oct. 1787; Arch. Aff. Etr., Paris, Corr. Pol., E-U.; transcripts in DLC). Moustier, who told TJ he had hoped his leaving Paris would speed up the decision to produce a general arrêt on American commerce, waited impatiently—and vainly—in the hope that he would be able to bear the decision to America (Moustier to TJ, 19 Oct. 1787). But the report on which Lambert based his findings was not submitted to him until mid-October, a few days before Moustier was obliged to sail, and the thorough minister took another six weeks studying it and preparing on the basis of it his letter to Jefferson of 29 Dec. 1787 and its enclosed arrêt.

This report (Document II) has been attributed to Boyetet, but he clearly could not have written such an analysis of French commercial policy for the eyes of the controller-general when it contained two very complimentary references to another memoire that he had unquestionably written—and one, incidentally, that restated and elaborated an idea proposed by Jefferson to Vergennes on 15 Aug. 1785 and later advanced by Lafayette as well. The reason for this mis-attribution is made clear by the physical make-up of the manuscript (see note to Document II). The author was certainly identified with the general position assumed by Jefferson and Lafayette and his recommendations were all that either of them could have asked. It was probably prepared by Pierre Samuel Dupont. Both Dupont and Boyetet were members of the Committee on American Commerce and both were *commissaires généraux pour les relations du commerce extérieur*, Dupont for the Northern commerce (where most of the American tobacco was received) and Boyetet for the Southern. Though both were in the same department and were in general agreement on the need of commercial reform, they took opposing positions with respect to the treaty of commerce between England and France of 1786, which Dupont promoted and Boyetet denounced. In the midst of Boyetet's extremely intemperate and public attacks, Dupont wrote him a remarkably kind and even affectionate letter, a fact which may take on significance in light of the tributes paid to Boyetet's memoire in Document II. Dupont was certainly closer to the free trade views of Turgot and Quesnay than was Boyetet (René Stourm, *Les Finances de l'Ancien Régime et de la Révolution*, Paris, 1885, II, 32ff.). Dupont and Jefferson were also intimate friends, and it was Dupont who had summarized the findings of the Committee on American Commerce for presentation at the meeting held at Berni in May 1786. Perhaps the best reason for attributing the authorship to him, however, is the fact that it was Jefferson who procured from La Boullaye, *Intendant* of the farmers-general, the statement of purchases of tobacco made by the farmers-general which he forwarded to Dupont about a fortnight before the report was presented to Lambert (TJ to Dupont, 6 Oct. 1787). Jefferson also sent the same statement to Vernes, and copies of it are annexed both to the report that the Editors think was written by Dupont and to the *Mémoire* that was unquestionably prepared by Vernes. If their attribution is correct, it is not surprising that the general conclusions support Jefferson's arguments in every respect. Indeed, in regard to the principle of reciprocity, the report recommends the adoption of Jefferson's argument as being appropriate and beneficial for the whole of French commercial policy. The developing conflict in the spring of 1788 over French policy respecting American commerce, and Jefferson's place in that conflict, cannot be properly understood without a knowledge of the fact that the new controller-general's thoroughgoing investigation brought forward a report whose general tenor, conclusions, and even phraseology were appropriated by Lambert in his letters to La Boullaye of 23 Oct. 1787 (Vol. 12: 259-62) and to Jefferson of 29 Dec. 1787. The latter and its enclosed arrêt, thus grounded on documents with the preparation of which Jefferson was so closely connected, reflect also his Observations on Calonne's letter, presented to Montmorin on 3 July 1787. In view of this it is perhaps not going too far to suggest that Jefferson was in effect, though not, of course, in a literal sense, part author of the letter to himself that was signed by the controller-general.

While the report naturally devoted a more prominent place to the tobacco trade than to that of any other commodity, both because of its magnitude and because of its "très urgent" situation in the fall of 1787, the passages on the privileges to be granted the American whale fishery came to have increasing significance in the spring of 1788. The attack on these privileges, with vigorous and responsive leadership within the ministry, began almost before the arrêt containing them was issued, resulting in the amending arrêt of 22 Feb. 1788 which, under the guise of an effort to curtail the right of *entrepôt*, struck a sly blow at the American fisheries. The connection between this hostility to the favors granted American fisheries generally and the special privileges granted to William Rotch & Sons, Nantucket whalemen who had settled a few "Nantuckois" at Dunkirk, has not been established, but it is certain that the favored position of the house of Rotch would have been impaired by these general provisions. For the period subsequent to the arrêt of 22 Feb. 1788, then, one of the most significant features of the report is its declaration that the general privileges to American fisheries were less disadvantageous to France than were those of a special character granted to the Nantucket firm, a declaration that prepared Lambert to set his face against new appeals made by Francis Rotch in May 1788, which he did effectively (see notes to TJ to Jay, 23 May 1788, and to TJ's *Observations on the Whale-Fishery*, under 19 Nov. 1788).

It was Jacob Vernes of the prominent tobacco firm of Jean Jacques Bérard & Cie. who bore the brunt of work in preparing the *Mémoire* (Document III; see also note to Vernes to TJ, 10 Apr. 1788). This document was completed sometime between 8 Jan., when the Avocat Perignon delivered his opinion, and 15 Feb. 1788, when Vernes sent the full printed text to Montmorin with this observation: "comme ces reclamations et leurs motifs sont intimement liés avec de très grands intérets de l'Etat, comme la détermination actuelle du Gouvernement va décider si nos rapports avec les Etats-Unis formeront une branche d'industrie languissante ou un commerce avantageux et brillant, j'ose solliciter de votre bonté une attention particulière à la décision de cette affaire que la situation des Négocians françois et Américains qu'elle intéresse, rend très pressante pour eux" (Vernes to Montmorin, 15 Feb. 1788, Arch. Aff. Etr., Paris, Corr. Pol., E.-U., Vol. XXXIII; transcripts in DLC). This appeal was reinforced by the Estates of Brittany who on the same day urged Montmorin's consideration of the need for protection for the merchants of L'Orient against the bad faith of the farmers-general. Their memorial was, in actual fact, little more than a recapitulation of the *Mémoire* and reaffirmed in other terms the several recommendations made in that document, concluding by urging upon the ministry considerate attention to the legitimate claims of the merchants and to "les Bornes de l'Independance de la ferme" as questions already decided by the resolutions of Berni "et enfin par la lettre de Mr. le Controlleur G[éné]al au Ministre americain du 29. Xbre dernier qui regle l'achapt des tabacs et promet de nouveau l'Execution de la Décision" (same). There can be little doubt that Lafayette, who had identified himself with the claims of the nobles of Brittany in the Assembly of Notables of 1787, and who would shortly again do so under dramatic circumstances (Gottschalk, *Lafayette, 1783-89*, p. 294, 387-92), helped engineer this powerful support for the attack on the farm.

Because of the length and repetitive nature of Documents II and III, which in large part form a stage in the development of the attack on the farmers-general beginning with Jefferson's letter of 15 Aug. 1785, these two documents are summarized rather than printed in full. But in the making of these summaries, no material facts or observations have been omitted that are not accounted for editorially (e.g., the documents which form the Appendix of the *Mémoire*). Direct quotations are employed, at times extensively, when the passages are not repetitive of facts or observations readily available elsewhere in this edition; and the phraseology of the summaries is in fact more nearly the authors' words in translation than they are the words of the Editors, though at times, for the sake of brevity, the Editors have selected a particular statement as illustrative or as summing up a longer passage.

I. Jefferson's Suppressed Article in His Observations on Calonne's Letter

6. It is reckoned that this nation employs 30. ships in the African trade, and that these take, one with another, 50 hogsheads of tobacco in part of their loading. The regulations for the protection of the farms forbidding them to take this tobacco from the ports of France, they are obliged to put into Lisbon, and there furnish themselves with the tobaccos of Brazil. It would seem that Magazins d'entrepot established in the principal ports[1] might be placed under such cautions of double keys &c. as to expose the farmers to no danger. This would save to France freight and commission on that quantity of tobacco, paiment in cash instead of commodities, and the deviation of 30 ships from the route of their voiage by putting in to Lisbon. It would at the same time and in the same proportion augment the demand for the tobaccoes of the United states.

MS (DLC); undated, but ca. 4 July 1787; endorsed by TJ, possibly at a later date: "Entrepots for tobo. for Africa." This fragment was once the lower part of the final sheet of TJ's Observations on Calonne's letter concerning American trade (see text, Vol. 11: 539-43), but it was detached from the MS (now at ViWC) probably by TJ in the course of composition, since the RC sent to Montmorin does not include it. No evidence remains on the top half of the sheet to show that the present fragment was a continuation of its text, but an examination of the PrC made from MS (ViWC) and to be found in DLC: TJ Papers, 25: 6203-7, shows that TJ also tore away the lower half of *its* final sheet, but in such a way as to leave remnants of easily identifiable ascenders of the letters in the passage: "6. It is reckoned that. . . ." Thus, aside from the continuance of the sequence of numbers and the substance, which prove that it belongs to TJ's Observations as originally written, this PrC contains a sort of catchword that keys it to the present fragment, which is widely separated from the MS to which it was originally appended (being now at TJ Papers, 233: 41598).

[1] Deleted at this point: "of the Atlantic."

II. Rapport sur le Commerce des Etats-Unis de l'Amérique avec la France

15 Oct. 1787

[*Introduction*:] The freedom of the United States and "la juste reconnaissance qu'ils ont dû concevoir pour la France à cette occasion" seemed to promise an expanded commerce between the new republic and its first ally. But this takes place slowly. Our fiscal arrangements, our laws and treaties, the complicated forms that have been used so long in the collection of duties, the variety of our tariffs, the restrictions imposed on most of our manufactures have slowed up and in many respects annihilated the effect of the reciprocal good will between the two nations. Although commerce of United States was worth 72 to 75,000,000^{tt} before the war, of which we could hope to have the better part, we are very far from receiving it.—Our traders have made some efforts, the Americans have had good will, the government has made some sacrifices, but expectations have not been realized, chiefly because too many branches of government operate separately on this commerce and because they have not been able to establish an effective and harmonious center for their operations. A committee of the Council has made a great study of this commerce, and some important decisions have been reached. These have been announced by government to Congress, along with the intention of taking up other matters on which decisions have not been reached. Yet both French and American merchants complain that promises made in the name of the king have not been met, and they press for decisions on the objects not yet determined. Whatever the plan may be that government will adopt to harmonize the different branches of administration involved in this commerce, it cannot be doubted that both political engagements and the national interest require "que l'on pourvoie provisoirement aux choses dont les Etats-unis d'Amérique auraient à se plaindre."

The object of this Mémoire is to point these out and to make known also what still remains to be desired for the mutual advantage of the two nations. The report will be divided into three parts: (1) The first will deal with the tobacco trade; the principal branch of American commerce; its history since the peace; the work of the committee; the resultant decision of the ministry; the complaints of merchants concerning its non-execution; the response of the farmers-general to these complaints; and the necessity of avoiding in future the tragic consequences of a total suspension of commerce. (2) The second will deal with other branches of American commerce on which the work of the Committee has led to a decision; the decision itself given and notified in the name of the king; the complaints that have risen on the ground that the promises contained in it were not executed: the question whether these promises were of a dangerous sort, what advantages they promised, and whether any of them are susceptible of modification. (3) The third will deal with objects on which no decisions have been reached. Each of these will include in full the acts and documents which must receive the attention of government, in order that this report may present "le recueil complet de tout ce que le Ministère peut avoir à lire ou à rechercher sur cette Matiere."

PART I. The American tobacco trade is subjected in France to a monopoly that is not even enjoyed by merchants—a purely fiscal monopoly whose agents can purchase only with money, which the sellers are free to use in this or neighboring countries for return cargoes. This position, unfavorable to a reciprocal commerce and unattractive to "les envoys de l'Amerique, a été empirée par une circonstance qui a excité beaucoup de réclamations."

When peace was declared, the farmers-general, having no supplies on hand, calculated that the needs of the Americans would force them to yield an abundant supply at low price. "Une politique assez Naturelle lui fit feindre de n'avoir pas de grands besoins." They gave no encouragement to the first captains to arrive with cargoes of tobacco, even treating them "avec une sorte de rigueur." The latter grumbled and went on to England. In America, the supply failed because of the war, the burning of warehouses, and the scarcity of cargo vessels. The farmers-general, forced to meet the demand, bought some cargoes at a considerable price, and made a contract with Alexander that could not be filled. An American house at L'Orient [*Williams & Bérard*] offered to supply its need at the average price of 42.^{tt} per quintal. Then, just as the return of planters to cultivation and the beginning of peace promised abundance of tobacco at low prices, Robert Morris proposed to furnish 20,000 hhds. per year for three years at an average price of 36.^{tt} This was below the market price in Europe, in consideration of which he obtained an advance of a million livres, plus a reduction from the legal tare of 15% to the real tare of 10%, which concealed under his apparent price of 36.^{tt} the hidden price of 37.^{tt} 16s. This advance enabled Morris to depress the price of tobacco, to take terms for final payment, and to carry on his commerce almost without spending a penny. The engagement of the farmers not to buy American tobacco from any one else, directly or indirectly, enabled Morris to give law to the American planters in respect to all tobacco destined for France, or a fourth of their total harvest. It was this exclusive privilege that "choqua principalement les Cultivateurs Américains, les Etats de Virginie, de Maryland et le Congrès." The French consuls in America remonstrated. The American minister to France and the Marquis de Lafayette pointed out that it was bad enough for the commerce of the two countries to have a company enjoy a monopoly of the sale in France and that it would be too much to give to an individual the monopoly of the purchase in America. "Ces reclamations exprimées avec force" drew the attention of the minister of foreign affairs who actively pressed the minister of finance to form a Committee to discuss the steps to be taken concerning this contract with Morris. The Committee was formed, held its first meeting 8 Feb. 1786, discussed a great number of questions, received from Lafayette a plan for a simple impost and tax on tobacco sold that would return to the king a revenue equal to that derived from the monopoly. This plan, also suggested by M. Jefferson and elaborated by M. Clavière, is based chiefly on the example of England and is still too far removed from the principles and established usages of our country to justify any hope that it could be adopted by government. It will require long discussion, reflection, and experience in eradicating the inconveniences believed to be inherent in the plan before even tentative approaches can be made to it. This monopoly on the sale of tobacco must, then, for the present be regarded as "une donnée invincible" on which it is necessary to arrange combinations and speculations in this branch of trade. Some bold and imaginative financiers [*in margin*: "Idée de M. Faulze"] have thought that the power resulting from the monopoly itself could enable France to engross the whole American tobacco trade by quadrupling her purchases and reselling the surplus to other nations. Their plan succeeded no more than the other. It can be expected that for a long time to come the existing arrangement will continue, with the farmers-general the only real buyers supplying what is actually needed and paying for it in specie. "On ne s'écartera pas de ce point de Vue dans la suite de cette exposition." Some important ideas presented to the Committee were premature and can be passed over; but those that led to results will be detailed. The contract with Morris was laid before the Committee.[1] . . . One of the first things that struck the

Committee was that the use of American and French cargo vessels was not required by this contract, but only given a simple expression of preference which compelled nothing: this was regarded as a grave defect. It was also noted that no obligation rested on Morris to take in return French produce and merchandise, and it was brought out that he was paid in bills of exchange on London, whence he took in return British merchandise. The farmers-general say that they had engaged Morris to make an experiment with French goods and that he had agreed to do so to the extent of 250,000.[tt] They offered to give bounties to other American traders whose tobacco they would buy *à prix défendu* and who would take French goods in return. The draft of an arrêt was prepared on this proposition, but it was abandoned because, as was noted, if the price was not regulated, the farmers would make the bounty illusory by passing its cost on to the merchant in the form of low bids, whereas, if the price were fixed, with the same tare as that allowed Morris, the farmers could not be required to pay the bounty since this would make such purchases even higher than those obtained of Morris, which were already too dear.—A merchant of L'Orient, present with the Committee, pointed out that the advantages given to Morris rendered illusory the seemingly low price he had offered, and he showed that the price of tobacco since the making of the contract had fallen, resulting in a loss to the farmers-general of one-sixth of the value of their purchases. In consequence, this loss to the king and the company deprived the royal treasury of 500,000[tt] per year and each farmer-general of about 12,000[tt] income. Yet the farmers-general who had made the contract actively opposed the cancellation that the interest of their company and the general view of the Committee seemed to demand. The Committee pointed out that Morris had in 1785 and up to that time delivered only a third of what he had promised, and thus the contract could be cancelled because of non-performance on his part. The farmers who had made the contract nevertheless still thought that the national honor required its being upheld. Morris' agent pointed out that he had advice of shipments that would almost complete the first year's quota; and although four and a half months remained of the first year, counting from the date of signing the contract in Europe, the majority felt that the first year could only begin with the signing in America, and thus Morris could not be charged with having failed in his engagement. Various means were proposed to keep the Morris contract from depriving other merchants and American planters of outlets in

France for their tobacco. The report of these measures and the different opinions of the Committee concerning them were made by M. Dupont at the extraordinary meeting held at Berni 24 May 1786. presided over by the minister of foreign affairs and the controller-general. This report is here inserted.[2] . . . The different opinions on the six proposals presented at Berni were set forth at great length, finally resulting in a decision "qui est devenu la Loi que l'on doit suivre et qui a été notifié Ministeriellement par ordre du Roi aux Etats-unis et inséré dans les Papiers publics. Il est très important de placer ici cette décision."[3] . . . This decision was officially announced to the farmers-general, to the American minister to France, to the French minister in America, and was published "dans toutes les gazettes Américaines."

Today the French and American merchants declare that, on the faith placed in this decision, great quantities of tobacco were shipped to France and the farmers-general paid for a considerable amount of it at inferior prices. The farmers-general countered with a statement from 1 Jan. 1786 to 3 Sep. 1787 of purchases which they believe supports the conclusion that they have more than fulfilled their obligation under the Berni decision. It shows that in this period 22,124 hhds. were purchased by the farm, of which only 13,033 fell under the terms of the Berni decision, and in consequence 9,091 were bought *à prix défendu*. The following observations on this were made by both French and American merchants.

They say that the decision led planters and merchants to believe that 12 to 15,000 hhds., or an average of 13,500, would be bought per year, or 1,124 per month, and their tobacco would be received and paid for on the same prices and conditions as those established for Morris; that on this expectation they made contracts and shipments; that nevertheless the figures of the farm itself show purchases of only 13,300 hhds. in fourteen months, or 931 hhds. only per month purchased in accordance with the terms of the decision; that, therefore, they fell short of their obligations by 2,727 hhds. They add that this account nevertheless favors the farmers-general because: (1) the list of purchases includes many lots bought in English trade and brought to France, whether from England or from America, in English vessels, which is "précisement contraire à l'esprit et à la lettre de la décision de Berni"; (2) the decision has not been faithfully executed in respect to the tare, since a legal tare of 15% applies to general commerce, while only 10% is borne by Morris. They say also that 3,650 hhds. of those reported by the farm were bought at Marseilles or Sète, which have no connection with the Berni decision nor to the engagement it produced, since Morris' contract did not extend to the Mediterranean supply as that had always been and must remain free; that, deducting these from the 19,683 hhds. purchased since the agreement, there remained a total of 16,033 hhds. apparently but not really purchased according to their promise, for a part came from England and 3,000 hhds. were bought at an inferior price—a price rendered still lower by the 5% differential in tare.

The farmers-general replied that its engagement applied only to the quantity to be bought, since the question of an inferior price for inferior quality had been foreseen by Article 5; that if they had bought 3,000 hhds. "dans les Ports de L'Océan" since the decision, at inferior prices and different conditions, this was due to inferior quality, as proved by the fact that the proprietors had not entered claims as they were entitled to do under the Berni decision, thus recognizing themselves the inferior quality of their offerings.

It is impossible today to tell whether this allegation is well founded. It is indeed true that several merchants complained to M. Jefferson and to the Marquis de Lafayette, and that they had asked advice of them. But none of them had appealed to the Council as authorized by Article 5, "nul d'eux n'y avait intérêt car la Ferme générale qui était obligée de prendre des Tabacs jusqu'à une certaine quantité mais non pas tels Tabacs eut donné naturellement la préférence à ceux qui ne lui auraient point fait de procès et le recours au Conseil n'eut servi qu'à prolonger indéterminement le moment de la vente des Tabacs."—There is some reason to believe that the farm obtained several shipments at inferior prices by leading hard-pressed owners to believe that its quota had been filled and that it would oblige them to wait unless they consented to sell at a lower price.

Thus situated between opposing allegations, it seems that all government can do to carry out the spirit of the Berni decision and give satisfaction to French and American merchants is to direct the farmers-general to continue to buy, in accordance with that decision, 1,100 hhds. per month up to the end of 1787; and to order at the same time that the facts both as regards purchases of English tobacco, or those brought in English ships, and the differential in tare, be verified; and that the farmers-general be held responsible for augmenting its purchases of tobacco coming directly from America on French or English vessels in proportion to its English purchases, "comme aussi de bonifier la différence de la Tarre aux vendeurs qui ne seraient point convenus avec elle de leurs marchés à prix défendu, et pour lesquels la décision de Berni et l'égalité avec M. Morris, sont la Loi."

As for those who sold *à prix défendu* and who have not appealed to Council for the determination of the quality of their tobacco, it is more than likely that they had reason to be discontented and disgusted: "Cela est affligeant pour les deux Nations; mais on ne Voit aucun moyen d'y apporter remede, le mal est consommé; la preuve de l'abus de la position s'il a eu lieu est impossible à acquerir." This applies to the past, but its principle should be adopted for those cargoes that arrive up to the end of the year. There remains, however, a more important object to be considered, one that merits the whole attention of the government of France and on which it is well that the two nations be forewarned.

To execute in good faith the contract with Morris and the Berni decision, would require that the farmers-general, instead of getting a supply for a year and a half as required by its agreement, fill their warehouses with more than two years' supply without making any new purchases. Even if it were rigorously required that the supply of a year and a half remain intact, the farm would still have a supply for six or seven months' consumption without any new purchases.

This excess supply has been made at a price at least one-sixth above the market value of tobacco, and this is a sacrifice that France has made out of friendship for America. It is true that M. Morris alone has profited from about five-sixths of this sacrifice that has been not less real on the part of the king and the farmers-general, and that the remaining sixth has been profitable to the planters and merchants of America, who moreover still feel the effects of the repercussions produced by M. Morris' profits.

It is, then, only just that when the farm is freed of its contract with Morris and its obligation under the decision of Berni, it should reduce its purchases and look for its profits from the lowered prices that cannot fail to be produced by such reduction on the one hand and "la concurrence établie entre tous les Vendeurs" on the other. The farm, without inconvenience to itself, could cease all purchases for six months, at least except those proposals made to it at very advantageous prices, and, as a commercial and financial company principally concerned with its own interest, it is clear that this is what it would naturally do.

It is equally clear, nevertheless, that this measure would be "tres funeste au Commerce de l'Amèrique et aux rapports entre les deux Nations."[4] Thus the contract with Morris, which, in order to avoid injustice to other merchants and planters, forced this oversupply, will be harmful even after its expiration by the sudden stagnation of commerce and the depreciation of prices that will inevitably follow. If the American tobaccoes should cease during six months to have any sale in France, it is clear that American shippers would find an outlet in England for their principal product, that they would almost wholly abandon our market, and that the sale of our national produce and merchandise would suffer accordingly. The political and commercial interest of the two nations demands that they foresee this revolution and that they forestall it. The following is the only means foreseeable of accomplishing this. It will still be onerous to the farmers-general and to the king because of the capital sums it will employ, but it will be less harmful in all respects than a suspension of commerce.

The tenure of the farmers-general will not expire for five years. During this time French consumption of American tobacco will amount to 105,000 hhds., or 21,000 hhds. per year. It will be sufficient if the farm has at the end of its tenure about 30,000 hhds. The farm has at present, or will have by the end of the year, a supply that exceeds this requirement by about 25,000 hhds. This, deducted from the 105,000 that will be consumed up to and including 1792, leaves only 80,000 to be purchased. The excess of 25,000 hhds. should be distributed over the five-year period, and moreover, the 80,000 hhds. should be similarly apportioned by monthly quotas among the five years.

It is necessary, then, to make a new arrangement, to be sanctioned by the king, under which the farmers-general would be required not to suspend their purchases, but to continue them "sur le pied *de Seize mille Boucauds* par année . . . ou *treize cent Boucauds* par mois en tout, et rèpartis selon les besoins tant dans les Ports de L'Ocèan que dans ceux de la Mediterrannèe." They must be required to prove every three months that they have actually bought about 4,000 hhds. brought directly to France by French or American vessels, and on condition that, if more is needed to meet the demand, they be required to make the additional purchases in the proportion of five-sixths coming directly from America and one-sixth from Europe. "De cette maniere le commerce ne sera point intèrompu, le dèbouchè du commerce libre et particulier sera même augmentè de *deux mille cinq cent Boucauds* par annèe; puisqu'il n'a du être selon la dècision de

Berni que de *treize mille cinq cent Boucauds*. Il aura la perspective d'augmenter encore de *cinq mille Boucauds* par année à commencer en 1793."

No law regulating price can be imposed on the farm. It would be imprudent to attempt to force them to follow the English market price "qu'on pourrait faire hausser en apparence par des manoeuvres illusoires." The Americans have desired that no more contracts such as that of M. Morris be made, and they are right. This is the first of their demands met by the decision of Berni. "Il a été déterminé une fois pour toutes que la concurrence reglerait les prix—il ne faut plus déroger à cette loi de la raison et du commerce." One thing that can be done henceforth, is in the spirit of our government and our existing legislation, and is part of a proposal placed before the Notables for the reform of laws and treaties. This is to establish an *entrepôt* in every port where there is a bureau of the farm, and thus open up to merchants who wish to sell leaf-tobacco, either to foreign nations or to the farmers-general, the possibility of buying tobacco and storing it in warehouses almost duty free until they have found outlets for it. This is an idea proposed by M. Boyetet, *commissaire général* of commerce, in a mémoire which he read to the committee to be submitted to the minister, but of which he has not supplied a copy to be included here.

"Il peut en résulter une petite concurrence d'achat favorable aux deux Nations et qui s'accroîtra de jour en jour en raison de ce que l'Entrepôt général établi en même tems que le Nouveau Tarif des droits de traites aura favorisé et étendu le commerce de speculation dans tous les ports de France."

PART II. *Other branches of American commerce on which the studies of the Committee led to a decision.*

This part of the Mémoire will be concerned with other aspects of American commerce which did not prove so formidably obstructive as that presented by the monopoly on the sale of tobacco in France and on which the Committee charged with studying the interests of the two nations met with more success. The work of the Committee in this respect could not be better summed up than in a letter written by M. de Calonne, on order of the king, to M. Jefferson on 22 Oct. last. "De toutes les Pièces qui doivent entrer dans ce Mémoire c'est la plus importante."[5] . . . This letter, written officially after the orders of the king had been taken on its contents, announcing the intentions of His Majesty and having been made public by being printed, became a regulation that could be revoked only by new conventions and new notifications. But this regulation must not be regarded as an onerous obligation. It has not been imposed lightly. It is, as pointed out, the fruit of eight months' work of the Committee in which matters were discussed with "beaucoup de soin et de profondeur." It must be examined article by article for the reasons that have produced it and the remarks to which these may give rise.

Produce of the Whale Fishery. For some time our whale fishery has not been carried on with success. The attempts that have been made lately with all the care possible have resulted in more than 60% loss. The English have only been able to maintain their whale fishery by bounties of 30 to 40%. They do this very sagaciously by means of their Loyalists in Halifax whom they employ to try to persuade the whalers of Nantucket to settle in that colony.

They have in consequence repulsed by heavy duties the products of the whale fishery brought by Americans to England, formerly their principal market, and at the same time have presented to them a prospect of all the privileges of the English fishery—provided they fix their domiciles at Halifax. This involved "au moins . . . quatre mille Matelots les plus habiles et les plus intrépides de l'univers." If these moved to Halifax, the English might in the next war man eight vessels more. If they remain at Nantucket, bound to us by interest, by alliance, and above all by the habit of finding in France the reward of their work or the market for the products of their fishery, to say nothing of the resentment built up by the way the English treat them today, we could hope to engage half of them in our service. "C'est donc une Escadre de huit Vaisseaux à ôter à l'Angleterre et une de quatre à nous assurer ou une différence de douze Vaisseaux à notre avantage qu'il est question de nous conserver. L'importance pour notre politique et pour notre commerce en est inappréciable."

The proposal to establish at Dunkirk some of these Nantucket families will not meet the object in view. They will not establish there a French fishery that is no longer congenial to Europeans; they will be given only the assurance of enjoying all of the privileges of the French fishery for that part in which the Nantucketers will be interested. "On croit, c'est passer le but d'une part et le mal remplir de l'autre."

It is not necessary to give all the advantages of the French fishery to that of Nantucket, still less to a part of that fishery, by an exclusive privilege. It will suffice to grant enough advantages to preserve the friendship of the two nations by a common interest, and to forestall among the Nantucketers the desire to emigrate, which would put them under the power of England, "et il ne faut refuser à aucun d'Eux ces avantages réduits à leurs justes bornes."

It is thought, then, "que sans *nationaliser* contre l'esprit de toutes nos Loix une partie des huiles de Poisson fabriquées par les Pêcheurs de Nantucket sous prétexte qu'ils ont en France un Associé," it will be well (1) to extend to them the same moderation of duties on fish oils granted the Hanseatic towns and which cannot be refused them anyway since the United States by its treaty with France has the right to demand that it be treated "comme les Nations les plus favorisées"; (2) to exempt from duty the products of the whale fishery, such as whalebone and spermaceti; (3) to reduce the duties on whale oil brought in French or American vessels to the level announced by the king in confirming to them the exemption on individual rights of manufacture. This will be an advantage for the American fishermen which the Hanseatic towns do not enjoy, but it relates to a commodity of the first importance for our industry and one that the Hanseatic towns themselves can no longer supply. It is moreover, very proper that we accord to our *allies* of America more advantages than to *our friends* of the *north* of Germany, for Hamburg, Lübeck, and Danzig will never be able in war to contribute to our strength, and have no obligation to do so.

This arrangement will be less disadvantageous for our French fishermen, who make other fish oils, than is the privilege "donné à la Maison *Roche* de Dunkerque." It will be more advantageous to the whole of the Nantucket fishermen. It will more than fulfill the engagements undertaken by the king. It will give to our allies "une marque particulière d'affection."

But in occupying ourselves with these means of opening in France a market for the products of the American whale fishery equally favorable for all, something difficult to believe is discovered.

It appears that in the middle of changing ministers, in one of those moments when the new minister has not yet had time to put himself on guard against the pretexts and sophistries with which unjust demands are given a plausible color, "le Sr. Portalés fabricant de toiles de coton et de toiles peintes," found means for obtaining for fifteen or sixteen years the exclusive privilege of manufacturing spermaceti candles, or, in other words, a monopoly of the purchase of all the spermaceti oil the Americans may be able to send to France. This individual has spoken publicly of this privilege as having been granted to him. Such a privilege, however, which makes him master of the price, would be more onerous to American commerce and would more effectively repulse it than the duties that this commerce has borne, or that might still be imposed on it. In the face of this monopoly, the suppression of these duties would only produce profits for Pourtalés, and would be of no advantage to France or to America. Occasionally exclusive privileges have been granted for new manufactures in order to create new industries, and the best informed persons on administrative matters think nevertheless that it would be better to encourage new inventions by other means. But this is not a new industry. The art of fabricating candles or tapers with fatty substances is known to all the world, excepting perhaps the textile manufacturer to whom the exclusive privilege of manufacturing them has been granted.

It is without doubt useful to establish this industry, since it will be one means of making up for the excessive scarcity of tallow and since it opens up one more branch of commerce between us and our allies who, in general, lack means of paying for our merchandise and are thus forced to restrict their purchases of them. But the more advantageous it is to open up this branch of commerce and to favor this fabrication to be carried out by French hands, the more unreasonable and unjust it will be to concentrate it in a single hand, and in a hand notoriously inexpert at this kind of industry. "Il n'y a rien de plus dangereux pour les Gouvernemens que ces sortes d'opérations auxquelles il est impossible de trouver une bonne raison; car alors le Public s'acharne à y en chercher de mauvaises et la plus grande récompense d'une Administration pure se trouve perdue. Il suffit sans doute d'avoir dénoncé au Ministere cette méprise et ce danger pour que l'un et l'autre cessent de subsister."

Rice. Rice not imported from the Levant was subject, under the former rates, to a duty of only 11¼d. per quintal, and that from the French colonies to 1s.6½d, with the normal duty of sols per livre included in both cases. These duties will not be augmented under the new tariff, and will even be diminished somewhat. They cannot be regarded as an obstacle to importation, and so no new regulation in respect to them need be made.

Potash. Potash is a raw material for use in the making of saltpetre, glass, bleaches, and in the liming of grains. Its importation was formerly prohibited in regions where the salt-tax prevailed, but this prohibition was difficult to enforce. The manufacture of powder and the other articles mentioned account for a great consumption of potash. The interests of this industry, as well as the interest of America, require that the duties on potash be abolished or be made nominal, "et que la promesse faite au nom du Roi ait son execution."

Beaver fur. Beaver skins and fur have been exempted from entry-duties since the arrêt of 12 Feb. 1760 and, by the decision of 9 Nov. 1784, have been free of internal duties as well. The promise made on this subject thus contains nothing new, and there is no reason to change it. The interest of our hat-makers requires this even more than the interest of American commerce does.

Raw hides. The admission of this item, so necessary for the work of our tanneries, should be encouraged. It is one of those articles on which the new schedule of tariffs reduces the duties to a nominal level. There can be no inconvenience, then, in allowing this merchandise to enjoy the advantages which have been promised to Americans should they send any to France.

Masts and timber. Masts and timbers for shipbuilding have been exempted from entry-duties since the last century, but not when these materials are intended for domestic construction. It can be seen how impossible it is to tell on its arrival whether a beam or a plank will be used in the construction of a ship or a house, and this ridiculous inconsistency in our law will be altered in the new tariff. There appears, then, no reason for setting aside, in respect to this item, the promise that the king has caused to be made.

Ships of American construction. It is to be noted that only the ships' hulls are made in America, because lumber is plentiful and cheap, and that, since labor is high in America, all of the rigging is supplied in Europe, most of it being drawn at present from France. It follows that, in facilitating the sale of American ships, the king assures employment to the French makers of rigging and tackle. The purchase of American-built hulls, which are much lower in price than those made in France, tends, moreover, to procure for French ship-owners the advantage of being able to operate more economically and thus to compete better with foreign nations. The suppression of the 5% duty on the purchase of these ships is, then, in every sense a benefit bestowed by the king on our ship-owners and our carrying-trade. It would not be reasonable to deprive them of it.

Trees, plants, and seed. It is so useful to naturalize foreign trees that one cannot regret the suppression of the duties on their introduction. This tendency must, then, continue to be respected.

Arms and gunpowder. In times of ignorance and barbarism the exportation of every sort of arms was severely prohibited. It was apparently thought that if these were sold to foreigners, none would remain for the defense of the realm; and our most modern laws have servilely repeated this prohibition against the exportation of arms, even the most ancient and useless. We can congratulate ourselves that the progress of enlightenment finally permits us to add the manufacture and the export of arms to our other manufactures and commerce. The administration of powder has already given, with considerable profits and success, an example of the advantages of selling this great means of defense to foreign countries; and it cannot be imagined that there can be any thought of diminishing what the king has promised our allies in respect to this item.

Books and paper. No paper is required to pay export-duty except wall-paper. This is a manufacture at which we excel, and its market should expand greatly in America. One cannot regret the encouragement that the king promises to this branch of export trade.

As for books, these are already exempt from duty.

It has been represented that the exemption of export-duty and even the restoration of internal duties on paper and cardboard, so far as the export of printing papers is concerned, was harmful to our printing industry and our booksellers, who are obliged to meet the whole of these duties on books printed in the interior of the realm and who in consequence find it more profitable to print abroad. There was provided, then, in this respect, a general change which consisted in requiring payment of export-duty on papers to be used in printing and restoring that on paper and cardboard in printed books. But when this change shall have taken place with respect to other nations, there can be no inconvenience in permitting the Americans to enjoy an exception which has been promised them, for labor is so dear there that there is no reason to fear that books can be printed there in order to be brought into France, and it will be useful to us if American newspapers are printed on paper of our manufacture.

Conclusion of Part II. An examination of each of the articles mentioned in the letter written to M. Jefferson by order of the king has shown that the American demand for the execution of the promises made to them is not only founded on "le droit des Gens, mais aussi conforme à l'interêt de la France qu'à celui des Etats-unis. On ne peut donc leur refuser de passer en Loi les Stipulations qui leur ont été annoncées et d'assurer leur execution à compter du jour où les envois des Marchandises Américaines y denommées arrivées en France, ont pu être importées en vertu d'expeditions faites sur la parole du Roi, après qu'elle a été rendue publique en Amerique."

PART III. *Other branches of French and American commerce on which there has been as yet no decision.*

The letter of M. De Calonne decides only the points on which the Committee established to study the most advantageous commercial measures for the two nations had caused an arrêt to be issued. M. Jefferson has made some observations on the articles requiring further decisions. These observations and the provisional response of the controller-general in a letter to M. le Comte de Montmorin of 6 Sep. 1787 are here given in full.[6] . . . This provisional letter of M. Lambert does not eliminate the need for discussing M. Jefferson's observations.

§i. *Regulation of admiralty duties.* The idea of regulating admiralty duties by the number of masts or the draught of a vessel has at first glance an appearance of simplicity. It has been proposed and rejected in England. M. Jefferson is certainly right in proposing the burthen of a vessel as a more just measure. There are very accurate means of measuring tonnage. It may be decided, then, that the regulation on the admiralty duties will be to reduce them to a single one and to establish them on the basis of tonnage.

§ii. *The tariffs of the new admiralty duties.* M. Jefferson observes that the principle posed for augmenting the admiralty duties on foreign ships is based on the fact that most foreign nations require similar duties of us and proportionately higher than ours. He here lays stress on the principle of reciprocity in order to show that in several of the American states there are no such duties, and that in others they are very light. It thus follows that the Americans ought rather to expect a diminution, as they have been led to hope, than an augmentation which the principle of reciprocity would not justify. "Son observation semble parfaitement fondée et l'on croit que la règle à cet égard doit être vis à vis de toutes les Nations et de chaque Etat particulier, la réciprocité la plus éxacte; afin d'engager chaque Etat et chaque Nation à diminuer les droits sur cette navigation en raison de ce que son Gouvernement voudra que nous accueillions la sienne." It is true that the tariff will be more complicated to calculate since it would contain almost as many articles as flags; but it would be just, "et en peu de tems il ramenerait à l'uniformité les Nations qui auraient voulu repousser notre navigation, et qui nous verraient opposer à la leur un obstacle pareil. Celles qui pour echapper à cette juste reciprocité voudraient prendre un Pavillon qui ne Serait pas le leur ne le pourraient sans des faux frais ordinairement plus onéreux que la différence du droit, et sans s'exposer de plus aux peines des fausses déclarations. Il y a donc lieu de croire que les Droits d'Amirauté seraient assez-promptement baissés chez toutes les Nations, et s'y établiraient à un juste niveau."

What M. Jefferson says concerning flax, hemp, and furs is equally applicable to the commerce that we carry on with the peoples of the North of Europe, and there is no reason to make any exception. "La réciprocité des droits sur la navigation présente veritablement la seule régle."

§iii. *Fish oils.* On this subject, reference must be made to what has been said concerning it in the observations on the different articles of the letter written to M. Jefferson by order of the king. The Hanseatic oils enjoy a diminution on the entry-duties, but have always paid the duties of manufacture in the provinces in which these are established. Thus the exemption of American whale-oil is a particular favor.

It will be still more advantageous to the Americans to exempt from duties whalebone, spermaceti, and whale-oil when shipped directly to France on their own or French vessels, and to require them to pay only the same duties that the Hanseatic towns pay on the oils of all other kinds of fish also brought on French or American vessels. "C'est un arrangement qui parait devoir convenir également aux deux Nations."

As for the period for the execution of the engagements made with the Americans, one should refer to the conclusion of the second part of this Mémoire.

§iv. *Rice.* Everyone is in complete agreement on this article.

§v. *Potash.* M. Lambert has responded to M. Jefferson's observations relative to the local duties of Rouen by announcing his desire to see them moderated. If Rouen refuses, American potash will take another route, and will not be sold less in France. Rouen alone will lose the product by its duty. This is a powerful reason to facilitate its suppression or moderation.

§vi. *Turpentine, tar, and pitch.* The new schedule of tariffs moderates the duties on these merchandises as being useful naval stores. Thus the views of M. Jefferson "doivent être remplies par une législation qui doit incessamment paraitre. On ne verrait aucun inconvénient à ce que le ministère en prit avec lui l'engagement conforme au Plan général des droits de traites."

§vii. *Other favors for American commerce of which some are already decided by government, and others appear to be of a nature not to be refused.* It is to be regretted that M. Boyetet has not kept a copy of a Mémoire that he read to the Committee, and sent subsequently to the controller-general, containing some excellent ideas on American commerce. It is the only important document lacking in the present statement, but it can be annexed from the files of the controller-general's office. Since it is not now available, this article will be limited to some measures yet to be taken in favor of American commerce and these may or may not include those proposed by M. Boyetet.

The new plan of regulations for duties includes the establishment of the right of *entrepôt* for every kind of merchandise in every port of the realm where there is an office of the farmers-general, and to this will be added open transit for all articles destined for the interior that are not prohibited or subject to heavy duties.

As a result, all of these ports will share the principal advantages of the free ports; the Americans will be able to deposit their merchandise there without paying duty and for a simple and extremely moderate *droit d'entrepôt*; and they will also be able to find there an assortment of every imaginable kind of merchandise that other nations will likewise have brought to these ports.

"Cette grande vue politique et commerciale doit être regardée comme le plus puissant attrait pour multiplier les rélations de navigation et de commerce entre l'Amèrique unie et la France. Il n'est pas impossible d'y en ajouter un autre."

It was proposed to the Committee that bounties be granted on French merchandise that the Americans should take in exchange for tobacco. An arrêt was even drafted for accomplishing this. This idea should be reconsidered for all French manufactures that are in competition with those of other countries and are carried from France to America in French or American vessels. These bounties could vary according to the nature of the merchandise from 2 to 4% ad valorem. This is a work that will demand very close attention to regulate the rate and quota of each article of merchandise. But if it is considered that it will not be necessary to apply this system to the whole of our commerce with America, and that it will be sufficient to apply it only to those articles of merchandise with which we do not enjoy a decided advantage; if it is further considered that our wines, brandies, vinegars, oils, soaps, dried and candied fruits, salts, papers, books, prints, cambrics, linens, fashions, silks, and draperies of the first quality have no need of it, it will be seen that, supposing our commerce with America worth 30,000,000₶ per year, only about a third of this, or 10,000,000₶ in value, will be eligible for bounties. It may be concluded, then, that the cost of stimulating and sustaining this commerce would cost not more than 100,000 écus per year.

It cannot be doubted that this expense would be returned to the king with interest by the augmentation of duties of every sort which would be produced by the growth of commerce and the increased consumption of goods to which this stimulus would give rise.

Résumé général. If the government of France obliges the farmers-general to fulfill faithfully up to the end of this year what was enacted by the decision at Berni, and to continue afterwards to purchase for five years 1,300 hhds. of American tobacco *à prix défendu*; if it revokes the monopoly granted for the manufacture of spermaceti candles and makes that manufacture free; if it exempts from duty spermaceti and whalebone derived from the American fishery; if it accords to whale-oil the same reduction of entry-duty and the exemption of duty on manufacture that have been granted the Hanseatic towns; if it extends to all other fish oils brought hither by French or American vessels the same privileges granted those brought from the Hanseatic towns; if it applies to rice, potash, beaver skins and fur, timbers, American ships, arms, powder, and paper the favorable terms announced by the king, making them effective from the date at which they were known in America long enough to determine shipments; if relative to the admiralty duties and to turpentine, pitch, and tar, it does what M. Jefferson asks; if to these favors it adds those of the right of *entrepôt* to all merchandise in all of the ports and of transit for most of them through the country; if it adds export bounties on about a third of the commodities that Americans carry away from France—it cannot be doubted that these advantages, "ajoutant au sentiment qu'inspire la memoire des Services passés ne doivent établir entre les deux Nations un Commerce très actif, et les plus solides rélations de bienveillance et d'amitié reciproques."

MS (Arch. Aff. Etr., Paris, Mémoires et Documents, E.-U., Vol. IX; photostats in DLC); in a clerk's hand, consisting of the following: table of contents, p. [i]-[xv]; main body of the report, p. 1-140; an annexed document, being the same detailed state of purchases made by the farmers-general as that summarized in Vol. 12: 212 in the note to TJ to Dupont, 6 Oct. 1788 (and employed also as Appendix IX of Document III of the present series), p. 141-8. Following this there is a single numbered leaf (p. 149) which is blank except for the following: "Mémoire de M. Boyetet." It was this notation, occurring as it does on what appears to be a final covering page of the report, that naturally led Waldo G. Leland, *Guide to Materials for American History in the Libraries and Archives of Paris*, Washington, 1943, II, 963, to describe it as having been written by Boyetet. But, as the above text shows, the author meant this caption to apply to another document that could be annexed from the files of Lambert's office—a document that Boyetet wrote and that the author of the present document praises at two points, regretting that it was not at hand to be inserted in its proper place and suggesting that it be annexed later.

1 The text of the contract with Morris (and its implementing contract with Le Normand) is here omitted; it is printed above, Vol. 9: 586-8.

2 The summary of the six propositions (p. 35-62 of the MS) is here omitted; these propositions are summarized and discussed in Vol. 9: 459.

3 The text of the decision of Berni is here omitted; it is printed above, Vol. 9: 597-8.

4 The marginal notation at this point reads: "et le Commerce avec l'Amerique serait perdu."

5 The text of Calonne's letter to TJ of 22 Oct. 1786 is here omitted; it is printed above, Vol. 10: 474-6.

6 TJ's Observations and Lambert's comment thereon are omitted here; their texts are printed above, Vol. 11: 539-41; Vol. 12: 162-3.

III. *Mémoire pour des Négocians de L'Orient, Intéressés au Commerce des Etats-Unis; Contre La Ferme Générale*

[*Introduction*:] "Les Négocians de la ville de l'Orient, occupés du commerce des Etats-Unis, sont forcés de réclamer à la fois la justice et la bienveillance du Gouvernement. C'est sur la foi de la protection annoncée par le ministere et d'une décision du Conseil du Roi, qu'ils ont exposé et leur crédit & leur fortune, par les avances qu'ils ont faites aux Américains.

"L'intéret de l'Etat est intimement lié à celui des Exposans, La conservation ou la perte d'un commerce précieux, celui des Etats-Unis, dépendent des mesures qu'on va prendre. En ce moment les plus légeres meprises seroient dangereuses; car on est rarement le maître de rappeller une branche de commerce détournée; et celle des tabacs d'Amérique présente un intérêt d'autant plus important pour nous, qu'en l'abandonnant, la France la porte à l'Angleterre.

"Aussi dès l'époque de la paix les Ministres ont-ils paru animés du même esprit, pénétrés des mêmes principes sur l'importance du commerce des Etats-Unis; et se sont-ils empressés, chacun dans leur département, d'adopter les premieres dispositions qui pouvoient l'attirer et le fixer en France.

"Mais le Privilege exclusif de la Ferme Générale pour la branche des tabacs, la principale de ce commerce, ayant fait tomber entre les mains de cette Compagnie l'exécution des plans des Ministres, ils n'en ont pu suivre ni assurer les effets. Quelques étendues & éclairées qu'aient été leurs vues patriotiques sur les avantages que la nation devoit retirer de l'indépendance de l'Amérique, elles sont venues se retrecir et s'éteindre dans les Bureaux de la Ferme. Là, les plans ministériels, fondés sur des principes généraux d'esprit public, ont été sans cesse contrariés par un esprit d'economie du moment, par des mesures et des intentions d'intérêt particulier.

"C'est de cette contradiction que sont nés les maux dont les Exposans souffrent depuis long-temps. Dès le commencement de la paix, les Américains appellés par le ministre, ont été éloignés par la conduite de la Ferme Générale. Elle est venue ensuite, par un traité secrétement conclu avec un seul particulier Américain, rompre toutes les liaisons commencées entre tous les individus des deux nations; fermer expressement les ports ouverts aux Américains par des franchises dispendieuses, et arrêter par le fait toutes les exportations de marchandises de France pour les Etats-Unis.

"Enfin, lorsque par une décision du Conseil du 24 Mai 1786, l'Administration instruite par les représentations du commerce est intervenue, et qu'après de longues et contradictoires discussions, la Ferme Générale a pris l'engagement de recevoir des particuliers Américains une certaine quantité de tabacs à des prix et conditions fixées; lorsque cet engagement pris avec la sanction du Roi a été deux fois publié en France et en Amerique par la voie des Ministres et Consuls; lorsqu'enfin, par diverses exemptions de droits et autres avantages accordés à notre commerce par les Etats-Unis, et par diverses exportations considérables qu'ils ont faites de marchandises de nos fabriques, la France a reçu le prix des faveurs accordées au commerce d Amérique, par la décision du Conseil; la Ferme Générale refuse de recevoir les tabacs venus dans les Ports de France, en vertu de cet engagement sacré qu'elle élude. Elle n'y a satisfait que partiellement jusqu'à ce jour: pour le remplir, il lui reste encore à recevoir plus de treize millions de livres pesant de tabac, et cependant elle laisse gémir les Exposans sous le poids d'un engorgement de tabacs arrivés depuis plus d'un an. Sans doute elle veut les forcer à les lui vendre à une grosse perte: elle sait bien qu'elle est maîtresse de leur sort, qu'elle est en France le seul consommateur de tabac; et elle ne répond seulement pas à leurs répresentations et à leurs plaintes. Elle contraint ainsi les Exposans à recourir à la justice & à la protection éclairée du Gouvernement.

"Ils viennent réclamer l'exécution de la décision du Conseil et de l'engagement public de la Ferme contracté en présence des Ministres du Roi. Ils demanderont justice d'après les Etats de cette Compagnie même: et après avoir rendu sensible par un fidele exposé des faits la triste influence sur le commerce du Royaume, de l'esprit qui, depuis la paix, et dans trois époques différentes, a dirigé cette Compagnie dans l'exercice de son privilege relativement aux Etats-Unis, ils oseront proposer pour l'avenir un remede facile et simple qui semble actuellement être devenu indispensable."

[*Section*] 1. Before the American revolution, England obliged colonies to bring their produce to her ports and to export from them all manufactures received in return. Few articles were exempted from "la loi de ce double monopole." Great Britain sold to the rest of Europe the major part of American import, which amounted in 1770 to £3,347,819 sterling, tobacco alone accounting for £906,550. "Sans ce commerce, la possession des Etats-Unis fût devenue onéreuse à l'Angleterre; leur défense et leur administration lui ont toujours été fort dispendieuses."

[*Section*] 2. Our relations with America have included differing points of view, some entering upon them with enthusiasm, others with disdain and deprecation. The government, above such exaggerated impressions, sought to render the newly-independent states useful to the nation. After a war of five years, what would Great Britain lose by the independence of the colonies if she was able to retain their commerce and be free of the cost of administering them? It was then up to France to deprive her rivals of the greatest portion of American commerce. The government then seized the first moment of peace to draw Americans toward France. Bounties being effective, but too expensive, they chose the means of establishing packet-boats, of establishing entrepôts in the ports of France for tobacco and other produce, and, in response to their request, of making free ports of Bayonne and L'Orient. During the war France had been given promise of what the American commerce could become in future. In 1782 their vessels had exported 19,000,000[tt] worth of merchandise from L'Orient alone. But with the peace the Americans began to obtain the same merchandise from other nations and especially from England, "où une longue habitude, d'anciennes dettes et des liaisons individuelles les rappelloient." A strong interest was needed to draw them to France, and happily one existed in the fact that Americans could sell a part of their productions in French ports promptly and with less expense than elsewhere. France consumes 20 to 25 hhds. of tobacco of about 900 to 1,000 pounds net weight; she consumes wheat and flour, rice, fish, oil, potash, furs, wood, tar, charcoal, &c. Bringing these products to French ports, Americans are more or less forced to carry back French merchandise, for port expenses and, in winter, the delay of a single day causing inactivity for their vessels for as long as three months would keep them from seeking return cargoes in England. Because of this, the Americans, though preferring the salt of Portugal and England, have exported salt heavily from Brittany, along with "draps, toiles, indiennes, soyeries de nos fabriques, des thés, nankins, et autres articles des Indes" which they formerly got in London. Also, they have carried away brandy from different ports, and from Marseilles in particular "vins, huiles, savons, fruits et autres denrées" formerly furnished by Spain and Portugal. The Americans, too, occupied with clearing and improving the land, cannot pay for their imports except with their own produce and facility for such payment must be provided if France wishes to sell them her merchandise. But the ministry had a still more pressing interest in drawing Americans to French ports: this lay in France's undeniable need for some of the American produce. "Ce besoin autrefois nous rendoit tributaires de l'Angleterre, et si nous ne le transformions point en un cours de commerce d'échanges, nous allions inévitablement payer aujourd'hui ce même tribut à l'Amérique." The knowledge of this position of the United States vis-à-vis France and England; the certainty that exports of French merchandise could begin only with favored

American imports; the desire to avoid throwing away the fruits of an onerous war—it was these things that determined the conduct of the ministry toward Americans. Packet-boats would cement these bonds with a regular correspondence. Free ports would draw all sorts of merchandise "par la liberté si chère à cette nation, et par la célérité de la réexpédition de leur navires." Entrepôts in other ports would provide useful advantages. On this base the ministry rested the commerce that it wished to create, after which it could be left to itself. Happy effects were promised, but the care needed by a free commerce did not suffice for a non-existent commerce. For, in the most considerable branch of this commerce, tobacco, the farmers-general enjoy an exclusive privilege which forced the Americans to take law from them and to accept whatever price they fixed. Thus when government withdrew its favors, the Americans fell under the hand of the farm. Thus by refusing the tobaccoes they had brought hither, or by offering a lower price than that paid by our rivals, the farm, in spite of all of the effort of the ministry, could destroy the single interest that had attracted the Americans to our ports. Thus the farm, so long as it remained an absolute and independant master of this branch of commerce, could annihilate the measures of the ministry. Let us see the use that the farm made of this independence, and how its principles and conduct have, at different periods, opposed those of the administration.

[*Section*] 3. §I. The tobacco plantations in America were ruined during the war, their equipment burned by the British, their merchant vessels destroyed. In the years 1783 and 1784 following the war tobacco was very dear in Europe and in the United States. Despite this, the farmers-general consistently offered lower prices than those of Holland or England; even when tobacco was selling from 40 to 60 livres per quintal, they sent an agent to America under contract to buy, delivered in France, at 30 livres. The result of a conduct so contrary to the true principles of commerce was inevitable: the Americans went to London and Amsterdam. The agent, unable to purchase at 30 livres, obtained tobacco in Europe, infinitely inferior in price and quality. In Sep. 1784 the parliament of Brittany took strong measures against the defective snuff being retailed, whereupon the farmers-general, fearing exposure of the real cause, hastened at great expense to purchase from England and Holland several cargoes that its own measures had forced away from France. At the end of 1784 the farm made a contract with Robert Morris engaging to buy from him annually 20,000 hhds. of tobacco in 1785, 1786, and 1787 at 36 livres per quintal, to receive them on arrival, to reduce the tare from the normal 15% to the actual weight of the casks, to advance a million livres without interest, to limit the places of receipt to Bordeaux, Morlaix, Dieppe, and Le Havre, and, without requiring it, to favor American and French vessels. This contract bore all the evidence of being hastily entered upon, since it sacrificed the interest of the farm itself: it rendered the farm liable without assuring it of supplies. For one of two things was bound to occur: either tobacco would continue to be rare and dear in America, or an abundant harvest would cause the price there to fall. If the first, the farm stood to lose 5 or 600,000 livres per year if it held Morris to the scrupulous execution of his contract, no clause of which obliged him to do so to his loss. If the second, the farm could obtain tobacco in America, without a contract, at a lower price than that stipulated in its obligation to Morris. In either hypothetical case, the farm stood to lose. Morris' conduct proves this. He counted on a prompt decline of price in America, but tobacco continued dear in 1785 and, instead of 20,000 hhds., he obtained only 4,783, mostly inferior. By Aug. of 1786 he had got only 4,362 of the quota for that year, or a total of only 9,145 instead of the 32,000 due in that period, but a lowering of price enabled Morris toward the end of 1786 to buy a total of 20,884 hhds. In 1787, with an abundant harvest and a low price, he furnished the quota of 20,000 hhds. But the farm now permitted him to ship on the deficit of 1785, so that, in the last 16 months it received from him 51,000 hhds. as compared with 9,000 in the first twenty months. This indulgence, the motives for which are unknown, has suddenly filled the warehouses and at a higher cost to the farm than the market would have borne. These are the advantages the farm has drawn from its contract.

But if the true interest of the farm itself was forgotten in the making of this contract, "que dire de la froide indifférence qu'on y marquoit pour ceux de la nation, et de l'étrange contradiction qu'il venoit opposer à toutes les vues connues du ministère?" (1) The ministry wished to draw Americans to our ports and thus create an opportunity for exports of French merchandise. But the contract with Morris forced them to foreign ports, and he, compensated by drafts on Europe negotiated in America, never had any interest in taking his return in French merchandises. Thus an expenditure of 20,000,000 livres produced no exports from France. (2) The free ports created by the ministry on the choice of Americans were interdicted to Morris for delivery of his tobacco; the farm had designated other ports in the contract. (3) The object of creating packet-boats for easy and quick communication between merchants was nullified for three years in this respect, for Morris on one side and the farm on the other "remplaçoient en totalité les deux Nations." (4) For three years, very probably because of this contract, an American flag was not seen once in our ports. Morris, not being required to ship on French or American vessels, must have preferred the ships of the Dutch, the Swedes, and others whose economical navigation lowered freight costs.

Such was the contract that has had such troublesome results for the state. We make no deductions concerning the spirit which moved the farm; but in our state of ignorance as to the causes which created a contract onerous alike to the farm and the state, "la précipitation dont nous l'avons accusée ne paroitra pas sans doute une sévère interprétation." They claim to have obtained the verbal approval of the minister of finance, but, even so, this would not change its nature or its effects. "Un exposé aussi secret que le fut le traité, l'aura sans doute déterminée."

§II. If Morris had executed his contract in 1785, the alienation of other American merchants would have been the inevitable result. But, witnessing his failure, the merchants sent several cargoes. By treating them equitably, the farmers could have somewhat repaired the damage caused by their contract. But, seeing them in port with tobacco, they tried as in the beginning of peace to force a quick and heavy reduction of price. They concealed their needs, refused to give contract prices, bought only the tobacco that met their own tests of price, condition, and quality, and thus forced the price down 20% below that offered Morris. An enormous loss resulted to the owners, and 6 to 7,000 hhds. accumulated in L'Orient alone. Complaints were made to the minister. They called for the annulment (résiliation) of the contract by government, which they thought justified by Morris' failure to execute his part and "par l'état de pénurie" in which this had left the farm. In Aug. 1785 their consul general in France presented to the controller-general the memoire sub-joined (Appendix No. I). Government chose a committee of magistrates and members of different departments of administration, at the meetings of which the farmers-general were present. They answered verbally and in writing to the complaints offered, and the matter was long discussed. This committee sent to the controller-general on 8 Apr. 1786 a resolution calling for the annulment of the contract as being disadvantageous to the two nations. The farm, feeling the effect of the unfavorable light in which it appeared, offered premiums to encourage imports of American tobacco, whereupon the committee added to its resolution the wise observation that, whether enforced or annulled, such premiums would be without object, a judgment justified by the fact: for while this was being offered to the ministry on the one hand, the farmers-general on the other continued to offer inferior prices for the cargoes in port. The committee reassembled at Berni in the presence of the minister of foreign affairs and the minister of finance. The farmers-general strongly opposed annulment of the contract, and preferred the only terms that could end its pernicious effects: to buy tobacco brought by Americans and to end the odious differences in treatment complained of. This was in effect ministerially announced to America by terms of the decision of Berni and by a letter from the controller-general to the American minister on 22 Oct. 1786 (Appendix, No. II).

The minister thought he could then leave this commerce to itself. But, solemn and precise though the Berni decision was, it could become effective only if loyally executed. This execution was left to the farmers-general who had made the contract with Morris and who had so recently defended it.

§III. The decision of Berni produced "chez les Americains la plus vive sensation." The very day that it was published in Virginia—the province that produces most tobacco—the legislature passed a law exempting French wines and brandies from a considerable duty. Their vessels, expedited to France, met the same old obstacles. Proof of the invariable system followed by the farm is to be found in a circular letter issued by it on 19 June 1786 to its officials concerning the Berni decision—a letter made known to commerce only by "un heureux hasard" and given in full in the Appendix (No. III). This letter orders execution of the agreement and states that, "Dans l'impossibilité . . . de fournir au payement de tous les tabacs, existans dans les divers ports," the farm will fix each month the quota of purchases it will be possible to make in each port; that, nevertheless, cargoes now in port that are known not to have come from America directly and in French or American bottoms will not receive Berni benefits; that such cargoes, as well as new arrivals in this class, will fall "*dans la classe ordinaire pour les achats à prix défendus, et les allouances d'usage dans le commerce*"; and that if consignees desire to expedite the sale of cargoes coming directly from America and in French or American vessels, "il conviendroit de nous en informer."—Nothing could show more clearly than this letter the handicaps placed by the farmers-general on the execution of the Berni decision. The supposed "*impossibilité de fournir au payement*" is only a pretext; the real design is to force the consignees by these delays to make propositions to the farm "*a prix défendus, et avec les allouances.*" These "*allouances*" [*as explained in footnote*] allow a 5% profit to the farm by a charge for tare in that amount above the actual weight of the casks (the tare required of Morris); thus, in addition to losing on the low prices, the consignees lost 5% on the weight of their tobacco.

This was the disposition of the farm one month after the Berni decision! It has kept faithfully to it. It began with heart-breaking delays for vendors whose tobaccoes had long lain in warehouses. It lowered its prices on pretexts of inferior quality, though it is public notoriety that commerce generally furnished better tobacco than Morris. It paid at up to three months' exchange, whereas Morris was paid at one month. It wholly ceased buying at L'Orient, where Americans were most active, so that about 5,000 hhds. in the warehouses accumulated charges and tied up funds for their unfortunate owners. It has long since resumed buying in other ports; the motive for this discrimination is not known.

The farm claims that a glut of the market and scarcity of funds dictate this conduct. But it can find warehouses and funds for tobacco whose consignees wish to expedite the sale and make propositions "*à prix défendu, et avec les allouances d'usage*"; for the 16,000 hhds. in excess that it has been kind enough to receive from Morris; for a cargo bought recently "à prix défendu" at Bordeaux that was negotiated for at Havre at 30 livres. The farm has presented a state of purchases (Appendix No. IX) from private merchants in 1786 and 1787 to show how it executed its agreement. Assuming this state to be without error, it shows that the farm bought 16,573 hhds. under the terms of the decision, which is far from the 27,000 hhds. required, and that it bought 5,551 hhds. "à prix défendu."

Is this the way in which the intention of the minister should be carried out? "La décision, deux fois publiée, a attiré en France des tabacs d'Amérique: étoit-elle ou n'étoit-elle pas un engagement sacré envers leurs propriétaires? En quoi consisteroit donc la foi publique?" By its conduct the farm has desolated and alienated a commerce "très-important pour l'Etat"; it has forced French merchants to protest the drafts of owners of tobacco drawn to France by its engagement; and it has left unexecuted their orders for the export of French merchandise. The farm cares nothing for complaints about these things and often treats them with silence. Proof of it exists in a letter written to the farm by a house in L'Orient and never answered.

[*Section*] 4. §I. The exports and imports from L'Orient will justify the wise policy adopted at the beginning of peace to favor American commerce. Appendix No. IV shows exports from Jan. 1785 to 1 May 1786 of 2,100,000£; No. V, from 1 May 1786 to 1 July 1787 (according to figures prepared by officers of the farm for the minister), shows 89 American or French vessels brought in tobacco or other produce worth 4,372,241£; No. VI shows that they reëxported French manufactures or produce or items of Oriental trade worth 1,369,486£ (reëxports of foreign manufactures accounted for an additional 17,277£; purchases by captains and crew, 311,500£; ships' port charges 355,000£; and, in addition, reëxports of tobacco to Holland and the North, 200,000£, and "par les Interlopes Irlandois et Ecossois," 500,000£). These exports would be even greater if the farm had not refused to receive tobacco that has been at L'Orient for more than a year.

But, important though they are, these direct exports are not the only advantages that attend a commerce with the United states: "Interlopes" from Ireland and Scotland come to L'Orient for certain kinds of tobacco, and they come with greater frequency in proportion to the imports: in 1784 there were 5 Irish and Scottish ships; in 1785, 16; in 1786, 30; and in 1787, from 1 Jan. to 30 Apr., 28. They bring little merchandise and pay for four-fifths of their exports in foreign gold, another fifth in salt provisions and butter. Their ships are small and carry on this commerce with great activity. These 79 vessels (Appendix No. VII) exported tobacco, brandy, and other objects worth 905,000£. Thus one trade which attracts another has produced in this period a total value of exports of 5,259,263£ from L'Orient alone. "Que seroit-ce si avant et depuis la decision, toutes les opérations des Américains n'y eussent pas été contrariées! Si leurs navires n'eussent pas été retardés; si de prompte ventes à la Ferme leur eussent permis de disposer de leurs fonds à leur volonté, et de renouveller leurs expéditions."

It is known that considerable exports have been made from other ports, but full details are lacking. In May and July 1787 three full cargoes of wine, brandy, fruit, and other items left Marseilles. The 60,000 hhds. of tobacco imported under the Morris contract have cost 19 to 20,000,000£ to the realm and have produced no exports worth mentioning. If, instead, they had been imported by commerce, exports worth at least 10 to 12,000,000£ would have resulted, judging from figures presented for L'Orient. This is a net loss for the state, for the farm paid in specie, not in merchandise. English manufactures benefited. Morris negotiated most of his drafts there, and this contributed not a little to continue to hold down the rate of exchange with England, which for some years has been disadvantageous to France. Even if the farm had profited 2 or 3,000,000£, would this have compensated the state for a loss caused by this pernicious contract? But the contract was burdensome even for the company, and no such profit resulted. Its faults are irremediable, but five years' troublesome and consistent experience points to a better future. It shows that a commerce as important as this with the United States must continue to be under the immediate hand of the minister; that its fate cannot be allowed to depend on the opinions or the procedures of a private company with an exclusive privilege, since in a thousand circumstances and sometimes even against its own interest, it is able to oppose the general interest. We turn now to the future aspect under which this commerce, relieved of its handicaps, appears to the eyes of the administration.

§II. "L'importance de ce commerce ne se borne pas pour nous aux seules exportations du Royaume. La France consommant une forte grande quantité de tabacs, est de plus très-avantageusement placée pour devenir l'entrepôt de ceux qu'elle ne consomme pas. Si les Américains sont bien traités en France, ils y apporteront toujours leurs tabacs avec empressement: ils seront sûrs d'y trouver un débouché annuel considérable & une vente prompte.

"Or, comme les acheteurs viennent nécessairement où il y a le plus de marchandises, parce que c'est là que se trouvent les assortimens et le bon marché; cette affluence des cargaisons Américaines forcera les Flammands, les Hollandois et les autres nations du Nord, dont la consommation moins forte que la nôtre se borne à certaines especes de tabacs, à venir les choisir dans nos Ports, ou à y porter leurs ordres.

"Ils y viendront comme les Irlandois y viennent. Il s'est déjà exporté diverses parties de tabac du port de l'Orient pour la Hollande et pour le Nord. D'un autre côté, par une réaction ordinaire et naturelle, l'affluence des acheteurs augmentant pour les Américains la facilité des ventes et la célerité des opérations, ils préféreront nos Ports aux Ports étrangers qui ne leur offriront point le même attrait. Peu à peu la France deviendra le centre et l'entrepôt du commerce du tabac. A cette branche s'en joindront d'autres qu'elle aura nécessairement attirées; car, on l'a déjà dit, ces branches se touchent. Tout ceci est annoncé par la position des choses et par l'expérience de tous les tems; et ce n'est point par une autre marche que les nations les plus commerçantes se sont approprié les branches d'industrie et de commerce auxquelles elles ont dû leur prospérité.

"La Ferme Générale recueillera elle-même des avantages durables d'une affluence de tabacs bien décidée. La certitude de ses approvisionnemens; le choix des qualités; le bon marché constant qui en résultent, suites naturelles d'une conduite fondée sur les véritables principes en matiere de grand commerce, valent bien, sans doute, les bénéfices passagers, que, par une marche moins ouverte et des ventes forcées, on peut momentanément arracher aux Américains.

"Le commerce du riz particuliérement, branche très importante d'exportation d'Amérique, ne pourra nous échapper s'il est protégé par le Gouvernement.

"Ce n'est donc point un objet de détail et de petite importance que les Supplians osent recommander à l'attention du ministere. Il est d'autant plus pressant dans ce moment cù notre traité avec l'Angleterre frappe si désavantageusement sur nos manufactures et sur notre commerce; dans ce moment où toutes les nations s'efforcent de reprendre les branches d'industrie qui leur appartiennent."

[*Section*] 5. The memorialists offer to submit authentic and original proofs to any persons the minister may designate that the tobacco surrendered to the farm up to now and that remaining unsold at L'Orient are the property of merchants and citizens of different states and towns in the United States; that these owners shipped the tobacco here in consequence of the decision of the Council of State and by the dispositions announced by the minister of the king—taking the course that government desired this commerce to take. The fate of the memorialists is linked with that of the owner because of advances made by them. "Sans ces avances la plupart des Americains ne pourroient envoyer leurs productions en France. La Ferme a été obligée d'avancer un million au sieur Morris. Les retards apportés par cette Compagnie à l'achat des tabacs et l'espoir qu'ont eu les Exposans de les voir bientot cesser, les ont engagés à satisfaire aux besoins des Propriétaires Américains, et à laisser grossir leurs avances jusques à de très-fortes sommes. Leur crédit et leur fortune y sont engagés, et l'inexécution de la décision du Conseil pese ainsi sur eux d'une maniere aussi cruelle que sur les Américains mêmes. Si le ministere ne les tire pas de cette situation; s'il ne s'établit pas un nouvel ordre de choses, les négocians de France n'oseront plus faire d'avances aux Américains; et ce sera pour cette nation une autre cause d'éloignement, non moins décisive que celles que nous avons décrites. Cette inaction forcée de leurs fonds cause aux Supplians un tort irréparable: elle les a empêchés de les employer à d'autres branches d'industrie, ou à hâter les progrès de celle-ci.

"On peut voir dans la Lettre déjà citée (cotée no. 8.) adressée à la Ferme Générale en Juillet 1787, comment elle a été instruite de la triste position où elle réduit les Exposans par le refus des tabacs du commerce; elle a su que le crédit et la fortune d'honnêtes négocians y étoient engagés. Qu'il leur soit permis d'exprîmer ici l'impression douloureuse et la juste surprise qu'a dû leur causer dans leur position la froide indifférence avec laquelle leurs représentations directes à la Ferme ont été accueillies. Si ces reclamations étoient mal fondées, cette Compagnie ne leur devoit-elle aucune explication, mais seulement un silence dédaigneux? Au reste, ce silence même sous lequel la Ferme cherchoit à rester enveloppée, ne prouve-t-il sa propre conviction intérieure sur la justice des réclamations du commerce? Si cette Compagnie n'a pas osé mettre par écrit quelques explications sur sa conduite, c'est qu'elle étoit bien sûre d'avance qu'après une réfutation facile, elles deviendroient pour elle un motif de condamnation.

"Cependant tandis qu'elle refusoit les tabacs de la décision, la Ferme recevoit et payoit à leur arrivée tous les tabacs du sieur Morris, elle lui laissoit excéder de quinze ou seize mille boucauds les bornes de son traité pour la derniere année. Il sembloit qu'elle cherchat à désespérer ainsi le commerce pour éloigner enfin sa concurrence, et pour préparer par son éloignement et par le dénuement de tabacs qui en seroit la suite, la justification d'un nouveau contrat. (Car c'est sous le point de vue du dénuement où elle s'étoit trouvée de tabacs en 1784, qu'elle avoit fait excuser à Bernis l'existence de son traité; et c'est ce qui explique cette phrase justificative insérée dans le préambule de la décision. Le comité . . . informé des circonstances dans lesquelles ce traité a été passé). . . .

"Mais permettra-t-on à la Ferme Générale de rejetter sur le commerce par des procédés désastreux pour lui, les inconvéniens de l'excès de faveur versé par elle sur le sieur Morris. Elle a eu des magasins et des fonds pour les tabacs de ce fournisseur si inexact, dont les valeurs vont se convertir en achats de marchandises Angloises. Peut-elle en manquer pour les tabacs nationaux!

"La Ferme ne peut alléguer contre le commerce le défaut de fonds et de magazins. Quant aux fonds, elle a déjà reculé de deux mois les termes des payemens au commerce, sans le dédommager par des intérêts pour ce retardement arbitraire: elle n'ignore pas qu'il se preteroit sans difficulté à quelque prolongation sur l'échéance des lettres de change, rachetée par un intérêt au cours de la place. A l'égard des magasins, cet obstacle se réduit à huit ou dix sols par mois, que coûte pour chaque boucaud le loyer des mêmes magasins dont se sert le commerce.

"Les exposans doivent faire remarquer que le port de l'Orient est victime de l'inexecution de la décision du Conseil, depuis beaucoup plus long-tems que les autres ports. Au mois de Juin dernier la Ferme recevoit encore les cargaisons entrées dans d'autres ports à des dattes bien posterieures tandis qu'elle n'avoit pas reçu des exposans un seul boucaud sur le nombre de 4000 arrivés à l'Orient depuis la date du premier Octobre 1786.

"Cependant c'est le port dont la position a toujours de préference attiré les Américains, & qu'ils annonçoient eux mêmes pouvoir devenir un jour le centre de leur commerce en Europe. Ainsi non-seulement le commerce des Etats-unis a été mal accueilli par la Ferme, mais de plus c'est précisément dans le port où il se portoit naturellement, où il se seroit le plus facilement étendu, qu'elle l'a le plus défavorablement traité.

"Cette inégalité de traitement contrarie et l'équité et les principes de bonne administration en matière de commerce. Il est de principe que le commerce attiré par certaines convenances de position et d'intérêt, ne se détourne point forcément; qu'il faut lui laisser à lui-même le soin de juger de son intérêt, de ses convenances et des lieux où il les peut trouver. Très-surement les Américains seront meilleurs juges à cet égard que la Ferme Générale; et lors qu'elle aura maltraité leur commerce dans un port, elle ne doit pas prétendre qu'en les accueillant moins mal dans un autre, elle dédommage l'Etat.

"En voilà assez sans doute pour démontrer l'impérieuse nécessité de la nouvelle et constante intervention du Ministère que les exposans oseront solliciter, aprés avoir préalablement conclu à l'exécution des engagemens de la Ferme pris avec la sanction de sa Majesté, et en présence de ses Ministres.

"Sans doute cette compagnie ne se persuade point qu'en lui accordant à bail la vente du tabac, le Roi ait pu aliéner le droit de diriger d'une manière avantageuse à l'Etat un commerce d'importance du premier ordre, lorsqu'il est prouvé que sans cette surveillance il pourroit totament se détruire.

"Dès que le privilége de la Ferme Générale la fait devenir administratrice en quelque partie susceptible de rentrer dans l'ensemble des opérations de l'Etat, ne reste-t-elle pas de plein droit sous la main des Ministres du Roi, seuls Administrateurs du Royaume?

"Ces principes adoptés au commencement de 1786, par l'érection d'un comité d'Administration, ont été confirmés par la décision du 24 Mai 1786; leur nécessité est aujourd'hui consacrée par une double expérience.

"Aureste on a vû si l'intérêt propre de la Ferme, n'éxige pas qu'on l'empêche de faire des traités, et d'éloigner les propriétaires d'une denrée dont elle a un besoin absolu, et dont elle pourroit même un jour fournir la moitié de l'Europe, si par sa constitution elle n'étoit pas constamment et inévitablement entrainée à appliquer au commerce des principes fiscaux. . . . Les Exposans, avant de conclure, doivent prévenir le Gouvernement sur l'explication que la Ferme Générale pourroit donner à la décision, relativement au terme auquel elle doit commencer. La décision du Conseil ordonnoit que la Ferme recevroit 12 à 15000 boucauds de tabac par an, aux mêmes prix et conditions stipulés par le traité du sieur Morris. Elle fut prononcée le 24 Mai 1786, mais les plaintes du commerce duroient depuis six mois, et il souffroit depuis plus long-tems. Les mémoires avoient été remis en Décembre 1785. La décision fut retardée par le temps fort long que la Ferme prit pour répondre; par les discussions qu'elle occasionna; par les intervales des séances; mais les tabacs n'en étoient pas moins accumulés depuis plusieurs mois.

"En jurisprudence, les droits et les dommages sont adjugés du jour de la demande et non du jour du jugement. Si un principe contraire pouvoit être admis en cette affaire et dans toute discusion du commerce avec la Ferme Générale, l'intérêt qu'elle auroit à les faire traîner en longueur, deviendroit aussi pernicieux que le mal même: prolonger pour elle, seroit gagner sa cause; puisque le commerce lassé et dépourvu des moyens d'attendre, est enfin réduit à céder. La décision a donc évidemment porté sur les tabacs qui étoient accumulés depuis près d'un an dans les ports. La Ferme Générale l'a reconnu elle-même, puisqu'elle a commencé à exécuter la décision par ces mêmes tabacs.

"Enfin, l'esprit et la lettre de la décision du Conseil, ayant été bien évidemment de traiter le commerce particulier à l'instar du contrat de M. Morris, dont on vouloit ainsi amortir les fâcheux effets; il n'est pas douteux que l'année de la décision ne soit pour les particuliers ce qu'est pour le sieur Morris l'année du traité. Or, puisqu'il avoit toute l'année 1786 pour fournir les vingt mille boucauds, (et l'on sait qu'il a porté bien plus loin cette liberté) le commerce que lui associoit la décision, avoit indubitablement l'année entiere pour fournir les 12 à 15000 boucauds fixés. Si le Conseil avoit eu une intention contraire, la décision eût été différemment exprimée; elle eût désigné numérativement la totalité des tabacs que devoit fournir le commerce; elle n'en eût pas laissé la fixation à faire arbitrairement dix-neuf mois après par la Ferme Générale. Elle a donc eu à acheter 12 à 15000 boucauds en 1786 et 12 à 15000 boucauds en 1787. Ce seroit l'un dans l'autre 13500 boucauds par an, et en totalité vingt-sept mille boucauds que la Ferme a pris l'engagement de recevoir du commerce, aux prix et conditions du traité du sieur Morris et de vaisseaux Americains ou François.

"CONCLUSIONS. Les Exposans produisent sous le No. 9, l'état fourni par la Ferme Générale, des tabacs qu'elle a reçus des particuliers en 1786 & 1787, avant et depuis la décision du Conseil du 24 Mai 1786. D'après lequel elle auroit reçu aux prix de la décision 16573 boucauds de tabacs.

"Mais il y a sur cet état quelques erreur, et les Exposans y trouvent 3122 boucauds contraires à l'engagement exprimé par la décision, ainsi que 597 boucauds qui pourroient être admis seulement après les détails que la Ferme devroit donner sur leur origine.

"L'état des reprises des Exposans se trouve joint aux Pieces justificatives sous le N°. 10. Il en résulte que la Ferme, qui selon son engagement devoit recevoir du commerce en 1786 et 1787 27,000 boucauds de tabac, n'a récellement reçu aux termes de la décision que 12,854 bouc. [*which, together with 597 hhds. whose origin is in doubt, leaves a*] Déficit dans l'exécution de la décision du Conseil, et que la Ferme doit encore recevoir du Commerce 13,549 bouc. . . .

"En conséquence, les Exposans osent conclure à ce que vu les lenteurs et retards volontaires qui oppriment le commerce depuis si long-temps; retards que la Ferme fait sur-tout peser avec une inégalité marquée sur les Exposans, puisqu'elle a reçu dans les autres Ports les tabacs arrivés jusqu'en Mai ou Juin, et qu'elle leur laisse sur les bras des tabacs arrivés depuis un an, ce qui les met dans une situation fâcheuse et pressante: le ministere veuille bien ordonner.

"1°. Que la Ferme Générale recevra provisoirement dans le port de l'Orient et sans délai la quantité de 3500 boucauds de tabacs, par ordre de dates d'arrivée, et aux termes de la décision du Conseil du 24 Mai 1786, et qu'elle justifiera avant la fin du présent mois de Janvier des ordres donnés par elle à cet égard.

"2°. Qu'elle complettera l'exécution de la décision de Bernis par l'achat dés 10,049 boucauds qui resteront à recevoir (sauf à ajouter la quotité de 597 boucauds douteux) et que cet achat se fera dans tous les ports indifféremment, sans préférence, en suivant les dates d'arrivées pour l'ordre de réception, de maniere que les tabacs arrivés par exemple à l'Orient en Novembre, ne soient reçus qu'après ceux qui seroient arrivés en Octobre à Bordeaux ou ailleurs, et vice versa, ce dont elle justifiera avant la fin de Février 1788, par des états détaillés des arrivées et des ordres qu'elle aura donnés à ses préposés pour chaque port.

"3°. Que les propriétaires des tabacs retardés seront autorisés à ajouter à leurs factures 45 sols tournois par boucauds, par chaque mois de retard que leur a fait supporter la Ferme sur les tabacs arrivés depuis la décision, pour représenter les intérêts et le magasinage; en déduisant cependant deux mois depuis la date de l'arrivée.

"Et que si quelque besoin momentané porte M M. les Fermiers-Généraux à prolonger le terme des lettres qu'ils fourniront en payement au-delà du terme du traité, ils en bonnifieront l'intérêt aux vendeurs au cours de la place.

"4°. Et attendu que la démonstration des pernicieux effets du traité du sieur Morris pour la Nation, après avoir été reconnue par le vœu du Comité et par la décision du Conseil, a été portée depuis par les faits jusqu'a l'évidence. On demande que d'après l'article premier de cette décision, il soit sevérement défendu à la Ferme Générale de faire aucun traité du même genre, mais même, sous quelque prétexte que ce soit, de donner aucune suite ou prolongation à ce traité terminé depuis le premier Janvier 1788; ni de recevoir dorénavant à plus haut prix ou plus célérement que ceux de tout autre particulier, les tabacs de ce Négociant ou de tout autre. Les faveurs dont l'a comblé la Ferme ont déjà trop coûté à l'Etat.

"Comme le traité du sieur Morris est expiré le premier Janvier, et attendu que la loi doit être réciproque, il paroît juste en même tems de proposer, que si la quantité de tabacs du commerce qui se trouveront arrivés dans les divers ports jusqu'au 31 Décembre 1787 n'est pas assez considérable pour completter les 27,000 boucauds fixés par la décision, la Ferme n'en sera pas moins sensée avoir rempli son engagement, dès qu'elle aura reçu tous les tabacs entrés dans les ports jusqu'à cette même époque.

"5°. Que pour assurer l'exécution de l'article ci-dessus, il soit ordonné que dorénavant et comme l'explique l'article 2 de ces conclusions, la Ferme Générale ne pourra dans ses achats de tabacs Américains intervertir l'ordre des dattes d'arrivées dans tous les ports pris ensemble, de maniere que tous les tabacs arrivés dans un mois dans les divers ports de France, seront reçus avant ceux qui entreront dans quelque port que ce soit dans le mois suivant.

"Ainsi, le commerce Américain ne sera plus contrarié. Il se portera de lui-même où l'attireront les convenances qui peuvent le fixer. Sans cette régle la Ferme seroit encore la maitresse de faire souffrir la majeure partie du commerce dans un ou deux ports propres aux Américains en feignant d'en favoriser une portion dans les places qui leur conviennent le moins.

"6°. Les arrangemens ci-dessus nécessitent une fixation de prix faite d'avance. On sent que l'obligation d'acheter imposée à la Ferme, devient illusoire si elle reste maitresse des prix; ce seroit rouvrir la porte aux procédés arbitraires, aux préférences et aux traités secrets; mais aussi il se trouve divers inconvéniens à le fixer publiquement long-tems à l'avance, comme le traité y avoit obligé le ministere à l'epoque de la décision. Il ne faut pas que la fixation de prix en Europe puisse influer sur ceux des Etats-Unis.

"Il est un moyen aussi simple que juste de concilier les droits de tous et les intérêts de l'Etat.

"C'est d'arrêter ce prix tous les quatre mois à un taux équitable, d'après le cours de l'étranger, et de la même maniere que se fixent les prix des denrées coloniales pour le droit du Domaine d'Occident.

"7°. Enfin, vu l'importance de cette branche d'administration, et la nécessité prouvée de surveiller continuement l'exécution des plans du ministere. Les Exposans osent humblement proposer qu'il soit désigné tel conseil ou comité permanent d'administration spécialement chargé de veiller à l'exécution fidelle de la décision du 24 Mai 1786, ainsi que de celles qui pourront suivre, comme aussi de rendre provisoirement et célérement justice au commerce. Ce comité présideroit à la fixation des prix.

"Sans un tel établissement, quelques ordres que le ministere donne à la Ferme, le commerce sera toujours languissant. Ses maux par de tardifs redressemens ne seront jamais réparés; les plaintes, les débats renaîtront sans cesse; les Négocians François découragés refuseront des avances aux Américains; ceux-ci s'éloigneront; et la France perdra totalement un commerce intéressant qu'il semble facile de conserver et d'étendre.

CONSULTATION. Perignon, "Avocat aux Conseils du Roi," to whom the foregoing memorial was submitted, finds, in an opinion of 8 Jan. 1788, that the demands of the merchants of L'Orient are the natural and necessary consequences of the decision of Council of 24 May 1786; that the interest of the state, as well as the interest of the merchants, requires that that decision be fully executed; that the exclusive contract between the farmers-general and Morris was prejudicial to the state and to the farm itself; that equity requires the purchases as stipulated in the decision of Berni be carried out in all ports without discrimination, according to the date of arrival of cargoes; that, nevertheless, since the farm had suspended purchases at L'Orient earlier than elsewhere, justice requires that the farm receive without delay a proportionate quantity from that port; that 3,500 hhds. would appear to be a moderate and justifiable quantity; that both reason and facts produced have shown that the farm's delays caused a real injury to commerce; that the merchants of L'Orient, therefore, are entitled to ask reimbursement of the farm for interest and warehouse charges for those cargoes affected by such delays; that they should be authorized to add a certain sum to the cost of each hogshead for each month of delay, though, since no cargo can ever be sold immediately on arrival, the merchants should agree that "les mois de retard" be begun two months after the arrival of the cargo; that the other conclusions of the merchants are considered to be well founded; that the administration should regulate the price to be paid the consignees of tobacco at stipulated periods of each year, for example every four months, in order to avoid the harm resulting from fixing prices long in advance; that the merchants have proposed only one means of doing this with information about causes and circumstances affecting this branch of commerce, namely, the establishment of a permanent committee or council of administration charged with supervising the execution of the decision of Berni, with the rendering of prompt and provisional justice to this commerce, and with the fixing of equitable prices; that, in consequence of the facts set forth in the memorial, it could not be doubted that government would soon see under its eyes, under the protection of this committee, an interesting branch of commerce developing rapidly. "Accoutumés à apporter leurs tabacs dans nos ports, les Américains y verseront toutes les productions de leurs climats, ils emporteront nos denrées en retour et la France se trouvera l'entrepôt du commerce le plus florissant et le plus utile."

The following letter of 20 Oct. 1787, from one of the first houses of Philadelphia to a firm of L'Orient, received since the printing of the present *Mémoire*, will make better known than any argument the dispositions that the conduct of the farmers-general has given rise to in the United States: "We shall be happy to serve your views as to consignments when in our power. But whilst the Farmers refuse Tobacco from individuals and discourage their shipping it, as they have lately done, there can not much commercial inter course be expected between the two countries, especially when, as of late, they disregard such obligations as that of the committee of Berni, and leave many on this side the dupes of the confidence reposed in them. We hope to hear some favorable change has taken place in this matter. . . ."

PIECES JUSTIFICATIVES

No. I.

Paris, le 26 Août 1785.

"MEMOIRE donné par M. Barclay, Consul général des Etats-unis de l'Amerique, à Monseigneur le Contrôleur général.

UN Contract pour la livraison des Tabacs à Ferme, tel que celui qu'on dit avoir été conclu, c'est-a-dire, pour une quantité à peu près égale à la consommation de deux ou trois ans, doit verser naturellement tout le Commerce des Tabacs entre l'Amérique et la France dans les mains de deux ou trois individus, car il est à présumer que lorsque ce contract sera connu en Amérique, personne, à l'exception de ceux qui sont engagés par ce Contract, n'osera charger du Tabac pour la France, vu le peu d'espoir que l'on aura d'en trouver un débit raisonnable; ce principe de monopole doit être injurieux à la France à tous égards: car le débouché étant, pour ainsi dire, fermé ici par ce Contract, les Américains se trouveront dans la nécessité d'envoyer leurs Tabacs ailleurs, et par le retour de leurs bâtimens recevront les Marchandises provenantes des Manufactures de ce Pays, au lieu de celles de la France. Il est possible et même probable que ceux qui ont fait ce Contract, prennent quelques denrées Françoises en retour, mais il est certain que la quantité en seroit infiniment plus conséquente, si ce commerce étroit libre et ouvert.

"Le monopole du Tabac en France en entraînera un second en Amérique, et le Commerce réciproque des deux Etats sera restreint aux personnes seules qui ont fait le Contract. Cette circonstance sera suivie d'une rivalité (il est à craindre, peu favorable aux Fabriques de France) entre les contractans, qui seuls tireront des Fabriques Françoises, et le Commerce en général; car ces derniers tireront leurs denrées des endroits où ils trouveront un débit pour leurs Tabacs, et useront de tous leurs moyens pour s'en assurer un débouché en préférence. On peut même craindre que les lettres de change tirées de l'Amérique pour le Tabac contracté, ne soient remises en Angleterre pour l'achat de leurs Fabriques, ce qui ne pourroit qu'ajouter au désavantage entre la France et l'Angleterre, déjà trop onéreux, puisqu'il perd dans ce moment près de 10 pour 100.

"Il étoit à présumer qu'en conséquence de la franchise accordée à l'Orient et autres Ports, que la France auroit été un dépôt général de Tabac pour toute l'Europe; car les Américains, assurés dans le principe d'un débouché considérable, auroient, par la concurrence, fourni bien au-delà des besoins de la Ferme: elle auroit eu le choix; les prix, par cette concurrence, auroient été modérés, le surplus auroit passé à l'étranger, et le débouché des Fabriques de France auroit été infiniment conséquent.

"Il est mortifiant d'ajouter que ces avantages précieux sont perdus sans ressource par le Contract en question.

No. II. The decision of 24 May 1786 [*omitted here; for text, see* Vol. 9:586-8].

No. III. Circular letter of the farmers-general to its officers [*omitted here; see summary of salient points above*].

Nos. IV, V, VI. Tables of exports and imports for L'Orient [*omitted here; for summaries, see text above*].

No. VII. Table of exports to Ireland and Scotland [*omitted here; see summary above.*]

No. VIII. Letter from a commercial house of L'Orient to the farmers-general in July 1787 [*omitted here; this is the letter from Messrs. Bérard & Cie. of 14 July 1787, printed in* Vol. 12:78-82].

No. IX. State of purchases made by the farm from commercial houses and individuals from 1 Jan. 1786 to 3 Sep. 1787 at eleven ports [*omitted here; for summary, see* Vol. 12:212].

No. X. Memoire on tobacco received by the farmers-general in 1786 and 1787 [*omitted here; see summary of salient figures above*].

The above summary is based on the copy sent by Vernes to TJ; it is now in DLC (see Sowerby, No. 3610) and has two pagination sequences: p. [1]-62, the text of the *Mêmoire*, and p. [1]-30, the *Pièces Justificatives* (designated above as Appendix); the following imprint appears on p. 60 (p. 61-2 being blank when the form was first completed, but afterwards having the letter from Philadelphia of 20 Oct. 1787 added to these pages): "[Paris] De l'Imprimerie de L. F. Prault, Imprimeur du Roi, Quai des Augustins, à l'Immortalité. 1788" (a variant of Prault's imprint appears on p. 30 of the second sequence). This (TJ's own copy) in DLC is bound up with another copy, together with Lafayette's *Résumé De l'Avis . . . au Comité*, the reply of the farmers-general, and Lafayette's rebuttal in three parallel columns, the whole being bound in contemporary French calf with the label: "American Commerce" (the binder erred in placing the eight folding sheets of tabulations—No. IX of the *Pièces Justificatives*—in incorrect sequence and after p. 24 instead of following p. [22], which is blank and the page on which No. IX belongs); see Sowerby, No. 3610. Another complete copy of the *Mêmoire* is in Arch. Aff. Etr., Paris, Corr. Pol., E.-U., Vol. XXXIII, accompanying the covering letter from Vernes to Montmorin of 15 Feb. 1788. A MS version, representing an early stage of the text of the *Mêmoire*, is in Arch. Aff. Etr., Mémoires et Documents, IX; photostats in DLC.

From William Carmichael

DEAR SIR   Madrid 14 April 1788

I received on the 26th. Decr. your favor of the 13th[1] of that month. I have endeavoured in vain to decypher by means of the cypher which Mr. Barclay left with me the three first lines of your letter of the 14th June 1787. Nor have my efforts been more successful in my attempts to decypher that of Sep. 25th altho' I have tryed every method perscribed for that Effect. I therefore take it for granted that Colonel Franks must have made some mistake in the delivery of the Cypher. In the course of this I will merely for the sake of conviction employ some phrases of my cypher of which you may divine the Sense, should not our cyphers correspond as I really am persuaded they do not. It is a vexatious circumstance for me, as it has not only deprived me of your sentiments and information but occupied uselessly some hours almost every day for several weeks in endeavours to break the Shell that I might enjoy the kernel. Patience is a very necessary virtue here and I am constrained to practise it *porfuezza* in its fullest sense. Our new constitution has employed some part of the Idle Moments of the Corps Diplomatic and others here. The general conclusion seems to be that, if adopted, it will give energy and consequently respectability to our confederation. The first view of its outlines I own, revolted me and perhaps I wrote too soon and too freely my sentiments thereon to America. Had I been in [*Maryland*][2] I should in all probability have been of the sentiment of Paca and the other you mention. At all Events I would have been for a fair discussion and not as some have done, insisted on accepting or rejecting it in toto. However dangerous may be delay I confess that I think a Removal of the principal Objections which separate states may make to its acceptance, by the Convention which Congress, as you suppose, may in that case assemble, has my strongest approbation. A general approbation will effectually disappoint the hopes of our Enemies of being able to divide us and encourage others to form connections from a firm assurance of our respectability. The rapidity and success with which our western lands have been sold astonishes the Corps diplomatic here and all reflecting persons. It was a peice of Intelligence which I circulated with much pleasure, perhaps there was some malice in my satisfaction when I observed the Effect it had on the countenances of the B. M. and of some of his partizans. That Minister labours incessantly to encourage the Pacific disposition of this Court, on the other hand, I am persuaded the F. E. takes all the pains in his power to inspire a jealousy of the hostile Intentions of G. B. and its Allies. From many Circumstances I am induced to beleive there is at present a very good understanding between the two latter. The C. F. B.'s language is pacific and I am convinced that nothing but a conviction of the hostile views of the B. C. can make him deviate from the system which he has formed of Rendering to the Nation over the councils of which he presides that internal Vigor and happiness which it had in great measure lost from the maladministration of Many of his Predecessors in Office. There are still however accounts of Armaments in the Sea Ports and altho' these are sometimes Contradicted, it is more than probable that such preparations are making as will enable this court, if necessary, to show Europe at a short notice, the Respectability of its maritime Force. Indeed it seems necessary that such precautions should be taken at this Crisis.

The Turkish Embassador left this court without being regretted by any one except some Ladies whom curiosity or other motives Induced to frequent his Society. He was a petulant and childish character. His Mission hath cost however considerably to this Court. I have sent the amount to Congress to shew what we may expect from Similar Connections. The Algerines seem at length contented. In truth they ought to be. The Sums they have received from hence ought to deter our councils from ever having recourse to the same mode of pacification. I have received no letters from thence for a long time. The plague has broke out again and it is apprehended that it may be as fatal as in the last year. I have received no answer to the Letters I have written Mr. Jay relative to the support of our Captives. Since the Orders given by Mr. Lamb while there, I have taken nothing upon myself on their account. You will have been advised of the proceedings of the Assembly of the Accionista of the Bank of St. Charles and the result of its decisions. Nothing can be more contrary to our Ideas, than the manner in which their deliberations were conducted. If I thought it a subject which would interest you, I would enter into the most minute details as I beleive I am au fait on this head. The inclosed Gazette containing an ordinance prohibiting the importation by foreign vessels of Many articles essential to their commerce, unless in what are styled here priveledged ports, hath excited the Attention of the Corps Diplomatic. Its execution is delayed for six months. As we can claim no exemption from treaty, I observe the reclamations made against it by others, if they Succeed, I then may interest myself. Also, as I have written promises, that America shall be treated as the most favored Nation, until a Commercial Treaty fixes the footing on which we are to be with this Country. It is reported that France is negotiating if it has not concluded a commercial Convention. I have endeavoured to discover whether there is any truth in this Report, but without success, unless it be called such to know that in the ports, the French are not treated at present with more favor than Heretofore. Various reports have been circulated here that the Kentucke people had descended the River Missisippi with the Intention of Attacking the Spanish Settlements and these originate as far as I have been able to trace them from G.B. I have been told that the Minister has expressed his uneasiness and displeasure on the receipt of this news. I have taken Measures to be ascertained of the truth of this Circumstance and shall be probably able to advise you before the close of this Letter, for wishing to have a secure opportunity of writing I have been led into an unpardonable delay, expecting every instant to have it in my power to explain to you fully and freely my Sentiments. I have spoken to Campomanes and several others on the subject you mention respecting the plan of cutting thro' the Isthmus of Panama. These Gentlemen have all assured me, that it has been only Ideal, that no particular survey has been Made for this purpose, for that the face of the Country and the apparent obstacles had discouraged the Government from an Expence that the Nature of the Local seemed to indicate would be Useless. Campomanes has promised me to make very particular inquiries on this head and I will endeavour to prevail upon him, if his Occupations will permit him, to favor me with his Sentiments in writing on this Subject. Ulloa is not here at present. When I last saw him, he appeared much broken in mind and Body. I have yet received no remittances from America and my situation would be deplorable if my personal credit was not good here. With this advantage however it is distressing, for the sense of obligations and the necessity of having recourse to others, without any given time for repayment preys upon my spirits. I have written to my Brother to sell or Mortgage a tract of Land, to enable me to sustain my Career here, until Congress shall think proper to recall or to support me regularly and have given bills at long date of payment to Merchants here to receive no advances from them until, these bills are accepted. I have written thrice to Mr. Jay since the month of June last on the necessity of remittances, but I have no answer. I suppose in fact that there are no funds. Mr. Littlepage wrote me from New York some time previous to his departure for Europe that he had directed his Guardian to pay the ballance due me to Messrs. Hoe and Harrison at Alexandria, in consequence of this advice I inclosed his Obligation to my Attorney to receive the money that these Gentlemen should pay on his accompt not only for the amount of that obligation but for what else he might credit me for in the note which I supposed he had left with his Guardians. Of Course his subsequent application to me in Europe with offers of repayment could not be attended to by me until I knew whether I had been paid in America or not. I now know that on the first of Feby 1783 no offers of reimbursing me in America had ever been made. I therefore can now pray him to pay to your order (since you permit me to take this Liberty) what he thinks I advanced for him, without Interest, because when I gave him the Money which he calls a trifle, I distressed myself to serve him without any interested view whatever. I shall write him on the Subject. I have just received the inclosed Letter for you from Monsr. Chiappe. I was in some pain at his long silence since I dispatched the Ratification. It appears however that we are still in favor. I have seen the Emperor's Diatribe against G. B. He wants money and I suppose England will give it him or make this rupture a pretext for arming a Squadron for the Mediterranean. The Armaments continue here. They are too small for great Objects and too great for Little ones. I still persist in thinking that Spain before the end of June will be able to send 30 sail of the Line to sea. The British Minister is uneasy, but he has no instructions as yet to demand the reason of these Armaments and I beleive as far as I can judge he will leave this disagreable task to Mr. Eden. [*Maryland*] has not acceded to the Constitution, [*Massachusetts*] has. The [*majority*] seem pleased with it, what says [*you*?] I dare not ask you to excuse my long Silence. I have given you the true motives and I intreat you to believe me.

With great Respect and Esteem Yr. Excys. Obliged & Hble. Sert,

WM CARMICHAEL

RC (DLC); partly in code. Enclosures: (1) Probably Francisco Chiappe to TJ, 6 Mch. 1788. (2) The enclosed gazette has not been identified. See also Carmichael to TJ, 5 June 1788.

[1] Thus in MS; it should have read "15th."

[2] This and subsequent words in italics and in brackets (supplied) are written in code and have been conjecturally decoded by the Editors. This code (Code No. 13) was the one that David Franks left with Carmichael in Nov. 1786; see note to TJ to Carmichael, 25 Sep. 1787.

From Stephen Cathalan, Jr.

Marseilles, 15 Apr. 1788. Forwards a letter just received for TJ from Giuseppe Chiappe; will be glad to transmit any letters TJ may wish to send to Chiappe. Hopes TJ has received through John Turnbull the meteorological observations of Marseilles; would like to know what he should pay the copyist. The farmers-general have purchased a cargo of Virginia tobacco at Sète at 34.tt15s and have given orders to purchase all unsold tobacco at Marseilles at 33tt; one cargo was sold there at that price but Cathalan and the other merchants are holding their supplies; they have been informed from America that no tobacco will be shipped from there for a long time; if the farmers-general are forced to prove purchases of 4666 hhds. in the next month they will have to buy at Marseilles; the merchants rely on TJ's negotiations with Lambert. An arrêt has recently been published which annuls the privileges granted in the arrêt of 29 Dec. 1787 in regard to duties on fish oils; he has not seen a copy of the new regulation but if the report is true he will suffer a loss on a shipment of such oil which he received on 28 Jan. Asks TJ to inform him what changes have really taken place and whether he can secure the benefits of the regulations of 29 Dec. 1787 which were in full effect on the date the shipment was received. Has sent his power of attorney to Philadelphia for the collection of the debt due him from Thomas Barclay in accordance with law in the United States. They have news from Turkey but nothing more recent than the previous month.

RC (DLC); 4 p.; endorsed. Enclosure: Giuseppe Chiappe to TJ, 6 Mch. 1788.

From John Bondfield

Bordeaux, 19 Apr. 1788. Acknowledges TJ's letters of 22 Feb. and 3 Mch.; forwarded TJ's letter to Pichard; hearing nothing from Pichard, wrote him and received the enclosed reply. The "Vins d'hautbrion belonging to Monsr. Le Cte. De fumel" are esteemed as next in quality and a few hogsheads of this of the 1784 vintage are available. Has received "two Cases vin de frontignac from Mons. Lambert" which he will forward to Moustier in New York. The "check occationd by the overstock of Tobacco" at Bordeaux the previous fall having given "another channel to the American Navigation, it may be twelve months before any imports of consiquence come this way"; nevertheless, the "market at present presents the most favorable sales."

RC (DLC); 2 p.; endorsed. Enclosure (MHi): Pichard to Bondfield, Libourne, 13 Apr. 1788, asking him to inform TJ that he has no "vin de la fitte de l'année 1784"; that he is sorry and hopes to serve him in the future; that he would have written TJ immediately if "Mr. Jefferson avoit datte sa lettre et meut envoye son adresse"; and that, though he had some "vin de la fitte de lannee 1786," it was not yet potable.

To William Short

⟦*19 Apr. 1788.* Recorded in SJL Index. Not found; the letter may have concerned the matter of the conference with Lambert that Vernes had discussed in his letter to TJ of 10 Apr. 1788, which TJ received at Strasbourg on 16 Apr.⟧

From Abraham Baldwin

Sir New York 20th April 1788

Your favour of the 7th of Feby., with the enclosure from Mr. Fanning, was duly received.

In the letter to Mr. Fanning, which I do myself the honour to enclose, I have given him all the information he will need for the security of his surveys. It must undoubtedly have occurred to you, Sir, that the present unexplained state of our southern and western boundary must have rendered it improper for the state of Georgia to do any thing respecting the private right of soil to the lands on the Missisippi. Many applications have been made, but the general assembly has never done any thing, but what appear[ed] necessary to prevent the present settlers in that country, from becoming our enemies from the apprehension that we might deprive them of their possessions.

My expectation is that the state of Georgia will soon[1] make a cession of their western territory to congress. They have long only waited an issue of our present great national question, whither they might expect protection in return.

It did not appear necessary to state either of these reasons to Mr. Fanning, as the measures to be pursued by him, for securing his ancient surveys of land in that territory, will probably be much the same, whether his titles are to be obtained from the state of Georgia or from the united States. With the greatest respect and esteem I have the honour to be, Sir, your most obedient humble servt.,

ABR BALDWIN

RC (DLC); endorsed. The enclosed letter to Fanning (missing) was forwarded by TJ in his to Fanning, 29 July 1788.

The FAVOUR here acknowledged was TJ's to the Georgia delegates in Congress, 7 Feb. 1788.

[1] At this point TJ inserted an asterisk and wrote at the bottom of the page: "They have done this. See New York journal. Mar. 17." It is surprising that Baldwin should not have known of the Georgia cession at this date. Writing from New York on 16 Apr. 1788, Rufus King said: "Georgia has ceded upwards of Thirty Millions of acres of land lying between the 31st and 33d degrees of lat. and between the Apalachicola and the Mississippi to the United States, on condition that nine or more states ratify the new constitution"; the news of Georgia's conditional cession was certainly known in Congress at the time Baldwin wrote (C. R. King, *Life of Rufus King*, I, 326; Burnett, *Letters of Members*, VIII, No. 830, note 3; No. 831). *The New-York Journal, and Daily Patriotic Register* for 17 Mch. 1788 carried the following notice: "Augusta, Feb. 19. *Extract from the Proceedings* of the present House of Assembly . . . February 8. Yesterday the honorable general assembly of this state adjourned. . . . During their session they passed the following laws: . . . An Act to empower the delegates of this state in Congress assembled to sign, seal, and deliver, a deed of cession to the United States of certain western territory belonging to this state."

From Espinay de Laye

Lyons, 20 Apr. 1788. Is writing on behalf of Alexandre Berger, a merchant of Lyons and a member of "une Tres Bonne Et ancienne famille dans le Commerce," who wishes to go to Richmond and would like a letter of recommendation and the necessary passports. Is sending this letter by a brother of "M. le prieur D'Arnas," his neighbor, whom TJ saw "dans ma Terre en Beaujolois" and to whom TJ gave a copy of "L'histoire de vos provinces." Knowing Berger's family and also knowing TJ's "maniere de penser" and his "amour a obliger," asks TJ to assist Berger, "Soit par vos conseils, Soit par des lettres de Recommandation." Believing TJ is interested in his personal affairs and those of his son, informs him that his son has just been made a captain of cavalry "dans le Regiment Dauphin"; hopes TJ will see his son and aid him with his advice. Mme. de Laye joins in sending compliments and in the hope that they may again see TJ in their home; also sends his compliments to TJ's kinsman who lives with him and reminds him of "la promesse qu'il m'a faite de me venir voir."

RC (ViWC); 2 p.; in French; endorsed.

The reference to TJ's kinsman is doubtless to William Short who visited the Château de Laye in the autumn of 1788 (see Short to TJ, 24 Sep. and 2 Oct.1788).

From James Madison

Dear Sir Virginia Orange April 22. 1788

Being just acquainted by a letter from President Griffin that Mr. Paridise is in N. York and proposes to sail in the first packet for France I drop you a few lines which will go by that conveyance if they arrive in N. York in time; which however I do not much expect.

The proposed Constitution still engrosses the public attention. The elections for the Convention here are but just over and promulged. From the returns (excluding those from Kentucky which are not yet known) it seems probable, though not absolutely certain that a majority of the members elect are friends to the Constitution. The superiority of abilities at least seems to lie on that side. The characters of most note which occur to me, are marshalled thus. For the Constitution, Pendleton, Wythe, Blair, Innis, Marshal, Doctr. W. Jones, G. Nicholas, Wilson Nicholas, Gabl. Jones, Thos. Lewis, F. Corbin, Ralph Wormley Jr. White of Frederik, Genl. Gates, Genl. A. Stephens, Archd. Stuart, Zachy. Johnson, Docr. Stuart, Parson Andrews, H. Lee Jr. Bushrod Washington considered as a young Gentleman of talents: against the Constitution, Mr. Henry, Mason, Harrison, Grayson, Tyler, M. Smith, W. Ronald, Lawson, Bland, Wm. Cabell, Dawson.

The Governor is so temperate in his opposition and goes so far with the friends of the Constitution that he cannot properly be classed with its enemies. Monroe is considered by some as an enemy, but I believe him to be a friend though a cool one. There are other individuals of weight whose opinions are unknown to me. R. H. Lee is not elected. His brother F. L. Lee is a warm friend to the Constitution, as I am told, but also is not elected. So are Jno. and Man Page.

The adversaries take very different grounds of opposition. Some are opposed to the substance of the plan; others to particular modifications only. Mr. H——y is supposed to aim at disunion. Col. M——n is growing every day more bitter, and outrageous in his efforts to carry his point; and will probably in the end be thrown by the violence of his passions into the politics of Mr. H——y. The preliminary question will be whether previous alterations shall be insisted on or not? Should this be carryed in the affirmative, either a conditional ratification, or a proposal for a new Convention will ensue. In either event, I think the Constitution and the Union will be both endangered. It is not to be expected that the States which have ratified will reconsider their determinations, and submit to the alterations prescribed by Virga. and if a second Convention should be formed, it is as little to be expected that the same spirit of compromise will prevail in it as produced an amicable result to the first. It will be easy also for those who have latent views of disunion, to carry them on under the mask of contending for alterations popular in some but inadmissible in other parts of the U. States.

The real sense of the people of this State cannot be easily ascertained. They are certainly attached and with warmth to a continuance of the Union; and I believe a large majority of the most intelligent and independent are equally so to the plan under consideration. On a geographical view of them, almost all the counties in the N. Neck have elected fœderal deputies. The Counties on the South side of James River have pretty generally elected adversaries to the Constitution. The intermediate district is much chequered in this respect. The Counties between the blue ridge and the Alleghany have chosen friends to the Constitution without a single exception. Those Westward of the latter, have as I am informed, generally though not universally pursued the same rule. Kentucky it is supposed will be divided.

Having been in Virga. but a few weeks, I can give you little account of other matters, and none of your private affairs or connections, particularly of your two nephews. The Winter here as every where else in the U.S. was very severe, which added to short crops of corn, threatened a great scarcity and high price. It is found however that neither of these evils has taken place. Corn may be purchased for 2 dollars, and even 10s. per barrel. Tobacco is as low at Fredb. as 18/ per Ct. and not higher at Richmond than 22 or 23/. There is at present a very promising spring, especially in the article of fruit. The night before last was so cold as to produce an alarm for the vegetation of all sorts; but it does not appear that any thing less vulnerable than young cucumbers has been injured.

I shall ask the favor of Mr. Griffin to send you by Mr. Paridise, or if he should be gone by some other hand, the debates of the Conventions in Penna. and Massachussetts, and any other publications worth your reading.

I am Dear Sir your affect. friend & Servt.,

Js. Madison Jr.

RC (DLC: Madison Papers); endorsed.

From De Rieger

[*Paris, after 22 Apr. 1788*] Announces that he has had an audience with the king and royal family, on Tuesday, 22 Apr., "en Sa qualité de Ministre Plénipotentiaire du Duc de Wurtemberg."

RC (DLC); without date, but probably written soon after the audience announced; at foot of text: "Aux arcades du Palais Royal No. 123. Côté de la ruë des Bons enfans."

From William Shippen

My dr. Sir — Philadelphia 22d. April 1788.

I am much obliged and flatterd by your great attention to my son; The obligation will be much increased if you will honor me with a few lines expressive of your opinion of his figure and improvement. I am more anxious to hear of him from you than any man in Europe because you are the best judge, and I am sure you will not *flatter* the hopes of a fond Father.

The Delegations to the Convention of Virginia and Maryland are said to be in favor of the new Constitution, but there will be a powerful opposition in each State, but from a Minority. Mr. Madison and Col. Innis are opposed to Mr. Henry and Mr. Mason. Mr. Shippen will show you the whole delegation.—If he should not be in Paris please to forward the enclosed to the Hague or Amsterdam. Present my affectionate compliments to Miss Jefferson and believe me to be My dr. Sir wth the greatest esteem Your most obedient & very humbl. Servt., W. Shippen jr

RC (DLC). Enclosure not found.

From Edward Carrington

Dear Sir — New York Apl. 24. 1788

I was but a few days ago honoured with your favor of the 21. December. Having been absent on a trip to Virginia ever since the 1st. of Jany. I was alike cut off from it, and an opportunity of writing you. Massachusetts, Jersey, Pensylvania, Deleware, Connecticut and Georgia, have adopted the Constitution. New Hampshire has been in convention upon it, but finding that a Majority had assembled under instructions or promises to vote in the Negative of whom a sufficient number were converted to turn the scale, an adjournment has taken place until June for the purpose of getting such clear of their fetters, and it is not doubted by the Friends of the measure, that this will be effected so that a ready adoption will be the consequence of their reassembling. New York, Maryland, Virginia, North Carolina and South Carolina are to deliberate between this and July; in Maryland and South Carolina no doubt is entertained as to the adoption. In New York and Virginia very active opposition is made and the event is uncertain. In the latter it will depend much upon the ideas entertained in convention as to the issue in N. Hampshire, whose reassembling is to be after the meeting in Virga. I am certain that a great Majority of our Convention, will be for adopting upon being ascertained that nine states will adopt, as much worse apprehensions are held from the event of a disunion, than from any thing that is in the constitution.—We have a party that is truly antifederal headed by Mr. Henry, but it will be limitted to a few, unless the federalists who are for amendments, should, from a mistaken view of the probability of the measures being carried into effect by Nine States, be drawn into steps favouring the antifederal scheme.—Mr. H—— does not openly declare for a dismemberment of the union, but his Arguments in support of his opposition to the constitution go directly to that issue. He says that three confederacies would be practicable and better suited to the good of America, than one. God forbid that I should ever see the trial made. Virginia would fall into a division from which she might add to her burthens, but could never derive aid of any kind.

North Carolina is to sit after Virginia, and it is probable, will follow her. Of Rhode Island we say nothing when speaking of American politics.

Of the States which have adopted Jersey and Deleware were unanimous. Georgia we hear was also unanimous. In Pensylvania the Majority was about two thirds and the Minority continue much discontented. In Connecticut the Majority was about two thirds, the Minority acquiescing. In Massachusetts the Majority was small the Minority acquiescing. The debates of this convention have been published, a Copy whereof you will receive herewith.

It would have afforded me much pleasure to have seen your sentiments fully upon this Subject but Mr. Madison having gone to Virga. before my return to this City, I have not seen your letter to him as yet. You ask "would it not have been better to assign to Congress, exclusively, the Article of imports for federal purposes, and to have left direct Taxation exclusively to the States." It is probable that the former, aided by the Land Office, might have cleared off the present debts of the Union, and supported the current expences of Government during peace, but in a case of War, other resources must be brought into practice, and with a view to such an event, some coercive principle must have been established whereby the federal Government should act with effect, and had this not been interwoven in its civil administration, a military one must occasionally have been put in practice upon delinquent states. The former will never be excercised but when necessary, and then in a way not odious or inconvenient to the people. The latter must forever be both odious and inconvenent, let the occasion be what it may.

I feel sensibly for your situation with our numerous and too justly discontented foreign Creditors. Nor do I see a prospect of relief before the New Government shall get into operation, which must still require some time. The proposition for filling up the Loan in holland provided the Broker be suffered to retain 180,000 Guilders the interest of certain certificates in his possession of our domestic debt, will not be acceded to by Congress, and yet I do not see upon what ground we are to expect that loans will be made upon the common principle. I should myself be for acceding, because it appears that it would preserve our Credit until it is probable the new Government would commence, this I think so great an object, that I would not stand on a precise adherence to Systems. We have at present not a competent Congress to act in the Case, but from the Sentiment of the members attending, and those of the Board of Treasury, I am convinced the terms would not be accepted. I hope the views of our Creditors are turned upon the revolution which is about to take place with us, and that they may be induced to continue their patience until time shall produce the issue. I apprehend that amongst the first measures of the new Government, will be that of negotiating Loans for the purpose of satisfying the foreigners to whom the U.S. are indebted, as it will require some time to bring into practice the resources from which money is to be derivd.

I am happy that my information in the case of Commodore Jones apprised you of the hazards you might have run, and I am at the same time pleased that you fell on the expedient of acting safely without disappointing him. The business of the prize money which was paid under your direction is fully understood by Congress, and I believe every one else whose attention has been called to it.

I am much obliged by your information upon European politics.

It is true we ought not to entangle ourselves in the affairs of others, when we can avoid it, but keeping clear of them depends, in some measure, upon knowing their circumstances and views. I will venture one idea upon European politics. It would seem that the Turks should meet with support against Russia from other powers in addition to France. Russia has already a vast Territory which is peopling fast; she is also growing in naval force. Suppose she should get Turkey with those seas which belong to it, would she not be dangerous to the rest of Europe? I have the Honor to be Dr Sir with the most perfect respect & Esteem Your Most obt. Servt.,

Ed. Carrington

P.S. I have not a list of the Returns for the Virginia Convention or I would send it to you. It contains many obscure characters whom you would know nothing of. It is unfortunate that in this great business the passions instead of the Reason of the people were called into operation. This circumstance renders the issue then the more uncertain because a great proportion must act from the influence of a few Men whose popular talents may be exerted.

RC (DLC); endorsed. This letter was carried by John Paradise (see Carrington to TJ, 14 May 1788), who also carried THE DEBATES OF THIS CONVENTION, being a copy of *Debates, resolutions, and other proceedings, of the Convention of the Commonwealth of Massachusetts convened . . . for the purpose of assenting to and ratifying the Constitution recommended by the Grand Federal Convention*, Boston, 1788 (Sowerby, No. 3008).

To Maria Cosway

Paris Apr. 24. 1788.

I arrived here, my dear friend, the last night, and in a bushel of letters presented me by way of reception, I saw that one was of your handwriting. It is the only one I have yet opened, and I answer it before I open another. I do not think I was in arrears in our epistolary account when I left Paris. In affection I am sure you were greatly my debtor. I often determined during my journey to write to you: but sometimes the fatigue of exercise, and sometimes a fatigued attention hindered me. At Dusseldorp I wished for you much. I surely never saw so precious a collection of paintings. Above all things those of Van der Werff affected me the most. His picture of Sarah delivering Agar to Abraham is delicious. I would have agreed to have been Abraham though the consequence would have been that I should have been dead five or six thousand years. Carlo Dolce became also a violent favorite. I am so little of a connoisseur that I preferred the works of these two authors to the old faded red things of Rubens. I am but a son of nature, loving what I see and feel, without being able to give a reason, nor caring much whether there be one. At Heidelberg I wished for you too. In fact I led you by the hand thro' the whole garden. I was struck with the resemblance of this scene to that of Vaucluse as seen from what is called the chateau of Petrarch. Nature has formed both on the same sketch, but she has filled up that of Heidelberg with a bolder hand. The river is larger, the mountains more majestic and better clothed. Art too has seconded her views. The chateau of Petrarch is the ruin of a modest country house, that of Heidelbourg would stand well along side the pyramids of Egypt. It is certainly the most magnificent ruin after those left us by the antients. At Strasbourg I sat down to write to you. But for my soul I could think of nothing at Strasbourg but the promontory of noses, of Diego, of Slawkenburgius his historian, and the procession of the Strasburgers to meet the man with the nose. Had I written to you from thence it would have been a continuation of Sterne upon noses, and I knew that nature had not formed me for a Continuator of Sterne: so I let it alone till I came here and received your angry letter. It is a proof of your esteem, but I love better to have soft testimonials of it. You must therefore now write me a letter teeming with affection; such as I feel for you. So much I have no right to ask.—Being but just arrived I am not au fait of the small news respecting your acquaintance here. I know only that the princess Lubomirski is still here, and that she has taken the house that was M. de Simoulin's. When you come again therefore you will be somewhat nearer to me, but not near enough: and still surrounded by a numerous cortege, so that I shall see you only by scraps as I did when you were here last. The time before we were half days, and whole days together, and I found this too little. Adieu! God bless you! Your's affectionately,

TH: JEFFERSON

PrC (ViU).

When TJ SAT DOWN TO WRITE to Maria Cosway at Strasbourg, where he spent less than two full days, he was probably overcome less by STERNE UPON NOSES than by the climb to the top of the steeple of the cathedral, which he believed to be "the highest in the world, and the handsomest," but which he advised travellers to tackle as "the last operation of the day, as you will need a long rest after it" (see under 19 June 1788). But the association of noses and Strasbourg is another indication of the thoroughness with which he knew his Sterne. "Slawkenbergius's Tale" of the man who arrived in Strasbourg from the Promontory of Noses and precipitated a revolution in the affairs of the city because of the curiosity of the inhabitants about the size of his nose is to be found in *Tristram Shandy*, Book III, ch. xxxi-xlii, Book IV (Laurence Sterne, *Works and Life*, W. L. Cross, ed., New York, 1904, V, 103-96).

From William Gordon

Sir London Apr. 24. 1788

In a late letter to the Marquis de La Fayette I mentioned my design of writing soon to your Excellency. The reason of my having been so long silent was, that I might be able to acquaint you, that the second volume of the History was printed, which I can at length do. You was pleased generously to offer me your friendly assistance for the procuring a similar consideration for an early copy of the work, to what you obtained for Dr. Ramsay; I am therefore encouraged at the present period to apply for your aid; and design if it meets with your approbation to send you the two volumes for your inspection; and should they be honored, as I hope will be the case, with your recommendation, the bookseller will probably be willing to allow me for them what your Excellency may think reasonable, in order to an immediate translation, with an engagement to be furnished with the 3d and 4th as soon as printed off. The Marquis having obligingly hinted at a translation, I observed to him that you had mentioned the like but without intimating any thing more, so that your special proposal is not known to him. You will judge upon the propriety, or impropriety of communicating to him particulars, when you take notice of having heard from me on the subject. Pray present all the compliments to him on my behalf; and instruct me in the proper form of inserting his title and name among my subscribers, of which I am not master at present. He has honored me with a subscription for a dozen sets. If I mistake not you was a considerable sufferer by Tarleton's needlessly cruel ravages: wish to have some general account thereof in order for Insertion. I remain with great esteem Your Excellency's very humble servant,

William Gordon

Direct for me at No. 1. Orange Street Red Lion Square.

RC (DLC); endorsed; below endorsement TJ noted the following for his reply: "M.F's titles Tarlton's ravages subscribe 6. sets translation"; there are also three diagrams of unknown significance on the MS.

From John Jay

Dear Sir New York 24th. April 1788

Since the 3d. November last I have been honored with your Favors of the 19th. 22d. and 24th. September, 8th. and 27th October, 3d and 7th November, 21st and 31st December and 5th. February last—all of which have been laid before Congress; but they have given me no Orders respecting the Subjects of them.

The State of my Health was for a long Time such as to oblige me to omit some good Opportunities of writing to you fully. It is not yet perfectly re-established; but I am nevertheless so far recovered, as to have Reason to hope that the approaching Season will moderate, if not wholly remove my remaining Complaints.

Since the rising of the late Convention at Philadelphia, Congress has done but little Business, and I apprehend that will continue to be the Case while the Fate of the proposed Constitution remains undecided. You will perceive from the public Papers that it has given Occasion to Heats and Parties in several of the States.

The late commercial Arrangements of France relative to the United States, will tend to render the Connection between the two Countries more intimate. They bear Marks of Wisdom and Liberality, and cannot fail of being very acceptable. It is to be regretted that the mercantile People in France oppose a System, which certainly is calculated to bind the two Nations together, and from which both would eventually derive commercial as well as political Advantages.

It appears to me that France has not a single Ally in Europe on which she can fully depend, and it doubtless would be wise in her to endeavor so to blend her Interests with ours as if possible to render them indissoluble. This in my Opinion can only be done by giving us all the Privileges of Frenchmen, and accepting in Return all the Privileges of Americans. If they could bring themselves to adopt this Idea, their Schemes of Policy respecting us would be greatly simplified; but the Spirit of Monopoly and Exclusion has prevailed in Europe too long to be done away at once, and however enlightened the present Age may appear when compared with former ones, yet whenever ancient Prejudices are touched, we find that we only have Light enough to see our Want of more. Toleration in Commerce like Toleration in Religion gains Ground it is true; but I am not sanguine in my Expectations that either will soon take place[1] in their due Extent. I have the Honor to be &c:

JOHN JAY

FC (DNA: PCC, No. 121). Dft (NK-Iselin); with some deletions and interlineations, one of which is noted below. This letter was carried by John Paradise.

[1] At this point Jay wrote, and then deleted: "even in France."

From William Short

[*Paris, 24 Apr. 1788.* Recorded in SJL Index. Not found.]

From the South Carolina Delegates in Congress

SIR New York April 25th. 1788.

We receiv'd by the Juno from Havre your Excellency's Favor of the 13th Jany. last, accompanied by a Letter and a Cask of Rice to be forwarded to Mr. Drayton in Charleston. The Letter was forwarded on the day it came to us, but the rice cou'd not be sent by the same Conveyance. It is, however, now on board a Vessel ready to sail for that place, and we are hopeful it will arrive before the sowing Season is too far advanced to give it a Trial. As Citizens of South Carolina we beg Leave to express our thankful Acknowledgements for your Attention to the Interests of that State.

We have the Honor to be with the most perfect respect Your Excellency's Obedt. humb. Servts.,

DL. HUGER
JOHN PARKER
THOS. TUD. TUCKER

RC (MHi); endorsed: "S. Carolina Delegates of"; in Tucker's hand, signed by the delegates.

From Jean Jacques Peuchen

EXELLENCE! Cologne le 25e. Avril 1788.

Tout de suitte après la reçeption de la Lettre obligeante, que Votre Exellence eutes la grace de m'ecrire de Frankfort, je me suis dabord rendu chès le Maitre Serrurier, pour voir si les deux Poëles en question n'etoient pas encore vendû; heureusement je les trouvai encore sur les memes plaçes, ou Nous les avons quitté, et je fis sur le champ le marché avec lui, à la reserve, qu'il devoit changer le Buste d'homme en vase antique, ce qu'il m'accorda d'abord. Après donc qu'il les a arrangé en Ordre, je les ai fait mettre dans des fortes Caisses, et embarqué dans le Bateau du Capitaine Ryswyk, à l'addresse de Mrs. Nicolas & Jacob van Staphorst pour la Voiture de ƒ4½—rendu à Amsterdam.

Mais Votre Exellence sera peutetre etonnée, que les Ornements et la Main d'oevre pour les polir est si cher, Car le prix de 4½ sols la livre ne s'attend que brût, comme ils sortent de la fonderie.

Ci joint V: E: trouvera son Compte Speçifié, traduit de l'allemand en françois, telle que je viens de lui payer, montant à 95 Ecûs 47 Sols. ce qui font, à *f*1½ florins d'hollande par Ecû—143 florins et 14 sols. Crt. d'hollande, lesquelles je tirerai selon Vos ordres sur Mrs. Staphorst.

J'ai fait mettre aussi 4 ℔ couleur de fer, et une grosse Brosse dans les Caisses: avec lesquelles on lui rend son Lûstre, qu'ils perderont surement en Routte, moyenant un peu d'eau de Vie, que l'on applique à la Brosse. Et comme aparement Vous ne connoitrés pas la façon des Pierres, sur lesquelles nous plaçons ces fourneaux dans Nos Chambres, également arrangé à l'antique, et qui lui donne son ornement complette, j'ai fait mettre dans chaque caisse le juste dessein en gros papier, afin que Vous puissiés les faire faire Chès Vous par un Maçon habile.

J'espere que V: E: les reçevera en Son Tems, toute à fait à Votre Satisfaction, et si en tout cas çelà donnera Lieu que les Poëles seront introduit en Amerique, je Vous prie Monsieur de Vous souvenir de moi; car ayant des forges moi meme, ou j'ai etabli une pareille fabrique, je serai à meme de pouvoir façilitér beaucoup les Prix, peutetre au dela de 10 à 15 pour Cent au brût.

Me recomandant toujours en toute Occasion dans Votre Graçieuse Souvenir, et suis avec une Consideration des plus distingués de Votre Exellence le très hble. & obeisst. Serviteur,

Jean Jacques Peuchen

RC (MHi); endorsed.

The enclosed statement of costs "du Maitre Serrurier Göbell" showed that "le plus grand Poele" weighed 323 ℔s. and contained such ornaments as "deux Rosettes & 12 Boutons . . . une figure devant le poële . . . Guirlande attaché à la collonne . . . une grande vase, orni avec 3 tetes des femmes, entourés des Perles, & un Bouquet en fleurs . . . deux Bouchoirs"; and that "le petit Poele, egalement surmonté d'une joli Vase," weighed 175 ℔s. and had more modest ornaments: "Deux Rosettes . . . une guirlande . . . une Vase orné d'un Bouquet . . . un Medaillon . . . deux Bouchoirs . . . 4 Livres, couleur de fer" (Tr in French, MHi).

To Madame de Tessé

Paris April 25. 1788.

I am sorry, Madam, on the return from my journey, to be obliged to accost you with a letter of condolence on our common misfortunes. But Botany is the school for patience, and it's amateurs learn resignation from daily disappointments. I had the honour of telling you that after many little efforts to procure you supplies of plants in detail, I had at length got a friend, returning from hence to Virginia, to undertake to send me the whole of your catalogue, and that I thought he would not fail. He did not. He made the collection of which I have now the honour to inclose you his list. He put it on board a vessel coming to Havre in the month of December, so that according to all probability it should have arrived here in February in good time. But before the vessel could sail, the river in which she laid, was frozen up, and so continued a month. When she arrived at Havre, she was obliged to leave the port within twelve hours, during which time the plants could not be taken out. She went to Dunkirk, and delivered them to the American agent there, who immediately wrote to me; [bu]t I was gone to Amsterdam, and the plants have by this circumstance been detained a month at Dunkirk. He wrote me word he would forward them as I should direct; but thought they could not come by land safely. I suspect from this circumstance that they are packed in earth, and for another reason also, which is, that moss is not to be had in the part of Virginia from which they come. There are four boxes, and if they be packed with earth they will probably be too heavy to come by the Diligence. But on this I am desirous to receive your orders as I am doubtful myself what would be the best method of bringing them. The person in whose hands they are will do any thing we please with them, but I believe we must say particularly to him what we would have done, as he is a merchant, and not a gardener nor even an Amateur in our way. It will be with great pleasure I shall receive and execute your commands on this subject, and after asking permission to present here my respects to Madame de Tott and Monsieur de Tessé, to add assurances of my regret that my wishes and endeavors to do what may be grateful to you should be so often unsuccessful, and to tender the homage of those sentiments of respect and attachment with which I have the honour to be Madam Your most obedient & most humble servant, TH: JEFFERSON

PrC (CSmH). Enclosure not identified.

From William Duer

New York, 26 Apr. 1788. Asks TJ to deliver a letter to Daniel Parker which is enclosed.

RC (MHi); addressed and endorsed; signed by Duer as secretary to the commissioners of the treasury. The enclosed letter to Parker has not been found.

From Madame de Tessé

a châville ce 27 avril [1788]

Vous arrivés, Monsieur, pour Repandre des bienfaits et le plus grand de tous est sans doute votre presence. Je suis bien empressée den jouir et si vous m'accordiés la grace de diner chés moi mercredi à Paris, le petit voyage que j'y vais faire loin dêtre considéré comme une privation ainsi que jai coutume denvisager tout le tems que j'enleve a la campagne me paroîtra infiniment heureux. Puisque vous ordonnés que je décide la manière quon doit prendre pour faire arriver les plans de virginie retenus a dunkerque je prononcerai qu'ils doivent aller par mer au havre et du havre ici par la seine, en observant de ne les point faire arriver à Paris, ce qui revient a des Retards et a des droits tout a fait inutiles, mais de les faire arreter par le correspondant du havre au Pecq près de st. germain en se servant de l'adresse cy jointe. Mon jardinier anglois assure que si les plans n'ont pas trop souffert ils peuvent être plantés avec succes a la fin de may. Il paroît qu'il y a quelques graines. Si elles sont dans une boîte separée ces graines pourroient être envoyées par la diligence en même tems qu'on feroit partir les plans par une autre voie. Votre bonté non seulement autorise, mais exige tous ces détails sans quoi je Rougirois dy entrer. Me. de Tott et Mr. de Tessé aussi empressés que moi de vous exprimer leur reconnoissance, esperent que vous cederes à ma priere pour mercredi et je veux absolument me flatter de vous assurer bientôt moi même de tous les sentimens avec lesquels jai l'honneur dêtre, Monsieur, votre tres humble et tres obeissante servante,

NOAILLES DE TESSÉ

RC (DLC); year supplied in date line from internal evidence and TJ's letter to Mme. de Tessé of 25 Apr. 1788 to which this is a reply; endorsed; below the endorsement TJ made the following notes: "plants beef china letters for Warville."

MON JARDINIER ANGLOIS was one Cyrus Bowie, according to information in a file of papers concerning removal of specimens from the gardens at Chaville to the Museum of Natural History in Paris in 1792-3, preserved in the Bibliothèque Centrale du Muséum d'Histoire Naturelle, MSS. No. 306.

To Cabanis

MONSIEUR à Paris ce 28me. Avril 1788.

Monsieur Lambert de Frontignan, par une lettre en datte le 22me. Fevrier m'avoit prié de vous payer la somme de 129.tt pour cent bouteilles de vin qu'il avoit envoyé à Monsr. le Comte de

Moustier en Amerique par mon ordre. Malheureusement sa lettre n'etoit pas encore arrivée la 3me. Mars quand je suis parti de Paris pour les Païs bas et l'Allemagne. Je la trouve ici à mon retour qui n'est que de 4. ou 5. jours. Je vous envois cette somme là Monsieur, et je vous prie d'etre assuré que ce n'auroit souffert un moment de retard si ce n'avoit eté pour mon absence, et d'agréer les sentimens d'estime et de consideration avec lesquelles j'ai l'honneur d'etre Monsieur votre tres humble et très obeissant serviteur,

TH: JEFFERSON

PrC (MHi).

Dr. Lambert's letter of 22 Feb. 1788 has not been found. TJ made the following entry in his Account Book under 28 Apr. 1788: "pd Cabanis banker for Lambert of Frontignan 100. bottles of wine sent to the Count de Moustier 129.ᵗᵗ" A draft for this sum was evidently enclosed in the present letter.

To Francis Coffyn

SIR

Paris April 28. 1788.

Your favor of March 22[1] arrived during my absence on a journey to Amsterdam from which I am but lately returned. I thank you for your attention to the 4. boxes of plants and have to ask the favor of you to send them by the first conveiance by sea to Havre to the care of M. Limozin. I have reason to believe there are some seeds also. If these are packed in a separate box I will beg of you to send them (that is, the seeds) by the Diligence immediately, or indeed if they are in the same boxes with the plants, if you can get at them readily without disturbing the plants I will thank you to pack them in a box and send them by the Diligence, because there is not a moment to lose for putting them into the ground. Be so good as to write me the amount of the expences these things may cost you, and tell me if you have any correspondent at Paris to whom I may pay it. If not, I can send it to you by Mr. Rotch who is here from Dunkirk. I am with very great esteem Sir Your most obedient humble servant,

TH: JEFFERSON

PrC (MHi).

[1] Thus in MS, an error for 23 Mch.

To La Blancherie

SIR

Paris April 28. 1788.

Having left Paris the 3d. of March on a journey through the Low countries and Germany, your favors of Mar. 9. and 25. have awaited an answer till my return which was only 4. or 5. days ago. I should with great pleasure have undertaken to forward the memoir to Doctr. Franklin which you mention in that of the 9th. had you not found an occasion before my return, and I shall with chearfulness do the same with the papers which you propose to send him thro' me. I met with Mr. Adams at Amsterdam, and we spoke on the subject of his subscription to your institution. As he had subscribed but for three years, and had paid one, he considered himself as justly called on for the remaining two years only. The fact was that even for those years the papers had come to him very irregularly and at a great expence of postage. I have now the honour to send you eight Louis from him. I send you also a copy of my notes on Virginia, which you express a desire of seeing, and of which I beg your acceptance. They are very slight sketches on a subject, which fully detailed would have filled volumes. I have the honour to be with sentiments of the most perfect esteem and regard Sir Your most obedient & most humble servt,

TH: JEFFERSON

PrC (DLC). Enclosure: Copy of *Notes on Virginia*—probably the edition in French.

TJ made the following entry in his Account Book under this date: "pd. M. de la Blancherie for Mr. Adams 192.^{tt}"

From Benjamin Vaughan

DEAR SIR Jeffries Sq: London, April 28, 1788.

Presuming upon your kindness on a former occasion, I beg leave to have the honor of introducing to your acquaintance Mr. Baillie, nephew of the late Dr. William Hunter and who at present participates in the possession of his valuable cabinet. I take this liberty at the desire of a friend whom I esteem without having the pleasure of knowing Dr. Baillie, though not without being assured from his character that you will have satisfaction in shewing him your kind attentions, and derive pleasure from his conversation.

I have the honor to be, dear sir, Your respectful & obedt. humble servt. BENJN. VAUGHAN

RC (DLC); endorsed.

From Carra

MONSIEUR Paris ce 29 avril 1788.

J'ai L'honneur de vous envoyer un exemplaire du mémoire du Sr Cazeau qui n'a point été publié ni communiqué encore à personne qu'à M. Le Mis. de la fayette, par la raison que nous sommes convenus d'attendre votre retour, pour conférer sur cette affaire. En conséquence je vous prie de vouloir bien nous donner cette semaine un rendez vous pour mercredi ou jeudi prochain, et j'aurai L'honneur d'en prévenir M. Le Mis. de La fayette que je dois voir Mardi prochain, ainsi que le Sr. Cazeau. J'attends votre réponse aujourdhui s'il est possible, et je suis avec les sentimens de la considération la plus respectueuse Monsieur votre très humble & très obéissant serviteur

CARRA

rue de La michodiere a coté d'un chapelier près le jardin de Richelieu

RC (DLC); 2 p.; in French; endorsed; several diagrams on verso, comparable and probably related to those on verso of Gordon to TJ, 24 Apr. 1788, the significance of which is at present unknown.

The MEMOIRE DU SR CAZEAU was forwarded by TJ to Jay, 23 May 1788 (see note there).

From William Carmichael

DEAR SIR Aranjuez 29 April 1788

I had the honor to address you after a long silence the 14 Inst. You will receive that Letter by the same Conveyance as this. On the 18th. Inst. I received advice from the Board of Treasury that a remittance of three thousand dollars had been made me to a house at Amsterdam. This credit enabled me to take the feild. I came here the 23d. On that day the Russian Minister, who had received a courier the 21st. communicated to this court the Empresses intention of sending a fleet to the Mediterranean. Inclosed you have the Answer of this court to that Communication. On the 25th. I had a conference with the Ct. de Florida B. relative to the late reports of hostilities which were supposed to have been commenced by the Kentucke People. He Assured me that he had no official Advice on this subject, and our Conversation ended in contradicting all that had been asserted to have been said by him to a certain foreign Minister and with Assurances of the strongest nature of his Majestys desire to cultivate a lasting harmony between the two Countries. I cannot repeat all the particulars of this Conversation. I must observe to you however that packet boats will sail six or seven times in the year from Corrunna to New York. On the 22d. Inst. 7 sail of the Line sailed from Cadiz to be joined by two more from Ferrol. I have no time to mention the Conjectures of others. I still think that Spain wishes to be prepared for all Events and that she acts in some degree if not altogether in concert with France. Mr. Eden is expected at Madrid the 2d of this[1] Month. We shall see what this Colossus of Negotiators will be able to do. His Sentiments on our head are already communicated to the Minister and some of the principal Persons of the Nation Indirectly. The Courier is waiting. You will therefore excuse my conciseness and pardon me for a silence which has proceeded only from a desire of writing you fully by an opportunity which has failed me from the Indisposition of a Countryman for some months here.

I have the honor to be with great respect & Esteem Yr. Exys. Most Obedt. Hble Servt, Wm. Carmichael

RC (DLC). Enclosure (DLC): Copy, in Spanish, of Floridablanca's letter to Stefan Zinovieff, Russian ambassador at Madrid, 27 Apr. 1788, informing him that he had presented to the king Zinovieff's communication announcing the projected operations of a Russian squadron in the Mediterranean and requesting permission for its vessels to enter Spanish ports in case of necessity; and stating that, if such vessels were obliged to enter, they would find such a reception as humanity dictated, but that, because of Spain's treaty of peace with Turkey which stipulated strict neutrality in case that power became engaged in war with Russia, the king hoped the commander of the squadron would not allow the vessels under his command to enter Spanish ports except in case of absolute necessity.

Carmichael gave additional PARTICULARS OF THIS CONVERSATION in his report to Jay, 29 Apr. 1788, in which he stated that the rumors of hostilities "by the inhabitants on the western waters against Louisiana . . . said to be secretly excited and encouraged by the United States" had not been officially reported to Floridablanca, who was "far from entertaining a suspicion of Congress encouraging any enterprise of that nature" and who reported that "the person most active in exciting the Americans of the western hostilities was an Englishman, whose name he did not then recollect" (*Dipl. Corr., 1783-89*, III, 363-7; with this letter Carmichael also enclosed a copy of Floridablanca's letter of 27 Apr. 1788 to the Russian ambassador; translation printed in same, III, 367).

[1] Thus in MS.

From Maria Cosway

London 29 of April

At last I receive a letter from you, am I to be angry or not? I think when we go to question and doubt it is a good syng, tho' I dont know whether it is in favor of you or the Manner in which you appollogies. Many Contradictions will make me answer article by article your letter; My hand for writing made you Open my letter in preferance to all the others you received on your arrival, I am not obliged *to you* for this distinction. Sympathy, and remorse have my acknoledgements. Afterwards lett me tell you I am not your debtor in the least. The fatigue of your journey the different occupations the & & & & prevented your writing, I agree, but how could you led me by the hand all the way, think of me, have Many things to say, and not find One word to write, *but on Noses*? No, this I cannot put up with, it is too bad, and what is worse it is not indolence, it is what I must add to my Misfortunes, and I never thought your name was to be on *that* list. You say my letter was angry, You acknowledge it is a proof of esteem, but you prefer softer testimonies of it. Give me the example if you please. Am I to adress a stranger in such confidential terms? who writs to me so short and scarse as possible? Oh I wish My dear friend I could announce to you our return to Paris! I am afraid to question My Lord and Master on this subject; he may not think or like to refuse, and a disappointed promise of this kind would be too cruel to me. I cannot bear it. I should be doubly Miserable all the Summer; but why dont you Come? Your friend Mr: de la Luzerne is here, Mrs. Church, we should go to see Many beautifull villas, enjoy all the best England can afford and make the rest up with our own Society; we shall not have a Numerous Cortege, I promise to Make Myself and my Society according to your own wish. At home we may do it better, if I come to Paris I may do more what I please this time. There are but four people I could wish to pass all my time with. Is this too great a Number? when *you* are One, even if you dont guess the others I am Sure you would not object to. I long to return. I left a bad impression in the atmosphier. I was worse then myself, and realy so bad that Sometimes I hardly knew Myself. I am Much better now, and My Constant occupations for these three Months past keep me in better health or they keep me in better spirits, and that is the Most dangerous Malady I can have. If you want to hear what Italian Singing is, come to London. Marchesi is here and the Most wonderfull Singer I ever heard. The Opera is good but for want of equal performers with him it is rather dull as the whole spectacle depending on one person, makes the rest appear tiresome. We shall have a New One very soon and wonders are expected.

I cannot announce the portrait of a friend of mine in my Study yet, Trumbull puts me out of all patiance. I allways thought painting slow work, 'tis dreadfull now.

How is Mr: Short? Pray remember me to him in the kindest Manner, the beauty he lost his heart by is here keeling every body with her beweching Eyes.

Say many things to Madme: de Corney. I love her very Much and I will add that word to her Husband too. When you see any body I know speak of me if they are agreable t'will improve the subject, if they love me I shall be recalld to your remembrance with partiality. I would wish to deserve and nourish the good Opinion you have of me from your own Sentiments, inforce it by those you esteem, and oblige you from a return of the affection & friendship I feel for you to allow without bounds you will allways be deficient to MARIA COSWAY

Mr. Cosway presents his Compliments.

RC (ViU); addressed: "A Monsieur Monsieur Jefferson à la Grille de Chaillot a Paris"; endorsed; postmarked: "[A]P 29 88" and "ANGLETER[RE]"; seal attached.

From Framery

Copenhagen, *29 Apr. 1788.* Encloses a packet which came from M. Dechezaulx, French consul at Bergen, for John Paul Jones. Jones departed from Copenhagen on 15 Apr. for Elsinore and left that place on 18 Apr. by land for St. Petersburg. Before his departure Jones asked that the packet from Dechezaulx be sent to TJ. Framery has advanced for postage "*6 Rixdalers*, *4. marcs*, *12 Schelings* (*30.*tt *10s. de notre monnoie*)," which he asks TJ to pay to Frin & Cie., bankers in Paris. Takes this opportunity to offer his services to TJ.

RC (DLC); 2 p.; in French; signed: "framery Sécrétaire Legation de S. M. très chrétienne"; endorsed. The enclosed packet for Jones has not been identified, but it probably pertained to the matter of the two English prizes taken by the *Alliance* in 1779; since TJ caused William Short to make copies of the enclosures in Jones's letter of 8 Apr. 1788, it is possible that at this time he also had Short transcribe the following, press copies of which, in Short's hand, are in DLC, and all of which pertain to this subject: Dechezaulx to Benjamin Franklin and others, under dates of 14 Sep. 1779, 26 Oct. 1779, 4 Jan. 1780, and 11 Apr. 1780 (DLC: TJ Papers, 4: 587-8, 620-2, 624-6, 686-7; 5: 720-1). See also TJ to Bernstorff, 19 June 1788.

From La Blancherie

Paris, *29 Apr. 1788.* Acknowledges TJ's letter of 28 Apr., the work on Virginia, and the payment of 196.tt[1] for John Adams. Will send Dr. Franklin's copies of his weekly publication to TJ to be forwarded. Would appreciate learning from TJ "des details sur l'etablissement d'un jardin botanique accordé au Roi dans la nouvelle Jersey"; would also like to have any "gazettes Anglo-Américaines" which have information about industry, arts, or agriculture "dans ces contrées." Will announce TJ's *Notes on Virginia* in his publication at the first opportunity, and is pleased to have this opportunity to do honor to him. Is about to depart for London, and would gladly undertake any commission for TJ there.

RC (DLC); 2 p.; in French; endorsed. Enclosure (DLC): Receipt, dated 28 Apr. 1788, for 192[tt] received from John Adams through TJ for "Sa contribution des années 1785. et 1786 aux frais de l'établissement de la Correspondence générale et gratuite pour les Sciences et les Arts, a titre d'associé Protecteur."

[1] An error for 192[tt], the amount mentioned in the enclosed receipt and also the amount entered in TJ's Account Book under 28 Apr.

From Antoine Terrasson

Sir — Paris 29th April 1788.

I have the honour to inclose to your Excellency some English and french papers relating the Enterprize of a canal in the state of South carolina and a writing from marquis De La fayette desiring a conversation on the matter at your leizure. As I am a stock holder and I have been elected one of the Directors in March of Last year, what you can verify by the news papers of that time, I have some mind to get a sufficient sum of money to carry the Enterprize in execution, since we have been obliged by the circumstances of the country to suspend it tho' an excellent one very safe and very advantageous for the south and nort carolina and the undertakers too: You can judge of the credit it deserves by the Names of the subscribers.

I am with Great respect your most humble and most obedient Servant,

Terrasson

Hotel De valois Cul de sac de la fosse aux chiens

RC (MoSHi); endorsed. Enclosures not found; they pertained to the canal between the Santee and Cooper rivers, which was 22 miles long, rising by a series of three locks 34 feet to a summit and then descending by seven locks 69 feet to the Cooper river. The Santee Canal originated on 10 Nov. 1785 when a group of South Carolinians gathered at the State House in Charleston to consider plans and agreed to petition the legislature for a charter incorporating them as a company and authorizing a capital of 1,000 shares at £100 sterling each. Col. John Christian Senf, with whom TJ had been associated while governor of Virginia, was the engineer who designed the canal (F. A. Porcher, *History of the Santee Canal*, Charleston, S.C., 1903).

From Ezra Stiles

SIR | Yale College Apr. 30. 1788.

Last Summer I received two Letters from you, one of Decr. 24. 1786 and another of Sept. 1786, One of them thro' the Hands of Mr. Trumbull, which passed a long Circuit before it reached me. I immediately wrote an Acknowledgment of the Recipt of these obliging Letters and of the Books which accompanied them, as gave me very particular Pleasure. At the same Time I received a Letter from the Marquiss de Chastellux with a Copy of his American Travels which also gave me great Satisfaction. I am ashamed that any of our Countrymen should take Umbrage at some of his free and humorous Remarks upon our American customs, especially when the most of them are very judicious, and the greater Part of his Travels are most excellent. Your Letter of Sept. 1786 contained so many curious Things in natural Knowledge that I not only took the Liberty to suffer a Copy or Extract to go into the public prints, but communicated it last Octo. to the newly formed Connecticutt Society of Arts and Sciences.

Mr. Barlow, Author of the Vission of Columbus, will present you with this. I need say nothing further to commend him to your Civilities and Benevolence, than that he is an American of an ingenious and worthy Character. I think the new Constitution will take place. Wishing you every Blessing, I have the Honor to be, Dr. Sir, Yr. most obedt very hble Servt, EZRA STILES

I have been enraptured with your Notes on Virginia which Colo. Humphry was so obliging as to lend me. I have read it again and again with new Delight.

RC (DLC); addressed, in part: "His Excellency Thomas Jefferson Esq LL.D Minister Plenipotentiary &c Paris favored by Mr. Barlow"; endorsed.

TJ's LETTER OF [1] SEPT. 1786 was printed in part in the *American Museum*, II (Nov. 1787), 492-3, having doubtless been copied from the PUBLIC PRINTS to which Stiles communicated it.

From Imbert de la Platière

Paris [*Apr. 1788*]. Is sending TJ the first volume of "L'histoire Générale des femmes des nations les plus inconnues" which follows naturally "la Galerie universelle des hommes Célèbres" for which TJ had subscribed. If, after reading this first number, TJ approves of it, he hopes he will be allowed to send the successive issues as they appear each month.

RC (DLC); 2 p.; in French; endorsed. Without date, which has been supplied from an entry in SJL Index for a letter received "88 Apr." Enclosure: Probably *La Belle Laure, amante de Pétrarque*, Paris, 1787, the first of La Platière's biographies of women (*B. N. Cat.*, under Imbert de la Platière; see also La Platière to TJ, 22 Dec. 1787).

From Meier & Cie.

L'Orient [*Apr. 1788*]. Ask TJ to intercede for them with the officials of the farmers-general at St. Esprit, near Bayonne, who charged full duty on 40 casks of whale oil which were part of a shipment of 100 casks sent from their free port on 1 Dec. 1787 by the *Don de Dieu*, Captain Lescanvis, notwithstanding that a certificate from the L'Orient "Bureau de Ville" of the same date stated that the oil was of 598 casks, part of a larger consignment 13,359 Veltes received by them 18 Sep. 1787 for the account of Elias H. Derby of Salem, and transported thence in the American ship *The Three Sisters*, Captain Daniel Saunders. In accordance with the decree of 29 Dec. 1787, the duty should have been only 7[lt] 10s. per barrel of 520 ℔s. with an additional 10s. for each extra pound. The officers of the farmers at Bayonne are unwilling to concede this favor granted by the court for the encouragement of commerce with the United States. Their pretext is that the oil was not delivered there directly from America, but went first to L'Orient, a free port, making it subject not only to full duty but also to "droits de fabrication." The latter duty would have been levied even if the oil had gone directly to Bayonne. The correspondent of Sevenne Fils ainé of L'Orient, the firm to which the oil was sold with the understanding that only the above-mentioned duty would be charged, points this out in a letter, extract of which is enclosed. Oil from the same source has been shipped to other ports under similar circumstances without encountering any such difficulties. Request that TJ see that justice is done and that Derby is reimbursed for the surplus duty levied. Though the ship and cargo were officially declared to be of American origin, nevertheless neither Derby nor Saunders knew that a certificate of origin from the French consul at Boston should have accompanied the other papers. They have accordingly written to Derby to forward them such a certificate.

RC (ViWC); 2 p.; in French; endorsed; undated and date supplied from internal evidence and an entry in SJL Index for a letter of "88 Ap." which is the only entry for a letter received from this firm (see TJ's reply, 29 July 1788). The enclosed extract of a letter from Sevenne Fils has not been found, nor has the certificate which was apparently sent with this letter and returned in TJ's reply been identified.

From Richard Price

[ca. Apr. 1788?]

Dr. Price presents his best respects to Mr. Jefferson, and takes the liberty to introduce to him (Mr. Ashburnham) the young person who is the bearer of this note. He is virtuous, sensible and worthy; and any little notice that it may not be inconvenient to Mr. Jefferson to take of him will be well bestow'd. His business at Paris is only to employ himself there for a few weeks in learning the French language, in order afterwards to return to his father who is the governor of Bombay in the East Indies.

The Book and Pamphlet which accompany this note Dr. Price presents to Mr. Jefferson, not from any opinion of their value, but merely as a testimony of the high respect which he always feels for Mr. Jefferson, and of his gratitude to him for the Satisfaction and instruction he has received from Mr. Jefferson's Notes on the State of Virginia.

RC (MHi); no date or place, but evidently written some time before TJ wrote Price on 11 July 1788. SJL Index records this and one other undated letter from Price in 1788, both of which preceded Price's letter of 26 Oct. 1788 and the second of which has not been found. Enclosure: Presumably Price's *A Review of the Principal Questions in Morals* (3rd edn., London, 1787); see Sowerby, No. 1248. The pamphlet has not been identified.

To Cyrus Griffin

SIR — Paris May 1. 1788.

The bearer hereof, Monsieur de la Vallée is recommended to me as a gentleman, of worth, wealth, and high connection. Meaning to visit our country I take the liberty of asking leave to introduce him to the notice and civilities of your Excellency, and to assure you that your attentions will be highly gratifying to him and to his respectable connections in this country. I avail myself with pleasure of the same occasion of renewing assurances of those sentiments of high respect & esteem with which I have the honour to be Your Excellency's most obedient & most humble servant,

TH: JEFFERSON

PrC (DLC); at foot of text: "His Excellency Cyrus Griffin President of Congress."

MONSIEUR DE LA VALLEE is not to be confused with Gilles de Lavallée, a French textile manufacturer whom TJ had recommended to friends in America in 1785 (see note to Lavallée to TJ, 14 Aug. 1785); he was Chastel de la Vallée, whom Thomas Lee Shippen introduced to his father as "the brother of a lady who is dear to my best most lovely and most amiable friend Madame de Foucault. He will have delivered to my sister a letter of introduction and I beg you to be civil to him for my sake" (T. L. Shippen to William Shippen, Paris, 6 May 1788; DLC: Shippen Family Papers).

To Francis Lewis

Sir Paris May 1. 1788.

The bearer hereof, Mr. Berger, merchant of Lyons, proposes to go to America with a view either to establish himself there or to extend his commercial connections. His particular line is that of silk, and he is recommended to me as a person of worth, and of a firm and antient house of commerce at Lyons. This recommendation comes to me from the Marquis d'Espinay a very worthy gentleman of that place. As no person can give him better counsel than yourself in the mercantile line, so I am sure there is no one more disposed to guide the steps of a stranger, and to avail him of the knowledge you possess in that line. Permit me therefore Sir to ask for him your notice and counsel, and to procure for him such acquaintance as you think may be useful. Accept at the same time a renewal of the assurances of that esteem & attachment with which I have the honour to be Sir Your most obedient & most humble servt., Th: Jefferson

PrC (DLC); at foot of text: "Mr. Lewis. New York." For the recommendation by Espinay, see his letter to TJ of 20 Apr. 1788.

To James Madison

Dear Sir Paris May 1. 1788.

The bearer hereof, Monsieur de Warville, is already known to you by his writings, some of which I have heretofore sent you, and particularly his work sur la France et les etats unis. I am happy to be able to present him to you in person, assured that you will find him in all his dispositions equally estimable as for his genius. I need only to ask your acquaintance for him. That will dispose you to shew him all the civilities and attentions which may render his time agreeable in America, and put him into the way of obtaining any information he may want. I am gratified, while rendering him this service, to procure to myself the occasion of repeating to you those sentiments of esteem & attachment with which I am Dear Sir Your sincere friend & humble servant,

Th: Jefferson

PrC (DLC). See TJ to Brissot de Warville, 27 May 1788.

To Edmund Randolph

SIR Paris May 1. 1788.

The bearer hereof, the Chevalier de Saint Trys, passing hence to America, and meaning to visit Virginia, I take the liberty of recommending him to the notice and civilities of your Excellency, and of praying you to introduce him to such a line of acquaintance as may be agreeable and useful to him. Tho' not particularly honoured by a previous acquaintance with him, I have sufficient assurances of the worth and respectability of his character to satisfy you that your good offices will be well placed on him. Permit me at the same time to renew to you assurances of the great esteem & respect with which I have the honor to be Your Excellency's Most obedient & most humble servt, TH: JEFFERSON

PrC (DLC); at foot of text: "His excellency Edmund Randolph governor of Virginia."

To Charles Thomson

DEAR SIR Paris May 1. 1788.

The bearer hereof is Mr. Warville who is already probably known to you by his writings, and particularly that on France and the United states. He is moreover a person of great worth, politically and morally speaking, and his acquaintance will give you great satisfaction. Permit me therefore to introduce him to the honour of your acquaintance, and to ask for him those attentions and civilities which you are ever ready to shew to worth and talents: and to repeat the assurances of those sentiments of esteem & attachment with which I am Dear Sir Your friend and servant,

TH: JEFFERSON

RC (DLC: Thomson Papers); addressed: "Mr. Charles Thomson Secretary of Congress at New York. Favored by Mr. Warville."
PrC (DLC). See TJ to Brissot de Warville, 27 May 1788.

To Charles Thomson

DEAR SIR Paris May 1.

The bearer hereof Monsieur le Chevalier de Saint-Trys is strongly recommended to me by Monsieur de Meusnier author of the part of the new Encyclopedie which relates to Economie—politique et diplomatique, of which I sent a copy to Congress. I am sufficiently assured of his worth to take the liberty of recommending him to your notice, and civilities, which will be greatly gratifying to him, as an introduction to you particularly was asked by M. de Meusnier and himself. A further inducement is to multiply occasions of repeating to you assurances of the sincere esteem & respect with which I am Dear Sir Your friend & servant,

TH: JEFFERSON

PrC (DLC).

To the Commissioners of the Treasury

GENTLEMEN Paris May 1. 1788.

In a letter which I had the honour of writing to Mr. Jay on the 30th. of Aug. 1785. and which announced to him the final settlement of the prize money due to Capt. Jones's squadron, and the order of the Marechal de Castries that the money should be paid into his hands, I mentioned that that order could not be obtained but on my undertaking that, if it should appear there had been any French subjects on board the Alliance their portion of the prize money should be paid by our banker in Paris. In consequence of this undertaking a Mr. E. MacCarthy applied to me some time ago for his share amounting to 731ᵗᵗ-3. Capt. Jones happened to be here: he told me the claim was just, that MacCarthy was on board the Alliance and was a French subject (being a Lieutenant in their service) and he pointed out to me his name on the roll. I therefore have paid the bill he drew on me to that amount, which I shall carry into my account. I thought it proper to notify this to you to prevent the danger of a double paiment and have the honour to be with sentiments of the most perfect esteem & respect Gentlemen Your most obedient & most humble servt,

TH: JEFFERSON

PrC (DLC); at foot of text: "The honble. The Board of Treasury."

From Francis Coffyn

Dunquerque, *2 May 1788*. Acknowledges TJ's letter of 28 Apr. 1788. No ships being available for Le Havre, has sent the four boxes of plants overland "by the way of St. omer to the care of my friends Messrs. Broucq freres of that place," recommending that they forward them immediately. Hopes they arrive safe; expenses too trifling to notice.

RC (MHi); endorsed; in SJL Index TJ incorrectly attributed this letter to Zaccheus Coffyn.

To John Rutledge, Jr.

Friday May 2. 1788.

Mr. Jefferson's compliments to Mr. Rutledge. He had not decided about going to the review tomorrow, and therefore it needs a much less sacrifice than he is disposed to make to Mr. Rutledge to abandon the little idea he had of going. He has but two horses which can be well rode. Mr. Short will naturally expect one, and Mr. Rutledge shall have the other.

RC (NcD); addressed: "A Monsieur Monsieur Rutledge à Paris."

THE REVIEW TOMORROW: On 3 May 1788, at the Plain of Sablons, the regiments of French and Swiss Guards, headed by the Count of Artois, were reviewed by the king (*Gazette de Leide*, 20 May 1788).

To George Washington

SIR — Paris May 2. 1788.

I am honoured with your Excellency's letter by the last packet and thank you for the information it contained on the communication between the Cayahoga and Big beaver. I have ever considered the opening a canal between those two watercourses as the most important work in that line which the state of Virginia could undertake. It will infallibly turn thro the Patowmack all the commerce of Lake Erie and the country West of that, except what may pass down the Missisipi. And it is important that it be soon done, lest that commerce should in the mean time get established in another channel. Having in the spring of the last year taken a journey through the Southern parts of France, and particularly examined the canal of Languedoc through it's whole course, I take the liberty of sending you the notes I made on the spot, as you may find in them something perhaps which may be turned to account some time or other in the prosecution of the Patowmac canal. Being merely a copy from my travelling notes, they are indigested and imperfect, but may still perhaps give hints capable of improvement in your mind.

The affairs of Europe are in such a state still that it is impossible to say what form they will take ultimately. France and Prussia, viewing the Emperor as their most dangerous and common enemy, had heretofore seen their common safety as depending on a strict connection with one another. This had naturally inclined the Emperor to the scale of England, and the Empress also, as having views in common with the Emperor against the Turks. But these two powers would at any time have gladly quitted England to coalesce with France, as being the power which they met every where opposed as a barrier to all their schemes of aggrandizement. When therefore the present king of Prussia took the eccentric measure of bidding defiance to France by placing his brother in law on the throne of Holland, the two empires immediately seised the occasion of solliciting an alliance with France. The motives for this appeared so plausible that it was believed the latter would have entered into this alliance, and that thus the whole political system of Europe would have taken a new form. What has prevented this court from coming into it, we know not. The unmeasurable ambition of the Emperor and his total want of moral principle and honour are suspected. A great share of Turkey, the recovery of Silesia, the consolidation of his dominions by the Bavarian exchange, the liberties of the Germanic body, all occupy his mind together, and his head is not well enough organised to pursue so much only of all this as is practicable. Still it was thought that France might safely have coalesced with these powers, because Russia and her, holding close together, as their interests would naturally dictate, the emperor could never stir but with their permission. France seems however to have taken the worst of all parties, that is, none at all. She folds her arms, lets the two empires go to work to cut up Turkey as they can, and holds Prussia aloof neither as a friend nor foe. This is withdrawing her opposition from the two empires without the benefit of any condition whatever. In the mean time England has clearly overreached herself. She excited the war between the Russians and Turks, in hopes that France, still supporting the Turks, would be embarrassed with the two empires. She did not foresee the event which has taken place of France abandoning the Turks, and that which may take place of her union with the two empires. She has allied herself with Holland, but cannot obtain the alliance of Prussia. This latter power would be very glad to close again the breach with France, and therefore, while their remains an opening for this, holds off from England, whose fleets could not enter into Silesia to protect that from the Emperor.—Thus you see that the old system is unhinged, and no new one hung in it's place. Probabilities are rather in favour of a connection between the two empires, France and Spain. Several symptoms shew themselves of friendly dispositions between Russia and France, unfriendly ones between Russia and England, and such as are barely short of hostility between England and France. But to real hostilities this country would with difficulty be driven. Her finances are too deranged, her internal union too much dissolved, to hazard a war. The nation is pressing on fast to a fixed constitution. Such a revolution in the public opinion has taken place that the crown already feels it's powers bounded, and is obliged by it's measures to acknowlege limits. A states general will be called at some epoch not distant. They will probably establish a civil list, and leave the government to temporary provisions of money, so as to render frequent assemblies of the national representative necessary. How that representative will be organised is yet incertain. Among a thousand projects, the best seems to me that of dividing them into two houses of commons and nobles, the commons to be chosen by the provincial assemblies who are chosen themselves by the people, and the nobles by the body of noblesse as in Scotland. But there is no reason to conjecture that this is the particular scheme which will be preferred. The war between the Russians and Turks has made an opening for our Commodore Paul Jones. The Empress has invited him into her service. She ensures to him the rank of rear-admiral, will give him a separate command, and it is understood that he is never to be commanded. I think she means to oppose him to the Captain Pacha on the black sea. He is by this time probably at St. Petersburg. The circumstances did not permit his awaiting the permission of Congress, because the season was close at hand for opening the campaign. But he has made it a condition that he shall be free at all times to return to the orders of Congress whenever they shall please to call for him, and also that he shall not in any case be expected to bear arms against France. I believe Congress had it in contemplation to give him the grade of Admiral from the date of his taking the Serapis. Such a measure now would greatly gratify him, second the efforts of fortune in his favor, and better the opportunities of improving him for our service[1] whenever the moment shall come in which we may want him.

The danger of our incurring something like a bankruptcy in Holland, which might have been long, and even fatally felt in a moment of crisis, induced me to take advantage of Mr. Adams's journey to take leave at the Hague, to meet him there, get him to go on to Amsterdam, and try to avert the impending danger. The moment of paying a great sum of annual interest was approaching. There was no money on hand; the board of treasury had notified that they could not remit any, and the progress of the loan which had been opened there, had absolutely stopped. Our bankers there gave me notice of all this, and that a single day's failure in the paiment of interest would have the most fatal effect on our credit. I am happy to inform you that we were able to set the loan a going again, and that the evil is at least postponed. Indeed I am tolerably satisfied that if the measures we proposed are ratified by Congress, all European calls for money (except the French debt) are secure enough till the end of the year 1790. by which time we calculated that the new government might be able to get money into their treasury. Much conversation with the bankers, brokers, and money holders gave me insight into the state of national credit there which I had never before been able satisfactorily to get. The English credit is the first, because they never open a loan without laying and appropriating taxes for the paiment of the interest, and there has never been an instance of their failing one day in that paiment. The Emperor and Empress have good credit, because they use it little, and have hitherto been very punctual. This country is among the lowest in point of credit. Ours stands in hope only. They consider us as the surest nation on earth for the repaiment of the capital. But as the punctual paiment of interest is of absolute necessity in their arrangements, we cannot borrow but with difficulty and disadvantage. The monied men however look towards our new government with a great degree of partiality and even anxiety. If they see that set out on the English plan, the first degree of credit will be transferred to us. A favourable occasion will arise to our new government of asserting this ground to themselves. The transfer of the French debt, public and private, to Amsterdam is certainly desireable. An act of the new government therefore for opening a loan in Holland for this purpose, laying taxes at the same time for paying annually the interest and a part of the principal will answer the two valuable purposes of ascertaining the degree of our credit, and of removing those causes of bickering and irritation which should not be permitted to subsist with a nation with which it is so much our interest to be on cordial terms as with France. A very small portion of this debt, I mean that part due to the French officers, has done us an injury of which those in office in America cannot have an idea. The interest is unpaid for the last three years; and these creditors, highly connected, and at the same time needy, have felt and communicated hard thoughts of us. Borrowing as we have done 300. thousand florins a year to pay our interest in Holland, it would have been worth while to have added 20 thousand more to suppress those clamours. I am anxious about every thing which may affect our credit. My wish would be to possess it in the highest degree, but to use it little. Were we without credit we might be crushed by a nation of much inferior resources but possessing higher credit. The present system of war renders it necessary to make exertions far beyond the annual resources of the state, and to consume in one year the efforts of many. And this system we cannot change. It remains then that we cultivate our credit with the utmost attention.—I had intended to have written a word to your Excellency on the subject of the new constitution, but I have already spun out my letter to an immoderate length. I will just observe therefore that according to my ideas there is a great deal of good in it. There are two things however which I dislike strongly. 1. The want of a declaration of rights. I am in hopes the opposition of Virginia will remedy this, and produce such a declaration. 2. The perpetual re-eligibility of the President. This I fear will make that an office for life first, and then hereditary. I was much an enemy to monarchy before I came to Europe. I am ten thousand times more so since I have seen what they are. There is scarcely an evil known in these countries which may not be traced to their king as it's source, nor a good which is not derived from the small fibres of republicanism existing among them. I can further say with safety there is not a crowned head in Europe whose talents or merit would entitle him to be elected a vestryman by the people of any parish in America. However I shall hope that before there is danger of this change taking place in the office of President, the good sense and free spirit of our countrymen will make the changes necessary to prevent it. Under this hope I look forward to the general adoption of the new constitution with anxiety, as necessary for us under our present circumstances.

I have so much trespassed on your patience already by the length of this letter that I will add nothing further than those assurances of sincere esteem & attachment with which I have the honor to be Your Excellency's most obedient & most humble servant,

TH: JEFFERSON

RC (DLC: Washington Papers); endorsed by Washington: "From The Honble. Thos. Jefferson 3d. May 1788." PrC (DLC). Enclosure: "Extract from notes made on a journey through the south of France 1787," accompanied by an engraved map of the canal of Languedoc (both in DLC: Washington Papers); the passages extracted from TJ's travel notes are indicated in Vol. 11: 446-54; see also descriptive note, Vol. 11: 463.

Washington's LETTER BY THE LAST PACKET was that of 1 Jan. 1788. As shown by John Adams' letters to his wife, the idea of establishing a loan on the expectation that by the end of the year 1790 THE NEW GOVERNMENT MIGHT BE ABLE TO GET MONEY INTO THEIR TREASURY was TJ's, and the present detailed report to Washington was no doubt equally calculated on his part in order to enlist the powerful support of the one who was expected to occupy the presidency. When Abigail Adams wrote to TJ on 26 Feb.

1788, neither she nor Adams had any real expectation that TJ would be able to journey to Holland in time; she learned of it "by letters received from France," rejoiced "in the Idea of your having Met again before you leave Europe," and sent her "most respectfull compliments to Mr. Jefferson." Adams soon discovered that TJ had pressing business to urge upon him: "I thought myself dead . . . as a Public Man," he wrote Abigail, "but I think I shall be forced, after my decease, to open an additional Loan. At least this is Mr. Jeffersons opinion and that of Mr. Van-staphorst. . . . I am very impatient at this unforeseen delay, but our Bankers as well as Mr. Jefferson think it absolutely necessary for the Public." Adams saw the need for such a loan quite as clearly as TJ, and was doubtless pleased to be urged to perform a duty that was far more within his competence than within TJ's, but he could not refrain from teasing Abigail, as he often did so charmingly: "I must therefore submit, but, if in Consequence of it you should meet Southwesters on the Coast of America, and have your voyage prolonged three weeks by it, remember it is all your own Intrigue, which has forced me to open this Loan. I suppose you will boast of it as a great Public Service. Yours forever John Adams" (8? Mch. 1788; MHi: AMT). And on 14 Mch. 1788 he wrote again: "Mr. Jefferson is so anxious to obtain Money here to enable him to discharge some of the most urgent demands upon the United States and preserve their Credit from Bankruptcy for two years longer after which he thinks the new Gov't will have Money in their Treasury from Taxes; that he has prevailed upon me to open a new Loan, by Virtue of my old Power.—I was very much averse to this but he would take no denial" (same).

[1] TJ first wrote, then deleted, "against," knowing well that Washington would guess the eventuality that he had in mind.

To James Madison

DEAR SIR Paris May 3. 1788.

Mine of Feb. 6. acknoleged the receipt of yours of Dec. 9. and 20. Since that, those of Feb. 19. and 20. are come to hand. The present will be delivered you by Mr. Warville, whom you will find truly estimable, and a great enthusiast for liberty. His writings will have shewn you this. For public news I must refer you to my letter to Mr. Jay. Those I wrote to him from Amsterdam will have informed you of my journey thither. While there, I endeavored to get as well as I could into the state of national credit there: for tho' I am an enemy to the using our credit but under absolute necessity, yet the possessing a good credit I consider as indispensible in the present system of carrying on war. The existence of a nation, having no credit, is always precarious. The credit of England is the best. Their paper sells at par on the exchange of Amsterdam the moment any of it is offered, and they can command there any sum they please. The reason is that they never borrow without establishing taxes for the paiment of the interest, and they never yet failed one day in that paiment. The Emperor and Empress have good credit enough. They use it little, and have been ever punctual. This country cannot borrow at all there. For tho' they always pay their interest within the year, yet it is often some months behind. It is difficult to assign to our credit it's exact station in this scale. They consider us as the most certain nation on earth for the principal; but they see that we borrow of themselves to pay the interest, so that this is only a conversion of their interest into principal. Our paper for this reason sells for from 4. to 8. per cent below par on the exchange. And our loans are negotiated with the patriots only. But the whole body of money dealers, patriot and Stadholderian, look forward to our new government with a great degree of partiality and interest. They are disposed to have much confidence in it, and it was the prospect of it's establishment which enabled us to set the loan of last year into motion again. They will attend stedfastly to it's first money operations. If these are injudiciously begun, correction, whenever they shall be corrected, will come too late. Our borrowings will always be difficult and disadvantageous. If they begin well, our credit will immediately take the first station. Equal provision for the interest, adding to it a certain prospect for the principal, will give us a preference to all nations, the English not excepted. The first act of the new government should be some operation whereby they may assume to themselves this station. Their European debts form a proper subject for this. Digest the whole, public and private, Dutch, French and Spanish into a table, shewing the sum of interest due every year, and the portions of principal paiable the same years. Take the most certain branch of revenue, and one which shall suffice to pay the interest and leave such a surplus as may accomplish all the paiments of the capital at terms somewhat short of those at which they will become due. Let the surpluses of those years in which no reimbursement of principal falls, be applied to buy up our paper on the exchange of Amsterdam, and thus anticipate the demands of principal. In this way our paper will be kept up at par, and this alone will enable us to command in four and twenty hours at any time on the exchange of Amsterdam as many millions as that capital can produce. The same act which makes this provision for the existing debts, should go on to open a loan to their whole amount, the produce of that loan to be applied as fast as received to the paiment of such parts of the existing debts as admit of paiment. The rate of interest to be as the government should privately instruct their agent, because it must depend on the effect these measures would have on the exchange. Probably it could be lowered from time to time. Honest and annual publications of the paiments made will inspire confidence, while silence would conceal nothing from those interested to know.

You will perceive by the Comte rendue which I send you, that this country now calls seriously for it's interest at least. The non-paiment of this hitherto has done our credit little injury, because the government here saying nothing about it, the public have supposed they wished to leave us at our ease as to the paiment. It is now seen that they call for it, and they will publish annually the effect of that call. A failure here therefore will have the same effect on our credit hereafter as a failure at Amsterdam. I consider it then as of a necessity not to be dispensed with that these calls be effectually provided for. If it shall be seen that the general provision before hinted at cannot be in time [to comply with the first calls of this country];[1] then it is the present government which should take on itself to borrow in Amsterdam what may be necessary [for them].[1] The new government should by no means be left by the old to the necessity of borrowing a stiver before it can tax for it's interest. This will be to destroy the credit of the new government in it's birth. And I am of opinion that if the present Congress will add to the loan of a million (which Mr. Adams and myself have proposed this year) what may be necessary for the French calls to the year 1790. the money can be obtained at the usual disadvantage. Tho' I have not at this moment received such authentic information from our bankers as I may communicate to Congress, yet I know privately from one of them (Mr. Jacob Van Staphorst who is here) that they had on hand a fortnight ago [near][1] 400,000 florins, and the sale [of bonds][1] going on well. So that the June interest which had been in so critical a predicament was already secured. If the loan of a million on Mr. Adams's bonds of this year be ratified by Congress, the applications of the money on hand may go on immediately according to the statement I sent to Mr. Jay. One article in this I must beg you to press on the Treasury board. That is an immediate order for the paiment of the three years arrearages to the French officers. They were about holding a meeting to take desperate measures on this subject when I was called to Holland. I desired them to be quiet till my return, and since my return I have pressed a further tranquillity till July by which time I have given them reason to hope I may have an answer from the Treasury board to my letters of March. Their ill humour can be contained no longer, and as I know no reason why they may not be paid at that time, I shall have nothing to urge in our defence after that.

I do not know *Warville's*[2] *business in America. I suspect him* to be *agent* of a *company* on some *speculation of lands. Perhaps you might connect him usefully* in what *yourself and Monroe* had *proposed.*

You remember the Report drawn by Governor Randolph on the navigation of the Missisipi. When I came to Europe, Mr. Thomson was so kind as to have me a copy of it made out. I lent it to Dr. Franklin and he mislaid it so that it could never be found. Could you make interest with him to have me another copy made and send it to me? By Mr. Warville I send your pedometer. To the loop at bottom of it you must sew a tape, and, at the other end of the tape, a small hook (such as we use under the name of hooks and eyes.) Cut a little hole in the bottom of your left watch pocket. pass the hook and tape through it, and down between the breeches and drawers, and fix the hook on the edge of your knee band, an inch from the knee buckle. Then hook the instrument itself by it's swivel-hook on the upper edge of the watch-pocket. Your tape being well adjusted in length, your double steps will be exactly counted by the instrument, the shortest hand pointing out the thousands, the flat hand the hundreds, and the long hand the tens and units. Never turn the hands backward. Indeed it is best not to set them to any given place, but to note the number they stand at when you begin to walk. The adjusting the tape to it's exact length is a critical business, and will cost you many trials. But, once done, it is done for ever. The best way is to have a small buckle fixed on the middle of the tape, by which you can take it up and let it out at pleasure. When you chuse it should cease to count, unhook it from the top of the watch pocket and let it fall down to the bottom of the pocket. I am to pay to Dr. Ramsay (if he requires it) 936 livres Tournois for a bookseller here. I take the liberty of writing to him that you will answer his draught to that amount. I communicate to him at the same time a proposition from the bookseller to furnish it in books. If he accedes to this, no draught will be made on you. Otherwise I must beg the favor of you to honour his bill and charge it to me. I send you the captain's receipt for the boxes of books forwarded some time ago. My absence prevented the receipt's going to you sooner. I am with sentiments of the most sincere esteem & attachment Dr. Sir your affectionate friend & servt,

Th: Jefferson

Neckar des opinions religieuses
Mirabeau aux Bataves
Volney sur la guerre des Turcs
Meilhan sur l'esprit et les moeurs
} now sent you by Mr. Warville.

RC (DLC: Madison Papers); partly in code; docketed above date-line by Madison: "Recd Augt. 1. 88." PrC (DLC); lacks several interlineations made by TJ in RC after PrC was executed (see note 1 below); accompanied by MS of text *en clair* of coded portion on separate sheet, in TJ's hand. Enclosures: (1) The "captain's receipt for the boxes of books forwarded some time ago" was the bill of lading furnished by Captain Charles Jenkins of the *Juno* that had been transmitted by Limozin to TJ, 11 Jan. 1788 (MHi). (2) *Compte rendu au Roi, au mois de mars 1788, et publié par ses ordres* (Paris, Imprimerie royale, 1788); see note to TJ to Jay, 4 May 1788.

1 This and other passages in brackets (supplied) were interlined in RC by TJ after executing PrC.

2 This and subsequent words in italics are written in code and were in part decoded interlineally by Madison; his decoding has been verified by the Editors, employing the text *en clair* and Code No. 9.

To John Jay

SIR — Paris May 4. 1788.

I had the honor of addressing you in two letters of the 13th. and 16th. of March from Amsterdam, and have since received Mr. Remsen's of Feb. 20. I staid at Amsterdam about 10. or 12. days after the departure of Mr. Adams in hopes of seeing the million of the last year filled up. This however could not be accomplished on the spot. But the prospect was so good as to have dissipated all fears; and since my return here I learn (not officially from our bankers but) through a good channel that they have received near four hundred thousand florins since the date of the statement I sent you in my letter of Mar. 16. and I presume we need not fear the completion of that loan, which will provide for all our purposes of the year 1788. as stated in that paper. I hope therefore to receive from the treasury orders in conformity thereto that I may be able to proceed to the redemption of our captives. The purposes of the years 1789. and 1790 as stated in the same paper will depend on the ratification by Congress of Mr. Adams's bonds of this year for another million of florins. But there arises a new call from this government for it's interest at least. Their silence hitherto has made it be believed in general that they consented to the nonpaiment of our interest to them, in order to accomodate us. You will perceive in the 75th. and 76th. pages of the Compte rendu which I have the honour to send you that they call for this interest and will publish whether it be paid or not; and by No. 25. page 81. that they count on it's regular receipt for the purposes of the year. These calls for the 1st. days of January 1789. and 1790 will amount to about a million and a half of florins more, and if to be raised by loan, it must be for two millions, as well to cover the expences of the loan, as that loans are not opened for fractions of millions. This publication seems to render a provision for this interest as necessary as for that of Amsterdam.

I had taken measures to have it believed at Algiers that our government withdrew it's attention from our captives there. This was to prepare their captors for the ransoming them at a reasonable price. I find however that Capt. Obrian is apprised that I have received some authority on this subject. He writes me a cruel letter, supposing me the obstacle to their redemption. Their own interest requires that I should leave them to think thus hardly of me. Were the views of government communicated to them they could not keep their own secret, and such a price would be demanded for them as Congress probably would think ought not to be given lest it should be the cause of involving thousands of others of their citizens in the same condition. The moment I have money, the business shall be set into motion.

By a letter from Joseph Chiappe, our agent at Mogadore, I am notified of a declaration of the Emperor of Marocco, that if the States general of the United Netherlands do not before the month of May send him an Ambassador to let him know whether it is war or peace between them, he will send one to them with five fregates and that if their dispositions be unfavorable, these frigates shall proceed to America to make prizes on the Dutch and to sell them there. It seems to depend on the Dutch therefore whether the Barbary powers shall learn the way to our coasts, and whether we shall have to decide the question of the legality of selling in our ports vessels taken from them.

I had informed you in a former letter of the declaration made by the court of Spain to that of London relative to it's naval armament, and also of the declaration of the Count de Monmorin to the Russian minister here on the same subject. I have good information that the court of Spain has itself made a similar and formal declaration to the minister of Russia at Madrid. So that Russia is satisfied she is not the object. I doubt whether the English are equally satisfied as to themselves. The season has hitherto prevented any remarkeable operations between the Turks and the two empires. The war however will probably go on, and the season now admits of more important events. The Empress has engaged Commodore Paul Jones in her service. He is to have the rank of rear-admiral, with a separate command, and it is understood that he is in no case to be commanded. He will probably be opposed to the Captain Pacha on the Black sea. He received this invitation at Copenhagen, and as the season for commencing the campaign was too near to admit time for him to ask and await the permission of Congress, he accepted the offer, only stipulating that he should be always free to return to the orders of Congress whenever called for, and that he should in no case be expected to bear arms against France. He conceived that the experience he should gain would enable him to be more useful to the U.S. should they ever have occasion for him. It has been understood that Congress had had it in contemplation to give him the grade of rear admiral from the date of the action of the Serapis, and it is supposed that such a mark of their approbation would have a favourable influence on his fortune in the North. Copies of the letters which passed between him and the Danish minister are herewith transmitted. I shall immediately represent[1] to Count Bernstoff that the demand for our prizes can have no connection with a treaty of commerce, that there is no reason why the claims of our seamen should await so distant and incertain an event, and press the settlement of this claim.

This country still pursues it's line of peace. The ministry seem now all united in it; some from a belief of their inability to carry on a war; others from a desire to arrange their internal affairs, and improve their constitution. The differences between the king and parliaments threaten a serious issue. Many symptoms indicate that the government has in contemplation some act of high-handed authority. An extra-number of printers have for several days been employed, the apartment wherein they are at work being surrounded by a body of guards who permit nobody either to come out, or go in. The commanders of the provinces, civil and military, have been ordered to be at their stations on a certain day of the ensuing week. They are accordingly gone: so that the will of the king is probably to be announced thro' the whole kingdom on the same day. The parliament of Paris, apprehending that some innovation is to be attempted which may take from them the opportunity of deciding on it after it shall be made known, came last night to the resolution of which I have the honour to inclose you a manuscript copy. This you will perceive to be in effect a Declaration of rights. I am obliged to close here the present letter, lest I should miss the opportunity of conveying it by a passenger who is to call for it. Should the delay of the packet admit any continuation of these details, they shall be the subject of another letter to be forwarded by post. The gazettes of Leyden and France accompany this. I have the honour to be with sentiments of the most perfect esteem & respect, Sir, your most obedient & most humble servant, TH: JEFFERSON

RC (DNA: PCC, No. 87, II). PrC (DLC). Enclosures: (1) Correspondence between Jones and Bernstorff, as described in note to Jones to TJ, 8 Apr. 1788, q.v. (2) Declaration of the parlement of Paris, 3 May 1788, stating that the attempts against the nation in the persons of their magistrates evidently proceeded from opposition by the parlement to two disastrous imposts and other matters of ministerial policy; that the fatal project of the minister to annihilate the principles of the monarchy leaves the nation no other recourse than a declaration by the parlement of the principles it is obliged to maintain and will never cease to support; that France is a monarchy governed by "la loi suivant les Loix"; that among these are some which are fundamental and which embrace and consecrate such rights as the male succession to the throne, the right of freely granting subsidies through the Estates General regularly convoked and assembled, the customs of the provinces and irremovability of the magistrates, the right of the provincial parlements to refuse to register royal acts not conformable to the constitutive laws of the provinces and the fundamental laws of the state, the right of each citizen to be accused only before judges by law appointed, and that right of the citizen without which all other rights would be useless—the right to appear immediately before a competent judge when arrested by any authority whatsoever; that the parlement protests against every attempt that may be made to violate these principles and unanimously declares that, being bound by oath, its members can in no way deviate from them; and that the members, unable to consent to any innovation in these principles or to take part in any deliberative body not made up of the same persons and clothed with the same legislative rights, will, in case of being dispersed by force and of being no longer able by itself to maintain these principles, entrust its security to the king, the peers of the kingdom, the Estates General, and each of the orders singly or combined which make up the nation (Tr in DNA: PCC, No. 87, II, in French, accompanied by a translation by John Pintard). (3) A copy of the *Compte rendu au Roi, au mois de mars 1788, et publié par ses ordres* (Paris, Imprimerie royale, 1788).

It is important to note that, while TJ was undoubtedly correct in thinking the ministry's SILENCE HITHERTO HAS MADE IT BE BELIEVED IN GENERAL THAT THEY CONSENTED TO THE NON-PAIMENT OF OUR INTEREST TO THEM, IN ORDER TO ACCOMODATE US, the publication of the *Compte rendu* was not a sudden determination but was undertaken by the zealous new controller-general, Lambert, at precisely the moment TJ, Lafayette, Bérard, and their other collaborators were pressing so zealously to have the French government support the assurances given by it in 1786 to encourage American commerce. TJ evidently did not know on 6 Oct. 1787, the day he transmitted to Dupont the statistics on purchases of tobacco so reluctantly given up by the farmers-general on Lambert's insistence, that on that same day Lambert wrote to Montmorin noting with pain, in an account just submitted to him, that the United States was "fort arrièré" in its engagements to France; that, for arrearages of interest and for advances made in 1786 and 1787 for payment of interest on the Holland loan of 1781, the United States was obligated to pay France, 1 Oct. 1787, some 1,800,000,ᵗᵗ which the king would have to remit to Holland; and that on 1 Jan. 1788 the United States would owe (1) an arrearage of interest at 5% for four years on a loan of 18,000,000,ᵗᵗ or 3,-600,000ᵗᵗ; (2) another 1,500,000ᵗᵗ representing the first payment on this loan; and (3) interest at 5% since 1 Jan. 1784 on another loan of 6,000,-000,ᵗᵗ or 1,125,000,ᵗᵗ making a total of 8,025,000.ᵗᵗ Lambert urged Montmorin to give this matter his attention and particularly to inform him what could be expected concerning the first item of 1,800,000ᵗᵗ for which the royal treasury would be in advance by the end of the year. Montmorin replied that he had given Moustier instructions necessary to pursue this matter in his capacity as minister to the United States (Lambert to Montmorin, 6 Oct. 1787, and Montmorin's reply, 4 Nov. 1787, in Arch. Aff. Etr., Paris, Corr. Pol., E.-U., Vol. XXXII; transcripts in DLC).

Thus, while TJ set off post-haste to Holland early in March to make arrangements for the impending obligations that the Amsterdam bankers had warned would fall due in June, ministerial preparations were under way for the solemn warning posted in the *Compte rendu.* It is not without significance that the first of the commissioners authorized by an arrêt of 16 Feb. 1788—the day after Vernes' *Mémoire* against the farmers-general was submitted to Montmorin (see Vernes to TJ, 10 Apr. 1788, note, and succeeding documents)—to examine the state of the loan-contract between the United States and France of 25 Feb. 1783, was Saint-Amand, one of the representatives of the farmers-general at the Council of Berni and a vigorous opponent of the measures there adopted. As translated by John Pintard from THE 75TH. AND 76TH PAGES of the *Compte rendu*, this examination of the debt concerned three charges: (1) a loan of 18,000,000tt reimbursable in 12 years, reckoning from 1787 at the rate of 1,500,000tt per annum with interest at 5%; (2) a loan of 10,000,000tt made in Holland, reimbursable in 10 years, reckoning from 1787 at the rate of 1,000,000tt per annum with interest at 4%; and (3) a loan of 6,000,000tt reimbursable in six years, at the rate of 1,000,000tt per annum reckoning from 1797 with interest at 5% (accompanied by a tabulation showing date of reimbursement, capitalization of the three charges according to fixed periods, interest according to fixed periods, and the general totals per annum, the whole to be liquidated by 1803; DNA: PCC, No. 87, II). Saint-Amand and his three fellow-commissioners appended this statement: "The first Reimbursement was to have taken place in 1787. It has not yet been made: untill this was done it was thought proper only to carry into the receipts the interest of the advances made to the U. States of America.—This interest amounts to Livres 1,600,000. Account will be annually rendered of what shall have been paid, as well in capital as interest." In accordance with this, the commissioners listed under item NO. 25. PAGE 81. the sum of 1,600,000tt as anticipated income for the year (Pintard's translation; same).

The GOOD CHANNEL through whom TJ learned of the progress of the Holland loan was Jacob van Staphorst (see TJ to Madison, 3 May 1788). The GOOD INFORMATION about the Spanish declaration to the Russian ambassador came through Carmichael (see his to TJ, 29 Apr. 1788). CHIAPPE's letter was that of 26 Feb. 1788 and the CRUEL LETTER from O'Bryen may have been that of 25 Oct. 1787 or that of 1 Mch. 1788, both of which are recorded in SJL Index and both of which are missing (it was probably the latter). The PASSENGER who was to call for this letter was probably one Ford (called "Faure" by Limozin; see under 22 May 1788). TJ later asked that the letters and packets brought to Le Havre by Ford to catch the May packet be entrusted to Brissot de Warville, who was sailing by a private vessel (TJ to Limozin, 4 and 17 May 1788).

[1] TJ first wrote, then deleted, "write"; his representation was made in person.

To André Limozin

SIR Paris May 4. 1788.

The bearer hereof, Mr. Ford, will have the honour of delivering you a packet from me, which contains gazettes &c. to be sent by the packet boat which will sail in a few days for New York. I ask the favor of you to receive and keep it till it shall be called for by a passenger who will go from this place and whom I propose to charge with that and my letters.

On my return here a few days ago, I found your letter of the 9th. of April, and one from Mr. Coffyn of Dunkirk informing me my boxes of plants were arrived there and in his care. I immediately wrote to him to send them back to Havre addressed to you, and I must beg the favor of you to send them by water as soon as they arrive, not to Paris, but to Monsieur Blard, Commissionaire au Pecq sous St. Germains en Laye, addressed to Madame la Comtesse de Tessé á Chaville prés Versailles.

By your letter to Mr. Short I find that some salt beef was arrived at Havre which had been sent me from Hamburg by Messrs. Parish and Thomson, and that it could not be received without a passport. But to obtain a passport requires application to so many bureaus, and so much delay, that I always prefer abandoning things of small value where they cannot be got without this ceremony. It is what I mean to do as to the beef. With respect to the China cups and saucers it was too late when I arrived here to write to Messrs. Van Staphorsts on the subject. I should be unwilling to lose them, yet unwilling also to ask a passport. Perhaps a moderate fee to the Customhouse officer may relieve the difficulty. I apprehend Messrs. Van Staphorsts will give you previous notice of the vessel they send them by.

I find matters here in the same pacific state in which I left them. The armament of Spain is very puzzling indeed; but there is no symptom that this country expects to be engaged in war.

I am with very great esteem Sir Your most obedient & most humble servt, TH: JEFFERSON

PrC (MHi). See Coffyn to TJ, 22 Mch. 1788, and TJ's reply, 28 Apr. 1788. The PASSENGER to whom TJ proposed to entrust his letters was Brissot de Warville.

From John Rutledge, Jr.

Paris, 6 May 1788. Asks TJ, on receipt from Messrs. Bérard of "the money which Messrs. Brailsford & Morris have desired them to remit to you," to deposit it with Messrs. Boyd & Ker, who are forwarding this letter.

RC (DLC); endorsed by TJ: "Rutledge John Junr." Enclosed in Boyd, Ker & Co. to TJ, 9 May 1788.

To David Ramsay

DEAR SIR Paris May 7. 1788.

It is time to give you some account of your affairs with the bookseller Frouillé. They stand thus.

Price agreed on for the copy for translation	900. livres Tourn.
9 copies (out of 50) of the English work received from Dilly and sold @ 12.ᵗᵗ	108
	1008
Cr. By a dozen copies of the translation sent you @ 6.ᵗᵗ	72
Balance now paiable to you	936. livres

I delivered to him your letter wherein you pointed out exactly the papers which should be omitted in the translation, and the alterations of the text in order to accomodate the work to foreigners, who are not interested in minute details. This would have reduced the work to one volume, halved the expence and increased the sale, so that he might have probably made a good job of it. But his translator persuaded him the whole would be desired: that there was a general objection against purchasing a garbled work, and so he undertook to publish it complete. The consequence is that he loses by it, as he supposes, about 2000 livres: and he desired me to represent this to you, and to tell you that he submits himself to you, whether he should be spared by you any thing out of the sum of 900.ᵗᵗ contracted for, and if this cannot be done, whether you would not consent to take it in books which would ease him. I told him I could not refuse to convey to you his representations, but that you were certainly bound neither in justice nor honour to make any abatement: I told him the loss you had sustained in this work by the impediment to the sale in England: but that as to the proposition to take it in books, perhaps that might be acceded to by you, as you might want books, or your neighbors who would pay you the cash for them. If this should answer your purpose, Frouillé is an honest man and will furnish at as moderate prices as any body: I only advise in that case that you call for French books only, as classical and foreign books are excessively dear here. I would superintend his purchases. But in this you are as free as if the proposition had never been made: insomuch that if it is more convenient to you to receive the money, you have only to draw on Mr. Madison in New York for 936 livres, as I have desired him to pay your draught to that amount out of the monies of mine in his hands.

The war between the Turks and two empires goes on. This country will not engage in it. She is so convulsed by her internal difficulties that she could scarcely carry on a war. The king and the parliament are bidding against each other for the good will of the nation, which will by this means obtain valuable improvements in it's constitution. I am with great & sincere esteem & attachment Dr. Sir your most obedient & most humble servt,

TH: JEFFERSON

PrC (DLC).

To Antoine Terrasson

SIR Paris May 7. 1788.

I have read with attention the papers on the subject of the canal of the Santee and Cooper rivers, and shall be glad to do any thing I can to promote it. But I confess I have small expectations for the following reason. Genl. Washington sent me a copy of the Virginia act for opening the Patowmac. As that canal was to unite the commerce of the whole Western country almost, with the Eastern, it presented a great view. The general detailed the advantages of it, and it had the weight of his name, and was known to be under his immediate direction. It was pushed here among the monied men to obtain subscriptions but not a single one could be obtained. The stockjobbing in this city offered greater advantages than to buy shares in the canal. I tried whether they would lend money on the security of the canal, but they answered they could get as good an interest by lending to their own government, with a douceur in the outset, and would have their money under their own eye, more at their command and more sure as to the paiment of interest. However if you find any opening and can point out to me how I may be useful in promoting it I shall do it with infinite pleasure. I have the honour to be with sentiments of the most perfect esteem Sir your most obedt. & most humble servt,

TH: JEFFERSON

PrC (DLC). Though not mentioned as an enclosure, the PAPERS ON THE SUBJECT OF THE CANAL may have been returned with this letter; these papers had been sent to TJ in Terrasson's letter of 29 Apr. 1788, q.v.

From John Trumbull

DR. SIR London 7th. May 1788.

Give me leave to present to you Mr. Thos. Duché, Son of Mr. Duché of Phila. who is nigh you at Chaillot for his health:—you will find him a very amiable and well instructed young man:—He has ask'd my advice of the route he should take to return to England and I have recommended him to come by Strasbourg, Manheim, Dusseldorp, Flanders and Holland: as this tour will give him a Sight of a very fine part of France and Germany, and of many collections of Paintings (for he is a brother of the brush.):—As you have just made exactly this tour you are much better able to advise and inform in the article of expence and the manner of travelling than I am, and you will oblige me very much by giving him your opinion on this subject, as well as by any civilities you may shew him while He remains near you. I am Dear Sir, most gratefully, Your Friend & Servant, JNO. TRUMBULL

RC (DLC); endorsed.

As a friend of Trumbull, student of Benjamin West, and nephew of Francis Hopkinson, Thomas Spence DUCHÉ must have been received by TJ with the cordiality that he extended to all young American travellers; but as the son of the Rev. Jacob Duché, who had regarded the Declaration of Independence as a mistake, who had appealed to Washington to cease hostilities against England, and who had lived for a decade in London as a Loyalist, he must have been received with less than wholehearted enthusiasm. Five years earlier young Duché's father had written to Benjamin Franklin: "My Son, who is now in his 20th year is a Pupil of my good Friend West, and most enthusiastically devoted to the Art, in which he promises to make no inconsiderable Figure. As he is my only Son, and a good Scholar, I wished to have educated him for one of the learned Professions. But his Passion for Painting is irresistible. West feeds the Flame with the Fuel of Applause: and his great Example has excited in my Boy an Ambition to distinguish himself in his Native Country, as his Master has distinguished himself here. The late Revolution has opened a large Field for Design. His young mind already teems with the great Subjects of Councils, Senates, Heroes, Battles—And he is impatient to acquire the Magic Powers of the Pencil to call forth and compleat the Embryo Forms" (Duché to Franklin, 22 Apr. 1783, PPAP; quoted by Albert Frank Gegenheimer, "Artist in Exile: Thomas Spence Duché," PMHB, LXXIX [1955], 3-26, at p. 9). Since this was an object that Trumbull himself had in contemplation, and one, too, that had great appeal for TJ, Trumbull's introduction takes on added interest. TJ usually gave the utmost attentions and hospitality to ambitious young Americans, and continued to follow their pursuits with interest, as his letters to Thomas Mann Randolph, Jr., Thomas Lee Shippen, John Rutledge, Jr., John Banister, Jr., and others testify. But evidently his interest in young Duché, who was undeniably an able artist, terminated with his laconic response to Trumbull on 18 May 1788. One of TJ's steadfast principles was that political differences should not be allowed to intrude upon social relationships, but, while it is difficult to believe that such differences could ever have caused him to be inhospitable, it is easy to believe that an American artist ambitious to portray the great scenes of the American revolution would evoke a more cordial enthusiasm in TJ if he bore the name Trumbull than if he bore the name Duché. This was neither to employ political principles in judging an artist's work nor to condemn a son for an act of disloyalty on the part of the father: it was merely to exercise the right of choosing between the congenial and the less congenial. Yet TJ must have found young Duché attractive and intelligent, as all of Duché's family and acquaintances evidently did, and, if political subjects seemed uninviting for discussion at the Hôtel de Langeac in May, 1788, TJ may have found his own deep interest in music and paleontology suggesting safe and congenial subjects with one who dabbled at composing, and who, at the age of sixteen, had been recorded in the minutes of the Library Company of Philadelphia as the donor of a "petrified Clam" (same, p. 25). Duché's travels

FOR HIS HEALTH proved unavailing; he died of tuberculosis on 31 Mch. 1790, leaving at an early age a few canvases that prove how talented he was (five of these are reproduced in connection with Gegenheimer's essay, cited above).

From William Carmichael

DEAR SIR Aranjuez 8th May 1788

Mr. Symond delivered me on the 3d instant *your*[*s*][1] *of the 1st. of Feb.* The *cypher inclosed in that letter has enabled me to profit altho' late of information: I shall in*[*close*] the one *left with* [*me*] *by Mr. Barclay and Mr. Franks, and trust* [*mine*] to the care of Mr. Symond, in order that you may have it in your power by seeing the paper to discover the reason of this extraordinary *mistake.* I regret exceedingly that this circumstance should have so long interrupted an intercourse which would have been both agreable and useful to me. *I have no advice of an official nature* [*from*] *America for many months* [. . .]:[2] The Pacquet brought me by Mr. Symond consisted of old newspapers and a scrap of paper announcing that they were forwarded from the office in the Absence of Mr. Jay. *That paper is dated* the *8 November.* I had the honor to address you last week by a Russian Courier to which I have very little to add, except that by a Letter which I have since received from one of our Captains at Algiers, I find, they have abandonned the protection of Spain; In consequence perhaps of what I mentioned to the Spanish Consul, in conformity to your Ideas, that the United States would not indemnify him for what the Dey might think proper to exact in case of the Death of one or more of them while under his protection. I have done all in my power to serve these Unfortunate People. I pity their situation and hence can bear with more patience their reproaches. I send you the inclosed Letter, in order that you may see the manner of thinking of one of them. They have sent me Many Letters and by the way of Marseilles which to me were exceedingly expensive, especially at a time, when as Yr. Exy. knows I was obliged to live on my own personal credit here. Their Letters I have not only forwarded with care, but have written to their relatives to tranquillize them as well as I could, on the situation of their Friends in Captivity. Mr. Eden arrived here the 6th, an Indisposition prevented him from having an audience of the Minister yesterday. This day he waited upon him at twelve and I suppose will be presented on Saturday. I imagine he will imploy that coquettry here which he pretends the Court of France practises for some time with those of Vienna and

Petersburg. But *our Cte.*[3] will teach him that honesty is the best Policy. *The minister is of a suspicious nature as are most of his whom* I *have known.*—A high reputation for *abilities in another puts one on their guard*, when an exertion on the *part* of *each is* to *take place*. Hence the *person* on the *defensive* is disposed to chuse his *arms* his own *ground &c.* Perhaps this being the case Mr. Eden *may meet* with [*an*] *adversary &c.* like a [. . .][4] *fellow* of whom I have heard who *fought* in *retreat* until his unweildy Antagonist *out* of breath was constrained to call a *parley when* he insisted *he would fight* no more until the *other stood firm*. The other in reply assured him that until he *had* fought him *over six acres*, he would never make a *stand* as that had been invariably his manner when he received a *challenge*. Of course our hero retired with the poor consolation of having sweated in the feild of Battle to no purpose. In a very short time I shall have the honor of making my remarks to you on what is yet in embrio. I mentioned the sailing of the Squadron from Cadiz the 22d. I amongst others wished to know its destination. Several who have spoken on this subject to the Minister, have assured me that he had invariably ans'd that it was merely a squadron of evolution to try the sailing of some late constructed vessels. Mr. L——n last night on his honor Assured me that *he had*[3] received no instructions to ask any questions on this Subject but that the Minister had given him the same Assurances as those Above mentioned. Yesterday I was told by the *ambassador of Portugal their minister had assured him* that it would soon enter into the Mediterranean. I can only repeat the title of the Comedy much ado about Nothing and I cannot persuade myself that the Object held to view is the real one, altho' I have seen and see so many Absurdities every day that on these points I ought not to be sceptical; I write these particulars to you merely that by comparing language *you may draw*[5] *something from the court where* you *are* for I presume the *motives are well known there*. I must observe however that *this fleet is to go to* the *westward with provisions* for *4 months*. I am just Informed that the Ct. de Florida Blanca has told Mr. Eden this day that the Squadron is to cruise to the Westward and then to enter into the Mediterranean. I have written to you in cypher in some parts of my Letter merely to shew you that I am happy at the Idea of having it in my power to render the Intercourse more frequent as nothing will give me greater pleasure, than the hope of meriting your confidence and esteem. You will set me right in some mistakes which you see I have made. By Mr. Symond I mean to send you one or two publications which I hope will interest your curiosity, I flatter myself that I shall hear from you now and then, for it is almost the only Consolation I receive. With sentiments of the highest Respect & Esteem I have the honor to be Yr. Excys Obliged & Most Humble Sert,

WM. CARMICHAEL

RC (DLC); partly in code. The enclosed letter from one of the captives at Algiers has not been identified, but it is true that, as Carmichael here explained, they had sent him MANY LETTERS; some of these had been forwarded to TJ, but others remained among Carmichael's papers, of which a selection is now to be found among the supporting documents for the claim of Alphonsa F. A. Blake, Carmichael's daughter, (e.g., Isaac Stephens to Carmichael, 30 Nov. 1785 and 14 Feb. 1787; Richard O'Bryen to Carmichael, 6 Dec. 1785 and 14 Sep. 1787; DNA: HR 27 A–G 7.4, nos. 38, 40, 41, 42). OUR CTE.: The Count de Floridablanca. MR. L——N: Robert Liston, British minister at the Court of Madrid. Presumably Carmichael intended to enclose the cipher-key LEFT . . . BY MR. BARCLAY AND MR. FRANKS, but did not do so: it was forwarded later (see Carmichael to TJ, 18 May 1788).

[1] This and subsequent words in italics (except as otherwise noted) are written in code and were decoded interlineally by TJ, who soon discovered that Carmichael was not overstating the case in referring to SOME MISTAKES . . . I HAVE MADE. TJ, in an attempt to straighten out Carmichael's garbled coding, filled in several words and syllables interlineally, giving both the correct symbol and his conjectured reading; the Editors have verified his decoding from a partially reconstructed code (Code No. 11) and have given in square brackets (supplied) some of their own conjectures for words not encoded by Carmichael but evidently intended; for words or parts of words garbled by Carmichael but not conjecturally decoded by TJ; or for the right word encoded in the wrong form (e.g., *my* for *mine*). TJ himself may have made an error in decoding (see note 5) and in two instances neither TJ nor the Editors were able to penetrate Carmichael's garbling except on the basis of tenuous conjectures (see notes 2 and 4).

[2] At this point Carmichael wrote the symbols *1077* and *1097*, the former for *never* and the latter for the punctuation mark for *semi-colon*; TJ interlined both decodings but gave no conjectural decoding of his own. Carmichael may have intended only to punctuate the sentence, but chose 1077 in error, then chose the correct 1097, and then failed to delete the former.

[3] These two words are not written in code, but are underscored in MS.

[4] Carmichael wrote the symbol *1081* for *nar*, which TJ decoded, but for which he gave no conjectural reading. The symbol *1181* in Code No. 11 stands for *ile*; possibly Carmichael meant to refer to a VILE FELLOW.

[5] TJ decoded this as if Carmichael had written the symbol for *constitu* and the letter *w*; he was correct as to the latter, but erred as to the former.

To Francis Hopkinson

DEAR SIR Paris May 8. 1788.

I am now to acknolege the receipt of your favor of Dec. 14. and to apologize for a delay that has happened in the sending the vinegar you desired. I gave a memorandum to one of my servants to enquire of the Chevalr. de la Luzerne's maitre d'Hôtel what kind of vinegar it was. He was out of town, the thing was forgotten for some time, at length recollected and the enquiry made. It was what they call Vinaigre à l'estragon. I have now sent 3. dozen bottles to M. Limozin at Havre to be forwarded to you by the first ship for Philadelphia, and must beg your acceptance of it from me. Should you wish to procure supplies hereafter I would observe to you that it costs from 24 to 45. sous the bottle according to it's quality and that what I send you is of the best quality. I think I described to you in a letter of the year 1786. a stop invented for the Harpsichord by one Walker in England, which he calls the Celestini. I have received a harpsichord with this stop, and can assure you that on full trial it proves a charming thing. The sound is between that of the Harmonica and of the organ (heard at a distance.) It is fit for such music only as suits the Harmonica. I have lately seen a very simple improvement of the Harmonica. It is only a bit of thin woollen cloth of the length of the axis and of such breadth that, one edge being pasted on the edge of the case in front, the other may reach a little more than half way over the glasses. This is wetted, lais on the glasses as they revolve, and receives the touch of the fingers. It spares the trouble of perpetually wetting the fingers, and produces a more agreeable tone. I think the artist mixed a little vinegar with the water for wetting it. His object in this was the preservation of the cloth. I am anxious to know what progress you make with the Bellarmonica, which I think, if it can be made perfect, will be a great present to the Musical world. Will you be so good as to tell me how your method of quilling the harpsichord, and also your 2d invention for substituting leather for the quill, stand the test of experience?—I must trouble you to enquire for a M. Tillier another of the wandering sons of this country whose case I inclose to you. I am in hopes it will give you less trouble, as he is supposed to be in Philadelphia.—I think I have sent you as far as the 22d. livraison of the Encyclopedie. We have now to the 26th. I shall send you in the course of the summer the four last with such others as shall be come out in the mean time. The war of the Turks and two empires goes on. The affairs of Holland seem settled. There is no immediate appearance of war in any other quarter. This country is fully occupied by her domestic dissensions. The king and the parliament are quarelling for the oyster. The shell will be left as heretofore to the people. This it is to have a government which can be felt; a government of energy. God send that our country may never have a government, which it can feel. This is the perfection of human society. Adieu my dear friend & believe me to be your's affectionately,

Th: Jefferson

P.S. Present me in friendly terms to Dr. Franklin and Mr. Rittenhouse.

PrC (DLC). The enclosed statement of the case concerning ANOTHER OF THE WANDERING SONS OF THIS COUNTRY was evidently a copy of a document in DLC: TJ Papers, 27: 4601 (in French, undated), stating that a M. Tillier, a young man from Berne, had gone to Philadelphia a few years earlier, met a merchant named Biddle, married his sister, become associated with him in an unsuccessful business venture, and failed to let his family in Switzerland know anything of his affairs or to reply to inquiries. Almost at the time TJ forwarded this inquiry, Rudolph Tillier was on his way to Europe with his wife, Sarah Biddle Penrose Shaw (this was her third marriage), who, on passing through Paris, soon reported that "his Excellency Mr. Jefferson was very polite" to them (see Hopkinson to TJ, 17 July 1788; Carrington to TJ, 10 Aug. 1788; PMHB, XXXVIII, 103).

TJ's MEMORANDUM TO ONE OF MY SERVANTS has not been found. The servant was probably Petit (the others at this time were Espagnol, Patier, Boileau, Nomeni, James Hemings—the last a slave—and a garçon); in Petit's accounts covering this period there were several extra articles, among which was the following entry for the week of 4—10 May 1788: "Vinegar . . . 87.[tt]" For TJ's description of the STOP . . . FOR THE HARPSICHORD and for Hopkinson's request for THE VINEGAR, see their respective letters of 9 May 1786 and 8 July 1787.

To William Shippen

DEAR SIR Paris May 8. 1788.

I duly received your favor of Dec. 5. and have been made happy by the acquaintance of your son who has past some time with us in Paris. I have been absent a part of it, in Holland, so that I have seen less of him than I could have wished; but I have seen enough to attach me to him very sincerely, and assure you he will answer all your expectations and your wishes. I inclose you a letter from him. He left us yesterday with Mr. Rutledge for Bruxelles. He seemed disposed to follow in some degree a route which I proposed to him. That is to say, after seeing the Austrian and Dutch Netherlands, to take for his guides thro' Germany the rivers Rhine and Danube, making, in his transit from the one to the other, an excursion to Geneva. To quit the Danube at Vienna, and go on to Trieste and Venice, thence to the bottom of Italy, come up it again, pass the Alps at Nice, follow the Mediterranean to Cette, then pass the Canal de Languedoc and the Garonne to Bordeaux, and thence either return to Paris or take wing for America as he pleases. He will thus have seen the best parts of the Netherlands, Germany, Italy, and France, and return satisfied that no part of the earth equals his own country. He will return charged, like a bee, with the honey of wisdom, a blessing to his country and honour and comfort to his friends, in this number I hope to be classed by him, by you, and by Mrs. Shippen, being with sentiments of esteem & attachment, as sincere as they are antient, Dear Sir, Your affectionate friend & humble servant,

TH: JEFFERSON

RC (DLC: Shippen Family Papers); at foot of text: "Doctr. W. Shippen." Enclosure: Thomas Lee Shippen to William Shippen, 6 May 1788 (DLC: Shippen Family Papers), a brief note which informed his father of their intended departure the next day, but which he opened after sealing in order to "relate . . . what has been agitating Paris for the two last days." The account that young Shippen gave was from a different vantage point than that exhibited in TJ's official dispatch to Jay of 4 May or in the oft-quoted passage of his letter to Hopkinson of 8 May. In part it reads: "On Saturday last the 3 of May the Parliament of Paris passed a spirited resolve by an unanimous vote, 9 peers being present of which Messrs. les Presidens De Premini & De Boulonnais were the authors. On Monday lettres de cachet were issued to apprehend these gentlemen. They had the address to elude the pursuit of the King's officers by different stratagems—The former suspecting the consequence of his open behaviour in the Parliament, ordered his coach and six to be made ready, and immediately escaped by a private way to the Palace —a place hitherto held sacred as a sanctuary to all who take refuge in it. The officers thought themselves sure of their prize having the coach and six in their possession, and gave the patriot time to escape. The other disguised himself in his valet's livery, and arrived at the Palace nearly at the same time where they joined counsels and convogued the Parliament. They came, 21 peers were of the number and about 400 persons of rank and high office. They had not long been sitting in debate, the Parliament within and their friends without the great chamber when a body of French guards to the number of 900 invested the Palace, whose orders were to allow no person to come in nor any one to go out. They were consequently confined in close custody all the night and some of the oldest Peers in France who had been most accustomed to soft repose were obliged to sleep upon the hard benches. In the morning, at 10 oclock of Tuesday the officer of the guards followed by a file of men their guns doubly loaded with ball entered the great chamber of justice, and demanded in an authoritative tone of voice that Messrs. De Premini and De Boulonnais should be given up, upon which the Parliament cried out with one voice Nous [som]mes tous De Premini and De Boulonnais. [Qu'est-ce] ce que c'est que vous demandez de [nous?] The officer then opened an order from the King commanding him to seize the before named gentlemen wherever they should be found meme au milieu de la grande chambre. They then came forward—were carried ignominiously in a hackney coach to the Lieutenant de Police, and are sent to a desart island in the Mediterranean. It is said to be the first instance of the sacredness of the Parliament house being violated, and the silence of the people on the occasion, tho' it is acknowledged to be the most arbitrary stretch of power that has been almost ever made, by all who hear of it, shews how fit they are to be ruled despotically. While the guards were surrounding the Palace and the idle people of the neighborhood were surrounding the guards, the rest of Paris were as still and tranquil as if their rights had not been in jeopardy—I confess I am not sanguine in my hopes of a revolution in France in favor of liberty."

From Nicolas & Jacob van Staphorst

Amsterdam 8 May 1788

We are honored with your Excellency's respected Favors of 7 Ulto. from Frankfort and 18 ditto from Strasburgh, the latter advising your draft on us ƒ426. Holld. Cy. in favor of Mr. Jean de Turckheim, Which shall be discharged and placed to the Account of the United States. Similar Reception awaits Mr. Peuchen's Bill for a Couple of Stoves which we will with greatest pleasure receive and forward to Mr. Limozin at Havre; To whose address We have loaded the Three Cases you left with us, upon the Ship De Jonge Bernardus Capt. Claas Arends Koen. Next Post will carry the Bill of Lading, in which We have inserted the Cases as containing Des Meubles pour son Excellence Thos. Jefferson Ministre plenipotentiare des Etats Unis auprés de la Cour de Versailles, To avoid any difficulties that might otherwise occur at the Custom House.

We congratulate your Excellency, upon the Success We have had with the Undertakers, justifying the Assurances we gave you, that the June Interest would undoubtedly be provided for. We were desirous of engaging the Undertakers further, but they strongly dissuaded pushing the Matter at this Moment, flattering us that after Payment of the Interest and upon the Arrival of good News that might shortly be expected from America, the remaining Bonds would be readily called for. Being firmly of the same Opinion, We delivered a Written proposal to Messrs. Willinks, to supply your Excellency with Funds immediately, to face all the Objects you wished to settle during this Year, except the ƒ60m for a particular purpose, that we could not know if you wanted so soon. They replied, they had no idea of coming under Advances themselves, to relieve those Persons who had already assumed them, and to our Representation that there was a fair nay almost certain Prospect of our speedy Reimbursment, they answered that was an additional reason, why Mr. Grand and others could wait, since if we received the Money soon We could pay it soon, And that for their Part they would not subject themselves to Advances. So determined even were they, that it required much difficulty of persuasion to bring them into the Plan. They write Your Excellency upon this date in conjunction with us, which we hope will fulfill Your Excellency's purposes, altho' it falls short of our Wishes, to enable you to discharge speedily, Objects that We join you in deeming it for the Honor and Credit of the United States, not to suffer to remain longer unpaid. Your Excellency may rely upon our continued Attention, to making you Remittances as Monies shall come in. We are very respectfully Your Excellency's Most obedient & very humble servants,

Nic. & Jacob van Staphorst.

We have paid Mr. J. J. Peuchen of Cologne his assignment upon us ƒ143.14 Cz. for Your Excellys. Accts.

RC (DLC); in a clerk's hand, except signature in hand of Nicolas van Staphorst; addressed; endorsed.

TJ's letter of 18 Apr. 1788 FROM STRASBURGH has not been found and is not recorded in SJL; it was obviously a mere letter of advice concerning the draft in favor of MR. JEAN DE TURCKHEIM. The PARTICULAR PURPOSE for which 60,000*f* were needed was the redemption of the Algerine captives (see TJ to Jay, 16 Mch. 1788, Enclosure I, note 3).

From Willink & Van Staphorst

Amsterdam, 8 May 1788. Have succeeded in arranging for sale of enough bonds of the United States to pay Carmichael the amount designated, to take care of TJ's "disposals and other incidental calls," and then, after paying the June interest, to leave a surplus of 40,000 guilders Holland currency in their hands available to TJ's requisition; "We trust the Payment of this Interest and some good news from America may give a spring to the Credit of that Continent and enable us to place the remaining Bonds of the Million negotiated last year." Funds will then be available for the expenses of the different legations. Dumas' claim for arrears has been met by payment in bonds without prejudice to the June interest or to other claims upon Congress; an additional premium of 1% has had to be paid to the "First Undertakers" of the loan to induce them to supply the money earlier than they were obligated to.

RC (DLC); 2 p.; in a clerk's hand, except signatures; endorsed.

From Boyd, Ker & Co.

Paris, 9 May 1788. Enclose a letter from John Rutledge, Jr., asking TJ to pay them any money received for his account from Jean Jacques Bérard & Cie. of L'Orient.

RC (DLC); address below signature: "Rue d'Amboise No. 4." Enclosure: Rutledge to TJ, 6 May 1788.

To Madame de Bréhan

Paris May 9. 1788.

It was not till the month of March, my dear Madam, that we became assured of your safe arrival in America. In the mean time we had been alarmed by reports, to which we should have paid no attention in a case less interesting. No author for the tale could be named, no origin traced; yet those who loved you, and they are numerous, feared it might be true, because it was not impossible. And even now we learn that your passage was long and disagreeable, and that on your arrival, you have been attacked by a severe illness. All this however I hope is long ago passed over, and that at this moment you are enjoying good health and a clear sky: that you speak English so well as to shew how precious you are in society, and that my good country-women set a just value on your acquaintance, and endeavor to make you happy. The resources you have within yourself also will do this, and particularly that of painting. The season is now approaching when you will be able to go and visit the magnificent scenes which nature has formed upon the Hudson, and to make them known to Europe by your pencil. You know before this that we have lost your con-disciple Drouay. He was certainly a great loss as he had shewn himself capable of treading steadily in the steps of David. Presuming that your other friends write to you, I shall not give you either their news, or that of Paris, of which they are so much better possessed than I am. The confusion here at present is really distressing. Society is spoilt by it. Instead of that gaiety and insouciance which has distinguished it heretofore, all is filled with political debates into which both sexes enter with equal eagerness. It is even some consolation to me that you are not here, as I am sure you would be miserable. I am so, whose business it is to be a spectator only, and not a party.—I long to see you and to know what have been your sensations in the new position you have taken. I fear they have not been agreeable. To the disagreeable aspect of new customs, the perplexities of a foreign language, the insulated state in which it places us in the midst of society and the embarrasment it occasions when speaking or spoken to, have been added in your case a severe season and severe illness, which must have made disagreeable things appear still more disagreeable. Have patience, my dear friend. Search in every object only what it contains of good; view, in those whom you see, patients to be cured of what is amiss by your example, encourage in them that simplicity which should be the ornament of their country; in fine, follow the dispositions of your own native benevolence and sweetness of temper, and you will be happy and make them so. Above all things continue your partialities to him who values them beyond measure & who has the honour to be with sincere attachment & respect, Dear Madam, your affectionate friend & humble servant,

TH: JEFFERSON

PrC (DLC).

From Broucq, Frères & Soeurs

St. Omer, 10 May 1788. Forwarded yesterday from Coffyn of Dunkerque by "le voiturier nommé louis Lehieu d'angre Liévin en Artois 4 caisses **T◆J** plombées et cordées," weighing about 247 tbs., containing young plants or foreign shrubs, to be delivered in ten days. Total costs for *voiturier*, Coffyn, and themselves, 23[tt] 18s.

RC (DLC).

From Johann Ludwig de Unger

Salzliebenhalle, 10 May 1788. Thanks TJ for his letter of 16 Feb. 1788 and for granting the favor asked of him; says he is deeply affected by TJ's remarks "sur le Bonheur et les Avantages propres à l'Amerique." "Un tel Eloge de la Part de Votre Excellence est garant de la Prosperité de ces Contrees si interessantes a tant d'egard, et inspire en meme Tems des Voeux ardens pour la Durée de cette Prosperité avec tant d'autres. Ces Voeux tiennent etroitement a ceux que je forme pour la Conservation de Vos jours precieux, Monsieur. Puissies Vous etre jusqu'au Terme le plus eloigne le Soutiens et l'ornement de Votre Patrie."

RC (DLC); in French; 3 p.; endorsed.

To Anne Willing Bingham

Dear Madam — Paris May 11. 1788.

A gentleman going to Philadelphia furnishes me the occasion of sending you some numbers of the Cabinet des modes and some new theatrical peices. These last have had great success on the stage, where they have excited perpetual applause. We have now need of something to make us laugh, for the topics of the times are sad and eventful. The gay and thoughtless Paris is now become a furnace of Politics. All the world is run politically mad. Men, women, children talk nothing else; and you know that naturally they talk much, loud and warm. Society is spoilt by it, at least for those who, like myself, are but lookers on.—You too have had your political fever. But our good ladies, I trust, have been too wise to wrinkle their foreheads with politics. They are contented to soothe and calm the minds of their husbands returning ruffled from political debate. They have the good sense to value domestic happiness above all other, and the art to cultivate it beyond all others. There is no part of the earth where so much of this is enjoyed as in America. You agree with me in this: but you think that the pleasures of Paris more than supply it's want: in other words that a Parisian is happier than an American. You will change your opinion, my dear Madam, and come over to mine in the end. Recollect the women of this capital, some on foot, some on horses, and some in carriages hunting pleasure in the streets, in routs and assemblies, and forgetting that they have left it behind them in their nurseries; compare them with our own countrywomen occupied in the tender and tranquil amusements of domestic life, and confess that it is a comparison of Amazons and Angels.—You will have known from the public papers that Monsieur de Buffon, the father, is dead: and you have known long ago that the son and his wife are separated. They are pursuing pleasure in opposite directions. Madame de Rochambeau is well: so is Madame de la Fayette. I recollect no other Nouvelles de societé interesting to you, and as for political news of battles and sieges, Turks and Russians, I will not detail them to you, because you would be less handsome after reading them. I have only to add then, what I take a pleasure in repeating, tho' it be to the thousandth time that I have the honour to be with sentiments of very sincere respect & attachment, dear Madam, Your most obedient & most humble servant,

TH: JEFFERSON

PrC (DLC). Enclosure not identified, but for Mrs. Bingham's appreciation of previous numbers of the *Cabinet des Modes*, see her letter to TJ, 1 June 1787. The GENTLEMAN GOING TO PHILADELPHIA who carried these publications was Brissot de Warville.

From La Lande

College Royal, Paris, 11 May 1788. Requests TJ to forward enclosed letter to an American astronomer and, when he writes to Benjamin Franklin, to present his respects; "Les ministres ont ordinairement la Complaisance de favoriser la Correspondance qui interesse les Sciences."

RC (MHi); endorsed. Enclosure not identified; if the letter was directed to a particular astronomer in America, it was evidently not the Rev. James Madison or David Rittenhouse, the two persons whom TJ would probably have thought of first if the communication were intended for an undesignated astronomer (see TJ to Madison, 19 July 1788; Rittenhouse to TJ, 8 Nov. 1788).

From Thomas Digges

Dublin May 12 1788
No. 30 Essex Street

SIR

A Cotton manufactory having been lately set up in Virginia, not only patronizd by the State but encouragd by some of the leading Gentlemen in it, some artists from England as well as this Country are wishing to get to it; And altho I have been a little hurt since my arrival in Ireland through my endeavours to get some useful mechanicks to my home near Alexandria, (two or three of whom are *now* under rigourous trial in the Courts here for attempting to ship themselves with their Tools implements &ca &ca) I cannot refrain from troubling Your Excellency with this letter, merely introductory of Mr. Henry Wild now the leading mover of the late Major Brookes's Cotton Manufactory at Prosperous near Naas in this County. This Gentleman about the year 1782 made an effort thro the direction and advice of Doctor Franklyn, to whom He is well known, (and in which he was somewhat aided by me) to move with His Family &ca. &ca to Philadelphia; but on the point of his Embarkation he was forcibly and openly stoppd by an order from the Secretary of State, and Mr. Brookes above mentioned obtaind a large premium for getting Mr. Wild fixd at Prosperous as director and conductor of the principal and still most flourishing Cotton Manufactory in this Kingdom.

Mr. Wild, who is not only at the head of His trade as an Artist but an excellent scholar and man of genius, has long and still ardently wishes to settle in a Country, which from his principles in politicks and love of liberty, He looks to as far above his own, has brought his affairs to nearly that Crisis as to enable him to move from Ireland; and stands only in need of that advice and proper direction in his attempt which I would wish every honest and good Tradesman to possess before he wildly sets down in America.

You will oblige him very much Sir, and it will be rendering our State an acquisition to get such an able and accomplishd artist to settle in it, if You will favour myself, or Him, with a line mentioning what State the Cotton Manufactory is in, at what particular spot in Virginia it is fixd, what Engines or implements are most immediately necessary for him to take, The tradesmen such as spinners or weavers most wanted, who are the directors or patrons of the Work, where and to whom to apply on his landing—or any other directions which may strike You as most useful for Him. Mr. Wild is not only a perfect master, but can construct *every article of machinery* necessary for the Cotton Manufactory. I not only wish him success in it, but most ardently request You to add your advice and aid to Him in the further progress of His Plan.

I am with the highest Esteem Your Excellencys Most Obedt. & very Hble. Servt, THOS. DIGGES

P.S. My direction is to *No. 30 Essex St., Dublin*, And Mr. Wild will add his at the foot of this Letter and mention any other matters He may want to communicate, for I am obligd to send this letter to Him at Naas some 15 or 20 miles from hence. I would recommend that what You write Him may be directed to me; for as a Citizen and tradesman He may be much injurd if the substance of this correspondence should become known.

I can give Mr. Wild introductory Letters to my neighbour Genl. Washington and many others at Alexandria and thereabouts but I guess the manufactory is at or near Richmond.

There is a Mr. Jno. Linton a Printer and dyer of Cotton, a perfect master of his Trade who would also attend Mr. Wild to America.

RC (DLC); endorsed; addressed. Enclosure: See below.

This was the first, but by no means the last, effort made by Thomas Digges to introduce textile industry into Virginia in the latter part of the 18th century (see, for example, his letter to TJ, 28 Apr. 1791; Washington to TJ, 12 July 1791). Digges, a venturesome Marylander who was forever promoting schemes of this sort, as a resident of London was suspected of being a spy in the employ of both the British and the American governments during the revolution (but see Washington's favorable testimony in his letter of 27 Apr. 1794 to John Fitzgerald, *Writings*, ed. Fitzpatrick, XXXIII, 340-1). He may have been correct in asserting that a COTTON MANUFACTORY had been set up in Virginia under the patronage of the state, but no confirming evidence has been found among the works of Batchelder, Bishop, Mitchell, White, Woodbury, Clark, Bagnall, Baines, and others, though it was to be expected that desultory efforts to attract mechanics experienced in the use and construction of the new textile machines of England would be made in the southern and middle states as well as in New England (see Gilles de Lavallée to TJ, 14 Aug. 1785, note). TJ himself knew of no such manufactory in Virginia (see his reply 19 June 1788). There is much about Digges in Franklin Papers (PPAP) and the effort of HENRY WILD (Wyld) to establish a cotton manufactory in Philadelphia on the ADVICE OF DOCTOR FRANKLYN in 1782 is the subject of correspondence among Wyld, Franklin, and Edmund Clegg between 25 Dec. 1781 and 13 Dec. 1782 (same). Wyld's address does not appear AT THE FOOT OF THIS LETTER, but his letter of 20 May 1788 was probably placed under cover of this one.

There had been attempts to set up textile manufactures at the outbreak of the Revolution, some of them encouraged by public authority and one of these was "The Manufacturing Society in Williamsburg," which early in 1777 was advertising for "likely Negro lads from 15 to 20 Years of Age, and as many girls from 12 to 15 Years" and which actually set up a plant "within a few Steps of the Capitol Landing" and employed "an exceeding good Heckler, regularly bred to the business in England"; but this could scarcely have been the enterprise that Digges had in mind (*Virginia Gazette*, Dixon & Hunter, 7

Feb., 25 Apr., 16 May, 25 Aug. 1777; see also Brooke Hindle, *The Pursuit of Science in Revolutionary America, 1735-1789*, Chapel Hill, 1956, p. 205-6, 246).

From Jean Baptiste de Gouvion

SIR Paris may the 13th. 1788

I was told that you have some prospect that the interests due by the united states to the Foreign officers shall be pay'd at the end of July next; give me leave to represent to your Excellency that captain Castaign who is a native from Martinico is upon the point of returning there, he has been near four years solliciting in this country for employment without success. His means are exhausted. You would oblige him greatly if you would give him an order upon M. Grand to be pay'd of the three years interest due to him, it is but a trifle, and it shall be of a great help to him; if you can comply with our request we shall keep you the utmost secret to save you from being troubled by any other sollicitor. I am respectfully Sir your most obedient servant GOUVION

RC (DLC); endorsed. TJ evidently did not reply directly to Gouvion (there is no record of a reply in SJL Index), but he did write at once to Castaing; see letter following, which, being cast in general terms, was applicable to all of the French officers to whom arrearages of interest were due, and of which TJ may well have made one or more press copies for transmittal to Gouvion and others.

To Pierre Castaing

SIR Paris May 14. 1788.

I am sorry it is not in my power to procure you immediate paiment of the arrearages which you observe are due to you from the United states. Mr. Adams and myself have taken measures in Holland, which if approved by the Board of Treasury we think will not fail to ensure a paiment of all the arrearages of interest due to the foreign officers, and that this may take place as soon as the Board of Treasury shall send orders in consequence of my letter to them of March. 29. These orders cannot arrive sooner than the month of July; but by that time they may arrive. So that it is my opinion the paiment may be expected in July or August with a good degree of confidence. I can say nothing stronger in a case which does not in any degree depend on my will. The moment orders for paiment arrive they shall be announced to all the officers who are creditors, and whose addresses I presume are lodged in

Mr. Grand's office. I have the honour to be with much esteem Sir Your most obedt. humble servt., TH: JEFFERSON

PrC (DLC); at foot of text: "Captain Castaign."

From Edward Carrington

MY DEAR SIR New York May 14. 1788

Mr. Barlow of Connecticut will have the Honor to call on you with this letter. I have not the pleasure of a personal acquaintance with him but his Literary Talents have considerably distinguished him as a poetical as well as prose writer, and he is introduced to me as a Gentleman deserving your countenance. Permit me to recommend him to your attention and civilities. He conducts to the Marquis de La Fayette, the Eldest son of our illustrious Friend Genl. Greene, who is sent at the particular request of that Noble Man, to receive his education under his direction in France. I have given the little Fellow a few lines to you and directed him to deliver them in person. It is unnecessary for me to solicit for him the attention of one who so well knew his Father.

I had the pleasure to write you pretty fully on the 25th.[1] Ult. by Mr. Paradise, since which no event has taken place except the adoption of the Constitution in Maryland, by a Majority of 63 against 11. South Carolina is now sitting and the general countenance of intelligence from thence, is much in favor of the Measure. There seems to be no doubt entertained of an adoption by a considerable Majority. Would this be the case it will give eight States. Virginia being the next to set will meet under very critical circumstances, because upon her decision will, in my opinion, depend not the fate of the Measure, but whether some degree of convulsion shall, or shall not, attend its Maturation. It will have[2] gone too far to be retracted, and even Virginia herself, should she in the first instance reject, must afterwards come in. Indeed New Hampshire will certainly accede when she re-assembles, and compleate the Nine for giving action to the project, but a decision in the Negative in Virga. would, in one moment, give additional life to the Minority in Pensylvania, whose opposition has taken a stubborn stand, and the appeal may in that quarter, be to the sword, nor will I venture a conjecture upon the effect such an effort there, will have amongst the opposers in Virginia. I hope, however, that the possibility of a calamity of this sort, will have its effect on some of the more wise in the opposition, and incline them to adopt rather than run such a hazard. Should Virga. adopt, we shall at once have a Government, the issue of a thorough revolution, without the violent means which have uniformly been requisite for the like events elsewhere. I pray God we may exhibit to the world this instance of our superior wisdom and benevolence.

I do myself the pleasure to send you by Mr. Barlow a volume containing a Number of Periodical papers which have been written in this City upon the occasion of the Constitution. They are written, it is supposed, by Messrs. Madison, Jay and Hamilton. The Numbers run to as many more, the remainder are to form a second vol. which will be published in a few weeks. I will do myself the pleasure to send it to you as soon as it is done.

Mr. Madison, in a Letter which he wrote me a few days ago, requested me to obtain the first and second volumes of the Philosophical Transactions of the society in Philada. and forward them to you. Upon enquiry I find that the 1st. vol. is not in print, having been destroyed during the War. The second I have got the favor of Mr. Barlow to take with him for you. I am told the 1st. is to be reprinted. When it is done we will take care to forward it to you. During Mr. Madisons absence in Virginia I am aware of your dependance upon me for regular information upon the progress of the business of the constitution and shall omit no opportunity of writing.

I have the Honor to be, My dr. Sir with the most sincere regard Yr. Friend & Hble St.,

Ed. Carrington

RC (DLC).

Joel BARLOW OF CONNECTICUT—"an admirable man, of an excellent Character, and his Intentions are most pure," John Adams had written on 4 Sep. 1787 in explaining to the Russian ambassador that Barlow wanted to present a copy of the *Vision of Columbus* to the Empress (AMT:MHi)—arrived at Le Havre on 24 June 1788, ambitious to make his fame in literary circles and also to promote land sales for the Ohio Company. He remained in Europe seventeen years, achieved more success in the former object than in the latter, and emerged as a full-blown libertarian, as symbolized by the fact that it was he who, on Paine's imprisonment in Paris, took the manuscript of *The Age of Reason* and saw to its publication. He was the guardian on this trip of George Washington Greene, son of GENL. GREENE and godson of Washington, who was on his way, at Lafayette's desire, to be educated in France, just as Lafayette's Indian protégé, Peter Otsiquette, was returning to America. TJ, Short, Barlow, and Lafayette planned the education of young Greene, who was placed in the Pension Lemoine, across the street from the Hôtel de Langeac, where Crèvecoeur's two sons were already enrolled. Lafayette hoped that his own son, also a namesake and godson of Washington, would complete his education in America, but this well-intended cultural interchange had disappointing results: the turbulence of French politics detained young Lafayette, Greene was killed in a hunting accident soon after returning to America, and Peter Otsiquette soon sloughed off the astonishing veneer of French, English, and music that he had acquired, returned to the ways of his people, and became a hard drinker (Gottschalk, *Lafayette*, 1783-89, p. 404-5).—A more enduring part of American thought and culture that

Barlow brought to Paris was the first of the two-volume collection of essays by MESSRS. MADISON, JAY AND HAMILTON,—*The Federalist.* The copy of this first volume that Carrington sent (see TJ's comment to Madison, 18 Nov. 1788), if it survives, is not now identifiable; the copy that remains among TJ's books in DLC is one with an interesting provenance, for it bears on its two title-pages the signature of Elizabeth Schuyler Hamilton, wife of Alexander Hamilton, and above one of these signatures has the inscription: "For Mrs. Church from her sister." On a fly-leaf of this volume TJ wrote the following which may have been based upon conversations with Madison, but which is not wholly in accord either with Madison's claims or with the findings of historians:

"No.2.3.4.5.64. by Mr. Jay.

No.10.14.17.18.19.21.37.38.39.40.41. 42.43.44.45.46.47.48.49.50.51.52.53. 54.55.56.57.58.62.63. by Mr. Madison.

The rest of the work by Alexander Hamilton"

(see Sowerby, No. 3021 for a description and for illustrations showing Mrs. Hamilton's signature on one title-page and TJ's annotations). Alexander Hamilton, two days before his duel with Burr, "concealed," in a volume of *The Federalist* in Egbert Benson's office, being certain that it would be found, a list in his own handwriting containing his own attributions of authorship, though a few months earlier, in the full vigor of life and of political expectations, he had opposed the idea of identifying the author of each number in a new edition of *The Federalist*; this list reads: "Nos. 2,3,4,5,54, by J. Nos. 10,14,37, to 48 inclusive, M. Nos. 18,19,20, M.&H. jointly. All the others by H." On the basis of this Benson list, *The Federalist* was issued in 1810 as the second and third volumes of the collected works of Hamilton, assigning major credit to him for originating and executing the idea of *Publius*' essays and attributing to him authorship of sixty-three out of the total of eighty-five essays. Madison himself claimed, in a "true distribution of the numbers of the Federalist among the three writers," furnished by him in 1818 to Jacob Gideon who brought out an edition of *The Federalist* that year, to be author of twenty-nine of the essays, instead of the fourteen attributed to him in the Benson list. Ten editions published between 1818 and 1857 followed the Madison rather than the Hamilton designations, but with the Civil War the great classic suffered another sea-change as it had in the years immediately following Hamilton's death: Hamilton's list, rejected for forty years, was again restored to favor, a fact "directly correlated with the see-saw of prestige between these two interpreters of the Constitution, depending upon whether agrarian or capitalistic interests were politically dominant in the country," but helped along in the process by the prodding hand of Henry Cabot Lodge as editor of *The Works of Alexander Hamilton* (1884), whose acceptance of the Benson list was characterized by "self-contradiction, distortion of his data, and sins of documentary omission." Lodge's conclusion that "Hamilton's authority is shown to be six times as good as that of Madison" was, in spite of these defects and in spite of E. G. Bourne's shattering blows as early as 1896, nevertheless accepted by some usually careful modern scholars. This is no longer possible in the light of the brilliant essay by Douglass Adair, "The Authorship of the Disputed Federalist Papers," WMQ, 3rd ser., I (1944), 97-122, 235-64), from which the foregoing facts and quotations are drawn. Adair concludes that Publius "spoke with a Virginia accent in the controversial essays, and that James Madison undoubtedly wrote every number he claimed in the Gideon list." His conclusions, supported by irrefutable evidence and objective reasoning, should set at rest permanently the long, politically-tinged controversy. See also Madison to TJ, 10 Aug. 1788.

1 Thus in MS; it should be "the 24th."

2 Carrington first wrote "has," then deleted it and wrote "will have."

From Grand & Cie.

SIR Paris 14th May 1788

We have the honour to send you 7 Bills, firsts and seconds, on Messrs. Willink & Staphorst in Amsterdam, making together Bo ƒ36000 at 10 days from the16th Inst. Be pleased to send them back to us signed, with the letter of advice, and we will have the honour to advise you the proceeds after their negotiation. We are very respectfully Sir, your most obedient humble servants,

GRAND & CO.

RC (DLC); endorsed. The enclosed bills (not found) are described in TJ's LETTER OF ADVICE to Willink & Van Staphorst, 16 May 1788. TJ's Account Book under date of 14 May has the following entry: "Gave Mr. Grand bill on Willincks & Van Staphorsts for 36,000ƒ banco. This is to replace monies he had advanced for U.S. from the fund of Virginia, and from his own funds. So it need not be entered in my account with the U.S. These bills were dated the 16th inst."

To C. W. F. Dumas

SIR Paris May 15. 1788.

My first moments after my return having been necessarily occupied by letters which had come during my absence and which required immediate answers, I have not till now been able to resume my correspondence with you, and to inform you of my safe arrival here after a very agreeable tour through Germany. Our news from America comes down to the 14th. of March. At that time the state of the new Constitution was thus. It had been accepted in Massachusets by 187 Ayes against 168 Noes.

Connecticut	148	40
Pennsylvania	46	23
Delaware	22	0
New Jersey	39	0
Georgia	33	0
	475	231

The conventions of the other states were to meet as follows

Maryland	April 21.
S. Carolina	May 12.
Virginia	May. 26.
New York	June 17.

New Hampshire June.
North Carolina July
Rhode island has not called a convention.

I have received a letter from General Washington wherein he gives it as his opinion that Virginia will accede to it. Mr. Madison inclines to the same opinion. In fact if Maryland and S. Carolina should have adopted it, as there is great reason to believe, the motives will become very cogent on Virginia for accepting also. She will see that 8. states have already concurred, that New Hampshire and North Carolina will probably concur, that the opposition to be made by Virginia and New York would have little effect, and joined with Rhode island would even be opprobrious. So that probably she will follow the example set by Massachusets of accepting the constitution unconditionally, and instructing her delegates to join with those of Massachusets in urging future amendment. In this case the matter will be fixed by nine states at the close of this month or beginning of the next, and we may have the news by the last of June. It is very possible that the President and new Congress may be sitting at New York in the month of September. I have no other material news from America. Here all seems peace without and war within. A great deal of good is offered to the nation, but some think there is more evil in the form of the offer.—I have the honour to be with sentiments of the most perfect esteem and respect, Sir, Your most obedient & most humble servt.,

TH: JEFFERSON

PrC (DLC).

Except for the erroneous anticipation that NORTH CAROLINA WILL PROBABLY CONCUR, TJ's appraisal was remarkably close to that made on the preceding day in America by Carrington (see Carrington to TJ, 14 May 1788). TJ doubtless intended Dumas to make the substance of this letter known through the pages of the *Gazette de Leide*, and Dumas promptly did so: the letter, freely edited and adapted to its new purpose by Dumas, appeared in the *Supplément* for 3 June 1788 under the title "Extrait d'une Lettre de New-York du 14 Mars." Dumas did not alter TJ's facts or conclusions, but he did omit the names of Washington and Madison and substituted for the sentence in which they occurred the following: "Les Personnes les plus instruites sont persuadées, que l'Amérique-Unie est à la veille de voir bientôt ce grand Ouvrage consommé selon le voeu des Amis de la Patrie, notamment que l'Etat de Virginie, dont l'influence est à juste titre très-considérable dans la Confédération, suivra l'exemple des deux autres principaux Membres, Massachusett's et Pensylvanie." At the conclusion of the tabulation of votes for and against the Constitution in the six states that had ratified, Dumas added this observation: "Ainsi, comptant ensemble la masse des suffrages de six Etats il y en a eu 475. qui ont approuvé le Projet de la Convention-Générale contre 231. qui l'ont rejetté, par conséquent plus des deux tiers. L'on n'en peut tirer que l'augure le plus favorable pour l'acceptation universelle de la nouvelle Forme." Dumas also called this publication to Jay's attention in a letter in which he stated: "You will see by the Leyden Gazette of June 3d, and the supplement of the 10th, that I am using the surest means of keeping up the credit of the United

States in Holland; and I have the satisfaction to see that it succeeds, the more especially as that of all other countries, even of Holland itself, is falling. I must, however, remark, that the article headed *Philadelphia April* 23, in the supplement (No. 49) of the Leyden Gazette of June 17, is not mine, and that I know not who inserted it" (*Dipl. Corr., 1783-89*, III, 617-8; Dumas misdated both RC and FC [Dumas Letter Book, Rijksarchief, The Hague; photostats in DLC] as 10 June; the letter was probably written 18 or 19 June). For understandable reasons, Dumas sent this letter by way of Amsterdam instead of, as usual, by way of Paris for TJ to see; the letter "headed *Philadelphia April* 23" may have been a letter from one of Mazzei's correspondents: it contains the following reference to the Constitutional Society of which Mazzei was founder: "La Société Politique de Richmond, dans l'Etat de la Virginie, a pris, pour sujet de ses délibérations publiques, l'examen de la nouvelle Constitution: Après trois Séances de débats et de discussions, elle a été approuvée par une pluralité de 128. contre 15. voix"; the extract published was generally concerned with the progress of ratification of the Constitution.

To John Jay

DEAR SIR Paris May 15. 1788. Private

The change which is likely to take place in the form of our government seems to render it proper that during the existence of the present government, an article should be mentioned which concerns me personally. Incertain however how far Congress may have decided to do business, when so near the close of their administration, less capable than those on the spot, of foreseeing the character of the new government, and not fully confiding in my own judgment where it is so liable to be seduced by feeling, I take the liberty of asking your friendly counsel, and that of my friend Mr. Madison, and of referring the matter to your judgments and discretion. Mr. Barclay, when in Europe, was authorized to settle all the European accounts of the United states. He settled those of Doctr. Franklin and Mr. Adams, and it was intended between us that he should settle mine. But as what may be done at any time is often put off to the last, this settlement had been made to give way to others, and that of Beaumarchais being pressed on Mr. Barclay before his departure for Marocco, and having long retarded his departure, it was agreed that my affair should await his return from that mission. You know the circumstance which prevented his return to Paris after that mission was finished. My account is therefore unsettled. But I have no anxiety on any article of it, except one. That is the Outfit. This consists of 1.Clothes. 2.Carriage and horses. 3.Houshold furniture. When Congress made their first appointments of Ministers to be *resident* in Europe, I have understood (for I was not then in Congress) that they allowed them all their expences and a fixed sum over and above for their time. Among their expences was necessarily included their Outfit. Afterwards they thought proper to give them fixed salaries of 11,111⅑ dollars[1] a year; and again by a resolution of May 6. and 7. 1784. the '*salaries*' of their ministers at foreign courts were reduced to 9000 dollars to take place on the 1st. of Aug. ensuing. On the 7th. of May I was appointed in addition to Mr. Adams and Dr. Franklin for the negociation of treaties of commerce; but this appointment being temporary for two years only, and not as a resident, the article of Outfit did not come into question. I asked an advance of six months salary, that I might be in cash to meet the first expences, which was ordered. The year following I was appointed to succeed Doctr. Franklin at this court. This was the first appointment of a minister resident since the original ones under which all expences were to be paid. So much of the antient regulation as respected *annual expences* had been altered to a sum certain. So much of it as respected *first expences, or Outfit*, remained unaltered, and I might therefore expect that the actual expences for Outfit were to be paid. When I prepared my account for settlement with Mr. Barclay, I began a detail of the articles of Clothes, carriage and horses, and houshold furniture. I found that they were numerous, minute, and incapable, from their nature, of being vouched, and often entered in my memorandum book under a general head only, so that I could not specify them. I found they would exceed a year's salary. Supposing therefore that, mine being the first case, Congress would make a precedent of it and[2] prefer a sum fixed for the Outfit as well as the salary, I have charged it in my account at a year's salary. I presume there can be no question that an Outfit is a reasonable charge. It is the usage here (and I suppose at all courts) that a minister resident shall establish his house in the first instant. If this is to be done out of his salary, he will be a twelvemonth at least without a copper to live on. It is the universal practice therefore of all nations to allow the Outfit as a separate article from Salary. I have enquired here into the usual amount of it. I find that sometimes the sovereign pays the actual cost. This is particularly the case of the Sardinian Ambassador now coming here, who is to provide a service of plate and every article of furniture and other matters of first expence, to be paid for by his court. In other instances they give a service of plate and a fixed sum for all other articles, which fixed sum is in no case lower than a year's salary. I desire no service of plate, having no ambition for splendor. My furniture, carriage, apparel are all plain. Yet they have cost me more than a year's salary. I suppose that in every country and in every condition of life, a year's expences would be found a moderate measure for the furniture of a man's house. It is not more certain to me that the sun will rise tomorrow, than that our government must allow the Outfit in their future appointment of foreign ministers, and it would be hard on me so to stand between the discontinuance of a former rule, and institution of a future one, as to have the benefit of neither. I know, and have so long known, the character of our federal head, in it's present form, that I have the most unlimited confidence in the justice of their decisions. I think I am so far known to many of the present Congress as that I may be cleared of all views of making money out of any public emploiment, or of desiring any thing beyond actual and decent expences, proportioned to the station in which they have been pleased to place me, and to the respect they would wish to see attached to it. It would seem right that they should decide the claims of those who have acted under their administration, and their pretermission of any article might amount to a disallowance of it in the opinion of the new government. It would be painful to me to meet that government with a claim under this kind of cloud, and to pass it in review before their several houses of legislation and boards of administration to whom I shall be unknown: and being for money actually expended, it would be too inconvenient to me to relinquish it in silence. I anxiously wish it therefore to be decided on by Congress before they go out of office if it be not out of the line of proceeding they may have chalked out for themselves. If it be against their inclination to determine it, would it be agreeable to them to refer it to the new government by some resolution which should shew they have not meant to disallow it by passing it over? Not knowing the circumstances under which Congress may exist and act at the moment you shall receive this, I am unable to judge what should be done on this subject. It is here then that I ask the aid of your friendship and that of Mr. Madison; I am incapable of asking either of you to do any thing inconsistent with your judgments, with your sentiments or your offices. I only wish that that may be done for me which you think it is right should be done, and which it would be right for me to do were I on the spot, or were I apprised of all existing circumstances. Indeed were you two to think my claim an improper one, I would wish it to be suppressed as I have so much confidence in your judgments that I should suspect my own in any case where it varied from yours, and more especially in one where it is so liable to be warped by feeling. Give me leave then to ask your consultation with Mr. Madison on this subject, and to assure you that whatever you are so good as to do herein will be perfectly approved and considered as a great obligation conferred on him who has the honour to be with sentiments of the most perfect esteem & attachment Dear Sir, Your friend & servant,

TH: JEFFERSON

RC (NK-Iselin); endorsed. 1st PrC (DLC: Madison Papers). 2d PrC (DLC). Both RC and 1st PrC were enclosed in TJ to Madison, 25 May 1788.

MY FURNITURE, CARRIAGE, APPAREL ARE ALL PLAIN: Thomas Lee Shippen had noted a few months earlier, at court, that "Mr. Jefferson was the plainest man in the room, and the most destitute of ribbands crosses and other insignia of rank" (Smith to TJ, 9 Jan. 1788, note). TJ himself had been in Congress in 1784, had helped draft the instructions for the appointment of temporary commissioners to negotiate treaties of amity and commerce, and had witnessed, in the attempt of some to dispense altogether with ministers and to depend solely on consular establishment, what Gouverneur Morris at the time had called "that sort of despicable Saving which weak minds call Œconomy because they do not know what Œconomy is. Such folks [members of Congress] arm themselves with a few Ale House arguments against their Return Home and think they will become popular by rendering themselves ridiculous" (Morris to William Carmichael, 2 June 1784; DNA: HR 27A–G 7.4: Claim of William Carmichael).

1 After "fixed salaries," TJ first wrote and then deleted, "which I believe were 2500. guineas."

2 Preceding six words interlined.

From John Jay

Office for Foreign Affairs [*New York*], *16 May 1788.* Since his last of 24 Apr. 1788, has received no letters from TJ, and there has been no event of importance "except the Accession of Maryland to the Number of the States which have adopted the proposed Constitution. Until that business is concluded I apprehend that our national Affairs will continue much at a Stand." Barlow brings this and a packet of newspapers.

FC (DNA: PCC, No. 121).

From Dorcas Montgomery

SIR

Paris the 16th. [May] 1788

I beg ten Thousand pardon's for the Liberty I take, in recommending my Fatherless Son to your advice. The inclos'd writings I think very unjust, as my Son's personal Fortune is not more than eight Thousand pound's American money. If he complys with the inclosed agreement, He will be without any Cash. Mr. Pigott has acted by me a cruel, and ungenerous part, in Kidnaping my son into a marriage, and in making Him settle the principal of His personnal Estate upon His Daughter, and Her Children. I informed Mr. Pigott before my sons marriage that the Laws in Pennsylvania made a Provision for the Wife, by allowing Her one third of His Personal Estate. In that case my son's wife, would claim near Six Thousand pounds American money from my Son's real estate.—Mr. Pigott in *Pisa* insulted me basely, and took my son from me, and provided him with other Lodgings. Upon my being informed of the above, I sent for me son. He returned for answer He would not come, upon which I went to Mr. Pigott's and demanded him. His Daughter flew into a Chamber with Him and Lock'd the Door. I demanded my son of Mr. Pigott in a spirited manner, upon which He insulted me, and threatened me with the *Consul* of England, and that He would send me to prison. I defy'd him and his *English Consul*, with adding I had the protection [of the] Grand Duke. In one word I remain'd there from eight in the Evening until half after Eleven aClock, at night, in receiving nothing but abuse. I then inform'd him that I had Parents right, and that I should claim protection under the Civil Government. I accordingly went to the first magistrate, who was in his bed, but upon being inform'd that I was a Stranger, He rise. I simply repeated the facts. He ask'd me if I objected to my Son's marrying the young Lady. No, except their youth. He very politely beg'd me to return to my Lodgings, that my son should be with me in half an Hour, which was the case. He sent the next Day for my Son and Mr. Pigott, and give them a sever reproof.—I was quite a Stranger to the inclosed writing until two Days since when my Son shewed me the inclos'd. I advised him to propose friendly to Mr. Pigott to give a certain sum, and distroy the first writing. I am very sensible How much your time is employ'd, and beg a thousand pardons for the liberty I take.

I have the Honor to remain very respectfully Sir Your most. Obedt. & very Humble Servt. D. MONTGOMERY

RC (MHi); endorsed; recorded in SJL Index as written 16 May 1788. Enclosures: The INCLOS'D WRITINGS by Pigott have not been found, but their purport is clear, especially if viewed also in the light of TJ's letter to Pigott of 3 June 1788.

Robert Pigott (1736-1794), an eccentric reformer in dress and diet, whose daughter had married Robert Montgomery, had thought in 1776 that the American revolution meant the ruin of England, had sold his Chetwynd and Chesterton estates that were reputedly worth £9,000 a year, and had retired to the continent, where he became acquainted with Voltaire, Franklin, Brissot de Warville, and other figures of the Enlightenment. He created or adopted various fads—at one time or another being a zealous advocate of vegetarianism (though condemning bread), a crusader against hats as supposed symbols of ecclesiastical and political despotism, an admirer of James Graham and his electric bed, a gambler who once wagered 500 guineas with Sir William Codrington that his father would outlive Sir William's (not knowing that the elder Pigott had died a few hours before the bet was placed), and an enthusiast over the French revolution, even in its excesses (DNB).—Mrs. Dorcas Armitage Montgomery was married on 20 Aug. 1767 to Robert Montgomery of Christiana Bridge, Delaware, who died at the age of 27 on board his brigantine *Harmony* in the Bay of Gibraltar on 28 Apr. 1770, leaving her a widow with two children, Thomas (who also died in 1770) and Robert, at seventeen the husband of Pigott's daughter (from a communication from George H. Fairchild, the Historical Society of Pennsylvania, to the Editors, 2 Feb. 1956). Mrs. Montgomery corresponded with Franklin in 1781 about her son's schooling, thinking first to place him in or near Paris but finally concluding, possibly to her later regret, to settle in Geneva. From that place she entrusted Pigott with a letter to Franklin, wherein she described him as a friend to America (Mrs. Montgomery to Franklin, 21 Nov. 1781; PPAP). TJ possessed a copy of Pigott's address to the National Assembly entitled *Liberté de la Presse* (Sowerby, No. 2555).

To Edmund Randolph

Dear Sir Paris May 16. 1788.

Mr. Mazzei desires me to inclose his letter to you and to add my testimony to his of the necessities he is under. This I can do with truth, observing further that had I known of the sufferings he has gone through, they certainly should have been prevented. His situation really requires that his friends should strain his resources to the utmost and give him the benefit of them for his relief. The fear that he has lost every thing in the hands of Forster Webb depresses him extremely. It will be charity to relieve him from this fear if it is without foundation. If this be really to be added to his loss by Dohrman, the cruelty with which he is persecuted by fortune is deploreable.

With respect to M. de Rieux, I am afraid that good hopes are blasted. Not knowing him personally, but knowing his family here to be of wealth and distinction, having an esteem for his wife, and hearing that both were reduced to labour for subsistence, I introduced myself to the acquaintance of an aunt of his here whom I knew to be rich, and to have no child. I made her sensible of his situation, and that to relieve him from personal labour he must have at least six slaves, with cattle, horses &c. in proportion and that all this could cost 15000 livres. In fine she agreed to give him that sum: and she expected it would be laid out according to my calculation. I am told it has not been: and I wish she may never be told it. She had as good as promised me she would leave him twelve thousand guineas. But she is not more than 50. years old, and is healthy. The six negroes were to be the support of the family in the mean time.—I have taken the liberty of mentioning these circumstances to you, because I find Mr. Mazzei asks some attention to the case from you. This must be my apology. A further one is the pleasure I have in every occasion of assuring you of those sentiments of esteem & respect with which I have the honour to be Your Excellency's most obedient & most humble servt.,

TH: JEFFERSON

PrC (DLC); at foot of text: "His Excellency Edmund Randolph." The enclosed letter from Mazzei to Edmund Randolph has not been found, but his letter to Madison, 9 May 1788, concerning the DOHRMAN affair (printed in Garlick, *Philip Mazzei*, p. 121-2) is probably similar in substance.

To Nicolas & Jacob van Staphorst

GENTLEMEN Paris May 16. 1788.

The first moments after my return to Paris having been necessarily required by letters which had come during my absence and which called for immediate answers, it is not till now that I can have the pleasure of informing you of my return, of thanking you for your attentions and civilities while at Amsterdam, and of acknoleging the receipt of your favor of May 8. The bills of Mr. Turckheim and Mr. Peuchen, you will be so good as to charge in your account with the United States, as I shall credit them in mine.

I am happy that the loan has had the success you expected, and hope it will be filled up completely[1] by the time we receive orders for the two articles of Foreign officers and Algiers, from the board of Treasury. We shall probably receive at the same time the ratification of Congress for the million on the last bonds, so as to open that loan. In the mean time a new demand comes from this court for a regular paiment of our interest in future to them. This would require about three quarters of a million of florins per annum, and should Congress provide for that to the end of the year 1790. as we have proposed for the other European demands, it will require nearly two additional millions. On this I have asked their pleasure. I have the honour to be with very great esteem & attachment, Gentlemen, your most obedt. & most humble servt.,

TH: JEFFERSON

PrC (DLC).

[1] This word interlined.

To the Commissioners of the Treasury

Gentlemen Paris May 16. 1788.

In a letter of Mar. 29. which I had the honour of addressing you from Amsterdam, I stated to you what had passed till that date relative to our money affairs in Europe, and I inclosed you an estimate of these which looked forward to the end of the year 1790. I mentioned to you also that the prospect of filling up the loan of the last million was at that moment good, so that I thought you might be at ease as to the paiment of the June interest. I have now the pleasure to inclose you a letter from our bankers of the 8th. inst. wherein they inform me they have sold bonds enough to pay the June interest and have a surplus sufficient to replace the monies lent from the Virginia fund and by Mr. Grand. These advances were but momentary accomodations, made under the mistaken idea that the money was in Amsterdam ready to replace them, and it was not in idea to inscribe them on the roll of the debts of the United states, to take their turn of paiment. You will therefore I hope think me justifiable in having them replaced immediately as there is money enough now for that purpose over and above the June interest. The balance due to Gateau is for one of the medals I had your orders to have made, and has been due upwards of a twelvemonth. Mr. Short's salary I suppose included under your general order that the diplomatic calls shall be regularly paid by our bankers. So far then I shall venture to draw immediately, perhaps also for the little balance due to Ast, whose distresses call loudly for assistance. He has been obliged to carry his clothes to the pawn broker's to raise money for his subsistance. All the other articles of the estimate will await your orders, which you will therefore be pleased to give as you shall think proper.

The foreign officers had proposed a meeting, the object of which was, as I heard, to address Congress in terms which would have been very disagreeable, and at the same time to present a petition to the king claiming his interposition. This would have made a great deal of noise, and produced very disagreeable effects. This was a few days before I went to Amsterdam. I saw Colo. Gouvion the day before I set out, and desired him to quiet them till my return, explaining to him that one of the objects of my journey would be to enable you to pay them. I have since my return informed them of the prospect of paiment, and that your orders for that purpose may be hoped by the month of June—A letter from Obrian at Algiers shews me that he has had an intimation of my being authorised to redeem them, and imputes the delay to me. I have endeavored on the contrary to have it believed at Algiers that the public will not interest itself in their redemption, having been assured by the General of the religious order who is to act for us that if the Dey has the least expectations that the public will interfere, he will hold them at such prices as this order has never given, and cannot consent to give because of the precedent, and that in this case we shall lose the benefit of their agency. Under these circumstances it would be cruelty to the captives to let them know we are proceeding to their redemption. They could not keep their own secret, and the indiscretion of any one of them might for ever blast the prospect of their redemption. For I suppose it to be uncontrovertible that a regard to the safety and liberty of our seamen and citizens in general forbids us to give such prices for those in captivity as will draw on our vessels peculiarly the pursuit of those sea-dogs. It is for the good of the captives themselves therefore that we submit to be thought hardly of by them: but no time should be lost unnecessarily in proceeding to their redemption: nor shall a moment be lost after I shall be authorised by your order to receive the money. You perceive that by the extract from the letter of the bankers which I have the honour to inclose you, they expect to place speedily the rest of the bonds. I think I may venture to assure you they can do it at any moment if they are pushed. You know the misunderstandings which exist between those two houses. These are the cause of their not always saying as much as they might venture to say with truth.—There is an error in the estimate I sent you which must be explained. I omitted, when I set out from Paris, to ask Mr. Short for a state of the balance due him, and had always been ignorant of it, as the account remained between him and Mr. Grand. When making the estimate at Amsterdam, therefore, I was obliged to conjecture what that balance was, which I did from a very slight and mistaken circumstance as I now find. The balance due him, instead of being about 5000,tt as I had guessed, is 13,146.tt6 as you will see by his account now inclosed. I have the honour to be with sentiments of the most perfect esteem & respect, Gentlemen, Your most obedient & most humble servt.,

TH: JEFFERSON

PrC (DLC). Enclosures: Copies of Nicolas & Jacob van Staphorst to TJ, Willink & Van Staphorst to TJ, both of 8 May 1788; the copy of one (probably of the first since the full letter dealt in part with TJ's private accounts) was an extract; neither of the copies actually enclosed has been found, since the extant files of the Commissioners of the Treasury are very fragmentary. The enclosed statement of Short's account is also missing.

The ESTIMATE needing correction was that sent to the Commissioners in TJ's letter of 29 Mch. 1788 (text printed with TJ to Jay, 16 Mch. 1788). The LETTER FROM OBRIAN (missing) was probably the "cruel letter" mentioned in TJ to Jay, 4 May 1788 (see note there). The information given the foreign officers on the PROSPECT OF PAYMENT was set forth in TJ to Castaing, 14 May 1788; see also Gouvion to TJ, 13 May 1788, note.

To Willink & Van Staphorst

GENTLEMEN Paris May 16. 1788.

I am honored with your letter of the 8th. instant and in consequence thereof have this day drawn on you seven bills amounting in the whole to 36,000 florins banco in favor of Messieurs Grand & co. paiable at ten days date according to a letter of advice of this days date. These draughts are to cover the three articles of Virginia, Grand and Gateau as stated in the estimate I gave you. They are 500 florins short of that estimate. I find it will be more agreeable to Mr. Short and Mr. Ast to receive their draughts separately, and that that of Mr. Short will be considerably more than stated in the estimate. I had omitted at my departure from Paris to know from him his exact balance, and, when forming the estimate at Amsterdam, was obliged to insert it by conjecture. Instead of 5000 livres as there conjectured, it is 13,146.tt 6 sols. This excess beyond the estimate will be more than compensated in the two articles of Foreign officers and Algiers, whenever the Treasury board shall send you orders to pay them, as these two articles will be considerably below the estimate: so that on the whole it will only occasion a temporary variation. I shall take the liberty of drawing on you soon in favor of Mr. Short and Mr. Ast. The other articles must await the orders of the Treasury. I have the honor to be Gentlemen your most obedient & most humble servant,

TH: JEFFERSON

PrC (DLC). The ESTIMATE I GAVE YOU is the one referred to in note to the preceding letter.

To Willink & Van Staphorst

GENTLEMEN Paris May 16. 1788.

This serves to advise you that I have this day drawn on you for thirty six thousand florins banco divided into seven bills of exchange as specified below, paiable at ten days sight to the order of Messieurs Grand & co. which be pleased to honour and charge the same to the United states of America. I have the honour to be Gentlemen Your most obedient & most humble servt.,

TH: JEFFERSON

One bill for six thousand florins	6000*f*
One do. for five thousand eight hundred	5800
One do. for five thousand six hundred	5600
One do. for five thousand four hundred	5400
One do. for five thousand two hundred	5200
One do. for five thousand one hundred	5100
One do. for two thousand nine hundred	2900
	36,000

PrC (DLC). Although dated the 16th, this letter of advice was evidently written on the 14th and postdated as were the bills of exchange (see Grand & Cie. to TJ, 14 May 1788).

To John Bondfield

SIR

Paris May 17. 1788.

On my return from Amsterdam, I found here your favours of March 7. and April 19. of which I have now the honor to acknolege the receipt. The vin de Sauterne was also safely arrived. I had left directions for paiment of the bill for it, expecting you would have been so kind as to draw on me immediately for the amount. Whenever you shall do this, it shall be duly honoured; only be so good as to draw paiable at some days sight, to guard against the inconvenience of my being out of the house when the bill is first presented, which in the case of a bill from Lorient in one instance subjected me to a protest. I will also ask the favor of you to purchase for me from Monsieur le Comte de Fumelle 125 bottles of his vin d'Hautbrion of 1784. of which you say he has some hogsheads still, and to forward it by the way of Havre to the care of M. Limozin, or Rouen to the care either of Mr. Garvey or M. Montfort. Your bill for the amount of that also shall be duly honored.—I inclose you a letter from the Count de Montmorin on the subject of two strollers who call themselves Americans. If they be really such and are still in the hands of the Police I would trouble you to reclaim them, provided they can work their passage home on some ship. But if this will occasion any expence, they must remain where they are, as neither money nor authority has been put into my hands to send them home at the publick expence.

I have the honor to be with great esteem, Sir, your most obedient & most humble servt., TH: JEFFERSON

PrC (DLC). The enclosed letter from Montmorin on the subject of the TWO STROLLERS was evidently that of 25 Apr. 1788, which is recorded in SJL Index but has not been found. No draft of it or file copy has been found in Arch. Aff. Etr., Corr. Pol., E.-U., and there is no record of a reply by TJ.

From Edward Carrington

MY DEAR SIR New York May 17. 1788

My particular Friend Master George Washington Greene will have the Honor to deliver you this letter. Your acquaintance with his illustrious Father renders it unnecessary for me to solicit for him your attention and Countenance. He is sent to France at the age of about 12 years to be educated under the the direction of the Marquis De La Fayette. I have the Honor to be Dr. Sir Yr. Sincere Friend & Hl. St. ED. CARRINGTON

RC (DLC); endorsed. For a note on GEORGE WASHINGTON GREENE, see Carrington to TJ, 14 May 1788.

To André Limozin

SIR Paris May 17. 1788.

I had the honor of writing to you on the 4th. instant. Since that I have received a letter from Dunkirk informing me that my boxes of plants are coming on by land. You will not have the trouble therefore of receiving and forwarding them: and I am happy in every occasion of sparing you trouble, of which I am obliged to give you so much and so often.—Messrs. Van Staphorsts of Amsterdam, by a letter of the 8th. inst. inform me they have loaded my three cases on the ship De Jonge Bernardus (the young Bernardus) Capt. Claas Arends Koen, and have noted in the bill of lading that they contain 'des meubles pour S.E. Th. Jefferson ministre plenipotentiaire &c.' Perhaps this may give some facility to their entrance, tho' I doubt it. If nothing better can be done they might be plumbed and sent here, tho' that would not be so desireable as the introducing them by feeing the person who searches. —After these there will come from the same house boxes containing two cast iron stoves, which will occa[sion much di]fficulty [and wi]ll weigh six or seven hundred weigh[t. These boxes may come] either by water or by a waggon.—I [have also shipped] down the river to your care a hamper con[tainin]g 3. dozen bottles of vinegar addressed to Francis Hopkinson Philadelphia, which I will ask the favor of you to send by the first vessel which shall go from your port to Philadelphia. I also sent by a Mr. Ford some letters and packets for America to be sent by the packet boat. But as there is no packet boat under sailing orders, a gentleman (Mr. Warville) who goes from hence to Havre to take his passage in a private vessel will call on you for them in a few days. A Spanish squadron of 7 ships of the line has sailed from Cadiz. Their destination unknown. Sweden is arming 8. ships of the line and some frigates; Denmark doing the same. England is sending a squadron to Gibraltar to protect their trade against the Moors, and troops to her West and East Indies. France sends three regiments to the East Indies. Thus the nations are by little and little taking the position of war. Still I am satisfied that France will not engage in a war if she can avoid it, and there are no symptoms which threaten it this summer. She is likely to be sufficiently employed at home.

I have the honour to be with great esteem, Sir [your most obedient & most] humble servant, TH: JEFFERSON

PrC (DLC). An irregular hole, measuring about two by three inches, appears in the center of the manuscript, causing the loss of some words on recto and verso; the missing words have been conjecturally supplied in brackets.

The LETTER FROM DUNKIRK was that of Coffyn to TJ, 2 May 1788.

To Moustier

DEAR SIR Paris May 17. 1788.

I have at length an opportunity of acknoleging the receipt of your favors of Feb. and Mar. 14.[1] and of congratulating you on your resurrection from the dead among whom you had been confidently entombed by the news-dealers of Paris. I am sorry that your first impressions have been disturbed by matters of etiquette, where surely they should least have been expected to occur. These disputes are the most insusceptible of determination, because they have no foundation in reason. Arbitrary and senseless in their nature, they are arbitrarily decided by every nation for itself. These decisions are meant to prevent disputes, but they produce ten where they prevent one. It would have been better therefore in a new country to have excluded etiquette altogether; or, if it must be admitted in some form or other, to have made it depend on some circumstance founded in nature, such as the age or stature of the parties.—However you have got over all this, and I am in hopes have been able to make up a society suited to your own dispositions. Your situation will doubtless be improved by the adoption of the new constitution, which I hope will have taken place before you receive this. I see in this instrument a great deal of good. The consolidation of our government, a just representation, an administration of some permanence and other features of great value, will be gained by it. There are indeed some faults which revolted me a good deal in the first moment: but we must be contented to travel on towards perfection, step by step. We must be contented with the ground which this constitution will gain for us, and hope that a favourable moment will come for correcting what is amiss in it. I view in the same light the innovations making here. The new organisation of the judiciary department is undoubtedly for the better. The reformation of the criminal code is an immense step taken towards good. The composition of the Plenary court is indeed vicious in the extreme. But the basis of that court may be retained and it's composition changed. Make of it a representative of the people, by composing it of members sent from provincial assemblies, and it becomes a valuable member of the constitution. But it is said the court will not consent to do this. The court however has consented to call the States general, who will consider the plenary court but as a canvas for them to work on. The public mind is manifestly advancing on the abusive prerogatives of their governors, and bearing them down. No force in the government can withstand this in the long run. Courtiers had rather give up power than pleasures: they will barter therefore the usurped prerogatives of the king for the money of the people. This is the agent by which modern nations will recover their rights. I sincerely wish that in this country they may be contented with a peaceable and passive opposition. At this moment we are not sure of this. Tho' as yet it is difficult to say what form the opposition will take, it is a comfortable circumstance that their neighboring enemy is under the administration of a minister disposed to keep the peace. There are some little symptoms however lately, which look as if the war of the Eastern might gain upon the Western parts of Europe. Sweden has notified the court of Denmark it's intention to arm 8. ships of the line and some frigates. Denmark has in consequence determined to arm an equal force. Spain has sent 7. ships of the line with some frigates to sea. Their destination not yet known to the public. And she is going on with further naval armaments. England sends a squadron to the Mediterranean to protect her commerce against the Moores, and reinforcements of men to her West and East Indies. France sends three regiments to the East Indies, officers to Tippoo Saib's army, and receives an Embassy from this chief. Thus you see that things are insensibly taking the position of war, with professions of peace. Engage in war who will, may my country long continue your peaceful residence, and merit your good offices with that nation whose affections it is their duty and interest to cultivate. Accept these and all other the good wishes of him who has the honour to be with sincere esteem & respect Dear Sir your most obedient & most humble servant, TH: JEFFERSON

P.S. The hundred bottles of Frontignan are forwarded to Mr. Bondfeild at Bordeaux, who will send them to you.

PrC (DLC).

Moustier's entombment BY THE NEWS-DEALERS OF PARIS was broken by his arrival in New York after a voyage of 65 days, so enfeebled that Otto, reporting to Montmorin, thought the new minister would need a rest of several weeks to regain strength—a report which reached Montmorin almost a month after TJ's letter of 2 Mch. 1788. Otto said that Moustier was received by the citizens of New York "avec toutes les demonstrations de respect et d'attachement dues au representant d'une nation qui a rendu des services aussi essentiels aux Etats unis." But Moustier recovered quickly, and at once found himself ensnarled with the vexed question of the rights of immunity of consuls (see editorial note in connection with the Consular Convention, under 14 Nov. 1788) and with MATTERS OF ETIQUETTE. Moustier and Jay discussed the ceremonial reception of the new minister early in February, both in correspondence and in conversation. The former thought the ceremonial established in 1783 "susceptible de quelques observations surtout relativement a l'etiquette de la première visite aux membres individuels du Congrès." Nevertheless, he spoke confidentially to Jay and some others in order to make plain his deference to regulations that, he reported, Jay himself found offensive. On 12 Feb. Jay reported to Congress a letter from Moustier asking that "a Day be fixed for his *public* Audience, and intimating an Expectation that the Ceremonial will be the same as in the Cases of his Predecessors"; he advised that he had "perused and considered the Ceremonials heretofore used on such Occasions, and that they appear to him to put much less Distinction between an Ambassador and a Minister than the Laws and the actual Practice of civilized Nations have established," but that "considering the past and present state of American Affairs," he thought it "might not be so advisable to correct Mistakes relative to Matters of Ceremony and Etiquette at this Period, as when the proposed Plan of Government shall begin to operate" (JCC, XXXIV, 44-5). Congress set the day for 26 Feb., having first agreed to make the audience public and to follow precedent by distributing tickets to private individuals by allocating two to each member and eight to the president, but having rejected a committee suggestion that each member would be expected to distribute one of his tickets "to some Character more than ordinarily distinguished, the other at his Discretion" and also that Van Berckel and Gardoqui be given seats distinguishing them "from Persons less respectable in point of Rank" (JCC, XXXIV, 46, 51, 52, 54). On the appointed day Moustier was admitted to the chamber in which Congress met, and, before an audience composed of some sixty persons in addition to members of Congress, departmental heads, and foreign dignitaries, tendered his letter of credence signed by Louis XVI and Montmorin, delivered an address of customary felicitations, and heard one in reply by the president of Congress (texts printed in same, p. 64-5). Moustier informed Montmorin that he had tried to include in his discourse expressions of friendship and confidence, but that he thought it necessary at the same time to remind Congress gently of what the United States owed to the generosity of the king. He also drew an unflattering picture of Congress, but declared that that body could not be regarded as truly representative, since for some years the greater part of its members had been drawn from an inferior class, whether judged by wealth, position, knowledge, or talents, a fact which explained why the barren style of the president's response had not surprised him more, since it was the product of "des gens, qui dans leur petite sphere individuelle, se bouffisent de l'idée d'une parfaite egalité avec un Roi de France." He considered that his own address, which he expected to be printed in the multitude of gazettes that formed the sole reading of many Americans, as intended for the whole nation: Congress was only "un phantome de Souverain," unworthy of being compared with the members of the Federal Convention as representatives of the United States, and, unless the new Constitution were adopted, would be unable not only to discharge the national debt but even to raise the slender funds for government expenses. Montmorin agreed with this appraisal, approved Moustier's address and decision to abide by the disagreeable ceremonial ("Il faut convenir toute fois, que ce cérémonial est bien exigeant, et bien peu analogue à celui qui est reçu dans les Etats républicains en Europe"), and urged Moustier, while following his instructions to avoid intervening in American affairs, to make it very plain to Jay that this was out of respect for the independence of the United States as a sovereign nation and did not in any way reflect any indifference on the part of the king to the great issue being decided in America (Otto to Montmorin, 18 Jan. 1788; Moustier to Montmorin, 14, 27 Feb. 1788, the latter enclosing French texts of his address and the president's response; Montmorin to Moustier, 23 June 1788; all in Arch. Aff. Etr., Paris, Corr. Pol., E.-U., Vol. XXXIII; transcripts in DLC; the correspondence between Moustier and Jay concerning the audience is in *Dipl. Corr., 1783-89*, I, 245-53; see also Moustier to TJ, 13 Feb., 13 Mch., and 12 Aug. 1788). Congress reciprocated Moustier's impressions, at first with reserve and then with hostility. On the day after the audience, one delegate thought the new minister's "manner rather more lively than dignified, altho no decided opinion can be formed from a single interview, and that a public one." A few weeks later a member of the committee that had planned the audience reported to the governor of his state that "Mon'r le Comte de Moustier . . . is remarked to be not so courtly in his attention to congress as his predecessor." It was being rumored at that time, too, that Moustier was about to present a memorial on the French debt, a subject that "in the present condition of these states can only serve to disgust" (Samuel A. Otis to James Warren, 27 Feb. 1788; James White to Gov. Samuel Johnston of N.C., 21 Apr. 1788; Burnett, *Letters of Members*, VIII, Nos. 797, 831). Thenceforward Moustier's relations with Congress steadily deteriorated.

1 Thus in MS, an error for 13 Feb. and 13 Mch. 1788.

From William Carmichael

Dear Sir — Aranjuez 18th May 1788

Agreable to what I had the honor to mention you in a late Letter I now inclose you the Cypher delivered me by Colonel Franks. Mr. Symons will put it into your Exys. hands. This young Gentleman has behaved with the greatest propriety during his short residence here and I shall always be happy to render such civilities and services to persons who like this Gentleman come to me under your recommendation, as are in my Power. I have directed two or three late publications in Spanish to be put into

Mr. Symons hands for you and shall occasionally avail myself of similar conveyances to contribute to satisfy that thirst for general knowledge for which you are Distinguished. With high respect & Esteem I have the honor to be yr Exys. Most obedt. Hble. Servt.,

WM. CARMICHAEL

RC (DLC); endorsed. Enclosure (missing): Copy of the Adams-TJ-Barclay-Lamb code that had been left with Carmichael BY COLONEL FRANKS (see note to TJ to Carmichael, 25 Sep. 1787).

To Anthony Gerna

SIR

Paris May 18. 1788.

Not having heard from you since you left Paris I take the liberty of writing the present merely to ask whether I may expect from you the books of which I gave you a note. I also asked one of your catalogues of books printed in Dublin. Be so good as to send me a line in answer, inclosed to Mr. John Trumbull. No. 2. North street Rathbone place London. I am Sir your very humble servt.,

TH: JEFFERSON

PrC (DLC); at foot of text: "Mr. Gerna. Bookseller Dublin." Enclosed in TJ to Trumbull, this date.

The NOTE which TJ gave to Gerna has not been found; presumably it was written late in 1787: Gerna passed through Paris early in September and said that he would return in six weeks (Gerna to TJ, 8 Sep. 1787).

To John Stockdale

SIR

Paris May 18. 1788.

I must still refer you to my letters of Sep. 10. Oct. 10. Jan. 1. and Jan. 16. to which I have no answer except yours of Feb. 22. promising an answer. Lest your account should come during my absence in Holland and Germany, I remitted you from Amsterdam £15. sterling through Mr. Trumbul. I imagine you have not sent the books hearing that I was on a journey. To those desired in the letters above referred to be pleased to add the following.

Priestley's biographical chart & pamphlet.

Bell's Shakespeare. No. 50 & the subsequent ones. I have No. 49. & preceding.

Hargrave's Coke Littleton after folio 395. to which I have.

Monthly & Critical reviews after August 1787.

The Repository. printed by Justins. after No. 7. and continue to send me this as it appears.

Cumberland's Observer. neatly bound.

Nature displayed. In my letter of Octob. 10. I desired a copy of this work from Lackington's in 4. vols. If you have taken this, try to procure for me the 5th. 6th. and 7th. vols. also, which are sold separate. If you have not taken Lackington's copy, procure the work complete in 7. vols. for me.

Send the above by the Diligence. I must repeat my application for your account. I am Sir your very humble servant,

TH: JEFFERSON

PrC (DLC).

To John Trumbull

DEAR SIR Paris May 18. 1788.

The first moments after my return having been occupied by letters which required immediate answers, it is not till now I can acknolege your favors of Feb. 26. and Mar. 6. which came during my absence, and that of May 7. handed me yesterday by Mr. Duché. I omitted in mine of Mar. 27. from Amsterdam to tell you that I wished to pay Mr. Brown the same for Mr. Adams's picture as I had paid him for my own. You say mine does not resemble. Is it a copy? Because he agreed that the original should be mine, and it was that I paid him for. I find the Odometer too dear, and therefore will not order one. Has Oldham thought about the tea-vase? I would be willing to make some sacrifice of convenience to the beauty of the form. Of the degree you will be a good judge. On the adjoining leaf I give a catalogue of some books I would wish to have from Lackington bookseller Chiswell Street, Moorfeilds No. 46. 47. They are taken from his last catalogue. If Mr. Stockdale has books to send me, those from Lackington had better be sent to him to be packed in the same box and to come by the Diligence. Otherwise I presume Lackington will pack and deliver them to the Diligence. These books (if all still on hand) will amount to 46/ and with the Polyplasiasmos, the tea vase, and the Taylor will probably be nearly comprehended by the £15. (half of what I remitted you from Amsterdam) and £8. Mrs. Adams was to pay you which she did not know of when she made the remittance by Mr. Parker. I should have remitted a bill now, but that I wish it to comprehend Stockdale's balance which I do not know till I can receive a letter and his account. I now write him again on that subject and on that of books which I have asked from him so long ago as Octob. 10.—With respect to a Chariot I understood, I believe from you, that it was a custom with many persons in London to sell their chariot always after 2. years service. Now two years service, if moderate, will do little injury to a well built carriage, except as to the paint. If therefore such a one can at any time be found, of a genteel form, roomly, and substantially sound, for 50 guineas, I would prefer taking such a one, to the having one made; and I would ask the favor of you to make the purchase should such a one occur. As, on the incertainty of the purchase being made it would not be worth while to lodge the money with you, I think Mr. Lewis Tessier, banker, would be so good as to advance you the money for me (rather than let the bargain be lost) and take your bill on me which should be paid on sight. As to harness and how to get the carriage here, I should consider of it, on learning that the principal commission was executed. I presume there are shops where these carriages are to be seen collected, and mean to give you no other trouble than to direct your walks for exercise towards those shops. I should prefer taking the carriage as delivered by the owner, and before the workman has varnished it up, because in that varnish they know how to cover substantial defects.

I suppose Mrs. Church hears so often from hence that it is a work of supererogation to tell her Kitty is well. She is with us here at this moment, it being the family day. I am with great & sincere esteem Dear Sir Your friend & servant,

Th: Jefferson

P.S. Be so good as to forward the inclosed to Dublin.

Extracts from Lackington's last catalogue . . . for Th: Jefferson

292.	Ogilby's description of America. fol.	12s.6	12s.6d
299.	Procopius of the wars of the Persians, Vandals, Goths &c. by Holcroft. fol.		2s.3d
496.	Mascou's hist. of the antient Germans by Lediard. 2. vols. 4to.		8 0
781.	Dacugna's voiages in North America. 8vo.		1 6
988.	Hampton's Polybius 4. vols. 8vo.		14 6
1487.	Addison's travels in Italy. 12mo.		2
1769.	Gregory's comparative views. 12mo.		3
6075.	Martial Delphini. 8vo.		2 3[1]
			£2- 6- 0

Note where the particular number here mentioned happens to

be sold and there remains another of the same book and same edition, nearly corresponding in Price, let that be sent.

PrC (DLC). Enclosures: (1) TJ to Gerna, 18 May 1788. (2) TJ to Stockdale, 18 May 1788.

Trumbull's receipt for the £8. MRS. ADAMS WAS TO PAY is in MHi:AMT, and is dated 28 Mch. 1788.

[1] TJ also listed in a line below, and then deleted: "[. . .] Stirling's Virgil" @ 2s. 0d., altering the total sum accordingly.

To Stephen Cathalan, Sr.

SIR Paris May 20. 1788.

On my return from Holland and Germany I found here the letters you had done me the honor of writing me on the 26th. of March and 15th. of April, as also that by Mr. Turnbull, who I suppose had left Paris before my return, as I did not see or hear from him. You mention a declaration of the king's published at Marseilles and annihilating the favors granted on whale oil. I have made diligent enquiry and cannot find nor suspect that any such measure has taken place. I have not asked of the ministers, because I would wish, if I do mention it to them, to be able to tell them what has been the nature of the declaration published as if from the king at Marseilles. I will beg you therefore to give me information of the exact particulars of this declaration. In the mean time I think I may assure you no alteration of the arrêt of Dec. 29. has taken place except the taking the right of entrepot from our cod-fish.—I will beg the favor of you to do for me what you think right as to the copy of the meteorological journal. I approve perfectly of the sum of five guineas which you propose to pay to the copyist. The moment you inform me it is settled at that, I will pay the money to Sr. John Lambert for you. I paid him the former balance of 272tt-5 before I set out on my journey, but had not then time to give you notice of it. I will beg the favor of you to put the inclosed letter under cover to Capt. Obrian chez M. Logie Consul Anglois á Algiers, without saying a single word from what quarter it comes to you, as a suspicion of that might produce effects I wish to prevent.

I am desired by some gentlemen of South Carolina to procure to be sent to them some plants of the best species of Olive-trees. As Marseilles is the most convenient port for this, I must beg the favor of you to charge some gardener with the procuring and preparing these plants, and having them always in readiness to go by such vessel bound to Charleston as you shall be able to send them by. They lodge about 30. Louis in my hands to answer all expences, which will enable you to judge of the number to be sent. I would rather have so many sent as to exceed the sum rather than fall short of it, as I should wish to contribute five or ten guineas myself to the object. I suppose the plants cannot go till the fall or winter. There should also go a great quantity of the olives themselves, to be sowed on their arrival in Charleston in order to raise stocks whereon they may ingraft cuttings from the good plants. The same gardener may be charged to pack these olives properly. I presume Mr. Bernard could advise as to the best species of olive trees, and that he will be so kind as to do it. I shall have the honour of writing to him in a few days. I have that of being with my best respects to yourself & family, Sir, your most obedient & most humble servant,

Th: Jefferson

PrC (DLC). The enclosed letter to Richard O'Bryen has not been identified; this may possibly have been a letter from an American correspondent that TJ was merely forwarding, or it may have been a response by TJ to O'Bryen's "cruel letter" (see TJ to Jay, 4 May 1788), but no such letter is recorded in SJL Index; it should be noted also that it was against TJ's policy at this time to give the Algerian captives any reassurance of forthcoming attempts to redeem them, lest this create obstacles to doing so.

TJ's rough notes for this letter are jotted on the cover of Cathalan to TJ, 6 Mch. 1788, to which it is a response. Instead of writing to Bernard IN A FEW DAYS, TJ did not write until 12 Aug. 1788. TJ had forgotten that he had, in fact, notified Cathalan of paying Sir John Lambert for THE FORMER BALANCE before setting out on his journey (see TJ to Cathalan, 3 Mch. 1788).

To Van Damme

Monsieur — á Paris ce 20me. Mai 1788.

N'ayant point de vos nouvelles depuis mon retour á Paris, je prends la liberté de vous demander le progrés que vous avez fait dans les recherches dont vous avez bien voulu vous charger pour les livres que je vous ai prié de me procurer, et quand je pourrai en attendre l'expedition ou de la totalité, ou de telle partie que vous auriez pu trouver en attendant la reste.

J'ai l'honneur d'etre Monsieur votre tres humble et tres obeissant serviteur,

Th: Jefferson

RC (The Hague: Meermanno-Westrenianum Museum: Van Damme Papers); addressed: "A Monsieur Monsieur Van Damme libraire à Amsterdam." PrC (DLC).

From Henry Knox

Sir War Office May 20th. 1788.

I had the honor to receive your favor of the 6th. of February, and submitted a copy of it to His Excellency the President of Congress, but as a sufficient number of members have not been present, until within a few days past, nothing has yet been done on the business. But it is to be presumed that they will soon take into consideration the case of the unfortunate Pilot, and afford him such releif as the nature of his case appears to merit. I have the honor to be with the highest sentiments of Attachment & Esteem, Sir, Your Most Obedient & Humble Servant, H. Knox

RC (DLC).

To Amand Koenig

Monsieur Paris ce 20me. Mai 1788.

N'ayant point de nouvelles des livres que vous avez eu la bonté de vous charger de m'expedier le 18me. du mois passé, et craignant qu'ils peuvent etre ecartés quelque part, je prends la liberté de vous demander un mot d'information s'ils sont deja expediés ou quand ils seront expediés de Strasbourg.

J'ai l'honneur d'etre Monsieur votre tres humble et tres obeissant serviteur, Th: Jefferson

PrC (DLC); at foot of page: "M. Armand Koenig. libraire à Strasbourg."

To Vaudreuil

Monsieur le Marquis Paris ce 20me. Mai. 1788.

Vous m'avez fait l'honneur de m'envoyer des papiers relatives au nommé Monset qui s'est transporté en Amerique pendant la derniere guerre. Je les ai fait passer tout de suite à Monsieur Langdon, President de la nouvelle Hampshire qui a l'honneur de vous etre connu, et je m'empresse de vous addresser sa reponse ou vous verrez le resultat des recherches qu'il a fait. Ce m'auroit eté un plaisir veritable de pouvoir vous annoncer quelque chose plus avantageuse et plus agreeable aux personnes qui ont l'honneur de votre protection: mais nous n'en sommes pas les maitres. J'espere que vous y verrez au moins l'empressement avec lequel je cherche de vous temoigner les sentiments d'attachement et de respect avec lesquels j'ai l'honneur d'etre Monsieur le Marquis votre tres humble et tres obeissant serviteur, TH: JEFFERSON

PrC (DLC). The enclosed response from John Langdon concerning the MONSET case was probably that of 20 Dec. 1787 (missing). See Vaudreuil to TJ, 10 Aug. 1787; TJ to Vaudreuil, 10 Sep. 1787; and TJ to Langdon, 18 Sep. 1787.

To Gerard Walter

MONSIEUR Paris ce 20me. Mai. 1788.

N'ayant point de nouvelles de la porcelaine que vous avez eu la bonté de vous charger de m'expedier le 18me. du mois passé et craignant que ce peut etre ecartée quelque part, je prends la liberté de vous demander un mot d'information si elle est deja partie de Strasbourg, ou quand elle sera partie, et de vous assurer de la consideration avec laquelle j'ai l'honneur d'etre Monsieur votre tres humble et tres obeissant serviteur, TH: JEFFERSON

PrC (DLC); at foot of page: "Monsieur Gerard Walter negociant à Strasbourg."

From Henry Wyld

EXCELLENT SIR Prosperous May 20th, 1788

In addition to the desires of Mr. Diggs, will be obliged to you to inform me by letter what progress the wire Business hath made in America, whether you manufacture Cards for dressing Cotton and Wool? or import them? if the latter your Manufactures are precarious; how the stocking Hosiers are supplied with Cotton Thread, or whether the Manufacture any fine and superfine Cotton Stockings, or import what are used? Whether you have any stocking frame Makers, or whether there are any fine stockings of any denomination wrought there or not. How the weaving Business is carried on and in what state it is respecting cotton Goods Viz whether any kind of narrow cut Goods such as Corduroys Thicksets &c &c are brought to perfection, if not what stage the are stoped in, and how brought to market, likewise the narrow uncut Goods, that is to say Jeans Jeanetts Cantoons Baragons &c &c &c, how far you are advanced in the Manufacture of white Goods, that is, Calico Dimity &c &c and whether any attempt hath been made to manufacture Muslin. In short I will be obliged to you to be as explicit as possible on all the above subjects.

I need not observe to your excellency, that so long as you are beholden to a foreign Country for Artists, your manufactures are precarious, and all the Money paid by individuals for useful Fabricks manufactured at Home, is so much saved to the State; and I being informed of your real wants, will endeavour to procure helps for my-self, which you know will be an acquision to the state, but on that account would wish to be accommodated with a Vessel in which we could stow bulky substances, and bring over a few hands without expence, at some of the N.W. Ports of this Kingdome, but that I leave intirely to yourself and Mr. Diggs, to think of.

Respecting spinning Carding &c I think nothing of; as I flatter myself I shall equal Mr. Diggs report, and there is another person means to come along with me whose abilities are worthy the notice of any state, but the ship Indulgance will be almost absolutely necessary. I desire a speedy Answer directed to M. Henry Wyld, Prosperous Naas (add Ireland). I am Your Excellencies Most obedient Servant, HENRY WYLD

RC (MoSHi); endorsed. This letter was enclosed in Digges to TJ, 12 May 1788; that of Digges, but not that of Wyld, is recorded in SJL Index. TJ's reply of 19 June 1788 was addressed to Digges, but intended for both.

From André Limozin

MOST HONORED SIR Havre de Grace May 22nd 1788.

I am indebted to your both favors of the 4th and 17th instant. The first was deliverd to me by Mr. Faure with a small parcell containing Gazettes &c.

I am Striving to get leave from our Comptroller of this Custom house to forward you the hungd Beef sent to you from Hambro. Such trifles were not formerly refused. And I am certain that if you should take the trouble, to write few lines to the farmers Generals about it, they would immediately comply with your demand and in consequence send thier orders to their Collector here. But I have just now spoken to him. He gave me hint of a good Scheme which I hope will succeed, therefore you may be easy about it, and not take the least troubles.

Messrs. Van Staphorst have forwarded me the Bill of Lading for your China. I am very sory they have not acted agreable to the advice I had given them to have every thing outpacked and to leave it into the Captain's Cabbin to his Care. I dont see any other method but to forward you them by Land, plumbed and under the denomination of House furnitures for your Excellencys use. As to the Cast Iron stoves, I shall take care to forward you them by water if I can meet with a speedy opportunity, other wise I shall do it by Land.

I have received the hamper you mentionn for Mr. Francis Hopkinson which shall be sent to him by the first ship bound for Philadelphia. When Mr. Warville shall do me the honor to call upon me, I shall deliver him your papers, and will shew him Mr. Faure's Lodging in order that he may take back from his hands the Letters you had delivered him to be forwarded to America.

I am very glad to hear that there is no likelywood of a War breaking out suddenly by sea. For our Trade requires a Long peace to recover the heavy losses that [it][1] met with during last War. I have the honor to be with the highest regard Your Excellency's Most obedient & very Humble Servant,

ANDRE LIMOZIN

We have at present very little Trade with America.

RC (MHi); endorsed; addressed: "à Son Exellence Monsieur Thomas Jeffersson Ecuyer Ambassadeur des Etats unis de L'amirique a La Cour de Versailles, En Son Hôtel a la grille de chaillot, Paris"; postmarked.

1 This word (Limozin may have written "we") obscured by the postmark and supplied conjecturally.

From Nicolas & Jacob van Staphorst

SIR — Amsterdam, 22 May 1788

We have before us your Excellency's respected favor of 16th Inst. and sincerely congratulate you on your safe Return to Paris.

The further Sale of the remaining Bonds of the Loan of 1787 as well as the disposal of the Million signed by Mr. Adams when he was last here, will materially depend upon the News We may have from America. Should the New Government be adopted, it would certainly increase the Demand for them, but until the Organization shall be known, and its proceedings respecting the Public Debts be published, We cannot flatter your Excellency, We shall be able to raise Monies here for discharging the Interest due by the United States to the Court of Versailles. But after the aforegoing Objects shall have been settled upon the footing We trust they will, and their regular Operation be experienced for a short time, We cannot doubt the United States will have in their power to command the Funds here they may wish to negotiate.

Your Excellency will greatly oblige us, in the communication of any Intelligence you may have received respecting the Progress made in the Adoption of the new federal Government, and the probability when we may expect News, it will be agreed by a sufficient Number of States, to commence its Proceedings. The actual threatning Situation of European Politics, will we hope impress the reluctant States, with the Necessity of establishing such a Government for the Union, as may insure the Congress that Respect your Resources and happy local merits and will certainly have when the United States shall be represented by a firm and efficient Government.

We have likewise loaded in the Ship de Jeune Bernardus Capt. Claas Arendz Coen for Havre, the two Stoves received for your Excellency from Mr. Peuchen, The charges on which with the three Cases you left us, Your Excellency has herewith the Account of, For which We debit the United States ƒ18.

In consequence of your Excellency's promise to reimburse us One Hundred Guineas that Commr. Paul Jones asked of us upon Loan, provided he did not discharge it himself; We furnished him a Credit for that sum upon Copenhagen, Which he has disposed of. He has taken up the Matter as a Debt of Honor, assuring us he will take care We shall be paid, even if his Friend Doctr. Bancroft should not reimburse it to us, to which however he had strongly urged him. We have done the like and shall be glad the Affair may be thus settled; Otherwise We shall be under the Necessity to call upon your Excellency for directions to charge same to the United States. We are ever respectfully Your Excellency's Most obed. & very hble. Servs.,

Nic. & Jacob van Staphorst.

Note of Charges on 3 Chests received from His Excellency T. Jefferson Esqr. and 2 Chests received from J. J. Peuchen, Shipped by order of his Excy. to Mr. A. Limozin at Havre by de Jeune Bernardus, Claas Arends Koen Viz.

for freight of the 2. Chests from Cologne	ƒ 5.6
Boatage and Porterage	2.10
Exportation Duties and pasports	10.4
	ƒ18.—

RC (DLC); endorsed.

From Madame de Tessé

a châville ce 22 may.

Le caractere virginien s'est deployé Monsieur, dans la formation des quatre caisses de plans que je dois a votre bonté. Les épis de Maïs ont eté oubliés, j'ai cherché tres soigneusement dans la paille dont les plans etoient environnés et je n'en ai point trouvé de vestiges. Il ny avoit que deux ou trois petits paquets de graines si pourris quon na pu distinguer que le Gleditsia triacanthus. Mais en revanche la fortune qui devroit accompagner toutes vos demarches a bien servi cette fois votre bienfaisance pour les jardins de châville. Les arbres communs en france se sont trouvés dessechés et tous ceux que leur rarete nous rend infiniment précieux se sont conservés, tels que le Quercus Phellos, *The Dagger Leaf Oak* que je crois une très belle variete du Quercus Phellos, le sassafras le cornus florida, et l'azalea. Si ces deux superbes chênes sont communs dans le canton d'ou ces caisses sont parties il seroit bien a desirer que votre correspondant ait la complaisance d'en faire lever une centaine avec soin et den former une seule caisse sans y rien meler que des racines de sassafras qui tiennent peu de place. Depuis deux ans les graines de Liriodendron quon nous envoie de Philadelphie et de New York sont vuides damandes et par conséquent ne germent pas. Je vous conjurerois den faire venir une caisse entière de virginie recoltee avec soin, si vous aviés la bonte de me donner les details des frais que ces envois vous causent. Mais quoiqu'il soit glorieux de vous être obligée et que mon respect pour vous dans l'opinion de Mr. Short dut s'accommoder de vous avoir des obligations pecuniaires, je ne puis me defendre dy sentir un peu de repugnance et ma reconnoissance seroit plus entiere si vous aviés la bonte d'ordonner a votre homme d'affaires de me faire passer la notte de ce que vous avés paié pour moi et que vous voulussiés bien me permettre de le rembourser. Ce point de vue ma fait un tour auquel j'ay eté bien sensible en vous empechant de vous arreter chés moi la derniere fois que vous avés eté a versailles. Mr. de la Fayette a eté si agité ces derniers tems quil ny a pas eu moyen desperer de lui un arrangement solide avec vous. Cest ce qui ma empeché davoir recours a son amitié pour netre pas privée trop longtems de la satisfaction de vous exprimer, Monsieur, avec ma reconnoissance tous les sentimens dont je suis si vivement penetrée.

Me. de Totte me charge de vous rappeler son attachement. Nous demandons de n'etre pas oubliées de Mr. Short.

RC (DLC); unsigned and undated, but clearly written in 1788; see TJ's correspondence with Banister, under 7 Feb. 1787, 27 Sep. 1787, and 9 Aug. 1788; Coffyn to TJ, 23 Mch. and 2 May 1788; TJ to Limozin, 4 May 1788; Broucq, Frères & Soeurs to TJ, 10 May 1788—all of which, among others, help trace the peregrinations of the QUATRE CAISSES DE PLANS. See also Madame de Tessé to TJ, 7 Aug. 1788.

From Willink & Van Staphorst

Amsterdam, 22 May 1788. Following TJ's instructions of 16 May 1788, they have accepted the seven bills payable to Grand, but would have preferred "that Your Excellency had acquiesced to our Proposal of making you Remittances that We could easily have effected at short sight and more advantageously." Same applies to disposals in favor of Short and Ast. These will "exceed the Cash We shall have in hand as well as our Limits of ƒ40,000 at Command of Your Excellency"; but agree that these expenses ought not to be delayed further, in view of "the Dignity and Honor of the Government of the United States."

RC (DLC); 1 p.; endorsed; in a clerk's hand, except signatures of Wilhem & Jan Willink and Nicolas & Jacob van Staphorst.

To John Jay, with Enclosure

SIR Paris May 23. 1788.

When I wrote my letter of the 4th. inst. I had no reason to doubt that a packet would have sailed on the 10th. according to the established order. The passengers had all, except one, gone to Havre in this expectation. None however is sailed, and perhaps none will sail, as I think the suppression of the packets is one of the oeconomies in contemplation. An American merchant concerned in the commerce of Whale oil proposes to government to dispatch his ships from Havre and Boston at stated periods and to take on board the French courier and mail, and the proposition has been well enough received. I avail myself of a merchant vessel going from Havre to write the present.

In my letter of the 4th. I stated to you the symptoms which indicated that government had some great stroke of authority in contemplation. That night they sent guards to seize M. d'Epremesnil and M. Goislard two members of parliament, in their houses. They escaped and took sanctuary in the Palais (or parliament house.) The parliament assembled itself extraordinarily, summoned the Dukes and Peers specially, and came to the resolution of the 5th. which they sent to Versailles by deputies, determined not to leave the palace till they received an answer. In the course of that night a battalion of guards surrounded the house. The two members were taken by the officer from among their fellows, and sent off to prison, the one to Lyons, the other (d'Eprémenil) the most obnoxious, to an island in the Mediterranean. The parliament then separated. On the 8th. a bed of justice was held at Versailles wherein were enregistered the six Ordinances which had been passed in Council on the 1st. of May, and which I now send you. They were in like manner registered in beds of justice, on the same day nearly, in all the parliaments of the kingdom. By these ordinances 1. the criminal law is reformed, by abolishing Examination on the Sellette, which, like our holding up the hand at the bar, remained a stigma on the party tho' innocent; by substituting an Oath, instead of Torture, on the *Question prealable*, which is used after condemnation to make the prisoner discover his accomplices; (The Torture abolished in 1780. was on the *Question preparatoire*, previous to judgment in order to make the prisoner accuse himself.) by allowing Counsel to the prisoner for his defence, obliging the judges to specify in their judgments the offence for which he is condemned, and respiting execution a month, except in the case of sedition. This reformation is unquestionably good within the ordinary legislative powers of the crown. That it should remain to be made at this day proves that the monarch is the last person in his kingdom who yields to the progress of philanthropy and civilisation. 2. The organisation of the whole judiciary department is changed, by the institution of subordinate jurisdictions, the taking from the parliaments the cognisance of all causes of less value than 20,000 livres, reducing their numbers to about a fourth, and suppressing a number of Special courts. Even this would be a great improvement, if it did not imply that the king is the only person in the nation who has any rights, or any power. 3. The right of registering the laws is taken from the parliaments and transferred to a Plenary court created by the king. This last is the measure most obnoxious to all persons. Tho' the members are to be for life, yet a great proportion of them are from descriptions of men always candidates for the royal favor in other lines.—As yet the general consternation is not sufficiently passed over to say whether the matter will end here. I send you some papers which indicate symptoms of resistance. These are the Resolution of the Noblesse of Brittany, the Declaration of the Advocate general of Provence, which is said to express the spirit of that province; and the Arreté of the Chatelet, which is the Hustings-court of the city of Paris. Their refusal to act under the new character assigned them, and the suspension of their principal functions is very embarrassing. The clamours this will excite, and the disorders it may admit, will be[1] loud, and near, to the royal ear, and person. The parliamentary fragments permitted to remain, have already, some of them, refused, and probably all will refuse to act under that form. The Assembly of the clergy, which happens to be sitting, have addressed the king to call the States General immediately. Of the Dukes and Peers (38 in number) nearly half are either minors or superannuated; two thirds of the acting half seem disposed to avoid taking a part, the rest, about 8. or 9. have refused, by letters to the king, to act in the new courts. A proposition excited among the Dukes and Peers to assemble and address the king for a modification of the Plenary court seems to shew that the government[2] would be willing to compromise on that head. It has been prevented by the Dukes and peers in opposition, because they suppose that no modification to be made by the government[2] will give to that body the form they desire, which is that of a representative of the nation. They will aim therefore at an immediate call of the States general. They foresee that if the government is forced to this, they will call them, as nearly as they can, in the antient forms; in which case less good will will be to be expected from them. But they hope they may be got to concur in a Declaration of rights, at least, so that the nation may be acknowleged to have some fundamental rights, not alterable by their ordinary legislature, and that this may form a ground-work for future improvements. These seem to be the views of the most enlightened and disinterested characters of the opposition. But they may be frustrated by the nation's making no cry at all, or by a hasty and premature appeal to arms. There is neither head nor body in the nation to promise a succesful opposition to 200,000 regular troops. Some think the army could not be depended on by the government: but the breaking men to military discipline, is breaking their spirits to principles of passive obedience. A firm, but quiet opposition will be the most likely to succeed. Whatever turn this crisis takes, a revolution in their constitution seems inevitable, unless foreign war supervene, to suspend the present contest. And a foreign war they will avoid if possible, from an inability to get money. The loan of 120 millions of the present year is filled up by such subscriptions as may be relied on. But that of 80. millions, proposed for the next year, cannot be filled up, in the actual situation of things.

The Austrians have been succesful in an attack upon Schabatz intended as a preliminary to that of Belgrade. In that on Dubitza another town in the neighborhood of Belgrade, they have been repulsed and as is suspected, with considerable loss. It is still supposed the Russian fleet will go into the Mediterranean, tho it will be much retarded by the refusal of the English government to permit it's sailors to engage in the voiage. Sweden and Denmark are arming from 8. to 12 ships of the line each. The English and Dutch treaty you will find in the Leyden gazettes of May 9. and 13. That between England and Prussia is supposed to be stationary. Monsieur de St. Priest, the Ambassador from this court to the Hague is either gone or on the point of going. The Emperor of Marocco has declared war against England. I inclose you his orders in our favor on that occasion. England sends a squadron to the Mediterranean for the protection of her commerce, and she is reinforcing her possessions in the two Indies. France is expecting the arrival of an embassy from Tippoo Saïb, is sending some regiments to the East Indies, and a fleet of evolution into the Atlantic. Seven ships of the line and several frigates sailed from Cadiz on the 22d of April, destined to perform evolutions off the Western islands, as the Spaniards say, but really to their American possessions as is suspected. Thus the several powers are by little and little taking the position of war, without an immediate intention of waging it. But that the present ill humour will finally end in war, is doubted by no-body.

In my letter of Feb. 5. I had the honour of informing you of the discontent produced by our Arret of Dec. 29. among the merchants of this country and of the deputations from the chambers of commerce to the minister on that subject. The articles attacked were the privileges on the sale of our ships, and the entrepot for codfish. The former I knew to be valuable: the latter I supposed not so; because during the whole of the time we have had four freeports in this kingdom, we have never used them for the smuggling of fish. I concluded therefore the ports of entrepot would not be used for that purpose. I saw that the minister would sacrifice something to quiet the merchants, and was glad to save the valuable article relative to our ships by abandoning the useless one for our codfish. It was settled therefore in our conferences that an arret should be passed abridging the former one only as to the entrepot of codfish. I was in Holland when the Arret came out, and did not get a copy of it till yesterday. Surprised to find that fish oil was thereby also excluded from the entrepot I have been to-day to make some enquiry into the cause: and from what I can learn, I conclude it must have been a meer error in the clerk who formed the arret, and that it escaped attention on it's passage. The entrepot of whale oil was not objected to by a single deputy at the conferences, and the excluding it is contrary to the spirit of encouragement the ministers have shewn a disposition to give. I trust therefore I may get it altered on the first occasion which occurs, and I believe one will soon occur. In the mean time we do not store a single drop for re-exportation, as all which comes here is needed for the consumption of this country; which will alone, according to appearances, become so considerable as to require all we can produce.

By a letter of the 8th. instant from our bankers I learn that they had disposed of bonds enough to pay our June interest and to replace the temporary advances made by Mr. Grand, and from a fund placed here by the state of Virginia. I have desired them accordingly to replace these monies, which had been lent for the moment only and in confidence of immediate repaiment. They add that the paiment of the June interest, and the news from America will, as they trust, enable them to place the remaining bonds of the last year's million. I suppose indeed that there is no doubt of it, and that none would have been expressed if those two houses could draw better together than they do. In the mean time I hope the treasury board will send an order for so much as may be necessary for executing the purpose of Congress as to our captives at Algiers.

I send you herewith a Memoire of Monsieur Caseaux, whose name is familiar on the journals of Congress. He prepared it to be delivered to the king, but I believe he will think better, and not deliver it.

The gazettes of France and Leyden accompany this, & I have the honour to be, Sir, your most obedient & most humble servt.,

Th: Jefferson

P.S. May. 27. 1788. I have kept my letter open to the moment of Mr. Warville's departure (he being the bearer of it) that I might add any new incidents that should occur. The refusal of the Chatelet and grande chambre of Paris to act in the new character assigned them, continues. Many of the grandes bailliages accept, some conditionally, some fully. This will facilitate greatly the measures of government, and may possibly give them a favorable issue. The parliament of Toulouse, considering the edicts as nullities, went on with their business. They have been exiled in consequence. Monsr. de St. Priest left Paris for the Hague on the

23d. I mention this fact because it denotes the acquiescence of this government in the late revolution there.—A second division of a Spanish fleet will put to sea soon. It's destination not declared. Sweden is arming to a greater extent than was at first supposed. From 12. to 16. sail of the line are spoken of on good grounds. Denmark for her own security must arm in proportion to this.

RC (DNA: PCC, No. 87, II); with an unusual number of erasures, interlineations, and awkward phrases (e.g., "good will will be to be"), and in a stiffer handwriting than usual, possibly because of fatigue induced by the preparation of a large number of papers and letters for America (see TJ to Warville, 27 May 1788, note). PrC (DLC). Enclosures: (1) Unanimous resolution of the parlement of Paris, 5 May 1788, protesting the measures taken by the ministry in arresting Jean Jacques Duval d'Epresmésnil and Goislart de Montsabert as a substitution of despotism for law, as an attempt against the liberty of two of its members whose only crime was their zeal in defense of the most sacred rights of the nation, as a violation of the right to an immediate trial before competent judges, and as placing them and other magistrates and citizens under the immediate protection of the laws and the king, to whom an appeal was directed (Tr in French in an unidentified hand, accompanied by a translation by John Pintard; DNA: PCC, No. 87, II). (2) The precise form in which TJ sent the six ordinances enregistered at a *lit de justice* at Versailles, 8 May 1788, is uncertain and the copies appear not to have been preserved in DNA: PCC, but he probably sent a copy of *Discours du Roi, à l'ouverture du Lit de Justice, tenu à Versailles, le 8 mai 1788* (Sowerby, No. 2549). (3) "Arrêté de la Noblesse de Bretagne," undated, declaring "infâmes ceux qui pourroient acĉepter quelques places soit dans l'administration nouvelle de la Justice soit dans les administrations des Etats qui ne seroient pas avoués par les Loix Constitutionelles de la province" (Tr in same hand, with translation by Pintard; same). (4) "Discours de M. Maurel de Calessane 1er Avocat general au Parlement d'Aix *après la* lecture de l'edit portant creation de la cour plenière," formally opposing the registry of the new measure, declaring it to be destructive of the constitution, asserting it would be better to die than to accept such an "atteinte aux droits de notre patrie," and publishing their resistance to it in behalf of the king, to whom they give assurances of fidelity (Tr in hand of Short, with translation by Pintard; same; PrC of Tr in DLC). (5) "Arrêté du Chatelet" of Paris, undated, noting "avec la plus vive douleur les coups d'autorité multipliés contre les differentes cours du Royaume," the magistrates arrested, and the sanctuary of justice violated by armed guards; and, considering that the promulgation of ordinances, edicts, and declarations have been made without having undergone deliberation by the parlement, unanimously declaring that "elle ne peut ni ne doit faire proceder à la lecture, publication et enregistrement" of these ordinances, &c. (Tr in Short's hand; DNA: PCC, No. 87, II). (6) Though not specifically mentioning it as an enclosure, TJ evidently included as another paper indicating SYMPTOMS OF RESISTANCE an "Arrêté du Parlement de Dauphiné du 9 Mai," defending the constitutional rights of the country, denouncing the secret and simultaneous measures taken by the ministry as fatal to the nation, and declaring that the rights of the subject are not less sacred than those of the sovereign; that the monarchy cannot be preserved except on the basis of immutable laws securing to the citizens the liberty of their persons and property; that the nation has always guarded against the fatal effects of arbitrary power; that the right of consenting to imposts is as ancient as the monarchy, and can only be exercised in the States General; that long and unhappy experience has shown only too fully the facility of administration at committing the king's sacred word and then failing in the solemn engagements taken in his name; and that no officers of the parlement could, without betraying their oaths, take any place in administration without being regarded as traitors to the country (Tr in Short's hand, with translation by Pintard; DNA: PCC, No. 87, II; PrC of Tr in DLC). (7) Though likewise not specifically identified as an enclosure, a lengthy address presented 4 May 1788 by the parlement of Paris to the king was evidently included by TJ. It protested the king's answer of 17 Apr. 1788 as afflicting them greatly but leaving them with courage unabated; defended the prerogatives of the parlements as grounded in fundamental law which could not be contravened by royal or ministerial tendencies toward despotism; and concluded: "Pour votre Parlt. ces principes ou plutôt, Sire, ceux de l'état qui lui sont confiés, sont immuables. Il n'est pas en son pouvoir de changer de conduite. Quelquefois les magistrats sont appelés à s'immoler aux loix, mais telle est leur honorable et perilleuse condition qu'ils doivent cesser d'etre avant que la nation cesse d'etre libre" (Tr in Short's hand, with translation by Pintard; DNA: PCC, No. 87, II; PrC of Tr in DLC). (8) Communications from the emperor of Morocco to Giuseppe and Francisco Chiappe; see Chiappe to TJ, 6 Mch. 1788. (9) The memoire of Francis Cazeau, a former merchant of Montreal, which had been transmitted in Carra to TJ, 29 Apr. 1788, and which Cazeau had threatened to publish as an indictment of the good faith of the United States (see Short to Jay, 18 Mch. 1788), has not been found in DNA: PCC. But, sometime during 1788, Cazeau did present his complaint TO THE KING. His memoire, undated, was submitted to Montmorin and is in Arch. Aff. Etr., Paris, Corr. Pol., E.-U., Vol. XXXIII; transcripts in DLC. Its substance is similar to that which appeared ON THE JOURNALS OF CONGRESS in Mch. 1784 when TJ was present. In that memorial Cazeau stated that, in response to an appeal from the commander-in-chief of the American armies in 1775, he had supplied cloth and other articles to Arnold's expeditionary force and had purchased about 12,000 bushels of wheat for these troops, selling a part to the British contractor to allay suspicion; that he had been paid in paper money for the former, and, on the expectation of Arnold's return to Canada, he had retained the "flour middlings and bran" which had "spoiled for want of hands to take care of them"; that he had sent three batteaus with wines, spirits, and other articles which were plundered and destroyed; and that in consequence of his friendly acts in behalf of the United States, he had been imprisoned for over two years in Quebec, his property had been sequestered, and his family turned out of doors (JCC, XXVI, 147-9). (10) Again, though not specifically mentioned, TJ enclosed a printed copy of the arrêt of 22 Feb. 1788, printed herewith. Most of the foregoing were not actual enclosures, but were carried separately by Brissot.

It is possible that the opposition of the chambers of commerce to the arrêt of 29 Dec. 1787 that TJ had reported to Jay on 5 Feb. 1788 was less responsible for the new arrêt of 22 Feb. 1788 than the fact that Luzerne did not "manifest any partialities" toward America. Luzerne had not sent out the former arrêt until 26 Jan. and there was scarcely time for much opposition to develop before TJ knew that the terms of that arrêt were under attack within the ministry and that exceptions would be made to them. On 11 Feb. the controller-general, Lambert, invited TJ and Rayneval—and very probably others as well—to an evening conference at his home to discuss the observations that had been made on the arrêt (the invitation to Rayneval, on the same date and in the same terms as that to TJ, is in Arch. Aff. Etr., Paris, Corr. Pol., Vol. XXXIII; transcripts in DLC). Two days later TJ received a draft of the new arrêt from Dupont, but he was still in the dark as to the "real motives which produced this opposition" (TJ to Dupont, 15 Feb. 1788). On Saturday, the 16th, there was another conference held at Lambert's home. It included the following persons, all of whom very probably were at the conference on the 13th: TJ and Lafayette; the two *commissaires généraux* for commerce (Dupont and Boyetet) and their deputies from Marseilles, Normandy, and Brittany; Poujet and Chardon, who were in Luzerne's department and were especially concerned with fisheries; and La Porte and La Boullaye, councillors of state. Rayneval had been invited, but was not present. On Sunday, the 17th, Lambert reported to Montmorin the result of their deliberations, thus exhibiting the concern of the ministry by the extraordinary speed with which the new arrêt was pressed through to a quick conclusion. Although the terms of the new arrêt had been agreed upon and a draft of it made soon after the first meeting on the 13th, Lambert assured Montmorin that, on the 16th, they had examined all of the observations that had been made on the arrêt of 29 Dec. He further reported it as the *unanimous* conclusion of the conference that that arrêt would need no further modifications than those indicated on a projet that he then enclosed, on which he asked Montmorin to let him have his observations as soon as possible. "Je me suis attaché," he declared, "dans la rédaction à conserver l'unité des vües avec l'Arrêt précédent, afin que les Etats unis comprennent que cette explication n'apportera aucun retranchement réel à ce qu'ils avoient droit ou intérêt de prétendre ou d'espérer de la bienveillance du Roi, manifestée par l'arrêt dernierement expédié" (Lambert to Montmorin, 17 Feb. 1788; same). Montmorin was not so speedy in his reply as Lambert had been in preparing the arrêt; three weeks later he answered: "Il m'a paru que ce nouveau projet, en sauvant l'inconvénient de l'entrepot qu'il prescrit, étoit satisfaisant pour les américains" (Montmorin to Lambert, 10 Mch. 1788; same). Three days later Luzerne sent copies of the arrêt to the chamber of commerce at Marseilles, saying that the previous arrêt "ayant causé des inquietudes au Commerce, sur la facilité qui pourroit en résulter pour l'introduction de la Morue américaine en france, Sa Majesté a cru devoir interprêter cette disposition par un Second arrêt . . . qui excepte de ces entrepôts les poissons huiles et autres objets de pêche americaine" (Chamber of Commerce of Marseilles, Archives, ser. H., art. 82, "Commerce avec les Etats-Unis d'Amérique. Objets généraux. 1778-1793"; microfilm in TJ Editorial Files). Thus, though the arrêt is dated as approved in Council on 22 Feb., it was not actually issued until Montmorin gave his belated approval. By then TJ was in Holland and Short reported to Jay that the previous arrêt had been violently attacked and suffered "a slight alteration"; he believed no other would be attempted (Short to Jay, 18 Mch. 1788). It is evident from this that Short had not seen the arrêt, but it is equally evident from the context of his letter that he was aware the change was due to the "extreme jealousy of the ministry with respect to our fisheries . . . kept alive and augmented by some Americans settled at Dunkirk, who flatter them with the idea of employing seven thousand French fisherman in that business . . . provided other nations are properly discouraged." The primary object of the Nantucketers at Dunkirk was the whale fishery. Thus, whether Jay noticed it or not, Short revealed by indirection what was known to be in the arrêt long before TJ left for Amsterdam: the projet of an arrêt that Lambert said was unanimously approved by the conference at which TJ and Lafayette were present contained the repeated phrases referring to the exclusion of FISH OIL . . . FROM THE ENTREPOT: *it differs in no material respect from the arrêt as finally adopted* (see notes to the arrêt, printed herewith). It is possibly true that TJ did not get a *printed* copy of the arrêt UNTIL YESTERDAY, but it is certain that he could have got the official text several days before going to Holland, and may indeed have done so. The reasons for his not exhibiting the same concern for obtaining a copy that he had shown with respect to the arrêt of 29 Dec. 1787, when he went so far as to send a corrected proof copy to America, is clearly the one that he gave Jay early in February—that he thought "it better not to alarm our merchants with any doubts about the continuance" of the earlier arrêt. The new arrêt contained in its final passages an implied threat that the ministry might yield even further to the chambers of commerce, and TJ had observed to Jay in his letter of 5 Feb. 1788 that this "instability in the laws in this country is such that no merchant can venture to make any speculation on the faith of a law." His delay in sending the new arrêt was obviously calculated.

But on his lack of close attention to this relatively minor arrêt depended a more important matter. The exclusion of FISH OIL . . . FROM THE ENTREPOT, as TJ soon discovered if he did not know already, was very far from being A MEER ERROR IN THE CLERK WHO FORMED THE ARRET. It is very likely true, too, that THE ENTREPOT OF WHALE OIL WAS NOT OBJECTED TO BY A SINGLE DEPUTY AT THE CONFERENCES. There would have been no need to make such objection if, on the reading of the draft at the final meeting on the 16th, the crucial phrases of the arrêt ESCAPED ATTENTION ON IT'S PASSAGE, or received no comment, on the part of the person most concerned in protecting American interests—that is, the American minister himself. Poujet and Chardon, experienced bureaucrats, must have received TJ's silence with some satisfaction and reported it to Luzerne with even more. In February, TJ and Lafayette were clearly faced with a pressure that could not be withstood; in May, though TJ could easily have sent a copy of the arrêt in his dispatch of the 4th, he did not do so. Later in the month, the Quaker Nantucketers of Dunkirk engaged in the whaling trade were making another strong bid for support from the government and TJ was faced with the need of trying to recover ground lost by inattention on his part or by trickery within the ministry, and at the same time he was forced to prepare for the new attack; the underselling of both American and French oil by English merchants brought forth two memorials from Francis Rotch late in May (for a note on Rotch and the "Nantuckois" at Dunkirk, see under 19 Nov. 1788). The need to keep from alarming American merchants about the fate of the arrêt of 29 Dec. 1787 was mounting, and TJ was careful to point out that the attack on THE PRIVILEGES ON THE SALE OF OUR SHIPS enabled him to effect a compromise whereby the American minister tactfully saved the VALUABLE ARTICLE RELATIVE TO OUR SHIPS BY ABANDONING THE USELESS ONE FOR OUR CODFISH. This may have persuaded Jay, as it has historians, that there were concessions on both sides, but the evidence points to a single attack on American fisheries, not on the shipbuilding industry which under Article V of the arrêt was privileged to sell American-built ships in France duty-free. A copy of the arrêt of 29 Dec. 1787 in Montmorin's files bears in its margin two comments which may have resulted from Lambert's meeting of 13 Feb. 1788 and certainly resulted from the commercial protests against the arrêt. Only two of the articles of the arrêt are involved in these marginal notes, Articles II and X. Opposite the former is the following: "Cet article est sans inconvenient, parceque toutes les Nations étrangeres sont également assujetties au paiement des grands droits ou droits prohibitifs de l'arret du Conseil du mois de Juin 1763, dont la conservation a été votée dans l'Assemblée des Notables, à l'occasion du tarif uniforme." Opposite the latter is this: "Il n'en est pas de même de cet article. S'il laisse, comme il le paroit, la liberté d'entrepôser dans tous les Ports qui font le Commerce des Colonies, la morue verte ou Seche provenant de la pêche des Americains. Il en résulteroit des facilités que nous accorderions nous mêmes à notre préjudice, pour la Reéxportation de ces Morues à l'étranger et Surtout en Espagne, en Italie et en Portugal, paїs pour lequel la Finance accorde des primes au Commerce National. Celui-ci Seroit plus découragé par la présence et la concurrence de ces morues étrangères, qu'il ne Sera jamais excité par la faveur de la prime.—2.° Quelque précaution que l'on prenne, les déclarations Seront infidelles tant à la rentrée, qu'à la Sortie de l'Entrepôt. Il S'ecoulera toujours une quantité considérable de ce poisson étranger dans les provinces du Royaume; Et comme les Américains peuvent donner à moitié prix, la consommation du poisson de pêche National diminuera d'autant, les armemens tomberont, l'Ecole des Matelots S'anéantira; on Sent vivement ces préjudices par le contre coup de la franchise de Bayonne qui autorise de pareils entrepots et favorise tellement la fraude, que la Morue étrangère pénetre de là jusques dans le Languedoc. Il y a deux ans que les places de Commerce ne cessent de demander que cette franchise soit supprimée, pour ce qui concerne le poisson sec et salé; combien ces cris vont ils se renforcer, lorsqu'elle S'étendra à tous les ports, pour ainsi dire, du Royaume?—Il parait très important de prévenir le mal par une explication, qui excepte le poisson sec et salé de la Disposition de l'article 10. Il y va de la ruine ou de la conservation de la pêche francoise (Arch. Aff. Etr., Paris, Corr. Pol., E.-U., Vol. XXXII; transcripts in DLC). This was probably Rayneval's notation, showing the essential change that was desired. There was nothing in the marginal commentary opposite Article V. It is also to be noted that there was nothing in the comments concerning whale oil, or other products of the fisheries aside from cod. TJ, therefore, in laying emphasis upon a compromise whereby he yielded an unimportant article in order to save a valuable one, may only have employed a familiar diplomatic device by way of redeeming his promise to Dupont to "so represent the matter in my letters as that nothing shall be thought of it" (TJ to Dupont, 15 Feb. 1788). In achieving this legitimate purpose, he was able at the same time to cover his earlier failure to notice and to oppose the passages in the new arrêt concerning whale oil. He was now on guard, however, against Luzerne's unfriendliness, and when the same hostile forces in the Council aimed a more severe blow at the American whale fishery in the arrêt of 28 Sep. 1788 by the last-minute deletion of the critical word "European," without warning to TJ, he was quickly informed of the manoeuvre, suspected that it was the work of Luzerne, and acted promptly to overcome its effect.

Herein lay, presumably, one explanation for the opinion held of TJ by the minister of marine. Early in 1789 TJ presented Gouverneur Morris to Montmorin, Luzerne, and other ministers. Luzerne received Morris "with a degree of Hauteur I never before experienced." It was not until a year later, however, that Morris was given reason to believe that it was TJ rather than himself that had produced the chilly reception. "He speaks of Jefferson with much Contempt as a Statesman," Morris recorded in his diary on 6 Apr. 1790, "and as one who is better formed for the interior of Virginia than to influence the Operations of a great People." Morris said that he was "rather surprized at this Sentiment because Mr. Jefferson has in general excited favorable Ideas of his intellectual Faculties" (*A Diary of the French Revolution by Gouverneur Morris*, ed. Beatrix C. Davenport, Boston, 1939, I, 5, 476). Luzerne's contempt, evidently an attitude that was almost if not quite unique among French officials who had dealings with TJ, may have been due to the fact that he had felt the force of TJ's intellectual faculties as expressed in *Observations on the Whale-Fishery* and the arrêt of 7 Dec. 1788 which decisively defeated the hostile moves that the minister of marine had made against American whale oil. (See TJ to Montmorin, 23 Oct. 1788; TJ to Jay, 19 Nov. 1788, 11 Jan. 1789; TJ to Adams, 5 Dec. 1788.)

1 TJ first wrote "are" and then placed the two preceding words over it.

2 TJ deleted "court" and then interlined "government."

ENCLOSURE

Arret du Conseil d'Etat du Roi,

Qui excepte de l'Entrepôt accordé, par l'arrêt du Conseil du 29 décembre 1787, aux productions & marchandises des Etats-unis, les Poissons, Huiles & autres marchandises provenant de leurs pêchés.

Du 22 Février 1788.

Extrait des Registres du Conseil d'Etat.

LE ROI s'étant proposé d'accorder une protection particulière au commerce réciproque[1] de la France & des Etats-unis de l'Amérique, Sa Majesté a jugé qu'une des principales faveurs qu'Elle pouvoit faire à ce commerce, étoit d'accorder aux productions & marchandises des Etats-unis, l'Entrepôt pendant six mois, dans tous les ports de France ouverts au commerce des Colonies; & par l'article X de l'arrêt de son Conseil du 29 décembre 1787, Sa Majesté a assuré ces avantages[2] aux Etats-unis. Les expressions indéfinies de cette disposition ont inspiré des inquiétudes aux Commerçans du royaume, relativement à l'intérêt des pêches nationales, dont l'activité pourroit être également compromise par l'introduction en France des morues ou autres poissons, ainsi que des huiles de poisson ou de baleine provenant de pêches étrangères. Sa Majesté ayant également à cœur de tenir avec une fidélité inviolable les engagemens que sa bienveillance envers les Etats-unis lui a fait contracter, & de protéger les progrès des pêches nationales si intimement liés avec des intérêts encore plus importans, s'est fait rendre compte du peu d'usage qu'ont fait les Etats-unis, de la liberté qu'ils avoient, antérieurement à l'arrêt du 29 décembre 1787, d'entreposer les produits de leur pêche dans les ports francs du royaume, ainsi que des rapports des autres ports de France avec le commerce entre les Etats-unis & les Nations voisines des côtes francoises. Sa Majesté a reconnu, par ce compte, que l'entrepôt dans les ports François ne peut être presque d'aucun usage effectif, ni par conséquent d'aucun intérêt réel pour les Etats-unis, dont les pêches seront toujours plus avantageusement portées en droiture aux lieux de leur destination, voisins de la France, & que les bâtimens Américains qui apporteroient à Marseille, ou dans quelques ports François,[3] les poissons ou autres produits de leurs pêches, sous prétexte d'entrepôt & de destination étrangère, hors le cas des relâches forcées, ne pourroient presque jamais y être attirés, que par le desir d'en faire ensuite le versement frauduleux dans l'intérieur du royaume. Sa Majesté est assurée qu'une telle spéculation ne pourra jamais avoir le vœu, ni exciter l'intérêt des Etats-unis, & qu'Elle peut, sans aucune crainte d'affliger ses Alliés, procurer à cet égard une entière sécurité au commerce de son royaume. A quoi voulant pourvoir: Ouï le rapport du sieur Lambert, Conseiller d'Etat & ordinaire au Conseil royal des finances & du commerce, Contrôleur général des finances; LE ROI ETANT EN SON CONSEIL, interprétant l'article X de l'arrêt de son Conseil du 29 décembre 1787, a ordonné & ordonne que l'entrepôt continuera à être permis, aux termes dudit article, pour toutes les productions & marchandises des Etats-unis, autres néanmoins que les poissons & huiles, & autres marchandises provenant des pêches Américaines, à l'égard desquelles il en sera usé comme avant ledit arrêt du 29 décembre 1787, les formes duquel entrepôt seront, quant à présent, & jusqu'à ce qu'il en soit autrement ordonné, celles qui sont prescrites par les Règlemens pour les entrepôts réels; se réservant Sa Majesté, de modifier ces formes, d'y ajouter ou d'en retrancher, sur l'avis des Chambres du commerce, examiné en son Conseil, selon qu'il sera jugé convenable aux intérêts des deux Nations.[4]

MANDE & ordonne Sa Majesté à Mons. le Duc de Penthièvre, Amiral de France, aux sieurs Intendans & Commissaires départis dans les provinces, au Commissaire départi pour l'observation des Ordonnances dans les Amirautés, aux Officiers des Amirautés, Maîtres des ports, Juges des Traites, & à tous autres qu'il appartiendra, de tenir la main à l'exécution du présent arrêt, lequel sera enregistré aux greffes desdites Amirautés, lû, publié & affiché par-tout où besoin sera.

FAIT au Conseil d'Etat du Roi, Sa Majesté y étant, tenu à Versailles le vingt-deux février mil sept cent quatre-vingt-huit.

Signé LA LUZERNE.

LE DUC DE PENTHIEVRE, Amiral de France, Gouverneur & Lieutenant général pour le Roi en sa province de Bretagne.

VU l'arrêt du Conseil d'Etat du Roi ci-dessus & des autres parts, à nous adressé: MANDONS à tous ceux sur qui notre pouvoir s'étend, de l'exécuter & faire exécuter, chacun en droit soi, suivant sa forme & teneur; ordonnons aux Officiers des Amirautés de le faire enregistrer aux greffes de leurs siéges, lire, publier & afficher par-tout où besoin sera.

FAIT à Anet le vingt-huit février mil sept cent quatre-vingt-huit. Signé L.J.M. DE BOURBON. Et plus bas, Par son Altesse Sérénissme.

Signé PERIER.

Text from official printing bearing the imprint: "A Paris, De l'Imprimerie Royale. 1788." (DNA: PCC, No. 87, II); accompanied by an English translation by John Pintard. Another copy is in DLC: TJ Papers. The projet of the arrêt that Lambert sent to Montmorin on 17 Feb. 1788 is in Arch. Aff. Etr.,

Paris, Corr. Pol., E.-U., Vol. XXXIII; transcripts in DLC. Its text has been collated with the above and all differences are indicated in the notes below, where it is referred to as Dft. The draft that Dupont sent to TJ (acknowledged in TJ to Dupont, 15 Feb. 1788) has evidently not been preserved, a fact that may be significant in view of TJ's care in preserving such documents and in view of the interpretation advanced in the preceding notes to the covering letter for the present enclosure.

1 This word is not in Dft.

2 This reads in Dft: "cet avantage."

3 Dft reads instead: "ou dans quelqu'autre port françois."

4 Dft ends at this point.

From John Trumbull

DEAR SIR London 23d. May 1788.

I am this morning favor'd with yours of 18th May:—I am sorry to find from this, that one of your letters has miscarried, and the more mortified as it happens to be that which you mention to have written from Amsterdam containing a draft:—The only letter I have from you since one of three lines the 3d. March: mentioning your intention of leaving Paris on that tour is the present received this morning:—I beg you will therefore inform me immediately, whether you sent that letter by the Post: in which case I must search for it at the post office: or by Mr. Adams: who may in his hurry have carried it with him to America. You will likewise say who the draft was upon and drawn by whom, and when, and payable to whom, that I may inquire whether it has been paid, and stop it if it should in future come thro' other hands than mine. —Mr. Adams paid me the £8.0. of course: and this I have not expended for you: for the Taylor wishes your Bill to be larger before it is paid and won't give it me tho I have askd him two or three times—and Brown I deferr'd till I knew your intentions:—I believe what He means to send you of yourself to be the copy, and that Mr. Adams thus the original. They shall now be sent you with the Polyplasiasmos, your approbation of which I doubt, if your taste leads you to admire V. der Werf.

The Tea Vase. Oldham declares your Idea to be unreconciliable to any convenience without a total change of construction. Mrs. Church has made the attempt at Grays and some other Shops. They all agree that the *projection* of the robinet is of absolute necessity:—and that whatever form is substituted to the present straight one, still the projection must be preserved: so that all they can do is to exchange the present form for a serpent or something of that kind, which vomiting the water from his mouth, is rather more than less offensive, and at best is not your Idea. The only form, or the least objectionable to my mind is the Elephants Head and Trunk: if you think well of it I will try to have it executed, but you must expect they will charge high enough.

The Celestini—Walker has not yet quite satisfied himself with. He thinks he shall succeed, and promises you the first successful production.

Stockdale to whom I have deliver'd your letter promises to send the books and your account next week. Those you request of me from Lackington shall come at the same time. The other letter to Dublin goes by this Post.

The Chariot I will enquire about.—Mr. Church left us yesterday for Down Place, for the Summer. Was well as was Mrs. C. I hope the young ladies with you are so. I am with all Esteem your

JNO. TRUMBULL

RC (DLC); endorsed.

From Giuseppe Chiappe

EXCELLENCE Mogador Le 24e. May 1788.

A l'occasion que Je depeche pour Marseille un Batiment chargé de Retours pour cette Place, Je ne manquerois pas de continuer a V. E. le peu de nouvelles qui courent dans le Paÿs; L'Ambassade Hollandoise n'est pas encore paruë, ni non plus les Anglois se sont deçidés pour avoir libres autre fois les raffrechissements qui leurs ont êtés interdits pour Gibraltar des Ports de l'Arache, Tanger, et Tetuan; L'on attend de deux Cours les dernieres dispositions, et l'on croit fermement qu'elles seront satisfaisentes pour la continuation de la reciproque bonne armonie; Le 20e. du passé il est içi arrivée une Fregatte Portuguaise pour escorter la Fregatte de S.M.I. qui a êté raccomodée de fond en comble a Lisbone, et qui ne tardera a partir pour l'Arache se joindre aux autres Barbaresques qui doivent sortir pour quelque expedition; Je n'ay pas encore reçue la note des Presents envoyés par la Cour de Portugal a S.M.I. dans cette conjoncture, et Je ne manquerois pas d'en notifier V. E. tout de suite qu'elle me parvienne; S.M.I. est partie de Maroc le 6. du Courant pour Mequinez, l'ayant preçedée un Camp de Seize Mille Combattants de ses diverses Provinces, et l'on ignore encore sa veritable destination; Vôtre Nation Americaine continue a jouir des favœurs dont S.M.I. vœut la distinguer, et Je ne doute nullement qu'Elle aura toujours la preference; Je suis mortifié de me voir privé depuis long tems de quelque réponse de la part de

V. E. a qui J'ay écrit en diverses reprises, et toujours dans l'attente Je reitere a V.E. les offres sinceres de tous mes services, et J'ay l'honneur d'être très-profondement De Vre. Excellence Vre. très Humble & très Obeissant Servitœur, GIUSEPPE CHIAPPE

RC (MoSHi); endorsed.

To James Madison

DEAR SIR Paris May 25. 1788.

The inclosed letter for Mr. Jay being of a private nature, I have thought it better to put it under your cover lest it might be opened by some of his clerks in the case of his absence. But I inclose a press copy of it for yourself, as you will perceive the subject of it referred to you as well as to him. I ask your aid in it so far as you think right, and to have done what you think right. If you will now be so good as to cast your eye over the copy inclosed, what follows the present sentence will be some details, supplementory to that only, necessary for your information, but not proper for me to state to Mr. Jay.

Mr.[1] *Jay*. Tho appointed a minister resident at the court of *Madrid* he never was *received* in that character. He was continually passing from *Paris* to *Madrid* and *Madrid* to *Paris* so that he had no occasion to establish a houshold at either. Accordingly he staid principally in furnished lodgings. Of all our ministers he had the least occasion for an outfit, and I suppose spent almost nothing on that article. He was of a disposition too to restrain himself within any limits of expence whatever, and it suited his recluse turn.[2] Should he judge of what others should do, by what he did, it would be an improper criterion. He was in Europe as a voyageur only, and it was while the salary was 500 guineas more that at present.

J. Adams. He came over when, instead of outfit and salary, all expences were paid. Of rigorous honesty, and careless of appearances he lived for a considerable time as an oeconomical private individual. After he was fixed at *the Hague* and the salary at a sum certain, he continued his oeconomical stile till out of the difference between his expences and his salary, he could purchase furniture for his house. This was the easier as the salary was at 2500 guineas then. He was obliged too to be passing between *Paris* and *the Hague* so as to avoid any regular current of expence. When he established himself, his pecuniary affairs were under the direction of *Mrs. Adams*, one of the most estimable characters on earth, and the most attentive and honourable oeconomists. Neither had a wish to lay up a copper, but both wished to make both ends meet. I suspect however, from an expression dropped in conversation, that they were not able to do this, and that a deficit in their accounts appeared in their winding up. If this conjecture be true, it is a proof that the salary, so far from admitting savings, is inequal to a very plain stile of life, for such was theirs. I presume Congress will be asked to allow it, and it is evident to me, from what I saw while in *London* that it ought to be done, as they did not expend a shilling which should have been avoided. Would it be more eligible to set the example of making good a deficit, or to give him an Outfit, which will cover it? The impossibility of living on the sum allowed, reputably, was the true cause of his insisting on his recall.

Doctor Franklin. He came over while all expences were paid. He rented a house with standing furniture, such as tables, chairs, presses &c. and bought all other necessaries. The latter were charged in his account, the former was included in the article of houserent and paid during the whole time of his stay here; and as the established rate of hire for furniture is from 30. to 40. per cent. per annum, the standing furniture must have been paid for three times over during the 8. years he staid here. His salary too was 2500 guineas. When Congress reduced it to less than 2000, he refused to accede to it, asked his recall, and insisted that whenever they chose to alter the conditions on which he came out, if he did not approve of it, they ought to replace him in America on the old conditions. He lived plain, but as decently as his salary would allow. He saved nothing, but avoided debt. He knew he could not do this on the reduced salary and therefore asked his recall with decision.

To *him I*[3] succeeded. He had established a certain stile of living. The same was expected from *me* and there were 500 guineas a year less to do it on. It has been aimed at however as far as was practicable. This rendered it constantly necessary to step neither to the right nor to the left to incur any expence which could possibly be avoided and it called for an almost womanly attention to the details of the houshold, equally perplexing, disgusting, and inconsistent with business. You will be sensible that in this situation no savings could be made for reimbursing the half year's salary ordered to be advanced under the former commission and more than as much again which was unavoidably so applied, without order, for the purchase of the Outfit. The reason of the thing, the usage of all nations, the usage of our own by paying all expences of preceding ministers, which gave them the outfit as far as their circumstances appeared to them to render it necessary, have made me take for granted all along that it would not be refused to me; nor should I have mentioned it now but that the administration is passing into other hands, and more complicated forms. It would be disagreeable to me to be presented to them in the first instance as a suitor. Men come into business at first with visionary principles. It is practice alone which can correct and conform them to the actual current of affairs. In the mean time those to whom their errors were first applied have been their victims. The government may take up the project of appointing foreign ministers without outfits and they may ruin two or three individuals before they find that that article is just as indispensable as the salary. They must then fall into the current of general usage, which has become general only because experience has established it's necessity.—Upon the whole, be so good as to reflect on it, and to do, not what your friendship to me, but your opinion of what is right will dictate. Accept, in all cases, assurances of the sincere esteem & respect with which I am Dear Sir Your friend & servant,

TH: JEFFERSON

RC (DLC: Madison Papers); endorsed; docketed by Madison above the date-line: "Recd. Aug. 1. 88."; partly in code. PrC (DLC). Enclosure: RC and 1st PrC of TJ to Jay, 15 May 1788.

1 This and subsequent words in italics are written in code and were, in part, decoded interlineally by Madison; his decoding has been verified by the Editors, employing Code No. 9, and in two instances has been departed from: Madison's *Master Adams* and *Mistress Adams* were permissible decodings under the established key, but were not in accord with TJ's normal usage.

2 MS originally read: ". . . his recluse turn which is to avoid society"; after PrC was executed, TJ deleted in RC but not in PrC: "which is to avoid Society."

3 TJ first wrote out the words *him I* and then erased them, overwriting the code symbols but not really obscuring the original words.

From Amand Koenig

MONSIEUR Strasbourg ce 26 Mai 1788

Le 8 Avril j'ai eu l'honneur de vous envoyer par incluse de M. Prevost Libraire, Quai des Augustins, les livres mis de coté pour vous. Il y a longtems qu'ils sont arrivés à Paris, veuillez Seulement les faire prendre chez le dit Libraire. Si vous n'avez pas reçu la lettre qui vous donnoit avis de cet envoi, il faut que mon commis ait négligé de la porter à la poste, je vous demande mille pardon de cet oubli.

Je viens de recevoir de Leipzic *Euripidis Tragoediae T[om]us IIus.* Par première occasion j'aurai l'honneur de vous le faire tenir.

Je Suis avec un profond respect Monsieur Le plus humble de vos Serviteurs

AMAND KOENIG

RC (DLC); endorsed.

The relationship established by TJ with the Strasbourg bookseller was a pleasant one; TJ later declared that he found in Koenig's establishment "the greatest collection of Classics, and of the finest editions, I met with in Europe. I bought much of him on the spot, and much afterwards as long as I staid at Paris. It was as easy to drop him an order for a book, and it was sent by the Diligence as quick as I could get it almost from a bookstore of Paris. His prices were much lower, and his own arrangements with the Diligence took all expence and trouble off of the hands of his customers" (TJ to George Ticknor, 19 Mch. 1815). See illustration of Koenig's bookstore in this volume.

From George Mason

DEAR SIR Virginia, Gunston Hall May 26th. 1788.

My Son, John Mason, having entered into Partnership with Messrs. Joseph Fenwick & Compy., Merchants in Bourdeaux, where he will probably reside some Years, and intending to take his Passage in a Ship that will sail from Potomack River, about the last of June, I embrace the Opportunity of presenting you my Respects, and inquiring after Your Health; which it will always give me pleasure to be informed of.

This Letter will be forwarded by my Son, immediately upon his Arrival in Bourdeaux; and he will pay his Respects to You, in Person, as soon as he can conveniently go to Paris. I flatter myself You will find him a modest, chearful, sensible Young Man; and that his Integrity and Diligence will merit the Confidence of those, who may favour the Copartnership in which he is concern'd, with Consignments, or other Business in their Line. The Firm of the House will, I expect, upon his Arrival in Bourdeaux, be changed to Fenwick Mason & Compy.—Any good Offices which you may do the said House, or any Advice, which you may be pleased to give my Son, I shall esteem as the highest Mark of your Friendship.

I make no Doubt that You have long ago received Copys of the new Constitution of Government, framed last Summer by the Delegates of the several States, in general Convention at Philadelphia.—Upon the most mature Consideration I was capable of, and from Motives of sincere Patriotism, I was under the Necessity of refusing my Signature, as one of the Virginia Delegates; and drew up some general Objections; which I intended to offer, by Way of Protest; but was discouraged from doing so, by the precipitate, and intemperate, not to say indecent Manner, in which the Business was conducted, during the last Week of the Convention, after the Patrons of this new plan found they had a decided Majority in their Favour; which was obtained by a Compromise between the Eastern, and the two Southern States, to permit the latter to continue the Importation of Slaves for twenty odd Years; a more favourite Object with them than the Liberty and Happiness of the People.

These Objections of mine were first printed very incorrectly, without my Approbation, or Privity; which laid me under some kind of Necessity of publishing them afterwards, myself.—I take the Liberty of inclosing you a Copy of them.—You will find them conceived in general Terms; as I wished to confine them to a narrow Compass.—There are many other things very objectionable in the proposed new Constitution; particularly the almost unlimited Authority over the Militia of the several States; whereby, under Colour of regulating they may disarm, or render useless the Militia, the more easily to govern by a standing Army; or they may harrass the Militia, by such rigid Regulations and intollerable Burdens, as to make the People themselves desire it's Abolition.—By their Power over the Elections, they may so order them, as to deprive the People at large of any share in the Choice of their Representatives.—By the Consent of Congress, Men in the highest Offices of Trust in the United States may receive any Emolument, Place, or Pension from a foreign Prince, or Potentate; which is setting themselves up to the highest Bidder.—But it would be tedious to enumerate all the Objections; and I am sure they cannot escape Mr. Jefferson's Observation. Delaware—Pensylvania—Jersey—Connecticut—Georgia, and Maryland have ratifyed the new Government (for surely it is not a Confederation) without Amendments. Massachusets has accompanyed the Ratification with proposed Amendments. Rhode Island has rejected it. New Hampshire, after some deliberation, adjourned their Convention to June. The Convention of South Carolina is now sitting. The Convention of new York meets in June, that of North Carolina in July, and the Convention of Virginia meets on the first Monday in June. I shall set out for Richmond this week, in order to attend it.—From the best Information I have had, the Members of the Virginia Convention are so equally divided upon the Subject, that no man can, at present, form any certain Judgement of the Issue. There seems to be a great Majority for Amendments; but many are for ratifying first, and amending afterwards. This Idea appears to me so utterly absurd, that I can not think any Man of Sense candid in proposing it. I sincerely wish you Health, & every Felicity; and am, with the greatest Respect & Esteem dear Sir Your affecte. & obdt. Servt.,

G. Mason

P.S. Underneath is a Copy of the Resolutions which I introduced at the last Session of Assembly, upon the Subject of Paper Money, and which, being unanimously agreed to, I hope has given that iniquitous Project it's Death's-Wound.—Resolved that the present Scarcity of circulating Money has been, in a great Measure, caused by the general Fear and Apprehension of an Emission of paper Currency, inducing moneyed-men to lock up their Gold and Silver, prefering the Loss of Interest to the Risque of lending, or letting it out here.

Resolved that Money, by the common Consent and Custom of commercial Nations, is and ought to be considered as a Scale or Standard, by which to estimate the comparitive Value of Commodities, and that Nothing can be more improper and unjust, than to substitute such a Standard, as wou'd be more uncertain and variable than the Commodities themselves.

Resolved that an Emission of Paper Currency wou'd be ruinous to Trade and Commerce, and highly injurious to the good People of this Commonwealth; and that, by weakening their Confidence in the Laws and Government, corrupting their Manners and Morals, destroying public and private Credit, and all Faith between Man and Man, it wou'd increase and aggravate the very Evils it is pretended to remedy.

Resolved that the making paper Currency, or any thing but Gold and Silver Coin, a Tender, in discharge of Debts contracted in Money, is contrary to every principle of sound Policy, as well as Justice.

RC (DLC); endorsed; addressed: "His Excellency Thomas Jefferson Esquire American Minister at the Court of Versailles." Enclosure: Copy of "The Objections of the Hon. George Mason, to the proposed Fœderal Constitution. Addressed to the Citizens of Virginia," which appeared in the *Virginia Independent Chronicle* for 5 Dec. 1787 as copied from the *Virginia Journal and Alexandria Advertiser*, being reprinted as a pamphlet by Thomas Nicholas in Richmond late in 1787 or early in 1788 (Swem, No. 3515). The text is printed in P. L. Ford, *Pamphlets on the Constitution*, p. 327-32.

Almost at the very moment that Mason was describing the idea of RATIFYING FIRST, AND AMENDING AFTERWARDS as utterly absurd, TJ was expressing the opinion that this procedure was far preferable to his own, which was to have nine states ratify in order to insure adoption and then have the others, "by holding off, produce the necessary amendments" (see TJ to Carrington, 27 May 1788).

From Nathaniel Appleton

Boston, 27 May 1788. At request of his son Thomas, has shipped on TJ's account "Eight boxes of Spermaceti Candles, enclosed in one Case, on board the Sloop Phoenix Capt. Loring master bound to Havre de Grace and Rouen"; hopes TJ will find these of good quality; has sent several sizes, not knowing which would be most agreeable; has directed Captain Loring to lodge the case with Messrs. Le Couteulx & Cie., merchants at Rouen; thanks TJ "most sincerely for the kind notice you have been pleased to take of my son since his arrival in Paris." [*Subjoined:*] Invoice for candles shipped to TJ "on his Account and risque" shows that eight boxes, "Branded N. Appleton & Co.," contained 229¼ lbs. of candles net @ 2/6 and cost £28. 13s. 1d., plus 10/8 for the boxes and 2/6 for the case.

RC (MHi); 4 p.; addressed; endorsed.

To Brissot de Warville

Paris May 27. 1788.

SIR

I now trouble you with my packets for America, which are indeed unreasonably bulky. The larger one addressed to Mr. Jay contains chiefly newspapers, pamphlets &c. so may be disposed of as you please. That addressed to Mr. Madison is of the same nature, as are all the others except the smallest of the two addressed to Mr. Jay which contains my letters, and of which I ask your special care. The letters herein inclosed for Mr. Thomson and Mr. Madison I will desire you to deliver when convenient to yourself, being intended to procure to these gentlemen the honor of your acquaintance. Those to M. de Moustier and to Madame Bingham, you will be so good as to send to them on your arrival in New York and Philadelphia. I have now only to add my thanks for the trouble you are so kind as to undertake, and my wishes that you may find my country as agreeable as your love of liberty has led you to expect. Be so good as to present my affectionate friendship to Monsr. de Crevecoeur, to accept my prayers for a safe, speedy and pleasant voiage, and assurances of the esteem & respect with which I have the honor to be Dear Sir your most obedient & most humble servt.,

TH: JEFFERSON

PrC (DLC). Enclosures (or accompanying letters and packets): (1) TJ to Thomson, 1 May 1788. (2) TJ to Madison, 1, 3, and 25 May 1788, the last of which enclosed TJ to Jay, 15 May 1788. (3) TJ to Moustier, 17 May 1788. (4) TJ to Anne Willing Bingham, 11 May 1788. (5) A packet of letters for Jay (TJ to Jay, 23 May 1788 and its enclosures), and probably other letters for America, such as TJ to Commissioners of the Treasury, 16 May 1788, and TJ to Carrington, 27 May 1788. In addition to the large packets of newspapers, pamphlets, &c. for Jay and Madison, Brissot was also asked to carry the letters and packets previously taken to Le Havre by Ford, which included TJ to Jay, 4 May 1788, and which TJ had intended for the May packet (see TJ to Limozin, 17 May 1788, and Limozin's reply of 22 May).

To Edward Carrington

Dear Sir Paris May 27. 1788.

I have received with great pleasure your friendly letter of Apr. 24. It has come to hand after I had written my letters for the present conveiance, and just in time to add this to them. I learn with great pleasure the progress of the new Constitution. Indeed I have presumed it would gain on the public mind, as I confess it has on my own. At first, tho I saw that the great mass and groundwork was good, I disliked many appendages. Reflection and discussion have cleared off most of these. You have satisfied me as to the query I had put to you about the right of direct taxation. [My first wish was that 9 states would adopt it in order to ensure what was good in it, and that the others might, by holding off, produce the necessary amendments. But the plan of Massachusets is[1] far preferable, and will I hope be followed by those who are yet to decide. There are two amendments only which I am anxious for. 1. A bill of rights, which it is so much the interest of all to have, that I conceive it must be yielded. The 1st. amendment proposed by Massachusets will in some degree answer this end, but not so well. It will do too much in some instances and too little in others. It will cripple the federal government in some cases where it ought to be free, and not restrain it in some others where restraint would be right. The 2d. amendment which appears to me essential is the restoring the principle of necessary rotation, particularly to the Senate and Presidency: but most of all to the last. Re-eligibility makes him an officer for life, and the disasters inseparable from an elective monarchy, render it preferable, if we cannot tread back that step, that we should go forward and take refuge in an hereditary one. Of the correction of this article however I entertain no present hope, because I find it has scarcely excited an objection in America. And if it does not take place ere long,[2] it assuredly never will. The natural progress of things is for liberty to yeild, and government to gain ground. As yet our spirits are free. Our jealousy is only put to sleep by the unlimited confidence we all repose in the person to whom we all look as our president. After him inferior characters may perhaps[3] succeed and awaken us to the danger which his merit has led us into. For the present however, the general adoption is to be prayed for, and I wait with great anxiety for the news from Maryland and S. Carolina which have decided before this, and wish that Virginia, now in session, may give the 9th. vote of approbation. There could then be no doubt of N. Carolina, N. York, and New Hampshire.][4] But what do you propose to do with Rhode island? As long as there is hope, we should give her time. I cannot conceive but that she will come to rights in the long run. Force, in whatever form, would be a dangerous precedent.

There are rumours that the Austrian army is obliged to retire a little; that the Spanish squadron is gone to South America; that the English have excited a rebellion there, and some others equally unauthenticated. I do not mention them in my letter to Mr. Jay, because they are unauthenticated. The bankruptcies in London have recommenced with new force. There is no saying where this fire will end. Perhaps in the general conflagration of all their paper. If not now, it must ere long. With only 20 millions of coin, and three or four hundred million of circulating paper, public and private, nothing is necessary but a general panic, produced either by failures, invasion or any other cause, and the whole visionary fabric vanishes into air and shews that paper is poverty, that it is only the ghost of money, and not money itself. 100 years ago they had 20 odd millions of coin. Since that they have brought in from Holland by borrowing 40. millions more. Yet they have but 20 millions left, and they talk of being rich and of having the balance of trade in their favour.—Paul Jones is invited into the Empress's service with the rank of rear admiral, and to have a separate command. I wish it corresponded with the views of Congress to give him that rank from the taking of the Serapis. [I look to] this officer as our great future dependance on the sea, where alone we should think of ever having a force. He is young enough to see the day when we shall be more populous than the whole British dominions and able to fight them ship to ship. We should procure him then every possible opportunity of acquiring experience. I have the honour to be with sentiments of the most perfect esteem Dear Sir Your friend & servant,

Th: Jefferson

PrC (DLC). In DLC: Monroe Papers there is a PrC of a two-page Tr in TJ's hand consisting of extracts from his present letter to Carrington and from one to Cutting, for the identification of which see notes below and to TJ to Cutting, 8 July 1788.

TJ's query to Carrington about the RIGHT OF DIRECT TAXATION was in his letter of 21 Dec. 1787. J. B. Cutting, in England at this time, gave John Adams an excellent account of THE BANKRUPTCIES IN LONDON and of their impact on American relations; he reported that these had created much "commotion not only in the metropolis but nearly throughout the Kingdom. The failure of Fordyce in 1772 was a light business comparatively speaking. The engagements of the single House of Livesey & Co., whose paper circulated throughout the nation, are said to be [stopped] for no less a sum than fifteen hundred thousand pounds, not one half of which can ever be paid. The house of Potter & Lewis stopped payment on the same day for more than three hundred thousand. One of this last house was *it is said* committed to New Gate this last week on a charge of forgery. Both these houses have been playing a deep and dangerous game in the American market. It seems their intent was to monopolise the cotton and linnen branches entirely. With this view they have been pouring immense quantities of goods into every part of the United States for years past and it appears that their orders have been to sell almost at any rate. In various instances accordingly invoices have been disposed of thirty percent below prime cost, and thus has such incredible quantities of our specie been absorp'd and remitted hither, while our native and fair importers have found it impossible to buy abroad or sell at home without ruin.—In fine sir such a scene of wild speculation and extravagant and pernicious management both in England and elsewhere is now disclosed as astonishes everybody. Nor do the most sagacious people here pretend to predict the end of it. Everybody who has been concerned in circulating bills through all England is more or less affected, and new failures occur every hour. It is computed that at least three millions in private paper, which was unquestionable property to all mercantile intents and purposes one fortnight ago, is now annihilated. Upwards of forty thousand manufacturers in the County of Lancashire are destitute of employment, and ripe for mischief." Cutting added that these laborers were now lamenting their credulity in putting savings into the hands of bankers, and that both the minister and the Bank of England had been appealed to for assistance in the mounting crisis, but that neither of them "have, *can* or *dare* grant it." He concluded: "When the affair first commenced, the whole mischief was attributed to the perfidy of the merchants and people of America. But since the nature of the business has been developed, not a whisper of the kind vibrates. On the contrary the calumnies against the United States and her mercantile citizens begin to attenuate and expire. People of Candour and discernment begin to own that *one* of the causes of tardy payments from American debtors has been the *monstrous* conduct of a few British merchants themselves." This was a very brief attenuation, however; in a letter a few days later Cutting reported that "an American merchant and a *bankrupt* are become almost convertible terms in London. And in the present situation of our governments and the ruinous ballance of trade against us . . . how can it be otherwise? And what provokes my indignation in this business is that a swarm of adventurers from the United States and british swindling speculators . . . have been flung from the mercantile feculence of each country upon the other." He predicted that out of this crisis would come a "vast immigration of industrious and ingenious manufacturers" and mechanics who were standing on tip-toe ready to emigrate, but were held back by "the frightful stories that the Americans have no government capable of property or freedom, private or public, which are constantly circulated throughout Europe" (Cutting to Adams, 17 and 28 May 1788; MHi: AMT).

1 At this point TJ changed "was" to "is" by overwriting.

2 These two words interlined in substitution for "soon," deleted.

3 These two words interlined in substitution for "will," deleted.

4 PrC of extract mentioned above includes the whole of the matter enclosed in brackets (supplied), to which TJ prefixed the date-line and, at the close of this part of the extract, added: "To Colo. Edwd. Carrington."

From Sarsfield

28 may 1788

Voicy, Monsieur, ce qu'il vous faut pour M. Izard. Je vous l'envoie double pour que Vous puissiez En faire passer un à M. Izard. Je ne puis que vous répéter que cette Pension cy étoit preferée à L'autre Il y a peu d'années. Je ne crois pas qu'elle ait changé.

Vous connoîssez, Monsieur, mon Sincere Et Inviolable Attachement

RC (DLC); unsigned but in Sarsfield's hand. Sarsfield enclosed two copies of the prospectus of an engineering school, one of them for Ralph Izard, but neither has been found and the school has not been identified, though it was probably the Ecole des Ponts et Chaussées. See TJ to Izard, 17 July 1788.

To John Brown

Dear Sir Paris May 28. 1788.

It was with great pleasure I saw your name on the roll of Delegates, but I did not know you had actually come on to New York, till Mr. Paradise informed me of it. Your removal from Carolina to Kentuckey was not an indifferent event to me. I wish to see that country in the hands of people well-disposed, who know the value of the connection between that and the Maritime states, and who wish to cultivate it. I consider their happiness as bound up together, and that every measure should be taken which may draw the bands of Union tighter. It will be an efficacious one to receive them into Congress, as I perceive they are about to desire. If to this be added an honest and disinterested conduct in Congress as to every thing relating to them we may hope for a perfect harmony. The navigation of the Missisipi was perhaps the strongest trial to which the justice of the federal government could be put. If ever they thought wrong about it, I trust they have got to rights. I should think it proper for the Western country to defer pushing their right to that navigation to extremity as long as they can do without it tolerably; but that the moment it becomes absolutely necessary for them, it will become the duty of the maritime states to push it to every extremity to which they would their own right of navigating the Chesapeak, the Delaware, the Hudson or any other water. A time of peace will not be the surest for obtaining this object. Those therefore who have influence in the new country would act wisely to endeavor to keep things quiet till the Western parts of Europe shall be engaged in war. Notwithstanding the aversion of the courts of London and Versailles to war, it is not certain that some incident may not engage them in it. England, France, Spain, Russia, Sweden, and Denmark will all have fleets at sea, or ready to put to sea immediately. Who can answer for the prudence of all their officers? War is their interest. Even their courts are pacific from impotence only, not from disposition. I wish to heaven that our new government may see the importance of putting themselves immediately into a respectable position. To make provision for the speedy paiment of their foreign debts will be the first operation necessary. This will give them credit. A concomitant one should be magazines and manufactures of arms. This country is at present in a crisis of very incertain issue. I am in hopes it will be a favourable one to the rights and happiness of the people: and that this will take place quietly. Small changes in the late regulations will render them wholly good. The campaign opens between the Turks and the two empires with an aspect rather favourable to the former. The Russians seem not yet thawed from the winter's torpitude. They have no army yet in motion. And the Emperor has been worsted in two thirds of the small actions which they have had as yet. He is said to be rather retiring. I do not think however that the success of the Turks in the partisan affairs which have taken place, can authorize us to presume that they will be superior also in great decisions. Their want of discipline and skill in military manoeuvres is of little consequence in small engagements and of great in larger ones. Their grand army was at Andrianople by the last accounts, and to get from thence to Belgrade will require a month. It will be that time at least then before we can have any very interesting news from them. In the mean time the plague rages at Constantinople to a terrible degree. I cannot think but that it would be desireable to all commercial nations to have that nation and all it's dependancies driven from the sea-coast into the interior parts of Asia and Africa. What a feild would thus be restored to commerce! The finest parts of the old world are now dead in a great degree, to commerce, to arts, to science, and to society. Greece, Syria, Egypt and the Northern coast of Africa constituted the whole world almost for the Romans, and to us they are scarcely known, scarcely accessible at all. The present summer will enable us to judge what turn this contest will take.—I am greatly anxious to hear that nine states accept our new constitution. We must be contented to accept of it's good, and to cure what is evil in it hereafter. It seems necessary for our happiness at home; I am sure it is so for our respectability abroad. I shall at all times be glad to hear from you, from New York, from Kentucky or whatever region of the earth you inhabit, being with sentiments of very sincere esteem & attachment Dear Sir your friend & servant, TH: JEFFERSON

PrC (DLC).

To Nicolas van Staphorst

SIR Paris May 28. 1788.

I have this moment received a letter from Mr. John Trumbull of London informing me that the bill never came to his hands, which you were so kind as to draw on Herreis of London for £30. sterling or ƒ348.10 in my favor, on the 27th. or 28th of March. I remember that when I was addressing it to Mr. Trumbul, I could not recollect his address with certainty: and I think Mr. Hubbard was so kind as to undertake to put it under cover to your correspondent in London with a request to seek Mr. Trumbul out. I now suppose that I wrote the address of my letter wrong, that he has not been able to find Mr. Trumbul and that the letter therefore still is in his hands. I have accordingly desired Mr. Trumbul to call at Herreis's. But as I am not sure that it was to Herreis that Mr. Hubbard was so good as to inclose my letter, I have taken the liberty of entering into these details in order to ask your aid in investigating my bill of exchange. I have the honor to be with perfect esteem and respect Sir your most obedient humble servant, TH: JEFFERSON

PrC (DLC).

To John Trumbull

DEAR SIR Paris May 28. 1788.

I have this day received your favour of May 23. and in consequence have copied and inclose mine of Mar. 27. from Amsterdam. The bill it inclosed was drawn by Nicholas and Jacob Van Staphorst on Herreis of London either for £30. sterling or for 348 florins 10 sous; for I do not remember whether it was expressed in English or Dutch money. I indorsed it, and I believe made it expressly paiable to you. The bill must have been dated the 27th.

or 28th. of March. After I had written my letter and was about directing it, I could not recollect your address with certainty. I put it as well as I could therefore and got Mr. Van Staphorst to take it and put it under cover to his correspondent at London with a request to have it delivered to you. Probably the address has been so badly put as that he has not found you, and that the letter is still in his hands. It never entered my head to doubt whether it had got safe to you. Another circumstance made me suppose you had received it. This was an expression in a letter of Mrs. Cosway's which I supposed to allude to what I had said in my letter from Amsterdam, relative to her, and which thereafter I supposed you had shewn her. I hope you will find it still at Herreis's. Be so good as to let me know as soon as you can. In the mean time I write to Van Staphorst about it. I like the Elephant's head better than the strait spout. Do you remember how the Medusa's head of De Moutier's was made to answer? [. . .] in this. Kiss the hands of Mrs. Cosway and Mrs. Ch[urch for me.] Yours affectionate[ly,

TH: JEFFERSON]

PrC (DLC); signature and a few words torn away in lower right hand corner. Enclosure: Dupl (missing) of TJ to Trumbull, 27 Mch. 1788.

The LETTER OF MRS. COSWAY'S was that of 29 Apr. 1788. Trumbull had suggested THE ELEPHANT'S HEAD in his letter of 23 May 1788, which TJ must have just received. Late 18th-century craftsmen and artists helped set the convention in taste to which Trumbull and TJ here conformed in preferring an elephant's head and trunk to THE STRAIT SPOUT. An occasional variant was a serpent (see Trumbull to TJ, 23 May 1788) or the neck and head of a camel.

From Claudius de Bert

Le Havre, *29 May 1788*. The ship *Sally*, Captain Gilhison, belonging to Messrs. Henderson, Ferguson, & Gibson of Dumfries, Virginia, arrived a fortnight ago loaded with tobacco, is now taking in ballast, and "will saill hence in Seven or Eight days at farthest directly to Potomack." If TJ has any dispatches for America and will direct them to him at Le Havre, he will be pleased to deliver them to the captain and see that they are forwarded. Would be glad to take them himself but for an engagement with some friends not to leave France before 15 or 20 June—"and as that epoch will not be very distant from the one, at which you are expecting an answer from Congress, respecting our affairs, I should not be averse to defer my departure untill then provided the circumstances be still such, as will permit you to remain in the same opinion, you were in when I had the honor of seeing you at Paris."

RC (DLC); 2. p. endorsed; underneath signature: "chez Made. la veuve Becquet rue de la fontaine."

The AFFAIRS that De Bert referred to were the arrearages owed the French officers, and he probably had spoken to

TJ about the time that the latter was corresponding with other officers on this embarrassing subject on his return from Holland (see TJ to Castaing, 14 May 1788). Captain de Bert was one of the founders of the Society of the Cincinnati; he returned to America in 1789 (Lasseray, *Les Français sous les treize etoiles*, p. 129-30).

To Cambray

SIR Paris May 29. 1788.

The laws of the United states give no credit to the legalisation of an instrument of writing by their foreign ministers. They require that they should be legalised by affixing to them the seal of the city where the instrument is executed or acknoleged. On receiving your letter therefore, I sent the instrument it contained to your house with directions to the person having charge of your affairs there to apply to the Prevot des Marchands de Paris to legalise it and to affix the seal of his office. If I have not done exactly the thing you desired, it was to avoid you the disappointment of having your letters of procuration sent back from America for want of a due legalisation. I have the honor to be with sentiments of the most perfect esteem & attachment Sir Your most obedient & most humble servant, TH: JEFFERSON

PrC (DLC); at foot of page: "M. le Comte de Cambrai."

The nature of the document that Cambray desired to have LEGALISED is indicated in his letter to TJ of 9 June 1788. The present letter indicates that Cambray had written TJ at least one and perhaps two letters, and that TJ had written one to Cambray returning the INSTRUMENT; none of these letters has been found and none of them is recorded in SJL Index.

From William Carmichael

MY DEAR SIR Aranjuez 29 May 1788

I forwarded last week by Mr. Symons the paper mentioned in my last. I have received no letters from America since, but have seen a Philadelphia paper of the 7th of April, in which there is published an extract of a letter from General Washington expressive of his opinion that the Constitution would be adopted by the State of Virginia. *Here*[1] *the attention of our politicians have* of late *been much engaged* by the *armaments made in Sweden.* The *Russian minister* attributes them *to England which court* he asserts is *intriguing* every *where* to *embarrass* the *imperial courts. He thinks* or is led by his resentiment to suppose that so far from *promoting the ends proposed* their *present measures* will finally *bring about* an *alliance* which finally *will prevent them from* disturbing *others from a desire* of regaining their *former superiority*: I find that *he has* [had] a *long conversation* with the *minister* of *state* on this subject *who* wishes *to* prevent the *war* from becoming general, but *at present apprehends* that it will be impracticable if *Great Britain* persists in pursuing *it's underhand* Policy. I find from the *same quarter* that the *count* of *Florida Blanca hath spoken* to *Mr. Eden* seriously on the tendency of this kind of Policy, citing their intrigues with the *court* of *Sweden* and the Assistance afforded by them to the *Turks*, *contrary to their* assurances of *neutrality*. In the last mentioned instance he alluded to a *ship* of *800 and 50 tons from England* to *Gi*[*braltar*] which lately *sailed* from *thence* to *Constantinople* with *warlike stores*. This *ship* was formerly the *L'Oiseau*,[2] a *French frigate captured* last *war*. He told the Abovementioned person that *Mr.* [Eden] *had* little to *reply* to his *discourse* and in the *course* [of] the *conversation* said that *if Spain was forced into* a *war* He would go up to the neck into *it*, but that he wished *peace* and intreated the other not to *aigrir sa court*[3] by his *letter* to *Petersburg*. Such is the substance of what I have learnt. Please to compare it with what you have heard on these points and favor me with your Sentiments thereon. The *Russian adds that he expected* shortly to *know* the *sum furnished* to [*Sweden, and how*].[4] I must be allowed *to add for your government* that he and the one *at Paris are great enemies*.

The only representation made against the order which I inclosed you lately that I have heard of is by the Chargè des Affaires of Holland. I shall transmit to you it and the answer in my next if the person who has promised me the copies, keeps his word. Mr. Lardizabal often asks for you and desires me to present his respects to you. I suppose the Squadron mentioned in my former letters is by this time on its return to Port. I have seen a letter from the Missisippi which mentions some preparations made to oppose any Attempt that might be made to enter on the Territory of Spain in that part of the World by the People whom some Englishmen have been endeavouring to excite to hostility on the waters of the Missisippi. These preparations are made I suppose in Consequence of the information given by Congress to Mr. Gardoqui on this subject. Whenever an opportunity presents I beg you to mention me to the Ct. de Montmorin. You will shortly have the Dutchess of Vauguion and a part of the Family with you. The Ambassador accompanies his Lady as far as Bourdeaux. I have the honor to be with great respect & Esteem Your Excys. Obliged & Hble. Sert.,

WM. CARMICHAEL

RC (DLC); partly in code.

The RUSSIAN MINISTER at Madrid was Stefan Zinovieff, and the ONE AT PARIS, for whom he felt such enmity that Carmichael thought it necessary to put TJ on guard, was Ivan-Matvevitch Simoline. William Eden noted in his journal on 1 June 1788 that the wife of the French AMBASSADOR, "The Duchess de la Vauguyon, and her daughters, went away this morning on a leave of absence, and we suspect that they never mean to come back. They have been well liked here, and their absence will make a gap in the society" (*Journal and Correspondence of William, Lord Auckland*, London, 1860-2, II, 38). The order against which the CHARGE DES AFFAIRES OF HOLLAND made a representation was enclosed in Carmichael to TJ, 14 Apr. 1788, and, as promised, Carmichael reported further on the matter in his of 5 June 1788.

1 This and subsequent words in italics are written in code and were decoded interlineally—and with difficulty—by TJ; his decoding has been verified where possible by the Editors, employing a partially reconstructed key to Code No. 11. Carmichael not only possessed a faulty code, and used it erratically at times, but he also apparently inserted from time to time a superfluous symbol for additional security (see TJ to Carmichael, 3 June 1788, and also note 4, below). Matter in brackets (supplied) was not encoded by Carmichael and has been editorially inserted. Some of Carmichael's garbled encoding is conjecturally explained in the following notes.

2 Carmichael erred in encoding the name of this frigate; of the four symbols employed by Carmichael, TJ decoded only three—"l," "sea," and "w." (the last being interchangeable with "u").

3 The preceding three words are TJ's decoding. It is not clear whether Carmichael was consciously attempting to use French or merely erred in encoding. TJ evidently thought Carmichael meant to say *aigrir sa cour*, for he interlined the decoding thus in spite of the fact that the correct symbol for "ai" was "317," not, as Carmichael wrote, "1204." It is likely that Carmichael intended to make the passage read in the following sense: ". . . in the course of the conversation [Floridablanca] said . . . that he wished peace and intreated the other [Zinovieff] not to aigrir sa court by his letter [letters?] to Petersburg."

4 Carmichael wrote "146. 1140. 329." and TJ correctly decoded this as "President and now." It is possible that the last two symbols were intended to be superfluous, and it is almost certain that Carmichael meant to write, instead of the first symbol, "140."—the symbol for *Sweden*, a mistake he had already made in this letter in the phrase INTRIGUES WITH THE COURT OF SWEDEN, where "146." was given by Carmichael and was interlineally decoded by TJ as "Sweden"; the fact that TJ did not bother to correct the earlier misuse of "146." indicates that he allowed the context to suggest the correct reading without looking up the number in his cipher key. Carmichael clearly intended a new sentence to begin with the statement I MUST BE ALLOWED TO ADD, &c., so that the concluding words of the previous sentence, AND NOW, must be regarded either as intentionally superfluous or as an error made in encoding. If the latter is the case, then Carmichael may have intended to say: "The Russian adds that he expected shortly to know the sum furnished to Sweden, and how." It is impossible to determine which of these is the correct solution, but the Editors have accepted the latter as seeming to them to have a slightly higher degree of plausibility.

From Pierre Castaing

Paris, 29 May 1788. Encloses a response from Grand to his appeal for an advance of arrearages due by United States. Has tried in vain every means to avoid importuning TJ, but has no other recourse. "Vous etes trop bon patriote pour ne pas Faire un Effort en Faveur de quelqu'un qui s'est Sacrifié pour votre patrie." He is one of those who served longest: "J'ay pris les armes le premier jour de La révolution, et n'ay Cessé de servir jusqu'a la paix, pendant lequel Tems j'ay ete successivement volontaire, officier d'Infantairie, aide de Camp, guide, et enfin Captif pendant six mois, aux depens de ma Santé, de ma Fortune, et de ma jeunesse." He came to Paris to solicit compensation for his services and to await "L'effet des promesses du ministre de La guerre en ma Faveur. Je retourne a St. Domingue, ma Patrie, ou je dois etre employé par La protection de Monsieur le Marquis de La Fayette." But his finances will neither permit him to depart nor to remain until the end of July without exposing himself to the risk of disgrace. He will be forced to abandon both principal and arrears of interest "pour la modique Somme de Cent Louis d'or que l'on m'offre"; the certificate, amounting to £8826 principal and £1587 interest, is all that he has to show for nine years' service, and now, with the greatest regret, he is going to lose it at the very moment payment is expected. Renews his appeal to TJ to authorize Grand to pay arrearages only, or at least to ask some acquaintance to accept a bill of exchange at six months, which he will, on his word of honor, redeem by arrangements to be made at Bordeaux if the United States should not make the payment as expected. [*In postscript*:] TJ will note that Grand says if TJ will suggest some course of action, he will gladly concur.

RC (DLC); in French; 4 p.; beneath signature: "hotel de Boulogne. R. Croix des petits [champs]"; endorsed. The enclosed letter from Grand has not been found.

From Thomas Lee Shippen

My very dear Sir — Hague May 29th. 1788.

It is not more from a sense of duty than inclination that I devote the first moments after my arrival at this place to a complyance with the request which you were so good as to make upon my taking leave of you at Paris. For I gratify the one at the same time that I perform the other. Nothing flatters me so much as to acquire in any degree the esteem of those whom all the world esteem, and as the request you made me must have proceeded from sentiments which you entertained in my favor, I could not but have been flattered by it. But though that general Agent in human affairs—self love—has been instrumental in this business it is by no means the only incentive. The gratitude which your unbounded kindness exacts and the affection which your virtues have inspired me with, conspire to make my present occupation a most pleasing one. Besides, what can be more desireable than to correspond with those from whom you cannot fail of deriving instruction?

The excursions we have made from the direct road between Paris and the Hague and the time we have employed in examining the different places through which we passed have made our journey longer than we expected, and of course the month more advanced before our arrival here. The temptations which seduced us from our original plan were such as we could not resist nor have we cause now to complain of them. If the course we have taken is an unusual one, it has not been the less interesting on that account. On the contrary there is perhaps a greater satisfaction in seeing things in themselves curious, which have not attracted the general attention. For of those which have done so, you form a competent idea, from the continual accounts you hear of them from every body's mouth, whereas the others have la novelty and sometimes the surprize which they occasion to recommend them. We passed through Lisle Bruges Ghent Brussels Mecklin Antwerp Rotterdam and Delft, and remained 2 or 3 days in almost all of them. The decline of commerce in Flanders seems compensated by the flourishing state of agriculture there, and the Dutch cannot complain of the barrenness of their soil while they enjoy so superior advantages in commerce. However, the latter seem to have been considerably affected by the late disturbances. The flame of civil discord must always be hurtful to peaceable pursuits, and the merchants complain heavily of that which has lately been excited. In Rotterdam in particular, where I remained 4 or 5 days, I was informed that they had never suffered so severe a shock. Exchange is lower than it has ever been known, and inactivity and indolence have become the characteristicks of a people formerly the most industrious in the world.

Notwithstanding this, the Prince hugs himself in his own security, parades more and bows lower than ever. He thinks the people are made to minister to the pleasures of the Prince however limited in his power, and that it is by no means the duty of the Prince, to consult the happiness of his people. The orange cockades and triumphal arches, may poles, and Orange medals—inscribed Vivat Orange abound in all parts of the town, and the Prince snuffs up the incense as if a tribute due to his deservings. There is one instance however of successful resistance to the tyranny of the mob. The German Minister reverencing not only himself but his Imperial master absolutely refused wearing a yellow ribbon of any sort, declaring that he owed more to the dignity of his Court than to the folly of the multitude, and that he would not stoop to such base conditions, as long as he held a public station. In consequence of this, he was followed by about 200 people through the streets of the Hague and insulted by the most abusive language but, upon their threatening to throw him into the water, he went to the Court and asked for the Prince. Upon being shewn to him, he demanded as a right, not as a favor, that he would disperse the mob by whom he had been insulted and give him a passport which might protect him in future. The Prince could not refuse the one or the other and he walked the streets afterwards unoranged.

The Court sat off last night at 12 for Loowe one of the Princely Seats in Guelderland and where the Prince and Princess expect on the 11th. of June to embrace their brother and protector the King of Prussia while they thank him for all he has done and suffered for them.

This excursion of the Court renders this place insupportably dull and we are already nearly persuaded by the Swedish Chargé des Affaires to visit Amsterdam and the other places worth seeing in the Seven Provinces, and then to return here. In all events we shall not remain in the Netherlands more than 3 or 4 weeks during which time my address will continue au soin des Messieurs Wilhem & Jan Willink, Amsterdam.

I am in anxious expectation of the letter you were so kind as to promise me. Will you have the goodness to remember me to Mr. Short and the Marquis de la Fayette and to believe me with all possible consideration and respect your obliged and devoted friend,

T. Lee Shippen

RC (DLC); endorsed.

From C. W. F. Dumas

The Hague, *30 May 1788*. Contents of TJ's letter of 15 May and TJ's personal recollection of Dumas are equally precious to him; has communicated what appeared proper to friends of America at The Hague, Amsterdam, and particularly Leiden, where he hopes the *Gazette* will show what good use he tried to make of it. Stadtholder and family set off yesterday for Cleves, where the king of Prussia will join them the 10th for a day or two; they will return at the end of the month. Enclosed letter for Congress contains all Dumas knows of interest "pour nous." Hopes TJ will continue to send such good news as will come to him from America; and also from France, where he hopes "un bon, solide et prompt arrangement interne" will cause to be no longer applicable the energetic words with which TJ closed his letter: "here all seems peace without and war within." Must close in order to wait upon two young American gentlemen who have favored him with a visit; will inform TJ of the advice he thinks it necessary to give them for their sojourn here. [*Postscript dated 6 June 1788*:] TJ will have seen by the last "Supplément de Leide" the use he has made of the agreeable news sent him; he will with equal ardor seize every succeeding occasion provided by TJ to do the same: "Cela continue de faire un très-bon effet, specialement à Amsterdam, pour le crédit des Et. Un., tandis que celui d'autres nations, et notamment de la Hollande y baisse." There is a negotiation of this province for five million florins that has not, in the course of some weeks, succeeded—"ce qui est sans exemple." Thanks TJ and Adams for procuring for him at last payment of interest of his arrearages.

RC (DNA: PCC, No. 93, IV); in French; 2 p.; accompanied by translation by John Pintard. FC (Dumas Letter Book, Rijksarchief, The Hague; photostats in DLC); lacks one paragraph—that pertaining to the two young Americans (Shippen and Rutledge)—and the postscript (the "P.S. du 6e. Juin" that follows FC is actually a postcript of that date which belongs to the enclosed letter to Jay). Enclosure (same): Dumas to Jay, 28 May 1788, repeating a part of his dispatch of 10 May which had been forwarded via Amsterdam and stating that the courts still continue to pronounce atrocious sentences against the patriots, having ordered seven persons to be whipped at Amsterdam because their manner of wearing the cockade was thought improper; that St. Priest would arrive Sunday; that the French chargé d'affaires was giving a diplomatic dinner for Merode, the emperor's envoy, together with his secretary of legation, Bongé, chargé d'affaires of Sweden, D'Aguire, chargé d'affaires of Spain, and himself; that no others would be present in this small coterie which has met frequently during the winter at the French embassy and would probably continue to do so; that another coterie, much larger, had been gathering around the British ambassador; that [*in postscript dated 6 June*:] St. Priest presented his credentials on the 2d, and for two or three days after his arrival "la plus vile canaille, la juive surtout," assembled before the ambassador's house shouting insults because he and his servants do not wear Orange colors; and that he had presented Shippen and Rutledge to St. Priest. For the use made by Dumas of TJ's news in the SUPPLEMENT DE LEIDE of 3 June 1788, see note to TJ to Dumas, 15 May 1788.

From Homberg & Homberg Frères

Le Havre, 30 May 1788. Should the duties of 28s. 10d. and 10s. per livre imposed on spermaceti oil from America be levied on the gross weight, subjecting the barrels to the same duties as those on the oil? They and the customs are divided on this question.—Enclose customs receipts for 457 casks of oil totalling 180,947 ℔s. gross weight (net weight 150,790 ℔s.), cleared by them last January "du navire La Louise, Cap[itain]e Cotting venant de Boston pour Compte du Sieur Thos. Boilston," which shows that they were obliged to pay duties on gross weight. They do not think that this was the intent of government; on the contrary, everything supports the belief that the minister, in favoring American commerce by modifying the principal charges, intended to subject only the merchandise to the duties, not the accessories. If the contrary were so, would not the decree be explicit on the point?—They appeal then to TJ not only in order to recover the duties unjustly levied, but also to procure for commerce from government a definition of the limits stating what is equitably dutiable. "Nous espérons que votre Excellence s'y employera avec le zèle ordinaire qui l'a conduit dans tout ce qui a rapport à la prospérité des Etats unis de L'Amerique"; they hope TJ will inform them of the success of his appeal. [*In postscript*:] Ask him to return receipt when he has done with it.

RC (MHi); 4 p.; endorsed. Enclosure (missing) was returned, as requested, in TJ's response of 29 June 1788.

To John Jay

SIR Paris May 30. 1788.

A further delay of Mr. Warville enables me to acknolege the receipt of your letter of April 24. by Mr. Paradise. Nothing new has occurred since the date of my other letters which go by this conveiance: except that about one third of the Baillages have accepted their appointments. If the others pretty generally should do the same, and the Chatelet be brought over it will place government pretty much at their ease to pursue their other views of change. The only symptoms of violence which have appeared, have been in Britany, Provence and Languedoc. I have the honor to be with sentiments of the most perfect esteem & respect Sir Your most obedient & most humble servt., TH: JEFFERSON

RC (DNA: PCC, No. 87, II). PrC (DLC).

From Thomas Paine

May 1788

Your saying last evening that Sir Isaac Newtons principle of Gravitation would not explain, or could not apply as a rule to find the quantity of the Attraction of cohesion, and my replying that I never could comprehend any meaning in the term "Attraction of cohesion," the result must be, that either I have a dull comprehension, or that the term does not admit of comprehension. It appears to me an Athenasian jumble of words, each of which admits of a clear and distinct Idea, but of no Idea at all when compounded.

The immense difference there is between the attracting power of two Bodies, at the least possible distance the mind is capable of conceiving, and the great power that instantly takes place to resist separation when the two Bodies are incorporated prove, to me, that there is something else to be considered in the case than can be comprehended by attraction or gravitation. Yet this matter appears sufficiently luminous to me according to my own line of Ideas.

Attraction is to matter, what desire is to the mind but cohesion is an entire different thing, produced by an entire different cause. It is the effect of the figure of matter.

Take two Iron hooks, the one strongly magnetical and bring them to touch each other, and a very little force will separate them  for they are held together only by attraction.

But their figure renders them capable of holding each other infinitely more powerful to resist separation than what attraction can; by hooking them 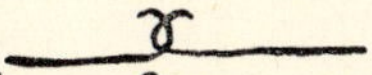 Now if we suppose the particles of matter to have figure capable of interlocking and embracing each other we shall have a clear distinct Idea between cohesion and attraction and that they are things totally distinct from each other and arise from as different causes.

The welding of two pieces of Iron appears to me no other than entangling the particles in much the same manner as turning a key within the wards of a lock, and if our Eyes were good enough we should see how it was done.

I recollect a Scene at one of the Theatres that very well explains the difference between attraction and cohesion.

A Condemned Lady wished to see her Child and the child its mother. This, call attraction. They were admitted to meet, but when ordered to part they threw their Arms round each other and fastened their persons together. This is what I mean by cohesion, which is a mechanical contact of the figures of their persons, as I believe all cohesion is.

Tho' the term "*attraction of cohesion*" has always appeared to me like the Athenasian Creed, yet I think I can help the philosophers to a better explanation of it than what they give themselves, which is, to suppose the attraction to continue in such a direction as to produce the mechanical interlocking of the figure of the particles of the bodies attracted.

Thus. Suppose a Male and female screw lying on a table and attracting each other with a force capable of drawing them together. The direction of the attracting power to be a right line till the screws begin to touch each other and then if the direction of the Attracting power to be circular, the screws will be screwed together, but even in this explanation, the cohesion is mechanical, and the attraction serves only to produce the contact.

While I consider attraction as a quality of matter capable of acting at a distance from the visible presence of matter, I have as clear an Idea of it as I can have of invisible things.

And while I consider cohesion as the mechanical interlocking of the particles of matter, I can conceive the possibility of it much easier than I can attraction, because I can by crooking my fingers see figures that will interlock, but no visible figure can explain attraction. Therefore to endeavour to explain the less difficulty by the greater appears to me unphilosophical. The cohesion which others attribute to attraction and which they cannot explain, I attribute to figure, which I can explain. A Number of fish hooks attracting and moving towards each other will shew me there is such a thing as attraction but I see not how it is performed, but their figurative hooking together shews cohesion visibly, and a handful of fish hooks thrown together in a heap explain cohesion better than all the Newtonian philosophy. It is with Gravitation, as it is with all new discoveries, it is applied to explain too many things.

It is a rainy morning and I am waiting for Mr. Parker, and in the mean time, having nothing else to do I have amused myself with writing this.

T Paine

RC (DLC). On the problem of dating some of the undated items written by Paine to TJ in 1788-1789, see Thomas W. Copeland, *Our Eminent Friend: Edmund Burke*, New Haven, 1949, p. 184, where the present letter is discussed in connection with three others that bear no date, all four of which are written on a paper described by Copeland as "a pale-green, over-sized sheet which so far as I know Paine did not use elsewhere," and all of which he thought may have been written in the spring of 1788, as the present one certainly was. This conclusion the Editors accept with respect to one of the three other undated items — that immediately following, which, like the present letter, is proved by internal evidence to have been written in Paris; but they are inclined to believe that an earlier date is indicated for the second—probably as early as late Jan. or early Feb. 1788 (see Paine to TJ, second item in this volume) and that a later date is indicated for the third—probably after 3 July 1788 and perhaps even as late as 1789. This last concerns Silas Deane and probably was a comment given by Paine to TJ after Foulloy had left with TJ for about twenty-four hours the letter-book and accounts of Deane, some of which TJ caused to be copied and the originals of which he purchased and sent to America in 1789 (see TJ to Foulloy, 4 July 1788; TJ to Jay, 3 Aug. 1788; TJ to Jay, 23 Nov. 1789). However, since Paine is not known to have been in Paris in 1788 after May of that year (same, p. 184) and since the memorandum conceivably could have been written even if the negotiations with Foulloy had not taken place, this last Paine item is also printed after the letter immediately following. Only one of these Paine items is accounted for in SJL Index—by an asterisk (indicating an undated letter) which occurs between the entries for those of 19 Feb. 1788 and 15 June 1788, thus confirming Copeland's conclusion as to one of these items but without identifying that one.

From Thomas Paine

Dear Sir [May? 1788]

I enclose you a Problem not about Bridgs but Trees, and to explain my meaning I begin with a fountain. The Idea seems far fetched, but fountains and Trees are in my walk to Challiot.[1]

Suppose Fig. 1st a fountain. It is evident 1st. That no more water can pass thro the branching Tubes than pass thro the trunk.

2d. That admitting all the water to pass with equal freedom, the sum of the squares of the diameters of the two first branches must be equal to the square of the diameter of the Trunk, also the sum of the squares of the four Branches, must be equal to the two, and the sum of the squares of the 8 Branches must be equal to the four, and therefore the 8, 4, 2, and the Trunk being reciprocally equal the solid content of the whole will be equal to the Cylinder Fig 2d of the same diameter of the trunk and height of the fountain.

Carry the Idea of a fountain to a Tree growing. Consider the sap ascending in Capillary tubes like the Water in the fountain, and no more sap will pass thro the Branches than pass thro the Trunk.

2dly. Consider the Branches as so many divisions and subdivisions of the Trunk as they are in the fountain, and that their contents are to be found by some rule, with the difference only of a Pyrimidical figure instead of a Cylindrical one.

Therefore to find the quantity of Timber (or rather loads,) in the Tree, figure 3d, draw a Pyramid equal to the height of the Tree as Fig. 4th, taking, for the inclination of the Pyramid, the diameter of the Bottom, and at any discretionary height above it which in this is as 3 & 2.

As sensible Men should never guess, and as it is impossible to judge without some point to begin at, this appears to me to be that point, and by which a person may ascertain near enough the quantity of Timber and loads of Wood on any quantity of Land, and he may distinguish them into Timber, Wood and faggots.

Yours &c. T P

RC (DLC); endorsed. On the problem of dating this memorandum, see note to preceding letter.

[1] Thus in MS. Paine meant *Chaillot*, a fact which establishes his presence in Paris at the time of writing this letter.

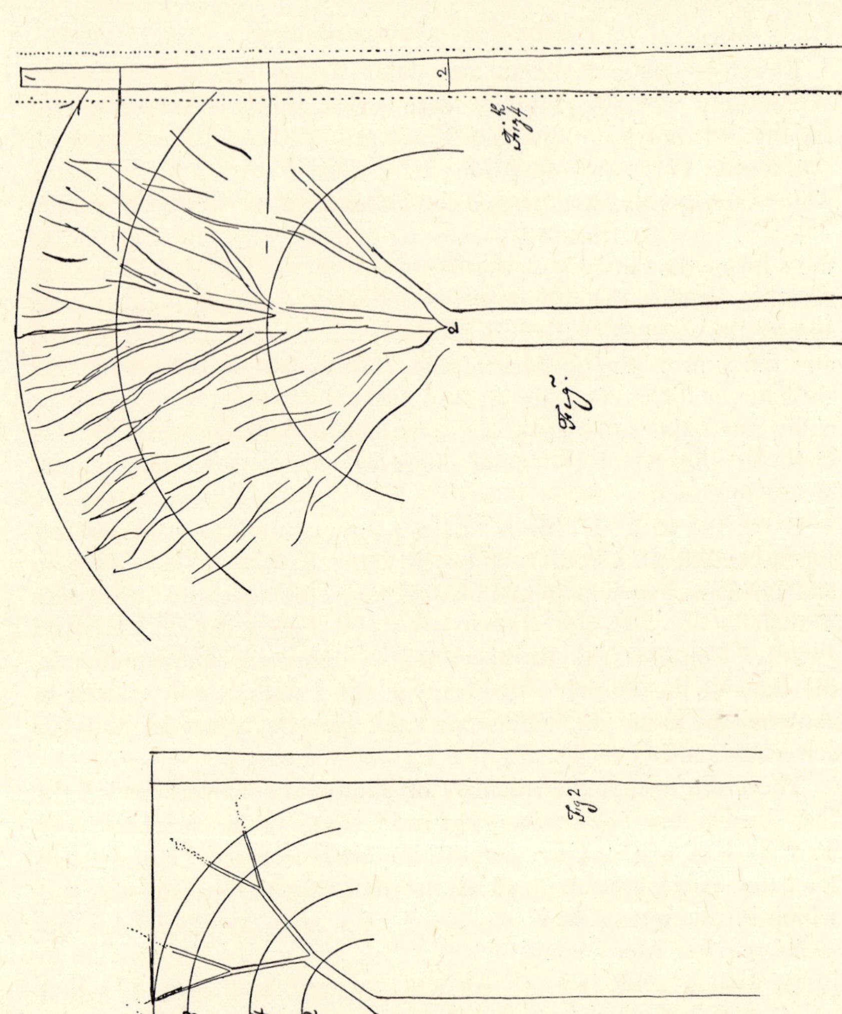

From Thomas Paine

Explanatory Circumstances

1st. The last dispatches are dated Octr. 6th. and Oct. 7th. They were sent by a private hand—that is, they were not sent by the post. Capn. Folger had the charge of them. They were all under one cover containing five separate Packets, three of the Packets were on commercial matters only. One of these was to Mr. R. Morris, Chairman of the commercial Committee, one to Mr. Hancock (private concerns) another to Barnaby Deane, S. Deane's Brother. Of the other two Packets, one of them was to the Secret Committee, then stiled the Committee for foreign Affairs, the other was to Richrd H. Lee. These two last Packets had nothing in them but Blank white French Paper.

2d. In Sepr. preceeding the date of the dispatches Mr. B—— sent Mr. Francis to Congress to press payment to the amount mentioned in the official Letter of Oct. 6. Mr. F—— brought a letter signed only by S. Deane. The Capn. of the Vessel (Landais) brought another letter from Deane both of these letters were to enforce Mr. B—— demand. Mr. F—— arrived with his letters and demand. The official dispatches (if I may so say) arrived blank. Congress had therefore no authoratative Information to act by. About this time Mr. D—— was recalled, and arrived in America in Count D'Estain's fleet. He gave out that he had left his accounts in France.

With the treaty of Alliance come over the Duplicates of the lost dispatches. They come into my Office not having been seen by Congress, and as they contain an injunction not to be concealed[1] by Congress, I kept them secret in the Office for at that time the foreign Committee were dispersed and new Members not appointed.

On the 5th. of Decr. 1778 Mr. D published an inflamatory piece against Congress. As I saw it had an exceeding Ill effect out of doors, I made some remarks upon it, with a view of preventing people running mad. This piece was replied to by a piece under the Signature of Plain truth, in which it was stated, that Mr. D—— though a stranger in France and to the Language, and without money, had by himself procured 30,000 Stand of Arms, 30,000 Suits of Cloathing and more than 200 pieces of Brass Cannon. I replied that these supplies were in a train of Execution before he was sent to France. That Mr. Deane's private letters, and his official dispatches jointly with the other two Commissioners contradicted each other.

At this time I found that Deane had made a large party in Congress, and that a Motion had been made but not decided upon for dismissing me from the foreign Office, with a kind of censure.

MS (DLC); endorsed by TJ: "Payne (Common sense)." On the problem of dating this memorandum see note to Paine to TJ, May 1788. Another circumstance that may argue for a later date is the endorsement on the present document: of the four Paine items written on similar paper and discussed in the note referred to, one has no endorsement, two are endorsed "Payne Thos.", and the present one is given an endorsement evidently to distinguish "Common sense" from Thomas Payne, the London bookseller with whom TJ established connections later in 1788 (see TJ to Thomas Payne, 1 Oct. 1788).

1 This word interlined in MS; Paine interlined the word "not" in the phrase "not to be concealed," perhaps intending to substitute "revealed" for the last but failing to do so.

To Pierre Castaing

SIR Paris June 1. 1788.

It is with real pain that I am informed of the difficulties of your present situation, and the more so as it is utterly out of my power to relieve them. There is neither authority nor money in the hands of any person here to discharge the arrearages of interest, nor do I know any person who is in the habit of purchasing those claims;[1] nor am I able to suggest to Mr. Grand any other arrangement for relieving you. I sincerely wish that you could defer disposing of your claims on the United states till orders can arrive from the Treasury board for discharging the interest, which may be expected in the course of the month of July. I have the honour to be with the most perfect esteem & regard Sir Your most obedient & most humble servt., TH: JEFFERSON

PrC (DLC).

1 At this point TJ wrote, and then deleted: "I cannot."

To Claudius de Bert

SIR Paris June 2. 1788.

I am honoured with your favor of May 29. and thank you for the information relative to the ship Sally. There is here an American family who are on the lookout for a passage to America. It consists of a gentleman (Mr. Montgomery), his mother, his wife, and two servants. I immediately communicated the information to them, and they in the instant began to prepare for their departure. They cannot fix the day, but they seem sure of being at Havre sometime between the 6th. and 10th. instant. If the vessel be not then gone, and they like her and can get a passage they mean to avail themselves of her, but do not chuse to enter into an engagement till they know something of the vessel. In the mean time they desire me to ask the favor of you to give us information what will be the day of her sailing, and whether they can have their passage on board her, the price &c. I beg your pardon for this trouble, but it is interesting to them. I am in hopes you can be so good as to write the answer by the return of the first post, in which case I can receive it the 6th. in the morning, and if they are ready, they may be at Havre in the course of that night.—I hope still to recieve orders from the Treasury by the last of July. I have the honour to be Sir Your most obedt. humble servt.,

Th: Jefferson

PrC (DLC).

From Richard O'Bryen

Algiers, 2 June 1788. "If any one is redeemed it is at a very exorbitant price. A few days ago an old Savoy Captain of a Merchant vessel was redeemed for the sum of 2150 Algerine Chequins, which is equal to £967.10 Sterling, and even with that price it was with much time the Dey was prevailed on to let him be redeemed; and I think that Sailors will be as high as £400. Sterling as they are very scarce here at present and much wanted to do the duty for the public."

MS missing. The text printed here, a Tr (DNA: RG 59) in the hand of a clerk of the Department of State, was extracted from the missing MS for use in connection with TJ's report of 28 Dec. 1790. PrC of another Tr by same clerk (DLC). At head of both: "No. 6. Extract of a letter from Richard O Brian to the Honble. Thomas Jefferson dated Algiers June 2d. 1788." Probably enclosed in Cathalan to TJ, 11 June 1788.

To William Carmichael

Dear Sir Paris June 3. 1788.

Your favors of Apr. 14. and 29. and May 8. have lately come to hand. That of Jan. 29. by M. de Molinedo had been left here during my absence on a journey to Amsterdam. That gentleman was gone, as I presume from my being unable to learn any thing of him. I had been led to Amsterdam in order to meet with Mr.

Adams and to endeavor in conjunction with him to take arrangements for answering the most pressing of our European calls for money till the end of the year 1790, by which time our new government will have been probably established, put under way, and enabled to draw money from it's own resources. We succeeded in obtaining enough to last to the end of the present year, and in arranging a plan for two years more if it shall be approved by Congress. In the estimate I gave in to our bankers was comprehended a sum to be drawn either monthly or quarterly, by yourself, Mr. Dumas, and myself: so that for the present year you need be under no further anxieties, nor, as I hope, for two more to come. You mention that you had been authorised to draw on a house in Amsterdam for 3000 Dollars. Whenever the term shall be expired to which that portion of salary was appropriated, if you will make your draught on Messrs. Willem & Jan Willink, Nicholas & Jacob Van Staphorst at Amsterdam, and send the first draught through me, I will write to them such an explanatory letter as may leave you under no future doubts, unless the dispositions already made at Amsterdam should be controuled by the Treasury board, which I have no reason to apprehend.—The cyphered words in your letter of Apr. 14. prove to me that Mr. Barclay left you a wrong cypher. In those of May 8. taken from the cypher I sent you, are several things which I cannot make out. From an expression in your letter I suppose some of these to have been intended, others I ascribe to the equivocal hand writing in the cypher, which I believe was by one of Mr. Barclay's clerks. I cannot always distinguish the letter e. from o. n. from u. t. from f. and sometimes from s. I observe you use repeatedly 1360. instead of 1363. which I presume to be an error of the copyist to be corrected in your cypher. I cite the following passage, drawing lines under the numbers I do not understand. '1001. 739. 1264. 1010. 1401. 1508. 1237. 1509. 950. 1509. 694. 861. 221. 742. 658. 233. 1017. 1077. 1097.'[1] and I do it that we may come to a perfect understanding of our cypher. The separating the numbers by a dot, as above, would add a facility to the decyphering of yours.—Mr. *Littlepage*[2] is *returned to Poland.* He expressed concern that you had not drawn on him, and appeared to me not to have a distinct idea of the sum, so that I think you will have to specify it to him. I will forward your letter to him whenever you shall be good enough to send it to me. —With respect to the *isthmus of Panama* I am assured by *Burgoine* (who would not chuse to be named however) that *a survey* was made, that a *canal* appeared very practicable, and that the idea was suppressed for *political reasons* altogether. He has seen and minutely examined the *report*. This *report* is to me a vast desideratum for *reasons political and philosophical*. I cannot help suspecting the Spanish squadron to be gone to S. America, and that some disturbances have been excited there by the British. The court of Madrid may suppose we would not see this with an unwilling eye. This may be true as to the uninformed part of our people: but those who look into futurity farther than the present moment or age, and who combine well what is, with what is to be, must see that our interests, well understood, and our wishes are that Spain shall (not forever, but) very long retain her possessions in that quarter: and that her views and ours must, in a good degree, and for a long time, concur. It is said in our gazettes that the Spaniards have sunk one of our boats on the Missisipi, and that our people retaliated on one of theirs. But my letters not mentioning this fact have made me hope it is not true, in which hope your letter confirms me. There are now 100,000 inhabitants at Kentuckey. They have accepted the offer of independance on the terms proposed by Virginia, and they have decided that their independant government shall begin on the 1st. day of the next year. In the mean time they claim admittance into Congress. Georgia has ceded her Western territory to the U.S. to take place with the commencement of the new federal government. I do not know the boundaries. There has been some dispute of etiquette with [*the*][3] *new French minister which has disgusted him*. The following is a state of the progress and prospect of the new plan of government.

The Conventions of 6. states have accepted it, to wit,

1. Massachusets by	187	Ayes against	168. Noes.
2. Connecticut	148.		40.
3. Pennsylvania	46.		23.
4. Delaware	22		0
5. New Jersey	39		0
6. Georgia	33		0
	475		231.

The other Conventions were to meet as follows.

7. Maryland.	April 21.
8. S. Carolina	May. 12.
9. Virginia	May. 26.
10. New York	June. 17.

11. New Hampshire June. 18.
12. North Carolina July.
13. Rhode island referred the question to their people.

About one third of these gave their votes, and of these there were about nine tenths against accepting the Constitution. In Maryland there was respectable opposition: yet it is thought they will accept. In S. Carolina there is scarcely any opposition. In Virginia the opposition is very formidable. Yet on the whole it is thought to have lessened and that that state will accede. New York is perhaps more doubtful: but if the 9. preceding states should have adopted it, this will surely induce her to do it. The New Hampshire convention met. Many of the delegates came instructed and determined to vote against it. The discussions brought them over to the side of the Constitution. But they could not vote against their instructions. They therefore asked an adjournment that they might go back to their constituents and ask a repeal of their instructions. Little doubt is entertained that they will accede.[4] The conduct of Massachusets has been noble. She accepted the constitution, but voted that it should stand as a perpetual instruction to their delegates to endeavor to obtain such and such reformations; and the minority, tho very strong both in numbers and abilities, declared viritim et seriatim that, acknowleging the principle that the Majority must give the law, they would now support the new constitution with their tongues and with their blood if necessary. I was much pleased with many and essential parts of this instrument from the beginning. But I thought I saw in it many faults, great and small. What I have read and reflected has brought me over from several of my objections of the first moment, and to acquiesce under some others. Two only remain, of essential consideration, to wit, the want of a bill of rights, and the expunging the principle of necessary rotation in the offices of President and Senate. At first I wished that when 9. states should have accepted the constitution, so as to ensure us what is good in it, the other 4. might hold off till the want of the bill of rights at least might be supplied. But I am now convinced that the plan of Massachusets is the best. That is, to accept, and to amend afterwards. If the states which were to decide after her should all do the same, it is impossible but they must obtain the essential amendments. It will be more difficult if we lose this instrument, to recover what is good in it, than to correct what is bad after we shall have adopted it. It has therefore my hearty prayers, and I wait with anxiety for news of the votes of Maryland, S. Carolina, and Virginia. There is no doubt that Genl. Washington will accept the presidentship, tho' he is silent on the subject. He would not be chosen to the Virginia convention. A riot has taken place in New York which I will state to you from an eye-witness. It has long been a practice with the Surgeons of that city to steal from the grave bodies recently buried. A citizen had lost his wife. He went, the 1st. or 2d. evening after her burial, to pay a visit to her grave. He found that it had been disturbed and suspected from what quarter. He found means to be admitted to the anatomical lecture of that day, and on his entering the room, saw the body of his wife, naked and under dissection. He raised the people immediately. The body in the mean time was secreted. They entered into and searched the houses of the Physicians whom they most suspected. But found nothing. One of them however, more guilty or more timid than the rest, took asylum in the Prison. The mob considered this as an acknolegement of guilt. They attacked the prison. The governor ordered militia to protect the culprit and suppress the mob. The militia, thinking the mob had just provocation, refused to turn out. Hereupon the people of more reflection, thinking it more dangerous that even a guilty person should be punished without the forms of law, than that he should escape, armed themselves and went to protect the physician. They were received by the mob with a volley of stones, which wounded several of them. They hereupon fired on the mob and killed four. By this time they received a reinforcement of other citizens of the militia horse, the appearance of which in the critical moment dispersed the mob. So ended this chapter of history, which I have detailed to you because it may be represented as a political riot, when politics had nothing to do with it. Mr. Jay and Baron Steuben were both grievously wounded in the head by stones. The former still kept his bed, and the latter his room when the packet sailed which was the 24th. of April.

You have no doubt seen the reformations proposed in this country. They are all good as to the matter, the manner alone being exceptionable. They say if the king can of his own authority abolish bad and erect good institutions co-eval with his own, he may do the reverse. When I said the changes were all good, I should have excepted the Cour plenière. The composition of that is undoubtedly vicious. If the minister will so far yeild to the public wish as to take the members of that court from the Provincial assemblies by free election, so that it shall become a representative of the nation, and will call the States general to ratify and establish it beyond the reach of the royal authority, this country will have made a vast stride towards political reformation. More than half the grand bailliages have accepted their offices. The Chatelet is disposed to accept, but their advocates still hold off. If these jurisdictions can be set a going, government will be relieved from the most embarrassing difficulty, and will, in my opinion, be able to go through with their measure.—Do you see Don Miguel de Lardizabal ever? If you do be so good as to present my compliments to him, and to remind him of my catalogue of books, in which he was so kind as to promise me his aid.

Mr. Young, the bearer of this is on the set-out, and in a very distant quarter from me. This obliges me to omit all other European details, and to assure you here of the sentiments of esteem & respect with which I have the honor to be Dear Sir Your most obedient & most humble servt, TH: JEFFERSON

PrC (DLC); partly in code, with accompanying MS bearing the text *en clair* in TJ's hand.

On TJ's earlier efforts to obtain Spanish books on America through Miguel de LARDIZABEL y Uribe, see Lardizábel to TJ, 30 May 1787, and TJ to Lardizábel, 6 July 1787. On the Chevalier BURGOINE and his relationship with Carmichael, see Carmichael to TJ, 29 Sep. 1786, 14 Apr. 1788; TJ to Carmichael, 25 Sep. 1787, note. The eyewitness of the RIOT . . . IN NEW YORK was John Paradise; see TJ to Shippen, 19 June 1788. Another eyewitness was Moustier, who sent a detailed report on the riot to Montmorin. Moustier thought that the riot proved "combien le peuple est peu accoutumé à obeir à un Gouvernement régulier et à quels excès il est capable de se porter pour parvenir à satisfaire sa volonté." His report differs considerably from that given by TJ—for example, he states that the militia turned out to defend the jail, and charged the mob with fixed bayonets, killing four; and that Steuben's wound was less serious than Jay's, both men having been struck in the forehead with paving stones, though Steuben's was a glancing blow. Moustier also stated that the chief justice had called for a grand jury investigation, both of those who were suspected of violating graves and of the mob that had insulted the magistrates; but he suspected that proof would be difficult: "par consequent il n'en resultera, qu'une epreuve de la fureur du peuple et du peu d'authorité des magistrats." Out of the excitement came a rumor that skeletons were bought in New York for the European market and shipped out on the French packet boats, one of which was then anchored at the quay. Moustier ordered her captain to make all possible resistance in case the mob attempted to board her. Some of her guns were charged with grape-shot. A crowd of about 400 men appeared for a moment some distance away, but then hurried off. Moustier had instructed the captain to harangue the mob in case an attack appeared imminent, and to offer to allow two of its representatives to inspect the interior of the packet. These measures, he reported, sufficed either because of the fear or the prudence of the people. He stated also that there were always British sailors in the port of New York who looked for occasions to insult the French, at which they had been only too successful even toward the officers commanding the packets; that the magistrates were too weak to prevent such outrages; and that there were several Englishmen in the mob, one of whom, a sailor, tried to force a window at the prison and received a bayonet thrust through the body (Moustier to Montmorin, 20 Apr. 1788, Arch. Aff. Etr., Paris, Corr. Pol., E.-U., Vol. XXXIII; transcripts in DLC; Montmorin received Moustier's dispatch on 25 May 1788). Concerning the Chevalier Bourgoing's assistance to TJ in procuring a copy of the proposals of a proposed canal across the ISTHMUS OF PANAMA, TJ wrote to Peter S. DuPonceau on 6 Nov. 1817: "While I resided in Paris I learned that a company of capitalists was formed there, to associate with others in Spain to undertake a navigable passage thro' the Isthmus of Darien, and that for this purpose they had presented a memorial to the Spanish government. The subject being interesting, I availed myself of my acquaintance with the Chevalier Burgoyne . . . to get a copy of the Memorial." Bourgoing procured a copy of these proposals, which were enclosed in the letter to DuPonceau and deposited in the archives of the American Philosophical Society; TJ docketed the manuscript as follows: "This Memoir was procured for me by the Chevalier Bourgoyne, author of the travels into Spain, while he was Chargé des affaires of France at Madrid. Th: Jefferson" (PPAP: Canals and Inter-Oceanic Communication; dated "â Paris le 30 Juin 1785," a date twice repeated in endorsements, but not in TJ's hand. See also Sowerby, No. 3899). If there was in actual fact a SURVEY made in consequence of these proposals, it does not appear that Bourgoing was successful in getting a copy of it for TJ, for if he had done so, TJ would almost certainly have included that REPORT also in his letter to DuPonceau.

1 This passage from Carmichael's letter was at first decoded interlineally by TJ as follows: "I have no advice of an ral fical ral owl e America for many months;." TJ's conjectural reading is that given in the letter itself; see Carmichael to TJ, 8 May 1788, especially note 2.

2 This and subsequent words in italics are written in code and are supplied from TJ's accompanying text *en clair*; TJ's encoding has been verified where possible from a partially reconstructed key to Code No. 11. He made a few minor errors, as, for example, in encoding Littlepage's name.

3 This word was not encoded by TJ; it is taken from the text *en clair*.

4 At this point TJ wrote, and then deleted: "And indeed we must hope that all come into it."

To Robert Pigott

[Paris, 3 June 1788]

Mr. Montgomery and his mother seem uneasy that such a sum *in cash* as 8000£ should be tied up in his hands by the marriage settlement. I apprehend this uneasiness may be removed and your daughter provided for more surely by settling lands of the value of 8000£ on her for life (if she survives her husband) and after both their deaths, on the children of their joint bed in such proportions as the survivor shall by deed or will direct. While this secures the estate to the children, it makes them in some degree dependant on their parents for the proportion which each is to have. To render a child independant of it's parents is to ruin it's education, it's morals, it's reputation and it's fortune.

The confidential manner in which I have been applied to on this occasion by the parties renders it my duty to them to make another observation and the perfect readiness to do what is right which I have observed in yourself and Mrs. Montgomery encourages me in doing it. Experience in England has established the proportion between the fortune brought to the husband by the wife and the Jointure settled on her and her children by him, so that no question is ever made on that. For every thousand pounds of fortune which the husband receives with her he settles a hundred a year on her for her life, if she survives him, and on her children by him, after the death of both parties. Your daughter bringing to her husband 3000£ fortune, the settlement on her should have been only of £6000 worth of lands or if you consider 8000£ as the proper provision for her, then you should have given her £4000 and Mr. Montgomery should settle on her 8000£ worth of lands supposed to yield 400£ a year, for her life, to go to his and her children after both their deaths.

Upon the whole, my idea of what should be done is this. That the 3000£ or 4000£ as you please should be paid to Mr. Montgomery on his arriving at age and confirming the marriage settlement, and that he should settle 6000£ or 8000£ worth of land on himself and his wife for their joint lives, then on the survivor for his or her life, then to the children of the joint bed in such proportions as the surviving parent shall by deed or will have directed: and that this be declared to be in lieu and satisfaction of Mrs. Montgomery's right of dower in her husband's lands, and of a distributive share of his personal estate.—I fear this opinion may appear to you officious. But having been consulted confidentially I cannot speak by halves. I feel myself bound to express the whole of my opinion if I express any part of it, and for this the parties have called on me. The infancy of the young [people] renders it a duty to take care of their interests equally and to declare what is the justice due to both. Both of them citizens of America, both enfants and both in a foreign country wherein I am in some degree charged with the interests of my fellow citizens, I feel myself placed in such a position of duty as will I hope apologize for the liberty I have taken, and entitle me to the pardon of yourself and Mrs. Montgomery to whom I send a copy of this letter. I have the honour to be with sentiments of the most perfect esteem & respect Sir your most obedient & most humble servant,

TH: JEFFERSON

PrC (MHi); undated, but an entry in SJL Index shows that TJ wrote to Pigott on 3 June 1788. The fact that there is no salutation and no date-line does not necessarily mean that the PrC is incomplete; the text, which is cast more in the form of a legal opinion than in that of a personal letter, appears to be complete. See Mrs. Dorcas Montgomery to TJ, 16 May 1788. TJ evidently made another PrC to be sent to Mrs. Montgomery, but neither it nor its covering letter (if there was one) has been found.

To Moses Young

Tue[sday] June 3. 1788.

Mr. Jefferson has the honour to present his compliments to Mr. Young. He is very sorry he was out of the way yesterday when he did him the honour of calling on him. He takes the liberty of troubling Mr. Young with a letter to Mr. Carmichael, which he would wish him to carry himself if he goes directly to Madrid and without making any long stay between here and there. But should he stop for 3. or 4. weeks any where he would beg the favor of him to forward it by post putting it under cover to some person at Madrid whose letters are not so liable to be opened in the post office and who could be relied on to send it to Mr. Carmichael. He has the honour of wishing him a good journey.

RC (MHi); MS torn so that part of date is missing. Enclosure: TJ to Carmichael, this date.

From Dubu de la Tagnerette

rüe ferou St Sulpice No. 10.
Paris. 4 Juin 1788.

MONSIEUR

Un objet important pour les Etats unis m'occupe. J'ay Eu l'honneur d'En faire part à M. le Mquis. de la fayette avéc quy J'ay l'honneur d'Etre lié depuis Vingt ans.

Il m'a adressé à vous, monsieur, Et J'ay desiré qu'il voulut bien vous Prévenir.

Il m'a remis une lettre, pour vous, Et J'ay l'honneur de vous demander si Dimanche vous series visible à Chaillot. Nous Traiterions à fond notre objet qui Exige de la Célérité par Rapport à notre gouvernement et à ses Besoins.

Je Suis avec Réspect, Monsieur Votre très humble et très obéissant serviteur DE LA TAGNERETTE

adm[inistrat]eur g[énéra]l des Postes

RC (MoSHi); endorsed. The OBJET IMPORTANT must have been Daniel Parker's proposal to transport mail in connection with his whale-oil ventures (on this, see TJ to Montmorin, 29 Nov. 1788).

From Claudius de Bert

SIR Havre de grace june the 5th 1788

I should have had the honour of answering your favour of the 2d. instant by yesterdays post had it not been delivred to me to late, having been absent from town great part of the day; I imediatly Communicated its Contents to Capt. gilkerson who Commands the vessel, and endeavoured to persuade him to wait for Mr. Montgomery and the ladies or their answer at least untill the Eight instant but had no success. He is still intending to sail to morrow the sixth, if the wind is fair, for fear of loosing the oportunity of a quick return, which has been particularly recomended to him by the owners of the vessel. Should the wind prove to be unfair on the sixth and afterwards, so as to prevent him from Sailing before the gentleman and ladies arrive at the havre, he would then be very willing to take them on board, he would even take it upon himself to wait for them a couple a days, Should he, before his Sailling receive intelligence of the certainity of their agreing the Ship, which by the Construction I put upon the letter, I most insured to him, but it would not satisfy him.

The ship is from 240 to 50 tons burthen and seems to be as Conveniently Calculated for half a dozen passengers, as Can be wished for, Considering her size. There will be several vacant Cabins too there being for the present only two passengers who have bespoke their passage. The price the Capt. asks is 500.[tt] for each of the ladies and gentlemen, and 150.[tt] for each of the servants.

I Shall be very glad Sir, if my information may arrive early enough, to be of any Service to your friend, and Shall always be very happy in executing whatever Commands you will be pleased to honour me with.

I do not loose all hopes yet to see the vessel stoped here for a few days longer, if the redoubling my instances with the Captain may prevail any thing, or if the least pretence of the winds being unsetled may furnish him with a justification towards the owners of the ship, he will certainly lay hold of it, to wait a few days, he being interested and inclined to do it. I Shall remain at my lodgings or leave such orders there as to be found at all times, during the preceeding days, in Case Mr. Montgomery would venture to dispatch an express; Should he get here before the vessel Sails, I Should then easily prevail on the Captain, to wait two or perhaps three days more according to his promisses. I have the honour to be with great respect Sir your most humble & most obedient Servant

De Bert

RC (DLC); endorsed.

From William Carmichael

My Dear Sir Aranjuez 5 June 1788

In a former Letter I had the honor to transmit you an ordinance published in March here, which seemed to alarm several of the Maritime Courts. I now inclose you a copy of an office presented by the Chargè Des Affaires of Holland on that Subject and the Answer given by the Ct. de F. B. I do not find that the Minister of any other court has made representations on this Subject. It is generally supposed (how true I know not) that the States General have been excited by the Policy of G. B. to instruct their Chargè des Affaires here to do what he hath done. It is beleived that the execution of this ordinance in many instances will be impracticable. If rigidly carried into Execution, Biscay will be greatly Affected by it. Perhaps it may *be*[1] *intended as a bugbear to compel them* to *admit* a *custom house*. This is a measure *long held* in *view tho difficult* to be accomplished. The Letters by this days post from Italy seems to confirm the accounts received of late of the advantages gained by the Turks in their various conflicts with the Austrians. Four sail of the Spanish Squadron of Evolution have returned into Port, three of which have been damaged by a gale of wind, it is said that they will again put to sea. There are no Letters from Algiers. I see that New Hampshire has rejected by a small Majority the federal Constitution. I have seen in a Hamburgh paper that Mr. L——ge had dissappeared. I hope on many accounts that this report is without foundation. I assure you that my own interest is the least motive of my concern. With very great respect & regard I have the honor to be Yr. Excys. Most Obedt. & Hble. Sert., Wm. Carmichael

RC (DLC); partly in code; endorsed. Enclosures: (1) C. Aubert, Aranjuez, 10 May 1788, to Floridablanca, making, in behalf of the Estates General, "les plus sérieuses représentations" against the restrictions imposed on foreign commerce, the effect of which would be to close absolutely to Holland produce all the non-privileged Spanish ports and thus to amount to a real prohibition, entirely contrary to the letter of treaties existing between Spain and Holland, particularly that of Utrecht, and upsetting the habits of commerce carried on under these treaties for a century and a half (Tr in DLC; in French; in Carmichael's hand). (2) Floridablanca to Aubert, 22 May 1788, replying to the foregoing and stating that the order is applicable to all nations; that those ports which by the treaty of Utrecht must be opened are subject to regulations for the entry of goods as established by each sovereign; that this may also be done by the States General, &c. (Tr in DLC; in Spanish; in Carmichael's hand).

Carmichael's former letter was that of 14 Apr. 1788, which also mentioned Mr. L——ge (Lewis Littlepage) and discussed Carmichael's own interest in regard to him.

[1] This and subsequent words in italics are written in code and were decoded interlineally by TJ; his decoding has been verified by the Editors with a partially reconstructed key to Code No. 11.

From Amand Koenig

MONSIEUR Strasbourg ce 5 Juin 1788

Ci joint je prends la liberté de vous présenter une notte d'Auteurs classiques que j'ai reçu depuis votre depart d'ici; comme vous avez temoigné que vous n'aimez point les *in folio et in 4°* je n'en ai pas mis sur cette liste. Tous ces livres sont in 8°, in 12° et plus petit format.

Virgilius Heynii vient de paroitre, mais l'éditeur n'en a point tiré d'Exemplaires sur papier fin.

Euripides Barnesii Tus. IIIus. est mis de coté pour vous. Je le joindrai aux Livres pour lesquels vous daignerez me donner vos ordres.

J'espere entre vos mains l'envoy que j'eus l'honneur de vous faire.

Je Suis avec un profond respect Monsieur Votre très humble & très obéissant Serviteur AMAND KOENIG

RC (DLC); endorsed. Enclosure (DLC: TJ Papers, 39: 6751-3): A 3-page "Liste de livres reliés nouvellement acquis, du format in Octova, &c.," listing sixty-eight titles, principally of the 17th century from the presses of Plantin, Jenson, Elzevir, Foulis, and others, and including works of Cicero, Euclid, Grotius, Hippocrates, Homer, Juvenal, Livius, Longinus, Lucretius, Plato, Sallust, Suetonius, Tacitus, Virgil, and others. For TJ's order, see his letter to Koenig of 29 June 1788. The EURIPIDES BARNESII, Vol. III, is in DLC and is described by Sowerby, No. 4527.

From André Limozin

MOST HONORED SIR Havre de Grace 5th June 1788

Since my former of the 22 May I am deprived of your favors. The young De la Croix Navy Prentice arrived with the New york Packet about three weeks ago deliverd me just now the inclosed for your Excellency. I have reprimanded him severely as a man of years is intitled to do a young lad for his carelessness.

I have handed the 2nd instant your Excellencys Papers to Mr. Warville agreable to the orders from your Excellency he was bearer of.

There is now but very little trade between this Place and the United States of America. I am with the highest regard Your Excellency's Most obedient & very Humble Servant,

ANDRE LIMOZIN

RC (MHi); endorsed. Enclosure not identified.

From Richard O'Bryen

[*Algiers, 5 June 1788.* Recorded in SJL Index. Not found.]

From John Trumbull

DR. SIR — London June 6th. 1788

I received yours of the 28th May and have enquir'd at Herries's for your Letter of March from Amsterdam and find that after having search'd for me ineffectually, as well they might, my little obscure corner not being expressly particularis'd in the address, they sent it back to Van Staphorsts in Amsterdam the 16th. of last month. Very probably therefore you will receive it before you do this.

In the mean time I have begun my enquiries about a Chariot, and am led to believe both from the prices of several which I have seen, and from the information of a very honest Coach maker, that Mrs. Church's wishd for the Job of building her a new one: —and therefore valued her's most uncommonly low. In fact I am assur'd that 50 Guineas must either have been an imposition on the part of the Coach maker who nam'd such a price, or he must have known some important defect in the carriage.—I will ascertain in a few days at what price such a Chariot as I think you ought to have may be had, and inform you precisely. You will then give me your Orders.

I will consult Mr. West about the Elephants head, and if we can decide upon a thing in any sort preferable to the common form it shall be executed for you.

Mrs. Church has left Town for the Summer. Mrs. Cosway is very well two days ago.

I am Dr Sir most respectfully your's, JNO. TRUMBULL

RC (DLC); endorsed.

From Benjamin Vaughan

DEAR SIR — Jeffries Sq:, London, June 6, 1788.

I should be perfectly ashamed of the liberty I have lately taken in giving a letter of introduction to you, had you not in some small degree favored me with encouragement. I presume for a double reason to give a letter in favor of my friend Mr. Dugald Stewart, as I am well convinced you will have considerable satisfaction in his acquaintance.

He is the son of the late Dr. Stewart of Edinburgh, and was joint Professor in Mathematics with him. When Dr. Adam Ferguson accompanied the commission of peace to America as its secretary, Mr. Stewart was suddenly requested to lecture to his class in Moral Philosophy; and the same when Dr. A. Ferguson afterwards received a paralytic stroke. He lectured not only with perfect applause, but had a much more numerous class than his friend. Professor Robison being afflicted with a complaint which disabled him from lecturing in Natural Philosophy, Mr. Stewart was again looked up to for supplying the chasm; and lectured in his room with as little preparation as before.

To these general talents, he adds great integrity and sentiment, and the universal esteem of his friends. I need not say that he is looked up to in Scotland. He is in particular the friend of Dr. Reid.

I have the pleasure to send you Lavater's Aphorisms and a little work upon Commerce.

I hope you received some instruments some time ago, and a letter which for its length required more apology than perhaps at the time I had leisure to add. I have the honor to be, with great esteem, Dear sir, Your respectful & faithful humble servt.,

Benjn. Vaughan

RC (DLC); endorsed.

Vaughan's other LETTER OF INTRODUCTION was that of 28 Apr. 1788. The LITTLE WORK UPON COMMERCE was evidently *New and Old Principles of Trade Compared; or a Treatise on the Principles of Commerce between Nations*, London, 1788, attributed to William Vaughan, brother of Benjamin Vaughan (TJ's copy bears on its title-page, but not in TJ's hand, "by William Vaughan"; Sowerby, No. 3548). The long letter which REQUIRED . . . APOLOGY was that of 26 Jan. 1787, enclosed in Vaughan to TJ, 5 Apr. 1788.

From Grand & Cie.

Paris, 7 June 1788. Transmits "le protet faute d'acceptation de la remise de £300. que Mr. Paradise nous a endossée sur Mrs. Rowles & Grimes." Ask whether TJ wishes them to send to him the draft itself.

RC (DLC); 1 p.; endorsed by TJ: "Paradise Grand."

From James Swan

Sir Havre de Grace 7th. June 1788.

I had the honor of writing the Marquis de la Fayette two days since, with proposals for furnishing a quantity of Salt beef, Pork and Butter, and live Sheep and Oxen for the use of the Kings Army and Navy in Europe, and the Islands. The present is only to request that so far as you shall find it for the advantage of America, you would promote the Contract. I am sure that to reflect upon the issue of such a business, the Minister can not long hesitate in accepting the offer. You will observe by the proposals, a Copy of which I have enclosed, that I propose taking 15℔ Cent in Merchandise and Manufactures the first year: but if it should be an object, and would promote or effect the Contract, and it was made an absolute condition, I would increase it to 25℔ Cent. Any step which Mr. Parker may have taken in an affair of the same nature this cannot interfere with, as we shall join in one Contract, or manage it in such a manner as not to have the two effected.

Should it be an objection that I have proposed no term of Credit and that one is required, I will comply with that also. To point out to you, who have thorough knowledge of the resources and capabilities of the United States and of every individual state, the benefit that would arise to New England in having this Contract, or a supply equal to it, effected, must be idle. It would give health and spirits to the sinking industry of the Farmer, who finding no just market for the produce of his labour is really so despondent thousands in consequence are deserting the old and finding new Settlements.

When necessary to attend that I may obviate any objections and respond to questions which may be made, I shall go to Paris. In the meantime and always I shall remain very respectfully with which I have the honor to be Sir Your mo. obedient & very humble Servt.,

James Swan

Mr. Mangon la Forest & Co. here or M. Quesnel, Comy. of Marine at Rouen [will] forward any Letters for me.

RC (DLC). Enclosure (DLC): A two-page document, in French, dated at Le Havre, 29 May 1788, and signed "Jam. Swan de Boston," submitting propositions to furnish to the government of France a quantity of salt pork and beef, livestock, and butter of New England for the royal army and navy in Europe as well as in the French West Indies, as follows: (1) 10 or 20,000 barrels of beef of the same quality and weight as that of Ireland, to be delivered in any port of France or of the islands after having been inspected and approved by an officer appointed to receive it, the part destined for the islands to be 5% cheaper than Irish beef; (2) 4,000 barrels of pork at the same price as that of Ireland, but of a quality very superior to it, "nos Porcs étant engraissés avec du Blee sauvage ou Maïs, ce qui leur rend la chair très excellente et très saine," to be delivered subject to inspection and approval as in the case of the beef; (3) cattle and sheep to be furnished royal troops and vessels in the islands in such quantity as is agreed upon and at a price lower than customary, in acceptable condition, except that, as the passage is long, the contractor will be allowed reasonable indemnity for any unusual loss of stock due to accidents of the sea, &c.; (4) 400,000 pounds of butter, delivered, inspected, and approved as in the case of Pork: "Le Beurre en Amérique est supérieur en odeur et en qualité a celui d'Europe, à cause des pasturages qui y croissant sur un terrain neuf ont plus de suavité et de Goût"; (5) these items to be delivered at stated periods; (6) on notification by the contractor to the French consul of shipment made from New England, he must be authorized to pay half immediately, either in specie or in bills of exchange on Paris at 90 days' sight, the remaining half to be paid after, and at the place of, delivery in the islands or in France, except that, on being paid for supplies delivered in France, the contractors will be obliged to take 15% of their payment in French merchandise or produce the first year and to have this amount augmented by 2½% each year up to the end of the contract, the supplies being augmented always in the same proportion; (7) ships carrying supplies to the islands will have the right to take on molasses or other permissive merchandise from the port in which they have unladed; (8) this contract to be valid only during time of peace, though, if the government demands it, the contractors obligate themselves to furnish the same quantities in time of war at a just and acceptable augmentation in price; and (9) in order to guarantee the execution of the contract on their part, the contractors will give "une caution françois de toute Solidité."

For a note on Swan, see Swan to TJ, 31 Jan. 1788. For TJ's response and possible influence on this contract, see TJ to Swan, 19 June 1788; and Swan to TJ, 7 July 1788; and the altered proposals under 19 July 1788.

From Cambray

Au Chateau de Villers aux Erables, par Montdidier, 9 June 1788. Acknowledges TJ's letter [of 29 May 1788]; regrets not having spoken to him in person about the desired certificate before leaving Paris. Since then a letter from the consul at Charleston "m'annonce avoir terminé mes interets avec l'assemblée de La Caroline pour mes arrerages"; but now, "pour que l'auditeur puisse faire mes comptes, il demande un Serment de ce que j'aurois pu recevoir. Je suis prêt à le faire, c'est la forme qui m'embarasse." Asks TJ's opinion, to which he would be glad to conform. "Je ne sçais pas si mon serment et ma parole d'honneur sous seing privé ne pourroit pas suffire. Il me semble que je ne sçaurois en faire davantage vis à vis d'un officier public."

RC (DLC); endorsed.

From Edward Carrington

My dear Sir New York June 9. 1788.

I had the honor to write you by the last packet by Mr. Barlow and Master G. W. Greene, since which South Carolina has acceded to the new Constitution by a great Majority. The inclosed papers contain the act, and some of the debates of the convention.

Virginia is now sitting, having met last Monday, but we have not yet received any intelligence as to the probable turn the business will take there. I am inclined to think the critical stage in which this convention meets the affair, will have much influence upon the opinions of many who set out in the opposition. In adopting they will certainly avoid commotion, and, at worst, accept a constitution upon which eight States have already agreed to hazard their happiness, and which may be amended, should it be found to operate badly; in rejecting they may produce commotion, with but little prospect of preventing the adoption. The five States who have not yet acceded, would never agree in their objects, and could even this be brought about, they must at last rather yeild to the 8, than these to the five; and it appears that the submission on either side must be intire, for should the 8 think of a compromise with the 5, there would be difficulty in agreing what points to yeild. These considerations will, I apprehend, have their effect in the convention of Virginia, and produce an issue different from that which might have taken place under other circumstances. I am happy to find that the five are so separated that there cannot be a possible effort, to Unite in an attempt to dismember the union. Had the southern States joined in opinion as to the constitution, I verily believe such a desperate step would have been tried, but it would have ended in their destruction, and perhaps that of all the others.

Mr. Madison and myself have sent you sundry Pamphlets and pieces which have been written by the Friends of the constitution; I have endeavoured to select from those which have been written on the other side, that which is reputed the best, to send you now, that you may fairly judge of the arguments brought forward amongst us pro and Con. The two Books enclosed contain a number of letters under the signature of the Federal Farmer, but the Author is not known. These letters are reputed the best of any thing that has been written in the opposition.

I hope by the next opportunity to be able to send you the second Volume of the Federalist. I have the Honor to be my dear Sir with great esteem yr. Sincere Friend &c &c. &c., Ed. Carrington

RC (DLC); endorsed. Enclosures: (1) [Richard Henry Lee], *Observations leading to a fair examination of the System of Government proposed by the late Convention; and to several essential and necessary alterations in it. In a number of letters from the Federal Farmer to the Republican*, New York, 1787 (Sowerby, No. 3020). The ACT, AND SOME OF THE DEBATES of the South Carolina convention were probably those printed in unidentified newspapers that Carrington enclosed.

To C. W. F. Dumas

Sir   Paris June 9. 1788.

I have the honor of inclosing to you a state of such articles of intelligence as I received by the last packet which may be interesting in Europe. I stated them for the publisher of an English and American gazette printed here in English once a week, which begins and deserves to be read. If you think any of these articles worth inserting in the Leyden gazette, you will be so good as to put them into the shape proper for that paper.—I have not thought it well to mention that in the fray at New York Mr. Jay, and Baron Steuben were among those wounded by the stones of the mob. Indeed the details of that affair must be still greatly abridged to bring it within the compass of the Leyden gazette.

I write you none of the news of this country, because if I did you would probably not receive my letter. I shall therefore only add assurances of the esteem & attachment with which I have the honor to be Sir Your most obedient humble servt.,

Th: Jefferson

PrC (DLC). TJ's enclosed STATE OF . . . ARTICLES OF INTELLIGENCE has not been found, but it included the account of the riot in New York that Dumas, who made two copies without suppressing anything, forwarded to Luzac at Leiden and to the Van Staphorsts at Amsterdam (Dumas to TJ, 20 June 1788); it was printed by Luzac in the *Supplément* to the *Gazette de Leide* of 27 June 1788, under the heading: "Extrait d'une Lettre de New-York du 30. Avril," and, like the similar account in TJ to Carmichael, 3 June 1788, was based upon letters from America (such as Madison to TJ 22 Apr. 1788, Carrington to TJ, 24 Apr. 1788) as well as the eyewitness account of John Paradise; like the letter to Carrington, it may also have included a general state of the progress of ratification but which Luzac possibly omitted from this issue of the *Supplément* because in that of 17 June 1788 he had published a similar account (one that Dumas informed Jay was not "his"). TJ's account of the riot as published by Luzac follows: "Il y a dix jours que notre Ville vit éclater dans son sein une Emeute populaire, qui eût pu devenir dangereuse, quoique n'offrant rien d'extraordinaire, ni dans sa cause ni dans ses circonstances.—Les Chirurgiens de New-York avoient eu depuis longtems la coûtume de s'instruire eux-mêmes dans leur Art et de l'enseigner à d'autres aux dépens du respect dû aux cendres des Morts: Ils enlevoient secrettement les Cadavres du Cimétière et les disséquoient dans des Leçons Anatomiques, en présence de leurs Elèves. Cette atteinte, portée à l'inviolabilité des Tombeaux, est un Acte punissable en vertu de la Loi Civile; mais jusqu'à présent il avoit été commis avec tant de dextérité et de circonspection, qu'on ne l'avoit point découvert. Malheureusement, la douleur conduisit l'un de ces jours les pas d'un Citoyen de New-York vers l'endroit, où peu auparavant son Epouse avoit été inhumée en sa présence: A sa grande surprise il apperçut des marques, que la terre avoit été remuée depuis l'enterrement. Aussi-tôt il soupçonna, que le Corps de la Défunte en avoit été enlevé: Il se rendit à l'Ecole Anatomique, trouva moyen d'être admis à la Leçon; et entrant dans la Salle le premier objet, qui s'offrit à ses yeux, ce furent les tristes restes de son Epouse, dépouillée de ses vêtemens, et à moitié disséquée. Voyant ainsi ses soupçons changés en certitude, et plus furieux encore que pénétré de douleur, il courut dans les Ruës, se plaignit à grands cris, et souleva en un clin-d'oeil tout le Petit-Peuple de New-York. Cependant les Chirurgiens, craignant les excès de la foule qui s'attroupoit, cachèrent le Cadavre; et le Peuple ne le trouva point dans la Salle de l'Ecole: Alors il alla faire des perquisitions dans les Maisons des Gens de l'Art, qu'il suspectoit davantage. Ces recherches ne furent pas plus heureuses; et le Corps disséqué avoit disparu. Peut-être l'affaire en seroit restée-là, parce que la multitude ne sçavoit point, à qui s'en prendre comme au vrai Coupable: Mais un des Chirurgiens, moins innocent du fait ou plus craintif que les autres, alla se rendre à la Prison, plus pour y chercher un asyle contre les violences, que sa conscience lui faisoit craindre, que pour subir la vindicte des Loix: L'événement ne répondit pas à son attente. La Populace, ne doutant plus qu'il ne fût le Spoliateur du Cadavre, attaqua la Prison et voulut l'en tirer à toute force: Le Gouverneur crut devoir intervenir, pour sauver ce malheureux: Il fit mettre la Milice Bourgeoise sous les armes: Mais celle-ci, jugeant que la Populace avoit un juste motif de vengeance, refusa d'agir. Dans cette extrêmité, des Citoyens d'un rang supérieur firent réflexion sur le danger, qu'il y auroit dans l'exemple d'abandonner un Accusé, quelque coupable qu'il pût être, à la punition, que voudroit lui infliger la multitude sans Forme ni Procès: Ils s'armèrent donc et investirent la Prison, où l'infortuné Chirurgien s'étoit retiré. La multitude les reçut, en leur envoyant une volée de pierres: Plusieurs d'entre eux furent grièvement blessés, dans ce nombre des Personnes de la plus haute considération. Il ne resta donc à ces Citoyens armés d'autre parti que de faire feu sur les Mutins: Il en fut couché quatre sur le carreau. Dans ces entrefaites un plus grand nombre d'Habitans notables avoient pris les armes, quelques-uns à cheval, pour rétablir le bon-ordre et rendre à la Justice son autorité. Dès qu'ils arrivèrent à l'endroit du Tumulte, le Peuple se dispersa; et c'est ainsi que se termina une affaire, dans laquelle il est difficile de se décider entre deux Partis, l'un agissant d'après l'impulsion d'une raison, qui calcule ses démarches, l'autre entrainé par le mouvement vif et subit d'un ressentiment, que dicte la Nature et qu'avouë l'Humanité.—Aujourd'hui la tranquillité est parfaitement rétablie."

TJ's final paragraph indicates that his letter was sent by post, a fact which may account for a subsequent publication in the *Gazette de Leide* which stirred TJ to write directly to Luzac and which prompted another account (see note to Dumas to TJ, 24 July 1788). The PUBLISHER was one Pissot, bookseller, whose ENGLISH AND AMERICAN GAZETTE, the *Général Advertiser*, had recently begun publication (see TJ to Hopkinson, 6 July 1788).

From John Jay

DR. SIR — Office for foreign Affairs 9th. June 1788

Since the Date of my last, Viz. the 16th. Ult: I have been honored with yours of the 13th. and 16th. March with the Papers which were enclosed with the last. They were immediately communicated to Congress, and the latter referred to a Committee, who not having as yet reported, it is not in my Power to say what Congress may probably think proper to do or order relative to the Subject of it.

You will herewith receive two Letters from Congress to his most Christian Majesty, together with Copies of them for your Information. You will also find enclosed Copies, from No. 1 to 20 inclusive, of Papers respecting the Claims of Francis Cazeau; which it is deemed expedient to transmit in Consequence of the Information communicated in Mr. Shorts Letter to me of the 18th. March last. Copies of an Act of Congress of the 2d. June Instant respecting de la Lande & Fynje, and of an Act of the 3d. Instant forming Kentucky into an independent State, will likewise be enclosed.

By the Newspapers herewith sent you will perceive that South Carolina has adopted the proposed Constitution. The Convention of this State will convene on Tuesday at Poughkeepsie; and as this City and County has elected me one of their Deputies to it, I shall be absent from hence until it rises. There is Reason to believe that the Majority of this Convention are decidedly opposed to the Constitution, so that whether they will venture to reject it, or whether they will adjourn and postpone a Decision on it is uncertain.

Accounts from Virginia and New Hampshire render it probable that those States will adopt it, and if so it may be presumed that North Carolina and even this State will follow the Example. Being exceedingly engaged in dispatching a Variety of Matters preparatory to my going out of Town, I must postpone the Pleasure of writing to Mr. Short by this Opportunity.

With great and sincere Esteem and Regard, I am &c.

JOHN JAY

FC (DNA: PCC, No. 121). Dft (NK-Iselin). Enclosures: (1) Two letters from Congress to Louis XVI, both dated 2 June 1788, in response to two from the king, both dated 30 Sep. 1787, and conveyed to Congress at the public audience held on 26 Feb. 1788 for the reception of Moustier, the first commending La Luzerne for his services as minister and the second accepting Moustier as his successor (the letters from Louis XVI and the responses are printed in JCC, XXXIV, 62, 195-6). (2) The documents numbered 1 to 20 and related to the claim of Francis Cazeau were sent by Jay in consequence of a resolution of Congress of 27 May 1788 directing him to send to TJ "a Copy of such Papers on the files of Congress as respect" Cazeau's claim, but these have not been identified nor the copies sent to TJ located; the claim extended back several years, as indicated in the note to TJ to Jay, 23 May 1788. (3) The ACT OF THE 3D. INSTANT FORMING KENTUCKY INTO AN INDEPENDENT STATE was not enclosed, and Jay was premature in supposing that it could be. What Congress did on 3 June was to appoint, in conformity with a report of the committee of the whole of 2 June 1788, a committee of one member from each state to report an act (the original reading was "a proper act") "for acceding to the independence of the said district of Kentucky and for receiving the same into the Union as a member thereof, in a mode conformable to the Articles of Confederation" (JCC, XXXIV, 194). This committee did not report until 3 July 1788, when John Brown reported a resolution to the effect that the "compact" entered into between Virginia and Kentucky be ratified and confirmed by Congress; that Kentucky be admitted to the Union as "an independent federal member" on 1 Jan. 1789; that it be "stiled the Commonwealth of Kentucky"; that Virginia be released from all federal obligations arising within the district of Kentucky after that date and from such part of her quota of the continental debt as should be apportioned to Kentucky "agreeably to the stipulations of the compact"; and that the district be admitted to representation in Congress from that date provided an accurate census should establish its population at 60,000 inhabitants. Nathan Dane of Massachusetts, seconded by Thomas Tudor Tucker of South Carolina (both of whom were, with Brown, members of the committee), thereupon moved to postpone Brown's resolution in favor of one stipulating that, whereas "nine states had adopted the Constitution . . . lately submitted to conventions of the people; and whereas a new confederacy is formed among the ratifying states and it is highly probable that the state of Virginia including the said district has already become a member of the said Confederacy," an act of Congress "in the present state of the government of the country severing a part of the said state from the other parts . . . and admitting it into the Confederacy formed by the Articles of Confederation and perpetual Union as an independent member" might be attended with dangerous consequences, besides being ineffectual in making the district a "separate member of the federal Union" formed under the new Constitution, Congress therefore deemed it "unadvisable to adopt any further measures for admitting . . . Kentucky into the federal Union as an independent member" but would recommend that this be done as soon as expedient under the new constitution. This substitute motion was carried by the vote of nine states against the unanimous vote of the Virginia delegates (Brown, Carrington, Griffin; JCC, XXXIV, 287-91). (4) A resolution of Congress of 2 June 1788 authorizing the Commissioners of the Treasury to negotiate and settle with De la Lande & Fynje the claims of the United States against that firm (JCC, XXXIV, 193-4).

MY LAST, VIZ. THE 16TH. ULT: In SJL Index there is an asterisk (indicating an undated letter) recording receipt of a letter from Jay between 16 May and the date of the present letter. This may have been an error, for TJ does not appear to have acknowledged such a letter in his communications to Jay. On the other hand, this may have been only a cover for a resolution of Congress of 20 Oct. 1787, approving Jay's report on the letter of Phineas Bond of 2 Oct. 1787 concerning the appointment of George Miller as consul for Great Britain in the states of North Carolina, South Carolina, and Georgia. A copy of this resolution is in DLC: TJ Papers, 34: 5797, and is endorsed by TJ: "recd Sep. 26. [1788?]."

From Burrill Carnes

⟦*Nantes, 10 June 1788.* Recorded in SJL Index, but not found. It is probable that this letter conveyed to TJ the information that Schweighauser & Dobrée would be willing to arbitrate the matter then in negotiation, a proposal on which TJ had asked Carnes to sound the opinion of Dobrée, and which, on receiving Carnes' favorable report, he formally advanced in his letter to Schweighauser & Dobrée of 27 June 1788. See TJ to Jay, 14 Nov. 1788.⟧

From Stephen Cathalan, Jr.

Marseilles, 11 June 1788. Acknowledges TJ's favor of 20 May; exactly as requested, he has forwarded to Logie under blank cover TJ's letter to O'Bryen. He now encloses one from Morocco. Has arranged with Bernard to pay copyist 60ᵗᵗ for doing the meteorological data. Sir John Lambert advised him that TJ had paid £272ᵗᵗ—5s. on Cathalan's account. Will procure plants of best species of olive trees "to the amount of 30 Louis or something more." "Nesmer a gardener of this Place, well known at Paris where he is till the end of this month, will be charged by me for the purchasing and packing them, as well as olives to be sowed." Will send them by Capt. Shewell if he returns. Fears that, "as they can't be got before the end of January . . . they will not be at Charles Town before March or april," too late to be planted. Bernard has promised to help in this.—Ambassadors of Tippoo Sahib arrived yesterday at Toulon; "a noble reception and festivals" have been prepared for them, and "We hope to see them here on their Journey to Paris."—All tobacco remaining in town was sold 15 May to "the Farmers General at 34^{tt} the Virginia and 31^{tt} the Maryland vu et agrée here, by their agent for the qualities, who has inspected here all the hogds. exactly, free of Damaged and carried and wheighed at Cette, while the damaged tobacco will be taken care of and deducted, the freight to Cette and risks at our own charges and payable in Bills on Paris at one month date after delivery there; Tare 15 pr. ct." Some of Cathalan's tobacco has been accepted at 34,^{tt} 32,^{tt} and 31.^{tt} "Would you believe that when arived at Cette the officers of the Manufactory of that Place, have refused of taking it, on pretence of bad quality &c. tho' they have been acquainted of the nature of the Treaty." His father has gone to Sète, and if they continue in their refusal, he will "suit them at Law, and the Farmers together; indeed they are all together bad Sort of People, and they do every thing to disgust adventurers to import of that article in France." Hopes they will show to minister and to TJ what quantity they have bought since beginning of January according to Lambert's letter of 29 Dec.; doubts if they have found enough tobacco in France to meet the requirement of the first four months; would be glad to hear of this from TJ for his guidance; believes that none will come this way from America before Sept.—By letters from Naples he learns that crops there are very poor; for this reason, wheat will not be supplied from Naples, the Adriatic, the coast of Salonica, and the Levant; hence "American wheat will have here good Proffit, because the Crops will be also here very Indifferent; I have advised of it my american friend, it would obtain at least 30^{tt} pr charge of 250℔. paris Wheight; we will want of Larger Supplies. You can advise of it your friends." Encloses copy of arrêt of 22 Feb. relating to duties on importations from fisheries of United States. "Here the oils pays no duties, but when carried at the first place of the Kingdom, they will pay directly the duty of 7^{tt}-10s. pr Cask of ℔. 520, with the 10s. pr. Livre; that has been told to me by the officers of the farms.—But this arret they say ought to be better explained, because the favor of the duty is only on the whale oil and not on the Cod fish oil, which will be" regarded as foreign oil, and it will "be easy for a Merchant to mix such oil with the whale oil, or declare it as such." Up to now, none has been "sent from hence to the Kingdom; they don't know yet, how it will be received at the first bureaux des fermes.—It is easy to you to have this matter well explained by Monsr. de Lambert." Has as yet had no offers for his oil, "on which I will loose great deal, and they pretend it is not feet for our taneries!" Sangrain's agent has no order for purchasing it; Cathalan wrote Sangrain three weeks ago, but has no answer. Caramand arrived yesterday at Aix for parliament. "The news we receive from Turkey are always older than those you receive at Paris." His mother is at Sète.

RC (DLC); 6 p.; endorsed. Enclosures: (1) Arrêt of 22 Feb. 1788; see TJ to Jay, 23 May 1788. (2) Probably O'Bryen to TJ, 2 June 1788.

From William Jones

Bristol. 11th June 1788.

It is now a long time since I had the honour of a letter from your Excellency, nor have I or my Agent in Virginia receivd a shilling in part of the large debt due from the Estate of the late Mr. Wayles.

The ballance of that Account proved, and sent out by Mr. Hanson (including Interest during the War) was £11,158:19:6[1] beside the Account of the African Ship Consignd Wayles & Randolph the ballance of which (with Interest also) was £6016.15.1. You must be sensible how I must suffer by such capital sums being witheld from me, and it is the more cruel, as it was from the unbounded Credit given by F. & J. to Mr. Wayles, that he was enabled to encrease his Estate so much, this he was sensible of and accordingly by his Will directed that our debt should be discharged before the Estate should be divided, from this I have been in hopes that you and the other Gentlemen would have made me some considerable payments long before this time.—That you suffered by the War, I am well convinced, but not so much as I have, still I have been obliged to discharge all the debts I owe here, tho' it has left me with little remaining.—Mr. Hanson writes me that Mr. W's Executors say they shall insist on cutting off the Interest during the War, as also the *Compound Interest* what they mean by that I know not, as no such charge was ever made, unless it is that we apply'd the remittances annually to the discharge of the former Years Interest, and the remainder, if any, to the discharge of the principal. This you must be sensible we have a legal right to do, otherwise a person owes me £1000. and makes me a remittance Yearly of £50, if I do not apply that to the discharge of the Years Interest, but deduct it out of the principal, the Person will still owe me £1000. and Interest the second Year to be chargeable only on £950. Thus in the course of 20 Years the original sum will still be owing and consist entirely of accumulated Interest on which no Interest can be charged. I admit if a Man owes me a Sum on which I charge him Interest, if he makes me no payment I shall add his Yearly Interest to his account but cannot charge him any Interest on the Interest, and this has been our uniform custom in all our Accounts.

From all this as well as from your Excellencys repeated declarations, I hope that you and the other Executors will make me some payments towards the discharge of the very large Sum which is now due to me from that Estate, and the witholding of which I assure you is attended with very great inconvenience and distress to me. Relying on Your Excellencys justice candour and humanity, I remain with great respect, Your Excellencys most Obedient & very Humb. Servt.

Tr (Vi: U.S. Circuit Court, Virginia District); in a clerk's hand; unsigned; salutation lacking; at head of text: "Coppy of a Letter from Wm. Jones to Thos. Jefferson Esqr." Recorded in SJL Index as received from "Jones Wm. (Bristol)." See TJ to Jones, 5 Jan. 1787 and 9 July 1788.

1 A state of the account by Hanson as of 19 Apr. 1783 (Vi: U.S. Circuit Court, Virginia District) shows a total of £11,248 1s. 10½d.

To Motture

[Paris, 11 June 1788]

[. . . in] justice des legalisations faites par leurs ministres [pour les?] etrangers. Nos loix, copiés sur ceux de l'Angleterre, demand[ent] que les actes quelconques soient legalisés par l'apposition du sceau de la ville où ils ont eté passés. Il faut, par example, que les actes faits á Paris soient legalisés par le sceau de la Prevoté de Paris, Monsieur le Prevot des marchands y mettant aussi sa signature. Au lieu donc, Monsieur, de vous envoyer ma legalisation des actes que vous m'avez fait l'honneur de me faire passer, laquelle ne vaudroit rien, je m'empresse de vous indiquer la legalisation seule valable chez nous, et de vous assurer des sentimens d'estime et d'attachement avec lesquels j'ai l'honneur d'etre, Monsieur, votre tres humble et tres obeissant serviteur, TH: JEFFERSON

PrC (ViWC); MS mutilated so that first part of letter is missing and first two lines of text printed here are faded and eaten away by acid in the ink. However, probably no more of the text is lacking than the salutation, the dateline, and perhaps one or two lines of text, a fact proved not only by the subject (see TJ to Cambray, 29 May 1788 for a comparable letter), but also by the notation "M. de la Motture" at the foot of the text, a designation that invariably occurred on the first page of TJ's letters. Date established by entry in SJL Index.

Motture, secretary of legation to the Sardinian ambassador, presumably sent the (missing) ACTES with a covering letter asking that they be authenticated, but no such letter has been found and it is not recorded in SJL Index. TJ evidently returned the documents with this letter.

From Robert Montgomery

SIR Havre 13th. June, 1788.

We arrived here 9th. Inst. and the Vessel for Virginia had sail'd the day before. Which we regret exceedingly, as the Character of the Vessel and Captain was good. We shall remain here Until the last of next week, to be inform'd of the determination of the French Packet.

Mr. Limousin was so kind as to call upon us yesterday, his Opinion is that there will Sail a Packet, in three or four weeks.

You was kind enough to offer us a Letter to your friend here, I shall much esteem the favour of your Sending me a line to Mr. Limousin as there is a probability that we shall remain here some time.

My Mother and Mrs. Montgomery join's me in Kind Compliments to you and Miss Jefferson, not forgeting Mr. Short. I have the Honor to remain very Respectfully Sir Your most Obedt. & very Humbl. Servt., ROBERT MONTGOMERY

RC (ViWC); endorsed.

For a general note on the Montgomerys, see note to Mrs. Montgomery to TJ, 16 May 1788. Thomas Lee Shippen, waiting in Paris in mid-April with John Rutledge, Jr., for "the return of Mr. Jefferson who is on a small excursion up the Rhine," since they did not "think it proper to go, without thanking this excellent man in person for all his civilities," reported to his father that "Mrs. Montgomery is just arrived and is very much indispos'd. I have only seen her once. Her son is married at Dunkirk to a Miss Pigott. The story is much too voluminous to put in a letter, if there were nothing else to put in it, but if you are curious to know it, I dare say her friends will be able to indulge you" (Thomas Lee Shippen to Dr. William Shippen, 15 Apr. 1788; DLC: Shippen Family Papers).

From Thomas Barclay

DEAR SIR Philadelphia 14 June 1788

I Beleive you will be much pleased to hear that I am going to Draw a Very Troublesom family from your Neighborhood. My Stay in America must unavoidably be longer than I intended, and therefore I think it Best that Mrs. Barclay and the Children join me here. I have not settled my accounts with Congress though they have been ready for Inspection for some time. The balance due to me from the public will be I Expect between Seventy and Eighty thousand livres, but there is an Arrangement to be made which requires nine States in Congress, and when so many are Collected, I shall push my affairs before them. All my thoughts are at present Engrossed in endeavors to put an End to my private Engagements. When this is done I shall fall into some line for the support of my family. My last Voyage to Europe has actually Cost me Twenty thousand guineas. I Beleive I have Enabled Mrs. Barclay to discharge her pecuniary obligations. There are others of an other Nature, which neither she nor I will Ever be able to get Clear of. With great Truth I can declare there is not one person on Earth to whom I am so much indebted as I am to you. I have not words to Express my sense of your Kindness therefore I will drop the Subject.—Eight States have adopted the proposed Constitution and it is generally believed Virginia will make the Ninth. With Every sentiment of Gratitude and Esteem I am Dear Sir Your affect. THOS. BARCLAY

RC (DLC); endorsed.

From Thomas Paine

DEAR SIR London June 15. 88

It is difficult to write about an affair while the event of it is depending because prudence restrains a man from giving an anticipated opinion, but as matters at present appear the Construction will take place here.

Perhaps the excess of paper Currency and the wish to find objects for reallizing it, is one of the motives for promoting the plan of the Bridge, but I can raise any sum of money that I please, if a Patent can be obtained for securing the construction. A Company has already offered themselves, but of this and other matters respecting it I will write you more fully by a future opportunity.

M. Quesnay goes from hence tomorrow morning, and I take the opportunity of mentioning just as much as is prudent to do.

Mr. Jones the Mathematical Instrument Maker, has returned me the Papers, he says that a subsequent improvement has taken place on the Air Pump, and by his account there has been a further very extraordinary improvement made at Amsterdam, but the principles he cannot inform me of.

Remember me to the Marquis de la Fayette. Your most Obliged friend & Hble Servant, THOMAS PAINE

RC (DLC); endorsed.

From Louis Joseph de Beaulieu

Beaucaire, 18 June 1788. Wrote to TJ two years ago about his situation as an officer who had fought the whole war, had shed his blood for the common cause, and had expended his small resources. "Mes blessures doivent etre un juste titre d'en recevoir la recompense."

To this TJ responded. Beaulieu appealed to Marbois, but he was ordered to Cap Français and he has received no response from him. Knowing no one in New York, he hopes TJ will accord his protection to "un ancien Serviteur des etats unis."

RC (DLC); in French; 2 p.; endorsed by TJ: "Beaulieu" and at foot of text: "See my letters of May 9. and 24. 1786." SJL Index records this and earlier letters, but no reply by TJ to the present one.

To André Limozin

SIR Paris June 18. 1788.

My last to you was of the 17. Ult. since which I have been honored with yours of May 22. and June 5. By a letter I have received from Messieurs Van Staphorsts at Amsterdam, I find they have shipt my two stoves on board the same vessel with the boxes of 'Meubles &c.' of which I am glad as it will give you trouble once only instead of twice. I find that you have been so kind as to call on Mrs. Montgomery and her son who went to Havre to obtain a passage to America in the ship Sally, but arrived too late. As they will probably stay at Havre till they can know of a certain passage either from thence or from some other port, I beg leave to recommend them to your further notice and civilities. They are wealthy citizens of Philadelphia of very clear circumstances, good connections and personal merit.—The Ambassador from Tippoo-Saïb arrived at Toulon the 10th. inst. where a magnificent reception was prepared for [him]. Notwithstanding the hostile appeara[nce] of the late naval [expedition] there are [circums]tances wh[ich] [lean tow]ards peace between [. . .][1] I believe. It [. . .]den[1] have been [. . .],[2] if she did not fear a bankru[ptcy . . .][3] France in a war during her prese[nt circumstances? I have the hono]r to be with great esteem & attachm[ent Your most obedient hu]mble servant,

TH: JEFFERSON

P.S. Not knowing Mr. Montgomery's address, I take the liberty of putting the enclosed under your cover.

PrC (DLC); MS torn and some words supplied conjecturally. Enclosure: TJ to Montgomery, 18 June 1788.

1 Eight or ten words torn away.
2 Six or eight words torn away.
3 Four or five words torn away.

To Robert Montgomery

SIR Paris June 18. 1788.

Your favor of the 13th. inst. came to hand the night before last. I am sorry to find you have missed your passage. Mr. De Bert had written to me on the subject on the 5th. inst. but by some means or other the letter did not get to my hands till the night of the 9th. which was the day you arrived at Havre. Not knowing your address at Havre I have taken the liberty of putting the present under cover to Monsieur Limozin and asked his attentions and services to you. The news of the day, so far as to be relied on, are the arrival of Tippoo Saïb's embassy at Toulon, and pacific dispositions in the Emperor, who has made overtures of peace to the Turks, as there is good reason to believe. The fermentation in this country is great. At Grenoble some of the military have been wounded, but amidst the exaggerations of two parties which render it so difficult for a neutral person to come at the truth, I rather beleive no person has been killed there. Be so good as to present my respects to the ladies and to accept assurances of the esteem with which I am Sir their & your most obedt. humble servt,

TH: JEFFERSON

PrC (ViWC); endorsed.

To William Frederick Ast, with Enclosure

SIR Paris June 19. 1788.

I have duly received your favor of the 1st. instant, and in answer can only observe that I am not authorized to settle your account, to decide on the balance due to you nor to order paiment in consequence. Mr. Barclay desired me to pay you specific sums, which you will see detailed on the back of the inclosed order which is for two thousand nine hundred and fifty three livres. I state them on the back of the order that when the account of Messrs. Willinck & Van Staphorsts shall be settled, the person settling it may see for what the order was drawn, and not carry it to my private debit. I do the same in all my draughts. I would advise you before you send off the inclosed order, to take a copy of it and send it to Mr. Barclay with your account. He is the person to decide what may be further due to you. I am with great esteem Sir Your most obedient humble servt., TH: JEFFERSON

PrC (DLC). Ast's FAVOR OF THE 1ST. INSTANT is missing and is not recorded in SJL Index.

ENCLOSURE

To Willink & Van Staphorst

GENTLEMEN Paris June 19. 1788.

Be pleased to pay to Mr. William Frederic Ast or order two thousand nine hundred and fifty three livres tournois arrears of salary due to him as clerk to Mr. Barclay Consul general of the United states of America, as stated on the back of this order for the information of the person who may at any time hereafter be appointed to settle your account with the United states. I am gentlemen Your most obedient humble servt, TH: JEFFERSON

Mr. Ast, in whose favor this order is, was Secretary to Mr. Barclay, Consul general of the U. S. of America in France. Mr. Grand having refused to pay draughts for money without the orders of Th: J. Mr. Barclay applied through Th: J. for paiments to Mr. Ast, as follows.[1]

1787. June 31.[2]	Mr. Barclay drew a bill on Th: J. in favour of Mr. Ast for		1800. livres
Aug. 2.	He advised Th: J. that he had drawn on him in favor of Mr. Ast for		495.
Nov. 30.	By letter from New York he desired Th: J. to pay Mr. Ast 25. guineas more		625.
	Subsequent charges by Mr. Ast which Th: J. knows to be just		
	Viz. Trunk to pack books, baling plumbing	15/ sterl.	
	Expence bringing trunk to Paris, cord &c.	12/6	33
			2953. livres

PrC (DLC); both the order on Willink & Van Staphorst and the statement of "specific sums" referred to in the covering letter are pressed on the same sheet, unlike the (missing) RC, which had the statement written on its verso. TJ retained another PrC of the statement only (DLC: TJ Papers, 36: 6131) that is identical with the one printed above, save as indicated below.

[1] In second PrC mentioned above the concluding part of this sentence reads: ". . . Mr. Barclay applied for paiments to Mr. Ast through Th: J."

[2] Thus in MS.

To Bernstorff

Paris June 19. 1788.

I had the honour of addressing Your Excellency by Admiral Paul Jones on the 21st. of January, on the subject of the prizes taken under his command during the late war, and sent into Bergen. I communicated at the same time a copy of the powers which the Congress of the United states of America had been pleased to confide to me therein, having previously shewn the original to the Baron de Blome envoy extraordinary of his majesty the king of Denmark at this court, and I furnished, at the same time to Admiral Paul Jones such authority as I was empowered to delegate for the arrangement of this affair. That officer has transmitted me a copy of your Excellency's letter to him of the 4th. of April, wherein you were pleased to observe that the want of full powers on his part were an invincible obstacle to the definitive discussion of this claim with him, and to express your dispositions to institute a settlement at this place. Always assured of the justice and honor of the court of Denmark, and encouraged by the particular readiness of your Excellency to settle and remove this difficulty from between the two nations, I take the liberty of recalling your attention to it. The place of negociation proposed by your Excellency meets no objection from us, and it removes at the same time that which the want of full powers in Admiral Paul Jones had produced in your mind. These full powers Congress have been pleased to honour me with. The arrangement taken between the person to be charged with your full powers and myself will be final and conclusive.

You are pleased to express a willingness to treat at the same time on the subjects of amity and commerce. The powers formerly communicated on our part, were given to Mr. Adams, Doctr. Franklin and myself for a limited term only. That term is expired, and the other two gentlemen returned to America; so that no person is commissioned at this moment to renew those conferences. I may safely however assure your Excellency that the same friendly dispositions still continue, and the same desire of facilitating and encouraging a commerce between the two nations, which produced the former appointment. But our nation is at this time proposing a change in the organisation of it's government. For this change to be agreed to by all the members of the Union, the new administration chosen and brought into activity, their domestic matters arranged which will require their first attention, their foreign system afterwards decided on and carried into full execution, will require very considerable length of time. To place under the same delay the private claims which I have the honour to present to your Excellency, would be hard on the persons interested: because these claims have no connection with the system of commercial connection which may be established between the two nations, nor with the particular form of our administration. The justice due to them is complete, and the present administration as competent to final settlement as any future one will be, should a future change take place. These individuals have already lingered nine years in expectation of their hard and perillous earnings. Time lessens their numbers continually, disperses their representatives, weakens the evidences of their right, and renders more and more impracticable his majesty's dispositions to repair the private injury to which public circumstances constrained him. These considerations, the just and honorable intentions of your Excellency, and the assurances you give us in your letter that no delay is wished on your part, give me strong hopes that we may speedily obtain that final arrangement which express instructions render it my duty to urge.

I have the honour therefore of agreeing with your Excellency, that the settlement of this matter, formerly begun at Paris, shall be continued there; and to ask that you will be pleased to give powers and instructions for this purpose to such person as you shall think proper, and in such full form as may prevent those delays to which the distance between Copenhagen and Paris might otherwise expose us.

I have the honour to be with sentiments of the most profound respect Your Excellency's most obedient & most humble servant,

TH: JEFFERSON

FC (DLC); in TJ's hand entirely, and endorsed by him: "Danish business"; at foot of first page: "son Excellence M. le Comte de Bernstorff, chevalier de l'ordre de l'elephant, ministre et Secretaire d'etat au departement des affaires etrangeres á Copenhagen." This has every appearance of being intended by TJ as the dispatch to be sent to Bernstorff, of which he took a PrC (DLC), but he evidently changed his mind and had Short prepare a translation in French to be sent instead. The RC of this translation is missing, but the first and third pages of a PrC made from it are in DLC in Short's hand (the fourth page consisted only of the complimentary close and TJ's signature). See Jones to TJ, 8 Apr. 1788, and note to Framery to TJ, 29 Apr. 1788.

To Cambray

SIR

Paris June 19. 1788

The assembly of Carolina requiring that you should renew on oath an account of the paiments you have received, the oath is necessary. There is in this country some officer of justice in every town authorized to administer an oath and make out a proces verbal of [fact]. I know because I once had occasion to take depositions here, and an officer (whose appellation I forgot) administered the oath; and it was certified under the seal of the city that he was the officer qualified to do it. Should you come to Paris before you comply with this formality, I shall with great pleasure attend to it, and advise you how to render it conformable to our laws tho' I apprehend the state of Carolina will not be scrupulous about forms. The oath is the essential. I have the honour to be with great esteem and attachment Sir Your most obedient & most humble servant, TH: JEFFERSON

PrC (DLC); endorsed.

To Thomas Digges

SIR Paris June 19. 1788

I have duly received your favor of May 12. as well as that of the person who desires information on the state of Cotton manufactures in America, and for his interest and safety, I beg leave to address to you the answer to his queries, without naming him.

In general it is impossible that manufactures should succeed in America from the high price of labour. This is occasioned by the great demand of labour for agriculture. A manufacturer going from Europe will turn to labour of other kinds if he find more to be got by it, and he finds some emploiments so profitable that he can soon lay up money enough to buy fifty acres of land, to the culture of which he is irresistably tempted by the independance in which that places him, and the desire of having a wife and family around him. If any manufacture can succeed there, it will be that of cotton. I must observe for his information that this plant grows no where in the United states Northward of the Patowmack, and not in quantity till you get Southward as far as York and James rivers. I know nothing of the manufacture which is said to be set up at Richmond. It must have taken place since 1783. when I left Virginia. In that state, (for it is the only one I am enabled to speak of with certainty) there is no manufacture of wire or of cotton cards; or if any, it is not worth notice. No manufacture of stocking-weaving, consequently none for making the machine: none of cotton cloths of any kind whatever for sale: tho in almost every family some is manufactured for the use of the family, which is always good in quality, and often tolerably fine. In the same way they make excellent haut stockings of cotton. Weaving is in like manner carried on principally in the family way: among the poor, the wife weaves generally, and the rich either have a weaver among their servants or employ their poorer neighbors. Cotton cost in Virginia from 12d. to 15d. sterling the pound before the war. Probably it is a little raised since. Richmond is as good a place for a manufactory as any in that state, and perhaps the best as to it's resources for this business. Cotton clothing is very much the taste of the country. A manufacturer on his landing should apply to the well informed farmers and gentlemen of the country. Their information will be more disinterested than that of merchants, and they can better put him into the way of disposing of his workmen in the cheapest manner till he has time to look about him and decide how and where he will establish himself. Such is the hospitality in that country, and their disposition to assist strangers, that he may boldly go to any good house he sees, and make the enquiry he needs. He will be sure to be kindly received, honestly informed, and accomodated in a hospitable way, without any other introduction than an information who he is, and what are his views. It is not the policy of the government in that country to give any aid to works of any kind. They let things take their natural course, without help or impediment, which is generally the best policy. More particularly as to myself I must add that I h[ave neither] the authority nor the means of assisting any persons in their passage to that country.

I have the honour to be with sentiments of the most perfect respect Sir Your most obedient & most humble servant,

TH: JEFFERSON

PrC (DLC). Enclosed in TJ to Trumbull, 24 July 1788.

To Jan Ingenhousz

DEAR SIR   Paris June 19. 1788.

I am late in answering your favor of Jan. 23. but it has not been possible for me to do it sooner. The letter to Doctor Franklin, after which you enquire, came to my hands on the 9th. of October. I sent it under cover with my own dispatches to our Secretary for foreign affairs at New York, and the Count de Moutier, who went minister from this country to America, was the bearer of it. His arrival in America was not known at Paris the beginning of March, when I set out from hence on a tour through Holland and Germany, and this is the first moment since my return at which I have been able to assure you that your letter is safely arrived at it's destination. Whatever others you may be pleased to have delivered me here for America I will answer for it shall go safely to their address in that country; and those your friends there may send to my care, shall always be delivered, as the present is, to the Count de Merci. Late letters from Doctor Franklin announce his health. We are told he is decided to retire this autumn from all public business. We are at present occupied in some amendments of our federal constitution, which I think will take place, and I have the happiness to inform you that our new republicks thrive well. Accept assurances of the esteem & respect with which I have the honour to be, Dear Sir, your most obedient humble servant,

TH: JEFFERSON

PrC (DLC).

In a notation on Ingenhousz' letter of 23 Jan. 1788, TJ stated that he did not know whether the communication to Franklin had been included in the public dispatches carried by THE COUNT DE MOUTIER or went by the November packet (Vol. 12: 530), a statement at variance with the assertion that Moustier WAS THE BEARER OF IT. TJ may have depended on memory in making the notation; possibly at the time of writing the present letter he referred to his correspondence and found that, more than a week after Moustier left Paris, he acknowledged receipt at Le Havre of the third packet addressed to Jay and placed in his care, proving that at least one packet was made up after TJ had received Ingenhousz' letter on 9 Oct. (Moustier to TJ, 19 Oct. 1787). Another discrepancy in this letter—that Moustier's arrival in America was not known at Paris THE BEGINNING OF MARCH—may also be a lapse of memory; but more probably it was merely the easiest way to avoid making a complicated explanation. TJ barely had time, in the press of business attendant on his sudden departure for Holland, to inform Montmorin of the news of Moustier's safe arrival, and in his haste he forgot to inform his friend Dupont, whose son was with Moustier on the vessel that had been feared lost (TJ to Montmorin, 2 Mch. 1788; TJ to Short, 29 Mch. 1788). The latter omission gave TJ "infinite affliction"; the failure to give Ingenhousz the mere line of information requested in his letter of 23 Jan.—a request amounting to not much more than the notation that TJ made on that letter—appears to be due not so much to the fact that it had NOT BEEN POSSIBLE . . . TO DO IT SOONER as to the fact that TJ may have been a bit annoyed by the scientist's premature anxiety.

To John Rutledge, Jr.

DEAR SIR Paris June 19. 1788.

Having omitted to ask you how I should address letters to you, I am obliged to put the present under cover to Mr. Shippen to the care of his banker at Amsterdam. Inclosed you will receive a letter lately come to my hands, as also such notes as I have been able to scribble very hastily and undigested. I am ashamed of them; but I will pay that price willingly if they may on a single occasion be useful to you. I will at some future moment find time to write the letters for Frankfort, Florence, Milan, Nice and Marseilles, which those notes will point out and lodge them on your route if you will be so good as to keep me always informed how and where I must send letters to you. I would suggest an alteration in the route I had proposed to you: that is, to descend the Danube from Vienna so as to go to Constantinople, and from thence to Naples and up Italy. This must depend on your time, and the information you may be able to get as to the safety with which you may pass thro' the Ottoman territories. It is believed the Emperor is making overtures for peace. Should this take place it would lessen the difficulties of such a tour. In the mean time this gleam of peace is counterbalanced by the warlike preparations of Sweden and Denmark known to be made under the suggestions of the court of London. In this country there is great internal ferment. [Bu]t I am of opinion the new regulations will be maintained. Perhaps the Cour pleniere may be amended in it's composition, and the States general called at an earlier period than was intended. We have no accounts yet of the decision of Maryland, S. Carolina, or Virginia, on the subject of the new confederation. Yet it seems probable they will accept it in the manner Massachusets has done: and I see nothing improbable in the supposition that our new government may be in motion by the beginning of November.—I must press on you, my dear Sir, a very particular attention to the climate and culture of the Olive tree. This is the most interesting plant in existence for S. Carolina and Georgia. You will see in various places that it gives being to whole villages in places where there is not soil enough to subsist a family by the means of any other culture. But consider it as the means of bettering the condition of your slaves in S. Carolina. See in the poorer parts of France and Italy what a number of vegetables are rendered eatable by the aid of a little oil, which would otherwise be useless. Remark very particularly the Northern limits of this tree, and whether it exists by the help of shelter from mountains &c. I know this is the case in France. I wish to know where the Northern limit of this plant crosses the Apennine, where it crosses the Adriatic and Archipelago, and, if possible, what course it takes through Asia. The fig, the dried raisin, the pistache, the date, the caper, are all very interesting objects for your study. Should you not, in your passage through countries where they are cultivated, inform yourself of their hardiness, their culture, the manner of transporting &c. you might hereafter much repent it. Both then, and now I hope, you will excuse me for suggesting them to your attention; not omitting the article of rice also, of which you will see species different from your own. I beg you to make use of me on all possible occasions and in all the ways in which I can serve you, not omitting that of money should any disappointment take place in your own arrangements. Mr. Berard's money was paid to Boyd Ker & co. as you desired. I have the honour to be with very great esteem Dear Sir Your most obedient & most humble servt,

TH: JEFFERSON

PrC (DLC). Enclosures: (1) The LETTER LATELY COME was probably from Rutledge's father, but has not been identified. (2) The NOTES . . . SCRIBBLED VERY HASTILY AND UNDIGESTED were a copy of those enclosed to Shippen in the preceding letter and are printed immediately following.

Jefferson's Hints to Americans Travelling in Europe

Old Louis or Dutch Ducats are the best money to take with you.

Amsterdam to Utrecht. Go in the Track scout on account of the remarkeable pleasantness of the canal. You can have the principal cabin to yourselves for 52 stivers. At Amsterdam I lodged at the Wapping van Amsterdam. I liked the Valet de place they furnished me. He spoke French, and was sensible and well informed,[1] his name was Guillaume or William.

Utrecht. The best tavern Aubelette's. A steeple remarkeable for it's height.

Nimeguen. Chez un Anglois au Place royale. The Belle-vue here is well worth seeing. The Chateau also. At this place you must bribe your horse hirer to put as few horses to your carriage as you think you can travel with. Because with whatever number of horses you arrive at the first post house in Germany, with that they will oblige you to go on through the whole empire. I paid the price of four horses on condition they would put but three to my chariot. On entering the Prussian dominions remark the effect of despotism on the people.

Cleves. The Posthouse. The road most used is by Xanten and Hochstrass. But that by Wesel and Duysberg is perhaps as short. Near Duysberg is the place where Varus and his legions were cut off by the Germans. I could find no body in the village however who could speak any language I spoke, and could not make them understand what I wished to see. I missed my object therefore, tho' I had taken this road on purpose. The Post house is the best tavern.

Dusseldorff. Zwey brukker Hoff. Chez Zimmerman. The best tavern I saw in my whole journey. In the palace is a collection of paintings equal in merit to any thing in the world. That of Dresden is said to be as good. This will be worth repeated examination. On the road from Dusseldorff to Cologne is a chateau of the elector, worth seeing. There is a famous one at Bensberg, which is off the road. I do not know whether it is best to go to it from Dusseldorff or Cologne. Being now in Westphalia take notice of the ham, and the hog of which it is made, as well as the process, price &c.

Cologne. At the Holy ghost. Chez Ingel. A good tavern. This place and it's commerce is to be noted. A good deal is carried on to America. It's quai resembles, for the number of vessels, a sea-port town. From hence the Cologne millstones are sent. But I could not satisfy myself where were the quarries; some saying near Andernach, others at Triers on the Moselle. Here begins the cultivation of the vine: and here too begins the Walnut tree in open fields.

Bonne. The court of England. The palace here is to be seen.

Andernach. A large collection of the Cologne mill stones. Enquire here from whence they are brought, and the price.

Coblentz. The Wildman ou l'Homme sauvage. A very good tavern. The tavern keeper furnished me with the Carte des postes d'Allemagne. I paid his bill without examining it. When I looked into it, after my departure I found he had forgot to insert the Map, and I had no sure opportunity of sending him the price. Pray pay him for me with this apology, and I shall reimburse it with thankfulness. He is very obliging. He accompanied me to a gentleman well acquainted with the vineyards and wines of the Moselle about which I wished to inform myself. He will recollect me from that circumstance.

Here call for Moselle wine, and particularly that of Brownberg and of the Grand Chambellan's crop of 1783. that you may be acquainted with the best quality of Moselle wine. The Elector's palace here is worth visiting, and note the manner in which the rooms are warmed by tubes coming from an oven below. The Chateau over the river to be visited. Remarkeably fine bread here, particularly the roll for breakfast, from which the Philadelphians derive what they call the French roll, which does not exist in France, but has been carried over by the Germans.

From Coblentz to Mayence or Frankfort the post road goes by Nassau, Nastaden, Schwalbach, and Wisbaden. It is as mountainous as the passage of the Alps, and entirely a barren desert. Were I to pass again, I would hire horses to carry me along the Rhine as far as a practicable road is to be found. Then I would embark my carriage on a boat to be drawn by a horse or horses till you pass the cliffs which intercept the land communication. This would be only for a few miles, say half a dozen or a dozen. You will see what I am told are the most picturesque scenes in the world, and which travellers go express to see, and you may be landed at the first village on the North East side of the river after passing the cliffs, and from thence hire horses to Mayence. Stop on the road at the village of Rudesheim, and the Abbaye of Johansberg to examine their vineyards and wines. The latter is the best made on the Rhine without comparison, and is about double the price of the oldest Hoch. That of the year 1775 is the best. I think they charge two florins and a half a bottle for it in the taverns.

Mayence. Hotel de Mayence. Good and reasonable. The ham of Mayence is next to that of Westphalia for celebrity.

Hocheim is a little village on the road to Frankfort. Stop there half an hour to see it's vineyards.

Frankfort. The Rothen house, or Red house chez Monsr. Dick. The son of the Tavern keeper speaks English and French, has resided some time in London, is sensible and obliging. I recommend here also my Valet de place, Arnaud. He is sensible, active, and obliging. He accompanied me to Hocheim, Mayence, Johansberg and Rudesheim.

Messrs. Dick pere et fils, are great wine merchants. Their cellar is worth seeing. You may taste at their tavern genuine Hoch, and of the oldest.

Francfort is a considerable place and worth examining in detail.

Major de Geismer may happen to be here. If he be, present yourselves to him in my name. If you shew him this note, it will serve to ensure you all the attentions you need. He can tell you what there is worth seeing. If he is not here you will find him at Hainau where he is now in garrison, and to which place you should make an excursion. I shall write to him soon and will prepare him for your visit. Near the village of Bergen, which may be seen from the road to Hanau, was fought the battle of Bergen between Marshal Broglio and Prince Ferdinand in 1759.

A quarter of a mile from Hanau is Williamsbath, a seat of the Landgrave of Hesse, well worth visiting.

Manheim. Cour du Palatin. Good tavern. At this place you must propose to make some stay. Buy the pamphlet which mentions the curiosities of the town and country.

The gallery of paintings is more considerable than that of Dusseldorp, but has not so many precious things. The Observatory worth seeing.

Excursion to Kaeferthall to see the plantation of Rhubarb and herd of wild boars.

Excursion to Dossenheim to see the Angora goats. They are in the mountains a few leagues beyond Dossenheim.

Excursion to Heidelberg. The chateau is the most imposing ruin of modern ages. It's situation is the most romantic and the most delightful possible. I should have been glad to have passed days at it. The situation is, on a great scale, what that of Vaucluse is on a small one.

Excursion to Schwetzingen to see the gardens. They are not to be compared to the English gardens, but they are among the best of Germany.

Note. Kaeferthall, Dossenheim, Heidelberg and Schwetzingen may be visited in a circle if more convenient.

Remark the boat bridges and manner of their opening to let vessels pass.

Carlsruh. This place is not noted in the post map, but it is a post station, and well worth staying at a day or two. The posts leading to it are Spire and Craben.

Carlsruh is the seat of the Margrave of Baden, an excellent sovereign if we may judge of him from the appearance of his dominions. The town seems to be only an appendage to his palace.

The tavern is (au Prince hereditaire) good and reasonable. Visit the palace and particularly it's tower. Visit the gardens minutely. You will see in it some deer of an uncommon kind, Angora goats, tamed beavers, and a fine collection of pheasants.

Strasburgh. à l'Esprit. The Cardinal de Rohan's palace to be seen. The steeple of the Cathedral which I believe is the highest in the world, and the handsomest. Go to the very top of it; but let it be the last operation of the day, as you will need a long rest after it.

Koenig, bookseller here has the best shop of classical books I ever saw.

Baskerville's types I think are in this town.

Beaumarchais' editions of Voltaire are printing here.

Here you will take a different rout from mine. The rivers Rhine and Danube will be the best guides in general. You will probably visit the falls of Schaffhausen.

At Ulm, if you find it eligible, you can embark on the Danube and descend it to Vienna.

From Vienna to Trieste. Examine carefully where you first meet with the Olive tree, and be so good as to inform me of it. This is a very interesting enquiry, for South Carolina and Georgia particularly. I have now orders from S. Carolina to send a large quantity of olive trees there, as they propose to endeavour to introduce the culture of that precious tree.

GENERAL OBSERVATIONS

Buy Dutens. Buy beforehand the map of the country you are going into.[2] On arriving at a town, the first thing is to buy the plan of the town, and the book noting it's curiosities. Walk round the ramparts when there are any. Go to the top of a steeple to have a view of the town and it's environs.

When you are doubting whether a thing is worth the trouble of going to see, recollect that you will never again be so near it, that you may repent the not having seen it, but can never repent having seen it. But there is an opposite extreme too. That is, the seeing too much. A judicious selection is to be aimed at, taking care that the indolence of the moment have no influence on the decision. Take care particularly not to let the porters of churches, cabinets &c. lead you thro' all the little details in their possession, which will load the memory with trifles, fatigue the attention and waste that and your time. It is difficult to confine these people to the few objects worth seeing and remembering. They wish for your money, and suppose you give it more willingly the more they detail to you.

When one calls in the taverns for the vin du pays they give you what is natural and unadulterated and cheap: when vin etrangere is called for, it only gives a pretext for charging an extravagant price for an unwholsome stuff, very often of their own brewing.

The people you will naturally see the most of will be tavern keepers, Valets de place, and postillions. These are the hackneyed rascals of every country. Of course they must never be considered when we calculate the national character.

Before entering Italy buy Addison's travels. He visited that country as a classical amateur, and it gives infinite pleasure to apply one's classical reading on the spot. Besides it aids our future recollection of the place.

Buy the Guide pour le voyage d'Italie en poste. The latest edition. It is the post book of Italy.

The theatres, public walks and public markets to be frequented. At these you see the inhabitants from high to low.

HINTS ON EUROPEAN TRAVEL 1788

OBJECTS OF ATTENTION FOR AN AMERICAN

1. Agriculture. Every thing belonging to this art, and whatever has a near relation to[3] it. Useful or agreeable animals which might be transported to America. New species of plants for the farm or garden, according to the climate of the different states.

2. Mechanical arts, so far as they respect things necessary in America, and inconvenient to be transported thither ready made. Such are forges, stonequarries, boats, bridges (very specially) &c. &c.

3. Lighter mechanical arts and manufactures. Some of these will be worth a superficial view. But circumstances rendering it impossible that America should become a manufacturing country during the time of any man now living, it would be a waste of attention to examine these minutely.

4. Gardens. Peculiarly worth the attention of an American, because it is the country of all others where the noblest gardens may be made without expence. We have only to cut out the superabundant plants.

5. Architecture worth great attention. As we double our numbers every 20 years we must double our houses. Besides we build of such perishable materials that one half of our houses must be rebuilt in every space of 20 years. So that in that term, houses are to be built for three fourths of our inhabitants. It is then among the most important arts: and it is desireable to introduce taste into an art which shews so much.

6. Painting, statuary. Too expensive for the state of wealth among us. It would be useless therefore and preposterous for us to endeavor to make ourselves connoisseurs in those arts. They are worth seeing, but not studying.

7. Politics of each country. Well worth studying so far as respects internal affairs. Examine their influence on the happiness of the people: take every possible occasion of entering into the hovels of the labourers, and especially at the moments of their repast, see what they eat, how they are cloathed, whether they are obliged to labour too hard; whether the government or their landlord takes from them an unjust proportion of their labour; on what footing stands the property they call their own, their personal liberty &c.

8. Courts. To be seen as you would see the tower of London or Menagerie of Versailles with their Lions, tygers, hyaenas and other beasts of prey, standing in the same relation to their fellows.

A slight acquaintance with them will suffice to shew you that, under the most imposing exterior, they are the weakest and worst part of mankind. Their manners, could you ape them, would not make you beloved in your own country, nor would they improve it could you introduce them there to the exclusion of that honest simplicity now prevailing in America, and worthy of being cherished.

At Venice Mr. Shippen will of course call on his relation the Countess Barziza.

Here the question must be determined whether you will go down the coast of the Adriatic and come up that of the Mediterranean; or go by Padua and Bologna to Florence and so down the coast of the Mediterranean and back again the same road to Florence.

On your return from Florence, the route will be Pistoia. Lucca. Pisa. Leghorn. Pisa. Lerici. la Spetia. Sesti. Porto Fino.

Nervi. Here you re-enter my tour. The gardens of the Count Durazzo at this place are extremely well worth seeing. They exhibit a very rare mixture of the Utile dulci, and are therefore peculiarly to be attended to by an American. Woburn farm in England is the only thing I ever saw superior, in this point, to Count Durazzo's gardens at Nervi.

Between Nervi and Genoa is a palace worth stopping to see. There is good architecture and a fine prospect. I forget to whom it belongs.

I am not certain that the road from Porto Fino to Genoa leads by Nervi. If it does not, it will be an excursion of only 4. or 5. hours from Genoa.

Genoa. Ste. Marthe is the tavern here, most in the English stile. But le Cerf (more in the French stile) is much the most agreeably situated. The back windows look into the port and sea.

Abundance, abundance to be seen here. The Description des beautés de Genes et de ses environs will give you all the details, but prefer a good selection to seeing the whole.

An excursion to Sestri, Pegli &c. See the Description des beautés de Genes. The Prince Lomellino's gardens at Sestri are the finest I ever saw out of England.

Do not be persuaded to go by water from Genoa to Nice. You will lose a great deal of pleasure which the journey by land will afford you. Take mules therefore at Genoa. Horses are not to be trusted on the precipices you will have to pass. I paid a livre of Piedmont per mile for three mules, and this included the driver's wages but not his etrennes. A livre of Piedmont is a shilling sterling. So it is 4 pence a mile for every mule. From Genoa to Nice is 125 miles, geometrical, viz. to Savona 30 miles, to Albenga 30. Oneglia 20. Ventimiglia 25. Monaco 10. Nice 10.

Noli. Here you see the Aloe on a precipice hanging over the sea. A fishing village of 1200 inhabitants. A miserable tavern, but they can give you good fish viz. Sardines, fresh anchovies &c. and probably strawberries; perhaps too Ortolans. They gave me all these on the 28th. of April.

Albenga. The most detestable gite, called a tavern, that I ever saw in any part of the earth, and the dearest too. A very fine extensive plain here, worth visiting.

Oneglia. } Considerable towns, a mile apart, worth giving
Port Maurice. } a day to. Your mules will be the better for this rest, and yourselves also. But you must have provided for this in your bargain at Genoa, or take mules at Genoa only to Oneglia and there take fresh ones.

St. Remo. The Auberge de la Poste a very good one. The rooms look into a handsome garden, and there are Palm trees under the windows. A half a day might be well given to this place.

Ventimiglia.

Bordighera. Very extensive plantations of Palm tree in the neighborhood of this place.

Menton. Fine Orange plantations.

Monaco. It is a little off the road, but worth going to see.

Nice. I lodged at the Hotel de York. It is a fine English tavern, very agreeably situated, and the mistress a friendly agreeable woman. There is another English hotel of equal reputation. The wine of Nice is remarkeably good. You may pass many days here very agreeably. It is in fact an English colony.

Call here on Monsr. de Sasserno, a merchant of this place and very good man. Be so kind as to present him my compliments and assure him that I retain a due sense of his friendly attentions. I was recommended to him by the Abbé Arnoud. I am persuaded he will give you any local informations you may have occasion for.[4]

Were you to go directly from hence to Marseilles you would see only what is least worth your seeing: while you would miss precious objects which require a circle to be made from this place. I propose the following circuit therefore to terminate at Marseilles.

Cross the Alps at the Col de Tende, hire mules and a carriage at Nice to take you to Limone, which is three days journey. You will probably be obliged to leave your carriage the 2d. or 3d. day; but your mules, in their return, will carry it back to Nice. There are many curious and enchanting objects on this passage. Watch where you lose and where you recover the Olive tree in rising and descending the several successive mountains. Fall down and worship the site of the Chateau di Saorgio, you never saw, nor will ever see such another. This road is probably the greatest work of this kind which ever was executed either in antient or modern times. It did not cost as much as one year's war. Descending the Alps on the other side you will have that view of the plains of the Po, and of Lombardy in general which encouraged the army of Hannibal to surmount the difficulties of their passage. Where they passed is not known at this day: tho' some authors pretend to trace it. Speckled trout on all the road from Nice to Turin.

Turin. Hotel d'Angleterre. Much to be seen here. Excursions to Moncaglieri, Stupanigi, Superga. Ask for Nebiule wine. Monferrat wines worth tasting. Cabinet of antiquities here worth seeing.

Excursion to Milan.

Vercelli. Hotel des trois rois. Wines of Gatina and Salusola. Here is made the best of the Piedmont rice. Mr. Rutledge should examine the husking mills, manner of cleaning, culture, produce, price, and manners of using it.

Novara. Fields of rice all along the road.

Milan. Albergo reale, the best inn. Buy the Nuova guida di Milano which will give you the details of what are to be seen. Add to them the Casa Candiani which I think is built since the publication of the book.

Excursion to Rozzano to see the Parmesan cheese made, and the management of their dairies. See their ice houses. Learn the method of storing snow instead of ice. Ask for Mascarponi, a rich and excellent kind of curd, and enquire how it is made. Go on from Rozzano to the celebrated church of the Chartreux, the richest thing I ever saw. Excursion to hear the echo of Simonetta. The Cathedral of Milan a worthy object of philosophical contemplation, to be placed among the rarest instances of the misuse of money. On viewing the churches of Italy it is evident without calculation that the same expence would have sufficed to throw the Appennines into the Adriatic and thereby render it terra firma from Leghorn to Constantinople. Fine excursion to the Lago di Como &c. Return to Turin.

From Turin cross the Alps at Mount Cenis, and go to Geneva

and Lyons. Not having travelled this road I can say nothing of it.

Lyons. The best tavern is on the Place de Bellecour. A good deal to be seen here. Do not be persuaded to go down by water; it is dangerous and you lose the view of the country.

Vienne. à la Poste. The tavern keeper capable of giving you some account of the antiquities here. The Pretorian palace[5] worth seeing, now used as a church and school room. The Sepulchral pyramid a little way out of the town is handsome.

A league below Vienne, on the opposite side of the river is Cote-rotie.

Tains. Do not go to the tavern at the Post house, the master of which is a most unconscionable rascal. There is another tavern before you get to that which has a better mien. On the hill impending over this village is made the wine called Hermitage, so justly celebrated. Go up to the hermitage on the top of the hill, for the sake of the sublime prospect from thence. Be so good as, for me, to ask the names of the persons whose vineyards produce the Hermitage of the very first quality, how much each makes, at what price it is sold new, and also at what price when fit for use. Be particular as to the white wine, and so obliging as to write me the result.

Montelimart. The country here is delicious.

Pont St. Esprit. To be seen.

Orange. A little before this you see the first olive trees. Some antiquities here.

Avignon. The Post house, a good tavern charmingly situated. It is called l'hotel du Palais royal, and is on the Place de la porte Pio.[6] The Hotel de St. Omer, more frequented, is disagreeably situated.

Taste the vin blanc de Monsieur de Rochegude, resembling Madeira somewhat.

A charming excursion to Vaucluse, about 20. miles from Avignon. It is worth climbing up to the Chateau which they pretend to be Petrarch's.

The tomb of Laura is to be seen in a church of Avignon.

Aix. The hotel St. Jaques a very good one. The bread at this place is equal to any in the world; the oil is also considered as the best. I had here an excellent valet de place named Flamand. A neat town, but little to be seen. Learn here the cultivation of the Olive.

Marseilles. Hotel des princes. Well situated and tolerably good. The hotel de Bourbon et de York at the end of the Course is in rather higher reputation. The commerce of this place is the most remarkeable circumstance. Visit the Chateau on a hill commanding the town, called Notre dame de la Garde. M. Bergasse's wine cellars. Excursion to the Chateau Borelli. Excursion by water to the Chateau d'If. Excursion to Toulon. Examine the cultivation of the Caper at Cuges and Toulon. Go on to Hieres which on account of it's orange groves is worth seeing. From Hieres there is a Chateau de Geans worth going to see. It belongs to the Marquis de Pontoives.

At Marseilles enquire into the cultivation and species of the dried raisin which could not fail to succeed in S. Carolina. Enquire also into the species of figs. Buy here a plan of the Canal of Languedoc in 3. sheets.

St. Remis. The tavern keeper here is an intelligent man. Some fine ruins about ¾ of a mile from this place.

Arles. A fine amphitheatre, and an abundance of Antient sarcophages, in the Champs elysées. Detestable tavern.

Pont du gard. On the road. One of the most superb remains of antiquity.

Nismes. The name of the hotel I lodged at the first time I was there was, I think, le petit Louvre, a very good inn. The 2d. time I lodged at the Luxembourg, not so good. The vin ordinaire here is excellent and costs but 2. or 3. sous a bottle. This is the cheapest place in France to buy silk stockings. The Amphitheatre here, and the Maison quarrée are two of the most superb remains of antiquity which exist. They deserve to be very much studied. The fountain of Nismes is also very curious. There is a book of the curiosities of the place. The cabinet de Segur well worth seeing.

Lunel. Remarkeable for it's fine Muscat wines. It is only a village.

Montpelier. This place is soon seen.

Frontignan. A village remarkeable for it's fine Muscat wine. M. Lambert medecin, will give you any information you desire on your calling on him *de ma part.* He is a very sensible man.

Cette. A place of growing commerce. Remarkeable as the principal seaport for the Canal of Languedoc. Here you may embark to pass through the Etang de Tau.

Agde. Here you may either go in the post boats which pass from hence to Thoulouse in 4. days, or you may hire a small boat and horse and go at your leisure, examining every thing as you go. I paid 12 livres a day for a boat, a horse and driver. I was 9 days going, because I chose to go leisurely.

Bezieres. A wine country. It is here in fact that they make most of the wine exported under the name of Frontignan.

Carcassonne. Near this place (to wit, at la Lande) you see the last olive trees.

Castelnaudari. It takes a day to go and visit the sources of the water which supply the canal of Languedoc, to wit, St. Feriol, Escamaze, Lampy. Here you hire horses and a guide. It gives a day's rest too to your boat horse. Observe that after you leave Cette, you can get no butter for your breakfast through the whole canal, and rarely eatable bread. A stock of butter and biscuit should be laid in at Cette.

Toulouse. Here ends the canal. From hence you may go down the Garonne by water, or go post. You pass near Langon and Sauterne, remarkeable for their fine wines.

Bordeaux. The best tavern is the hotel d'Angleterre, chez Stevens & Jacob. A place of great commerce. There are some remains here of an antient circus of brick. You will before have had occasion to remark the size and texture of the antient brick. The different kinds of their wine to be enquired into, the owners of the best vineyards, prices of the wines of all qualities &c. brandies. Remark the elm trees on the Quai des Chartrons. From Bordeaux to Blaye you may go by water.

Rochefort. The tavern is le Bacha.

Rochelle.

Nantes. I suppose the new tavern by the theater is now ready. If not, you will be puzzled for lodgings. If you chuse to see l'Orient it should be by way of excursion, returning to Nantes and taking the road up the Loire. Observe the subterraneous houses in the banks.

Tours. The tavern is le Faisan. This place worth seeing. An excursion to the chateau of Monsr. de la Sauvagere, at Grillemont 6. leagues from Tours on the road to Bourdeaux, now belonging to M. d'Orçai, to verify the fact of the spontaneous growth of shells related by Voltaire in his Questions Encyclopediques art. Coquilles, and by M. de la Sauvagere in his Recueil de dissertations. This last is the important source of enquiry, and probably you may find the book at Tours, tho' it is very rare.

Chanteloup. Well worth seeing and examining.

Blois. Orleans. Paris.

MS (DLC: Shippen Family Papers); entirely in TJ's hand; consisting of five sheets labelled "No. 1" to "No. 5," the first four of which have 4 p. of text each, and the last only 1 p.; with numerous deletions and interlined phrases and sentences which reflect the hasty composition referred to in the letters to Rutledge and Shippen, 19 June 1788. This is the copy that TJ enclosed in the letter to Shippen. PrC (DLC); with some variations from the MS as indicated in notes below. PrC of Tr (NcD); in the hand of William Short; consists of four sheets labelled "No. 1" to "No. 4," the first three having 4 p. of text each, and the last only 2 p.; Short copied from MS rather than from its PrC, for his text incorporates all of the changes that TJ made in MS after he had executed PrC (see notes below, where this is referred to as Short's PrC to distinguish it from TJ's PrC). This is perhaps the copy that was enclosed in TJ to Rutledge; if so, Short must have retained the original Tr (missing) for his own use when he set out to join Shippen and Rutledge on the Italian portion of their journey.

It is obvious, from the state of TJ's MS and from its arrangement, that these notes were "scribbled very hastily and undigested" (TJ to Rutledge, 19 June 1788) and were designed to overtake the two young men for whom they were especially intended before they departed from Holland. They had delayed their trip in Paris awaiting TJ's return, and, now that he was back, duties were so pressing that he could not find time to forward the promised letters of introduction. But it does not follow from this pressure and this particular purpose that TJ failed to pursue his characteristic course of adapting a special device to a general purpose. These hints were in part a distillation of his two travel journals of 1787 and 1788, both of which remained in his files and, if serving the purpose of Shippen and Rutledge had been his only aim, TJ could have sent the original to one and its press copy to the other without suffering any loss. But midway in the course of this hasty digesting of hints from his own travel journals, TJ began to set down general observations—applicable still to any traveller anywhere—and to make particular generalizations for the American traveller in 18th century Europe. Thus TJ, while doubtless regretting the hasty composition and the general form, could still want to save a copy against the need to serve other young Americans that might seek his advice in future.

TJ's advice to BUY DUTENS . . . BUY ADDISON'S TRAVELS . . . BUY THE GUIDE POUR LE VOYAGE D'ITALIE EN POSTE . . . BUY THE NÜOVA GUIDA DI MILANO was one that he himself had followed. He already possessed, or acquired on his own travels, the following in addition to numbers of other maps, travels, and guide books: Louis Dutens, *Itinéraire des Routes les Plus Fréquentées, ou Journal de Plusieurs Voyages aux Villes Principales de l'Europe, depuis 1768 jusqu'en 1783*, 4th edn., Paris, 1783, giving distances in English miles from one post to another, measured by odometer, the number of hours required to travel between posts, weights, measures, money, post hire, &c. (Sowerby, No. 3869); Joseph Addison, *Remarks on several Parts of Italy, &c. In the Years 1701, 1702, 1703*, London, 1745 (Sowerby, No. 3908); *Guide pour le Voyage d'Italie en Poste*, Turin, 1786 (Sowerby, No. 3907); *Nuova Guida di Milano*, Milan, 1787 (Sowerby, No. 3911).

See Elizabeth Cometti, "Mr. Jefferson Prepares an Itinerary," *Journ. Southern History*, XII (1946), 89-106.

1 Following this TJ wrote, and then deleted: "but I cannot remember."

2 TJ interlined this sentence in MS after he had made his PrC; it is in Short's PrC.

3 This word was omitted by TJ in MS and, of course, it is not in his PrC; Short supplied it in his PrC.

4 This paragraph as added by TJ in MS after he had made his PrC; it is in Short's PrC.

5 TJ first wrote, and then deleted, "an antient temple," interlining the reading as above.

6 This sentence was inserted in MS at foot of the page and keyed to the text by an asterisk; Short's PrC includes it in the text as above.

To Thomas Lee Shippen

DEAR SIR Paris June 19. 1788.

I have been honoured with your favour of May 29. and take the first possible moment of acknowleging it, and of inclosing such notes as my recollection has suggested to me might be of service to you on your route. They have been scribbled so hastily and so unformally that I would not send them, did not a desire of accomodating yourself and Mr. Rutledge get the better of my self love. You will have seen in the Leyden gazette the principal articles of intelligence received from America since you left us, and which I have furnished to Mr. Dumas for that paper. The account of the riot in New York was given me by Mr. Paradise who was there at the time, and who, with his lady, is now here. You may perhaps meet them at Venice. Mr. Jay and Baron Steuben were wounded with stones in that riot. Genl. Washington writes me word he thinks Virginia will accept of the new constitution. It appears to me in fact from all information that it's rejection would drive the states to despair, and bring on events which cannot be foreseen: and that it's adoption is become absolutely necessary. It will be easier to get the assent of 9 states to correct what is wrong in the way pointed out by the constitution itself, than to get 13. to concur in a new convention and another plan of confederation. I therefore sincerely pray that the remaining states may accept it, as Massachusets has done, with standing instructions to their delegates to press for amendments till they are obtained. They cannot fail of being obtained when the delegates of 8 states shall be under such perpetual instructions.—The American newspapers say that the Spaniards have sunk one of our boats in the Missisipi, and we one of theirs by way of reprisal. The silence of my letters on the subject makes me hope it is not true. Be so good as to keep me constantly furnished with your address. I will take the first moment I can to write letters for you to Baron Geismar for Frankfort, Febroni at Florence, the count dal Verme and Clerici at Milan, Sasserno at Nice, Cathalan at Marseilles, which at this it is impossible for me to do. I beg you to make on all occasions all the use of me of which I am susceptible and in any way in which your occasions may require, and to be assured of the sentiments of sincere esteem & attachment with which I have the honour to be, Dear Sir, Your most obedient & most humble servt,

TH: JEFFERSON

RC (DLC: Shippen Family Papers); at foot of first page: "T. Lee Shippen, esq." PrC (DLC). Enclosure: See TJ to Rutledge, this date.

On the articles furnished by TJ to THE LEYDEN GAZETTE, see note to TJ to Dumas, 9 June 1788, and Dumas to TJ, 20 and 24 June 1788. The letters of introduction promised are indicated in the note to TJ to Francis dal Verme and others, 13 July 1788.

To James Swan

Sir Paris June 19. 1788

I have been honoured with your favor of the 7th. inst. That of March 1. came a day or two after I had left this place for Amsterdam, and this is the first moment since my return which very pressing occupations would permit me to take [it] up. I have no question but that the functions of Consul would be discharged by you with all possible attention and propriety. As yet no Convention is settled for the establishment of Consuls. This has prevented their being named hitherto: Mr. Barclay's nomination having been only as an additional qualification to his Commission for settling our accounts in Europe. When a Convention shall have been executed, the nomination of Consuls will be made by Congress themselves. It is a question also worthy your attention whether Honfleur would not be preferable to Havre. It has been for some time in contemplation with this government to render Honfleur a free port, with a particular view to encourage the American commerce to go there, and the reports hitherto made on the subject give it a great preference over Havre.

With respect to the contract for supplies of beef, I wish most ardently those supplies could be brought from America. It would be of great advantage to those states who have at present the fewest objects of exportation. I shall gladly lend any aid I can to the treaties that shall be set on foot for that purpose. Mr. Parker has turned his attention to it, and perhaps you would do well to join in your propositions. I observed to him that there would be a powerful motive opposing itself, in the mind of government, to these propositions. Ireland supplies them at present, and takes in return their wines and brandies. We take returns in money to be laid out in London. The commodities we draw from France are very inconsiderable indeed. An answer to this objection should be prepared. Any proposition which shall be made to government in this head will probably be referred to the officer employed to procure these supplies, and his prospect of personal advantage in the change, will [influ]ence his report.

I have the honour to be with much respect Sir Your most obedient humble servant, Th: Jefferson

PrC (DLC). For a note on Swan's proposed contract for supplies of beef, see Swan to TJ, 7 June and 7, 19 July 1788.

From C. W. F. Dumas

Monsieur La haie 20e. Juin 1788.

Mon premier soin a été, de faire et envoyer deux copies des interessantes nouvelles que V.E. m'a bien voulu transmettre dans sa faveur du 9e. courant, l'une pour la Gazette de Leide, pour laquelle même je n'ai pas trouvé un iota[1] à supprimer; l'autre pour nos Amis d'Amst[erda]m.

L'émeute du bas-peuple à N. York prouve, que par-tout où bonne Justice n'est déniée à personne, elles sont toujours un mal intolérable quelque sensation qui puisse en être le motif.

Puisque je courrois risque de ne pas recevoir les Lettres de Votre Excellence, j'aime mieux, en attendant que tout soit bien, qu'Elle ne me parle que d'Elle-même, de nos Etats, et de leur accord successif et final pour la nouvelle organisation provisionelle.

Je suis avec le plus vrai respect De Votre Excellence le très-humble & très obéissant serviteur C W F Dumas

RC (DLC); endorsed. FC (Dumas Letter Book, Rijksarchief, The Hague; photostats in DLC). Dumas wrote a dispatch to Jay on this same date, but did not follow his usual practice of sending it as an enclosure to his letter to TJ, probably because it contained the following: "Je crois devoir prevenir V.E. que l'Arte. Philade. 23 Av. dans le Suppt. No. 49 de Leide 17 Juin, n'est pas de moi, et que j'ignore d'où il est tiré; mais que j'en ai fourni un autre, que je m'attends de voir paroître la semaine prochaine" (Dumas to Jay, 20 June 1788; same). The article that appeared in the *Supplément* for 17 June 1788 may have been supplied by Mazzei (see note to Dumas to TJ, 30 May 1788), but the other piece that Dumas allowed Jay to think he had furnished was TJ's interessantes nouvelles enclosed in his letter to Dumas, 9 June 1788; see note there. The copy made by Dumas pour nos amis d'Amsterdam was probably sent to Nicolas van Staphorst.

[1] FC reads "une syllabe."

From John Trumbull

Dr. Sir London June 20th 1788

Your letter from Amsterdam reach'd me safe three days ago sent by Van Staphorst to Parker.

I have received the £30 inclos'd. Our account stands thus

Recd. of Mr. Jefferson	
By Mrs. Adams	£ 8. 0. 0.
By Herries & Co.	30. 0. 0.
	£38. 0. 0.

Paid for do.	
Polyplasiasmos picture	£ 1.11. 6.
for Mr. Short at Woodmasons	0. 8. 0.
do. for gloves	0.10. 0
Books at Lackington's	1. 0. 9.
Paper &c. at Woodmason's	0.18. 6.
Stockdale	15. 0. 0.
Cannon the taylor	5.10. 0.
Brown	10. 0. 0.
	£34.18. 9.
Remains in my hands	3. 1. 3
	£38. 0. 0.

The Polyplasiasmos picture will come with those from Brown, which are not quite ready:—The books from Lackington (which are only Polybius—16/6—Addison 2/. and Martial 2/3, the others you mark'd being sold) are at Stockdales as well as the paper &c &c from Woodmason's, to go with his books. He has promis'd so often that they should go the next Diligence that I don't believe his promise of sending them tomorrow. If I find they are not gone I shall beg Mr. Parker to put the paper in his trunk as he goes in two or three days to Paris.

I have extended my inquiries about a Chariot and am satisfied that such a bargain as that of Mrs. Church is not to be found in London. Among all the Repositories and Coachmakers I find nothing that I would think of sending you for less than 70 Guineas. There is one for that price offers at this moment much superior to any other of the same price and I have been half tempted to exceed your Orders:—At any rate I would wish you to renew your orders the first post, and expressly to say how far I must go:—For 50. I really see nothing which I can think of buying:—I was so tempted with what I saw to-day that I call'd on Mr. Lewis Tessier to shew him your letter in which you suppose He will advance the money on my Draft on you at Sight:—But his answer was that of a London Merchant, a direct refusal:—He cannot pay any thing, but on the Draft of Mr. Grand,——and to tell you the truth I am too poor, so that to my poverty and his incivility you owe my obedience to your orders.

I am most gratefully yours Jno. Trumbull

RC (DLC); endorsed.

TJ's LETTER FROM AMSTERDAM was that of 27 Mch. 1788, which had gone astray (see Trumbull to TJ, 6 June 1788). The receipt of Mather BROWN for £10 "paid by the Hand of Mr. Trumbull" for "A Portrait of Mr. Adams," dated 2 July 1788, endorsed by Trumbull, is in MHi. LEWIS TESSIER, London banker, was the one to whom John Adams had written two years earlier, saying that TJ, coming away from Paris suddenly, had forgotten to obtain a letter of credit from Grand; that he would need only small sums; that Adams did not doubt Tessier would furnish these on TJ's draft; and that TJ would present the letter in which Adams made himself responsible (Adams to Tessier, 17 Mch. 1786; MHi: AMT). On the occasion when Adams spoke, Tessier furnished TJ with much more than small sums—indeed, in all about four times as much as Trumbull required (Account Book, Mch.-Apr. 1786).

From Etienne Clavière

rue Grange aux belles derriere l'opéra
Paris le 21 Juin 1788

MONSIEUR L'AMBASSADEUR

Je fais travailler aux comptes que je dois mettre sous vos yeux avant de les envoyer à mon ami de Warville; j'ai été retardé par mille Causes involontaires. Mes chiffres sont prettes, il ne faut plus que les ranger. Mandez moi, s. v. p. s'il partira bientot un Paquetbot pour New Yorck afin que je connoisse le tems que j'ai devant moi.

J'ay l'honneur d'etre avec une haute estime Monsieur l'Ambassadeur Votre très humble et très obeïssant serviteur

E CLAVIERE

RC (DLC); endorsed.

To — —

Paris June 22. 1788.

DEAR SIR

I take the liberty of introducing to your acquaintance the Marquis de Valadie, bearer of this letter, a gentleman of distinguished family in this country. A genuine love of liberty, a desire of freeing himself from the shackles which the laws and manners of Europe impose, and a predilection for our country, tempt him to pay it a visit. You will find him well informed, sensible, honest and plain as a republican, all of which are titles to your notice and civilities to which give me leave to add the recommendations of him who has the honor to be with great esteem & respect Dr. Sir Your most obedt. & most humble servt,

TH: JEFFERSON

PrC (DLC).

From Chamillard

pavillon poyré Rue Satory
Monsieur Versailles 22 juin 1788.

J'ay raporté à M. Le Comte de Montmorin, ainsy qu'à M. le Comte de la Luzerne, les dispositions où vous Etiés de suivre auprès de M. le Baron de Blome les Intérêts des Equipages des deux frégates que les Danois ont rendu au Gouvernement Anglois, et le dezir que vous aviéz que le ministere françois secondât vos demarches à cêt égard. Ces deux Ministres m'ont autorizé, à agir de concêrt avec vous, Monsieur, dans cêtte negociation; J'attendray donc que vous veuilliéz bien me faire sçavoir le jour et le moment qui vous conviendront, pour me rendre a Paris, à l'effêt de concerter une Entrevüe avec M. le Baron de Blome, d'après ce que vous auréz résolu à ce Sujêt.

Je suis avec Respect, Monsieur, Votre tres humble et tres obeissant Serviteur CHAMILLARD
Lieutenant-Colonel d'Infanterie

RC (MoSHi); endorsed.

From André Limozin

Le Havre, 22 June 1788. Articles mentioned in TJ's of 18 June not yet arrived from Amsterdam; Limozin has delivered TJ's letter to Montgomery and called on Mrs. Montgomery. "I have taken the freedom to present her My Son and to invite her to take tomorrow at my house with her Children a Family's Dinner." She has accepted, and Limozin regrets he cannot be of the company "because some very important business which cant be postponed on account of the Season (St. Johns Time) oblige me to sett of for one of my Country Estates which the Teneur of the Manner is leaving." Will invite her again and ask her to "look upon my house as if it was her own . . . since she is worthy of your Excellency's recommendation." Grateful for TJ's "kind informations" and asks their continuance.

RC (MHi); endorsed.

From John Rutledge, Jr.

Dr Sir Hague June 22d. 1788.

I trust you will have received, before this reac[h]es you, my letter from Amsterdam, dated, if I mistake not, the 13th. inst.;

since that time we have not had any thing new in this Country. The attentions of People have been very much turned towards france and engaged in contemplating the issue of her actual Situation. The account of the late revolt in Dauphiny has occasioned very great joy in this place where british influence greatly prevails. It is, I think, very much to be lamented that matters have been carried to such extremities. It will do much harm without any possibility of doing good. The form of the french government seems accomodated to the genius of the french People. The ebullitions of Liberty therefore can only be temporary: and may disturb but cannot direct the Government. Inclosed your Excellency will receive a Letter which some days past came under cover to me. My letters, dated the 7th. of April, mention the Indians in Georgia being very troublesome. They have encroached upon the Lands of the Georgians, plundered many Inhabitants and committed Murders not far from Savanna. The Planters have all erected Forts on their Estates and armed their Negroes for defending them. The Governor has offered a reward for every Indian head. The Assembly have raised a body of regular Troops, and, like antient Carthage, marched them into the their Enemy's Country in order to draw them from their own. The troops were raised on very good terms. They are to be paid, as the Romans were, with conquered lands. Be pleased to make my Compliments to Mr. Short and believe me to be dr Sir with the most lively Sentiments of friendship and regard, Your very much obliged friend & hble Servt.

J. RUTLEDGE Junior

I have this moment received Letters from Charleston dated April 17th. They mention that the election came on the preceeding day for Delegates to the Convention, that they had not received returns from the Country but that in the City and the neighbouring Districts the Elections had been made with very great judgement and that it was very certain that the new Constitution will be accepted.

RC (DLC); endorsed; addressed. The enclosure has not been identified, but it was almost certainly the letter from John Rutledge, Sr. to TJ, 6 Apr. 1788, which was written at the same time that Rutledge wrote his son advising him to accept TJ's advice about his European tour.

Rutledge's LETTER FROM AMSTERDAM has not been found and is not recorded in SJL Index.

To Nicolas & Jacob van Staphorst

GENTLEMEN Paris June 22. 1788.

I have duly received your favor of the 22d. May and will take care of your indemnification for the 100 guineas furnished Admiral Paul Jones, should he not otherwise reimburse you which I would beg you to press on him, as may be convenient and decent. I note the disbursement of ƒ18 on account of the stoves from Cologne. As there are already several small advances for which I have troubled you, and one or two others will occur soon, I would prefer including them in one order, so as to avoid multiplying little debets in your account against the U.S. If you approve of this, I would ask you to state them in a separate account against me, and when I shall have drawn an order in favor of Mr. Van Damme for books, which I expect to do soon, I will desire you to sum all my little articles together, and carry them in a single one to the debet of the U.S.

Since mine of May 28. on the subject of the bill of exchange for £30. miscarried,[1] Mr. Trumbull has been to Sr. Robert Herreis's where they informed him, that having sought him in vain, they had returned you the letter. If you will be so good as either to send it back to John Trumbull No. 2. North street, Rathbone place London, or to send me a duplicate of the bill of exchange, I will be obliged to you, and have the honour to be with sincere esteem & attachment Gentlemen your most obedt. humble servt,

TH: JEFFERSON

PrC (DLC).

[1] TJ may have intended to write ". . . the bill of exchange for £30. that miscarried"; his ambiguous remark above is clarified by the fact that MISCARRIED applied not to TJ's letter of 28 May 1788, but to the bill of exchange, which had been enclosed in TJ to Trumbull, 27 Mch. 1788 (see note there).

From M. Amoureux

L'Orient, 23 June 1788. Only received on 4 June the letter John Paul Jones wrote him from Copenhagen 8 April last, directing him to sell immediately and at the best price some merchandise belonging to him and remaining in Amoureux' hands, and to remit the proceeds to TJ. Has just succeeded in selling a good part of this merchandise, "mais au terme de six mois, parcequ'il y avoit beaucoup d'objets qui ne sont propres que pour l'hiver." Nevertheless, since by his agreement with Jones he is answerable for the credit of the buyers, he can, if desired, remit at once.—Offers TJ his "Services les plus devoués"; he is always gratified to be useful to those interested in the prosperity of the United States, "ou j'ai de bons et respectables amis, et dont le sort ne peut jamais me devenir indifferent."—It has been rumored here for several days that the franchise enjoyed by this port since 1784 would before long be transferred to Port Louis. Since this could not take place without TJ's knowing it in advance, he would be very grateful if, in his answer, TJ would inform him whether this rumor "est réellement fondé"; it is a point very interesting to those having relations with the United States.

RC (DLC). PORT LOUIS: A small port just below L'Orient on the Bay of Biscay.

From Edward Bancroft

Charlotte Street, Rathbone Place
June 23d. 1788.

DEAR SIR

During the last twelve months I have from time to time, constantly flattered myself with the hope of shortly seeing you in Paris, and my journey has been as constantly retarded; I think however that it certainly will take place in the month of August next. But in the mean time I beg leave to introduce your Notice the Bearer Mr. Dobyn an Irish Gentleman who is very well recommended to me; and who, having by an exercise of Friendship exposed himself to a considerable loss has come to the resolution of selling his Paternal Estate in Ireland and removing to America, with a considerable number of his Tenants whose attachment will lead them to accompany him thither. He wishes however to obtain such advice and information as will enable him to prosecute this plan in the most advantageous manner and I have advised him to visit Paris, and address himself to you, as being better qualified than any other person, to direct his future steps, which your distinguished benevolence will I am sure incline you to do. And I doubt not but he will prove himself worthy of the favours you may bestow on him, and which I venture to sollicit in his behalf.

Mr. Paradise informs me of his being with you and that no words can sufficiently express the kindness which you have exercised to him.

I shall have occasion in two or three days to trouble you with a few Queries from the society for abolishing slavery, which your generous Philanthropy will doubtless engage you to answer.

The Easterly winds which have long prevailed have prevented all Arrivals from America for several weeks so that we have no news from thence so late as you must have received by the French Packet.

If there be any service which I can possibly render you here, I beg you will give me an opportunty of manifesting my sense of the many Favours you have conferred on me, and the respectful Attachment with which I have the honor to be Dear Sir Your most faithful and most Devoted Humble Servant

EDWD. BANCROFT

RC (DLC); endorsed.

From Leray de Chaumont

MONSIEUR Passi ce 23 Juin 1788

J'ai l'honneur de remettre à votre Excellence, copie du compte des déboursés des Sieurs Gourlade & Moylan pour la frégate l'aliance en 1780. Votre Excellence verra au bas de cette copie qu'il me fut donné des ordres pour pourvoir à cette avance, et que vos Etats en doivent Compte à la Marine de France. Le Ministre avait décidé antérieurement que toutes les dépenses de relache de cette frégate ne pouvaient être a la charge de la Marine du Roi; mais votre prédécesseur M. Franklin se trouvant alors très a l'étroit pour les fonds, je fis des réprésentations aux quelles on eut égard. Tant que j'ai été à même, Monsieur, de rendre les Services les plus essentiels à votre pais, je l'ai fait avec un zele qui ne s'est pas démenti. J'y ai absorbé toute ma fortune qui était immense, et je suis réduit a en recouvrer les débris pour satisfaire mes créanciers. Si les Etats unis m'eussent seulement payé avec exactitude les rentes de leurs billets de Loan office, ils m'auraient épargné des frais qui me ruinent journellement; mais depuis 1777. que je leur ai fait des prêts, je suis encore a toucher un Sol des interêts. Voila mon Etat. Si votre Excellence veut Savoir quels sont les services que j'ai rendus à Sa Nation, c'est en lui exposant, que j'ai envoyé des vaisseaux chargés de tout ce qui pouvait être le plus utile aux armées et aux peuples des Etats unis. Un de mes Capitaines, le Chevalier Roche, commandant ma frégate l'union, parut à Charlestown et y devança M. le Marquis de la Fayette. Ce même Capitaine repassa en Europe dans la fregate qui apportait M. et Made. Jay. Sans lui cette frégate serait périe en Mer et M. Gerard qui y était pourrait l'attester. J'ai fait passer par voie de la Martinique aux Etats unis des quantités de poudres de guerre dont ils avaient grand besoin, et ce fut M. Rt. Morice qui les reçut. J'ai envoyé quantité de batimens chargés de sel avec ordre de le distribuer a bas prix, et à ce sujet mes intentions ne furent pas remplies; parce qu'un de ceux à qui ils ont été adressés ne s'est occupé que de son interêt particulier, en vendant ce Sel fort cher au peuple: j'en fus doublement faché. Des Corsaires américains avaient fait des prises sur les Anglais et les amenerent à Nantes avant que nous fussions déclarés en faveur de la Nation américaine; on rendit ces prises aux anglais. Alors, je fis des réclamations et le Gouvernement m'autorisa a en rendre la valeur aux propriétaires de ces Corsaires, ce que j'exécutai au Sçu de toute l'Amérique. Je ne bornai pas cette rentrée a la rendre en papier monnoie: c'est en argent dur que je la fis payer. Si je m'étais permis de profiter des circonstances, j'aurais gagné plus d'un milion sur cet objet. Enfin, Monsieur, tout ce que j'ai envoyé pour secourir l'Amérique a été converti en papier monnoie et en billets de Loan-office. Si j'eus fait négocier ces papiers, j'en eus augmenté le discrédit et j'aurais peut être rendu aux Anglais le plus grand service; mais au contraire, j'ai donné des ordres dans le tems de le garder, parceque mes espérances étaient fondées sur vos succès et sur la reconnaissance de votre païs. Je ne mets pas, Monsieur, au nombre des services que j'ai rendus, l'avantage d'avoir reçu dans mon asile tous les députés des Etats-unis, le plaisir que j'en ai ressenti a été ma récompense, d'autant que l'opinion que j'ai méritée inspirait une grande confiance à tous ceux qui avaient a traiter avec eux.

Je n'entre dans ces détails avec votre Excellence, que parce que le hazard m'en offre l'occasion. Je désirerais cependant, Monsieur, que mon fils qui est à Philadelphie, fut traité pour mes affaires en proportion des services par moi rendus; et alors je le reverrai consolé de tous les malheurs qui ont accablé ma famille.

J'ai l'honneur d'être avec respect Monsieur Votre très humble et très obeissant Serviteur LERAY DE CHAUMONT

RC (MoSHi); endorsed. Enclosure not found.

From Maria Cosway

London 23 June

I will write two words, to show you I can write *if I please* but as I dont please I shall say no More, as I wait to hear from you. If my silence is of consequence, you will easily be sensible that yours is Very much so with me, but [I] must have patience, oh I break my first intention.

So addio M. Cosway

Should I have wrote so much if Mr. Trumbull had not Come to ask me to send a letter by a person who is going to see you? Ask yourself if you deserve it? Or if it is not only a spontanous inclination, or irrestibility to this temptation, tho' you neglect me, I force myself to your recolection.

RC (ViU); endorsed: "Cosway Maria."

From André Limozin

Le Havre, 25 June 1788. Wrote on 22d. Had hoped to enjoy company of Mrs. Montgomery, "but . . . a misfortunate illness prevented her from performing her promise." Her son kindly accepted his son's pressing invitation. "I would not have your Excellency to be too uneasy about the State of health of these Ladies, for My son assures me that they were at the Play the very same day in the Evening."—An American ship, *The Mary*, Capt. Huston "arrived last night from Norfolk. As she will go back to America Mrs. Montgomery will I suppose take her passage with her family on board of her." The enclosed came on her for TJ. [*In postscript*:] New York packet brought for TJ "a very small Package . . . . I am afraid it is Smoaking Tobacco." It is sealed; he dares not open it without TJ's permission or forward it without knowing contents; and he desires TJ's orders on it.—Mr. Barlow of Connecticut asks him to let TJ know that "he is arrived here, that he hath great many dispatches for your Excellency which he expects to deliver you in few days."

RC (MHi); endorsed. The enclosed letter was almost certainly that from Martin Osler, French consul at Norfolk, to TJ, 10 Mch. 1788 (missing, but see TJ to Guiraud & Portas, 28 June 1788), which TJ received at the same time he received the present letter.

From John Trumbull

Dr. Sir London 25th. June 1788.

By the Diligence which leaves this to-morrow morning you will receive from Stockdale a Box with books, and the paper &c. from Woodmason's. I said in a letter of last friday that the paper would come with Mr. Parker, but this conveyance will reach you probably as soon:—In that letter I told you of a Carriage for £70 which had attracted my wishes, because its goodness could be depended upon: in fact it is as good as new:—The Cranes and Springs have been us'd enough to prove them, the wood of the carriage is entirely new, and the Body very little the worse for service.

It is painting a colour I have desir'd and this with new Harness Cloth &c. is included in the price, and will be ready in 6 or 8 days: —When if I receive your Orders, it is your's; if not it will remain for any other buyer.

I likewise gave you our account. I enclose a line from Mrs. Cosway. Mrs. Church is at Down place, very well. I am your

JNO. TRUMBULL

RC (DLC); endorsed. Enclosure: Maria Cosway to TJ, 23 June 1788.

From Van Damme

Amsterdam
Ce 25 Juin 1788.

MONSIEUR!

Je Demande Pardon par Retardement des Expedition des Livres, Jusque Adjourd'ui Acheté de Vostre Comte. Ce est le Cause par le Petit Partie, Trouvable dans les premiere Tems de Vostre Voÿage a Paris.

J'ai le Honneur de a Vous Expedier a Vostre Addresse, les Livres selon les Facture incluse, dans une petit Caisse, Marqué **T.I. Libri** dans bon Estat. Consiste, Ensemble ƒ148.11: L'Argent Courant de Hollande.

Le Premiers sont selon Vostre Note, Et Trouvé Chez De Búre.

Le Seconde Separation, sont selon Vostre Note, Et Trouve dans L'Catalogue 2. Vol: Octavo, Et qui est en Vente Publique, *Septembre* prochain. L'Catalogue est ici incluse dans L'Caisse.

Le Troisieme Separation, sont les Livres, Acheté par Vous meme, dans nostre Maison, Et quelques autre Livres de Vostre Part.

En L'Esperanse de Vostre Nouvelles, en Regarde autre Commissions des Livres, je suis dans tout les occasions, Tres Parfaitement, Monsieur, Vostre Tres Humble Et Tres Obeist. Serviteur,

PR. VAN DAMME

P.S. Vostre autre Commissions que reste, je Expedie d'icelle, dans peu de Tems.

ENCLOSURE

Aschetė pour le Comte de Mr. Jefferson

1788.	De Bure No. 4771. Arrianus. Graec. et Lat. Amst: 1757. 8vo.	7–10–
	4856. Appianus Alexandrinus. Graec. et Lat. 1670. 2 Vol. 8vo.	12– :–
	4909. Savillii, in Tacitum. Elzevir. 1649. 12°.	3–15–
	2572. Aristophanes. Graec. et Lat. 1670. 16°.	5–10–
	4107. Alciphronis, Epistolae. Graec. et Lat. Lipsiae. 1715. 8vo.	5–10–
	4122. Symmachi, Epistolae. Lugd. Bat: 1653. 12°.	1–12–
	1788. Hippocratis, Opera Omnia. Graec. et Lat. Lugd. Bat. 1665. 2 Vol. Exempl. Hitidiss. 8vo.	34– :–
	1804. Corn. Celsus. Lugduni Tornaesius. 16°.	3–10–
Apicius Coelius, de Opsoniis. Etc. Amst: 1709. 8vo.		4–10–
Ant. van Dale, Dissertationes super Aristea. Amst. 1705. 4to.		7–10–
Dictionarÿ. English and Dutch. 2 Vol. 4to.		14–10–
Frontini, Strategematum. Lugd. Bat. 1675. 12°.		2–10–
Gellii, Noctes Atticae. Elzevir. 12°.		4–16–
A. Grotii, Mare Librum. Lugd. Bat. Elzevir. 1633. 16°.		2–10–
S. Seldeni, Mare Clausum. Elzevir. 1636. 16°.		2–12–
Th. Hobbes, De Cive. Elzevir. 1647. 12°.		2–10–
Hippocratis, Aphorismi. 1732. Et 1748. Graec. et Lat. Et un autre Livre Grec. 16°.		4–10–
Strada. De Bello Belgico. Romae. 1648. 2 Vol. 12°.		4–10–
Aurel: Prudentius. Elzevier. 1667. 12°.		7–10–
B. Brissonius, De Ritu Nuptiarum. Lugd. Bat. 1641. 12°.		3–10–
Sulpitius Serenus. Lugd. Bat. Elzevir. 1605. 12°.		4–10–
J. H. Meibomii, De Flagrorum Usu in Re Veneria. 1770. 16°.		2–10–
		141–15–
	Caisse, Emballage, Expedition, Etc.	4– 6–
		146– 1–
	Catalogus Librorum. 2 Vol. 8vo.	2–10–
		148–11–

RC (DLC); endorsed. Enclosure (same).

From John Brown Cutting

DEAR SIR London 26 June 1788

Since the departure of our late Minister from this court I have been detained here merely by private engagements. I have not however abstain'd from scrutinizing some portion of the public measures of this Country, especially that section of them during the last part of the present session of parliament which includes, a few among their many, views upon the United States. For assuming the liberty to disclose to you a hint or two of this sort I do not feel the necessity of apology. Far from imagining I shall incur rebuke as for officiousness, I am confident you will accept the motive as a justification for the zeal. I trust that whenever even the most inconspicuous citizen of our country conceives aught detrimental to its great interests meditated by foreigners, which by communicating to the higher official personages of the union, he may possibly contribute to frustrate he will always deem it his duty to approach them, nor hesitate to speak where silence might misbecome a republican.

Concerning some of the purposes for which Ministry here have calculated the british southern whale fishery bill (a copy whereof Mr. Parker will give you with this letter) I have already written to Mr. Adams. On the same topics I have now the honour to address you. [The public objects manifestly intended to be accomplish'd by its operation are important. Among the principal ones which this Government mean to effect I select the following: 1. To distance all competition in the fisheries, monopolize the oyl trade, and nourish a national nursery for seamen. 2. To defeat both as to France and to America that mass of growing benefits which might otherwise result from your Edict of Decr. 1787. 3. To extirpate a (suppositious) projected settlement of american whale fishermen in France. 4. Toestablish such a settlement on the coast of Scotland. (Vid. Bufoy's Speech.) 5. To check the growth or perhaps suffocate the germ of our rising marine in the west. 6. To diminish the maritime force of France, or hinder its augmentation. To these public may be superadded the private views of anglo-american merchants, some of whom expect a liberal remittance from Nantucket as an immediate adjunct of the plan, beside the consequent advantages from the conversion of forty foreign bottoms into domestic ones, and fixing in Britain forever the best of human implements for executing and extending so productive a commerce.

These private purposes stimulated the first application to government for this new bill to depopulate Nantucket, and impoverish our best national resource. Lord Hawksbury (late Mr. Jenkinson), who succeeds to that secret influence with the sovereign which his patron the Earl of Bute bequeathed to him on his political demise, encouraged and brought forward the Scheme from its earliest suggestion in March, soon after that indiscreet promulgation of the French edict of Decr. He drew the heads of the act himself. From the board of trade whereof he is president it came recommended. It was adopted and was only approved by that junto of the privy council who agree upon the substance of all great acts ere they assume even an embrio-shape in the Commons. Being hostile to America it met the applause of the Monarch. It was hurried through a Committee by Mr. Grenville, the Subconductor of Hawksbury's commercial Systems, and from that moment to the last form of its enaction, discussion at large of its merits was evaded, and all disclosure of the chief objects it is intended to effectuate, was studiously stifled and prevented.

If the plan prospers it is to be extended occasionally whereby a palsy may be infused into the stoutest sinew of the United States; while Britain gains an accession of strength. By the complete success of the first experiment only she obtains nearly five hundred of the most vigorous skilful and undaunted seamen ever seen on the face of the Ocean.

It is for France to consider how far her most essential interests are involved with ours in this business. Surely her government must discern that at this moment much of the oyl which she is consuming flows in from hence, while the british merchant after payment of all her burthens on the article, receives a handsome profit from the french consumer. Nor does the extent of the mischief here terminate—Since a rival power in the mode of gathering this same oyl not only sustains and nourishes a vast marine but eventually from the pockets of the french people swells the stream of public revenue!][1]

I must not now enlarge upon these subjects, as Mr. Parker waits for this letter.

Dr. Shippen informs me, dating May 12th that Maryland has adopted the new national government, and that South Carolina was expected to ratify the same in about ten days from the period of his thus announcing it. There is in London a very accurate list of the names of the State Convention, which I imagine is now assembled in Virginia, marked by a member of that body, with the supposed determination of each individual on the great question. The majority in favour of adopting is but small, according to this statement. Among those who are *for* the measure Governor Randolph it seems has marked his own name in the margin. I have not seen this paper; but the account I have reason to believe genuine.

I am with perfect respect and esteem Your Excellency's Most Obedt. Servt.
JOHN BROWN CUTTING

RC (DLC); endorsed. PrC of Extract (DLC); bearing caption "Letter from a person in London dated June 26. 1788."; see note below.

For a note on the BRITISH SOUTHERN WHALE FISHERY BILL, see TJ to Montmorin, at end of July 1788. See also Cutting to TJ, 17 Oct. 1788 and TJ's *Observations on the Whale-Fishery*, under 19 Nov. 1788. On BUFOY'S SPEECH, see Cutting to TJ, 7 Oct. 1788.

[1] Brackets in MS. The matter enclosed in brackets represents the whole of the text of the Extract. This Extract (all save the final paragraph of which is printed in Mass. Hist. Soc., Procs., 2d ser., XVII [1903], p. 501-2) was evidently prepared by TJ for enclosing in the undated letter to Montmorin that TJ wrote ca. July 1788 but never sent (see at end of July 1788).

To Ferdinand Grand

SIR
Paris June 26. 1788.

Mr. Paradise having sent the letter of advice relative to his bill of exchange to one of his friends in London to negotiate, it will not be necessary for you to trouble yourself till we know the result. Should he not receive the money therein, I will replace at the end of the month the 2400.tt you have been so kind as to advance him.

I had desired Mr. John Trumbull, if he met with a very good second hand carriage to be bought cheap in London, to buy it for me. And as it was incertain whether one might occur, I did not think it worth while to send him the money, supposing he might either obtain a fortnight's credit, or if he could not, I desired him to ask of Mr. Teissier to furnish the money for which I undertook to send him your bill by the return of the same post. Mr. Trumbull lately met with a carriage to his mind, but as it could only be bought for ready money, he could not purchase it for me. I suppose it was on that occasion he applied to Mr. Teissier. As it is possible he may find some other occasion of making the purchase advantageously for me, and you are so kind as to offer me your services herein, I will ask the favor of you to give me a letter of credit on Mr. Teissier in the name of Mr. John Trumbull for such sum not exceeding eighty guineas as he may apply for. I do not ask a bill of exchange, because it is incertain whether the money will be called for at all, and because in the mean time it would be lying dead. In the case of the bill of exchange of somewhere about 100 guineas you were once so kind as to furnish me with to purchase a harpsichord in London, the money lay dead in the hands of my friend eighteen months before it was called for. I would for this reason prefer a letter of credit in the present case;

and should the money be actually applied for, I will immediately replace it, by paying Mr. Teissier's bill on you for it with the usual expences. I am with great esteem Sir Your most obedt. humble servt,
TH: JEFFERSON

PrC (DLC); endorsed.

From Willink & Van Staphorst

Amsterdam, 26 June 1788. Inform TJ that they "have now in hands about Ten Thousand Guilders in favor of the United States," which they stand ready to remit on TJ's directions if he wishes to dispose of it.

RC (DLC); in a clerk's hand, signed by a member of each firm: "Wilhem & Jan Willink Nics. & Jacob van Staphorst"; endorsed.

To Blome

SIR
Paris June 27. 1788.

I have the honor now to inclose you the letter for his Excellency the count de Bernstorff which you were so kind as to undertake to forward. I sincerely wish the effect of it may be that you may be charged with the settlement of the affair which is the subject of it. It would assure to us a candid and speedy arrangement. Permit me to add to these wishes the assurances of respect & attachment with which I have the honor to be, Sir, Your most obedient & most humble servant,
TH: JEFFERSON

PrC (DLC). Enclosure: TJ to Bernstorff, 19 June 1788.

To Madame d'Houdetot

à Paris ce 27me. Juin 1788.

C'est aujourdhui, Madame la comtesse, le premier jour depuis plusieurs semaines que des affaires m'auroient permis de sortir de chez moi. J'avois le projet de m'en profiter pour aller vous rendre mes devoirs à Sanois. Mais un tems pluvieux me defende d'avoir cet honneur la d'aujourdui, et d'autres engagemens pour les quatre jours à venir. Monsieur Short croit que vous devez quitter Sanois lundi prochain; ainsi ce ne pourroit etre qu'après votre retour que je scaurai vous y presenter mes respects. J'attendrai avec impatience ce moment la, et m'en profiterai avec empressement.

J'ai eu l'honneur, Mardi dernier, de rencontrer Monsieur de Lalive votre neveu à Versailles, et hier il m'a fait celui de me faire visite. C'est un jeune homme charmant, et dont la physionomie donne les preventions les plus favorables. Tout le monde lui a trouvé une figure bien interessante. Il m'a confirmé les nouvelles de votre prochain depart de Sanois.

Vous a-t-on dit, Madame, que la Prusse et l'Angleterre ont signé leur traité d'Alliance le 13me. du courant? et que le roi de Suede a donné une declaration motivée des raisons pour lesquelles il s'est armé, qui a un peu l'air d'une declaration de guerre contre la Russie? La premiere nouvelle est sure, la derniere assez bien fondée, quoique la declaration n'a pas eté encore vue ici. Si la Suede commence la guerre il seroit bien à craindre que la France n'y soit impliquée à la longue. Je fais des voeux bien sinceres que ce n'arrive pas, avant qu'elle aura bien arrangé ses affaires internes. Un fois arrangée, je ne vois pas que cette combinaison des nations occidentales de l'Europe fera d'autre effet que de se banqrouter, la partie censée riche, par la partie connue pauvre.

J'ai l'honneur d'etre avec les sentiments de respect et d'attachement les plus sinceres, Madame votre tres humble et tres obeissant serviteur TH: JEFFERSON

P.S. A quatre ou cinq jours d'ici il y aura une occasion bien sure pour ecrire en Amerique.

PrC (DLC); endorsed.

To Schweighauser & Dobrée

GENTLEMEN Paris June 27. 1788.

In my letter of Feb. 16. I had the honour to inform you that your vouchers, with their verification by Mr. Carnes, were not yet come to hand, and in that of March 3. that I had at length received them, but was in that instant obliged to set out to Holland. Since my return I have been so pressed by other business, that it has been impossible for me to undertake so voluminous a collection of papers till within these few days. I have now gone through them, and am ready to proceed with you to a decision, which I propose to you to have made by way of arbitrators to be named with the joint consent of both parties. I should wish them to be persons having experience and knowlege both in law and commerce, and rather of a neutral nation. Among the refugees from Holland now at Paris, such characters can[1] be found.

If you concur in this mode of settlement, I suppose it will be necessary for you or Mr. Dobrée to come to Paris: that he bring with him full powers to settle this matter finally both as to Puchelberg and Mr. Schweighauser's representatives; that he produce a main-levée as to our stores and the key of the warehouse to be delivered to the arbitrators and by them to me, if they award in favor of the U.S. so that I may take possession of the stores clear of impediment from the tribunals of this country, or to be restored to you if they award in your favor. These preliminaries are indispensable before I can proceed. You will send also the original vouchers to be delivered in like manner.

The orders of the navy board, and Dr. Franklin's letters you will of course see to be necessary so far as they relate to the subject in dispute, and come provided with them and such other documents as you may have occasion for, so that we may finish the business in as few days as possible. But do not come, if you please, till you shall have advised me of your readiness, and received my answer, that no accidental circumstance may expose you to delay, in Paris.

I am with great esteem and attachment Gentlemen Your most obedient & most humble servt, TH: JEFFERSON

PrC (DLC). Tr (Arch. Aff. Etr., Paris; Corr. Pol., Angleterre, Vol. 566); in Short's hand; enclosed in TJ to Montmorin, 11 Sep. 1788. Tr varies in a few phrases from PrC.

TJ's suggestion that the arbitrators be drawn from a neutral nation and specifically from AMONG THE REFUGEES FROM HOLLAND NOW AT PARIS was not made without knowledge of the fact that such refugees (e.g., Adrian van der Kemp, who had only recently left for New York, and J. G. Diriks, who was still in Paris) belonged to the Patriot party in Holland and were therefore almost certain to possess a friendly bias toward the United States, a fact of which Schweighauser & Dobrée were also undoubtedly aware.

1 Tr reads "may be found."

From John Bondfield

SIR Bordeaux 28. Juin 1788

I have to acknowledge the receipt of your favor of the 17 Ulto.

Under the Guard of the Prevost I found the Men mentioned in the Letter of Le. Cte. de Montmorin. One of them was an Englishman who had no claim to the protection of America, the Other an Irishman but who served part of the Campaign in the American Army and say's married in Virginia. This man I took out and obtaind a passage on board the ship Comte d'Artois Capt. Young bound to Norfolk. A Vessel from Baltimore stranded on our Coast has thrown a number of Seamen on our hands which until opportunity offers to get them passages or ship them in some of our outward-bound West Indiamen lays on me a charge that is rather heavy. Publick funds in cases of this nature ought to contribute. Captain Cain in the Ship Marquis de la Fayette takes four tho' his Ships Company is more than Compleat, in navigation which requires the strictest Economy Every charge is considered. Extra provisions of two months at least for every Extra hand is felt, and my applications supported by the Laws of humanity are Imposts which the Publick ought to Support by an allowance ℔ head to every Captain who should receive on board seamen thus situated to indemnify the provisions.

The 125 Bottles of Haut Brion shall be shipt by the first Ship that sails from hence for Rouen or Havre. Inclosed is a Bill of Loading for two Cases of Muscat forwarded to the care of Geo. Clymer of Philadelphia to whom I have wrote to dispose of them agreable to orders he may receive from Le Cte. de Moustier.

This part of the Kingdom ferments but has not committed any Act, restraind by respect for the Cheifs.

I have the Honor to be Sir Your most Obedient Humble Servt.

JOHN BONDFIELD

RC (DLC); endorsed. The enclosed bill of lading has not been found.

From Grand & Cie.

Paris, 28 June 1788. In accordance with TJ's request of 26 June, they transmit letter of credit for £80 sterling and ask that he acknowledge receipt of it. They will also follow TJ's wishes respecting Paradise's letter of credit for £300 remaining in their hands.

RC (DLC); in French; 2 p. TJ's letter acknowledging receipt of the letter of credit has not been found.

To Guiraud & Portas

GENTLEMEN Paris June 28. 1788.

According to your desire in a former letter, I wrote to Mr. Oster Consul of France in Virginia, on the subject of your ship le David. I now inclose you his answer received last night. He does not explain why the government of Virginia refused to suffer the Captain and crew to be sent back: but I presume it is on the general principle that our laws do not give up criminals to any nation to be punished, but punish them themselves. If the Captain is able to repay you any damages, you can pursue him civilly in Virginia. I have the honor to be gentlemen Your most obedt. & most humble servt,

TH: JEFFERSON

PrC (DLC). The enclosed letter from Martin Oster to TJ, 10 Mch. 1788, is listed in SJL Index but has not been found; it was in response to one that TJ WROTE TO MR. OSTER on 20 Oct. 1787.

To André Limozin

SIR

Paris June 28. 1788.

I think I recollect to have written, about a year ago, to Virginia for a small package of tobacco of a particular quality made on my own estate. It was intended for a friend in France who makes his own snuff and was curious to try tobacco of the first quality. This may be the package which you are so kind as to mention in your letter of the 25th. instant. I am in hopes there are in the same package one or two ears of Indian corn (Maïs) of a particular kind, which I also wrote for, and which I am anxious to receive. Be so good as to open the package. If there be tobacco in it, and it occasions any difficulty I would not wish you to give yourself trouble about it, but rather to abandon it. When I wrote for it, I supposed the prohibitions extended only to the sale of tobacco.

A treaty of alliance between England and Prussia was signed on the 13th. instant. Sweden is believed to have given out a declaration of the reasons of her arming, which has very much the air of a declaration of war against Russia. We have not yet seen it here. It would not be unexpected to hear that she has commenced hostilities. She is subsidized by England, and if she does begin a war, we must beleive it to be on the instigation of England with a view to bring on a general war. This power with Denmark and Holland ranging themselves on the side of England, destroys the equilibrium of power at sea, which we had hoped was established. I am with great esteem, Sir, your most obedt. humble servt,

TH: JEFFERSON

PrC (DLC).

To Chamillard

Sir Paris June 29. 1788.

I have duly received the letter of the 22d. instant with which you were pleased to honour me. I have written to the Count de Bernstorff, Minister for foreign affairs at the court of Denmark to propose his empowering some person here to arrange our demand against them. I presume they will authorise the Baron de Blome to do it. As soon as they shall have sent full powers to him or any other person, I will do myself the honour of letting you know it, and be glad to be availed of your information and aid in the business. I have the honour to be with much regard, Sir Your most obedt. and most humble servt,

Th: Jefferson

PrC (DLC); at foot of text: "M. Chamillard, Lt. Col. d'infanterie. Pavillon poyné rue Satory á Versailles."

To Homberg & Homberg Frères

Gentlemen Paris June 29. 1788.

I have now the honour to return you the paper you were so kind as to inclose me on the subject of whale oil. Immediately on the receipt of it, I asked the opinion of the Redacte[ur] of the Arrêt of Dec. 29. whether the duty should be paid on the gross or nett weight. His answer was that it had [been] his intention, in wording the Arret, to have the duties [paid] on the weight of the oil only, not on that of the barrel. [But on] examining the expression he had used, he found [that some] doubt might be raised by those disposed to doubt. He the[n re]commended to me to ask an explanatory decision of the counci[l, which I] shall do, but not immediately; as there will be some other matters a while hence, and I would wish to make one trouble only for them, out of many. I am obliged to you for informing me of this matter, as I always shall of all others concerning our commerce which may arise; & have the honour to be, Gentlemen, Your most obedient humble servt,

Th: Jefferson

PrC (DLC); MS mutilated so that some words are missing and have been conjecturally supplied. Enclosure missing; see Homberg & Homberg Frères to TJ, 30 May 1788.

To Amand Koenig

MONSIEUR à Paris ce 29me. Juin 1788.

J'ai reçu en bon ordre les livres que vous avez eu la bonté de m'expedier, et aussi la lettre du 5. Courant que vous m'avez fait l'honneur de m'ecrire avec la catalogue. Je ne trouve sur cette catalogue que deux articles que je vous demand[erai] c'est à dire

Demetrius Phalereus de elocutione. Gr.lat. Foulis. 1743. 3.[tt]

Menandri et Philemonis reliquiae. Gr.lat. Amstel. 1709. 7[tt]–10.

Ayez la bonté de m'envoyer en meme tems

Aesopi fabulae Gr.Lat. Haupmanni. 8vo. Platonis opera Gr.Lat. 12.vols. 8vo. Aristophanes Bronchii – – – la 3me. volume d'Euripides Barnesii 4to.	les memes editions que j'ai acheté chez vous. Brochés.

Comme je n'ai point de correspondence à Strasbourg, je vous demanderai la permission d'en payer le montant à votre correspondant ici M. Prevost, ou à telle autre personne que vous aurez la bonté de m'indiquer. J'ai l'honneur d'etre Monsieur votre tres humble et tres obeissant serviteur TH: JEFFERSON

PrC (DLC); endorsed.

To John Trumbull

DEAR SIR Paris June 29. 1788.

A delay of the post office put it out of my power to answer your's of the 20th. by the first post. I now inclose you a letter of credit on Mr. Teissier for eighty pounds sterling. This will cover the cost of the Tea vase after paying for the carriage if it be not sold before your receipt of this. If it be, you may hereafter at your leisure perhaps find another. You judged rightly in supposing I did not mean to limit the price absolutely to 50 guineas. Knowing that it often happened that from caprice or some other cause people sold their carriages for much less than their worth, I wished to avail myself of any such caprice which might come in your way, so that my object is a great, or at least a good bargain.—When you shall have made the purchase if any known person should be coming, perhaps they will pay the expence of horses for the use of the carriage, or half the expence, I paying the other half. If no such conveiance occurs I have thought it would be best to send it by water to Rouen, but not to put it on board the vessel till a day or two before she sails: because those vessels lie months in the river, taking every thing offered them, till they can make up their load.—Present me affectionately, and most affectionately to Mrs. Church and Mrs. Cosway. Kitty is now with us, and well. She kisses this letter and charges it to deliver the kiss purely and faithfully to her Mama.—No news from Stockdale. I am done with him irrevocably. Adieu Your's affectionately,

TH: JEFFERSON

PrC (DLC).

From André Limozin

⟦*Le Havre, 30 June 1788.* Recorded in SJL Index, but no letter of this date has been found. There is in MHi, however, a remnant of what may be this letter; it is unsigned, but is endorsed "Limozin" by T.J. It reads: "I was forgetting to mention to your Excellency that I have received Mr. Wm. Shorts Letter dated the 1rst instt. and that of his friend Mr. Fulwar Skipwith dated the 4th instt. with 4 inclosed for America which agreable to his desires I have forwarded. I have charged your account with the postage for them, amounting to 10 Lvrs. 7 Sous." Limozin again mentioned the amount of the postage on Short's letters in a letter to TJ of 6 Oct. 1788, q.v.⟧

From Nicolas & Jacob van Staphorst

Amsterdam, 30 June 1788. Acknowledge TJ's letters of 28 May and 22 June. Request in former concerning letter to Trumbull anticipated by N. Hubbard's having transmitted it to Daniel Parker to be given to TJ. Enclose "Second of our draft for £30 Stl." On 21 Apr. account of United States charged *f*426 for TJ's draft to Turckheim and *f*143.14 for that to Peuchen. Other items will be consolidated in one debit, as requested.—"We have already pressed Admiral Paul Jones to reimburse us the 100 Guineas" furnished under TJ's guarantee, and will renew request as soon as they learn of his return to St. Petersburg, when they presume "He will be equally able and willing to discharge this Debt of Honor."

RC (DLC); endorsed. Concerning the SECOND OF OUR DRAFT see TJ to Trumbull, 27 Mch. 1788, note.

From John Paradise

[*Paris, ca. June 1788.*] In answer to TJ's note, he states that the "true form of addressing a letter to his daughter is A Madame la

Comtesse Barziza née Paradise a Bergame par Milan"; Count Barziza and others "give her the title of excellency to which she has no right, until her name be enrolled in the golden book." As to the marriage settlement, he refers TJ to Mrs. Paradise's letter.

RC (MHi); endorsed; undated, but presumably TJ's NOTE (missing) was written in anticipation of his letter to Lucy Paradise, 8 July 1788. Neither TJ's inquiry nor the present note is recorded in SJL Index. See Shepperson, *John Paradise and Lucy Ludwell*, p. 315-9.

To John Banister, Jr.

DEAR SIR　　　Paris July 2. 1788.

The bearer hereof, Mr. l'Olive, having intended a voyage to Virginia the last year, I gave him a letter of introduction for Colo. Bannister your father. Having since understood that Colo. Bannister was gone to the West Indies, I now take the liberty of addressing Mr. L'Olive to your acquaintance. You will find him perfectly worthy of it in every respect, and your attentions will be more precious to him as he does not speak English. I will ask them therefore as a favor to me, and as he cannot here decide his route from Petersburgh, so as to enable me to give him letters of introduction on the road he may go, I will ask that favor of you, and beg you to receive my acknolegements for it, and assurances of the esteem with which I am Dear Sir Your friend & servant,

TH: JEFFERSON

PrC (DLC). TJ's letter of introduction of 1787 FOR COLO. BANNISTER has not been found.

From Jacob Gerrit Diriks

Paris, "Audessus des Bains des Dames Palais Royal," 2 July 1788. Since interview with TJ this morning, M. Tegelcan says he can furnish 4,000 to 5,000 guilders on the loan office certificate from Congress "If Your Excellency would be so kind as to testify, that the Bills are good and will be paid with the Interest . . . in one or two Years." Is much in want of cash, and begs TJ to grant this favor to convince Tegelcan "that he has nothing to fear, and that the Loan office certificates are Solide."

RC (DLC); endorsed.

Diriks (1752-1805) was a Dutch Patriot who had served in Surinam under his father, an artillery officer in the Dutch army, and had occupied various posts in the Pennsylvania Line and in the Continental Army during 1777-1778, being pursued by the ill health that had come upon him in Surinam; in 1787 he served as colonel of the Patriot forces in Gelderland and, upon the triumph of the Stadtholder, escaped to France, where he was made a captain in the French army on the day before the present letter was written (communication from H. Hardenberg, The Hague, 23 July 1956).

To Jacob Gerrit Diriks

Sir Paris July 2, 1788.

As a private individual and citizen of America I can with propriety and truth deliver it to you as my firm belief that the loan office certificate you shewed me, and all others of the same kind will be paid, principal and interest, as soon as the circumstances of the United states will permit: that I do not consider this as a distant epoch, nor suppose there is a publick debt on earth less doubtful. This I speak as my private opinion. But it does not belong to me to say that it will be paid in two years, or that it will be paid at all, so as by the authority of my affirmation to give to it any new sanction or credit. The board of treasury or Congress can alone do this. You will be sensible therefore Sir, of the impropriety, and even the hazard, of my going out of the line of my office so far as to undertake, or to aver, that these certificates will be paid within one or two years. On every occasion where I can do it of right, I shall be happy to render you every possible service, being with sentiments of perfect esteem, Sir Your most obedt. humble servt. Th: Jefferson

PrC (DLC).

From Gallimard

Trévoux en Dombes, 2 July 1788. Asks TJ's advice and protection in moving with his family to the United States; inquires "si, avec votre secours, je pourrois obtenir dans l'un des états unis d'amérique, une Concession de terrein de bonne qualité et en un lieu où l'air soit sain? Dans lesquels des états unis j'aurais à choisir pour me fixer? et quelles seraient les conditions de la Concession." Has enough money to pay for "chevaux, bestiaux, instrumens d'Agriculture, frais de constructions, et autres qu'exige un pareil deffrichement.—Je ne suis forcé par aucune mauvaise affaire à quitter la France: Je suis receveur des Domaines du Roi et fais en sorte de remplir cette place de maniere à etre exempt de tout reproche. Ce qui me détermine donc à passer en Amerique, est l'envie de suivre mon goût pour l'Agriculture si par cette voye, je puis ameliorer ma fortune. La place que j'occupe dépend de l'Administration generale des Domaines du Roi; ainsi vous pourriez, Monsieur, si vous le désirez, prendre auprès de cette compagnie des informations sur mon compte, mais alors je vous serais obligé de ne point lui laisser pénétrer mon dessein, parcequ'elle pourrait voir de mauvais œil que je me propose de la quitter."

RC (DLC); endorsed.

To Edmund Randolph

Sir — Paris July 2. 1788.

The bearer hereof, Monsieur L'Olive, proposing [to] pass thro' Virginia, I take the liberty of presenting him to your Excellency's acquaintance, and notice. He is a very wealthy and worthy citizen of this country, and will justify by his merit the attentions you will be so good as to shew him. He has the disadvantage of not speaking our language, and I do not know whether your Excellency may supply that by speaking his. I shall hope it however as his good sense would powerfully recommend him to you. I am happy in every occasion of repeating to you assurances of the great esteem and respect with which I have the honor to be, Your Excellency's most obedient & most humble servt,

Th: Jefferson

PrC (DLC); endorsed; at foot of text: "His Excellency Governor Randolph."

To John Trumbull

Dear Sir — Paris July 2. 1788.

In mine of the 29th. June by the last post I inclosed you Mr. Grand's letter of credit for £80. on Mr. Teissier. By your favor of the 25th. handed me to-day by Mr. Parker I see there is a probability that the carriage you had in view will not have been disposed of before the letter of credit reaches you, so that the opportunity of making the purchase will not be lost. I consulted with Mr. Parker about the best mode of bringing it. He sais that if a traveller comes in it, no duty is paid, and that there are very frequent occasions of sending it by travellers who for the use of the carriage to Paris will gladly undertake to deliver it here clear of all expence; that he himself shall go to London and return again to Paris in the course of six weeks, and will be glad to bring it. I think it best therefore to abandon the idea of sending it by water, and to wait for Mr. Parker, unless any known person shall be coming sooner, who will bring it clear of expence. I thought it necessary to mention this to you by this post. A box is arrived for me at the Douane which I presume to be from Stockdale. I give you abundance of thanks for all the trouble you take for me and am with very sincere esteem Dr. Sir Your friend & servt,

Th: Jefferson

P.S. Be so good as to receive the whole 80£ from Mr. Teissier. Should it not be all wanting for the carriage it will be ready for other purposes.

PrC (DLC).

From John Ledyard

Sir [Before 3 July 1788]

When men of genius want matter of fact to reason from it is bad, though it is worse to reason without it: it is the fate of genius not to make, or to misapply this reflexion, and so it forms theories: humble minds admire these theories because they cannot comprehend them, and disbelieve them for the same reason.

Simplify the efforts and attainments of all the antient worlds in science and it amounts to nothing but theory: to a riddle: the sublime of[1] antient wisdom was to form a riddle: and the delphic god bore the palm: Men had then great encouragement to do so: they were made priests phrophets, kings and gods: and when they had gained these distinctions by riddles it was necessary by riddles to preserve them.

Men have since tho but very lately and not yet universaly sought impartialy for truth and we now a days seek truth not only for its own enchanting beauty, but from a principle tho not more valuable yet more generous viz. the pleasure of Communicating it to one another. The soothsayers, magicians, phrophets, and priests of old would think us as errant fools as we think them knaves.

In my travels I have made it my rule to compare the written with the living history of Man, and as I have seen all kinds of men so I have not hesitated to make use of all kinds of history (that I am acquainted with) in the comparison: and I give in many cases as much credit to traditions as to other history: implicit credit to none nor implicit credit to inferrences that I myself draw from this comparison except rarely; and then I am as sure as I want to be. Thus I know and feel myself above prejudice. Moses, Albugassi and the writers of the last 20 years are all alike to me as to what I am seeking for: I would only understand if I could what man has been from what he is: not what he may be hereafter tho all mention the tale. I would also know what the earth has been from observing how it is at present: not how it may hereafter be tho all mention also this tale. You know how ignorant and plain a Man

I am, but I declare to you that in this temper of mind and from the information incident to the extent and nature of my travels I find myself at my ease concerning things which some cannot and others will not believe that are of considerable importance; and I will tell you in a very few words what some of them are—I wish I had time to mention them all, or if I do that it was more in detail.

Sir I am certain (the negroes excepted because I have not yet personaly visited them) that the difference in the colour of Men is the effect of natural causes.

Sir I am certain that all the people you call red people on the continent of America and on the continents of Europe and Asia as far south as the southern parts of China are all one people by whatever names distinguished and that the best general one would be *Tartar*.

I suspect that *all* red people are of the same family. I am satisfied myself that America was peopled from Asia and had some if not all its animals from thence.

I am satisfied myself that the great general analogy in the customs of Men can only be accounted for but by supposing them all to compose one family: and by extending the Idea and uniting Customs, traditions and history I am satisfied that this common origin was such or nearly as related by Moses and commonly believed among all the nations of the earth. There is a transposition of things on the globe that must have been produced by some cause equal to the effect which is vast and curious: whether I repose on arguments drawn from facts observed by myself or send imagination forth to find a cause they both declare to me a general deluge. I am yr. Excellencys most humble & most gratefull friend,

LEDYARD

RC (DLC); undated, but endorsed by TJ: "Ledyard John. recd. July 3. 1788. Paris." SJL Index, which usually carries in the letters-received column an asterisk to indicate undated letters, has an asterisk between entries for 4 July and 15 Aug. 1788; such entries in SJL Index refer to the dates that letters were written, not received, and the appropriate asterisk for an undated letter is usually, but not always, placed in proper chronological sequence in SJL Index. In view of these facts, it is possible that Ledyard, who was in London in May-July 1788, wrote TJ a (missing) letter from that place on 4 July 1788; that the asterisk for the present letter, received on 3 July, was misplaced; and that the present letter therefore may have been written from some point in Ledyard's trek across Siberia, being received in Paris sometime after Ledyard arrived in London.

[1] This word repeated in MS.

To Thomas Paine

Dear Sir Paris July 3. 1788.

The inclosed being part of a newspaper published here I thought you would like to see it, and therefore cut it out and inclose it. I have no doubt that the author of it has had you in view when he wrote it: and perhaps, when you return it may be worth while to see what he offers to shew. I have had conversations on your business since you left us, and find you will not be able to get a step forward without an estimate. Indeed I doubt whether any thing be meant to be done: at any rate your proposal is only taken up as the handmaid to another object, and will be executed only in t[he] case it shall be found to ensure that. A Frenchman neve[r] sais No: and it is difficult for a stranger to know when he means it. Perhaps it is the longest to be learnt of all the particularities of the nation. If therefore you can do any thing where you are, do not lose the occasion.—Have you been enchanted by the magician Merlin? I presume you have. I do not write you news, because you would never receive the letter if I did, as it goes thro' the post offices of the t[wo] countries. I am with great & sincere esteem Dear Sir Your friend & servant,

Th: Jefferson

PrC (DLC). Enclosure not found.

From the Commissioners of the Treasury

Board of Treasury
July 3d 1788

Sir

You inform us in your letter of the 7th of Feby last, that Mr. Ast (Secretary to the Consulate) was at L'Orient; and that, "whether he comes up with the papers of Mr. Barclay's Office, or sends them, that they shall be received, sealed up, and taken care of." Though these expressions imply strongly that Mr. Ast will do the one, or the other, yet it does not clearly appear that you have communicated our order to him and required the delivery of these papers in consequence of it.—It is therefore our wish that these papers may be taken under your protection, and sealed up as you propose; if this is not done when, this letter arrives.—Their careful custody we concieve of great moment to the Public; and in this point of view we have no doubt of your attention to this object.

We are Sir Your obedt. Huml. Servts.

Samuel Osgood
Walter Livingston
Arthur Lee

RC (DLC); in a clerk's hand, signed by each of the commissioners.

From Richard Claiborne

London, 4 July[1] *1788.* Introducing a Mr. Cole, to whom he has mentioned his lands in Virginia and his aim as to sales or settlements, "and as he is a residenter, of large property in Germany, from which Country it was the advice of Your Excellency to me to procure Settlers," Claiborne would be glad to have TJ give Cole his "general sentiments" on such property—his lands are in "Monongalia, Harrison, Jefferson, and Fayette Counties, and lie on Chat, Hughs's, Little Kenhaway, Green, and Ohio Rivers"—and on "other advantages peculiar to the Country." [*In postscript:*] Offers to TJ "the sincere compliments which are so justly due to you upon this memorable day."

RC (MoSHi); endorsed; addressed in part: "Hon'd by Mr. Cole"; MS mutilated by breaking of seal, so that some words and letters are lost.

The Rev. John Murray (1741-1815), founder of Universalism in America, wrote from Gloucester, England, to an unidentified correspondent on 23 June 1788: "A Major Cleyburn (who was Aid to General Greene) has been some time in England endeavouring to dispose of Lands, and has in his possession sundry scroles of Parchment signed by Mr. Jefferson, but, having, I presume, no other dependance I left him in Prison for debt" (NjMoW). If Claiborne was in fact imprisoned, he was soon released. Murray was himself trying to attract settlers from England to Ohio. The "sundry scroles" were evidently land grants signed by TJ as governor.

1 The date-line, written below the signature and above the postscript, has the day of the month underscored: "London *4th July* 1788."

To Foulloy

Monsieur Foulloy having delivered to me two books of Silas Deane, to wit his letter book of 1777. and his Daybook of accounts from 1776 to 1780. which he has as a pledge from Silas Deane for the sum of a hundred and twenty guineas. I promise to return to him those books, or to be answerable to him for the sum for which he holds them as a pledge; the books to be redelivered on his demand tomorrow evening. Given under my hand this 4th. day of July 1788.

Th: Jefferson

PrC (DLC). Entries in SJL Index show that TJ wrote Foulloy on 3 and 9 July and received letters from him on 7 and 8 July 1788. The entry for 3 July may be a mistaken reference to the present document, which is more properly a receipt than a letter; in any case, no such letter of 3 July 1788 has been found. See TJ to Jay, 3 Aug. 1788.

To Francis Hopkinson

DEAR SIR Paris July 6. 1788.

A printer here has begun to print the most remarkeable of the English authors, as that can be done here much cheaper than in England or even Ireland. He supposes America could take off a considerable number of copies, and has therefore applied to me to find a sure correspondent for him. Being unacquainted with the printers of Philadelphia and the booksellers, yet satisfied that that would be the best place for him to have a correspondent, I must ask of you to recommend one and to hand to him the inclosed proposals, and the piece of a volume which we send as a specimen. An Octavo volume will cost here 96 sous, which are exactly 4/ sterling, bound and, with the abatement of 10. per cent about 3/8 sterl. The same in London would cost 7/. Above all things let the correspondent be solid in his circumstances. If young Mr. Beach has begun to exercise his destined calling of a printer, he would be the best correspondent for Pissot for many reasons; one is that Pissot is personally known to him, having been the bookseller of Dr. Franklin.

I am with very great & sincere esteem Dr. Sir Your most obedient humble servt, TH: JEFFERSON

PrC (DLC).

YOUNG MR. BEACH was Benjamin Franklin Bache, grandson of Benjamin Franklin, who lived at Passy with Franklin and was taught printing by him. Enclosure not found, but the PRINTER HERE was one Pissot, a bookseller in quai des Augustins who had just established a weekly newspaper, *Général Advertiser*, which included "tout ce que les Papiers, Journaux, Magasins et Pamphlets Anglois et Américains fournissent de plus intéressant sur les affaires de la Grande-Bretagne et des Etats-Unis de l'Amérique" (*Journal de Paris*, 26 May 1788). See Hopkinson to TJ, 23 Oct. 1788; Franklin to TJ, 24 Oct. 1788.

Jefferson's Affidavit Concerning John and Lucy Ludwell Paradise

We, Thomas Jefferson, Minister plenipotentiary for the United States of America at the court of Versailles certify to all whom it may concern:

That we are personally and well acquainted with the family of

Mrs. Lucy Paradise, wife of John Paradise esquire, with their connections and condition:

That the said Lucy was born in the state of Virginia, in the lawful wedlock of her parents, of a Christian family, and educated in the Christian religion:

That her father, the honourable Philip Ludwell esquire was a native of the same state of Virginia, was a member of the Royal Executive council, of the General court the supreme judicature of the state, and a Visitor of the College of Williamsburg of public foundation:

That her grandfather, the honourable Ludwell esquire, was President of the said state, that is to say, the vicegerent and representative of the king during the absence of the governor, and in cases of inter-regnum:

That her great grandfather, the honourable Philip Ludwell esquire, was Governor of the neighboring state of Carolina, that is to say, the immediate Vicegerent and Representative of the king, in ordinary and extraordinary:

That her mother was of the family of Grymes: her uncle on the mother's side, the honourable Philip Grymes esquire was Receiver general of the king, a member of the Royal executive council, and of the General court the supreme judicature of the state:

That her grandfather on the same side, the honourable Grymes esquire, was Secretary of the state, a member of the Royal executive council, and of the General court the supreme judicature thereof:

And that her ancestors in general, both on the side of the father and mother, have been of the most distinguished in that country from it's first settlement, for their wealth, and the honours and offices they have filled:

That in that country no distinction of ranks has ever been admitted at all, much less to be made hereditary:

And all this we certify of our own knowlege, so far as the facts are of our own times, and so far as they are of earlier times, we have learnt them from the public records and history of the state, and from the constant uncontradicted reputation of that country, of which we are native born.

With respect to the said John Paradise esquire, heretofore resident in the kingdom of Great Britain, lately removed to Virginia and become of our personal acquaintance, we can certify his personal worth only, which is great, and his condition, which is that of a gentleman, and citizen of the state of Virginia, invested with all the rights of that character, capable of all the offices and honours of that country, and received a Visitor of the same College of Williamsburg of which his father in law, Philip Ludwell before named, was a Visitor. His family is unknown to us but by reputation, which has represented it as well distinguished by wealth and office in England.

Given under our hand and seal at Paris in the kingdom of France this 6th. day of July in the year of our lord 1788.

TH: JEFFERSON

PrC (DLC); at foot of text: "John Paradise." An entry in SJL Index for 6 July 1788 may refer to this document or to a (missing) letter of transmittal. The original of the affidavit, with seal attached, is stated by Shepperson, *John Paradise and Lucy Ludwell*, p. 479, to be in the possession of Miss Philippa Ludwell Barziza of Texas.

From Thomas Lee Shippen

MY DEAR SIR   Spa July 6 1788

Your agreable letter of the 19th of June with the excellent remarks which accompany it, was presented to me 2 days ago only, on the road between Amsterdam and Spa. It had been forwarded by Messrs. Willincks to the Hague at the time when I was coming from that place to Amsterdam and was sent by the banker of Mr. Rutledge to his correspondent at Liege who delivered it to me. Your observations could not possibly have been better calculated for my purpose, nor have reached me at a more favorable time. They embrace every subject to which I was desirous of turning my attention, and come at the moment when I am passing through the countries which are the scene of them. To tell you that I admire the amiable modesty which blinds you to the merit of this little performance, no less than the performance itself, and both extremely, would be to ill express the very high sense I have of it, and it would be utterly impossible to express to you one half the gratitude I feel, for your having sent it. The style and manner of the work shall form the model of my future attempts, and when I am experiencing the advantages of it I shall always think of you Sir with thankfulness. My journey from Amsterdam to this place has been rather agreable, and I find myself now in the most delightful residence in the world. I have written to Mr. Short on the subject of both in detail, and if you are desirous of entering into it, he will have the goodness of informing you. Your attention and goodness make me suppose it possible that you would interest yourself in our lesser transactions, though I cannot justify to myself the occupying of your valuable time in relating them to you. Your advice on the subject of our future travels appears to me so excellent, that it must be something very extraordinary which can prevent me from pursuing it. On the day after tomorrow we proceed by Aix la Chapelle to Cologne and thence up the Rhine according to your Itinerary. From Strasburg I shall have the honor of writing to you again, and my address will be poste restante at that place until the 12th of this month only. After that time you will please to send any letters which you may have for me to the care of the Post master at Berne.

Of the riot I had heard with regret, and rejoiced at its sudden extinction. It appears from all accounts that it was by no means an alarming affair.

The reasons you assign for the adoption of the new constitution in America after the example of Massachusetts appear to me to be the most conclusive I have met with, and I join with you Sir in praying with all my heart that the remaining States may accept it. The conjuncture seems to call loudly for the event, and I think much depends upon its being carried into execution immediately.

Your letter gave me the first information I have received on the subject of the affair on the Missisipi, and your opinion decides mine with respect to what we ought to wish for on the occasion. Otherwise I should have thought that *golden* advantage at least might have been derived from a war with Spanish America.

The letters you promise us will be the most invaluable tokens of your remembrance and regard and will always be received as such with gratitude.

A punctual attention to the few commissions with which you have honored me, and a constant and ardent zeal of being employed in your service, are the only returns which are in my power now to make for all your kindness, but you may always confide in me as your most devoted and affectionate servant.

THOS. LEE SHIPPEN

P.S. My father desires me in all his letters to thank you for him and to assure you of his inviolable attachment.

RC (DLC); endorsed. Dumas was also involved in the circuitous routing of TJ's LETTER OF THE 19TH: On 1 July Dumas wrote to Rutledge at Spa, enclosing two letters for Shippen (Dumas Letter Book, Rijksarchief, The Hague; photostats in DLC).

From Cordon

Paris, 7 July 1788. Yesterday, as ambassador of the king of Sardinia, he had his first audience with the king and royal family.

RC (DLC); addressed; in French; 2 p.

From Foulloy

Paris, 7 July 1788. Could not call on TJ this morning as promised because he was forced to go to Versailles again, not having finished yesterday with Rayneval; hopes to "see the End of it this time," and "if Extraordinary affairs do not Happen," will call on TJ tomorrow morning between ten and eleven.

RC (DLC); endorsed.

From Teresa Murphy

[*7 July 1788.* Recorded in SJL Index, but not found.]

From James Swan

SIR Havre 7th July 1788

I have had the honor of your Excellencie's favor of the 19th. Ulto. and am fully satisfied as to the Consular business, that it is best for me to wait the establishment of the new Constitution. I think it probable I shall renounce the idea, as I certainly will not go to Marseilles, and my family never would content themselves at Honfleur.

With respect to the Contract for Beef &c. the Marqs. la Fayette has presented the proposals I made, and hinted to me, that it would be well for me to appear at Paris between the 15th. and 25th. instant to answer to some objections. I shall then have the honor and satisfaction of paying my respects to your Excellency, and hope with your influence and his, that something may be done. I shall be prepared to remove the objections of Ireland taking wine and Brandies in return for their beef, being more advantageous than my proposals, and a proper influence on the officer who procures the Supplies, I have no doubt of succeeding in.

When at Paris I shall propose a Contract for Royal masts, which I am well able to furnish.

Should Mr. Parker be in Paris, I think it would be well for him to tarry till the talk be over with the Administrators. He has entered into this business, and wishes to promote it, and to unite our Views in one Contract.

I have the honour to be with the most perfect respect & esteem Your Excellencies Most obed. & very huml. Servt.,

JAM. SWAN

RC (DLC); endorsed. On the aid that TJ gave Swan in support of the proposed CONTRACT FOR BEEF, see Swan to TJ, 7 June and 19 July 1788.

To Barziza

Paris July 8. 1788.

The letter of March 15. which Your Excellency did me the honour to write me arrived during my absence on a journey through Holland and Germany, and since my return my attention has been necessarily engaged by objects of business which had accumulated during my absence. The friendly reception of Mr. and Mrs. Paradise in Virginia, which you kindly ascribe in some measure to my letters, was in truth owing to their merit alone, which had been too well previously known to need any testimony from me. My only merit consisted in wishes to serve them. This I shall long preserve, as it is the necessary effect which their virtues must produce on the minds of all who know them. I sincerely congratulate your Excellency on their safe arrival in France, and on your prospect of seeing them in the course of the present season in Venice, where their happiness will be perfectly reestablished by being witnesses to that of your Excellency and of your worthy spouse their daughter. That this may long continue and increase is the sincere prayer of him who has the honour to be with sentiments of the most perfect respect & attachment, Your Excellency's most obedient & most humble servt,

TH: JEFFERSON

PrC (DLC); at foot of text: "H. E. Count Barziza."

To Lucy Paradise Barziza

MADAM Paris July 8. 1788.

The letter of March 15. which you did me the honor to address me, came during my absence on a journey through Holland and Germany, and my first attentions after my return were necessarily called to some objects of business of too pressing a nature to be postponed. This has prevented my acknoleging, so soon as I could have wished, the honour of receiving your letter. The welcome reception which Mr. and Mrs. Paradise met with in Virginia was due to their own merit, which had been well known there before their arrival, and to the esteem for your family entertained in that country. You could experience the same, Madam, were any considerations to tempt you to leave for a while your present splendid situation to visit the transatlantic seat of your ancestors. Heaven has already blessed you with one child, for which accept my sincere congratulations. It may perhaps multiply those blessings on you: and in that event your family estate in Virginia may become a handsome and happy establishment for a younger child. It will be a welcome present to a country which will continue to think it has some claims on you. I felicitate you on the prospect of seeing Mr. and Mrs. Paradise at Venice. The happiness of your situation, your virtues and those of the count Barziza will contribute to re-establish that tranquillity of mind, which an unhappy loss has disturbed and continues to disturb. Sensibility of mind is indeed the parent of every virtue: but it is the parent of much misery too. No body is more it's victim than Mr. Paradise. Your happiness, your affections, and your attentions can alone restore his serenity of mind. I am sure it will find repose in those sources, and that your virtues and those of the count Barziza will occupy his mind in thinking on what he possesses rather than on what he has lost, and induce him to deliver himself up fully to your affections. I wish to you, Madam, a continuance of all those circumstances of happiness which surround you, and have the honour to be with sentiments of the most perfect esteem & respect Madam your most obedient & most humble servt., TH: JEFFERSON

PrC (DLC); at foot of text: "The Countess Barziza."

To John Brown Cutting

DEAR SIR Paris July 8, 1788.

Your communications of the 26th. Ult. instead of needing apology from you, require thanks from me, which I most cordially give you. I shall make a due use of them here, and trust they will have some effect. You cannot do me a greater favor than by a continuance of your communications while you remain in London, of which I will endeavor to profit my country.—Mr. Barlow of Connecticut arrived here by the last packet which sailed from N. York on the 26th. of May. He says Colo. Smith arrived there the 24th. The first vessels will probably bring us news of the accession of S. Carolina and Virginia to the new Confederation. The glorious example of Massachusets, of accepting unconditionally, and pressing for future amendment, will I hope reconcile all parties. The argument is unanswerable that it will be easier to obtain amendments from nine states under the new constitution, than from thirteen after rejecting it.[1] As our information here is much less quick than at London, you will much oblige me by dropping me a line of information as the accession of the other states becomes known to you. We expect daily to hear that the Swedes have commenced hostilities against the Russians. I am in hopes every thing here will turn out well. I am with great esteem Dr. Sir your most obedt. humble servt.,

TH: JEFFERSON

July 11. Since writing this letter I receive from America information that S. Carolina has acceded to the new constitution by a vote of 149 against 72. I hope Virginia will now accede without difficulty.

RC (MHi: AMT); endorsed; addressed: "Mr. John Brown Cutting No. 2. North street Rathbone place London. Favored by Mr. Parker"; postscript written in margin. PrC (DLC). PrC of Extract (DLC: Monroe Papers); in TJ's hand, comprising that part of TJ's letter to Carrington, 27 May 1788, as indicated in note to it, and that part of the present letter as indicated in the note below. See also TJ to Donald, 7 Feb. 1788; Monroe to TJ, 12 July 1788; Madison to TJ, 24 July 1788.

[1] The preceding three sentences, together with the postscript, comprise the whole of the extract from the present letter in the composite PrC of Extract described above.

From Foulloy

Paris, 8 July 1788. Since the purpose of his return to England would be in part to enable him to call in the funds owed him by Deane by putting in the hands of the minister the two books he holds as security —an extreme course he views with much repugnance because it might injure his own country; since TJ proposed to write to Congress; and since it is impossible for him to await the reply, having lost heavily in two bankruptcies, he will return the books and wait, provided TJ will now send him fifty louis d'or. TJ's reply, which he expects by the bearer, will determine the course that he will take.

RC (DLC); in French; 2 p.; endorsed; at foot of text in TJ's hand: "hotel St. Pierre rue d'Anjou près de la rue Dauphine." TJ's proposal to write to Congress may have been made either in conference or in a missing letter of 3 July 1788; in any case, a month elapsed before he wrote to Jay. See TJ to Foulloy, 4 and 9 July 1788.

From Gautier

ce Mardi 8 Juillet

Mr. Gautier prie Monsieur Jefferson d'agréer ses Obéissances et a l'honneur de lui envoyer le Catalogue des Classiques de Deux Ponts; avec les prix à Strasbourg. Les Negocians qui le lui en-voyent lui font espérer la même remise qu'aux libraires, savoir 25 pC., soit ¼ du prix. La collection des Latins, sera bientot complette, celle des Grecs sera continuée, et après Thucydides on donnera Pausanias, Xenophon, Aristote &c. Le prix du transport p[our] Paris est d'environ 8 à 10 livres par Cent pesant.

RC (DLC); endorsed.

From William Gordon

London July 8. 1788
No. 1 Orange Street Red Lion Square

SIR

I trouble you afresh from an apprehension that either your Excellency did not receive my letter of February, or that your answer has miscarried. I mentioned in my letter my having delayed to write, till I had gotten forward in printing; and informed you that I had finished the two first volumes, and should be obliged to you for your friendly assistance in the way you had proposed, by procuring from some bookseller a gratuity for an early copy, as in the case of Dr. Ramsay's History. I have now completed the third volume, and am about 100 pages in the fourth. The three volumes could be sent over immediately, that so the translation might be commenced. The sum you mentioned as granted for Dr. Ramsay's would go far toward paying for engraving the maps, and is therefore an object with me. Whether an increase of it should be asked on account of the four volumes I leave to your determination: but your friendship in this business would confer a lasting obligation on, Sir, Your Excellency's most obedient & humble servant, WILLIAM GORDON

Mr. Trumbull has I apprehend by this time conveyed in company with some pictures intended for you, the Marquis de la Fayette's picture of general Washington, which the marquis intended for my service in case of my having an engraving of the general. Intreat your care as to it's being safe delivered.

RC (DLC); endorsed by TJ: "Gordon Wm F's picture."
Gordon erred in assuming that he had written a LETTER OF FEBRUARY, and TJ accepted the error; he had actually written on 24 Apr. 1788; see TJ to Gordon, 16 July and 2 Sep. 1788.

From John Rutledge, Jr.

Dear Sir Spa July 8th: 1788

Your agreeable letter of June 19th: was not received by me untill my arrival at this place. Mr. Willincks who forwarded it says that it reached Amsterdam the Evening of the day on which I left it. I thank you very much and sincerely for the Notes which came inclosed. I prize them exceedingly and am very sensible to your goodness in writing them. The alteration which you propose I shall make in my route, that is, to descend the Danube from Vienna so as to go to Constantinople, and from thence to Naples I think (provided it will be safe to pass through the Ottoman territories) will be much more eligible than going, as I intended, from Vienna to Trieste and entering Italy by Venice. This however must depend on Circumstances, for altho' it is certain that negotiations for Peace are on foot it does not seem certain that an accommodation will immediately take place. Since I had the pleasure of writing to you from the Hague, from which place I forwarded you a letter from my father, I have received Letters from Charleston dated the last of April. They mention Marylands having accepted the new Constitution and say that its adoption in our State may be regarded as a thing certain. Much do I thank you my dear Sir for your hints respecting the olive Tree, I am well convinced how great a circumstance its introduction into our State will be and shall myself pay much attention to its culture and Climate.

I shall leave this heavenly place the day after Tomorrow for Aix la Chapelle. At Coblentz I certainly will lodge at l'homme Sauvage and shall as you desire remind him of the Map which in his Bill he had forgotten. At Frankfort I shall avail myself of the Opportunity your Notes afford me of making the acquaintance of Major Geismer who you have been so good as to say you will prepare for my Visit. I expect to be at Geneva soon in August; letters directed there Poste Restante will find me. I shall be made very happy in receiving them and in the interim am, Dr. Sir, with the sincerest wishes possible for your health and happiness Your affectionate friend & much obliged Servt.,

J. Rutledge Junr.

RC (DLC); endorsed.

From Van der Schreul

[8 July 1788. Recorded in SJL Index, but not found.]

From Etienne Clavière, with Enclosure

MONSIEUR L'AMBASSADEUR Suresne le 9. Juillet 1788

J'ay l'honneur de vous envoyer les tableaux relatifs à l'extinction de la dette américaine en profitant de l'avantage des rentes viagéres. J'ai cru que si une telle affaire pouvoit avoir lieu ce ne seroit jamais que par un marché précis où toutes les chances douteuses seroient rendues certaines. C'est là proprement le métier de la Compagnie d'Assurance sur la vie. Je ne sai si vous jugeres que ces tableaux méritent d'aller au Congrès, ne fut-ce que comme objet de Curiosité; je ne les enverrai pas à mon ami Warville que vous n'ayes eu la bonté de m'en dire votre Sentiment. D'ailleurs je ne sai comment écrire, et je me proposois de vous prier de vouloir bien joindre ma lettre à vos dépêches. Il y aura dans tout ceci des Circonstances qui empêcheront la négociation. De votre coté la confédération ne s'avance pas, et ici les choses tendent à augmenter tous les jours le discredit. Cette derniere circonstance ne devroit cependant pas arrêter l'affaire, mais plutot la favoriser: vous en sentés les raisons.

J'ay l'honneur d'être avec beaucoup d'estime, Monsieur l'Ambassadeur, Votre tres humble & tres obeïssant Serviteur,

E CLAVIERE

RC (DLC); bound with TJ's copy of Clavière's *Compagnie Royale d'Assurances. Prospectus de l'établissement des assurances* (Paris, 1788), and described in Sowerby, No. 2458, as being the covering letter for several MSS similarly bound. (One of these MSS, however, is a rough draft of the proposal that TJ had transmitted to Jay in his letter of 12 Nov. 1786, the translated text of which is printed in Vol. 10: 520-3; the fact that this draft is in Clavière's hand confirms the conjecture there advanced that it was Clavière who informed TJ of the proposal of a Dutch company to purchase the American debt to France.) The other MSS bound with this copy of *Compagnie Royale d'Assurances* were in fact enclosed in the present letter and are as follows: (1) "Tableau du Resultat de £3,400,000 de Rentes Viagères constituées sur Cent Têtes choisies, employées à acquitter les Payemens annuels que les Etats Unis doivent faire pendant Seize Ans, suivant qu'ils sont portés dans le Compte Rendu des Finances de France de l'Année 1787, pour acquitter une Dette de £34,000,000," a table presented in two parts and based on the supposition that the United States would manage the intricate operation and in addition that "les Etats Unis se procureroient par quelque moyen la Somme de 34,000,000, pour acheter le Viager." (2) A "Second Tableau, Servant à montrer le developpement de l'exécution d'un Marché fait entre les Etats Unis et la Compagnie Royale d'Assurances sur la Vie, établie à Paris. Marché par lequel, la Compagnie s'engageroit à faire annuellement le Payement de la Dette des Etats unis, telle qu'elle est passée dans le Compte Rendu des finances de France de 1787, et dans le même nombre d'Années. Le Tableau indique aussi les Sommes que le Congrès seroit obligé de remettre annuellement à la Compagnie et la difference de ces Sommes, comparées à celles qu'ils doivent payer suivant le Compte Rendu." In addition to the tables, this MS carried the following explanation: "On suppose que £3,570,000 de Rentes Viagères seroient achetées sur le pied de £10. 10s. de Rentes pour £100 de Capital, et couteroient par consequent £34,000,000. Que les frais d'achatat, de Constitution, et en général de la Manutention de toute cette affaire doivent être evalués à 2½%, £879,291. Que les frais de perception des Rentes pendant 16 Ans, monteroient a 1% sur les Rentes les quels frais escomptés sur le pied de 6% l'an, font une valeur actuelle de 292,350."; thus the United States "seroient débiteurs à l'interet de 6% l'an, jusqu'au Remboursement £35,171,641." In consequence,

"Il en coutera aux Etats unis pour acquitter leur Dette et les Intérets suivant le Compte rendu £46,100,000
Il ne leur en Couteroit par l'Operation du Viager que 34,828,063

Difference au profit des Etats unis £11,271,937
Interêt Composé de cette Difference jusqu'à la Seizième année à 5% 8,146,951

Total de l'Epargne en faveur des Etats Unis 19,418,888."

(3) "Tableau du Remboursement annuel d'une Somme de £35,171,640, pour être accompli dans l'espace de Seize Ans, avec l'interêt à 6%." The three foregoing enclosures are in a clerk's hand, in tabular form. The fourth enclosure is printed below.

ENCLOSURE

Observations sur le Tableau en deux parties

On voit par ce tableau que les 3,400,000[tt] de rentes viagères sur des Têtes choisies, emploïées à payer annuellement pendant seize années, la Dette des Etats-unis, laisseroient des la huitième année, un capital excédant la dette et les interets de 26,272,507.[tt] desquelles separant l'escompte pendant huit ans, il resteroit 16,432,087,[tt] qui peuvent être considérées comme le bénéfice net de l'opération, au moment où les rentes seroient achetées, destinées au payement de la Dette, et les excédens vendus; ensorte que les Etats-unis ne débourseroient reellement, pour acquitter leur Dette de trente quatre millions, que l'excédent de cette somme sur £16,432,087

C'est à dire que pour payer 34 millions, ils ne débourseroient réellement que 17,567,913

34,000,000

Mais ces calculs doivent être modifiés par les observations suivantes.

1.° Cette opération ne peut pas être faite sans fraix. Elle exige 1.° un Emprunt de 34 millions au moins; une livraison de Contrats, et des remboursemens annuels, soit de l'Emprunt soit des interets. 2.° Un emploi du produit de l'Emprunt en viager. Pour faire cet emploi, il faut acheter le viager, choisir les Têtes, retirer les contrats, procurer les certificats de rentes. 3.° Il faut ensuite retirer les rentes, vendre les excédens du viager; et comme on ne pouroit éxécuter cette vente le meme jour, ni de la meme manière, il faut que certaines opérations soient remplacées par d'autres équivalentes. 4.° Il se pouroit même qu'il y eut des avances à faire pendant un ou deux ans, à cause du Déficit des rentes comparées aux payemens annuels de la Dette. Tout cela entraine comme l'on voit une Manutention assez compliquée. Elle demande de l'intelligence, de l'exactitude, du zèle et de la fidélité: ce qui n'est pas à trouver pour rien.

2.° Les Etats-unis, quoique réunis par une Convention fédérale propre à leur donner le plus grand credit, trouveroient difficilement des prêteurs qui leur fournissent une somme de trente quatre millions. Peut-être même que s'ils étoient Certains de la trouver, ils jugeroient plus convenables à leurs rapports politiques d'employer tout de suite cette Somme à s'acquitter envers la france, qu'à faire une Spéculation quelqu'avantageuse qu'elle put leur être.

3.° Enfin quoique le produit des rentes viagères soit determiné par une probabilité très voisine de la certitude, les Etats-unis auroient sans-doute de la répugnance à entreprendre une grande Spéculation dont le resultat seroit fondé sur la vie de Cent individus. Il est sans exemple que l'événement n'ait pas repondu aux Calculs faits d'avance sur la probabilité de la vie humaine; mais il faut avoir souvent et long-tems réfléchi à cette matière, pour se livrer à ces probabilités. C'est l'histoire de la Navigation.

Ces Observations expliquent pourquoi l'on ne presente point le Tableau en deux parties, comme une Spéculation que les Etats-unis doivent faire; mais uniquement comme la baze sur la quelle reposent des propositions qui, en réduisant le bénéfice des Etats unis, rémédieroient aux divers inconvéniens de la Spéculation, telle que le Tableau en deux parties la présente.

On a donc fait un second Tableau. Celui-ci offre le développement du marché que les Etats-unis pouroient faire avec la Compagnie Royale d'assurances sur la vie, pour acquitter par son moyen la Dette énoncée dans le Compte rendu des finances de france pour l'année 1787, et dans le même nombre d'années.

1.° Par ce marché la Compagnie seroit autorisée à acheter au nom et pour le Compte des Etats-unis, trois millions Cinq cent Soixante et dix mille livres de Rentes viagères. On suppose qu'elles ne couteroient pas plus de 34. millions.

2.° La dite Compagnie acheteroit les dites rentes, les constitueroit sur cent têtes de jeunes filles, et en feroit la perception; le tout à ses fraix.

3.° La Compagnie garantiroit la vie des Têtes, de manière que le revenu général seroit fixé sur un pied certain.

4.° Elle se chargeroit de revendre les excédens de rente de la manière qu'elle jugeroit à propos, et à ses risques et perils.

5.° Elle s'engageroit envers les Etats unis et envers le Gouvernement de france à acquitter la Dette des premiers dans le nombre d'années, et sommes énoncees, dans le Compte rendu des finances de france pour 1787.

6.° Les Etats unis, de leur côté, seroient tenus de faire payer exactement à la Compagnie chaque année, et pendant seize ans consécutifs, les Sommes indiquées dans le Tableau cy-après, les quelles Sommes montent ensemble à 34,828,068 livres; ensorte que l'économie des Etats unis dans ce marché seroit de £11,271,932. outre l'interêt de ce qu'ils auroient à payer de moins chaque année.

Dans le cas où les rentes viagères necessaires à cette opération couteroient moins de 34 Millions de livres, les Sommes annuelles payables par les Etats unis seroient reduites dans la proportion de ce qui auroit été dépensé de moins que 34 millions; si elles coutoient plus, ces Sommes seroient augmentées aussi à proportion.

Telles sont les principales conditions de marché que les Etats unis pouroient faire avec la Compagnie Royale des assurances sur la vie. On y ajouteroit de part et d'autre toutes les autres conditions qui paroitroient necessaires, et qui découleroient de la nature même du marché. On ne s'est pas attaché à les rechercher, parcequ'elles ne sont point essentielles pour déterminer le marché. En en mettant la baze sous les yeux du congres, ainsi que le Développement de son éxécution, on Lui offre tout cequi peut le déterminer, quant au calcul. Il ne sauroit etre difficile de convenir ensuite de tout cequi importeroit à la Sureté des Contractans.

MS (DLC); see note to covering letter, above.

It is difficult to believe that one so well acquainted with American institutions as Clavière was could have been unrealistic enough to suppose that TJ would place these proposals SOUS LES YEUX DU CONGRES, even as an object of curiosity. TJ had long known that Clavière and a group of Dutch bankers had approached the French ministry with the hope of purchasing the American debt at a heavy discount, and had transmitted information of this to Jay, urging late in 1786 that there was "no time to lose" if Congress desired to forestall such private speculations by making its own loan in Holland and liquidating the debt to France on its own terms, an object that TJ earnestly recommended just as, on an earlier occasion, he had urged Virginia to buy up its own state debt in order to forestall speculators (see TJ to Jay, 26 Sep., 12 Nov. 1786). But it is significant that when Clavière's close friend and associate, Brissot de Warville, departed for America, TJ did not know what his real object was, though he suspected (correctly) that it related to land speculation. This ignorance of Brissot's agency was due to the very good reason that the principals desired that it be kept secret. "His views in going to America," wrote Parker to Andrew Craigie, "are principally to obtain a perfect knowledge of the funds and the land in the western Territory. The representations that he will make to his friends in Europe will determine them respecting the purchase of the Funds. As he is a literary man . . . he will pass unsuspected in America of having any design to buy the Funds. . . . If he should recommend them to his connections they will make large purchases, all of which he proposes to confine entirely to you and Col. [William] Duer." Parker hoped to confine this operation "so that we shall be all united in one general interest" and he urged Craigie to introduce Brissot to "all your friends in congress" (Parker to Craigie, 2 June 1788, quoted in Eloise Ellery, *Brissot de Warville*, Boston, 1915, p. 433-4). Parker, too, had experienced many good offices at the hands of the American minister, but this secret speculative operation, aimed both at the American domestic debt and at the debt due France, was withheld from TJ. A few weeks earlier TJ had written urgent letters officially and privately to suggest a policy of debt management that would sustain American credit, forestall speculation, and guarantee that the government under the new Constitution would be able to begin operations with a sound credit in Europe (TJ to Madison, 3 May 1788; TJ to Jay, 4 May 1788; TJ to Washington, 2 May 1788). The policy that he recommended was, moreover, characteristically aimed at public benefit and grounded on the hope that a candid, open approach would inspire confidence: "Honest and annual publications of the paiments made will inspire confidence, while silence would conceal nothing from those interested to know" (TJ to Madison, 3 May 1788). The policy that he opposed was such a private, non-competitive, secretly-arranged negotiation as Parker favored, and the observation that "silence would conceal nothing from those interested to know" had an ironic twist in the speculation embarked upon by Clavière, Parker, Stadnitski, and Cazenove—for that speculation included among its principals William Duer and Samuel Osgood (the latter as secret partner), both members of the Board of the Treasury (Merrill Jensen, *The New Nation*, p. 385-6). This fact not only helps explain the need for secrecy, but puts in a clearer light the "note of moral superiority" in the report of the Commissioners of the Treasury on TJ's letter of 26 Sep. 1786 to Jay (see note to that letter, and Malone, *Jefferson*, II, 188-89). Further, it suggests that the present fanciful scheme may have been intended to occupy the attention of Congress, to prolong debate, and to serve as a screen for activities going on under the immediate eyes of Congress. If this conjectured object was in contemplation, the adventurers failed, for TJ pigeonholed the proposals and the operators went on to their own unsuccessful conclusion, brought about in large part because they came to mistrust each other; because Robert Morris and Gouverneur Morris soon entered the scene; and because the Dutch bankers had already laid the groundwork for their own ultimate success among the several competitive groups. These facts, too, put in perspective the urgent appeal that TJ again repeated after two years. In his letter to Jay of 3 Aug. 1788 TJ again returned to the "momentous object" of preventing a speculative transfer of the American domestic debt to Europe. Speculations had already begun in France, he reported, and if this debt were to be retained at home "there is not a moment to lose; and I know no means of retaining it but those I suggested to the Treasury board in my letter . . ." of 29 Mch. 1788. Save as an example of his consistent public purpose and as a contrast to private profit-seeking, TJ's long effort was a failure, and the words would return to exacerbate his sensitive nature when Alexander Hamilton made a "tortured" use of the original proposal of 26 Sep. 1786 (see TJ to Washington, 2 Mch. 1793).

To Foulloy

Sir | Paris July 9. 1788.

I had the honour of observing to you in our first conference that I had no authority to purchase the books you offered for the United states; but still that there was a possibility they might be so interesting to them as to induce me to risk myself by making the purchase, tho out of my line of duty. On examination of them however I found them by no means sufficiently interesting to be purchased at the price proposed, nor to induce me to hazard a purchase without orders. I will write to Congress on the subject, describing to them the contents of the books, but can by no means without their orders give such a sum as fifty Louis d'ors for them. You may be assured of hearing from me immediately on receiving their orders should they think proper to give me any on the subject. I have the honor to be Sir your most obedt. humble servant,

Th: Jefferson

PrC (DLC).

TJ's professing to find the books not sufficiently interesting to warrant his risking himself BY MAKING THE PURCHASE may be taken only as a sort of bargaining stratagem: actually, he had found the Deane manuscripts intensely interesting, both personally and publicly, and had caused extracts to be made of them during the short while they were in his possession. See Paine to TJ, at end of May 1788; TJ to Jay, 3 Aug. 1788; TJ to Foulloy, 4 July 1788; Foulloy to TJ, 4, 7, July; Meunier to TJ, 18 Dec. 1788.

To William Jones

SIR Paris July 9. 1788.

In my letter of January 5. of the last year, I informed you that I had received information from the gentlemen to whose management I had left my estate, that the proceeds of a sale they had made, with the profits of the estate to the end of the year 1786. would clear it of other demands so that I might begin the discharge of a debt to Kippen & co. and my part of Mr. Wayles's debt to you: that I was therefore desirous of arranging with you such just and practicable conditions as might place both our minds at ease: and I proposed that you should relinquish the claim to interest during the war (8. years) and in proportion as I should pay my third acquit me, pari passu, as to the other two thirds: that on my part I would take on myself the loss in the papermoney deposited in the treasury of Virginia, would pay interest incurring before and since the war, and would remit 400£ sterling annually till my third should be thus paid. In your answer of Feb. 25. 1787. you said that you had sent a copy of my letter to Mr. Hanson, your agent in Virginia, that you were apprehensive if you released any part of Mr. Wayles's estate, that you should release the whole: but that so soon as you should hear from your agent you would immediately write to me. I was in constant expectation therefore of receiving a letter from you in full answer to my propositions till your's of June 11. 1788. came to my hands, in which you observe 'it is now a long time since you had a letter from me.' By this I should infer that some intermediate letter from you had been written to me and had miscarried: for I have certainly received none from you of any date between those of Feb. 25. 1787. and June 11. 1788. which I hope will justify my silence and expectation.

My impatience to begin the paiment of my debt to you had occasioned me to make my propositions of Jan. 5. immediately on receiving the information from the managers of my estate which is therein mentioned. They very soon after contradicted that information, observed that some inaccuracies in the Steward's accounts had made them conclude too hastily that they should be clear of all other debts by the end of the year 1786, and in fact I have found that so slender have been the crops made that they have not yet cleared it of those debts. Nevertheless having made the proposition to you of a fixed annual paiment I will not recede from it: and to guard against all possibility of failure I have desired they will rent my whole estate, lands, slaves, and stocks, at fixed sums of hard money, as I had formerly done a part of it. According to the rents then given me, the whole should now bring in 1000£ currency of Virginia (dollars at 6/) a year clear of all charge. They write me lately that advantageous offers are already made for a part, and I have hopes this operation will take place at the close of the present year. Whenever therefore you shall accede to what I have proposed I will advance the annual paiments to you to three fifths of the profits of the estate (for I find that Kippen & co. should receive two fifths, and not one third only as I had before conjectured). These I presume will make 600£ currency a year to you, leaving 400£ a year for Kippen & co. I will do more. I will immediately direct the sale of my lands in Goochland and Cumberland for which I was offered before the war 3000£ currency, and they have been since increased in value by a neighboring purchase of £500. of which money you shall receive three fifths, and, if you chuse, the bonds of the purchasers to that amount shall be made to you and not to me. You doubt whether a release to me as to the other two thirds of the debt will not in law effect a release of those two thirds. It would not by our laws: however if your doubt on that head continues, I will undertake to obtain from the other two gentlemen an express agreement against that operation of the law. I have lately received from Mr. Eppes a letter by which I find he has the same anxious desire to pay off his proportion of this debt which I have: and I have no doubt he will agree to terms similiar to what I propose. He writes me word that he and Mr. Hanson differ so much in opinion that they shall be unable to settle on the balance which is due, and he desires me to undertake to settle it with you. I will proceed with you to that settlement when you please: and suppose we can do it by letter. To avoid postage on voluminous packages they can be sent to me by private conveiance if addressed to the care of Mr. John Trumbull No. 2. North street, Rathbone place London. What I have hitherto said must be considered as confined to Mr. Wayles's particular account, as rendered to us before the war, and not to extend to the negro ship on which you propose a claim in your letter of June 11. 1788. We never had an idea that Mr. Wayles's estate was in any manner interested in that concern. The consignment was to him and Richd. Randolph jointly. He died before any monies were collected. The authority survived to Randolph, so did the profits, and of course the whole obligation. We could not have called on a single creditor for paiment. Unless therefore there be some obligation on the part of Mr. Wayles of which I am not apprised, I do not apprehend we have any thing to do with it. Had we supposed ourselves liable, we should certainly have taken half the bonds out of Randolph's hands.

I shall expect your further explanation of this claim, and that you will be so good as to answer me as to my propositions relative to Mr. Wayles's own debt. I am with very great esteem Sir your most obedient humble servt., TH: JEFFERSON

PrC (DLC); at foot of text: "Mr. William Jones. Bristol." The RC (missing) was enclosed in TJ to Trumbull, 24 July 1788. Tr. (Vi: U.S. Circuit Court, Virginia District); in a clerk's hand; unsigned, with minor textual variations.

Jones's ANSWER OF FEB. 25. 1787 has not been found.

From La Lande

au College royal le 9 juillet 1788

MONSIEUR

Pardonnés si j'abuse encore de votre indulgence et de votre politesse pour obtenir un Eclaircissement qui interesse un de mes parens:

M. De Meurnand, qui a servi les etats unis, m'a chargé de sa procuration pour recevoir la rente qui lui est due. M.de Bouvignon lui a ecrit que vous esperiés recevoir des ordres pour faire payer ces interets dans ce mois-ci. Souffrez que je vous supplie de me faire savoir par un simple billet s'il y a quelque Esperance prochaine.

Permettes aussi que je vous demande vos ordres pour l'angleterre ou je suis sur le point de me rendre et que je vous prie de presenter mes respects à mon illustre confrere qui

Eripuit cælo fulmen, mox Sceptra tyrannis

Je suis avec respect Monsieur Votre tres humble et tres obeissant serviteur DE LA LANDE
de fac. des Sciences

RC (MHi); endorsed.

La Lande's ILLUSTRE CONFRERE was Benjamin Franklin. It was in 1778 that Turgot coined what has been called "the most famous of modern Latin epigrams: *Eripuit cælo fulmen sceptrumque tyrannis* (He snatched the lightning from the sky and the sceptre from tyrants)"; there "had been versions of almost the same thought and image before Turgot and his own may have been: *Eripuit cælo fulmen mox sceptra tyrannis* (meaning that as Franklin had wrested the lightning from heaven he would soon wrest the sceptre from George III)," but the commoner version became almost universal (Van Doren, *Franklin*, p. 606).

To Francis Eppes

DEAR SIR Paris July 10. 1788.

Your favor of Dec. 29. 1787. came to hand May 24. and that of April 4. on the 30th. of June. I will chearfully take the settlement with Jones off your hands, and do it as well as it can be done here. I wrote to him yesterday that I would proceed to settlement when he pleases. I should desire to take as our basis the *last account* current received by Mr. Wayles during his lifetime: because to that period we may consider his account as approved by Mr. Wayles. Then I must ask you to furnish me immediately 1. a list of all the tobaccoes shipped by Mr. Wayles posterior to those credited in that *last account*, with the accounts of the sales of them rendered by Jones. 2. A list and vouchers for the tobaccos shipped, after Mr. Wayles's death, of the produce of the estate before it was divided. 3. A list and vouchers of the tobaccos shipped by us separately to be credited to Mr. Wayles's account. I shipped one crop only, to wit, the first made after the division. I think it was about 40 hhds. the only vouchers for which are in the inspectors books at Richmond and Manchester. 4. A note of any hard money paiments made him by yourself or Mr. Skipwith. 5. A list of paper paiments deposited in the treasury under the sequestration law. John Randolph's debt was deposited as it was received in paper money. I made some deposits in my own account towards F. & Jones's debt. They were of monies I had received for debts contracted before any paper money was issued: but I meant and still mean to use them only in terrorem, to oblige him to a settlement on principles of substantial justice. The conditions I have offered for myself are 1. that he shall abandon interest during the war, eight years: 2. that for every hundred pounds I pay, he shall consider my part of the estate as absolutely discharged of 300£. 3. That I would pay interest incurred before and since the war: 4. that I would take on myself the papermoney deposits I had made; and lastly that I would make him such and such annual paiments till my third should be fully paid. Yourself and Mr. Skipwith will be so good as to inform me whether you will agree to similar terms, or what others you would propose. I am, like you, on a bed of thorns till I am cleared of debt. I therefore accede to your advice of selling my Cumberland lands, Elkhill and Smith's, and will beg of yourself and Mr. Lewis to do it. As I never proposed to sell them, I never had a direct offer for them but I had indirect overtures from which I concluded I might have 1500£ a peice for each of the two first before any paper money had been issued. It will be proper that no deed be demandeable till the paiments are actually made, and that, on failure to pay, they may be resold without application to Chancery. The deed for the Cumberland lands must recite expressly that that part is sold for the paiment of Mr. Wayles's debts, the deed of settlement, recorded in the General court, authorising a sale for that purpose only. I promise to Jones three fifths of the money arising from that sale and shall promise McCaul the other two fifths: as also to divide the rents and produce of my estate in the same proportion. If these should be proportioned to what I formerly rented my estate in Albemarle for, I hope in a reasonable time to be cleared of incumbrance without any further sales:—As to all demands for securityship, as they can be made on the pretence of law only and not of any moral obligation, I should be for treating them very differently from Mr. Wayles private debt. That is a debt of justice and should be honestly paid, because we have the property bought by him with that money. But we have not the property bought by the money for which he was security only. Let those pay who have it. We may conscientiously avoid it by every possible means. As to that for the Negro ship, I never yet saw any thing which could oblige us in law to answer it. The consignment was to Messrs. Wayles and Randolph jointly. On Mr. Wayles's death then the trust survived to Randolph alone, so did the right to sue on the bonds, so did the profit, and so did all the risque and responsibility. This is the case, unless the ordinary effect of the law has been changed by any express agreement on the part of Mr. Wayles, of which I never saw any evidence. I hope therefore that this cloud will dissipate. I have called on Jones for an explanation of the foundation of this claim.——In order to settle the price of our last shipments of tobacco to Jones, I shall get my friend James Maury of Liverpool to go, at our expence, to Bristol and satisfy himself what tobaccoes sold for there at the times ours

PrC (CSmH); incomplete, but probably lacking no more than one page, which may have had on it little more than the complimentary close; endorsed by TJ, evidently late in life: "Eppes Fras."—a fact which indicates that a concluding page, if made at all, was missing before 1826, since TJ customarily endorsed on the verso of the final page of a letter. Enclosed in TJ to Madison, 31 July 1788; see Madison to TJ, 17 Oct. 1788.

Eppes' letters of 29 Dec. 1787 and 4 Apr. 1788 are listed in SJL Index, but have not been found.

From Grand & Cie.

Paris, 10 July 1788. Acknowledge receipt from TJ of reimbursement of 2400,[tt] advanced to Paradise on TJ's order, by draft on Willink & Van Staphorst of 2 July 1788 for *f*2291.13.8 Banco.

RC (DLC); endorsed on recto by TJ: "Paradise John. Note of June 24. 1788. for 2400.[tt]" and, on verso, "Mr. Grand's receipt for 2400.[tt]" This receipt is written on verso of Paradise's acknowledgment, of which only the following remains: ". . . on Thursday May 29th. 1788, upon the same bill of three hundred pounds sterling, Mr. Paradise gratefully. . . ."

From George Wythe

DEAR SIR Williamsburgh 10 of July 1788

The books, which you sent last september did not arrive here until this day. They shall be distributed according to your appointment. For my part of them i owe many thanks but indeed, my good sir, such presents are too costly. P. Carr still attends me daily. I think him well advanced in the greek and latin languages. Your directions for prosecution of his studies will be profitable to him and me too. The convention for discussing the american government sat almost two weeks. The result of their deliberations is inclosed with this. The general assembly also sat part of the same time. Their meeting was occasioned by a refusal of the judges to execute an act for establishing district courts, which passed the preceding session. Mr. Paradise was pleased with the country and people here. But, after he heard of his daughter's death, the desires of all among us who knew him, could not prevale upon him to remain longer. To write is difficult, and sometimes a little painful; caused by a weakness in my right[1] thumb. I should suppose it to be a gout, which i had slightly once in the foot, but that there is yet no swelling. This infirmity must apologize for the rarity and shortness of my letters. But for the same reason yours will be more acceptable: if any circumstances can make them more acceptable. I am dear sir your obliged humble servant, G. WYTHE

RC (DLC); endorsed; date-line is repeated at foot of text. The enclosed resolution of the Virginia Convention of 25 June 1788, presumably in broadside or newspaper form, reads as follows: "We the Delegates of the people of Virginia, duly elected in pursuance of a recommendation from the General Assembly, and now met in Convention, having fully and freely investigated and discussed the proceedings of the Fœderal Convention, and being prepared as well as the most mature deliberations hath enabled us, to decide thereon, Do in the name and in behalf of the people of Virginia, declare and make known that the powers granted under the Constitution, being derived from the people of the United States may be resumed by them whensoever the same shall be perverted to their injury or oppression, and that every power not granted thereby remains with them and at their will: that therefore no right of any denomination, can be cancelled, abridged, restrained or modified, by the Congress, by the Senate or House of Representatives acting in any capacity, by the President or any department or officer of the United States, except in those instances in which power is given by the Constitution for those purposes: and that among other essential rights, the liberty of conscience and of the press cannot be cancelled, abridged, restrained or modified by any authority of the United States. With these impressions, with a solemn appeal to the searcher of hearts for the purity of our intentions, and under the conviction, that, whatsoever imperfections may exist in the Constitution, ought rather to be examined in the mode prescribed therein, than to bring the Union into danger by a delay, with a hope of obtaining amendments, previous to the ratification: We the said Delegates, in the name and in behalf of the People of Virginia, do by these presents assent to, and ratify the Constitution recommended on the seventeenth day of September, one thousand seven hundred and eighty seven, by the Fœderal Convention for the Government of the United States; hereby announcing to all those whom it may concern, that the said Constitution is binding upon the said People" (*Journal of the Convention of Virginia*, Richmond, Augustine Davis, 1788, p. 28-9). Wythe may have enclosed one of the copies ordered to be printed by the Convention, for which a voucher was issued 3 July 1788; none of these copies is known to have survived (Swem, "Va. Bibliog.," No. 7596).

On the BOOKS . . . SENT LAST SEPTEMBER, see TJ to Wythe, 16 Sep. 1788.

[1] This word interlined in substitution for "left," deleted.

From Stephen Cathalan, Sr.

the 11th. July 1788

An Algerian Privateer having been distroy'd by a napolitan man of war, 2 Months ago, at the due distance from the land out of Toulon, the Crew Went on Shore, and all the Services in that occasion were rendered to them.

Notwithstanding that, the recqsur[1] Capn. being returned to Algiers, has declard that the man of war was a french one, and our Scadron of observation crusing out of algier, the officers were forbiden of Landing or making any Fresh provisions.

The Dey of algiers has asked, to our Consul there, extravagant reparations. This has given information to our Board of Trade and our Court, of those misintelligences, adding that war will ensue. We are expecting here the event. We hope that on that conjuncture[2] the Scadron will not Leave the Mediterranean to protect our vessels.

If the warr takes place, Your Colour will be more safe, because we will have forces to prevent their Crusing.

I have thought this Information worth of your attention.

American wheat will be sold at very advantageous prices here till next Spring. Philadelphia would obtain over 32[tt] pr. charge at Least.

No more tobacco remains unsold here, when you will know the quantity purchased by the farmers since the 1st. January, I will be much obliged to Communicate it to me.

RC (DLC); though containing neither salutation nor signature, this communication—which was evidently sent by private hands rather than by post—seems to be complete, the date-line being placed immediately at the foot of text; endorsed by TJ: "Cathalan"; in the hand of Stephen Cathalan, Jr.

1 This word doubtful; "rescued" may have been intended.

2 This word doubtful.

From John Brown Cutting

Sir London July 11. 1788

I am to congratulate you upon the adoption of the new national constitution of our country by the State of South Carolina. I cannot ascertain the precise numbers of the Convention, but the main question was carried by a majority of sixty six members, not without warm debate. I have mutilated a couple of newspapers which contain nothing beside the intelligence stamp'd on the columns cut out. From the specimen of eloquence and argument impressed on one of them a fair estimate may be formed of the talents of the Minority. That of Maryland exhibited proofs of riper ability. It seems to me (if it were not rash either to form or offer any opinion at this distance) that some of the gentlemen warmly opposed to an acceptance of the plan (in the back counties of Virginia) have diffused their objections throughout those of the two Carolinas which are most remote from the atlantic shores. In North Carolina violent contests at the election of members for their State Convention by a few of those tramontane districts have resulted. In one instance the operation of those intrigues to which I refer probably induced a majority of the voters to bestow their suffrages on men extremely obscure and unfit from excessive ignorance, as is alledged, to discuss or decide upon so great a question. In consequence of this conception the election was interrupted by those who wished men more enlightened, or as the phrase is, more *fœderal.* And by force of club law, their antagonists were defeated. I understand that North Carolina but for such forceful zeal in several parts of the Country wou'd not have exhibited a Convention so united in support of national system as is now the promise. The prospect now is that they will ratify at any rate. In apology for electioneering violences in that state, which few considerate citizens of our union will approve or attempt to justify, it may be urged that among the whole thirteen there is not a community, the internal and ferocious disturbances of which more loudly exact the interference of national authority and controul, such as is meant to be delegated by the ratification thus eagerly sought. Already the conflicts for independent power between those who denominate themselves citizens of Frankland and the residue of their neighbours who adhere to the legitimate government have issued in blood: armed parties within these few months have assaulted each other in open warfare, besieged dwelling houses inflicting mutual and mortal wounds; and menacing future feuds with which if not over-aw'd or quell'd by legal authority confessedly paramount to both parties and in some measure constituted for this express purpose, the worst sort of unsubdueable anarcy might be expected to result.

When I contemplate such events and the probability that similar ones might be engendered in various quarters of the union unless a strong superintending power vest in the general government capable to curb individual licentiousness and suffocate the germs of future discord; I am not surprized at the energy of almost the whole body of our enlighten'd and leading characters in every state who otherwise wou'd seem actuated with an unecessary if not intemperate zeal in a great and a good cause. Thus a person who were superficially to peruse the proceedings even of the liberal and patriotic Convention of Maryland wou'd be led to imagine that the objections and arguments of the Minority were treated with too much levity and even disdain by the majority. Whereas a minute scrutiny into the *motives* and the *measures* of each party wou'd satisfy a candid enquirer. It is not a solecism to say that the opposition to a thorough reform of the fœderal government began in Maryland even before the agitation of the question in the general Convention at Philadelphia. Mr. Martin, the attorney general, who was primarily appointed to that office by Mr. Chase, was by the same influence deputed to represent the State after Messrs. Carrol, Johnson &c. &c. the first choice of the legislature declined quitting

Maryland even upon the important business of new-framing the national government. Mr. Chase having just before menaced the senate for rejecting a wide Emission of paper money and appealed to the people against them, they had joined in that general issue and cou'd not venture to relinquish to a violent and headstrong party their active influence in the senate as well as in the lower house at the very moment when it was so essentially needed to stem the torrent of the populace for the paper. Those Gentlemen therefore remained at home, convinced their fellow citizens of their superior rectitude and wisdom, and defeated that favourite measure of Mr. Chase: meanwhile Mr. Martin and Mr. John F. Mercer, a young gentleman whom you well know, went to the general Convention, opposed the great leading features of the plan which was afterwards promulged, withdrew themselves from any signature of it, and from the moment when it was proposed for ratification, in conjunction with Mr. Chase and his sure coadjutor Mr. Paca, exerted every effort to hinder its adoption. So far did Mr. Martin proceed in his avowed hostility, as even to detail in the face of decency, before the assembled Legislature of Maryland, the petty dialogues and paltry anecdotes of every description, that came to his knowledge in conventional committees and private conversations with the respective members of the Convention when at Philadelphia. I blush'd in my own bed-chamber when I read his speech on this side of the Atlantic. An hostility so premature and determin'd did certainly render those Gentlemen who waged it, obnoxious to many of their fellow citizens, who likewise recollected their warm conduct relevant to the bills of credit, which they had so recently urged Maryland to issue. When the Convention met on the 21st of April whatsoever proposition came from Messrs. Chase, Paca, Martin or Mercer was viewed with jealousy or disgust, and generally rejected, by a great majority. Nay so far did this disposition to neglect their sentiments prevail that even to their well grounded objections and most cogent arguments no reply was made—a great majority remained inflexibly silent or called for the main question which on Saturday the 26th. was carried by 63 to 11. After which Mr. Paca renewed a proposition which had been rejected the day before for the appointment of a committee to consider and report what amendments shou'd be recommended by the convention of Maryland, when 66 voted for such a committee. And accordingly Mr. Paca, Messrs. Johnson, S. Chase, Potts, Mercer, Goldsborough, Tighlman, Hanson, J. T.

Chase, W. Tighlman Lee, McHenry and Gale were appointed. Upon the following amendments the Committee agreed.

1. "That Congress shall exercise no power but what is expressly delegated by this constitution.

2. That there shall be a trial by jury in all criminal cases, according to the course of proceeding in the state wherein the offence is committed; and that there be no appeal from matter of fact, or second trial after acquittal: but this provision shall not extend to such cases as arise in the government of the land or naval forces.

3. That in all actions on debts or contracts and in all other controversies respecting property, or in which the inferior fœderal courts have jurisdiction, the trial of facts shall be by jury, if required by either party: and that it be expressly declared, that the state courts in such cases, have a concurrent jurisdiction with the fœderal courts with an appeal from either, only as to matter of law, to the supreme fœderal court, if the matter in dispute be of value of   dollars.

4. That the inferior fœderal courts shall not have jurisdiction of less than   dollars; and there may be an appeal in all cases of revenue, as well in matter of fact as law, and Congress may give the state Courts jurisdiction of revenue cases, for such sums and in such manner, as they may think proper.

5. That in all cases of trespasses done within the body of a county, and within the inferior fœderal jurisdiction, the party injur'd shall be entitled to trial by jury in the state where the injury shall be committed; and that it be expressly declared that the state courts, in such cases, shall have concurrent jurisdiction with the fœderal courts; and there shall be no appeal from either, except on matter of law; and that no person be exempt from such jurisdiction and trial but ambassadors and ministers privileged by the law of Nations.

6. That the fœderal courts shall not be entitled to jurisdiction by fictions or collusion.

7. That the fœderal judges do not hold any other office of profit, or receive the profits of any other office under Congress, during the time they hold their commissions.

8. That all warrants without oath or affirmation of a person conscienciously scrupulous of taking an oath, to search suspected places or to seize any person or his property, are grievous and oppressive; and all general warrants to search suspected places, or to apprehend any person suspected, without naming or describing

the place or person in special, are dangerous and ought not to be granted.

9. That no soldier be enlisted for a longer time than four years, except in time of war, and then only during the war.

10. That soldiers be not quartered in time of peace upon private houses without the consent of the owners.

11. That no mutiny bill continue in force longer than two years.

12. That the freedom of the press be inviolably preserved.

13. That the militia shall not be subject to martial law, except in time of war, invasion or rebellion."

Thus far there was a concurrence in opinion either unanimously or by a considerable majority of the Committee. But when the following amendments were laid before the committee, a majority negatived the same.

1. That the militia unless selected by lot or voluntarily enlisted shall not be marched beyond the limits of an adjoining State, without the consent of their legislature or executive.

2. That Congress shall have no power to alter or change the time place or manner of holding elections for senators or representatives, unless a state shall neglect to make regulations, or to execute its regulations, or shall be prevented by invasion or rebellion; in which cases only Congress may interfere, until the cause be removed.

3. That in every law of Congress imposing *direct* taxes, the collection thereof shall be *suspended* for a certain reasonable time therein limited, and on payment of the sum by any state, by the time appointed, such taxes shall not be collected.

4. That no *standing army* shall be kept *up in time* of *peace* unless with the consent of two thirds of the members present of each branch of Congress.

5. That the president shall not command the army in person, without the consent of Congress.

6. That no treaty shall be effectual to repeal or abrogate the *constitutions* or *bills* of *rights* of the states or any part of them.

7. That no regulation of commerce or navigation act, shall be made, unless with the consent of two thirds of the members of each branch of Congress.

8. That no member of Congress shall be eligible to any office of profit under Congress during the time for which he shall be appointed.

9. That Congress shall have no power to lay a *poll* tax.

10. That no person conscienciously scrupulous of bearing arms in any case, shall be compelled *personally* to serve as a soldier.

11. That there be a responsible council to the president.

12. That there be no national religion establish'd by law, but that all persons be equally entitled to protection in their religious liberty.

13. That all imposts and duties laid by Congress shall be placed to the credit of the state in which the same be collected, and shall be deducted out of such states quota of the common or general expences of government.

14. That every man hath a right to petition the legislature for redress of grievances in a peaceable and orderly manner.

15. That it be declared, that all persons entrusted with the legislative or executive powers of government are the trustees and servants of the public; and as such accountable for their conduct. Wherefore whenever the ends of government are perverted, and public liberty manifestly endangered, and all other means of redress are ineffectual, the people may, and of right ought, to reform the old, or establish a new government; the doctrine of non resistance to arbitrary power and oppression, is absurd, slavish, and destructive of the good and happiness of mankind."

The introduction of these articles, especially the 7th and 13th, alarmed and gave offence to many of those among the majority who suspected the motives of Mr. Chase and his particular associates to be sinister and altogether hostile to any effectual plan of national government. And on Monday the 29th while the Committee were sitting the Convention upon motion resolved, "That this Convention will consider of no propositions for the amendment of the fœderal government, except such as shall be submitted to them by the Committee of thirteen." Upon which the Committee being sent for by the Convention, a majority of them determined, that they wou'd make no report of any amendments whatsoever. The Convention then immediately adjourned sine die.

Since which William Paca, Messrs. S. and J. T. Chase and John F. Mercer, members of the Committee, and Messrs. Martin, Cockey, Harrison, Love, Cromwell Pinkney and 2 Ridgley's members of Convention, have appeal'd to the public, complaining of the Convention, defending their own conduct and asserting that they "consider the proposed form of national government as very defective, and that the liberty and happiness of the people will be endangered if the system be not greatly changed and alter'd."

I have undertaken this local detail because I thought it might not be unentertaining to you especially if you have seen no other narrative of the proceedings in Maryland except that which in a Boston paper of May 23 I transmitted to you through Mr. Parker. I have also inclosed for the same purpose of amusing the manly proceeding of a Virginia Court of appeals. Without knowing the particular merits of the cause, I may venture to applaud the integrity of Judges who thus fulfil their oaths and their duties. I am proud of such characters. They exalt themselves and their country, while they maintain the principles of the constitution of Virginia and manifest the unspotted probity of its judiciary department. I hope you will not think me too *local* or *statically* envious when I mention that a similar instance has occur'd in Massachusetts. Where when the legislature unintentionally trespassd upon a barrier of the Constitution the Judges of the supreme Court solemnly determin'd that the particular statute was unconstitutional. In the very next session there was a formal and unanimous repeal of the law which perhaps was unnecessary.

I have just heard from New York that Mr. Jay who was reported to be mortally hurt in the late *anatomical* riots there is in tolerable health. Mrs. and Col. Smith arrived at Halifax on the 7th of May. They were in New York on the 20th. Mr. Adams had not arrived in Boston on the 1st of June. Mr. Hancock is again elected Governor and General Lincoln Lt. Governor of Massachusetts. I have no letter from Col. Smith himself.

The people of the district of Kentuckey having met in Convention agree to accept their independance conformably to the terms of the Virginia Ordinance passed some time since. They are to organize and legislate on the 1st of January 1789.

If a good private opportunity occurs soon I will transmit you a pamphlet or two lately written in various parts of the Union. The most inferior I have perused upon the fœderal government is attributed (erroneously I believe) to Mr. St. George Tucker. Judge Hanson of Maryland treats the same topic well. But Mr. Maddison, (who I am assured is the *genuine* author of the two volumes of essays signed *publius* and heretofore given to Col. Hamilton of New York) it is agreed transcends every politician who has attempted to explain or defend any system of fœderal Polity.

To the contents of my last by Mr. Parker I have nothing to add nor have I aught to subtract from truths which are undeniable. In three weeks I expect to embark for Charlestown and intreat the honor of your commands. Labouring as I do in this Island under the misfortune of excessive ignorance concerning all affairs on the continent I ought to supplicate a single letter from you at least that when I arrive in Carolina I may not be wholly empty of such information as Mr. E. Rutledge or any other of your friends might expect one to convey from Europe if not orally yet in writing.

This day his britannick majesty is expected to put an end to the present session of parliament in a satisfactory and pacific speech to both houses. Much of the past three weeks has been consumed in framing a bill to regulate the transportation of slaves from Africa to the West India Islands. The attempt or supposed attempt to interfere in a branch of commerce so lucrative and extensive excited great alarm and warm opposition among the individuals interested in the same, who are against every species of innovation. Few acts have undergone more mutation or remark from their origin to ultimate legitimacy; altho but an extemporaneous measure to accomplish an humane object. Some rational and superior system of legislation will I hope be devised by our country gently to prepare the negroes for that reception of their natural rights which might be effected without distracting society or extinguishing property!

With suitable apologies for the prolixity of this letter I am with great respect & much attachment Your Excellency's Most Obedt. Servant, JOHN BROWN CUTTING

If after perusal of the Carolina intelligence Mr. Short (to whom my best compliments are offerd) wou'd inclose it in a line to Mr. Rutledge to remain in the poste office at Strasbourg till call'd for he will amuse one friend and oblige another.

RC (DLC); endorsed. The MANLY PROCEEDINGS OF A VIRGINIA COURT OF APPEALS that Cutting enclosed are referred to in Wythe to TJ, 10 July 1788; the account that Cutting sent has not been found, but it probably was a newspaper report.

The PAMPHLET OR TWO LATELY WRITTEN IN VARIOUS PARTS OF THE UNION that Cutting promised to send were probably those discussed in the text and were related to the debate over the adoption of the Constitution. Cutting—possibly earlier—had sent to TJ two pamphlets by Tench Coxe, one being *An Address to an Assembly of the Friends of American Manufactures, convened for the Purpose of establishing a Society for the Encouragement of Manufactures and the Useful Arts, read in the University of Pennsylvania, on Thursday the 9th of August 1787* (Philadelphia, Aitken, 1787), and the other *An Enquiry into the Principles on which a Commercial System for the United States of America should be founded; to which are added some political observations connected with the Subject. Read before the Society for Political Enquiries, convened at the house of his Excellency Benjamin Franklin, Esquire, in Philadelphia May 11th, 1787* (Philadelphia, Aitken, 1787). See Sowerby, Nos. 3622-3.

To Dugnani

Paris July 11. 1788.

I have the honor of sending your Excellency the second volume of the American Philosophical transactions which came to my hands yesterday. My correspondent writes me that the first volume cannot be bought at this moment, the depot in which they were kept having been destroyed during the war. But he adds that they propose to reprint the first volume and that he will take care to send me a copy for you as soon as it shall appear.

I have written to Havre to have the post office there examined for the packet which your Excellency supposes may have come there from America to your address, and will have the honor of communicating to you the information I shall receive. I have now that of assuring you that I am with sentiments of sincere esteem and respect Your Excellency's most obedient and most humble servant,

TH: JEFFERSON

PrC (DLC); at foot of text: "H. E. the Apostolical Nuncio."

The CORRESPONDENT was Edward Carrington; see his letter to TJ, 14 May 1788. If Cardinal Dugnani's supposition about the PACKET . . . FROM AMERICA was put in writing, his letter has not been found; TJ's letter WRITTEN TO HAVRE is that to Limozin, this date.

To Nicholas Lewis

DEAR SIR

Paris July 11. 1788.

Your favor of Aug. 20. 1787. came to hand some time ago; that of Apr. 15. 1788 I received last night. I had just written to Mr. Eppes on the subject of my affairs, and intended writing to you to-day. The opportune arrival of the last letter enables me to answer both at the same time. I am much pleased that you approve of my plan of hiring my estate. Besides that the profit will be greater, it will enable me to see a fixed term to my embarrasments. For the same reason I would prefer money to tobacco rents, because my engagements for annual paiments must be in money. Yet if you think the greater assurance of punctual paiments in tobacco overbalances the advantage of a fixed sum in money, I leave it to your discretion. One peice of information however I must give you, which is that there is no prospect that the European market for tobacco will improve. Our principal dependance is on this country, and the footing on which I have got that article placed here, is the best we can ever expect. In the leases therefore, tobacco of my own estate, or of the best warehouses cannot be counted on at more than from 20/ to 22/6 currency the utmost. But I am in hopes my dear Sir, that more can be obtained per hand than 12£ currency, which you mention. I found my hopes on these considerations. I rented to Garth & Mousley as well as I recollect for £11. Sterling a hand, tobacco then from 18/ to 20/ the hundred and the legal exchange 25. per cent. Tobacco is now ten per cent higher and legal exchange raised 5. percent. This entitles us at present to ask £15. currency a hand. I never knew exactly what Garth & Mousley made. They only told me in general that they had made about a good overseer's or steward's lay each: suppose this 75£ each and calculate it on the number of workers they had, and it will prove how much more worth is a working hand with the lands and stock thrown in, than without them. Add to this that there is the addition of Hickman & Smith's lands in Albemarle (about 1000 acres) and that the lands in Bedford are much better for tobacco than those of Albemarle were when Garth & Mousley rented them. I only mention these considerations to enable you to demonstrate to those who enter into conference on the subject that a higher sum than £12. currency may be reasonably asked; but not to tie you down, for certainly I had rather rent for £12. currency than not to rent at all. I think I suggested in my former letters the necessity of stipulating a right to distrain when the rent is not paid. It might be a still greater security to stipulate also that their tobaccos shall be delivered at certain warehouses in your name, so that you may receive the money from the purchaser when the tenant has failed to pay.—I come over to your advice, Sir, to sell my lands in Cumberland and Goochland, and have accordingly desired Mr. Eppes to join you in doing it. As to the prices, I leave it to your discretions. I never had a direct offer for those lands, because I never meant to sell them. But from overtures made before a shilling of paper money had issued, I supposed I could get 1500£ for Cumberland and the same for Elkhill. This was before I purchased Smith's. I have promised to Jones three fifths of what these lands shall sell for, and even that the bonds shall be given in his name, if he will acquit me so far, and on condition he will make a final settlement with me on the terms I have proposed. I shall immediately write to Mr. McCaul that he shall have the other two fifths, as well as two fifths annually of the rents and profits of my estate, the other three fifths of these being proposed to Jones. The check on the tenants against abusing my slaves was, by the former lease, that I might discontinue it on a reference to arbitrators. Would it not be well to retain an optional right to sue them for ill usage of the slaves or to discontinue it by arbitration, whichever you should chuse at the time?

I will now proceed to take notice of some of the debts mentioned in your letters. As to Mr. Braxton's I still think his memory has led him into error on the subject, and that my memorandum books of that date would correct it. You mention 'a considerable debt due to Dr. Walker not enumerated in my list.' I settled with Doctr. Walker just before I left Virginia, and gave my acknolegement of the balance I owed him which was £40-11-9 3/4. This is stated in the list of my debts which I left you, and which I presume escaped your notice, as I know of no other debt of money to Doctr. Walker, unless he should have taken an assignment from somebody. Be this as it will, I know his justice and honour so well that whatever he has demanded is right, and I would wish it to be paid of the first money possible. If it be no more than the balance I have named with it's interest, rather than he should be incommoded, if you have not the money, be so good as to obtain it by drawing a bill on me at 60 days sight, which shall be honored. My friend Mr. Donald can dispose of this draught for you. 'Coutts's demand.' 'Donald, Scott & co.' I doubt both. I do not even remember the name of such a house as the latter. My papers will perhaps throw light on these. They were alphabetically arranged, so as that any paper may be found in a moment. But most of all my memorandum books will shew. 'Doctor Read's account' is noted in my list £48-13-3 under the name of Colo. Bannister, because you will find among my papers Reid's account and his order to pay the money to Bannister. Since I left Virginia Colo. Bannister is fallen in my debt. If therefore he has not relinquished to Read his claim on me, you can get his receipt for the money, for which I will credit him in the account of what I have paid for him.

'Boden of Norfolk £14.' If this is for Phripp & Bowden for leather (I beleive) it may be right, by possibility, but I doubt it. 'Hierom Gaines for timber, work &c. £19.' Frank Gaines owed me a certain number of days work. I agreed to take in exchange for it work from his father, whom I wished to employ in searching timber, searching the lines of my order of council &c. I think there is no other claim of Hierom's against me, and of course that his services were to pay a debt. Before I left Monticello I made a point of settling every account I could get at, in order to state it in my list of debts. Where I could not settle the balance accurately, still I entered the name in the list I left you, as a note that there was something due. It is not probable that I could have overlooked Hierom Gaines's account and especially for such a sum. I have great confidence in Hierom's integrity, and therefore hope that by the aid of these circumstances you will be able to settle this matter rightly.

'Wm. Chisholm. £26.' This is in my opinion impossible. He left my estate in Goochland when the British came there. He was in such distress afterwards that if I had owed him money, it was impossible I should not have raised it for him by some means or other, and much more so that I should have omitted it in my list, and lost every trace of it in my memory.

'Johnson a carpenter thirty odd pounds for work many years ago.' I have forgot that ever such a person worked for me: but, if he did, that he has been paid is certain. I made a point of paying my workmen in preference to all other claimants. I never parted with one without settling with him, and giving him either his money or my note. Every person that ever worked from me can attest this, and that I always paid their notes pretty soon. I am sure there did not exist one of these notes unpaid when I left Virginia, except to Watson & Orr who were still at work for me.

The debts in Bedford to Robinson, Bennet, and Callaway I suppose have been contracted since I came away.

In general I will beg of you to refer to my Memorandum books. They are small books which I used to carry in my pocket. They are 6. or 8. in number. There is an alphabetical index of names to every one, so that all the entries respecting any one person may be found in a moment in them. They were made with such scrupulous fidelity that I shall not be afraid to justify them on the bed of death, and so exact that in the course of 15 years which they comprehend, I never discovered that I had made but one omission of a paiment. I do not mean to say that the accounts before questioned are not just decisively. I have not confidence enough in my memory to say that. But they should be examined under several points of view. They may be paper money accounts. They may have been transferred from some other person who has been paid. They may be due from some other person and the demand made on me without foundation. They may have been paid by me either directly or circuitously. The silence of my memorandum books as to a money paiment or receipt by me may be relied on as negative proof, and their entries of a paiment or receipt as a positive proof of that paiment or entry. Wherever credits have been transferred circuitously from one to another, and accounts discharged in that way, I did not always enter them, nor even generally. But as you know a great deal of business was done in this way, it should always be well enquired into as to any accounts presented since I came away and not enumerated in my list. My omission there is a presumption that the account has been settled some way: tho' I do not pretend it to be infallible. I only made out as exact a list as I could.

I am so desirous of proceeding to the hiring my estate that I would not detain my sawyers to finish my bill of scantling. Only be so good as to put what stuff is ready into perfect security. The bricks also which are ready made I would wish to have well taken care of, that I may not have occasion to make any on my return.

I shall continue to reflect on the debts before observed on and which are mentioned to me for the first time in your letter received last night. Probably my recollection will enable me to be more particular on their subject in my next letter. So that the settlement of them had better be a little delayed, if my memorandum books do not satisfy you.

I shall give orders at Havre relative to the bacon whenever it arrives. But in future it will not be worth while to send me any, because it's importation is prohibited, and I have never yet been able to obtain any article of this kind from the Custom house. I thank Mrs. Lewis kindly for the ears of corn and the seeds accompanying them which are safely come to hand. The homony corn is a precious present. The corn of this country and of Italy, as far as I have seen it, cannot be eaten, either in the form of corn or of bread, by any person who has eaten that of America. I have planted some grains which may perhaps come to maturity as we have still 3 months and a half to frost.—One word more on my leases. I think the term should not exceed three years. The negroes too old to be hired, could they not make a good profit by cultivating cotton? Much enquiry is made of me here about the cultivation of cotton; and I would thank you to give me your opinion how much a hand would make cultivating that as his principal crop instead of tobacco. Great George, Ursula, Betty Hemings not to be hired at all, nor Martin nor Bob otherwise than as they are now. I am sensible, my dear Sir, how much trouble and perplexity I am giving you with my affairs. The plan of leasing will in a great measure releive you. I know Mrs. Lewis's goodness too and her attentions to them. I tender you both the feelings of the most heart felt gratitude. My daughters are well and join me in affectionate remembrance to yourself, Mrs. Lewis and family. I pray you both to accept assurances of my sincere affection, and of the sentiments of esteem & attachment with which I am Dear Sir your friend & servant, TH: JEFFERSON

RC (Dr. O. O. Fisher, Detroit, Mich., 1950). Enclosed in TJ to Madison, 31 July 1788 (see Madison to TJ, 17 Oct. 1788). PrC (DLC).

Lewis' letter of AUG. 20 1787 is recorded in SJL as received 19 Dec. 1787, but has not been found; that of 15 Apr. 1788 is also missing.

To André Limozin

SIR Paris July 11. 1788.

His excellency Count Dugnani archbishop of Rhodes and Nuncio of the Pope at this court supposes that there may be in the post office of Havre a packet addressed to him from America. I have promised him I would ask the favor of you to have the post office examined and to forward the packet if it be there; which I have the honour now to request of you.

Since the date of my last no new occurrences have arisen which indicate either peace or war. We expect daily to hear that Sweden has commenced hostilities against Russia.

I have the honor to be with great esteem Sir Your most obedient humble servant, TH: JEFFERSON

PrC (DLC).

To Richard Price

DEAR SIR Paris July 11. 1788.

It is rendering mutual service to men of virtue and understanding to make them acquainted with one another. I need no other apology for presenting to your notice the bearer hereof Mr. Barlow. I know you were among the first who read the Visions of Columbus, while yet in Manuscript: and think the sentiments I heard you express of that poem, will induce you to be pleased with the acquaintance of their author. He comes to pass a few days only at London, merely to know something of it. As I have little acquaintance there, I cannot do better for him than to ask you to be so good as to make him known to such persons as his turn, and his time, might render desireable to him.

I thank you, my dear Sir, for the volume you were so kind as to send me some time ago. Every thing you write is precious, and this volume is on the most precious of all our concerns. We may well admit morality to be the child of the understanding rather than of the senses, when we observe that it becomes dearer to us as the latter weaken, and as the former grows stronger by time and experience till the hour arrives in which all other objects lose all their value. That that hour may be distant with you, my friend, and that the intermediate space may be filled with health and happiness is the sincere prayer of him who is with sentiments great respect and friendship Dr Sir your most obedient humble servant,

TH: JEFFERSON

PrC (DLC).

For a note on the VOLUME sent by Price some time back, see Price's undated letter printed above at end of Apr. 1788.

From John Trumbull

DR. SIR London July 11th. 1788

I have your two Letters, of the 29th. June (enclosing Mr. Grand's letter of Credit on Mr. Lewis Tessier for Eighty pounds Stg. which I have this day receiv'd and given duplicate Receipts for) and of 2d: July. The Carriage I had agreed for was sold before I got your answer: but I have good hope of meeting as good a bargain before Mr. Parker goes again to Paris.—Lackington had only Alfred's Orosius. That I have bought and will send you by an early conveyance. The Pictures you shall also have as soon as the Varnish is so dry as to bear the danger of Dust which they may encounter on the road.—I really am in despair with respect to the Tea Vase:—I can find nobody who will undertake it with much promise of success. Elegance the workmen can easily attain, but they all declare that it must be with a sacrifice of utility unless they depart wholly from the form which you justly admire:—I will not however abandon all hope, and will try further. I hope the box you heard of contain'd the books paper &c. from Stockdale. I am your

JNO. TRUMBULL

RC (DLC); endorsed.

Grand enclosed one of Trumbull's DUPLICATE RECEIPTS in his letter of 22 July 1788. TJ had just purchased Thibault's edition of OROSIUS from Froullé; see Sowerby, No. 87.

From Benjamin Vaughan

DEAR SIR Jeffries Square, London, July 11, 1788.

I request the favor of your attending to the interest of Mr. James Rumsey of Virginia, who wishes to obtain patents for a new boiler to the steam engine and for the application of steam to the purposes of navigation. These patents he wishes to be separate; and to have a caveat entered through your means, or such other steps taken, as shall prevent any person not duly authorized by him from taking out a patent, till he can apply for it, for the various French dominions.—Mr. Rumsey is patronized by Genl. Washington, Dr. Franklin, and other respectable persons, notwithstanding he has a competitor in Pensylvania; which is my apology for presuming to write to you upon this occasion, and for requesting the favor that no delay may be used; having myself no personal interest in Mr. Rumsey's success, except my regard for a person who seems to me possessed of modest merit.

Though Mr. Rumsey wishes for secrecy, yet after having mentioned this wish, there can be no difficulty in stating to you and relying on your prudence in the use of it, that his objects are expressed upon record here in the following words.

"A Boiler to a steam engine, consisting of, or having connected with it, tubes or projections of homogeneous or varying forms, in which steam or fluids may be exposed to the action of fire throughout a great extent of surface:"—And "The application of the power of steam to the purposes of navigation, with or without the additional aid of the mechanical principles of *action and reaction*."

From your long silence, I am almost afraid of the miscarriage of my letters, in which case I shall hope for the honor of a line.

I have the honor to be, with great esteem, Dear sir, Your faithful & respectful humble servt., BENJN. VAUGHAN

Mr. Rumsay is at present in a favorable train of negotiation with Messr. Watt and Bolton, at Birmingham.

RC (DLC); addressed; endorsed.

From Dugnani

Paris July 12. 1788

I think you doubly, and to the book, what you have pleas'd to send me, and to the Eagerness, with which you have writ to Havre de Grace for find the letter, what I have speak you before. When the first volume will be reprint, be very glad if you procure me a Copy. I hope so as to packet to have got my aim by your goodness. I would will to know my duty for pay him immediately. I make bold to write to you in Englisch, but you have invited my, and the fortune favours the audacious. I am for ever with Sentimens of sincere estime & attachment, My dear friend your most obedient, & Most humble servant, DUGNANI A DE R

RC (DLC); endorsed: "Dugnani, Nonce Apostolique."

To Elizabeth Wayles Eppes

DEAR MADAM Paris July 12. 1788.

Your kind favor of January 6. has come duly to hand. These marks of your remembrance are always dear to me, and recall to my mind the happiest portion of my life. It is among my greatest pleasures to receive news of your welfare and that of your family. You improve in your trade I see, and I heartily congratulate you on the double blessings of which heaven has just begun to open her stores to you. Polly is infinitely flattered to find a name sake in one of them. She promises in return to teach them both French. This she begins to speak easily enough and to read as well as English. She will begin Spanish in a few days, and has lately begun the harpsichord and drawing. She and her sister will be with me tomorrow and if she has any tolerable scrap of her pencil ready I will inclose it herein for your diversion. I will propose to her at the same time to write to you. I know she will undertake it at once as she has already done a dozen times. She gets all the apparatus, places herself very formally with pen in hand, and it is not till after all this and rummaging her head thoroughly that she calls out 'indeed Papa I do not know what to say, you must help me,' and as I obstinately refuse this her good resolutions have always proved abortive and her letters ended before they were begun. Her face kindles with love whenever she hears your name, and I assure you Patsy is not behind her in this. She remembers you with warm affection, recollects that she was bequeathed to you, and looks to you as her best future guide and guardian. She will have to learn from you things which she cannot learn here, and which after all are among the most valuable parts of education for an American.[1] Nor is the moment so distant as you imagine. On this I will enter into explanations in my next letter. I will only engage, from her dispositions, that you will always find in her the most passive compliance. You say nothing to us of Betsy, whom we all remember too well not to remember her affectionately. Jack too has failed to write to me since his first letter. I should be much pleased if he would himself give me the details of his occupations and his progress. I would write to Mrs. Skipwith but I could only repeat to her what I say to you, that we love you both sincerely, and pass one day in every week, together, and talk of nothing but Eppington, Hors du monde and Monticello. And were we to pass the whole seven, the theme would still be the same. God[2] bless you both, madam, your husbands, your children, and every thing near and dear to you: and be assured of the constant affection of your sincere friend and humble servant, TH: JEFFERSON

PrC (CSmH).

1 Preceding three words are interlined.
2 Not capitalized in MS.

From Lafayette

Saturday [12 July 1788]

I thank You, My dear sir, on the Good News You Give me from S. Carolina. I Hope Virginia will not fail. Every thing Goes on well But the Point Relative to the Presidency which You and I Have at Heart. I Confess this Makes me Uneasy. Will the General Agree with You. The Moment He Adopts our Opinion, My fear is Gone.

Our Internal trouble did take a decided turn. The late Arrêt du Conseil Missed His object Because there was no time fixed for the Meeting of the National assembly. I am just summoned to Attend at six o'clock at the House of the deputies from Britanny.

Bonjour.

Will Mr. Short and You Break fast with me and Mr. Barlow on Monday that we may Confer on Master Greene's education.

RC (DLC); in Lafayette's hand, but without date-line or signature; endorsed by TJ: "Fayette Marq. de la." The date has been established by Gottschalk, *Lafayette, 1783-89*, p. 390, 404-5, from internal evidence.

The GOOD NEWS . . . FROM S. CAROLINA that TJ transmitted to Lafayette obviously came in the dispatch from Jay of 9 June, with newspaper accounts of the ratification of the Constitution by that state, and in Carrington's letter of the same date, both of which arrived in about thirty days from New York (see TJ to Shippen, 13 July 1788). TJ may have sent extracts of these letters to Lafayette, or may have written him a brief note, but no such communication from him at this time has been found.

To Alexander McCaul

Dear Sir Paris July 12. 1788.

An impatience to commence the paiment of my debt to you, induced me to convey to you, in the moment I received it, the joyful information from the managers of my affairs that by the end of the year 1786. they would be cleared of all other embarrasments, and I proposed to you at the same time arrangements for paiment. I have been not a little mortified by subsequent information from them that omissions in their accounts and failures in the collection of the amount of the sale they had made, removed the period of their disembarrasment to a later term: that they are not yet clear of the other debts and therefore will remit me nothing this year. My word however being engaged with you it shall be religiously fulfilled. I will therefore endeavor, by economies here, to make you this year's remittance. Had I known sooner of this disappointment, I would have[1] been prepared to make the remittance in the course of the next month. As it is I must avail myself of the condition contained in my propositions, which admitted some delay in certain cases: but in the present one, it shall not be long. In the mean while I will ask you to let me know to what house in London I shall direct the paiments when I am ready to make them; and whether I may divide the whole remittance of £200. into three or four portions if I find it more convenient to remit in proportion as I can spare.

To guard against the hazard of short crops I have directed my whole estate to be rented for a certain sum of money or tobacco, and I am pleased to be informed from Mr. Lewis that he will be able to rent the whole, and suppose the rents will amount to 1000£ currency a year, cleared of all expence. This will commence with the next year; and two fifths of the proceeds shall be annually and punctually paid to you. Besides this I have directed the immediate sale of my lands in Goochland and Cumberland, estimated at 3500£ currency of which two fifths shall also be paid to you. In short, my dear Sir, no efforts of mine shall be wanting to get through this debt as speedily as possible, and if the means already adopted should not suffice, others more effectual shall be adopted. I mentioned to you that my paiments should be divided between Jones of Bristol and yourself. As yet he has not met my proposals with the moderation and justice with which you have done it.

I am with sentiments of very sincere esteem & attachment, Dear Sir, your affectionate friend & humble servt.,

TH: JEFFERSON

PrC (DLC); endorsed. Enclosed in TJ to Trumbull, 24 July 1788.

1 This word supplied editorially, having been omitted by TJ.

To Anna Jefferson Marks

MY DEAR SISTER Paris July 12. 1788.

My last letters from Virginia inform me of your marriage with Mr. Hastings Marks. I sincerely wish you joy and happiness in the new state into which you have entered. Tho Mr. Marks was long my neighbor, eternal occupations in business prevented my having a particular acquaintance with him as it prevented me from knowing more of my other neighbors as I would have wished to have done. I saw enough however of Mr. Marks to form a very good opinion of him, and to believe that he will endeavour to render you happy. I am sure you will not be wanting on your part. You have seen enough of the different conditions of life to know that it is neither wealth nor splendor, but tranquility and occupation which give happiness. This truth I can confirm to you from longer observation and a greater scope of experience. I should wish to know where Mr. Marks proposes to settle and what line of life he will follow. In every situation I shall wish to render him and you every service in my power: as you may be assured I shall ever feel myself warmly interested in your happiness, and preserve for you that sincere love I have always borne you. My daughters remember you with equal affection, and will one of these days tender it to you in person. They join me in wishing you all earthly felicity and a continuance of your love to them. Accept assurances of the sincere attachment with which I am my dear sister your affectionate brother, TH: JEFFERSON

PrC (MHi); at foot of text: "Mrs. Anna Scott Marks."

To Hastings Marks

DEAR SIR Paris July 12. 1788.

My letters from Virginia informing me of your intermarriage with my sister, I take the earliest opportunity of presenting you my sincere congratulations on that occasion. Tho the occupations in which I was ever engaged prevented my forming with you that particular acquaintance which our neighborhood might have permitted, it did not prevent my entertaining a due sense of your merit. I am particularly pleased that Mr. Lewis has taken the precise measure which I had intended to recommend to him, in order to put you into immediate possession of my sister's fortune in my hands. I should be happy to know where you mean to settle and what occupation you propose to follow? Whether any other than that of a farmer? as I shall ever feel myself interested in your success and wish to promote it by any means in my power, should any fall in my way. The happiness of a sister whom I very tenderly love, being committed to your hands, I cannot but offer prayers to heaven for your prosperity and mutual satisfaction. A thorough knowlege of her merit and good dispositions encourage me to hope you will both find your happiness in this union, and this hope is strengthened by my knowlege of yourself. I beg you to be assured of the sentiments of sincere esteem & regard with which I shall be on all occasions Dear Sir Your friend & servant

TH: JEFFERSON

PrC (MHi).

From James Monroe

DEAR SIR Fredricksburg July 12. 1788

Altho I am persuaded you will have received the proceedings of our convention upon the plan of government submitted from Phila. yet as it is possible this may reach you sooner than other communications I herewith enclose a copy to you. These terminated as you will find in a ratification which must be consider'd; so far as a reservation of certain rights go, as conditional, with the recommendation of subsequent amendments. The copy will designate to you the part which different gentlemen took upon this very interesting and important subject. The detail in the management of the business, from your intimate knowledge of characters, you perhaps possess with great accuracy, without a formal narration of it. *Pendleton*[1] *tho much impaired* in *health* and in every respect in the *decline of life* shewed as much zeal to carry it, as if he had been *a young man*. Perhaps more than he discover'd in the commencement of the late revolution in his opposition to G. Britain. *Wythe acted as chairman to the committee of the whole and of course* took but little part in the debate, but was for the adoption relying on subsequent amendments. *Blair* said nothing, but was for it. *The Governor* exhibited a *curious spectacle to view: having refused to sign the paper every body* supposed *him against it.* But he afterwards had *written a letter* and *having taken a part which might be called rather vehement than active* he was constantly labouring to shew *that his present conduct* [was][2] *consistent with that letter* and *the letter with his refusal to sign: Madison* took *the principal share in the debate* for it. In which together with the aid I have already mention'd *he was somewhat assisted by Innes*, H. *Lee*, *Marshall*, *Corbin*, and *G. Nicholas as Mason*, *Henry and Grayson were the principal Supporters of the opposition.* The *discussion* as might have been expected where the parties were so nearly on a balance, was conducted generally with great order, propriety and respect of either party to the other, and its event was accompanied with no circumstance on the part of the victorious that mar[ked] extraordinary exultation, nor of depression on the part of the unfortunate. There was no bonfire illumination &c. and had there been I am inclin'd to believe, the opposition would have not only express'd no dissatisfaction, but have scarcely felt any at it, for they seemed to be governed by principles elevated highly above circumstances so trivial and transitory in their nature.

The conduct of Genl. Washington upon this occasion has no doubt been right and *meritorious*. All parties had acknowledged defects in the federal system, and been sensible of the propriety of some material change. To *forsake the honourable retreat to which he had retired* and *risque the reputation* he had so deservedly acquir'd, manifested a zeal for the publick interest, that could after so many and illustrious services, and at this stage of his life, scarcely have been expected from him. Having however commenc'd again on the publick theatre *the course which he takes becomes*[3] *not only highly interesting to him but likewise so to us: the human character is not perfect;* [*and*][4] *if he partakes of those qualities which we* have too much reason *to believe are almost inseparable from the frail nature of our being the people of America will perhaps be lost: be assured his influence carried this government; for my own part I have a boundless confidence in him nor have I any reason to beleive he will ever furnish occasion for withdrawing it.* More is to be apprehended *if he takes* a part in *the public councils* again *as he advances in age from the designs* of those *around him than from any dispositions* of *his own.*

In the discussion of the subject an allusion was made I believe in the first instance, by Mr. *Henry* to an opinion *you* had given on this subject, in a letter to Mr. *Donald*. This afterwards became the subject of much inquiry and debate in the house, as to the construction of the contents of such letter and I was happy to find the great attention and universal respect with which the opinion was treated; as well as the great regard and high estimation in which the author of it was h[eld]. It must be painful to have been thus made a party in this transaction but this must have been alleviated by a consideration of the circumstances I have mention'd.

From the first view I had of the report from Phila. I had some strong objections to it and as I had no inclination to *inlist* myself *on either side*, made no *communication* or positive *declaration* of *my sentiments* untill after the Convention met. Being however desirous to communicate them to *my* constituents *I* address'd the enclos'd letter to them, with intention of giving them a view thereof eight or ten days before it met, but the impression was delayed so long, and so incorrectly made, and the whole performance upon reexamination so loosely drawn that *I* thought it best to suppress it. There appear'd likewise to be an impropriety in interfering with the subject in that manner in that late stage of the business. I inclose it you for your perusal and comment on it.

You have no doubt been apprized of the remonstrance of the Judges to the proceedings of the Legislature in the passage particularly of the district court law, as likewise of its contents. The subject will be taken up in the fall. The legislature altho assembled for the purpose declin'd entering into it, because of the season of the year being anxious to get home about their harvest. For this purpose they passd an act suspending the operation of the district court law untill sometime in Decr. or Jany. next. Altho different modifications may be made of it yet I think the bill will be retained in its principal features.

I still reside here and perhaps shall continue to do so whilst I remain at the bar, especially if the district court law holds its ground. I hold a seat in the legislature and believe I shall do it for some time. The absence from my family is painful but I must endeavor to have them with me as much as possible. I hope you enjoy your health well. I have heard nothing to the contrary. I hope also that Miss Patsy and Molly are well. Short I likewise hope is in health. Remember me to them and believe me most affectionately your friend & servant, JAS. MONROE

RC (DLC); partly in code. Enclosures: Probably a copy of *Journal of the Convention of Virginia. Held in the City of Richmond, on the First Mon-*

day in June, in the Year of our Lord, One Thousand Seven Hundred and Eighty Eight (Richmond, Augustine Davis, [1788]), of which two hundred copies were issued at the close of the Convention (Swem, "Va. Bibliog.," No. 7586). A copy of this is in DLC: TJ Papers, 40: 6901, bearing many notations by James Madison, but, as these were added later, it is possible that this actually was the copy sent by Monroe and that Madison employed it at a later date. (2) James Monroe's *Some Observations on the Constitution, &c.*, a pamphlet that exists apparently in the one copy that is preserved in TJ's library (Sowerby, No. 3018) and on p. 3 of which TJ wrote "by Colo. James Monroe." This copy probably had a title-page originally; it has an errata list on p. 24; and it also contains a number of alterations in Monroe's hand. It is printed in Monroe, *Writings*, ed. Hamilton, I, 307-43, but Monroe's deletions, corrections, &c. are sometimes followed and sometimes disregarded, without indication in either case. These are not numerous, and for the most part are matters of phraseology.

It was on Monday, 9 June 1788, that Patrick Henry made his allusion to TJ's LETTER TO MR. DONALD of 7 Feb. 1788: "We are threatened with danger for the non-payment of our debt due to France. We have information come from an illustrious citizen of Virginia, who is now in Paris, which disproves the suggestions of such danger. This citizen has not been in the airy regions of theoretic speculation: our ambassador is this worthy citizen. The ambassador of the United States of America is not so despised as the honorable gentleman would make us believe. A servant of a republic is as much respected as that of a monarch. The honorable gentleman tells us that hostile fleets are to be sent to make reprisals upon us: our ambassador tells you that the king of France has taken into consideration to enter into commercial regulations, on reciprocal terms, with us, which will be of peculiar advantage to us. Does this look like hostility? I might go farther; I might say, not from public authority, but good information, that his opinion is, that you reject this government. His character and abilities are in the highest estimation; he is well acquainted, in every respect, with this country; equally so with the policy of the European nations. This illustrious citizen advises you to reject this government till it be amended. His sentiments coincide entirely with ours. His attachment to, and services done for, this country are well known. At a great distance from us, he remembers and studies our happiness. Living in splendor and dissipation, he thinks yet of bills of rights—thinks of those little, despised things called *maxims*. Let us follow the sage advice of this common friend of our happiness." This view of TJ's position takes on added interest in light of the fact that Henry was TJ's inveterate opponent. Edmund Randolph, the next day, replied to Henry: "In that list of facts with which he would touch our affections, he has produced a name (Mr. Jefferson) which will ever be remembered with gratitude by this commonwealth. I hope that his life will be continued, to add, by his future actions, to the brilliancy of his character. Yet I trust that his name was not mentioned to influence any member of this house. Notwithstanding the celebrity of his character, his name cannot be used as authority against the Constitution. . . . As far as my information goes, it is only a report circulated through the town, that he wished nine states to adopt, and the others to reject it, in order to get amendments. . . . That illustrious citizen tells you, that he wishes the government to be adopted by nine states, to prevent a schism in the Union. This, sir, is my wish. I will go heart and hand to obtain amendments, but I will never agree to the dissolution of the Union." But Henry, being well aware of the letter to Donald and of the fact that TJ had actually expressed the "wish with all my soul that the nine first Conventions" would adopt and equally so that the last four would "refuse to accede to it till a declaration of rights be annexed," refused to construe "the opinion of Mr. Jefferson, our common friend, into an advice to adopt this new government." Eight states had already ratified, and Henry's opponents had asserted that New Hampshire would certainly do so—as New Hampshire did while Virginia debated. "Where, then," Henry asked bluntly, "will four states be found to reject, if we adopt it? If we do, the counsel of this enlightened and worthy countryman of ours will be thrown away; and for what? He wishes to secure amendments and a bill of rights, if I am not mistaken. . . . His amendments go to that despised thing, called a *bill of rights*, and all the rights which are dear to human nature—trial by jury, the liberty of religion and the press, &c. Do not gentlemen see that, if we adopt, under the idea of following Mr. Jefferson's opinion, we amuse ourselves with the shadow, while the substance is given away? If Virginia be for adoption, what states will be left, of sufficient respectability and importance to secure amendments by their rejection? . . . Where will you find attachment to the rights of mankind, when Massachusetts, the great northern state, Pennsylvania, the great middle state, and Virginia, the great southern state, shall have adopted this government? Where will you find magnanimity enough to reject it?" The argument was telling, if disingenuous, and Madison, lacking the letters that TJ had already written which proved he had given up the idea expressed to Donald in favor of the Massachusetts plan for obtaining amendments, could only regret that Henry had "mentioned the opinion of a citizen who is an ornament to this state. . . . Is it come to this, then, that we are not to follow our own reason? Is it proper to introduce the opinions of respectable men not within these walls? . . . I believe that, were that gentleman now on this floor, he would be for the adoption of this Constitution. I wish his name had never been mentioned. I . . . know that the delicacy of his feelings will be wounded, when he will see in print what has and may be said concerning him on this occasion. I am, in some measure, acquainted with his sentiments on this subject. It is not right for me to unfold what he has informed me; but . . . he admires several parts of it, which have been reprobated with vehemence in this house. He is captivated with the equality of suffrage in the Senate, which the honorable gentleman (Mr. Henry) calls the rotten part of this Constitution. But, whatever be the opinion of that illustrious citizen, considerations of personal delicacy should dissuade us from introducing it here" (Elliot, *Debates*, Philadelphia, 1901, III, 152-3, 199-200, 314-5, 329-30). See also Madison to TJ, 24 July 1788.

[1] This and subsequent words in italics are written in code and were decoded interlineally by TJ; his decoding has been verified by the Editors, employing Code No. 9; two or three errors in encoding or decoding have been conjecturally corrected.

[2] This word supplied; Monroe not only omitted the verb but also erred in encoding *conduct* and *consistent.*

[3] Monroe encoded *fe* (887) for *come* (884).

[4] Monroe encoded *Massachusetts* (67) for *and* (673), and TJ so decoded it.

From Thomas Lee Shippen

Aix la Chapelle 12 July 88

Will you have the goodness my dear Sir to excuse the very great trouble I am giving you? In the middle of an inland journey I find a long letter filled to my father, and fear that if I let it go on, it will become too large for the Post to carry. In this emergency I know no way in which to ensure for my letter a safe and speedy conveyance but by sending it to you, and that is the only excuse I can offer for giving you the trouble. Have the kindness to give my respects to the Marquis and Mr. Short & believe me Sir, with great sincerity your devoted servant,

Thos. Lee Shippen

[P.]S. You will be surprized to find me still in this Country but the delights of Spa have been seducing for me to able to resist them.

RC (DLC).

To Francis dal Verme and Others

SIR Paris July 13. 1788.

The readiness with which you were so kind as to shew me what was most worth seeing in Milan and it's neighborhood when I had the honour of seeing you there, encourages me to address to you two of my young countrymen who will pass thro' Milan in a tour they are taking. The one is Mr. Rutledge, son of Governor Rutledge of South Carolina, the other Mr. Shippen of Philadelphia nephew of Mr. Lee late President of Congress. Their good sense, information and merit will do justice to any attentions your goodness will induce you to shew them.[1] The object of their journey being principally information, I will particularly ask of you to point out what is most worthy their notice and to procure them the facilities of seeing it. The sentiments you were so kind as to express towards my country as well as your natural goodness induce me to take the present liberty, and the rather as its furnishes me occasion of renewing to you assurances of the sincere esteem and profound respect with which I have the honour to be Dear Sir Your most obedient & most humble servt,

TH: JEFFERSON

PrC (DLC); at foot of text: "M. le Comte del Verme." As promised in his letter to Shippen on 19 June 1788, TJ on this date wrote other letters of introduction to Gaudenzio Clerici of Milan, Giovanni Fabbroni of Florence, André de Sasserno of Nice (in which he noted Mr. and Mrs. Sasserno's kindnesses to himself), Stephen Cathalan of Marseilles, and Geismar of Frankfort. Since these vary only in phraseology (with the exception of the last), they are not printed here; but see TJ to Geismar, following. The RC's were evidently enclosed in TJ to Rutledge and a duplicate set (evidently composed of second PrC's) was enclosed in TJ to Shippen, both of this date. PrC of the letter to Clerici is in DLC; PrC's of the letters to Fabbroni, Sasserno (in French), and Cathalan are in MHi.

Shippen and Rutledge, on the advice of Lafayette, had assumed military rank and uniforms as being safer and more economical, but TJ did not refer to them as "Captain" Shippen and "Captain" Rutledge as Short did in a letter of 31 May 1788 (Shepperson, *John Paradise and Lucy Ludwell*, p. 311).

[1] The corresponding sentence in the letter to Sasserno reads: "Ils meritent bien, par les qualités du coeur et de l'esprit, toutes les attentions que vous aurez la complaisance de leur faire, et ils auront besoin de vos conseils pour leur route."

To Geismar

MY DEAR SIR Paris July 13. 1788.

On my return to this place I found such a mass of business awaiting me that I have never been able to write a letter of which friendship was the only motive. I take the first moment to inform you that my journey was prosperous: that the vines which I took from Hocheim and Rudesheim are now growing luxuriously in my garden here, and will cross the Atlantic next winter, and that probably, if you ever revisit Monticello, I shall be able to give you there a glass of Hock or Rudesheim of my own making. My last news from America is very encouraging. Eight states have adopted the new constitution and we are pretty sure of three more. New York is a little doubtful, and Rhode island against it. But this will not prevent it's establishment, and they will come into it after a while.—I shall still hope you will take a little trip to Paris one of these days.—Mr. Rutledge, the son of Governor Rutledge of S. Carolina, and Mr. Shippen, son of Dr. Shippen of Philadelphia and nephew of the late President of Congress, being to pass thro' Franckfort, I have desired them to wait on you, in confidence that you will advise them what there is to be seen in that neighborhood and procure them the facilities of doing it, as well as shew them any other civilities their situation may need. This I pray you to do for those very worthy and sensible young men for the love of him who is with sincere esteem & attachment My dear Sir your affectionate friend & servt., TH: JEFFERSON

PrC (DLC). See note to preceding letter.

From André Limozin

MOST HONORED SIR! Havre de Grace 13th July 1788.

Agreable to the desires expressed in the Letter your Excellency hath honored me with on the 11th instant, I have sent directly one of my head Clarkes with a beseech to the Master of the Post office to examine thoroughly if no Letters from america directed to his Excellency Count Dugnany archibishop of Rhodes and Nuncio of the Pope at the Court of Versailles were left in his office. The Said Master answerd that altho' he was sure, that no Letters for the Said Excellency were left in his office, he would examine all the Letters in the presence of my Clarke, and there was not one neither from america nor from any other parts for the Said Count. The Said Master recommanded to apply to the General Post office at Paris. Whenever I shall be usefull either to your Excellency or to your Friends, I beg to not be Spared. Your Excellency is surely informed that our Minister hath order'd to not fitt out any more Packets for any part whatsoever. It will be a very great detriment for the business and the Connexions that our Port hath with

America. God grant that a general peace may take place: but I am very much afraid of the Contrary.

I have the honor to be with the highest regard Your Excellency's Most obedient & very humble Servant, ANDRE LIMOZIN

RC (MHi); endorsed.

To John Rutledge, Jr.

DEAR SIR Paris July 13. 1788.

Your favor of the 8th. instant is just received, and I have now the honour to forward you the letters I promised. I have written them jointly for yourself and Mr. Shippen, on the supposition you will continue together, but lest your plans should vary, I send duplicates also. As you seem to think of the route by Constantinople I have been examining Capper's account of the stages from Vienna to that place. According to him you should descend the Danube to Belgrade, and then strike off by Nissa, Sophia, Philipopoli (or Philibay) and Adrianople (or Aderne) to Constantinople. At Belgrade however it would be worth enquiry whether it is not better to descend the river to Nicopoli and then strike off to Philibay, and Aderne. Of all these you will form a better judgment as you proceed. From Constantinople I should suggest the following route, Salonica, Athens, Corinth, Sparta, and from the Morea to take your passage for Syracuse, and so up through Italy. By a letter which your father has done me the honor of writing me on the 6th. of April, he approves of my proposition of your going to Madrid and Lisbon rather than increasing your tour and stay in the Northern parts of Europe. If this meets your own ideas, you should not turn off from the route you have hitherto had in view, till you get to Bordeaux. Our connections with the Spaniards and Portuguese must become every day more and more interesting, and I should think, the knowlege of their language, manners, and situation, might eventually and even probably become more useful to yourself and country than that of any other place you will have seen. The womb of time is big with events to take place between us and them, and a little knowlege of them will give you great advantages over those who have none at all.—I imagine you have heard terrible stories of the internal confusions of this country. These things swell as they go on. Crescunt eundo. As yet the tumults have not cost a single life according to the most sober testimony I have been able to collect. Nine tenths of Paris believe that 200 were killed at Grenoble, where there was in truth but an officer wounded. I think it will end in calling the States general the next year, of which a late arret seems to give foundation of hope: but I see no reason to expect the re-establishment of the parliaments. We daily expect the arrival of Tippoo Saib's embassy here. To save repetition I refer you to Mr. Shippen for the American news I communicate to him. I always need and must always repeat apologies for the freedom with which I venture my advice to you. It proceeds from that very sincere esteem with which I am Dear Sir your affectionate friend & servt,

TH: JEFFERSON

PrC (DLC). TJ enclosed the various letters of introduction that he had written for Rutledge and Shippen, and a duplicate set (evidently press copies) in the letter to Shippen of this date; see TJ to Francis dal Verme, 13 July 1788.

CAPPER'S ACCOUNT: James Capper's *Observations on the Passage to India, through Egypt. Also by Vienna through Constantinople to Aleppo, and from thence by Bagdad, and directly across the Great Desert, to Bassora* (London, 3rd edn., 1785), which TJ had bought from Stockdale in 1786 (Sowerby, No. 3933).

To Thomas Lee Shippen

DEAR SIR Paris July 13. 1788.

In a former letter to Mr. Rutledge I suggested to him the idea of extending his tour to Constantinople, and in one of to-day I mention it again. I do not know how far that extension may accord with your plan, nor indeed how far it may be safe for either of you. For, tho' it has been thought there has been a relaxation in the warlike dispositions of the belligerent powers, yet we have no symptoms of a suspension of hostilities. The Ottoman dominions are generally represented as unsafe for travellers even when in peace. They must be much more so during war. This article thefore merits exact enquiry before that journey is undertaken.

We have letters from America to June 11. Maryland has acceded to the constitution by a vote of 63. to 11. and South Carolina by 149. to 72. Mr. Henry had disseminated propositions there for a Southern confederacy. It is now thought that Virginia will not hesitate to accede. Governor Randolph has come over to the Federalists. No doubt is entertained of New Hampshire and North Carolina. And it is thought that even N. York will agree when she sees she will be left with Rhode island alone. Two thirds of their convention are decidedly anti-federal. The die is now thrown, and it cannot be many days before we know what has finally turned up.

Congress has granted the prayer of Kentuckey to be made independant, and a committee was occupied in preparing an act for that purpose. Mr. Barlow the American poet is arrived at Paris.

We expect daily to hear that the Swedes have commenced hostilities. Whether this will draw in the other nations of Europe immediately cannot be foreseen. Probably it will in the long run. I sincerely wish this country may be able previously to arrange it's internal affairs.—To spare the trouble of repetition I am obliged to ask of yourself and Mr. Rutledge to consider the letter of each as a supplement to the other. Under the possibility however of your going different routes I inclose duplicates of my letters of introduction. After acknoleging the receipt of your favor of the 6th. inst. from Spa, I shall only beg a continuance of them, and that you will both keep me constantly informed how to convey letters to you: and to assure you of those sentiments of sincere esteem with which I have the honor to be Dear Sir your friend & servt,

TH: JEFFERSON

PrC (DLC). For the enclosed DUPLICATES OF . . . LETTERS OF INTRODUCTION, see note to TJ to Dal Verme, 13 July 1788.

From Madame Brissot de Warville

Arnouville près Gonesse, *14 July* [*1788*]. Asks TJ to forward by a safe hand the enclosed letter to her husband.

RC (DLC). Enclosure not found.

From Maria Cosway

London 15 July 1788

Is it possible that I write another letter before I have My answer from My two last! What can be the reason? It is either obstinacy, or Constancy in Me: but what does your silence Mean My dear friend! It seems that opportunities absolutly force themselves on you to recal me to your remembrances, should I have otherwise so much Courage or should I be so bold as to *insist* in a corrispondance! Mr: St: Andrè is Coming to Paris and ask's me particularly for a letter to you, when I think of you I forgit all formality I only remember your kindness, your friendship. You cannot change; it is only by chance (and that is seldom) if I dont think of you that I supose I could not write to any body that does not think of me;

then a string of *punctellios* and *formalités* stand frowning before me waiting for the happy time, which brings me letters to answer. Such is the situation of your Most affte:

Maria Cosway in waiting

RC (ViU).

MR: ST: ANDRE carried other things to Paris besides Mrs. Cosway's letter. On 21 July 1788 Trumbull wrote to Short: "Monsr. St. André is so good as to charge himself with two books:—Alfred's Orosius for Mr. Jefferson, which you will please to deliver to him:—and an odd volume of Herculaneum which Mrs. Church bo't at Froulier's and which she begs you will have the goodness to return to him and take in exchange the 6th. Vol. . . . Say to Mr. Jefferson with my best respects that as Mrs. Church informs me she sends him a Tea Vase, I shall hold myself discharg'd from that Commission untill I hear further from him,—that He shall recieve His pictures in a few days,—and his Chariot as soon as I can find such an one as I would wish to see him ride in" (DLC: Short Family Papers).

From Schweighauser & Dobrée

Sir

Nantes 15. July 1788.

We recieved in course your Excellency's obliging letter of the 27h. of last month and are very thankful for its contents. We immediately communicated it to Mr. Minier one of the partners of the late house (en Comandite) of Puchelberg & Co. in L'Orient and he shares our gratitude for your kind endeavours of bringing the affair of the Alliance to a final settlement. After many interviews and long conversations on your proposals of arbitrators he has persisted in telling us that he thought this required none except Your Excellency meant them to examine the account as directed by the resolve of Congress of the 23d. August 1781 which positively says "That it shall be examined and paid by the Minister Plenipotentiary of the United States at the Court of Versailles &c."

Convinced that the merchants you would name with us (altho' we know none in the class you mention) would be qualified to judge whatever in this affair would be laid before them, conscious of the justice of our claim and possessed of every voucher necessary we have done all in our power to make him acquiesce to the mode proposed, but to no effect. If this requires a greater decision he seems to think that it is better to submit it to our ordinary tribunals.

It is not in our power to take any thing on ourselves in this affair without his and M. Puchelberg's concurrence. To prevent them from seizing the Alliance and other effects in their way at the time these advances were made M. Schweighauser agreed to lend the house the sum disbursed till it would be paid by the U.S. Were we to act in the least point without the sanction of these associates in this affair they would take this as a plea to leave the whole to our charge.

As it might be that we have taken Your Excellency's letter in too general terms we will esteem it as a particular favor of you to mention on what points you mean the arbitrators should judge that we may be able to explain it to the gentlemen. We are with gratitude & most profound respect &c.

(Signed) SCHWEIGHAUSER & DOBREE

Tr (Arch. Aff. Etr., Corr.-Pol., Angleterre, Vol. 566); entirely in Short's hand. Enclosed in TJ to Montmorin, 11 Sep. 1788.

To William Gordon

SIR Paris July 16. 1788.

In your favor of the 8th. instant you mention that you had written to me in February last. This letter never came to hand. That of Apr. 24. came here during my absence on a journey thro' Holland and Germany, and having been obliged to devote the first moments after my return to some very pressing matters, this must be my apology for not having been able to write to you till now. As soon as I knew that it would be agreeable to you to have such a disposal of your work for translation as I had made for Dr. Ramsay, I applied to the same bookseller with propositions on your behalf. He told me that he had lost so much by that work that he could hardly think of undertaking another, and at any rate not without first seeing and examining it. As he was the only bookseller I could induce to give any thing on the former occasion, I went to no other with my proposals, meaning to ask you to send me immediately as much of the work as is printed. This you can do by the Diligence which comes three times a week from London to Paris. Furnished with this, I will renew my propositions and do the best for you I can, tho' I fear that the ill success of the translation of Dr. Ramsay's work, and of another work on the subject of America, will permit less to be done for you than I had hoped. I think Dr. Ramsay's failed[1] from the inelegance of the translation, and the translator's having departed entirely from the Doctor's instructions. I will be obliged to you to set me down as a subscriber for half a dozen copies, and to ask Mr. Trumbul (No. 2. North street, Rathbone place) to pay you the *whole* subscription price for me, which he will do on shewing him this letter. These copies can be sent by the Diligence. I have not yet received the pictures Mr. Trumbul was to send me, nor consequently that of the M. de la Fayette. I will take care of it when it arrives. His title is simply *le Marquis de la Fayette*. You ask, in your letter of Apr. 24. details of my sufferings by Colo. Tarleton. I did not suffer by him. On the contrary he behaved very genteelly with me. On his approach to Charlottesville which is within 3. miles of my house at Monticello, he dispatched a troop of his horse under Capt. Mc.leod with the double object of taking me prisoner with the two Speakers of the Senate and Delegates who then lodged with me,[2] and remaining there in vedette, my house commanding a view of 10. or 12 counties round about. He gave strict orders to Capt. Mc.leod to suffer nothing to be injured. The troop failed in one of their objects, as we had notice so that the two speakers had gone off about two hours before their arrival at Monticello, and myself with my family about five minutes. But Captn. Mc.leod preserved every thing with sacred care during about 18. hours that he remained there. Colo. Tarleton was just so long at Charlottesville being hurried from thence by news of the rising of the militia, and by a sudden fall of rain which threatened to swell the river and intercept his return. In general he did little injury to the inhabitants on that short and hasty excursion, which was of about 60. miles from their main army then in Spotsylvania, and ours in Orange. It was early in June 1781. Lord Cornwallis then proceeded to the point of fork, and encamped his army from thence all along the main James river to a seat of mine called Elkhill, opposite to Elk island and a little below the mouth of the Byrd creek. (You will see all these places exactly laid down in the map annexed to my Notes on Virginia printed by Stockdale.) He remained in this position ten days, his own head quarters being in my house at that place. I had had time to remove most of the effects out of the house. He destroyed all my growing crops of corn and tobacco, he burned all my barns containing the same articles of the last year, having first taken what corn he wanted, he used, as was to be expected, all my stocks of cattle, sheep, and hogs for the sustenance of his army, and carried off all the horses capable of service: of those too young for service he cut the throats, and he burnt all the fences on the plantation, so as to leave it an absolute waste. He carried off also about 30. slaves: had this been to give them freedom he would have done right, but it was to consign them to inevitable death from the small pox and putrid fever then raging in his camp. This I knew afterwards to have been the fate of 27. of them. I never had news of the remaining three, but presume they shared the same fate.[3] When I say that Lord Cornwallis did all this, I do not mean that he carried about the torch in his own hands, but that it was all done under his eye, the situation of the house, in which he was, commanding a view of every part of the plantation, so that he must have seen every fire. I relate these things on my own knowlege in a great degree, as I was on the ground soon after he left it. He treated the rest of the neighborhood somewhat in the same stile, but not with that spirit of total extermination with which he seemed to rage over my possessions.[4] Wherever he went, the dwelling houses were plundered of every thing which could be carried off. Lord Cornwallis's character in England would forbid the belief that he shared in the plunder. But that his table was served with the plate thus pillaged from private houses can be proved by many hundred eye witnesses. From an estimate I made at that time on the best information I could collect, I supposed the state of Virginia lost under Ld. Cornwallis's hands that year about 30,000 slaves, and that of these about 27,000 died of the small pox and camp fever, and the rest were partly sent to the West Indies and exchanged for rum, sugar, coffee and fruits, and partly sent to New York, from whence they went at the peace either to Nova Scotia, or England. From this last place I believe they have been lately sent to Africa. History will never relate the horrors committed by the British army in the *Southern* states of America. They raged in Virginia 6. months only, from the middle of April to the middle of October 1781. when they were all taken prisoners, and I give you a faithful specimen of their transactions for 10. days of that time and in one spot only. Expede Herculem.[5] I suppose their whole devastations during those 6. months amounted to about three millions sterling.—The copiousness of this subject has only left me space to assure you of the sentiments of esteem and respect with which I am Sir your most obedt. humble servt.,

Th: Jefferson

PrC (DLC).

TJ may have suspected, but tactfully failed to point out, that Gordon was in error in thinking he had written TJ in FEBRUARY LAST, for the description of the contents of that letter as given in Gordon's to TJ of 8 July 1788 shows that he was actually referring to his letter of 24 Apr. 1788. The account of the Tarleton raid and the damage done by Cornwallis at Elkhill was utilized by Gordon in his *History of the Rise, Progress, and Establishment, of the Independence of the United States of America*, London, 1788, IV, 402-3, though TJ's phraseology was at times altered, sentences were rearranged, some parts were suppressed (see notes), and Gordon did not indicate that the passages indirectly quoted were from TJ except insofar as he had stated in his general preface that his use of the form of letters instead of chapters was "not altogether imaginary, as the author, from his arrival in America in 1770, maintained a correspondence with gentlemen in London, Rotterdam and Paris, answering in general to the prefixed dates." It is curious that Gordon should have omitted those parts of TJ's letter that are indicated below and should have retained the severe strictures against Cornwallis, all of which were retained save that part about the seizure of slaves. Gordon succeeded in offending both English and American readers, and he revised the text accordingly in subsequent editions (Sowerby, No. 487). It would be a fascinating and highly instructive exercise in historiography to trace out the letters that Adams, Knox, and others, as well as TJ, wrote to Gordon and to compare what use was made by him of the various (and doubtless occasionally conflicting) accounts given by individuals. Gordon was writing what can only be regarded as contemporary history, and he seems to have made more use of correspondence with individuals than was customary.

1 TJ wrote, and then deleted, "entirely."

2 TJ first wrote ". . . who were then at my house," and then altered the passage by deletion and interlineation to read as above.

3 Gordon omitted the preceding three sentences.

4 TJ deleted the following at this point: "I conjecture that the."

5 Gordon omitted the preceding three sentences.

To André Limozin

SIR

Paris July 16. 1788.

I received last night your favor of the 13th. and am obliged to you for the search made in the post office for the Nuncio's packet. With respect to the subject of your private note, I think I had the honor, in some former letter, of informing you that no Consular convention was as yet settled with this country, and that till there should be one it was not probable any appointment of Consuls would take place, and whenever it should, it would probably be made by Congress itself. All this continues still true. The Consular convention however is at present under way, and I foresee nothing to prevent it's being soon concluded. Whenever it is, I shall, with that, send some observations to Congress on places and persons, and shall assuredly give a just representation of the services of their antient servants. In the mean time you might get your friends in the several states of America, to interest their respective delegates in the appointment for Havre.—The king of Sweden has ordered the Russian minister to quit his dominions, and there can be no doubt now of his engaging in the war. This increases the probabilities that this war will in the long run become general. You, who live in the sea-ports, can always judge when this government expects to be involved in it, by the stir in the king's shipyards: and of this I should always be glad to receive information from you.—The 12 deputies of Bretagne were arrested two days ago and sent to the Bastille. I am with great esteem, Sir, your most obedt. humble servt., TH: JEFFERSON

PrC (DLC).

To John Paradise

Paris Wednesday evening July 16. 1788.

Will any of your occasions for money, my dear Sir, admit of being put off a few days? Mr. Grand will indeed furnish the 50 Louis you desire, on my order; but it will be on the condition, always understood between him and me, that I repay it punctually the 1st. day of the next month. The 100 Louis he has before furnished you, I repaid him the 1st. day of this month. Since that I have been obliged to get him to remit 80 pounds for me to London, and I have a quarter's rent which became due yesterday. These anticipations, with current calls, will take the whole of the monthly sum I am authorized to draw, the 1st. day of every month. If any of your calls can be put off to the first week in next month, it will give me another month to provide the reimbursement. If they cannot, I will not let you suffer, but will give you an order for the whole or a part as you shall find indispensable, and will endeavor to find some expedient to reimburse Mr. Grand, without which it would be the last order of mine he would ever pay. Be so good as to write me candidly, my dear Sir, and to be assured of every help my limited means will permit, as well as of the sentiments of sincere esteem with which I am Dear Sir your affectionate friend & servant, TH: JEFFERSON

PrC (DLC).

To John Stockdale

SIR Paris July 16. 1788.

In my former letters I mentioned to you that not knowing exactly the balance I owed you when I set out from this place for Amsterdam, I had remitted from Amsterdam a bill of exchange to Mr. Trumbull praying him to pay you 15£ out of it. As I did not recollect his address, the letter was inclosed to Sr. Robt. Herreis, who not being able to find him returned it to my bankers in Amsterdam, with whom it lay till I learnt accidentally that Mr. Trumbul had never received. He writes me that he has now received it and paid you the £15. I have lately received from you two packages of books, and will now beg the favor of you to send me an exact state of my account, charging me with the copies of the Notes on Virginia you sent to be sold here, and for which I will account to you immediately tho but a small part of them are sold. In fact they are prohibited. Charge me also to the end of my year's subscription for the Monthly and Critical reviews, and the Repository, and so long be so good as to continue to send them to me, and no longer. As soon as I receive your account I will remit you the balance. I am Sir your very humble servt., TH: JEFFERSON

PrC (DLC).

It would be interesting to know when and by what authority *Notes on Virginia* was PROHIBITED from being sold in Paris, but no evidence of this fact has been found. If there was an actual prohibition, it must have been temporary, for TJ indicated to Short in 1790 that some copies still remained unsold in the hands of Froullé (TJ to Short, 6 Apr. 1790, enclosure).

From Thomas Appleton

Rouen, 17 July 1788. Director of customs at Rouen has ruled that "refin'd Spermacœti could not be refus'd" under second article of Arrêt, but that "he Conceived it impossible Candles could ever be included" and that, "as having never been particulariz'd in any previous arret they must be" subject to the 5% ad valorem duty levied on all foreign merchandise not enumerated. On examining candles, he found that "from having been loaded in with the Cargo and so plac'd that no air Could possibly Come to them they were very much Heated which has produc'd a great number of spots and specks in each Candle and so very bad is the color and appearance that if they should be landed, I am decidedly of opinion they would frustrate the design." Will therefore, with TJ's permission, return them to Boston by the same vessel, sailing in six days via L'Orient. [*In postscript*:] Captain of vessel has a few good candles at 3^{tt} the pound. Appleton's address is care of Messrs. Le Couteulx & Cie.

RC (DLC); 1 p.; endorsed.

To Brailsford & Morris

GENTLEMEN Paris July 17. 1788.

I have been less diligent in acknoleging the receipt of your favors of Oct. 31. Jan. 10. and Mar. 17. than in attending to their contents. They have been the subject of repeated conferences with Mr. Berard of this city, during which I have discovered a real desire in that house to dispose in the best manner possible of the rice you had been pleased to consign to them; and a mortification that they could do no better than they did. They were to have informed me exactly what they got for the rice, and I waited for that before I answered your letters, but they have not sent it. I fear the consignments have not yeilded much profit, but hope at the same time they have not produced loss, and that the probability of a more favorable demand than happened on this occasion may induce you to continue to endeavor at opening this channel of commerce. I wish you could find means of availing yourselves of the Paris market, which I am of opinion would greatly increase the profits. Mr. Berard is more capable of advising you on this head than I am; the rice should in that case come to Rouen, or at least to Havre: and as this would be less convenient to him than Lorient, the place of his establishment, perhaps he may not be willing to encourage it. If you discover any symptom of this, I shall be always ready to make any enquiries you may desire for your more particular information.

The bill you remitted me for 726. livres has been duly paid by Mr. Petrie, and I have given the necessary commission at Marseilles for preparing olives, and olive plants to be sent to Charleston as soon as the season will admit. This, I am answerd, will not be till the last of January.—Mr. Berard paid your draught, intended for young Mr. Rutledge, into the hands of his bankers here, Boyd, Ker & co.

I have the honor to be with every disposition to facilitate your commercial connections with this country, and with sentiments of perfect esteem, Gentlemen, your most obedient & most humble servt,

Th: Jefferson

PrC (DLC). Enclosed in TJ to Trumbull, 24 July 1788.

To William Drayton

Sir — Paris July 17. 1787 [i.e., 1788]

My letters of Jan. 13. and Feb. 6. informed you that I had sent to your address 1. a couffe of Egyptian rough rice by Capt. Shewell bound from Marseilles to Charleston. 2. another do. by the Juno capt. Jenkins bound from Havre to N. York. 3. a box with cork acorns and Sulla seed by the Packet from Havre to N. York. A letter from the delegates of S. Carolina dated New York Apr. 25. announced to me the safe arrival there of the 2d. couffe, and their hope of getting it to you before the seed time would be over.

I am now to acknolege the receipt of your favor of Nov. 25. 1787. which did not get to my hands till April 24. 1788. In consequence thereof I wrote to a Mr. Cathalan at Marseilles to engage a gardener to prepare a large number of olive plants, of those which yeild the best Provence oil, and to have them in readiness to be sent by any vessels which may occur, bound to Charleston: and besides this, to send a great quantity of olives to be sown in order to raise stocks. These stocks would yeild a wilding fruit, and worthless: they are only to serve therefore to engraft on from the plants which will go, and which will yeild cuttings. This is the quickest way of procuring extensive plantations, and it is the best also. Mr. Cathalan writes me word he will charge a gardener to do this, but that as the objects cannot be sent from Marseilles till the last of January, it will be March or April before you can receive them. Messrs. Brailsford & Morris have remitted to me 726. livre tournois for this object which have been duly paid. Mr. Rutledge, the son of Governor Rutledge, having lately set out from this place on a tour which will take in Italy and the South of France, I recommend to him to pay very particular attention to the character and culture of this tree, as also to the caper, date, fig, raisin, pistache, and also to the article of rice. I am in hopes he will be able to enrich you with much more particular details than it has been in my power to do.—I shall be happy to be further instrumental in promoting the views of the Agricultural society, and of executing their commands at all times. I have the honor to be with sentiments of the most perfect esteem & respect Sir Your most obedient & most humble servt,

TH: JEFFERSON

PrC (DLC). Enclosed in TJ to Trumbull, 24 July 1788.

From Francis Hopkinson

MY DEAR SIR — Philada. July 17th. 1788

The last Letter I received from you is dated Augt. 1st. 1787 and my last to you April 6th. 1788. I have a pretty large Collection of News Papers for you, waiting a convenient opportunity. Mr. Tillier, who takes this, goes from hence to New York to embark for France. I could not ask him to take Charge of the Papers as they are too bulky: but I have made up a Package of Publications, which I think more immediately interesting, and which I hope he will accommodate with a Place amongst his Baggage. You will perceive that our great object for near a Twelve Month past has been the Formation and Ratification of a new System of Federal Government. I sent you the Plan proposed by the General Convention, long ago. Since the World began, I believe no Question has ever been more repeatedly and strictly scrutenized or more fairly and freely argued, than this proposed Constitution. It has now been solemnly ratified by 10 States viz. New Hampshire, Massachusetts, Connecticut, New Jersey, Pennsylvania, Delaware, Maryland, Virginia, South Carolina and Georgia, New York now hesitating, North Carolina to determine the last of this Month, Rhode-Island has not even call'd a Convention but seems disposed to do it.—Whether *This* is the best possible System of Government, I will not pretend to say. Time must determine; but I am well persuaded that without an efficient federal Government, the States must in a very short Time sink into Contempt and the most dangerous Confusion. Many Amendments have been proposed by the ratifying States but discordant with each other. A Door is left open in the Constitution itself for Amendments; but so large a Concurrence is made necessary that it may be supposed none will be admitted but such as shall co-incide with *general* opinion and *general* Interest. The new System was long argued and powerfully opposed in Virginia; however, she made the 10th. assenting State, by a Majority of 11 in Convention. Nothing can equal the Rejoicings in the Cities, Towns and Villages thro'out the States on the late fourth of July in Celebration of the Declaration of Independence and the Birth of the new Constitution. The Papers are fill'd with Accounts of Processions, Toasts &c. As a Specimen, I enclose the Exertions of Philadelphia on this Occasion. Altho' the State of New York hath not ratified, and it is very doubtful whether she will or no, yet the City is making grand Preparations for an Exhibition on the 22d. It is confidently talk'd that if the Convention should reject, the City of New York, with Straten and Long Islands, will seperate themselves from the State and join the Union.

Our friend Dr. Franklin has been, and indeed yet is, ill with a severe Fit of the Stone; he has had no Ease but from daily Annodynes. I was fearful of the Event on Account of his great Age but he seems getting better, and will I believe rub thro' it for this Time. Mr. Rittenhouse is in but a poor State of Health. No p[hiloso]phical news very interesting. I long [to] hear from you.—

I [long] to see you. We [hear] of great Commotions in France. How is your Situation affected by them. I wish you was here during the Formation of our new Government. We shall be in Want of Men of Ability and Integrity to fill important Departments. Much will depend upon our first off-set.

With best Regards to Miss Jefferson & sincere Wishes for your Health & Happiness I am, Dear Sir Your truly affectionate Friend & humble servant,

FRAS HOPKINSON

RC (DLC); addressed in part: "Favour'd by Mr. Tilier." The specimen of THE EXERTIONS OF PHILADELPHIA ON THIS OCCASION that Hopkinson enclosed has not been found, but it clearly was a copy of his own "Account of the Grand Federal Procession" of 4 July 1788, which was published in the *Penna. Packet* and also the *Penna. Gazette* of 9 July 1788. Hopkinson was, if anything, guilty of understatement when he described this as "a spectacle as singular in itself as the occasion was extraordinary," for nothing quite like it had ever occurred in an American city. Even the fabulous *Meschianza* of 1778 was dwarfed by it; there were 87 divisions in the gigantic parade, consisting of floats, allegorical figures and groups, bands and military organizations, official delegations, and representatives of trades and professions. The float devoted to printing, bookbinding, and paper contained a complete printing press mounted on a platform drawn by four white horses. Mercury "in a white dress, ornamented with red ribbands, and having real wings affixed to his head and feet, and a garland of flowers round his temple," stood beside the press. As the procession, consisting of about five thousand persons, moved out from South and Third streets, an ode which Hopkinson had composed especially for the occasion and also "one in the German language, fitted to the purpose, and printed by *Mr. Steiner*, were thrown amongst the people. . . . Ten small packages, containing the above ode, and the toasts for the day, were made up and addressed to the ten states in union respectively, and these were tied to pigeons, which, at intervals, rose from Mercury's cap and flew off, amidst the acclamations of an admiring multitude." Later the entire procession and the spectators, numbering some seventeen thousand persons, gathered around the central float, the "New Roof, or Grand Federal Edifice"—the inspiration for which, of course, was derived from Hopkinson's own satire of the previous winter—and heard James Wilson deliver an address, after which there was a great dinner served with "American porter, beer, and cyder." Toasts were drunk to the people of the United States, the Federal Convention, General Washington, the King of France, the United Netherlands, the heroes "who have fallen in defence of our liberties," "May Reason, and not the sword, hereafter decide all national Disputes," and, finally, "The whole Family of Mankind." Each toast was announced by trumpets, and answered by the artillery—ten rounds to each toast—and these in turn were answered by salutes from the *Rising Sun*, at anchor in the river (Hastings, *Hopkinson*, p. 407-9). Hopkinson's earlier satire had used the allegory of the roof to point out the defects of the confederation, and he now composed a poem called "The New Roof: a Song for Federal Mechanics" in which he employed the same device to show the strength of the union; this poem appeared in the *American Museum* for July and Hopkinson may also have enclosed a copy of it in the present letter. One of its stanzas reads:

Come muster, my lads, your mechanical tools,
Your saws and your axes, your hammers and rules;
Bring your mallets and planes, your level and line,
And plenty of pins of American pine:
For our roof we will raise, and our song still shall be,
Our government firm, and our citizens free.

To Ralph Izard

DEAR SIR Paris July 17. 1788.

I have duly received your favor of Nov. 10. but it did not get to my hands till Apr. 24. With respect to the subject of rice, I should myself give the preference to that of S. Carolina. It is fairest to the eye, and, to my taste, equal in flavor to that of Piedmont. But so far as this market is concerned, we must attend to it's taste also. That decides 10. sous the French pound for Piedmont rice, and 8. only for that of Carolina, in the retail. I sent seed therefore to give an opportunity of making experiments on it. Besides the difference of price, it may perhaps discover other differences in it's favour, it may yeild more, be hardier, less liable to devastation, grow in poorer lands &c. If the reverse should be the case, it will be dismissed. The same may be said of the Egyptian rice which I have sent, and which would be preferred here to that of Piedmont, if it could be got. But the eternal wars of that country intercept it from the market. I presume the Agricultural society will have very exact experiments made of the three kinds.

I cannot but approve your idea of sending your eldest son, destined for the law, to Williamsburgh. The professor of Mathematics and Natural philosophy there (Mr. Madison, cousin of him whom you know) is a man of great abilities, and their apparatus is a very fine one. Mr. Bellini professor of modern languages, is also an excellent one. But the pride of the Institution is Mr. Wythe, one of the Chancellors of the state, and professor of law in the college. He is one of the greatest men of the age, having held without competition the first place at the bar of our general court for 25. years, and always distinguished by the most spotless virtue. He gives lectures regularly, and holds moot courts and parliaments wherein he presides and the young men debate regularly in law, and legislation, learn the rules of parliamentary proceeding, and acquire the habit of public speaking. Williamsburg is a remarkeably healthy situation, reasonably cheap, and affords very genteel society. I know no place *in the world*, *while the present professors remain*, where I would so soon place a son.

I have made the necessary enquiries relative to a school for your second son. There are only two here for the line of engineering. I send you the Prospectus of the best, which is so particular in it's details as to enable you to judge for yourself on every point. I will add some observations. I have never thought that a boy should undertake abstruse and difficult sciences, such as mathematics in general till 15. years of age at soonest. Before that time they are best employed in learning the languages, which is merely a matter of memory. The languages are badly taught here. If you propose he should learn the Latin, perhaps you will prefer the having him taught it in America, and of course to retain him there two or three years more. At that age he will be less liable to lose his native language, and be more able to resist the attempts to change his religion. Probably three or four years here would suffice for the theory of engineering, which would leave him still time enough to see something of the practice either by land or sea, as he should chuse, and to return home at a ripe age. Decide on all these points as you think best, and make what use of me in it you please. Whenever you chuse to send him, if I am here and you think proper to accept my services towards him, they shall be bestowed with the same zeal as if he were my own son.

The war in Europe threatens to spread. Sweden, we suppose, has commenced hostilities against Russia, tho' we do not yet certainly know it. I have hoped this country would settle her internal disputes advantageously and without bloodshed. As yet none has been spilt, tho' British newspapers give the idea of a general civil war. Hitherto I have supposed both the king and parliament would lose authority, and the nation gain it, through the medium of it's states general and provincial assemblies. But the arrest of the deputies of Bretagne two days ago, may kindle a civil war. It's issue will depend on two questions. 1. Will other provinces rise? 2. How will the army conduct itself? A stranger cannot predetermine these questions. Happy for us that abuses have not yet become patrimonies, and that every description of interest is in favour of rational and moderate government. That we are yet able to send our wise and good men together to talk over our form of government, discuss it's weaknesses and establish it's remedies with the same sang-froid, as they would a subject of agriculture. The example we have given to the world is single, that of changing the form of our government under the authority of reason only, without bloodshed.

I inclose herein a letter from Count Sarsfeild to Mrs. Izard, to whom I beg to present my respects. I am with great sincerity Dear Sir Your friend & servt, TH: JEFFERSON

P.S. I thank you for your attention to the newspapers. They do not come regularly, but I dare say it is not the fault of the printer. On the 10th. instant I received the Columbian herald for

January, February, March and April. They came by the packet, and, as I suppose, from the office for foreign affairs.

PrC (DLC). Enclosed in TJ to Trumbull, 24 July 1788. The enclosed PROSPECTUS has not been found, but on 28 May 1788 Count Sarsfield sent two copies to TJ, one of them for Izard; see note there.

To John Paradise

MY DEAR SIR July 17. 1788.

When your letter was delivered me this morning, my servant had just set out with one to you. I am uneasy till I hear from you and know what your wants may be which you wish to have furnished immediately, and which shall accordingly be furnished. Have you heard that the royal thunder has fallen on the Marquis de la fayette?

Your's affectionately, TH: JEFFERSON

PrC (DLC).

Paradise's LETTER has not been found, but see TJ to Paradise, 16 July 1788, the letter that TJ's SERVANT HAD JUST SET OUT WITH.

To John Rutledge

DEAR SIR Paris July 17. 1788

Your favors of Dec. 25. Jan. 19. Mar. 3. and Apr. 6. have been duly received, and their contents attended to in time. The 2400 livres remitted in that of Jan. 19. were paid to your son, and the further sum of £300. (I think it was) on account of Messrs. Brailsford & Morris, as mentioned in your letter of Jan. 19. was paid by Berard into the hands of Boyd, Ker & co. Mr. Rutledge's bankers here. In consequence of your approbation of his preferring the Southern to the Northern parts of Europe, expressed in your letter of Apr. 6. I have written to him, as I presume you had done yourself. My last letter from him was dated at Spa, the 8th. inst. He had passed from hence to Brussels, Antwerp, the Hague, Amsterdam, Utrecht, Nimeguen and Spa. He was to set out from thence on the 10th. and follow the course of the Rhine to Strasburg and Basle and then go to Berne. He would then get to the Danube and descend that to Vienna. At Vienna he would judge from enquiry whether he might safely and profitably descend that river further, or go directly thence to Trieste and Venice, and so make the tour of Italy, return along the Southern coast of France and the

Canal of Languedoc and the Garonne to Bordeaux, and thence go to Madrid and Lisbon. Rivers are generally the best guides for travellers, because they furnish the best lands, most considerable cities, and most flourishing commerce. I have recommended to him to make what stay he can at Madrid and Lisbon. Our connection with those countries must become every day more interesting. We cannot foresee whether it will be friendly or hostile. Even a moderate knowlege of them will give him great advantages over his countrymen who will know nothing of them. I have also pressed on him a particular attention to those objects of agriculture which he will see cultivated in the Southern countries of Europe, and worthy of being so in his own. These are the Olive, fig, raisin, caper, date, pistache, and to observe also the rice of those countries. It is a pleasure to me to be able to say to you with truth that I observe in him the best dispositions possible, a good judgment and much information. He is likely to be as much improved by this tour, as any person can be, and to return home charged, like a bee, with the honey gathered on it. Mr Shippen sets out with him on the same tour, and probably will continue through it. But I suppose he gives you all these details. I shall be very happy to be serviceable in every way possible as well for his own sake, as to give you further proofs of the sincerity of the esteem with which I have the honor to be Dear Sir your most obedt. & most humble servt,

TH: JEFFERSON

PrC (DLC). Enclosed in TJ to Trumbull, 24 July 1788.
Rutledge's FAVORS OF . . . JAN. 19. MAR. 3. have not been found.

To John Stockdale

SIR

Paris July 17. 1788.

I had written the preceding letter yesterday, but it had [not] yet gone out of my hands when I received yours of the 11th. inst. I must refer you to my letter of Oct. 10. 1787. for an explanation of the credit I state on the next leaf for Watson's Phil. III. as also for the maps. All I wished as to the maps was to avoid loss, which I shall not do, charging you 10d. a piece instead of 1/ a peice which had been at first understood to be the price. I wish you had sent your whole impression to Charlestown, Richmond, Philadelphia and Boston, as I believe it would have been sold immediately. As the work could not be bought there, the periodical papers retailed it out to the public by piecemeal till at length (as I am informed) a bad edition is printed, either without a map or with a slight sketch of one. My letter of yesterday will also explain to you my desire as to the Reviews and Repository. I put this letter under cover to Mr. Trumbull who will be so good as to pay you the balance of £13-12. Should I have mistaken the price of the Reviews and Repository yet to come, or that of the octavo edition of Phil. III. which was the one you sent me, he will be so good as to accede to your correction of those articles. I am Sir your very humble servt,

TH: JEFFERSON

Th: Jefferson to Mr. Stockdale Dr.

		£	s	d
1788. July 11.	To balance of account this day rendered	56	6	8
	To Monthly and Critical reviews from July to Decemb. 1788.		13	6
	Repository to Dec. 1788. viz. No. 11—16		6	
		57	6	2

Cr.

	£	s	d
By charge of Dec. 9. 1786 of Watson's Philip III in 4to 25/. instead of 2.v. 8vo. 16/	0	9	0
By pd. for 12. vols of Sandford & Merton & P. Grandison 13[tt]-4		11	
By use of map plate 1025 copies @ 10d	42	14	2
Balance due to Mr. Stockdale	13	12	0
	£ 57	6	2

PrC (DLC); slightly torn; TJ began a postscript and then erased it, leaving only faint traces of "P.S." and one or two words. This letter covered that of YESTERDAY, and both were enclosed in TJ to Trumbull, following.

Stockdale's letter OF THE 11TH. INST. is recorded in SJL Index, but has not been found; it transmitted a statement of TJ's account showing a balance due of £56 6s. 8d. For a note on TJ's copy of WATSON'S PHIL. III, see Sowerby, No. 180, Robert Watson's *The History of the Reign of Philip the Third, King of Spain*, 2 vols., 8vo., London, 1786.

To John Trumbull

DEAR SIR Paris July 17. 1788.

Your favor of the 11th. came to hand yesterday. With respect to the Vase it is not worth the trouble I have already given you. I will take it therefore as it is. Indeed I have ever found it dangerous to quit the road of experience. New essays generally fail: so I will leave to some body else to find out the manner of giving an elegant spout to that elegant machine.—I take the liberty of inclosing to you my letters to Stockdale, and of desiring you to pay him his balance of £13-12. Should you however have met with another carriage to be purchased, so as that this sum may not remain in your hands, be so good as to keep up the letters to him and write me back and I will immediately send another bill. It is for this reason I put his letters under cover to you, and open. It being the moment of post I am obliged to conclude only adding assurances of the esteem with which I am Dear Sir your friend & servt,

Th: Jefferson

PrC (DLC). Enclosures: TJ to Stockdale, 16 and 17 July 1788.

To Edward Rutledge

My dear Sir Paris July 18. 1788.

Messieurs Berard were to have given me a particular account of the proceeds of the shipments of rice made to them. But they have failed. I fear, from what they mentioned, that the price has been less advantageous than usual, which is unlucky as it falls on the first essay. If on the whole however you get as much, as you would have done by a sale on the spot, it should encourage other adventures, because the price at Havre or Rouen is commonly higher, and because I think you may by trials find out the way to avail yourselves of the Paris retail price. The Carolina rice sold at Paris is separated into three kinds, 1. the whole grains, 2. the broken grains, 3. the small stuff and sell at 10.^{tt} 8.^{tt} and 6.^{tt} the French pound, retail. The whole grains which constitute the 1st. quality are picked out by hand. I would not recommend this operation to be done with you, because labour is dearer there than here. But I mention these prices to shew that after making a reasonable deduction for sorting, and leaving a reasonable profit to the retailer, there should still remain a great wholesale price. I shall wish to know from you how much your cargo of rice shipped to Berard netts you, and how much it would have netted *in hard money* if you had sold it at home.

You promise, in your letter of Octob. 23. 1787. to give me in your next, at large, the conjectures of your Philosopher on the descent of the Creek Indians from the Carthaginians, supposed to have been separated from Hanno's fleet during his periplus. I shall be very glad to receive them, and see nothing impossible in his conjecture. I am glad he means to appeal to the similarity of language, which I consider as the strongest kind of proof it is possible to adduce. I have somewhere read that the language of the ancient Carthaginians is still spoken by their descendants inhabiting the mountainous interior parts of Barbary to which they were obliged to retire by the conquering Arabs. If so, a vocabulary of their tongue can still be got, and if your friend will get one of the Creek language, the comparison will decide. He probably may have made progress in this business: but if he wishes any enquiries to be made on this side the Atlantic, I offer him my services chearfully, my wish being, like his, to ascertain the history of the American aborigines.

I congratulate you on the accession of your state to the new federal constitution. This is the last I have yet heard of, but I expect daily that my own has followed the good example, and suppose it to be already established. Our government wanted bracing. Still we must take care not to run from one extreme to another; not to brace too high. I own I join those in opinion who think a bill of rights necessary. I apprehend too that the total abandonment of the principle of rotation in the offices of President and Senator will end in abuse. But my confidence is that there will for a long time be virtue and good sense enough in our countrymen to correct abuses. We can surely boast of having set the world a beautiful example of a government reformed by reason alone without bloodshed. But the world is too far oppressed to profit of the example. On this side the Atlantic the blood of the people is become an inheritance, and those who fatten on it, will not relinquish it easily. The struggle in this country is as yet of doubtful issue. It is in fact between the monarchy, and the parliaments. The nation is no otherwise concerned but as both parties may be induced to let go some of it's abuses to court the public favor. The danger is that the people, decieved by a false cry of liberty may be led to take side with one party, and thus give the other a pretext for crushing them still more. If they can avoid the appeal to arms, the nation will be sure to gain much by this controversy. But if that appeal is made it will depend entirely on the dispositions of the army whether it issue in liberty or despotism. Those dispositions are not as yet known. In the mean time there is great probability that the war kindled in the east will spread from nation to nation and in the long run become general. It began between the Turks and Russians. Then the Emperor entered into it, now the Swedes have taken side, and so probably it will go on from one to another. This country is in a desperate condition to meet a war. The only hope is that England will be as little able to get money, and that a bankruptcy will follow the declaration of war. They first excited the Turks to begin, and now have engaged the Swedes to enter into it. Whether they may not repent it however may well be doubted, and that they may repent it is the hearty prayer of him who has the honour to be with the most sincere esteem & attachment, my dear Sir Your friend & servt,

TH: JEFFERSON

PrC (DLC). Enclosed in TJ to Trumbull, 24 July 1788.

For the CONJECTURES OF YOUR PHILOSOPHER, see Rutledge to TJ, ca. 1 Apr. 1789 and its enclosure.

To the Rev. James Madison

DEAR SIR Paris July 19. 1788.

My last letter to you was of the 13th. of August last. As you seem willing to accept of the crums of science on which we are subsisting here, it is with pleasure I continue to hand them on to you in proportion as they are dealt out. Herschel's volcano in the moon you have doubtless heard of, and placed among the other vagaries of a head which seems not organised for sound induction. The wildness of the theories hitherto proposed by him, on his own discoveries, seems to authorize us to consider his merit as that of a good Optician only. You know also that Doctor Ingenhousz had discovered, as he supposed, from experiment, that vegetation might be promoted by occasioning streams of the electrical fluid to pass through a plant, and that other Physicians had received and confirmed his theory. He now however retracts it, and finds, by more decisive experiments, that the electrical fluid can neither forward nor retard vegetation. Uncorrected still of the rage of drawing general conclusions from partial and equivocal observations, he hazards the opinion that *light* promotes vegetation. I have heretofore supposed from observation that light affects the *colour* of living bodies, whether vegetable or animal; but that either the one or the other receive *nutriment* from that fluid must be permitted to be doubted of till better confirmed by observation. It is always better to have no ideas than false ones; to believe nothing, than to believe what is wrong. In my mind, theories are more easily demolished than rebuilt. An Abbé here has shaken, if not destroyed, the theory of de Dominis, Descartes and Newton for explaining the phaenomenon of the rainbow. According to that theory, you know, a cone of rays issuing from the sun and falling on a cloud in the opposite part of the heavens, is reflected back in the form of a smaller cone, the apex of which is the eye of the observer: thus.

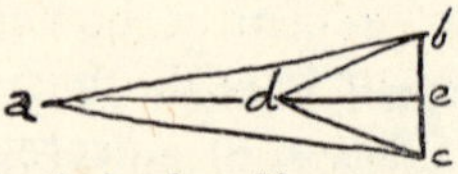

(a) the sun. (b) (c) the diameter of the rainbow (d) the eye of the observer. So that (d) the eye of the observer must be in the axis of both cones, and equally distant from every part of the bow. But he observes that he has repeatedly seen bows the one end of which has been very near to him, and the other at a great distance. I have often seen the same thing myself. I recollect well to have seen more than once[1] the end of a rainbow between myself and a house, or between myself and a bank not twenty yards distant, and this repeatedly. But I never saw, what he sais he has seen, different rainbows at the same time intersecting each other. I never saw coexistent bows which were not concentric also.—Again, according to the theory, if the sun is in the horizon, the horizon intercepts the lower half of the bow, from (e) to (c). If above the horizon, that intercepts more than the half, in proportion. So that generally the bow is less than a semicircle and never more. He says he has seen it more than a semicircle. I have often seen a leg of the bow below my level. My situation at Monticello admitted this, because there is a mountain there in the opposite direction of the afternoon's sun, the valley between which and Monticello is 500 feet deep. I have seen a leg of a rainbow plunge down on the river running through that valley. But I do not recollect to have remarked at any time that the bow was of more than half a circle. It appears to me that these facts demolish the Newtonian hypothesis but they do not support that erected in it's stead by the Abbé. He supposes a cloud between the sun and observer, and that through some opening in that cloud the rays pass and form an Iris on the opposite part of the heavens, just as a ray passing through a hole in the shutter of a darkened room, and falling on a prism there, forms the prismatic colours on the opposite wall. According to this we might see bows of more than the half circle as often as of less. A thousand other objections occur to this hypothesis, which need not be suggested to you. The result is that we are wiser than we were, by having an error the less in our catalogue; but the blank occasioned by it must remain for some happier hypothesist to fill up.

The dispute about the conversion and reconversion of water and air is still stoutly kept up. The contradictory experiments of Chemists[2] leave us at liberty to conclude what we please. My conclusion is that art has not yet invented sufficient aids to enable such subtle bodies to make a well defined impression on organs as blunt as ours: that it is laudable to encourage investigation, but to hold back conclusion. Speaking one day with Monsieur de Buffon on the present ardor of chemical enquiry, he affected to consider chemistry but as cookery, and to place the toils of the laboratory on a footing with those of the kitchen. I think it on the contrary among the most useful of sciences, and big with future discoveries for the utility and safety of the human race. It is yet indeed a mere embryon. It's principles are contested. Experiments seem contradictory: their subjects are so minute as to escape our senses; and their result too fallacious to satisfy the mind. It is probably an age too soon to propose the establishment of system. The attempt therefore of Lavoisier to reform the Chemical nomenclature is premature. One single experiment may destroy the whole filiation of his terms, and his string of Sulfates, Sulfites, and Sulfures may have served no other end than to have retarded the progress of the science by a jargon from the confusion of which time will be requisite to extricate us. Accordingly it is not likely to be admitted generally.

You are acquainted with the properties of the composition of nitre, salt of tartar and sulphur called Pulvis fulminens. Of this the explosion is produced by heat alone. Monsieur Bertholet by dissolving silver in the nitrous acid, precipitating it with lime water, and drying the precipitate on Ammoniac has discovered a powder which fulminates most powerfully on coming into contact with any substance whatever. Once made it cannot be touched. It cannot be put into a bottle, but must remain in the capsula where dried.—The property of the Spathic acid to corrode flinty substances, has been lately applied by a M. Puymaurin, of Toulouse, to engrave on glass, as artists engrave on copper with aquafortis.—M. de la Place has discovered that the secular acceleration and retardation of the moon's motion is occasioned by the action of the sun, in proportion as his eccentricity changes, or, in other words, as the orbit of the earth increases or diminishes. So that this irregularity is now perfectly calculable.—Having seen announced in a gazette that some person had found in a library of Sicily an Arabic translation of Livy, which was thought to be complete, I got the Chargé des affaires of Naples here to write to Naples to enquire into the fact. He obtained in answer that an Arabic translation was found, and that it would restore to us 17 of the books lost, to wit, from the 60th. to the 77th. inclusive: that it was in possession of an Abbe Vella at Palermo who, as soon as he shall have finished a work he has on hand, will give us an Italian and perhaps a Latin translation of this Livy. There are persons however, who doubt the truth of this discovery, founding their doubts on some personal circumstance relative to the person who sais he has this translation. I find nevertheless that the Chargé des affaires believes in the discovery, which makes me hope it may be true.

A country man of ours, a Mr. Lediard of Connecticut set out from hence some time ago for St. Petersburgh, to go thence to Kamschatka, thence to cross over to the Western coast of America, and penetrate through the continent to our side of it. He had got within a few days journey of Kamschatka, when he was arrested by order of the empress of Russia, sent back and turned adrift in Poland. He went to London, engaged under the auspices of a private society formed there for pushing discoveries into Africa, passed by this place, which he left a few days ago for Marseilles, where he will embark for Alexandria and Grand Cairo, thence explore the Nile to it's source, cross to the head of the Niger, and descend that to it's mouth. He promises me, if he escapes through this journey, he will go to Kentuckey and endeavour to penetrate Westwardly from thence to the South sea.

The death of M. de Buffon you have heard long ago. I do not know whether we shall have any thing posthumous of his.

As to political news, this country is making it's way to a good constitution. The only danger is they may press so fast as to produce an appeal to arms, which might have an unfavorable issue for them. As yet that appeal is not made. Perhaps the war which seems to be spreading from nation to nation may reach them. This would ensure the calling of the states general, and this, as is supposed, the establishment of a constitution. I have the honor to be with sentiments of sincere esteem & respect, Dear Sir Your friend & servant,

TH: JEFFERSON

PrC (DLC).

TJ's hope that the reported ARABIC TRANSLATION OF LIVY would prove to be true was doubtless tempered with a skepticism born of his earlier uncritical enthusiasm for James Macpherson's "translations" of the poems of Ossian (see Vol. 1: 96-7, 100, 101), of which Joseph Vella's "discovery" of the complete Livy was a rough parallel. TJ's request of his friend Pio, who was the CHARGE DES AFFAIRES OF NAPLES, may have been in writing, but it has not been found; however, an extract of the ANSWER from an unidentified person, dated 25 Dec. 1787, is in DLC: TJ Papers, 35: 6068. This extract, in Italian, was copied by TJ, and a translation of it reads as follows: "[It is] more than true, that there has been found in Sicily the Arabic translation of Titus Livius, and there is a certain Vella, most learned in that idiom, who is preparing to do a translation of it. There is more: the work which has been recovered is so voluminous as to give sound reason to hope that it may be a complete translation of all the works of this author, a thing which, if it be confirmed, enriches the commonwealth of letters by all that it lacks of him, and you and your friend well understand how interesting that is." Macpherson also was "most learned" in the idiom, but he was able to defend his position longer than Vella and he also was able to enlist more influential and enthusiastic supporters. Vella, under the protection of Archbishop Airoldi of Sicily, published in 1789 Volume I of his *Codice diplomatico di Sicilia sotto il governo degli Arabi, publicato per opera e studio de Alfonso Airoldi.* Five other volumes appeared, the sixth in 1792, printed with a font of Arabic type which Airoldi had obtained from Bodoni. From the very first doubts were expressed, and when Vella brought out at Palermo in 1793, under the sponsorship of the King of Naples, the first of two volumes of Arabic texts with Italian translation of manuscripts said to have been discovered at Fez, the doubts became conviction. Vella himself admitted the imposture and in 1796 was sentenced to imprisonment for fifteen years. TJ did not purchase either of his works.

1 Preceding three words interlined and possibly erased by TJ.

2 This word interlined in substitution for "the parties," deleted.

Swan's Proposals for Supplying American Beef, &c. to the French Government

Paris, 19 July 1788. "Jam's. Swan de Boston En faveur d'une association dans les Etats-Unis de l'Amérique," submits proposals for furnishing to the government of France a quantity of salt beef and pork, livestock, and butter from America for the troops and vessels of the king, in the colonies in America as well as in Europe as follows:

Ten to forty, or fifty, thousand barrels of beef of a quality equal to that of Ireland and of the same weight, to be delivered in some port of France or of the islands. This beef to be guaranteed to be the same quality as that of Ireland and consequently some may be delivered on trial. If it is necessary, an officer may be stationed in America to inspect all that will be taken on board either for the islands or for Europe, or only that found to be of good quality and well preserved by an inspector in the port of delivery will be unloaded.

Four to ten thousand barrels of pork of a quality guaranteed to be very superior to that of Ireland.[1] . . .

A quantity to be agreed upon of cattle and sheep to be delivered to the islands of France for the troops and vessels. "Les Troupes du Roi, et de Mer, et de Terre, qui ont été dans la Nouvelle Angleterre, savent bien que les Boeufs, et les Moutons en vie, sont bien supérieurs en qualité." They can be delivered at a price below that to which the islands are accustomed.[2] . . .

400,000 pounds of butter.[3] . . .

To guarantee the execution of the contract on their part, they will give "une caution Françoise de toute solidité." In contracts and trials made hitherto for shipment of American produce, no security has been given.

General conditions: delivery to be made at fixed periods, and wherever it is made, there will be an officer ready to make inspection of different articles and to do it without delay. Anyone attesting the receipt of such and such quantities will be able to authorize the purveyors to receive prompt payment in bills of exchange on the different departments or on the royal treasury.

Ships carrying provisions to the islands will have liberty to take on molasses and other merchandise at the port of unlading, but if this presents an insuperable difficulty it will not be insisted upon.[4] . . .

Price for salt provisions will be below that for such products of Ireland, and for livestock less than the customary price.

There will be fixed times of payment, to commence from the date of receipt of shipment, and although bills of exchange to be given in payment may be received after the date of the certificate of delivery, nevertheless, they will date from that time. Bills amounting to 15% the first year and 25% the second year to be withheld until certificates from the French customs are produced attesting that this amount has been shipped from France by, or for the account of, the purveyors, in brandy, wine, or manufactures of the realm.

Payment to be made in specie, but in order to encourage the use of French articles in America, "et pour commencer un commerce durable, et réciproquement avantageux," the contractors will hold themselves bound to take 15% of their payment in wines, brandies, and French products in the first year, 25% the second year, and each year afterward during the life of the contract an additional 2½%, the amount of supplies to be augmented in similar manner by an additional 2½% each year after the second year.[5] . . .

Remarques Générales.

L'on ne sauroit douter que la France aussi bien que L'Amérique ne desire de former un lien assuré et permanent. L'interêt du Commerce unit les Sauvages aux Civilisés, et soumet les ennemis dans l'alliance. Le lien d'intérêt est le plus fort qui puisse attacher une Nation à l'autre. Quoique l'Amérique et la France soient en tant que Nations dans une parfaite amitié, cependant le Commerce entre les deux a été troublé et éloigné par plusieurs causes, et ce sont principalement: 1o. les Américains n'etant point accoûtumés aux Manufactures de France. 20. Les Marchands des Etats Unis ayant du Crédit pour les Marchandises Angloises. On se propose de dissiper le premier par l'échange du produit de l'Amérique, pour les Vins, Eaux-de-Vie, et les Manufactures de France; et heureusement le dernier est actuellement entièrement detruit même avec les Anglois, ne se fiant à aucun qui n'est pas responsable, et en conséquence, seroit un bon Créancier à la France.

Si l'on observoit que les Américains sont accoûtumés aux Manufactures Angloises, et conséquemment ne voudroient point de celles des François, on pourroit répondre que les Contractants qui prendroient les Manufactures de France, auroient dans leur pouvoir, au moyen d'une certaine somme d'argent, d'obliger le Fermier à prendre en payement des Marchandises pour ses Boeufs, Porcs et Beurre, qui avec le tems estimeroit les Cottons, Draps &c. de France, comme sont actuellement ceux d'Angleterre, et même s'ils étoient de la même largeur et qualité, et pliés comme ceux-là, et au même prix, ils n'en pourroient pas faire la différence. Le Fermier une fois accoûtumé, le plus grand nombre de personnes le seroit aussi, car les Etats, où sont élevés les Bêtes-à-corne et les Cochons sont presqu'entièrement de cette classe d'hommes, et comme chacun a des Bestiaux à vendre chaque année, les Marchandises de France par ce moyen entreroient nécessairement presque toutes dans chaque Famille. Il n'a a pas d'autre moyen qui pût introduire l'usage de ces Manufactures si promptement, et si efficacément continuer la consommation.

Le Souscripteur a examiné personnellement les principales Manufactures en Normandie qui fabriquent ces articles que l'on employe en commun en Amérique, comme les Cottons, les Draps, les Toiles et la bonnéterie, enfin, pour assurer le Véritable intérêt des deux païs, et acquérir une connoissance nécessaire avant que ces propositions se fissent, dont il ose dire, qu'avec quelques réformes de peu de conséquence, en se conformant à la largeur, la foiblesse et le Glacé des Manufactures Angloises, lesquelles étant dressées, pressées, et pliées d'une manière particulièrement avantageuse, cache les fautes, et le besoin de force, que l'on ne trouve pas à présent dans les fabriques de Coton et de Laine de France, on pourroit les Vendre aussi bon marché, et l'on n'appercevroit aucune différence entre ceux Manufacturés en France et en Angleterre.

D'après un examen général sur les intérêts de la France et d'Amérique, il est evidemment de l'avantage de l'un, et de l'autre, de s'accorder ensemble, et dans ce moment que l'Angleterre a mis des entraves au peuple des Etats-Unis, par le découragement que l'on exerce continuellement contre l'importation de ses productions, et contre l'usage de ses Navigations; et quand il y a une Suspension du Crédit général des Américains, c'est l'instant où la France en saisissant l'occasion, recueilleroit tout aussi-tot de grands avantages.

Tandis que les Négotiants, Marchands et Fabriquants en France, ne connoissent point ceux qui sont responsables en Amérique, et en général qui n'ont aucune confiance dans le Commerce des Etats-Unis, un Contract de ce genre, sans hasarder un Sol du côté de la France, introduiroit pronptement un échange de denrées à un haut degré; et qui de la population actuelle qui s'accroit journellement, en peu de tems formeroit un revenu très considerable pour la Nation. Le nombre d'âmes des Etats-Unis double tous les Vingt ans; présentement il y en a près de trois millions et demi, dont la pluspart achètent la plus grande partie de leurs Vêtements.

J'eus occasion en faisant un Mémoire, ou Observations sur le Commerce entre la France et l'Amerique, (et qui fut traduit par le Consul Françoise à Boston, et envoyé au Maréchal De Castries lors de son Ministère) de faire un calcul de ces Manufactures de France, qui pourroient convenir à la consommation des Américains, et qui peuvent être fournis à aussi bon compte par ce Royaume que par l'Angleterre, et dans lequel je ne compris point les plus grossières lainés, ni aucune espèce de clincailles, comme fer, acier, &c., qui décidément sont meilleur marché dans ce paÿs que dans l'autre, et il se montoit à Cinquante deux Millions de Livres Tournois, et au delà par année: un commerce de cette importance donneroit de la vigueur à une Nation, et ranimeroit les esprits abbatus du pauvre laboureur et du Manufacturier découragé.

Il n'est pas nécessaire de remarquer qu'en tems de Guerre l'Angleterre coupe toute communication des vivres d'Irlande, et les Armées, et la Marine de France sont obligés de dépendre de l'ennemi pour les approvisionnements, ou être fournis par quelques autres à un prix énorme. Au contraire les provisions que l'on fourniroit d'Amérique seroient sûrs, et à bien meilleur compte que depuis plusieurs années.

Comment sont payés les Irlandois pour le Boeuf, &c., qu'ils vendent à la France? On me l'a dit, en Vins, et Eaux-de-Vie. Mais la chose est tout-à-fait contraire, et la Valeur est appliquée de la même manière, comme on l'a dit les Américains l'appliqueroient, nommément, pour les Marchandises Angloises. Par les Douanes d'entrée au Havre on y importa d'Irlande l'année dernière, dans ce petit port, un grand nombre de Mille Barils de Boeuf et de Porc, et de quart Barils de Beurre. Les propriétaires, ou les Vendeurs des quel, m'attestèrent unanimément le fait, que, (et ç'a toujours été le cas) il n'y eut pas une seule livre de la Valeur entière payée qu'en Lettres de Change sur Londres. Je suis très positivement informé que c'est la même chose dans tous les autres ports de France. Les Irlandois qui importent des Vins et des Eaux-de-Vie sont des hommes différents des Vendeurs de Boeuf; et ceux d'Angleterre et d'Irlande qui boivent les Vins et les Eaux-de-Vie de France (n'on obstant les impôts énormes) les payent en argent, et les boiroient quand même il n'y auroit pas seulement une livre de Boeuf pesant, porc ou beurre d'exporté en France dans une année. Où est donc la justice de l'objection, que l'Amérique prendroit la Valeur des provisions en argent de la France, et le payeroit à Londres contre des Marchandises, et que les Irlandois prennent le montant en Vins et Eaux-de-Vie? Est-ce que la proportion des Marchandises que l'on propose actuellement à recevoir en partie en payement ne seroit pas un avantage plus grand que celui qu'on en tire présentement en les recevant de Irlande, et la perspective du Commerce à venir avec l'Amérique, qui s'introduiroit par ce moyen, n'est-elle pas un objet de la plus grande conséquence pour la Nation Francoise?

L'on n'a pas besoin de faire mention de l'épargne générale, de l'utilité, et de la facilité des Contracts. Ils sont été trop utiles en tems de Guerre, en liant les individus à fournir, à tout hazard des approvisionements, et à donner trop peu d'embarras en tems de paix, pour qu'il soit nécessaire que le Souscripteur en dise quelque chose. La neutralité qu'on peut espérer que l'Amérique tiendra pendant plusieurs années, peut être une bonne raison pour qu'on puisse compter plus sûrement sur elle, que sur l'Irlande, qui nécessairement est engagée du Côté de la Grande Bretagne contre la France.

Soumis humblement
par Jam's Swan

MS (DLC); in Swan's hand; 14 p.; with a covering page bearing the following: "A Son Excellence Monsieur Jefferson Ministre Plenipotentiaire des Etats-Unis de l'Amérique de la Cour de Versailles de Son très obeissant et très humble Serviteur Jams. Swan." This is an amplification of Swan's original proposals of 29 May 1788, summarized above in note to Swan to TJ, 7 June 1788, and with some of the variations being indicated in the notes below; where the two proposals are substantially identical, their terms have not been repeated. MS (Archives Nationales, Paris, H1444, No. 251, Administration provinciale, Mélanges, Affaires diverses, 1765-1789); this is the text of the present proposals submitted by Swan to the French government, and in the same source are other documents concerning his efforts to sell supplies (e.g., grain) in 1788-1789.

There can be little doubt that TJ had something to do with the difference between Swan's original proposals of 29 May 1788 and those set forth above. TJ wished "most ardently" that such supplies could be brought from America, promised to lend what aid he could, and suggested that Swan ally himself with Parker (TJ to Swan, 19 June 1788). Thus the original proposal, signed by Swan only, was now signed by him in behalf of a company and the size of the contract was considerably enlarged; it was also designed better to protect the interests of the contractors, as, for example, in the provisions for settling by arbitration the reasonable indemnity for loss of livestock at sea and the augmentation of price during war. But the most important addition was in the general remarks; these are given above in full because, if not actually written in part by TJ, they certainly incorporated the basic ideas on commercial policy that he had been pursuing. More, the proposals now furnished an opportunity for habituating Americans to the use of French goods and for weaning them away from the consumption of English manufactures—for, as pointed out in these proposals, the American farmers supplying the provisions could be required to take French goods in return. This was a strategy that TJ had long promoted. He had certainly suggested the argument about trade with Ireland (TJ to Swan, 19 June 1788), and it is difficult to believe he did not suggest that contractors refrain from insisting upon the liberty to bring back molasses and other merchandise from the French West Indies after unlading their supplies, for he had for some time avoided pressing the ministry to open up the islands to American commerce, being convinced that it would not be granted and that, in case of war, France would be obliged to open up this commerce anyway (TJ to Jay, 6 Aug., 19 Sep., and 31 Dec. 1787). Also, the appeal to the argument that America could be expected to remain neutral in event of war with England and, especially, the statement that the population of America doubled every twenty years—a statement that TJ had made elsewhere on the very day that he wrote Swan in response to the original proposals (TJ's travel hints, printed under 19 June 1788)—seem both to bear the imprint of TJ's hand. This is not to argue, of course, that these general remarks do not also bear evidence of Swan's authorship. The reference to the personal inquiry about the products of Normandy and to Swan's own OBSERVATIONS SUR LE COMMERCE ENTRE LA FRANCE ET L'AMERIQUE is evidence of this (see note to Swan to TJ, 31 Jan. 1788). There can be little doubt, however, whether expressed in writing or in discussion, that these observations reflect consultations among TJ, Lafayette, Parker, and Swan in the period between 7 and 19 July 1788. Indeed, it had been Lafayette who, in 1784, suggested that Swan write his OBSERVATIONS.

1 The remarks concerning the superiority of American pork are omitted here as repeating those under item (2), note to Swan to TJ, 7 June 1788.

2 The omitted portion repeats item (3) of the same, except that provision is added here for the reasonable indemnity to be fixed by accepting the average of two estimates made by two persons to be chosen, one by each party.

3 The omitted portion repeats item (4) of the same concerning the good quality of American butter.

4 The portion omitted here repeats in part items (5) and (6) of note to Swan to TJ, 7 June 1788, though it varies in the stipulation that the augmentation of price during wartime is to be fixed in the manner described in note 2 above.

5 At this point in MS (p. 6) occur the date-line, the signature, and description of the company as quoted at the beginning, followed by the "Remarques Générales."

From André Limozin

Most Honored Sir! Havre de Grace 20th July 1788

I am very thankfull for the Contents of the Letter your Excellency hath honored me with the 16th instant which did not reach me before yesterday. Before to make any application in my behalf for the Consularship, I should be very glad to Know if your Excellency would approve my Steps for that purpose: for I should be very sory to do the least thing which should not be agreable to your Excellency, whose esteem is for me above all Consideration for the important Services America hath received from me since the year 1777. If they are Known to the present Members of Congress, I think my self more intitled to that Apointment than any body whatsoever.

Altho' there is not the least preparation neither here nor at Brest which could give[1] room to fear a War, I am afraid that if the Turks don't make peace, (and there is not the least prospect thereof) England will force us to not remain Neutrals, and to injoy much longer the blessings of peace. About 4 Months ago our Government had given very Strict orders to purchase all the sound oak timbers of any Size whatsoever which should be landed here, but since three weeks, these orders are altered, and reduced to take only the largest Size, and only what is very Sound [and] good. But I shall do my duty to acquaint your Excellency of what passeth here and in our Neighbourhood. I have the honor to be with the highest regard Your Excellency's Most Obedient & very Humble Servant, Andre Limozin

RC (MHi); endorsed; addressed; postmarked: "HAVRE"; and bearing on verso a few calculations in TJ's hand.

1 This word omitted in MS.

From John Polson

London. No 29 Villiers Street Strand
[ca. 20 July 1788]

Sir

When I had the honor of being Introduced to your Excellency at Paris in May 1785, you were so good as tell me that you would write to some Gentlemen in Virginia to know whether the Lands that were Granted to me as the Representative of my Brother William Polson Deceased (being 6000 Acres, he being a Lieutenant in the Virginia Troops before the Battle of the *Meadows* in the year 1754,) were Confiscated by any Law of the State of Virginia, Or whether I was at liberty to settle or dispose of them; and in the Month of Sepr. following, Your Excellency informed me that you had Written to Colo. Stephens, who was a Partner in the same Tract with me to know whether my share of the Land was Confiscated or not, and that you had also wrote to another Gentleman on the same Subject, but did not expect an Answer sooner than Christmass. Your Excellency may remember that I waited on you here in April 1786 and showed you the Virginia Gazette No. 349 dated 14 Jany. 1773 wherein Genl. Washington Advertises all the Officers and Soldiers that Served the Campagne of 1754 and their representatives that there Proportion of Land is laid out for them. My share is on the Kanhawa River near the Ohio, and I always paid my proportion of Every expence by my Attorney Mr. Alexr. Craig of Williamsburg Deceased. Your Excellency will confer a great obligation on me, if you will let me know whether my Lands are Confiscated or not, because if they are not, I will take some steps to have them either improved or Sold; and if I am unfortunate enough to have forfeited them for being a British Subject, for it can be only for that cause, for I was not employed in the war on the Continent, you will oblige me much by informing me of it, that I may have an Opportunity of Applying to the Commissioners appointed by Parliament for such Compensation as may appear to them to be equal to my loss. I am obliged to give in my losses in a few days, and if I have no authority to say that my Lands are Confiscated, I will receive nothing for them.

I hope your Excellency will excuse this liberty, as its a matter of consequence to me, and I have no other means of obtaining information. If the Lands of all British Subjects who did not join the American Army are forfeited, mine must of Course.

I have the honor to be with great respect Sir Your Excellency's Most Obedt & most Humble Servant, JNO. POLSON

RC (MoSHi); at foot of text: His Excellency——Jefferson Esqr."; undated, but SJL Index shows that TJ received a single undated letter from Polson in 1788; endorsed.

On 26 July 1788 Polson also wrote to Washington about his brother's claim to a share of the lands granted to the officers and soldiers of the Virginia regiment raised in 1754; see Washington's reply to Samuel Milford, 29 Sep. 1788 (*Writings*, ed. Fitzpatrick, XXX, 104-6). See also Polson to TJ, 13 May and 1 July 1785.

To Schweighauser & Dobrée

Sir — Paris July 20. 1788.

The resolution of Congress of Aug. 24. 1781. cited by Mr. Minier, directed that Joshua Johnson should examine and settle the accounts of Mr. Schweighauser against the frigate Alliance, and that their Minister plenipotentiary here should pay the balance that might be found due on the settlement of the said Johnson. Mr. Johnson refused to examine and settle the account, and to ascertain the balance. Their Minister then could not pay the balance found due by him, so that that resolution became of no effect.

Congress took up this subject again on the 16th. of Octob. 1786. and by their resolution of that date (a copy whereof I have the honor to inclose) authorized me to have this claim adjusted in such manner as I should judge most for the interest and honor of the United states, and that their property in your hands should be applied to pay the balance, if any should be found due, on such principles as should be agreed on between us. This is the resolution under which I act, and not that of 1781. I think the honor and consequently the interest of the United States requires that the claim in question be adjusted by sensible and honest men, indifferent to both parties.

In your letter of the 15th. instant you ask on what points I propose that the arbitrators shall decide? I answer, on all whereon we may differ in opinion. I do not know however that there is any difference of opinion except as to the articles furnished by Mr. Puchelberg to the Alliance. As to these, it appears to me that Mr. Puchelberg having furnished them without authority, and even against it, he is not entitled to reimbursement; but, if entitled, that the United States are not the debtor.

I will ask the favor of as early an answer as you can give me, and that it be definitive whether this matter shall be decided by arbitration, as that answer will determine my duty. I have the honor to be with great esteem, Sir Your most obedient humble servt,

Th: Jefferson

PrC (DLC). Tr (Arch. Aff. Etr., Paris, Corr.-Pol., Angleterre, Vol. 566); in Short's hand; enclosed in TJ to Montmorin, 11 Sep. 1788. Enclosure (PrC of Tr in Short's hand: DLC): The resolution of 16 Oct. 1786 was forwarded to TJ by Jay on 27 Oct. 1786 and is summarized above (Vol. 10: 490).

From Angelica Schuyler Church

Down Place July 21. 88

I send my dear Sir the little urn so long promissed and so long delayed, and hope you will accept the gift for the sake of the giver; it will sometimes at Monticello remind you of your friend.—Madame de Corny tells me you are going to America next spring. I shall also make that desired voyage, and see what my family and friends are doing. If I should meet you their I should be so happy to see you, and to introduce you to my father. I am very certain that you would please each other. Mrs. Cosway and I are enjoying the quiet of the country, she plays and sings, and we very often wish that Mr. Jefferson was here, supposing that he would be indulgent to the exertions of two little women to please him, who are extremely vain of the pleasure of being permitted to write to him, and very happy to have some share of his favorable opinion.

Adieu my dear Sir accept the good wish of Maria and Angelica. Mr. Trumbull has given us each a picture of you. Mrs. Cosway's is a better likeness than mine, but then, I have a better elsewhere and so I console myself.

I beg my compliments to the Young Ladies, I hope your *ward* improves, I will not thank you for your care, *I feel it* and sincerely your affectionate friend, ANGELICA CHURCH

RC (DLC); endorsed.

To Gautier

SIR Paris July 21. 1788

I am much obliged to you for the communication of the Deuxponts Catalogue of Greek and Latin books. There is nothing in it for which I have occasion except the 'L. Annaei Senecae Philosophi opéra. 4. vol. 7.[tt] 4.' If you have a correspondence there and can conveniently order this work for me, on condition it be an Octavo edition, I shall be obliged to you. I have their Plato which I like much. I wish they could be induced to print Diodorus Siculus and Dionysius Halicarnasseus in the same format. These are the only Greek authors of esteem which have never been printed but in large formats. There is indeed an Octavo edition of Diodorus printed at Basle. But it is of 5. books only out of 15 which remain, it is without a translation which is necessary for much the greater part of readers, and it is in an obsolete character, abounding with contractions now out of use, and little known, so that in fact it is worth nothing. Wesseling's edition of Diodorus, and Hudson's of Dionysius, exactly copied, but in Octavo format, would certainly meet with great success, the translation being printed on the same page with the original. Perhaps if you were to suggest this to the printers of Deuxponts, they might think it worthy their attention. I have the honor to be with great esteem & attachment Sir Your most obedient humble servt,

Th: Jefferson

PrC (DLC); partly faded.

From George Mason

Virginia Fairfax County,
Gunston Hall July 21st. 1788.

Dear Sir

I wrote You on the 26th. of May last, by my son John, Via Bourdeaux; to which I beg Leave to refer.

I intended to have given You the fullest Information in my Power upon the present gloomy State of American Politics, but the Ship, this Letter goes by, sails to-morrow; and I have had so severe an Attack of the Gout in my Stomach, for two or three Days past, that I have not been able to sit up, and now write in so much pain, that I must defer it, to another Opportunity. I enclose You however the last two or three Days proceedings of the Virginia Convention; which will shew You by how small a Majority, the new plan of Government has been ratified here.

I have desired Capt. James Fenwick (the Partner of the House in Bourdeaux, who transacts their Business here) to send over some Patterns of coarse Goods (as per List on the other Side) to his Brother and my Son; to see if such can't be manufactured in France, as cheap as in Great Britain: the Consumption of these Articles in the Middle and Southern States is immense; and nothing wou'd contribute more to encrease the commercial Intercourse between America and France, more than his being able to furnish them upon equal Terms with Great Britain. In this Light, perhaps it may be an Object worthy the Attention and Patronage of the French Ministry: if You think it so, and will write to my Son at Bourdeaux on the Subject, he will wait upon You at Paris, with the Patterns. You will observe that the coarse woolens are what we buy for our Slaves; most of the coarse french woolens I have seen are buttered with a great deal of Paste, or some such thing which shou'd be avoided; the nearer those woolens, to which our Slaves have been accustomed, are imitated, the better; the width too shou'd be minutely attended to, and must be full ¾th of an English Yard.

I am not able to sit up longer than to assure You, that I am, with the greatest Esteem & Respect dear Sir Your most obdt. Servt.,

G Mason

Patterns of the following Articles

white welsh plains or negroe's Cotton, nap'd and unnap'd
coarse half thicks—coarse Duffield or Bearskin
twill'd white Scotch plaiding—Dutch Blankets ⁶⁄₄ wide—15. in a piece
Scotch plaid Hose—Coarse Yarn Hose for negroes—Coarse felt Hats for Do.
ozenbrig thread—strong coarse Shoe thread—weeding and hilling Hoes
Sweed's falling Axes—flat pointed Nails—30d—20d—10d—8d. and 6d.
Sharp pointed 4d. Nails. N.B. the Axes must be well steel'd.

RC (DLC); endorsed. The enclosed LAST TWO OR THREE DAYS PROCEEDINGS OF THE VIRGINIA CONVENTION have not been found; Augustine Davis printed 200 copies of the journal of the convention of each day separately, and Mason probably enclosed such separates for the last days (Swem, "Va. Bibliog.," No. 7586). The present letter was enclosed in Mason's letter to his son, John Mason, of 2 Sep. 1788 (Rowland, *Mason*, II, 299-302).

From Grand & Cie.

Paris, 22 July 1788. Enclose Trumbull's receipt for £80 paid him by Tessier, who charged them, with expenses, £2037.3s.; they have debited TJ's account with this amount. Have had no advice yet on draft for £50 at 90 days deposited by TJ and forwarded by them for acceptance, but they will credit his account with proceeds.

RC (MHi); endorsed by TJ: "Grand's lre. That the £80 were paid to Trumbull That he will credit me Bannister's bill of £50." Enclosure (MHi): Receipt given to Lewis Tessier, signed by Trumbull in London, 11 July 1788, and "made double to serve but for one."

For the fate of the draft for £50, see TJ to Banister, 27 July 1788.

From the Commissioners of the Treasury

Board of Treasury
July 22d. 1788.

Sir

We have the honor of transmitting to you enclosed, a certified

Act of Congress of the 18th. Inst., relative to the papers belonging to the late Office of the Commissioner of Foreign Accounts. It is of great moment to the public that all these papers should be forwarded safely and without delay: we must therefore request your immediate attention to this Business.

Amongst the papers belonging to Mr. Barclay's Office, we consider all such as may have been delivered to him by Dr. Franklin, or any of the servants of the United States in Europe, although they may not relate to accounts actually settled by Mr. Barclay: that such papers were delivered, is stated in Dr. Franklin's Letter to this Board of the 31st. January last, an Extract of which you have enclosed.

We have no doubt that in the delivery of these papers you will use such precautions, as will enable the Board to ascertain (in case any of the packages containing them should be lost or opened) who is the person properly responsible for the same.

We have the honor to be with the greatest respect Your Excellency's Most Obedient Humble Servants,

Samuel Osgood
Walter Livingston
Arthur Lee

RC (DLC); in a clerk's hand; signed by each of the Commissioners. Enclosures: (1) Copy of resolution of Congress directing that "the Minister of the United States at the Court of France . . . transmit by such conveyance as he may judge most safe and convenient to the Treasury Board all the Books and papers which belong to the late Office of the Commissioners of Foreign Accounts" (DLC; clerk's copy; signed by Charles Thomson; endorsed by TJ: "Treasury board"). (2) Copy of a letter from Benjamin Franklin to Commissioners of the Treasury, 31 Jan. 1788, stating that, immediately on receipt of theirs of the 11th, enclosing one from Thomas Barclay, he had "ordered a fresh search to be made for the Papers . . . respecting the Vouchers of Mr. Ross's Accounts deposited in my Office when in France; and after the most careful and diligent examination nothing of the kind is found in my possession." Franklin added: "When I was about to leave that Kingdom, I ordered all papers relating to the public Accounts, and everything deposited with me as Consul (I having acted in that capacity before Mr. Barclay's arrival) to be put into his hands, which was done. I cannot therefore but be of opinion, that tho' he may not have taken notice of those vouchers, nothing having required his adverting to them, yet they will be found with the other Papers of his Office when they shall arrive in America" (DLC; clerk's copy; attested by William Duer).

To Benjamin Vaughan

Dear Sir — Paris July 23. 1788

Your favor of April 5. 1788. covering that also of Jan. 26.–87 did not miscarry; but I have been prevented answering it by a long journey through Holland and Germany, and by a necessary attention to some pressing matters in the first moments after my return. In fact, I was occupied on the subject of Hygrometers and preparing to write to you, when I received your favor of the 11th. inst. This requiring the first attention, I went immediately to the Marquis de Condorcet, Secretary to the Academy of arts and sciences, and spoke to him on the subject of the Caveat for Mr. Rumsey. He informed me that this was not their method of acting in such cases: that the best thing Mr. Rumsey could do would be to commit to paper a perfect description of his invention, expressed without any mystery, to seal this up with his own seal, and indorse on it the general title of his invention, to inclose this in a letter addressed 'à Monsieur Monsieur le Marquis de Condorcet, Secretaire de l'Academie des Sciences, à l'hotel de la Monnoie,' in which letter he will say that he means to come to France to ask an exclusive privilege for his invention as soon as his affairs will permit him, and praying that in the mean time the paper he incloses may be deposited in the office of the academy, unopened, but with an endorsement of the day on which it is received. The Marquis de Condorcet will comply with this request and Mr. Rumsey may rest most perfectly assured that his seal will remain unviolated. He will be at liberty also to withdraw it when he pleases. He will of course take care to find a safe conveiance from London to Paris for his letter. If, before the receipt of his letter, any application is made to the academy on the same head, the Marquis de Condorcet will give me notice of it.

I will now recur to the subjects of your letter of Jan. 1787. and first of all accept my thanks for Dr. Crawfurd's book which I had long desired, for the 7. Nos. of the Repository, which I like so well that I am become a subscriber for it, for De Luc's Hygrometer, and that of Mahogany on Dr. Franklin's principle and your plan. All these came while I was in Germany. The case of Magnets sent a twelvemonth sooner, I had desired Messrs. Nairne & Blount might ask paiment for of Colo. Smith, and I had desired Colo. Smith to pay for them, and supposed it done. But turning now to his account I do not find he has charged me with that paiment, so that if he made it, he has forgot to charge it, and consequently I am his debtor for it; if he did not pay it, then I am indebted to Messrs. Nairne & Blount, and will ask the favor of them to apply for it to Mr. John Trumbul No. 2. North street, Rathbone place, who will pay them. I have been a little at a loss with the Hygrometer of De Luc you were so kind as to send me. It is graduated from zero to 100, and I had understood these were his extremes. Those of De Saussure are the same. Yet, while this of De Luc, exposed to the open air has never fallen below 26. nor risen above 55. since it was in my possession, those of De Saussure have been generally, during the wet spell we have had, at about 90. Do you suppose any thing may have lessened the sensibility of the whale bone, or to what other cause must I ascribe the smallness of it's range? The manner in which Mr. Nairne has carried Dr. Franklin's idea into execution is estimable for it's simplicity, and simplicity in the hygrometer is peculiarly necessary. But it is liable to the objection you justly make that equal extensions of the wood are not equally indicated on the dial plate. The fillet of wood expanding in the direction of the tangent of the circle, the circle should be divided into portions corresponding to equal parts of the tangent, that is, the index should point out, not the angle it has moved over, but it's tangent. I think too that Mr. Nairne's fillet moving in grooves of wood, will be considerably resisted in it's motion, by the grooves which hold it. The fillet placed in a single groove in your manner is less resisted in it's motion, but the fillet being half buried in the groove is less exposed in that half to the influence of the atmosphere; consequently it dilates and contracts more slowly than the outer half, and necessarily becomes curved; it's indications become very false sometimes from this cause. I think too that it's dilatations must be expressed in numbers in order to give a result which shall be the just average of all our observations. For it is the result of all the observations to be made in Europe which is to express the ordinary humidity of it's atmosphere, and the result of all the observations to be made in America, which is to express the humidity of that atmosphere, and thus place the two in comparison. I have thought of the following plan, and a workman is now employed in executing it. a.b.c.d. is the stock of

mahogany, suppose 20. Inches long, and 2½ I. wide and thick. e.f.g.h. is the fillet of wood ⅒I. thick, 2I. lengthwise of the grain from e. to f. and 18.I. across the grain from e. towards g. I prefer beach because more sensible than mahogany. i.i.i. &c. are pullies fixed on the stock, in the grooves of which the edges of the fillet move, that it may meet less resistance in it's expansion and contraction. k.l. is a rack made fast to the end of the fillet e.f. which is moveable, while the end g. h. is made fast to the stock. m. is a toothed wheel the axis of which passes through a dial plate and carries an index n. o. to point out the degrees from 0. to 100. marked on the dial plate, these extremes of 0. and 100. to indicate the same state of dryness and moisture which the same numbers do on De Saussure's hygrometer. If, on experiment, I find this construction to answer, I will have four fillets cut of the same peice of wood, and adapted to so many instruments for comparative observations here, in England, and two different parts of America, and will take the liberty of presenting to you the one for England. I verily believe it will turn out in event that the atmosphere of our part of America is less humid than that of this part of Europe: and that this furnishes an instance the more wherein philosophers, as you justly observe, hasten to general conclusions from too few observations, and on false testimony of these observations. I must do the justice to those of your country to say they have given less than any others into the lies of Paw, the dreams of Buffon and Raynal, and the well-rounded periods of their echo Robertson.

From what I have seen of the climate of Europe, and what I have been able to learn of it from others, it seems to me that it's middle parts are covered by an almost perpetual bank of clouds, extending Northwardly beyond Copenhagen, but not so far as Stockholm, Eastwardly to Switzerland, Southwardly to a little beyond Lyons, and Westwardly to the Western coast of Ireland, and perhaps it is the same which is always hovering over the banks of Newfoundland. Should further enquiry confirm the fact it will be a curious question to examine why the middle parts of Europe should be subject to this general cloudiness while it's Northern and Southern parts enjoy a clear sky, as we do also in America? A considerable improvement in the Air pump has taken place in America. You know that the valves of that machine are it's most embarrassing parts. A clergyman in Boston has got rid of them in the simplest manner possible. The alteration he has made is described in the philosophical transactions of Boston. I put this description into the hands of a Mr. Jones, instrument maker in London, when I was there. But he has not tried it. I have since wished I had made an acquaintance there with Mr. Nairne, and communicated it to him. If he should wish to see the description, it is in the hands of Mr. Paine (Common sense) now in London who has withdrawn it for me from Jones. I have heard of an improvement made in this instrument at Amsterdam, but do not know what it is, and very much doubt whether it be as great as the one I have spoken of.—I have heard that they make in London an Odometer, which may be made fast between two spokes of any wheel, and will indicate the revolutions of the wheel by means of a pendulum which always keeps it's vertical position while the wheel is turning round and round. Thus [*see Fig. 1.*] I will thank you to inform me whether it's indications can be depended on, and how much the instrument costs. Should you sometimes see Lord Wycombe, and Dr. Price, I will trouble you to present my respects to them, begging you at the same time to accept assurances of the esteem & attachment with which I am Dear Sir Your most obedt. humble servt,

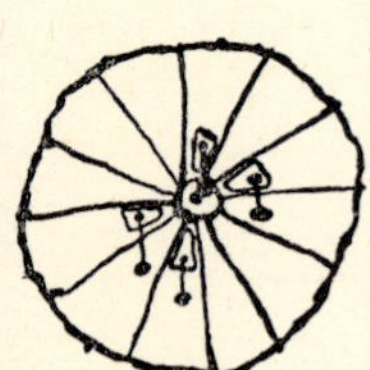

Fig. 1

TH: JEFFERSON

RC (Mrs. Langdon Marvin, Hallowell, Maine, 1947). PrC (DLC).

TJ's earliest opinion of THE LIES OF PAW may be found in his letter to Chastellux of 7 June 1785. Cornelis de Pauw (1739-1799) was the author of *Recherches Philosophiques sur les Américains, ou Mémoires intéressants pour servir à l'Histoire de l'Espece Humaine*, Berlin, 1771 (Sowerby, No. 3968). The CLERGYMAN IN BOSTON was the Rev. John Prince, whose "Account of an Air-Pump on a new Construction, with some Observations on the common Air-Pump," appeared in *Memoirs of the American Academy of Arts and Sciences*, I (1783), 497-519.

From William Carmichael

DEAR SIR

Madrid 24th July 1788

I received this day from Mr. Young Your Excellency's letter of the 3d Ultimo. The detention of that Gentleman on the road was much longer than he expected. I am happy to find that you have succeeded in making arrangements for our future support. As soon as I have examined the State of my accounts with Congress, I shall transmit to you the Amount of the ballance due me and draw in the manner you direct for what may be necessary for my support here. Ere this you will have received from Mr. Symonds the Cypher left with me by Mr. Barclay. In the one you sent me I have equal difficulty to distinguish the Letters you mention. I find that 1360 instead of 1363 has been appropriated to the *signification*[1] *of the latter*. I have corrected *this error* so that

I hope we shall soon come to a perfect good understanding. I did not draw upon Mr. *Littlepage* because I understood you was absent and that he was in such distressed circumstances, as to be constrained to quit Paris; I think I mentioned the latter Circumstance in one of my last Letters. However as he hath expressed a concern that I have not done this, I shall next post take the Liberty of inclosing you a letter for him and two sets of Exchange for the amount of what he himself acknowledges to have received in his Letter of the 3d of Novr. 1787 which you transmitted me in the Month of December: at the same time as you must know his situation much better than I can do, I beg you to act in consequence, for it is by no means my wish to distress him.

I have repeatedly applied to *Campomanes* who continues to talk of the *Canal* in question as a visionary Project. I wrote to a friend *at Cadiz* to question *Mr. Ulloa* on the same *subject*, but as yet I have no satisfactory answer [. . .][2] If the *survey* exists you may be assured that I will endeavour to have *a copy*. My last Letters from America (not official) dated the 26th of May confirm what you have been so good to mention in yours, since the date of which you have seen the accession of Maryland by a great Majority to the Constitution. Our Connections with this Country become more evident daily. You will have heard of the distruction of New Orleans by fire. It was so instantaneous that Little could be saved from the flames. I am informed that a Famine was apprehended in consequence and that a vessel was dispatched to Mr. Gardoqui for supplies of all kinds from North America. I have lately received letters from Algiers. It seems the Prime Minsiter has fallen a victim to his Ambition or riches, having been strangled by the Deys Order: He is succeeded by the Minister of Marine. The Regency seems disposed to quarrel with France I suppose with a view to exact a large sum of Money. Fifteen of our Unfortunate Countrymen survive, the Same allowance is continued to them, which I informed you I had authorized in the commencement of their Captivity and which Mr. Lamb confirmed. These Advances have been hitherto made by the Agents of this Court. I wish to know the Sentiments of Congress on the Subject and if practicable to be enabled to pay the Advances made hitherto. If your sentiments coincide with mine, I beg you to employ your Influence not only to refund the advances made, but to procure some little mark of notice to those who have behaved in a friendly manner to our distressed Countrymen. Dn. Miguel de Lardizabal dined with me on Saturday in Company with the first Under Secretary of State the Chevalier de Otamende and Andeaga who has in the same department the Correspondence with the Barbary States. Lardizabal always mentions you with the highest respect and some time ago spoke to me of the commission you had given him as difficult to execute: I shall remind him of it and engage him to write you on the Subject. I reserve for another occasion many particulars which I have not now leisure to communicate in the proper Manner and I intreat you to have the goodness to continue a correspondence which every day must become more interesting, If I can be allowed to be a judge of the designs of *our*[3] Enemies and of *those*[3] of the House of Bourbon with which they now find we are perfectly united. I have the honor to be with the highest respect Yr Exclys Most Obedt. & Obliged Hble Sevt,

Wm. Carmichael

RC (DLC); partly in code; endorsed. Enclosure not found.

[1] This and subsequent words in italics, except as noted, are written in code and were decoded interlineally by TJ; his decoding has been verified by the Editors, employing a partially reconstructed key for Code No. 11.

[2] At this point Carmichael wrote the following symbols: 707.1555.959. 1371.1611. which TJ correctly decoded as "4. yet 8. Tunis Mr. Barclay." Carmichael may have merely insterted these symbols to mislead, as he occasionally did, for otherwise the references to the SURVEY (see TJ to Carmichael, 3 June 1788, note) seem to be complete.

[3] This word is not in code, but is underscored in MS.

From Giuseppe Chiappe

Excellence Mogador Le 24e. Juillet 1788

Dans ma derniere du 24e. May que J'ay eû l'honneur d'êcrire à Votre Excellence, Je me proposois de l'informer ensuite de tout ce qui se passeroit à la Cour et dans le Paÿs à l'égard principalement des Anglois, et des Hollandois, et de la gite de S.M.I. au Nort a ses Provinces avec tant de Troupes qui faisoient soupsçonner une particuliere expedition. Je m'en aquitte avec bien du plaisir pour convaincre Votre Excellence de mon assiduité dans toutes les occasions qui se presentent, et non obstant que Je me trouve privé de l'honneur d'une seule réponse d'aprez bien des Lettres que J'ay écrites de toute part, Je continuerois de le faire avec la même exactitude. Quattre Frégattes Angloises détachées de l'Esquadre de la Mediterranée, et sous le même Comendant aprez avoir été à Tanger pour y depecher les Lettres a la Cour, ont parcourrue la Côte jusqu'a Mogador pour se faire voir, et par tout ont êtés reçues avec des marques sinceres de la meilleure correspondence. Les Lettres du Roy George n'en contestoient pas moins, et l'on est assuré que de part et d'autre l'on continuera dans la plus bonne armonie, non obstant que S.M.I. ne veuille pas plus se servir du Canal de Gibraltar pour faire passer ses Lettres, ni non plus accorder a cette Place les Provisions qu'Elle avoit coutume de tirer de ces Ports, mais l'on s'attend encore à l'eclaircissement de cet dernier refus, qui pourroit bien être revoqué dans peu de tems. Les Hollandois ont parus également à Tanger avec quattre de Leurs Vaisseaux de la Division de la Méditerranée. Un de ses Comandants chargé par SS:HH:PP: de l'Ambassade y est descendu, et en compagnie du Consul General de la Nation passera a la Cour aussi tôt qu'il en aura les ordres, et qu'il sera determiné le lieu de sa rencontre. En attendant S.M.I. est toujours campée aux environs de Mequinez d'ou il a fait partir ses Troupes augmentées jusqu'au nombre de 30. mille pour subjuguer des certaines Provinces Rebelles, et les ramener a leur devoir. Il tient encore la Campagne, mais les *plus sûres nouvelles* contestent que dans *peu de tems* le tout sera tranquil, et dans la plus grande subordination. Les Presents envoyés par la Cour de Portugal consistoient en Toileries très fines, Draps superbes de toute sorte, Velours, Soiries en Or, et fournitures très-riches en Pierreries precieuses. Cette Cour a obtenue la confirmation de l'extraction des Bleds avec les Droits *d'exportation* diminués comme auparavant, et aux conditions mêmes que la Cour d'Espagne. Votre Nation Americaine ne doit pas moins s'attendre à des predilections, vû que S.M.I. s'en est expliquée formellement, et il ne manque que la concurrence. D'aprez que Monsieur Barklay est parti pour Filadelfe Je n'ay pas reçu de Luy aucune Lettre, et J'ose recomander à Votre Excellence l'incluse pour Luy affin qu'elle Luy parvienne; et toujours rempli des sentiments de la plus haute estime, J'ay l'honneur d'être très profondement De Votre Excellence Le très-Humble et très-Obeissant serviteur GIUSEPPE CHIAPPE

RC (MoSHi); endorsed. Enclosure not found.

From John Brown Cutting

SIR [ca. 24 July 1788]

Since my last which Col. Trumbull had the goodness to inclose and superscribe I have been confined by severe indisposition; otherwise I shou'd have informed You by the last post that New Hampshire had adopted the new constitution by a large majority on the 24th of June. Altho I have not learned the particulars as to numbers &c. the fact may be relied upon. Beside the attestation of Capt. Thomson who brings the account a Mr. Dickason and other english merchants have letters from their correspondents announcing the event.

One hundred and forty of the Convention of Virginia met on the 2d of June and after having appointed Mr. Pendleton their President, resolved that no general or particular question shou'd be taken on the federal constitution until the same had been considered paragraph by paragraph. There was a rumour in New York on the 12th that Virginia had adopted it. But from the briefness of the interval from the meeting of the Convention and that date I doubt its authenticity.

On the 18th of June Mr. Adams was presented at the house of the Governor, where he resided by invitation after his arrival with the following address from the Legislature of Massachusetts.

"Sir

The return of yourself and family to the United States and to this your native state in particular is gratifying to all who recollect your many successful labours in the service of your country.

To the patriot citizens of a free commonwealth the affection of an enlightened people, will appear the most illustrious reward.

The Legislature of Massachusetts, just to the merit of all her citizens and particularly mindful of yours, participate in the public satisfaction which is manifest on your arrival: and in these congratulations the legislature are confident that they express the sentiments of the people."

To which Mr. Adams replied in these words:

"The kind and condescending congratulations of so illustrious a body as the legislature of Massachusetts on my arrival with my family in this my native country does me great honor and demands my most grateful acknowledgments.

If the dangers and fatigues which have fallen my share in the course of a memorable revolution h[ave] contributed in any degree to the acquisition or security of those inestimable blessings of Independence and Peace, of Commerce and Territory, of civil and religious Liberty which this highly favour'd nation now enjoys, the reflection on them will be a source of consolation to me to my latest period, and the candour and indulgence with which they have been received by my fellow citizens will ever be remember'd with gratitude."

Every mark of respect was manifested towards Mr. Adams on his arrival both by the government and by the people. The Governor had given previous orders to the commandant of Castle William to salute the vessel on board of which Mr. Adams was, whenever it shou'd pass: which was accordingly done: and immediately afterwards his Excellency dispatch'd the secretary of the Commonwealth in a public Yatch to proceed on board and in the name of the chief magistrate for the State welcome and congratulate Mr. Adams on his arrival, and to invite him to his house to receive there the compliments of his numerous friends. Thither accordingly as soon as he landed Mr. and Mrs. Adams proceeded amid the acclamations of many thousands who crouded the wharf where he landed and surrounded the carriage quite to the door of the Governor.

There is a gentleman just arrived from Virginia who left the Convention debating on the 11th of June. He says he attended several days and that nothing can exceed the teeming violence with which Mr. Henry and Col. Grayson combat the constitution, except the ability with which Mr. Maddison and Governor Randolph advocate it. Mr. Henry used such harsh language in reprobating the fickle conduct of the latter that the house compel'd him to ask that gentleman's pardon. No doubt was entertain'd in Virginia respecting the ratification by that State.

Very respectfully I have the honour to be Your Excellency's Mo Obedt Sert, J. B. Cutting

RC (DLC); addressed; endorsed; undated, but marked by an asterisk in SJL Index to show that it was received sometime between 11 July and 3 Aug. 1788; it certainly was received before TJ's letter to Dumas of 31 July 1788; see also postscript of TJ to Cutting, 6 Aug. 1788.

To John Brown Cutting

Dear Sir Paris July 24. 1788.

I am indebted to your favor of the 11th. instant for many details which I have not received otherwise. Notwithstanding a most extensive and laborious correspondence which I keep up with my friends on the other side the water, my information is slow, precarious and imperfect. The New York papers, which I receive regularly, and one or two correspondents in Congress, are my best sources. As you are desirous of having, before your departure for South Carolina, a sketch of European affairs, as they are seen from this position, I will give you the best I can, taking no notice of the 'bruits de Paris,' which, like the English newspapers, are but guesses, and made generally by persons who do not give themselves the trouble of trying to guess right. I will confine myself to facts, or well-founded probabilities, and among these must necessarily repeat a great deal of what you know already. Perhaps all may be of that description. The war undertaken by the Turks, unadvisedly as was conjectured, has been attended with successes which are now hastening the publick opinion to the other extreme. But it should be considered that they have been small successes only, in the partisan way; the probable event of the war can only be calculated after a great general action, because it is in that we shall see whether the European discipline has been over-rated, and the want of it in the Turks exaggerated. Russia certainly undertook the war unwillingly, and the emperor it is thought would now be glad to get out of it. But the Turks, who demanded a restitution of the Crimea, before they began the war, are not likely to recede from that demand, after the successes they have obtained, nor can Russia yield to it, without some more decisive event than has yet taken place. A small affair on the Black sea, which is believed, tho not on grounds absolutely authentic, is calculated to revive her spirits. 27. gun boats, Russian, have obliged 57. commanded by the Captain Pacha himself to retire after an obstinate action. The Russians were commanded by the Prince of Nassau, with whom our Paul Jones acted as Volunteer, and probably directed the whole business. I suppose he must have been just arrived, and that his command has not yet been made up. He is to be rear-admiral, and always to have a separate command. What the English newspapers said of remonstrances against his being received into the service, as far as I can learn from those who would have known it and would have told it to me, was false, as is every thing those papers say, ever did say, and ever will say.—The probability, and almost certainty that Sweden will take a part in the war, adds immensely to the embarrasments of Russia, and will almost certainly prevent her fleet going to the Mediterranean. It is tolerably certain that he has been excited to this by the court of London, and that he has received, through their negotiations, a large subsidy from the Turks (about 3. millions of Thallers) yet the meeting of the two fleets, and their saluting, instead of fighting, each other, induces a suspicion that if he can hinder the Russian expedition by hectoring only, he may not mean to do more. Should this power really engage in the war, and should it at length spread to France and England, I shall view the Swedish separation from

France as the event which alone decides that the late subversion of the European system will be ultimately ruinous to France. This power with the two empires and Spain was more than a match for England, Prussia and Holland, by land, and balanced them by sea, for on this Element France and Spain are equal to England and Russia to Holland. Sweden was always supposed on the side of France, and to balance Denmark on the side of England by land and sea; but if she goes over decidedly into the English scale, the balance at sea will be destroyed by the amount of the whole force of these two powers, who can equip upwards of 60. sail of the line.—There is a report, credited by judicious persons, that the Dutch patriots before their suppression, foreseeing that event, sent orders to the E. Indies to deliver Trincomale to the French and that it has been done. My opinion is either that this is not true, or that they will redeliver it, and disavow their officer who accepted it. If they did not think Holland and all it's possessions worth a war, they cannot think a single one of those possessions worth it.—M. de St. Priest has leave to go to the waters. Probably he will then ask and have leave to come to Paris, and await events.—The English papers have said the works of Cherburg were destroyed irreparably. This is a mathematical demonstration that they are not. The truth is that the head of one cone has been very much beaten off by the waters. But the happiness of that undertaking is that all it's injuries improve it. What is beaten from the head widens the base, and fixes the cone much more solidly. That work will be steadily pursued, and in all human probability be finally succesful. They calculate on half a million of livres, say 20,000£ sterl. for every cone, and that there will be from 70. to 80. cones. Probably they must make more cones; suppose 100. This will be 2. millions of pounds sterling. Versailles has cost 50 millions of pounds sterling. Ought we to doubt then that they will persevere to the end in a work, small and useful, in proportion as the other was great and foolish.

The internal affairs here do not yet clear up. Most of the late innovations have been much for the better. Two only must be fundamentally condemned; the abolishing, in so great a degree, of the parliaments, and the substitution of so ill composed a body as the cour pleniere. If the king has power to do this, the government of this country is a pure despotism. I think it a pure despotism in theory, but moderated in practice by the respect which the public opinion commands. But the nation repeats, after Montesquieu, that the different bodies of magistracy, of priests and nobles are barriers between the king and people. It would be easy to prove that these barriers can only appeal to the public opinion, and that neither these bodies, nor the people can oppose any legal check to the will of the monarch. But they are manifestly advancing fast to a constitution. Great progress is already made. The provincial assemblies, which will be very perfect representatives of the people, will secure them a great deal against the power of the crown: the confession lately made by the government that it cannot impose a new tax, is a great thing. The convocation of the states general, which cannot now be avoided, will produce a national assembly, meeting at certain epochs, possessing at first probably only a negative on the laws, but which will grow into the right of original legislation, and prescribing limits to the expences of the king. These are improvements which will assuredly take place, and which will give an energy to this country they have never yet had. Much may be hoped from the States general, because the king's dispositions are solidly good; he is capable of great sacrifices; all he wants to induce him to do a thing, is to be assured it will be for the good of the nation. He will probably believe what the states general shall tell him, and will do it. It is supposed they will reduce the parliaments to a mere judiciary.—I am in hopes all this will be effected without convulsions. The English papers have told the world, with their usual truth, that all here is civil war and confusion. There has been some riots, but as yet not a single life has been lost according to the best evidence I have been able to collect. One officer was wounded at Grenoble. The arrest of the 12. deputies of Bretagne a fortnight ago, I apprehended would have produced an insurrection; but it seems as if it would not. They have sent 18. deputies more, who will probably be heard. General Armand was one of the 12. and is now in the Bastille. The Marquis de la Fayette, for signing the paper which these deputies were to present, and which was signed by all the other Nobles of Bretagne resident in Paris (about 60, in number) has been disgraced, in the old fashioned language of this country; that is to say, the command in the South of France this summer, which they had given him, is taken away. They took all they could from such others of the subscribers as held any thing from the court. This dishonours them at court, and in the eyes and conversation of their competitors for preferment. But it will probably honour them in the eyes of the Nation.—This is as full a detail as I am able to give you of the affairs of Europe. I have nothing to add to them but my wishes for your health & happiness and assurances of the esteem with which I have the honor to be Dear Sir Your most obedt. & most humble servt, TH: JEFFERSON

RC (MHi: AMT); addressed: "Mr. John B. Cutting London." Enclosed in TJ to Trumbull, 24 July 1788. PrC (DLC).

From C. W. F. Dumas

MONSIEUR Lahaie 24 Juillet 1788

J'ai vu la Lettre que votre Excellence a écrite dernierement à Mr. Luzac, et Elle aura vu par son Supplément du 22, No. LIX, qu'il en fait fidele usage. Je lui avois déjà témoigné mon mécontentement sur l'insertion de la Lettre malintentionnée, prétendue de N. York du 26 Avril, tirée de certaine Gazette du 24 Juin,[1] et copiée dans son Supplément No. LIII, et prié de se tenir en garde contre de semblables pieces anonymes, tandis que je lui fournissois des intelligences plus sures, que je lui garantissois.

Une Lettre d'Amsterdam, du 21 du courant, m'apprend, "that by a Ship arrived the same day from N. York, there are Letters up to the 10th ulto. by which the appearances for the accession of the State of N. Yk. to the new federal plan are less flattering than before, the Members elected for that Convention being two thirds antifederalists. Yet there was a Chance, that if nine States had come in, N. York could do the like thro' policy"—[Nous ne nous en flattons pas trop]—"The accounts of Virginia and N. Carolina were promising, and all seem to think, the new Government would be decided upon the Beginning of July".

Nous espérions, les amis et moi, que 12 Etats s'y conformeroient, et nous sommes vraiment mortifiés qu'un Etat principal comme celui de N. Yk. tant pour le Commerce que pour son local, reste en défaut pour se faire ensuite tirer l'oreille par de longs pourparlers. Quoiqu'il en soit, dans mon opinion tout doit finalement tourner bien; et j'aime à me persuader, que le mois d'Août ne se passera pas sans que j'en reçoive la nouvelle positive, tant de Votre Excellence que de nos amis d'Amsterdam.

Vous verrez, Monsieur, par la Dépêche ci-jointe, combien de bonnes gens sont encore en ce pays sur le Lit de roses de Montezuma. Je me recommande à votre bon souvenir, et suis avec grand respect, de Votre Excellence, Le très-humble & très-obéissant serviteur, C W F DUMAS

RC (DLC); endorsed; brackets in MS. FC (Dumas Letter Book, Rijksarchief, The Hague; photostats in DLC). Enclosure (same): Dumas' dispatch to Jay, 18 July 1788, stating that the affair of the French ambassador would be held in suspense during his absence of some months in Lorraine; that someone had daubed the house of the United States with orange color during the night; that the disorders continue and two atrocious acts had occurred at Rotterdam—the murder of a tailor by the mob for having deposed against some seditious persons imprisoned by the late government, and the brutal and almost fatal attack on Captain Riemersma, a wealthy textile manufacturer, despite the fact that he wore an Orange cockade; that the attack on Riemersma was suspected of being planned and conducted by persons interested in English cotton manufactures; that Van Berckel's son had said some very unkind things of him to Shippen and Rutledge; and (in a postscript dated 20 July) that he enclosed the *London Courier* of the 16th containing the provisional treaty between Great Britain and Prussia, signed on 13 June (English translation printed in *Dipl. Corr., 1783-89*, III, 618-20).

TJ's letter to MR. LUZAC, publisher of the *Gazette de Leide*, has not been found and is not recorded in SJL Index. The LETTRE MALINTENTIONNEE that appeared in *Supplément* No. LIII of the *Gazette de Leide* for 1 July 1788 and inspired TJ's letter to Luzac enclosing a reply was in fact aimed at the account of the Doctor's Riot that TJ had drawn up and caused to be printed in *Supplément* No. LII of 27 June 1788; and aimed also at the piece appearing in *Supplément* No. XLIX for 17 June describing the favorable progress of ratification of the Constitution and the perfect harmony prevailing among the states (see note to TJ to Dumas, 9 June 1788). Luzac introduced this LETTRE MALINTENTIONNEE by saying that impartiality required its publication in view of the previous account in *Supplément* LII. This new piece included two items, both from New York, one dated 26 Apr. and one 30 Apr. 1788. The former stated that, although "la plûpart des bons Patriotes" were actively in favor of the Constitution, there were in some states powerful factions opposing any change in the system; that the latter feared the granting of too-great powers to Congress would cause a fall "de l'Anarchie dans le Despotisme"; that the public had never been more completely surprised than by the result in New Hampshire; that all of the friends of the Constitution had fully expected that state to adopt it, but the delegates, being given instructions to reject it, could find no other alternative than to adjourn to the third week in June, hoping thereby to win over more adherents to their side; that "Le Comté de Carlisle" in Pennsylvania had solemnly protested against the new form of government; that Rhode Island had rejected it; that New York could scarcely be counted upon to adopt; that only six states had ratified thus far, and, meanwhile, "le Congrès est dans un dénuëment complet: Ses Finances sont épuisées; et il s'y trouve rarement un nombre suffisant de Délégués pour délibérer sur les affaires publiques"; that the individual states continued to exercise, on their territory, all of the rights of sovereignty and to make laws which were scarcely consistent with engagements taken by Congress with foreign powers; that commerce, which at the beginning of peace had suffered a great shock, imperceptibly was being reëstablished, although it was less lucrative than before the war; that the weakness of the police in the principal cities had just been demonstrated in New York, where a mob of 1500 attacked the doctors, insulted the magistrates, and wounded several; that the governor was able to assemble only a few militia, but was repulsed, pulled by the hair—a fact specifically stated in one of Moustier's dispatches—and otherwise mistreated; that the "Populace vouloit absolument goudronner et emplumer les Médecins coupables; punition, qu'on inflige ordinairement en Amérique, et qui etoit connuë en France du tems des Croisades"; that the arrêt of 29 Dec. 1787 had produced a great sensation in America by the encouragements it gave to the commerce of the United States, which could only increase the bonds between the two nations. The "Extrait d'une Lettre de New-York du 30. Avril" stated that there had been some hope that Rhode Island would return to the fold, but this feeble ray had vanished when that state became the first formally to reject the Constitution; that, instead of calling a convention of deputies, the legislature had allowed the people to decide; and that on 24 Mch. 1788 the new Constitution had been rejected by a plurality of about 2700 to 200 votes.

The response to this in *Supplément* LIX of 22 July 1788 is there identified as coming "De Leyde, le 21 Juillet";

if Dumas is correct in saying that Luzac had made faithful use of TJ's letter, then the following, which appeared in this number, must have been substantially what TJ wrote: "Dans nos Feuilles précédentes nous avons annoncé, que six des Etats, qui composent l'Union-Américaine avoient déjà adopté la nouvelle Constitution Fédérative: sçavoir, ceux de Massachusett's, Connecticut, New-Jersey, Pensylvanie, Delaware, et Georgie; et que récemment celui de Maryland avoit suivi leur exemple par une pluralité de 63. contre 11. Voix. Nous pouvons dire aujourd'hui, qu'un huitième Membre de la Confédération vient de s'y joindre. C'est l'Etat de la Caroline-Méridionale. Le Projet de la Convention-Générale de Philadelphie y a été agréé par une pluralité de 149. contre 72. Voix. A la date des Avis, qui nous ont donné cette Nouvelle, la Convention de Virginie étoit assemblée pour le même objet: Si elle se décide egalement pour l'adopter, il y aura déjà le nombre de 9. Voix, qui est suffisant pour faire passer le Projet en Loi générale pour tous les Etats de l'Union. Ceux de New-Hampshire, New-York, et Nord-Caroline se seront probablement déjà déterminés aujourd'hui; mais l'on ne sçait pas encore si l'affirmative en faveur de la nouvelle Constitution y a réuni la pluralité ou la négative. Ainsi l'on s'abstiendra de faire des conjectures à cet égard, comme s'en est permis l'Auteur de l'Article de New-York du 26. Avril, inséré d'après la Gazette de France dans notre Supplément du No. LIII. Nous les hazarderons d'autant moins, qu'il pourroit en arriver à nos prédictions comme aux siennes; c'est-à-dire, qu'elles fussent démenties par l'évenement, presqu'au moment même que nous les aurions Communiquées au Public."

Although Dumas depreciated the accuracy of the anonymous pieces that appeared in *Supplément* LIII as coming from a "certaine Gazette," he knew, as did TJ, that these were drawn from the *Gazette de France*, a journal that for many decades had been the official organ of the French ministry and that had been openly acknowledged as such since 1762. This fact gave Luzac little choice in the matter except to publish. It also underscores the significance of the general tone of the articles, making necessary some comment on their origin and the attitude of the French ministry toward the American Constitution.

In DLC: TJ Papers, 33: 5714-5 there is an "Extrait des instructions données au Cte de Moustier le 30. 7bre 1787," in an unidentified hand and without any indication of the date or means by which it came into TJ's possession; this extract bears the following note at the head of its text: "Preuves du Machiavelisme et de la duplicité du Cabinet de Versailles." Accompanying this is a PrC of a translation in TJ's hand (without the note just quoted) which reads as follows: " 'The Ct. de Moustier will have seen in the correspondence of the Sr. Otto that the Americans are occupied with a new constitution. This object interests but weakly the politicks of the king. His Majesty thinks, on the one hand, that these deliberations will not succeed on account of the diversity of affections, of principles, and of interests of the different provinces, on the other hand, that it suits France that the U.S. should remain in their present state, because if they should acquire the consistence of which they are susceptible, they would soon acquire a force or a power which they would be very ready to abuse. Notwithstanding this last reflexion the Minister of the king will take care to observe a conduct the most passive neither to show himself for, nor against, the new arrangements on which they are occupied, and when he shall be forced to speak, he will only express the wishes of the king, and his own personal wishes, for the prosperity of the US.' " (A PrC of the French text is in MoSHi.)

The policy outlined in this instruction was, of course, but a continuation of Vergennes' consistent aim of maintaining the United States in a fairly impotent state so as to retain the new power more easily within the orbit of French influence. Moustier's dispatches of the spring of 1788 showed a faithful desire to execute his instructions, but at the same time the riot in New York, the treatment of French consuls in Virginia and elsewhere, the "absolument inerte" condition of Congress, its inability to give any weight to recommendations or requisitions, and a growing personal disaffection for the manners and customs of the people caused Moustier to hint that it would be worse to have thirteen weak sovereignties to deal with than one central government. In analyzing the views of those who supported and those who opposed the new Constitution, Moustier left little doubt of his own feelings of sympathy:

"La crainte du peu de sureté dans leurs proprietés agite tous ceux qui en possédent; l'avidité d'en acquerir ou de s'affranchir de leurs dettes excite un grand nombre d'opposans à la nouvelle Constitution. Ceux qui forment ce parti trouvent dans le papier monnoye un moyen de se liberer ou de s'enrichir, en forçant à accepter cette monnoye ideale, qu'ils créent et annulent à volonté, lorsqu'ils peuvent dominer dans les Legislatures des Etats. Ainsi l'on peut compter parmi les federalistes la plûpart des proprietaires et parmi les Anti-federalistes les Banqueroutiers, les gens de mauvaise foi, les necessiteux et des hommes qui ne pourroient exercer un pouvoir quelconque dans leurs Etats, qu'autant qu'il n'existeroit pas de Gouvernement général. Le commun du peuple se partage entre ses chefs. Il paroit jusqu'à present plus de moderation dans les federalistes que dans leurs adversaires. Mais il devient chaque jour plus embarassant de juger quelle sera l'issue de cette contention de pouvoir." It would be possible, he concluded, that a solid, united, durable government would be created, and equally possible that even the shadow of a body such as Congress would be dissipated. One could thus only speculate on one or the other of two hypotheses—that Congress would dissolve or that it would experience a new surge of life. "Vous jugerés d'apres celà, Monseigneur," he advised Montmorin, "que la partie n'est pas egale entre nous et quel avantage a M. Jefferson, qui peut toujours demander et solliciter, mais qui ne peut positivement rien promettre. Ce ministre est sans doute un excellent citoyen Americain et du nombre de ceux qui croyent qu'il est de l'interêt de sa nation d'etre très unie avec la notre, ce que je pense ainsi que lui, mais comme les faits prouvent que cette opinion n'est pas à beaucoup près généralement établie en Amerique, il me semble qu'il ne peut point y avoir de motif d'accorder aux Americains avec trop de facilitié, ni de quelque tems, aucune faveur ulterieure purement gratuite.—Si le nouveau Gouvernement s'etablit nous pourrons traiter avec lui a ce que je presume avec sûreté et avantage. Si le Congres se dissout où qu'il reste dans l'etat de foiblesse, où il est, je crois que nous serons obligés de traiter particulierement avec chaque Etat sur les objets de Commerce, puisque chacun s'avise de faire des loix à cet egard sans consulter ni ecouter le Congrès. Il est impossible dans les circonstances actuelles de rien entreprendre avec ce corps absolument inerte. En attendant je fais valoir, tant que je puis, les faveurs accordées par le Roi, les bonnes intentions de S.M., l'attachement de notre nation pour les Etats unis et j'entretiens de mon mieux les dispositions favorables, que je remarque dans quelques Americains" (Moustier to Montmorin, 8, 14, 15, 27 Feb.; 16, 25 Mch.; 20, 21 Apr. 1788; Arch. Aff. Etr., Paris, Corr. Pol., E.-U., Vol. XXXIII; transcripts in DLC).

These dispatches showing the difficulties of negotiating with a foreign power whose executive and legislative heads were all but non-existent coincided with the steadily-augmenting news arriving in Europe in late spring of 1788 to the effect that the new Constitution would be adopted. A reassessment of policy was required, and the ministry furnished Moustier with one: "Ce Seroit, M[onsieur], se livrer à une discution inutile que d'examiner si le changement qu'amena cette constitution nous conviendra ou non, et si nous devons faire ou non des demarches pour le prévenir dans l'etat où sont les choses. Nous devons nous en tenir au resultat, qui est: que si la nouvelle constitution est introduite, la confédération Américaine aquerrera une force et une énergie qu'elle n'a pas eues et qu'elle n'a pû avoir jusqu'à present; et que si la constitution ancienne est maintenüe la Rep. des 13. Etats-unis ne sera qu'un phantome, le congrès qu'un être de raison, et, comme vous l'observez, nous serons forcés de traiter de nos intérets avec chaque Etat en particulier.—La reserve qui vous a été prescrite sur cette matiére . . . a pour but la resolution invariable du Roi de ne point s'immicer dans les affaires intérieures des Etats-unis: cette reserve est un hommage que sa Mté. ⟨*doit*⟩ rend a leur independance, et non une preuve d'indifférence de sa part. Si, comme je n'en doute pas, vous vous êtes expliqué, dans ce sens avec Mr. Jay, vous l'aurez sûrement fait revenir de l'erreur où il vous a paru être." Montmorin was not surprised that Jay's views of Vergennes were not friendly, for Jay had always been suspected of having "un reste d'anglomanie, ou du moins peu d'affection pour la France, et son sentiment prédominant étoit sa jalousie contre Mr. Franklin." But the king and council had been "singulièrement étonnés" at Jay's opinion that the alliance between France and the United

States no longer existed. This was an opinion, Montmorin added, that needed to be corrected: the alliance was perpetual, the king had granted an accumulation of favors to American commerce, he had always taken and would not cease to take an interest in American prosperity, he would continue to contribute to it so far as possible without prejudice to his own interests. "Voila, M[onsieur], la doctrine que vous devez faire germer et que le conseil du Roi a été surpris de voir si mal établie. Quant à la nouvelle constitution vous vous abstiendrez de l'aprécier: mais vous pourrez dire que le Roi verra avec satisfaction toutes les dispositions qui seront propres a assûrer et consolider l'existence politique, la tranquilité et le bonheur des Etats-unis" (same). This reassessment of policy respecting the new constitution represented a considerable modification of that of the preceding autumn. The ministry might still wish to see the old system preserved, but by mid-year it became increasingly apparent that the new Constitution would be adopted; hence the directions to Moustier to correct Jay's ideas about the alliance and the need for continued caution in expressing views about the new government. This reassessment of policy was drafted by Rayneval on 23 June 1788. On the next day, the official organ of the ministry, the *Gazette de France*, published the news about chaotic conditions in America and about the discouraging prospects for the new Constitution—a report that Luzac felt obliged to publish as a counterweight to the optimistic account that had appeared in *Supplément* Nos. XLIX and LII, the latter certainly having been furnished by TJ. In view of these circumstances, it is difficult to avoid the conclusion that the anonymous debate carried on in *Suppléments* XLIX, LII, LIII, and LIX was in effect a newspaper discussion between TJ and the ministry, and that both were aware of the fact.

On this general subject of the French ministry's attitude toward the adoption of the Constitution, see C. A. Duniway, "French Influence on the Adoption of the Federal Constitution," *Am. Hist. Rev.*, IX (1904), 304-9. See also notes to TJ to Montmorin, 30 July 1788, and TJ to Dumas, 31 July 1788.

[1] FC reads: "tirée de la Gazette de Fce."

From Amand Koenig

MONSIEUR Strasbourg ce 24 Juillet 1788

En execution des ordres renfermés dans l'honneur de votre lettre du 29 Juin, je vous ai envoyé aujourd'hui par incluse de Mr. Prevost, Libraire, les livres et la notte ci contre, dont je vous souhaite bonne reception.

Demetrius Phalereus et *Aesopi fabulae gr. lat. Haupmanni* me manquent. Je ne pus non plus trouver ce dernier chez un de mes confreres. Quant au montant du petit envoi présent, veuillez le remettre seulement à Mr. Prevost.

Honnorez moi de la continuation de votre précieuse bienveillance. Je suis avec le plus profond respect Monsieur Votre très humble & très obéissant Serviteur AMAND KOENIG

Notte

1. Menandri & Philemonis reliquiere gr. lat. Amstel. 1709
1. Platonis opera. gr. lat. 8o. 12 Vol. broché
1. Aristophanes Brunickii 8. 9 vol. broché

RC (DLC); endorsed; addressed; postmarked "STRASBOURG."

From James Madison

DEAR SIR New York 24. July 1788

Your two last unacknowledged favors were of Decr. 20. and Feby. 6. They were received in Virginia, and no opportunity till the present precarious one by the way of Holland, has enabled me to thank you for them.

I returned here about ten days ago from Richmond which I left a day or two after the dissolution of the Convention. The final question on the new plan of Government was put on the 25th. of June. It was twofold 1. whether previous amendments should be made a condition of ratification. 2. directly on the Constitution in the form it bore. On the first the decision was in the negative, 88 being no, 80 only ay. On the second and definitive question, the ratification was affirmed by 89 ays against 79. noes. A number of alterations were then recommended to be considered in the mode pointed out in the Constitution itself. The meeting was remarkably full; Two members only being absent and those known to be on the opposite sides of the question. The debates also were conducted on the whole with very laudable moderation and decorum, and continued untill both sides declared themselves ready for the question. And it may be safely concluded that no irregular opposition to the System will follow in that State, at least with the countenance of the leaders on that side. What local eruptions may be occasioned by ill-timed or rigorous executions of the Treaty of peace against British debtors, I will not pretend to say. But altho' the leaders, particularly H——y and M—s—n, will give no countenance to popular violences[1] it is not to be inferred that they are reconciled to the event, or will give it a positive support. On the contrary both of them declared they could not go that length, and an attempt was made under their auspices to induce the minority to sign an address to the people which if it had not been defeated by the general moderation of the party, would probably have done mischief.

Among a variety of expedients employed by the opponents to gain proselytes, Mr. *Henry*[2] *first and after him Col. Mason introduced* the *opinions*, *expressed in a letter from a correspondent* [*Mr. Donald or Skipwith I believe*][3] and endeavored to turn the influence of your *name even against parts*, *of which I knew you approved.* In this *situation I thought it due to truth* as well as that it would be most agreeable to *yourself* and *accordingly took the liberty to state some of your opinions on the favorable side.* I am informed that copies or extracts of a letter *from you were handed about at the*

Maryld. Convention with a like view of impeding the ratification.

N. Hampshire ratified the Constitution on the 21st. Ult: and made the ninth State. The votes stood 57 for and 46. against the measure. S. Carolina had previously ratified by a very great majority. The Convention of N. Carolina is now sitting. At one moment the sense of that State was considered as strongly opposed to the system. It is now said that the tide has been for some time turning, which with the example of other States and particularly of Virginia prognosticates a ratification there also. The Convention of N. York has been in Session ever since the 17th. Ult: without having yet arrived at any final vote. Two thirds of the members assembled with a determination to reject the Constitution, and are still opposed to it in their hearts. The local situation of N. York, the number of ratifying States and the hope of retaining the federal Government in this City afford however powerful arguments to such men as Jay, Hamilton, the Chancellor Duane and several others; and it is not improbable that some form of ratification will yet be devised by which the dislike of the opposition may be gratified, and the State notwithstanding made a member of the new Union.

At Fredericksburg on my way hither I found the box with Cork Acorns Sulla and peas, addressed to me. I immediately had it forwarded to Orange from whence the Contents will be disposed of according to your order. I fear the advanced season will defeat the experiments. The few seeds taken out here by the President at my request and sown in his garden have not come up. I left directions in Virginia for obtaining acorns of the Willow Oak this fall, which shall be sent you as soon as possible. Col. Carrington tells me your request as to the Philosophical Transactions was complied with in part only, the 1st. volume, being not to be had. I have enquired of a Delegate here from Rhode Island for further information concerning W. S. Brown, but can learn nothing precise. I shall continue my enquiries, and let you know hereafter the result.

July. 26. We just hear that the Convention of this State have determined by a small majority to exclude from the ratification every thing involving a condition and to content themselves with recommending the alterations wished for.

As this will go by way of Holland I consider its reaching you as extremely uncertain. I forbear therefore to enter further into our public affairs at this time. If the packets should not be discontinued, which is surmised by some, I shall soon have an opportunity of writing again. In the mean time I remain with the sincerest affection Your friend & Servt.,

Js. Madison Jr.

P.S. Crops in Virginia of all sorts were very promising when I left the State. This was the case also generally throughout the States I passed thro' with local exceptions produced in the Wheat fields by a destructive insect which goes under the name of the Hessian fly. It made its first appearance several years ago on Long Island, from which it has spread over half this State, and a great part of New Jersey; and seems to be making an annual progress in every direction.

RC (DLC: Madison Papers); endorsed; partly in code.

On the use made of TJ's letter to Donald by THE LEADERS of the antifederalist forces in the Virginia Convention, Patrick Henry and George Mason, see note to Monroe to TJ, 12 July 1788. On 26 July Carrington wrote to Short, intending it for both him and TJ, and asking him "to make my apology to Mr. Jefferson, to whom Mr. Madison is writing pretty fully by the same conveyance [private hands, by way of Holland]. This will . . . supercede the necessity of my writing to him. By the June Packet I did myself the pleasure to inform Mr. Jefferson of the adoption of the Constitution by South Carolina as the eighth state. Since that N. Hampshire and Virginia have also acceded by small majorities—the Minorities however have acquiesced. . . . New York and North Carolina are now in session, the latter convened so lately that we have received no intelligence from her; she must doubtless follow Virginia implicitly. N. York has been sitting about 6 weeks. . . . A very great Majority have all along been decidedly in the opposition, but the situation of the business from the adoption of so great a number of states has been embarrasing to them. They have wished to reject, but know not how to do it. A conditional adoption has been brought forward in a variety of shapes, but all have even displeased the party projecting them, after a little consideration. Thus has the time of this assembly been spent. But it is expected that in a very few days, their deliberations will issue in an absolute adoption, attended with recommendatory amendments, nearly such as Virginia have agreed to. Mr. Hamilton Mr. Jay and Chancellor Livingston have conducted the federalist party. Governor Clinton a Mr. Lansing and a Mr. Smith have conducted the antifederalists. These have become established terms throughout the United States, to distinguish the supporters, and opponents of the Constitution.—We may now contemplate this Fabrick as erected, and permit me my dear Friend to congratulate you upon the event. So thorough a revolution was never before effected by voluntary convention, and it will stand as a lasting monument of a wisdom and congeniality peculiar to America. The system yet requires much to make it perfect, and I hope experience will be our guide in taking from or adding to it. There is however some reason to fear that alterations will be precipitated, so as to prevent some of the benefits which might result from trial. The opponents have acquiesced so far as to attempt nothing unconstitutionally, but, I apprehend it will now be their drift, to get into the Congress men who will promote the measure of a General Convention at too early a period. I am persuaded that could the Government operate uninterrupted for a few years, many of the visionary dangers which have been apprehended, would vanish, and in that time the real defects would be discovered and the remedies suggested" (DCL: Short Papers; docketed by Short as received 31 Aug. 1788).

[1] This word interlined in substitution for "discontents," deleted.

[2] This and subsequent words in italics are written in code and were decoded interlineally by TJ; his decoding has been verified by the Editors, employing Code No. 9.

[3] Brackets in MS.

To John Trumbull

DEAR SIR Paris July 24. 1788.

The inclosed letters containing matter which I could not permit to go through the post office of this country, I have waited for a private conveience which now offers. I put them under cover to you begging you will commit to the post office those to McCaul, Jones, and Digges, that you will give to Mr. Cutting the one directed to him, and also those for the two Rutledges, Izard, Drayton, and Brailsford & Morris if Mr. Cutting goes soon to Charleston. If not, I will beg the favor of you to find some sure hand to Charleston directly if possible, and if not then to New York, to be delivered to the Delegates for S. Carolina there. I have now written till I am all but dead, and will therefore only add assurances of the esteem with which I am dear Sir your friend & servt.

TH: JEFFERSON

PrC (MHi). The enclosures mentioned are to be found under the following dates: 19 June; 9, 12, 17, 18, and 24 July 1788.

To Charles Bellini

DEAR SIR Paris July 25. 1788.

Though I have written to you seldom, you are often the object of my thoughts, and always of my affection. The truth is that the circumstances with which I am surrounded offer little worth detailing to you. You are too wise to feel an interest in the squabbles in which the pride, the dissipations, and the tyranny of kings keep this hemisphere constantly embroiled. Science indeed finds some aliment here, and you are one of it's sons. But this I have pretty regularly communicated to Mr. Madison, with whom I am sure you participate of it. It is with sincere pleasure I congratulate you on the good fortune of our friend Mazzei, who is appointed here to correspond with the king of Poland. The particular character given him is not well defined, but the salary is, which is more important. It is of 8000 livres a year, which will enable him to live comfortably, while his duties will find him that occupation without which he cannot exist. Whilst this appointment places him at his ease, it affords a hope of permanence also. It suspends, if not entirely prevents, the visit he had intended to his native country, and the return to his adoptive one which the death of his wife had rendered possible. This last event has given him three quarters of the globe elbow-room, which he had ceded to her on condition she would leave him quiet in the fourth. Their partition of the next world will be more difficult, if it be divided only into two parts, according to the Protestant faith.—Having seen by a letter you wrote him that you were in want of a pair of spectacles I undertook to procure you some, which I packed in a box of books addressed to Mr. Wythe, and of which I beg your acceptance. This box lay forgotten at Havre the whole of the last winter, but was at length shipped, and I trust has come to hand. I packed with the spectacles three or four pair of glasses adapted to the different periods of life, distinguished from each other by numbers, and easily changed. You see I am looking forward to hope of a long life for you, and that it may be long enough to carry you through the whole succession of glasses is my sincere prayer. Present me respectfully to Mrs. Bellini, assure her of my affectionate remembrance of her, and my wishes for her health and happiness, and accept your self very sincere professions of the esteem and attachment with which I am Dear Sir your affectionate friend & servant,

TH: JEFFERSON

PrC (DLC).

From John Bondfield

SIR Bordeaux 25 July 1788

By the Brig Missoury arrivd yesterday from Philadelphia I received Letters from our friend Mr. Barclay with instructions to facilitate all in my power Mrs. Barclays return to America.

I write this Post to Mrs. Barclay advising her the arrival of the above ship and transmit her a remittance to discharge her engagements and defray her Expences to this Post where I shall retain the Vessel and hold her in readiness so soon as Mrs. Barclay can make it convenient to her and her family to come down.

The Deligence is the Conveyance the most expeditious and the least expensive. If Mrs. Barclay has nothing to occation a delay in Paris I have recomend her embracing the first Deligence so that by her early arrival here she may arrive on the Coast of America at a Good season.

I take the liberty to write you on the Subject being convinced it will give you pleasure and that whatever can promote by your good Councils to Mr. Barclay the measures most frugal and expeditious will be of service.

They write me from Philadelphia that they dayly expected to receve advice of Virginia Acceding to the Convention which will fix the Constition.

The farmers have not yet made any purchases from the private Importers. Some Cargoes have arrived sent by Mr. Morris but the sales have been made thro the Medium of Messr. Le Couteuls at Paris and the Conditions and Nature of the sales remain secret to the Agents here. A demand for Ireland and Russia serves at present to keep up the prices and gives vente for the Imports which have not been considerable this year.

A small vessel saild a few days past to Havre unknown to me that I omitted the opportunity to forward the two Cases of Claret all ready for shipping.

with due respect I have the honor to be Sir Your most Obedient Servant, JOHN BONDFIELD

RC (DLC); endorsed; on cover Barclay wrote and then deleted: "Madame Madme. Barclay," which may possibly indicate that he enclosed the letter to Mrs. Barclay in that to TJ, or, on the other hand, that he merely erred in writing the address.

To Collow Frères, Carmichael & Co.

GENTLEMEN Paris July 25. 1788.

A journey into Holland and Germany, and close occupation since my return, have prevented my having the honour of sooner answering your favors of the 19th. and 20th. of March which came here during my absence. I am sorry that the trees which came for me, on board the Portsmouth, should have been the occasion of any thing disagreeable between yourselves and Mr. Limozin. The difference of their being landed at Havre or at Dunkirk did not merit that. They came on to me very safely from this last place, and I can assure you that Mr. Limozin has never written a word to me on the subject of what passed on that occasion, and that it is not otherwise known to me than from your own letter. Your attentions to me on this, as well as on other occasions, have been highly satisfactory and flattering to me, and will always call for my sincere acknolegements, as well as assurances of the esteem & attachment with which I have the honour to be, Gentlemen your most obedient & most humble servt., TH: JEFFERSON

PrC (DLC); endorsed.

To J. P. P. Derieux

SIR Paris July 25. 1788.

I have duly received your favor of the 8th. of April, and am very happy that you have been able, with the succours of your relation here, to put yourself in so good a way. I have no right to take to myself any part of the merits. She was so well disposed that nothing was wanting but an explanation of your situation, and of the manner in which even a small aid would operate a great relief to you. There shall certainly be nothing wanting on my part to nourish her good dispositions towards you, and to improve them to your ultimate advantage. Her good health probably places her future donations at a great distance. I much approve your plan of commerce without either taking or giving an hour's credit to any person. This will enable you to take a very small profit on what you sell, to undersell every body else, and thus in time command a very extensive sale. It is a quick multiplication of small profits which makes the surest fortune in the end. It is prudent also to do a little in the farming way; especially if you can by that support your family, so as to convert the profits of your commerce continually into an increase of capital, and be thus providing future fortunes for your children, while your farm gives them present subsistence. This is practicable by a rigorous adherence to that simplicity of living to which your resolution seems fully adequate. To conform to our circumstances is true honor: and the only shame is to live beyond them. I am truly sensible, Sir, of the honour you do me in proposing to me that of becoming one of the Sponsors of your child, and return you my sincere thanks for it. At the same time I am not a little mortified that scruples, perhaps not well founded, forbid my undertaking this honourable office. The person who becomes sponsor for a child, according to the ritual of the church in which I was educated, makes a solemn profession, before god and the world, of faith in articles, which I had never sense enough to comprehend,[1] and it has always appeared to me that comprehension must precede assent. The difficulty of reconciling the ideas of Unity and Trinity, have, from a very early part of my life, excluded me from the office of sponsorship, often proposed to me by my friends, who would have trusted, for the faithful discharge of it, to morality alone instead of which the church requires faith. Accept therefore Sir this conscientious excuse which I make with regret, which must find it's apology in my heart, while perhaps it may do no great honour to my head, and after presenting me with respect and affection to Madame de Rieux, be assured of my constant dispositions to render you service, and of the sincerity of those sentiments of esteem with which I have the honour to be, Sir, your most obedient & most humble servant,

TH: JEFFERSON

PrC (DLC); endorsed.

Derieux' FAVOR OF THE 8TH. OF APRIL was actually an addition to his letter of 28 Jan. 1788, q.v. If TJ declined in writing THE OFFICE OF SPONSORSHIP that was OFTEN PROPOSED by his friends, such declinations have not been found. The present remarkably revealing letter is, so far as known, the first indication that his refusal to accept the Doctrine of the Trinity dated FROM A VERY EARLY PART OF MY LIFE.

[1] At this point TJ deleted "and therefore cannot."

From Grand & Cie.

[*Paris, 25 July 1788.* Recorded in SJL Index, but not found. It clearly was a covering letter for the return of the protested draft for £50 on Alexander Willock; see Grand & Cie. to TJ, 22 July, and TJ to Banister, 27 July 1788.]

To André Limozin

SIR

Paris July 25. 1788.

In answer to your favor of the 20th. I can assure you that your applications for the Consular appointment at Havre will be perfectly agreeable to me, and that I shall do the justice which is due to your attentions to the affairs of the United states in that port in the report which I shall send with the Consular convention as soon as that shall be finished. I will thank you to keep me informed of the orders of government and the proceedings and movements in your port from time to time which may be symptomatic of peace or war. Nothing new of that kind has arisen here since my last. I am with much esteem Sir your most obedient & most humble servt.,

TH: JEFFERSON

P.S. Has the bust of the Marquis de la Fayette come to your hands, or been shipped to Virginia?

PrC (DLC).

From André Limozin

MOST HONORED SIR

Havre de Grace 25th July 1788.

I had the honor of writing to your Excellency the 20th instant.

Captn. Koen is arrived from Amstl. with your China &c. That Master being chiefly loaded with East India Goods fitt for the Guinea trade which must be transboarded on Guinea Ships without being landed, being prohibited, the Custom house officers have kept a Steady Watch on that ship, therefore being no possibility to comply with your wish I have applyd to the Comptroller and have desired the leave that your articles might be forwarded to you plumbed, with acquit a Caution, and that the duties should be payd at Paris; in consequence of my application he hath written yesterday on that purpose to the farmers Generals and he doth not doubt in the least manner that my demand will be granted. I shall inform your Excellency of the issue thereof.

I have the honor to be with the highest regard Your Excellency's Most obedt. & very humble Servant, ANDRE LIMOZIN

RC (MHi); endorsed.
Goods that were PLUMBED were leaded and corded, that is, under seal.

To Van Damme

á Paris ce 25me. Juillet. 1788.

J'ai reçu, Monsieur, il y a deux jours, les livres que vous m'avez expedié, en assez bon etat, et je m'empresse de vous envoyer ordre pour le paiment. Vous la trouverez ci-jointe, addressée á mes amis Messieurs Nicholas et Jacob Van Staphorst. Je vous prierai de rayer des notes que je vous ai laissé les livres suivantes, que j'ai trouvé l'occasion d'acheter ailleurs depuis la date de mes notes, c'est à dire,

Senecae Philosophica.
Virgil Sedani.
Aristenaeti epistolae.
Aesopi fabulae.
Diodorus Siculus Graecé.
Juliani opera.
Suetonius.

Vous aurez la bonté de me fournir ce qui restera après avoir rayé de mes notes les livres que je viens de nommer, et j'attendrai cette fourniture d'ici au mois de Septembre, quand la vente, que vous m'annoncez, sera faite. J'ai l'honneur d'etre, Monsieur votre tres humble et trés obeissant serviteur, TH: JEFFERSON

RC (The Hague: Meermanno-Westrenianum Museum: Van Damme Papers); postmarked "P," set in a triangle; addressed: "A Monsieur Van Damme Libraire á Amsterdam." PrC (DLC). The enclosed draft has not been found, but see the letter of advice concerning it, following.

To Nicolas & Jacob van Staphorst

GENTLEMEN Paris July 25. 1788.

This serves to advise you that I have this day drawn on you in favor of Mr. Van Damme bookseller of Amsterdam for one hundred and forty eight florins eleven sous current of Holland for part of the books he was to furnish me, which be pleased to pay and place to my private account, until he shall furnish the residue when I shall consolidate the several little advances made for me into one order on the bankers of the United states. I have the honour to be Gentlemen Your most obedient humble servant,

TH: JEFFERSON

P.S. Has the vessel sailed yet from Amsterdam in which my stoves &c. were packed?

PrC (DLC).

From Thomas Appleton

SIR Rouen 26th. July 1788.

I receiv'd the letter which you did me the honor to write of the 20th. and have agreeably reship'd the candles. The Captain of the Vessel immediately upon his Arrival in Port enter'd his Cargo at the Custom House in which was included the Case. Altho' I knew this circumstance Yet as it had it not been landed, I concluded no duties would be demanded indeed the officer coincided with me in opinion: but I now find that not only the duty of entry is requir'd but also that of going Out of the Kingdom, both of which are equal and very extravagant. This being the situation I take the liberty of requesting Your Excellency's opinion, wether the duties should be paid, or if a discharge Can be procur'd from one of the farmer's General. As often as I have apply'd at the Office so various have been the duties requir'd which Convinces me, there is Not a precise article in any arret respecting this Kind of Merchandize.—It is not the amount which prevents me from immediately paying it: but I chose not to accede as it would then fix the right of demand in future, without Your approbation.

I have the honor to be with every Sentiment of respect Your Excellency's Most Obedient & Most Humble Servt.,

THOS. APPLETON

RC (DLC); endorsed.

TJ's LETTER . . . OF THE 20TH. is recorded in SJL Index, but has not been found (SJL Index gives its date as 22 July).

To John Banister, Jr.

Paris July 27. 1788.

I am sorry to inform you, my dear Sir, that the bill for fifty pounds sterling on Alexander Willock dated April 12. which you were so good as to remit me, was protested by that gentleman on the 18th. instant, of which I thought it necessary to give you immediate notice for your own security with respect to him, and shall therefore send you a duplicate of this letter by another conveyance. There is so little dependence on draughts made on mercantile people or by mercantile people that whenever those of the French minister or French consuls on the government can be obtained, they are preferable. This letter being intended merely for advertisement, I add nothing more than assurances of the esteem and attachment with which I am, Dear Sir, your sincere friend & humble servt,

Th: Jefferson

PrC (DLC); at foot of text: "John Bannister junr. esq."; endorsed.

The bill . . . on Alexander Willock was presumably enclosed in Banister's letter of 20 Apr. 1788, which is recorded in SJL Index but has not been found; see Grand & Cie. to TJ, 22 July 1788; TJ to Dunbar, 15 Dec. 1789.

To Angelica Schuyler Church

Paris, July 27. 1788.

Many motives, my dear Madam, authorize me to write to you, but none more than this that I esteem you infinitely. Yet I have thought it safe to get Kitty to write also, that her letter may serve as a passport to mine, and shed on it the *suave odeur* of those warm emotions it will excite in your breast. When we have long expected the visit of a dear friend, he is welcome when he comes, and all who come with him. I present myself then under the wing of Kitty, tho' she thinks herself under mine. She is here at this instant, well, chearful, and chattering French to her Doll, and her friend Polly. We want your presence to round the little family circle, to enliven the Sunday's dinner, which is not less a holiday to me than to the girls. We talk of you, we think of you, and try to enjoy your company by the force of imagination: and were the force of that sufficient, you would be with me every day. Worn down every morning with writing on business, I sally at 12. o'clock into the bois de Boulogne, and unbend my labours by thinking on my friends: and could I write as I ride, and give them my thoughts warm as they flow from the heart, my friends would see what a foolish heart it is. Kitty tells me you are at London; but why do you not tell me so yourself? for, I had rather learn it from you than from any body in the world. I presume then you see Mr. Trumbull, and that he tells you that your boasted artists of London are unable to disencumber our charming vase of it's spout, which gives it more the air of a brandy tub than of a form of fancy. He will tell you too that after plaguing him a great deal with this caprice, I have at length desired him to leave the dunces to their own ways, and to send me the vase as it is, spout and all. Our friend Madame de Corny has been country-mad ever since you were here. I suspect you bit her; for I know that this is your rage also, and that tho' you are in London now, your heart is always in the country. I wish you would let it come here sometimes. Why cannot you take a trip of a fortnight now and then to see Kitty? A week of that indeed would be spent on the road, but there would be a week left for us. You might be of great service to your friends in the Chaussée d'Antin at this moment; because after an examination of a thousand country-houses, some of which had one fault and some another, one at length is found which pleases Madame, but not Monsieur, and the contest is, which shall permit the other to sacrifice their taste on this occasion. Your mediation might help them over the difficulty. Come then, my dear Madam, to the call of friendship, which does not issue from the Chaussee d'Antin alone. Your slender health, requires exercise, requires amusement, and to be comforted by seeing how much you are beloved every where. Do not be afraid of breakings down on the road. They never happen when you know your carriage. If you will install me your physician, I will prescribe to you a journey a month to Paris. En attendant I am with sentiments of infinite esteem & attachment, Dear Madam your sincere friend and humble servant,

Th: Jefferson

RC (Boston, Mass., 1956: Property of several descendants of Gen. Charles J. Paine). PrC (CSmH). The enclosed letter from Catherine Church to her mother has not been found.

To Maria Cosway

Paris July 27. 1788

Hail, dear friend of mine! for I am never so happy as when business, smoothing her magisterial brow, says 'I give you an hour to converse with your friends.' And with none do I converse more fondly than with my good Maria: not her under the poplar, with the dog and string at her girdle: but the Maria who makes the Hours her own, who teaches them to dance for us in so charming a round, and lets us think of nothing but her who renders them *si gracieuses*. Your Hours, my dear friend, are no longer your own. Every body now demands them; and were it possible for me to want a memorandum of you, it is presented me in every street of Paris. Come then to see what triumph Time is giving you. Come and see every body stopping to admire the Hours, suspended against the walls of the Quai des Augustins, the Boulevards, the Palais royal &c. &c. with a 'Maria Cosway delint.' at the bottom. But you triumph every where; so, if you come here, it will be, not to see your triumphs but your friends, and to make them happy with your presence. Indeed we wish much for you. Society here is become more gloomy than usual. The civil dissensions, tho' they have yet cost no blood and will I hope cost none, still render conversation serious, and society contentious. How gladly would I take refuge every day in your coterie. Your benevolence, embracing all parties, disarms the party-dispositions of your friends, and makes of yours an asylum for tranquility. We are told you are becoming more recluse. This is a proof the more of your taste. A great deal of love given to a few, is better than a little to many. Besides, the world will derive greater benefit from your talents, as these will be less called off from their objects by numerous visits. I remember that when under the hands of your Coëffeuse, you used to amuse yourself with your pencil. Take then, some of these days, when Fancy bites and the Coeffeuse is busy, a little visiting card, and crayon on it something for me. What shall it be? Cupid leading the lion by a thread? or Minerva clipping his wings? Or shall it be political? The father, for instance, giving the bunch of rods to his children to break, or Jupiter sending to the frogs a kite instead of the log for their king? Or shall it be something better than all this, a sketch of your own fancy? So that I have something from your hand, it will satisfy me; and it will be the better if of your own imagination. I will put a 'Maria Cosway delint.' at bottom, and stamp it on my visiting cards, that our names may be together if our persons cannot. Adieu, my dear friend, love me much, and love me always. Your's affectionately,

TH: JEFFERSON

PrC (ViU).

From André Limozin

Most Honored Sir Havre de Grace 27th July 1788

I had the honor of writing to your Excellency the 25th instant to which I beg leave to crave reference.

I take the freedom to beseech of your Excellency the favor to give me an advice upon the following matter. One Mr. James Swan of Boston wrote to me the 12th of this month to inform me that he was to be appointed Consul at Marseille, but that he had apply'd to Congress that his appointment should be alterd, and in consequence should be for Normandy. That at his arrivall at Paris he had found Letters mentionning him my house as one of the most responsable of the Kingdom, that I was a Merchant of an extensive Knowledge [and] experience, and understanding perfectly well all the different Branches of trade in consequence whereof he should wish to be in correspondence with me and to give me the preference of the large Consignments which he is to receive in Salt Provisions made up in New England such as Beef Pork and Butter; for which reason he should be glad to Know what advances I should be willing to make upon such Consignments, and to what extent?

I Answerd him that I had seen sundry parcells of these provisions imported from New England, that they were neither properly Cured nor Suitably packd up and that they could not Keep long, upon which observations I received this day from him the answer of which I inclose a Copy.

If that Gentleman designs to establish himself here, I need not give him informations which would turn out in a short time to a great deteriment for me. It would be lending him arms to pull my house down, because I receive yearly Considerable Consignments from Ireland in the Said articles and I cant tell if his promise is Sincere or not. For which reason having so many instances of the friendship your Excellency favors me with I take the freedom to Claim your good advice; and to ask if you are acquainted with the Said Gentleman and what Confidence I can pay to his word. Your Excellency may intirely rely on my discretion and prudence. I have the honor to be with the highest regard Your Excellency's Most obedient & very Humble Servant, Andre Limozin

RC (MHi); endorsed. Enclosure (Tr in clerk's hand, MHi): James Swan to Limozin, dated at Paris, 24 July 1788, reading as follows: "Your favor of the 15th. instant came duely to hand, and if you wish to Serve my Country, and to open a [trade] I have with New England, a considerable part of which may Center with you, you will write me as to the Packing, Cutting and every thing which could make our Beef Pork and Butter Vendable with you, for as we have as good Salt, and as good Beef, and Can have as good Packers, as they have in Ireland, it is impossible in the Nature of things, that ours Shall not be equally in demand as the Irish. Indeed, in the Islands ours is preferr'd, because not So old consequently not So Salt. If you will please to write me here Soon I shall be glad to receive it, as I am preparing Letters for New England in answer to those received on this Subject and I shall tarry[1] but a little time here. . . ." For Swan's proposals, see under 19 July 1788.

[1] Limozin's clerk wrote "carry," but Swan presumably meant, if he did not write, "tarry."

From John Rutledge

Dear Sir Charleston July 27th. 1788

Not knowing, particularly, where the inclosed may find my Son, (which I presume you do) I take the Liberty of requesting you to have it safely conveyed to him, as soon as may be.

I am, with great Esteem & Regard, dr. Sir Yr. obliged hble servt.,

J: Rutledge

RC (DLC); endorsed. Enclosure not found, but it was probably one of the letters to John Rutledge, Jr. mentioned in TJ to Short, 21 Nov. 1788.

From Gaudenzio Clerici

Châlon-sur-Saône, *28 July 1788*. For more than forty days he has promised himself the pleasure of paying his respects to TJ and announcing his determination to return to America; but the bad state of his health prevents him from realizing this pleasure. Had a pleasant passage from Genoa to Nice; on the way from Nice to Avignon he contracted a fever which he supposed ephemeral and not sufficient to delay his departure. However, he was scarcely able to continue as far as Antibes, where his illness developed into a pleurisy; for two weeks his life was in peril; only slightly recovered, and weakened by frequent bloodlettings, he resumed his voyage, only to suffer a relapse. He was overcome at Avignon by a second fever, as violent as the first, which again delayed him sixteen days and resulted in heavy expenditures for a doctor and useless medicine. Since the trip was a comfortable one by water, he then dragged himself as far as Châlon but lacks the courage to subject himself to being huddled in a diligence and jostled about for four successive days, without interruption or repose, if he were not being quickly deprived of money and facing a situation of being in a strange land, unable to proceed or retrace his steps. Asks TJ to send him six or eight louis by the next post to maintain him until he can safely proceed to Paris. Has written to his relatives in Italy, from whom he expects prompt assistance as soon as he reaches Paris; asks pardon for his impertinence which is occasioned only by necessity.

RC (DLC); 4 p.; in Italian; endorsed.

Under date of 31 July 1788 TJ's Account Book shows that he "lent Gaudenzio Clerici 78.tt"

To John Brown Cutting

Sir Paris July 28. 1788.

When I had the honour of writing you on the 24th. inst. the transactions on the Black sea were but vaguely known. I am now able to give them to you on better foundation. The Captain Pacha was proceeding with succours to Oczakoff as is said by some (for this fact does not come on the same authority with the others), the authentic account placing the two fleets in the neighborhood of each other at the mouth of the Liman, without saying how they came there. The Captain Pacha with 57 gunboats attacked the Russian vessels of the same kind, 27 in number, the right-wing of which was commanded by Admiral Paul Jones, the left by the Prince of Nassau. After an obstinate engagement of 5. hours, during which the Captain Pacha flew incessantly wherever there was danger or distress, he was obliged to retire, having lost 3 of his vessels, and killed only 8 men of the Russians. I take this account from the report of the action by the Prince of Nassau which the Russian minister here shewed me. It is said in other accounts that all the balls of the Turks passed over head which was the reason they did so little execution. This was on the 18th. of June, and was the forerunner of the great and decisive action between the two main fleets which took place on the 26th. The Russian fleet commanded by Admiral Paul Jones, the Turkish by the Captain Pacha, of which the result only, and not the details are given us. This was that the vessels of the Turkish Admiral and Vice Admiral and 4 others were burnt, that is to say 6. in all. Two others were taken, and between 3 and 4000 prisoners. The Captain Pacha's flag was taken, and himself obliged to fly in a small vessel, his whole fleet being dispersed. The Prince Potemkin immediately got under march for Oczakoff to take advantage of the consternation into which that place was thrown. These facts are written by Prince Potemkin from his headquarters to Prince Gallitzin the Russian Ambassador at Vienna, who writes them to their minister here, who shewed me the letter. The number of prisoners taken render it probable that the Captain Pacha was on his way to the relief of Oczakoff with transports, as a less authentic report sais he was. We are not told authentically what was the force on each side in the main action of the 26th. but it is supposed to have been of about 15. ships of the line on each side besides their smaller vessels: but the evidence of this is vague and the less to be relied on as we have known that the Russians were much inferior in numbers to the Turks on that sea.—A war of a less bloody kind is begun between the Pope and king of Naples, who has refused this year to pay the annual tribute of the hackney as an acknolegement that he holds his kingdom as feudatory of the Pope. The latter has declared him to stand deprived of this kingdom, but gives him 3. months to consider of it. We shall see what will be made of this farce. I have written this supplement to my other letter, in hopes it may still find you at London. I am with much esteem, Dear Sir, your most obedt. humble servt.

TH: JEFFERSON

PrC (DLC).

To John Trumbull

DEAR SIR Paris July 28. 1788.

The inclosed letter to Mr. Bannister being of importance to me, as covering notice of a protested bill of exchange, I must ask the favor of you to send it by some vessel going into James river, or by the packet under cover to the Delegates of Virginia in Congress if the packet be not sailed. The packets of this country being discontinued I shall be obliged to trouble you sometimes with my American letters, till a proposition for their reestablishment, now under consideration, shall be decided on. I refer you to Mr. Cutting for the details communicated to him in the inclosed letter, of two actions between the Russians under the command of Admiral Paul Jones, and the Turks commanded by the Captain Pacha, which took place on the 18th. and 26th. of June, in the first of which was inconsiderable, but the last a compleat and signal victory by the Russians over the Turks, in which the last had 6. ships burnt, 2 taken, and between 3 and 4000 prisoners, the Captain Pacha escaping in a small vessel. I am my dear Sir Your's affectionately,

TH: JEFFERSON

PrC (DLC). Enclosures: (1) TJ to Banister, 27 July 1788. (2) TJ to Cutting, 28 July 1788.

For Daniel Parker's PROPOSITION . . . NOW UNDER CONSIDERATION to re-establish the packets, see TJ to Montmorin, 29 Nov. 1788. See also Swan's proposals concerning salt beef and pork, under 19 July 1788.

To M. Amoureux

SIR Paris July 29. 1788.

Admiral Paul Jones having only desired me to receive his

money, without saying how I should dispose of it, there is no occasion for you to remit it to me till the expiration of the 6. months credit you have given on the sale. But in the mean time I shall be glad to be informed what will be the exact sum you will remit that I may ask his orders in the first letter I write him. As you are interested in his welfare, I congratulate you on the splendid victory he has lately obtained over the Captain Bacha[1] on the Black sea.

I know that the Farmers general have wished to take away the Franchise of Lorient and fix it on some place where it would not be used. But I have no reason to believe his majesty's ministers have given them reason to expect such a transfer, which undoubtedly would be considered as injurious to the United States. I am Sir your most obedt. humble servt., TH: JEFFERSON

PrC (DLC). 1 Thus in MS.

To Thomas Appleton

SIR Paris July 29. 1788.

The first article of the Arret of Dec. 29. permits expressly the importation of Spermaceti on paying the duty of 7^{tt}-10 the Quintal and 10. sols the livre, and the general laws of the kingdom allow the importation of cotton spun for cambric at 20^{tt} the Quintal. I should think it adviseable to tender these duties: if they demand any others, they should produce the law authorizing it. I suppose there must be some speedy and summary way of deciding on contested demands of duty. It would be desireable to know what would be the course of a legal contestation of these duties and what the cost, as these might decide whether the trouble and risk would be too great for the object. If you will be so good as to make this enquiry and communicate the result to me I will consult on it with a friend here and write you on the subject. I am, Sir, with great esteem Your most obedt. & most humble servt.,

TH: JEFFERSON

PrC (DLC).

To Nicolas Darcel

SIR Paris July 29. 1788.

I do not accept the inclosed bills of exchange because I am not the person to whom they are addressed. I am named Minister plenipotentiary of the U.S. for transacting their affairs with the court of France, but with nothing to do in any other matter. These bills are directed to the Commissioners of the U.S. at Paris, that is to say to Doctr. Franklin, Mr. Deane and Mr. Lee who were appointed by a special Commission to borrow money, and to pay it to the order of the Treasurer of the U.S. As long as any of these gentlemen remained in France these bills were paid the moment they were presented. No one was ever delayed. Dr. Franklin, the last of these Commissioners left France in 1785. having staid here five years after the date of these bills, and been always ready to pay them. The books too, in which the paiments were entered, are all carried to America. It is there then that the bills must be presented, and there alone that it can be known whether the 1st. 2d. or 4th. have not been paid. Probably they have been paid, as they surely were if demanded within the first five years, and it is not probable they would have been kept up eight years unpresented. I have the honor to be Sir your most obedt. humble servt.,

Th: Jefferson

PrC (DLC). Enclosures not found.

To James Fanning

Sir Paris July 29. 1788.

I have now the honour to inclose you the letter of Mr. Baldwin of Georgia on the subject of your lands. In consequence of what he says I should think it adviseable for you to renew your applications to Messrs. Shoolbred and Moody to induce them to act as your attornies in this business. I shall always be ready to take care of your letters and to give you any other assistance in my power. I have the honor to be Sir Your most obedt. & most humble servt.,

Th: Jefferson

PrC (DLC). The enclosed letter from Abraham Baldwin to Fanning has not been found; it was transmitted in Baldwin's letter to TJ of 20 Apr. 1788.

To Gallimard

Sir Paris July 29. 1788

In answer to your favor of the 2d. instant I have the honour to inclose you a pamphlet containing the advice of Doctr. Franklin to persons proposing to emigrate to America. No person is better qualified than him to give advice on this subject. At the same time I would recommend to all those who propose to remove thither, to go there themselves before they carry their family, or even sell off their property here, that they may see whether the country, it's inhabitants and their manners are to their mind, and judge for themselves what part of the country may best suit their views. Having no charge from the United states on this subject I can only add assurances of the sentiments of regard with which I have the honour to be Sir Your most obedient humble servt.,

TH: JEFFERSON

PrC (DLC); at foot of text: "M. Gallimard receveur des Domaines du roi á Trevoux en Dombes." Enclosure: Copy of Benjamin Franklin's *Information to those who would remove to America* (Franklin, *Writings*, ed. Smyth, VIII, 603-14), a pamphlet that TJ caused to be reprinted for such uses as the present, not only because it saved needless repetition in writing but also because of its cogent views. Franklin had written this essay to disabuse those who intended to settle in America and who had "formed, thro' Ignorance, mistaken Ideas and Expectations of what is to be obtained there," and to "prevent inconvenient, expensive, and fruitless Removals and Voyages of improper Persons." The European image of an America populated by rich but ignorant inhabitants who were eager to reward strangers "possessing Talents in the Belles-Lettres, fine Arts, &c."; having an abundance of civil and military offices to dispose of that the natives were not capable of filling; possessing "few Persons of Family among them" and being disposed to yield great respect to "Strangers of Birth"; and having a government that encouraged emigrants not only by paying their expenses of transportation but by giving them "lands gratis . . . with Negroes to work for them, Utensils of Husbandry, and Stocks of Cattle"—this picture he characterized as the product of "wild Imaginations." On the contrary, America was a country of a "general happy Mediocrity," where there were few so miserable as the poor of Europe, few that were rich, few great landholders, few tenants, &c. Strangers who had no other quality to recommend them than birth or station might find that of value in Europe, but "it is a Commodity that cannot be carried to a worse Market than that of America." The kind of emigrants needed were "hearty young Labouring Men, who understand the Husbandry of Corn and Cattle," who could employ themselves briefly at high wages to accumulate the eight or ten guineas required to buy a hundred acres of fertile soil near the frontiers "and begin their Plantation, in which they are assisted by the Good-Will of their Neighbours, and some Credit. Multitudes of poor People from England, Ireland, Scotland, and Germany, have by this means in a few years become wealthy Farmers, who, in their own Countries, where all the Lands are fully occupied, and the Wages of Labour low, could never have emerged from the poor Condition wherein they were born." Artisans, people with moderate fortunes, servants and apprentices were also needed. The general mediocrity of fortune in America prevented idleness and vice, encouraged morality and religion. "Atheism is unknown there; Infidelity rare and secret; so that persons may live to a great Age in that Country, without having their Piety shocked by meeting with either an Atheist or an Infidel." Aimed at the lower classes, the essay that had begun as an effort to correct a distorted image ended by becoming one of the most forceful promotional tracts on America ever written.

TJ's Account Book has the following entry under 20 Sep. 1788: "pd for reprinting Dr. Franklin's Advice to emigrants 18f16 U.S." TJ evidently enclosed one of these copies, and it appears that his reprinting was (as indicated on a note on verso of half-title) made from the translation of Franklin's essay as published in Pt. iv, ch. vii, of Mazzei's *Recherches Historiques et Politiques sur les Etats-Unis de l'Amérique Septentrionale*. What appears to be the only recorded copy of this separate printing is TJ's copy in DLC, on the half-title of which TJ wrote: "par Mazzei." See Sowerby, No. 2567. The title reads: *Avis à ceux qui voudroient émigrer en Amérique.*

The response that John Adams gave to similar appeals differed, as was to be expected, from those of Franklin and TJ: "I am not come to this Country, sir," he answered one would-be emigrant, "to solicit emigrations to the United States of America, nor to offer any Kind of Encouragement to such as wish to go.—All the world knows that my Country is open to strangers. But she offers no rewards or assistance. Those who love liberty, Innocence, and Industry are sure of an easy, comfortable Life, but they must go there to obtain it at their own Cost and Risque. . . . It is by no means my business to carry on or to convey the Correspondence of Gentlemen at a distance who are total strangers to me, and therefore I pray that this intercourse may cease" (Adams to John Wooddrop, Glasgow, 3 Feb. 1786). It was characteristic of the new nation that its ambassadors should have spoken with such divergent voices, and a sign of its strength that it saw no need to compel them to speak other than their conscience and intelligence directed.

To John Jay

SIR Paris July 29. 1788.

Having received the inclosed letter[1] from Julien Laurent claiming his wages as Volunteer on board the Bonhomme Richard, I have the honour of forwarding it to you, supposing it will of course be referred to the proper office to take order on. I have the honour to be with sentiments of the most perfect esteem and respect Sir Your most obedient & most humble servt.,

TH: JEFFERSON

RC (DNA: PCC, No. 87, II). PrC (DLC). Enclosure: According to entry in SJL Index, Laurent wrote TJ on 11 Mch. 1788, but his letter (here enclosed to Jay) has not been found.

[1] A marginal note in a clerk's hand contains the following: "Sent to the Board of Treasury 11th. June 1789."

To Julien Laurent

á Paris ce 29me. Juillet 1788.

J'ai reçu, Monsieur, votre lettre au sujet des appointements qui vous sont redues en qualité de volontaire sur le corsaire le Bonhomme Richard. Mais comme je ne suis pas chargé de decider sur ces reclamations, ni de les payer, je m'empresserai d'envoyer votre lettre á Monsieur Jay, Secretaire des affaires etrangeres pour le Congrés pour demander la-dessus les ordres du bureau á qui ce appartient, et je vous en avertirai le moment qu'elles me sera annoncées. Je suis, Monsieur, votre tres humble serviteur,

TH: JEFFERSON

PrC (DLC); at foot of text: "M. Julien Laurent á Angers." VOTRE LETTRE: See note to TJ to Jay, preceding.

To Meier & Cie.

GENTLEMEN Paris July 29. 1788.

Your favor on the subject of the duties demanded at Bayonne on the oils of Mr. Derby came here during my absence on a journey to Holland which has occasioned a delay of the answer. It appears perfectly reasonable that oils which came from America directly to Lorient and were sent from there to Bayonne should pay the Hanse duties only, as having come from the United States to France directly, according to the regulations. The practice of the other ports of France to require the Hanse duties only, which you mention to me to have been done as to other parts of the cargo of oil sent to other ports, is a proof that the law of the land is such. But as the laws have doubtless provided a summary and speedy decision of contested claims of duty, the ministers would consider an application to them as irregular in a case where a regular decision is provided. So also if their regulations require the certificate of their consul in the port from whence the oil was shipped. The standing regulations of the law must be complied with. Our merchants know that these rules are never departed from with us. I inclose you the certificate which came in your letter, and have the honor to be Gentlemen your most obedt. humble servt.,

TH: JEFFERSON

PrC (DLC). Enclosure: See note to letter from Meier & Cie. to TJ, ca. Apr. 1788.

To John Polson

SIR Paris July 29. 1788.

Soon after your application to me I wrote to Genl. Stephens, near Winchester, and also to Mr. Joseph Jones in King George county, on the subject of your lands, but have received no answer from either, and therefore can give you no information whether they are confiscated or not. I should think it adviseable for you to write to both those gentlemen for information, referring them to the letters I have written to them; and that as being the representative of an officer, you might also write to Genl. Washington from whose punctuality you may be assured of an answer. Conveiances from England occur more frequently than from hence to America: nevertheless if you think that my forwarding your letters, with a line covering them, may be of service to you, I will willingly do it. I am Sir Your most obedt. humble servt.,

TH: JEFFERSON

PrC (DLC). For TJ's earlier letters ON THE SUBJECT OF YOUR LANDS, see TJ to Jones and to Adam Stephen, 19 June 1785.

From John Trumbull

DEAR SIR London July 29th. 1788.

I am afraid I have been guilty of an omission. In looking over some of your letters I find your request to have the address of the best classical bookseller, to which I beleive I never gave you any answer:—I enquir'd however in time, and am assur'd that *Payne* at the King's Mews [Gate] is as good as any if not the best.

I have your letters to Stockdale now in my [hands] having been very busy since I recev'd them [but I will] deliver them, pay him, and take his final Receipt [the] first day I pass his door.—I do not yet find another carriage to my mind. But I have no doubt but I shall in time for Mr. Parkers return:—He is indeed ill at present as well as Mrs. P. with a kind of Influenza which has afflicted many people of late, and among the rest Mr. Barlow and Cutting. They are recover'd.

You have been inform'd of the accession of New Hampshire, the ninth State to the new Constitution. We hope every day to learn that Virginia has also.

I am to thank you for your politeness to my friend Mr. Duché, and this in his name, as well as my own:—He return'd a few days ago in very fine health.

The City of Westminster is at this moment in high enjoyment of the glorious liberty of Old England. Open Alehouses, broken heads, and bloody noses are the delicious accompaniments of the Election. The Opposition are in triumph with the prospect even of the victory which they are likely to obtain over the Monarch and the minister:—Lord Townshend their man will doubtless be successfull.

I am dear Sir, with the highest respect Your obligd Servant,

JNO. TRUMBULL

RC (DLC); MS torn and some words supplied conjecturally.

To Mary Barclay

DEAR MADAM Paris July 30. 1788.

I have just recieved a letter from Mr. Barclay and another from Mr. Bondfeild by which I find it probable you will be setting out immediately for America. I am to dine at Chatoux tomorrow, and will do myself the honour of waiting on you either in the forenoon, or after dinner, to know whether there is any thing in which I can be serviceable to you before your departure. Should Mr. Barclay's remitances not answer as fully as he expected, be so good as to calculate what may be wanting, and to count on every assistance in my power. I have the honour to be with very sincere esteem Dear Madam Your most obedt. humble servt.,

TH: JEFFERSON

PrC (MHi). For the letters from BARCLAY and . . . BONDFEILD, see Barclay to TJ, 12 June 1788, and Bondfield to TJ, 25 July 1788.

To Maria Cosway

MY DEAR DEAR FRIEND Paris July 30. 1788.

Cease to chide me. It is hard to have been chained to a writing table, drudging over business daily from morning to night ever since my return to Paris. It will be a cruel exaggeration, if I am to lose my friends into the bargain. The only letter of private friendship I wrote on my return, and before entering on business, was to you. The first I wrote after getting through my budget was to you. It had gone off on the morning of the last post, and in the evening of the same day, your's of the 15th. was brought here by I know not whom, while I was out. I am incapable of forgetting or neglecting you my dear friend; and I am sure if the comparison could be fairly made of how much I think of you, or you of me, the former scale would greatly preponderate. Of this I have no right to complain, nor do I complain. You esteem me as much as I deserve. If I love you more, it is because you deserve more. Of voluntary faults to you I can never be guilty, and you are too good not to pardon the involuntary. Chide me then no more; be to me what you have been; and give me without measure the comfort of your friendship. Adieu ma tres chere et excellente amie.

TH: J.

PrC (ViU).

To C. W. F. Dumas

SIR Paris July 30. 1788.

Your favor of the 24th. has just come to hand, and that of the 20th. of June had never been acknoleged. I congratulate you on the news just received of the accession of New Hampshire to the new Constitution which suffices to establish it. I have the honor to inclose you details on that subject, as also on the reception of Mr. Adams, which you will be so good as to reduce to such a size as may gain them admission into the Leyden gazette. We may take a little glory to ourselves too on the victory obtained by the Russians under the command of our Paul Jones, over the Turks commanded by the Captain Pacha, and we may be assured, if it has been as signal as the Russians say, that Constantinople will be bombarded by that officer. Why did the Swedish fleet salute the Russian instead of attacking it? It would make one suspect that their whole movements had in view to divert the Russian fleet from going round if it could be done by hectoring without engaging in the war, well understood that Turkey pays, and England guarantees them against all events. It is scarcely possible however that all these things can pass over without a war. I think the internal affairs of this country will be settled without bloodshed. I have the honour to be with very great esteem & respect, Sir Your most obedt. humble servt., TH: JEFFERSON

PrC (DLC). Enclosure not found, but it was clearly a repetition in part of the news about New Hampshire's ratification of the Constitution which Dumas had received as early as 26 July and had already taken steps to detail for the *Gazette de Leide* and which appeared in *Supplément* LXII for 1 Aug. 1788 (Dumas to TJ, 7 Aug. 1788), reading in part: "Extrait d'une Lettre de New-York du 28. Juin. 'La Nouvelle Constitution Fédérative de la République Américaine a passé la crise de son acceptation; et déja il est sûr, qu'elle sera établie. La Convention de l'Etat de New-Hampshire, revenuë des idées défavorables, qu'elle avoit suivies dans sa première Session, en a agréé le Projet par une très-grande pluralité, le 23. de ce mois. C'est le neuvième Etat, qui a accédé à cette Forme; et par conséquent, en vertu de la Loi commune passée à ce sujet, elle commencera bientôt de sortir son plein et entier effet pour tout le Corps de la Confédération: Mais il est très-probable, que le nombre des Etats, qui y auront consenti de plein gré, ne restera pas à neuf.'" The article went on to state that the happiest augury occurred when Edmund Pendleton was elected president of the Virginia Convention, which assembled on 2 June, for "Mr. Pendleton, comme l'un des Citoyens les plus zélés pour le bien général de la Patrie, est aussi un des plus fermes Partisans de la Constitution Fédérative." This, as well as letters from Virginia, justified the expectation that Virginia would ratify by "une grande majorité" and this example would decide the question for North Carolina, since that state would not wish to oppose the opinion of other Southern states. The same conclusion might be drawn for New York in consequence of New Hampshire's election, since the former would not like to be alone with Rhode Island in opposing "un Projet, reconnu pour sage et avantageux par tous les autres Membres de l'Union-Américaine"—and even in Rhode Island itself the town of Providence had protested the resolution "prise par ce qu'on peut nommer le Petit-Peuple du reste de cet Etat."

One can only conjecture, in the absence of TJ's enclosure, how far his presentation of the news from New Hampshire and Virginia varied from that of Dumas; it is doubtful whether TJ risked predicting that Virginia would ratify by a great majority and it is almost certain that he did not comment on "le Petit-Peuple" of Rhode Island. But it is not necessary to conjecture about that part of his enclosure concerning Adams' arrival in America. As published in *Supplément* LXVIII for 22 Aug. 1788, it reads as follows: "Extrait d'une Lettre de Portsmouth dans le Nouveau-Hampshire du 25. Juin. 'Mr. Jean Adams, ci-devant Ministre-Plénipotentiaire des Etats-Unis de l'Amérique près du Roi de la Grande-Brétagne et près des Etats-Généraux des Provinces-Unies, arriva le 18. de ce mois à Boston, de retour du long séjour, qu'il a fait en Europe. La reception, qu'on lui a faite, a été aussi distinguée, qu'on la devoit et à son mérite personnel et aux services signalés, qu'il a rendus à sa Patrie. A son entrée dans le Havre, il fut salué par l'Artillerie du Fort Castle-William. Le Secrétaire de la République de Massachusetts-Bay alla à sa recontre avec le Yacht de l'Etat, pour recevoir Mr. Adams. Plusieurs milliers de Citoyens bordoient la rive, témoignant par des cris rédoublés leur joye de voir heureusement revenu parmi eux un Concitoyen, si cher à l'Amerique. Au Milieu de leurs acclamations, il fut conduit à l'Hôtel du Gouvernement, où il logea, et où toutes les Personnes notables de la Ville et des environs vinrent le complimenter. Comme l'Assemblée-Legislative de Massachusetts-Bay étoit Séante alors, elle lui envoya une Députation, qui lui adressa un Discours, dont voici la Traduction avec la Réponse de Mr. Adams.'" Following this there appeared a translation of the address and response as quoted by TJ from Cutting's letter of ca. 24 July 1788. For TJ's object in publishing this account of Adams' reception, see his letter to Adams, 2 Aug. 1788.

To André Limozin

SIR Paris July 30. 1788.

I know nothing myself of the person who was the subject of your letter of the 27th. except a mere slight personal acquaintance. But I have been told that he has been very unsuccesful in commerce, and that his affairs are very much deranged. I own I wish to see the beef trade with America taken up by solid hands, because it will give new life to our Northern states. In general they do not know how to cure it. But some persons of Massachusets have not very long ago brought over packers and picklers from Ireland, and the beef cured and packed by them has been sent to the East Indies and brought back again, and perfectly sound. We may expect the art will spread. Is the Irish beef as good as that of Hamburgh? If I had supposed Irish beef could have been got at Havre I would not have sent to Hamburgh for beef. I suppose that which came for me cannot be introduced.

You have heard of the great naval victory obtained by the Russians under command of Admiral Paul Jones over the Turks commanded by the Captain Pacha. We cannot see as yet whether this will hasten peace. The Swedish fleet having saluted instead of attacking the Russian, makes us suspect these movements of the king of Sweden may be a mere peice of Hectoring to frighten Russia from her purpose of sending her fleet round if he can do it without actually entering into the war. He is paid by the Turks. Nothing else new. I am Sir with great esteem your most obedt. humble servt., TH: JEFFERSON

P.S. The new constitution of America is now confirmed by 9 states, New Hampshire having agreed to it on the 24th. of June.

PrC (DLC).

TJ's acquaintance with James Swan, THE SUBJECT OF YOUR LETTER OF THE 27TH. was indeed slight, but what he neglected to tell Limozin was that he himself had assisted in the drafting of Swan's proposals so as to make them more conformable to what might be required by the French government and more likely to achieve a purpose that TJ had much at heart (see note to Swan's proposals, under 19 July 1788).

To Montmorin

SIR Paris July 30. 1788.

I have the pleasure to inform your Excellency that the new Constitution proposed for the United states is finally established by the vote of nine states. New Hampshire acceded to it certainly on the 24th. of June, and I have great reason to conclude that Virginia had done it some days before, in which case the vote of New-Hampshire would be the tenth.

I have the honour to be with sentiments of the most perfect esteem & respect your Excellency's most obedient & most humble servant, TH: JEFFERSON

RC (Arch. Aff. Etr., Paris, Corr. Pol., E.-U., Vol. XXXIII); docketed: "M. de R[ayneval]." PrC (DLC); lacks signature, which may have been clipped away during TJ's lifetime, for, on the same line with the final part of complimentary close and evidently written after the page was clipped, TJ put at foot of text (not in RC): "Count de Monmorin."

If the conjectural conclusion advanced in the note to Dumas to TJ, 24 July 1788, is valid, this notification to Montmorin takes on additional meaning, and so, perhaps, does the news in the following letter to Dumas about the prohibition of the distribution of the *Gazette de Leide* in Paris.

To C. W. F. Dumas

SIR Paris July 31. 1788.

I had the honour of writing to you yesterday, and after sending my letter to the post-office, received a notification that the distribution of the gazette of Leyden here was prohibited. The purpose of the present therefore is merely to ask the favor of you to make interest with your friend Luzac to send me the paper by post during the interval of it's prohibition. If put under a common letter cover, and addressed as a letter to me, it will come safely. I had rather pay the expence of the postage than lose the benefit of that paper, which in fact I think the only one in Europe worth reading. Your interference herein will much oblige Sir Your most obedt. & most humble servt., TH: JEFFERSON

PrC (DLC). See note to preceding letter to Montmorin; it is perhaps significant, in the light of the conjecture there referred to, that both the letters of 9 June and 30 July 1788 and their enclosures sent by TJ to Dumas for the *Gazette de Leide* went by post. It may also be significant that in the present letter TJ did not think it necessary to tell Dumas why its distribution by post had been prohibited in Paris.

To C. W. F. Dumas

SIR Paris July 31. 1788.

I was mentioning to-day to my friend the Count Diodati, minister plenipotentiary for the Duke of Mecklenberg-Schwerin, that I had asked the favor of you to have the Leyden gazette sent to me by post, during the suspension of it's distribution here, and he asked of me to procure at the same time the same benefit for him, being disposed as myself to pay the postage rather than be without the paper. I must therefore beg the favor of you to do this favor for him at the same time you are so kind as to give the orders for me, having his paper put under a common letter-cover and addressed à Monsieur le comte Diodati ministre plenipotentiaire du Duc de Mecklenbourg Schwerin, á Paris, rue de la Michodiere. Whatever may be necessary to be paid for him and for me, Messrs. Van Staphorst will be so good as to answer it to your Draught. I have the honor to be with very great esteem & respect Sir Your most obedient & most humble servt., TH: JEFFERSON

PrC (DLC).

From C. W. F. Dumas

MONSIEUR Lahaie 31e. Juillet 1788

Esperant que ma Lettre du 24e. Courant, avec une Dépeche pour le Congrès, est bien parvenue à V.E., J'ai l'honneur de lui acheminer ci-joint un Postcrit à la même Dépeche. Je n'ai rien à ajouter à ce que Votre Excellence y lira, sinon, que l'avis de l'accession de l'Etat de N. Hampshire, et de l'Election de Mr. Pendleton pour présider à la Convention de 140 Députés, qui a commencé ses séances en Virginie le 2e. Juin, m'est venue d'Amsterdam, par Lettre de nos amis du 26; et que celui de veiller à la sureté de nos Navigateurs et Pêcheurs, et de se garder contre toute surprise, me paroît ne devoir pas être méprise. Je suis avec grand respect De Votre Excellence Le très-humble & très-obéissant serviteur

C W F DUMAS

RC (DLC); endorsed. FC (Dumas Letter Book, Rijksarchief, The Hague; photostats in DLC). Enclosure (same): Postscript to Dumas' dispatch to Jay, 26 July 1788, enclosing answer of the Estates General to the French ambassador's note of the 16th; stating that he had just learned of New Hampshire's ratification of the Constitution and the probability that Virginia would do so; announcing the beginning of hostilities in Finland; suggesting that he be empowered, as soon as the new Congress begins its sessions, to communicate the fact officially; requesting that he be furnished with a letter of credence as chargé d'affaires so as to obviate any difficulty the Estates General might pose by saying Dumas was no longer in office since Adams had taken leave; and enclosing a resolution of the Estates General of 24 June 1783 showing that Dumas and their secretary had exchanged ratifications, in Adams' absence, of the treaty of amity and commerce between the United States and the Netherlands (translation printed in *Dipl. Corr., 1783-89*, III, 620-3). The passage in Dumas' letter to Jay concerning the progress of the ratification of the Constitution parallels in substance and, in part, in phraseology the account that he had caused to be published in *Supplément* No. LXII of the *Gazette de Leide* of 1 Aug. 1788.

To James Madison

DEAR SIR Paris July 31. 1788.

My last letters to you were of the 3d and 25. of May. Yours from Orange of Apr. 22. came to hand on the 10th. inst.

My letter to Mr. Jay containing all the public news that is well authenticated, I will not repeat it here, but add some details in the smaller way which you may be glad to know. The *disgrace*[1] *of the Marquis de la fayette* which at any other period of their history would have had the worst consequences for *him* will on the contrary mark him favourably to the nation at present. During the present administration he can expect nothing, but perhaps it may serve him with their successors whenever a change shall take place. No change of *the principal*[2] will probably take place before the meeting of the States general *tho' a change is to be wished*, *for his operations do not answer the expectations formed of him. These had been calculated on his brilliancy in society. He is very feebly aided too. Montmorin is weak tho a most worthy character. He is indolent and inattentive too in the extreme. Luzerne is considerably inferior in abilities to his brother whom you know. He is a good man too, but so much out of his element that he has the air of one huskanoyed. The garde des sceaux is considered as the principal's bull dog, braving danger like that animal. His talents do not pass mediocrity. The archbishop's brother and the new minister Vildeuil*[3] *and Lambert have no will of their own. They cannot raise money for the peace establishment the next year without the states general much less if there be war, and their administration will probably end with the states general. Littlepage* who was here as a *secret agent for the King of Poland* rather *overreached himself.* He wanted more money. *The King*[4] furnished it more than once. Still he wanted more, and thought to obtain a high bid by saying he was called for *in America* and asking leave to go there. Contrary to his expectation he received leave: but he went to *Warsaw* instead of *America* and from thence to join the *Russian army.*[4] I do not know these facts certainly, but collect them by putting several things together. *The King*[4] then sent an *antient secretary* here, in whom he had much confidence, to look out for a *correspondent, a mere letter writer* for him. A happy hazard threw *Mazzei* in his way. He recommended him, and he is appointed. He has no *diplomatic character* whatever, but is to receive *Eight thousand livres a year as an intelligencer.* I hope this *employment* may have some permanence. The danger is that he will over-act his part.—The *Marquis de la Luzerne* had been for many years *married* to his *brother's wife's sister secretly. She* was ugly, and deformed, but sensible, amiable, and rather rich. When he was *named ambassador to London* with 10000 *guineas a year*, the *marriage* was avowed, and he relinquished his *cross of Malta* from which he derived a handsome revenue, for life, and very open to advancement. *She* staid here, and not long after *died.* His real *affection for her* which was great and *unfeigned* and perhaps the loss of his *order* for so short-lived a satisfaction has thrown him almost *into a state of despondency.* He is *now here.*

I send you a book of Dupont's on the subject of the commercial treaty with England. Tho' it's general matter may not be interesting, yet you will pick up in various parts of it such excellent principles and observations as will richly repay the trouble of reading it. I send you also two little pamphlets of the Marquis de Condorcet, wherein is the most judicious statement I have seen of the great questions which agitate this nation at present. The new regulations present a preponderance of good over their evil. But they suppose that the king can model the constitution at will, or in other words that this government is a pure despotism: the question then arising is whether a pure despotism, in a single head, or one which is divided among a king, nobles, priesthood, and numerous magistracy is the least bad. I should be puzzled to decide: but I hope they will have neither, and that they are advancing to a limited, moderate government, in which the people will have a good share.

I sincerely rejoice at the acceptance of our new constitution by nine states. It is a good canvas, on which some strokes only want retouching. What these are, I think are sufficiently manifested by the general voice from North to South, which calls for a bill of rights. It seems pretty generally understood that this should go to Juries, Habeas corpus, Standing armies, Printing, Religion and Monopolies. I conceive there may be difficulty in finding general modification of these suited to the habits of all the states. But if such cannot be found then it is better to establish trials by jury, the right of Habeas corpus, freedom of the press and freedom of religion in all cases, and to abolish standing armies in time of peace, and Monopolies, in all cases, than not to do it in any. The few cases wherein these things may do evil, cannot be weighed against the multitude wherein the want of them will do evil. In disputes between a foreigner and a native, a trial by jury may be improper. But if this exception cannot be agreed to, the remedy will be to model the jury by giving the medietas linguae in civil as well as criminal cases. Why suspend the Hab. corp. in insurrections and rebellions? The parties who may be arrested may be charged instantly with a well defined crime. Of course the judge will remand them. If the publick safety requires that the government should have a man imprisoned on less probable testimony in those than in other emergencies; let him be taken and tried, retaken and retried, while the necessity continues, only giving him redress against the government for damages. Examine the history of England: see how few of the cases of the suspension of the Habeas corpus law have been worthy of that suspension. They have been either real treasons wherein the parties might as well have been charged at once, or sham-plots where it was shameful they should ever have been suspected. Yet for the few cases wherein the suspension of the hab. corp. has done real good, that operation is now become habitual, and the minds of the nation almost prepared to live under it's constant suspension.[5] A declaration that the federal government will never restrain the presses from printing any thing they please, will not take away the liability of the printers for false facts printed. The declaration that religious faith shall be unpunished, does not give impunity to criminal acts dictated by religious error. The saying there shall be no monopolies lessens the incitements to ingenuity, which is spurred on by the hope of a monopoly for a limited time, as of 14. years; but the benefit even of limited monopolies is too doubtful to be opposed to that of their general suppression. If no check can be found to keep the number of standing troops within safe bounds, while they are tolerated as far as necessary, abandon them altogether, discipline well the militia, and guard the magazines with them. More than magazine-guards will be useless if few, and dangerous if many. No European nation can ever send against us such a regular army as we need fear, and it is hard if our militia are not equal to those of Canada or Florida. My idea then is, that tho' proper exceptions to these general rules are desireable and probably practicable, yet if the exceptions cannot be agreed on, the establishment of the rules in all cases will do ill in very few. I hope therefore a bill of rights will be formed to guard the people against the federal government, as they are already guarded against their state governments in most instances.

The abandoning the principle of necessary rotation in the Senate, has I see been disapproved by many; in the case of the President, by none. I readily therefore suppose my opinion wrong, when opposed by the majority as in the former instance, and the totality as in the latter. In this however I should have done it with more complete satisfaction, had we all judged from the same position.

Sollicitations, which cannot be directly refused, oblige me to trouble you often with letters recommending and introducing to you persons who go from hence to America. I will beg the favour of you to distinguish the letters wherein I appeal to recommendations from other persons, from those which I write on my own knowlege. In the former it is never my intention to compromit myself, nor you. In both instances I must beg you to ascribe the trouble I give you to circumstances which do not leave me at liberty to decline it. I am with very sincere esteem Dear Sir Your affectionate friend & servt., TH: JEFFERSON

RC (DLC: Madison Papers); partly in code. PrC (DLC); accompanied by a one-page MS containing the text *en clair*, in TJ's hand, of most of the passages in code.

Pierre Samuel Dupont's book on THE COMMERCIAL TREATY WITH ENGLAND was his *Lettre à la Chambre du Commerce de Normandie; sur le Mémoire qu'elle a publié relativement au Traité de Commerce avec l'Angleterre* (Rouen, 1788); see Sowerby, No. 3617. Condorcet's TWO LITTLE PAMPHLETS were evidently his *Lettres d'un Citoyen des Etats-Unis, à un français, sur les affaires présentes* (Paris, 1788) and *Sentimens d'un Républicain, sur les Assemblées Provinciales et les Etats-Généraux* (Paris, 1778); Sowerby, Nos. 2467-8. TJ's opinion that La Luzerne, minister of marine, was SO MUCH OUT OF HIS

ELEMENT THAT HE HAS THE AIR OF ONE HUSKANOYED was a sentiment that the minister reciprocated at least in part, for La Luzerne told Gouverneur Morris in 1790 that TJ was "better formed for the interior of Virginia than to influence the Operations of a great People" (*A Diary of the French Revolution by Gouverneur Morris*, ed. Beatrix C. Davenport, Boston, 1939, I, 476). HUSKANOYED: Subjected to the practice among the Indians of Virginia of preparing young men for the duties of manhood by means of solitary confinement and the use of narcotics (OED, wherein the present letter is quoted as an example of the use of the word).

[1] This and subsequent words in italics are in code and were decoded in an unidentified hand (presumably that of a 19th century editor); the text of encoded passages is that of the Editors' decoding, employing Code No. 9, verified by the text *en clair.*

[2] Decoding in RC reads "principle," but TJ referred, of course, to the principal minister, Montmorin.

[3] Thus in text *en clair.*

[4] Preceding two words not in text *en clair.*

[5] TJ first wrote "suppression," and then altered the word by overwriting to read as above.

From Thomas Lee Shippen

MY DEAR SIR Strasburgh July 31. 1788.

Every stage of my journey has reminded me of you, and the remembrance has always been accompanied with gratitude and regard. And it was but natural that it should be so, since every stage has given me the sense of a new obligation, and how could I regard but with thankfulness and affection the goodness which was the author of it? At Dusseldorff I examined the gallery of paintings which you so judiciously recommend to my attention with infinite delight; I prevailed upon its inspector to lock me up in it for a whole forenoon, (not lest any possible attraction should be able to draw me out of it before it was necessary that I should go but because he had business to attend to in town and could not leave the door open) but instead of being satiated or even satisfied at the end of that time, I was only the more eager to pursue the gaze. In the afternoon I ran to it again and after quite exhausting the patience of the inspector and almost all the time too that I had determined to devote to Dusseldorff I tore myself away in pure compassion to my guide and a fair companion whom he had brought with him for company, and who did not seem quite satisfied that I should admire on canvas with so much enthusiasm what I might have found alive on her cheek more worthy of admiration, pronouncing to myself with great vehemence of asseveration that there could not be a greater collection of pictures on earth. It is rare indeed Sir, and cannot be examined with too much attention. The St. John of Raphael, the *annunciation* of Guido and the *last or great judgment* of Rubens (as it is called) are most to be wondered at, but there is a Magdalen of Carl Dolce, a Madonna of

Zannetti, and a vierge à sept douleurs by Guido (Cenni I think) which touched me more sensibly. However just in their designs and forcible in their expression may be the painters of the Flemish school, there is a delicacy an inexpressible softness in the Italian paintings of high note, which I never find among them, and which I am always enraptured with, when I meet it. Thus you see Sir I am become an Italian before I have reached Italy.

We were well entertained by Mr. Zimmerman at the Hotel des deux Ponts, and went to see a society which either must have escaped your attention, or which did not appear to you worthy of reco[mme]ndation. I mean the Society of La Trappe. It is to be seen at the distance of 2 miles from Dusseldorff and we walked to it before breakfast. We had heard so many strange stories of their rigid abstinence from all worldly enjoyments, of their invariable and undisturbed silence from the time of their becoming what they call Professors and of their employing so many minutes in every day in scratching up their own grave with their fingers, that I was not a little surprized to find them a fat jolly, wicked set of rogues who pray devoutly to be sure as it seems 7 times a day and sing very loudly *pendant office*, but in the intervening hours are allowed to work in the gardens, to walk into town (by the permission of the Prelate of the order,) to talk eat and drink as much as they please, and to indulge themselves in all licentiousness. There are some restraints about eating meat in the Hall, and about talking to each other either in their cells or in chapel, but they are very trifling impediments to a headlong indulgence of their passions which they appear to take every opportunity of indulging. They are about 28 in number 15 peres and 13 freres and undergo a constant diminution. They are all Germans except one who is a Frenchman about 50 years old and who seems as desperate an old offender as I ever saw, and to have an utter contempt for the particularities of his order. Notwithstanding my dissappointment I was not sorry that I devoted 2 hours to the visit, for I have always held that to be disabused of a false idea was next to being possessed of a just one.

We breakfasted at Benrath the pretty castle of the Elector Palatine a few miles from Dusseldorff and amused ourselves exceedingly 2 hours in running over his grounds and apartments there. They seem to vye with each other in taste and beauty. We dined at Bensberg the other seat of this magnificent Elector which we found it more convenient to visit on our way to Cologne than in an excursion from that place. The former put us 7 or 8 miles out of our way, the latter would have been an extraordinary ride of 12 miles. Here we saw as you must have done Sir with great pleasure three rooms adorned with some of the finest Weenixs in the world. This painter seems always to have succeeded better when employed in the service of a prince than in any other circumstances. All the pictures that I saw of his in Holland were far inferior to these I just mentioned and to some which you find in two collections of the Elector of Cologne. The prospect from this palace could not certainly have failed striking you Sir with admiration and delight. How vast, how rich, how beautiful! The time however that I was in the carriage between Bensberg and Cologne was spent in mournful reflections and satire making up human nature. Here said I, have I seen in 2 days four superb palaces all belonging to one prince who has not seen one of them for many years and in a reign of 46 years has made no use of them at any time. In the erection of these four palaces how many millions must have been expended which might have been applied to public uses or to the relief of the helpless or unfortunate; to the reward of unprotected merit, or the storing with new productions the receptacles of Science! And what end do they answer? They beautify uninhabited heights and are objects of wonder to curious passengers; and when the Prince who possesses them is led by caprice to quit his Paternal seats to inhabit his more remote dominions, he has a choice of habitations. Yet the Princes who have built them have been both models of admiration and esteemed worthy of all praise. How hard it is Sir to be obliged to believe that as we acquire the power, we lose the will of doing good on a large scale! There are most certainly great and beautiful exceptions to this rule, but I am afraid we shall not find them in Courts. The more I see of them the more I am drawn to your opinion that they are composed of the weakest and wickedest part of mankind.

We found the commerce of Cologne worthy of remark; it is very considerable, but carried on chiefly with Holland. That which they have with America is generally done by the way of Amsterdam or Rotterdam and through the merchants of those places. They send down the Rhine, cloths, silks, wine, mill stones and *Cologne water* and receive tobacco, rice, cheese &c. &c. in return. It is also a remarkable town for its power, its privileges and its independence. It has been engaged in former years in wars with the Elector of its name, and obeys no laws but what are of immemorial usage, or enacted by itself. We met with a gentleman here named Hüpsch who shewed us a curious collection of natural and exotic productions. He was very civil to us on account of our Country. He gave us some little Treatises too of his own composition, on manure, on the means of destroying insects that are hurtful to the grain, the inoculation of cattle and other subjects of œconomy which promise well. They are written in German, I think of translating the most material things in them while I am in Switzerland, and if I find any thing worthy your notice, I will have the honor of communicating it to you. We saw a palace of the Elector of Cologne at Bruhl of great taste and beauty built about 50 or 60 years ago, and another at Bonn of more considerable size, and grandeur. From the appearance of his possessions, it does not seem at all wonderful that the Emperor should have taken so much pains to procure them for his brother. At a place called Remagen 15 miles from Bonn we saw the vine for the first time and it was some leagues further that we saw the walnut tree in any considerable plenty. There were several vessels lading with stones of different sorts at Broh[l] 9 miles from Remagen and 9 on that side of Andernach. Upon enquiring of several Germans whom I saw near the place I was informed that both the large and small stones were found in that neighbourhood but at Andernach I sent for the principal dealer in the genuine mill stones of the Country and he furnished me with a written paper in German of which this is the translation.

				Rix-Dollars
Mill Stones	@	17 feet diameter	of the best sort a piece	65=208[tt]
Do.	@	Do.	of the 2d. best sort	60=192
Do.	@	Do.	of the middling sort	55=176
Do.	@	Do.	of the common sort	50=161
Do.	@	16 feet diameter	of the best sort	40=128
Do.	@	Do.	of the middling sort	37=118.8

These are all the sorts that can be procured and these the terms. They appear to me to be extravagant, tho' I confess I do not know much about it. I enquired particularly whether it was for each stone or whether a pair that the price was marked, and they assured me it was for each stone. I have put the Rix dollars into livres tournois according as they pass in the country where I made the enquiry. There is also a note in my memorandum which mentions that for the prices marked the stones will be delivered at Cologne. The address in German is Johsep Host in Andernach. Ober Mandigh and Nieder Mandigh are the places where the best are found the one distant 4½ and the other 3 miles from that part of the Rhine which flows by Andernach.

We still punctually followed your directions Sir. At Coblentz we found the Wild man a very civil one to us, and having no true Brownberg in the house, he sent out and got some for us. It is the best Moselle I ever drank. He was very much pleased to hear that you remembered him and as grateful for the re-imbursement of the post map. He remembered you fron the circumstance of your going to examine the vineyards or at least the man who was instructed about them, and not at all from that of your owing him the money. It came to 5/6.

Your advice in all things had proved hitherto so excellent that we determined to pursue it in mounting the Rhine tho' every body we spoke to on the subject threw impediments in our way. There was no road for more than 5 or 6 miles up that a carriage could go pass, when you got there you could not find a boat, and when you were put down on the other side the cliffs, you could not have horses to go on with and if we concluded to go entirely by water, the expense would be trebled, and the inconveniences innumerable; and our delay very great. These were the representations they made us. I was not to be dissuaded by their endeavors and Rutledge consented to hire a boat at 2 guineas and a half to take us to Mentz. Every yard we went we had a new object of delight; the scenes are romantic beyond every thing; the mode of travelling easy and convenient. We sat in our carriage, made notes as we went along and were extremely happy that we had pursued your plan. It delayed us a little, but we were amply repaid. On our way we lodged at Reidesheim and breakfasted the next morning on samples of Johannesberg wine. What a delicious liquor Sir it is! But I found it too expensive for us to think of importing it. The price on the spot is between 5 and 6 shillings sterg. a bottle by the Stück which holds about 4 pipes.

Of Franckfurt Carlsruhe &c. I shall have the pleasure of writing to you from Switzerland. I meant to have written of them fully from this place, as also to write to my friends in America and to Mr. Short but I have been so long on the top of the steeple here and am in so great haste to proceed to Basle that I fear I shall not be able to do either. In that event have the goodness Sir to inform Mr. Short that I have received his note, and thank him for it, and to present him with my best wishes. Will you be so good Sir as to let me know at what time of the month you have the most occasion to send letters to America? Excuse the length of my letter

John Trumbull's sketches of the Rhine in the vicinity of Mainz. (See p. xxviii.)

"Maria: not her under the poplar . . . ." (See p. xxix.)

"but the Maria who makes the Hours her own . . . ." (See p. xxix.)

Sir if you please; it is drawn out to a greater length than I intended tho' I have not said half I meant to have said or attempted [to] declare to you how much I am your devoted & obliged friend & servt.,

THOS. LEE SHIPPEN

P.S. Tomorrow morning we proceed to Switzerland. [*In margin of first page*:] I send one letter Sir to your care.

RC (DLC); endorsed. Enclosure (DLC: Shippen Family Papers): Thomas Lee Shippen to his father, Dr. William Shippen, 31 July 1788, in which he spoke gratefully of TJ's assistance: "My journey from Amsterdam has been delightful, variegated, and improving. . . . We proceeded in a German carriage which we purchased [at Aix-la-Chapelle] thro' Dusseldorff, Cologne and Bonn to Coblence whence we went up the Rhine in a boat to Mentz. This we did by Mr. Jefferson's advice. This good gentleman had just returned from making my tour as far as Strasbourg when I left Paris, and he then promised me to write to me what was most remarkable and worthy of my attention in the journey. At Liege I received his letter and with it some valuable extracts from the journal he had kept during his journey. This has been thus far my constant guide, and no man can have a better one. . . . Being in the neighbourhood of Hairsault where the Landgrave of Hesse Cassel keeps his court in Summer, we were prevailed upon by Major Geismar to whom Mr. Jefferson introduced us, to be presented at Court. We were well received and dined there, the young Princesses very curious to know every thing about our regiments, our service and our Country."—The two young travellers, at Lafayette's suggestion, had adopted military uniforms as being safer, cheaper, and more effective as passports to good society; thus they travelled as Major Shippen and Captain Rutledge, a device that may have caused embarrassment in framing replies to the questions of the young princesses of Hesse-Cassel but also brought compensations: "At Hairsault we were greatly patronized. They have every reason to think the Americans good soldiers and good soldiers are respected and honored throughout all Germany above all other men. The Prime Minister's lady took a particular liking to your son on account of his being an American. She is a violent enthusiast you must know in favor of universal liberty, and she triumphs in the reflection that one Country in the world large and respectable as ours is should have had virtue and wisdom enough to prize it as we have done. She glories in our revolution." Young Shippen's letter to his father, however, contrasted with that to TJ by being concerned less with what he had seen on the tour than with his anticipation of what lay ahead: "Mr. Short secretary to Mr. Jefferson and a most sensible agreeable man joins us at Ulm and goes with us down the Danube to Vienna. So far our journey is determined. There is no doubt after that but Short and Rutledge will proceed on from Vienna by land to Trieste, and so to Venice, Rome and Naples. There is nothing on earth at this moment that I desire so much as to be able to accompany them. But I have my doubts. Every body I have seen on the Continent tells me that Rome contains more monuments of the fine arts than all the world besides, that it is indispensible to visit Rome. Mr. Jefferson wishes it exceedingly. I am sure you have no objection but one." The one obstacle was caused by the fact that every place he had stopped between Paris and Strasbourg had been "so excessively dear, and my stay at each of them . . . so much prolonged beyond my expectations." His mode of living in Switzerland for the next two months, where he expected to study civil law and Spanish, would determine whether this obstacle could be surmounted.

WEENIXS: Paintings of Jan Weenix (1640-1719), court painter of the Elector Johann Wilhelm of the Palatinate for ten years (*Encyclopedia of Painting*, Bernard S. Myers, ed., N.Y., 1955).

To Montmorin

Sir [ca July 1788]

I have the honor to inclose for your Excellency's information a letter I have received from a person in London on the subject of the act lately passed by the British parliament for the encouragement of their whale fishery, as also the act itself. The writer of the letter is in a situation to know tolerably well what passes. He is attentive and worthy of credit. This act has two distinct objects. 1. To enable their fishermen by enormous bounties to undersell those of all other nations. 2. To present to the American fishermen a counter-invitation to come and settle at the new fishery they are endeavoring to establish on the Western coast of Scotld. rather than at Dunkirk. On the first subject I would beg leave to observe that the premiums given by the British government to their fishermen en-able them to undersell even in the ports of France the French fishermen who are aided by smaller premiums and the Americans who are aided by their poverty alone, and that there is reason to believe that the present supplies of oil now coming from England into France are made partly at least at the risk of that government with a view to beat down the French and American competition and to usurp to themselves the sole possession of that nursery of seamen.[1] These two advantages of premium and government security operate against the fishermen of France. There is a third which affects the Americans alone; British whale oil being liable in the ports of France to pay a duty ad valorem, they do in fact by the means of false estimates, introduce their oil for about one half or two thirds of the fixed duties paid by Americans.

Do the Commercial treaties of France permit an exclusion of all European whale oil from her ports? This would affect the Hanse towns in name only, because they meddle little in the whale fishery, and could willingly accept a light equivalent. It would affect capitally the English and Dutch, whose marine it does not seem the interest of this country to aliment. If their whale oil cannot be excluded, altogether[2] would not this purpose, and many others of great value be effected by a general law, subjecting merchandize of every nation and of every nature to pay additional duties in the ports of France, exactly equal to the premiums given on the same merchandize by their own nation? This would not only counterwork the effect of premium in the instance of their whale oils, but defeat their whole system of Drawbacks by the aid of which they make themselves the center of commerce for all the world. It is for the wisdom of his majesty's ministers to judge whether the remedies here suggested, or any other can be applied to this evil. There seems to be real cause at present to apprehend that this manoeuvre of the British government will be succesful and will enable their fishermen to supplant both the French and Americans in the ports of France.[3] The British oil comes at this moment in sufficient quantities to supply your demands and it undersells both the French and american fisheries which therefore lie in the ports unsold.

While false estimates encourage the English competition on one hand, false constructions of the law by the officers of the Douanes oppress that of the Americans on the other. The Hanseatic treaty uses these terms, 'Huiles et graisses de baleine, et d'autres poissons embarquer du poids de 520. livres, 7 livres 10 sols ensemble les sols pour livre,' by which clearly 520 ℔. of oil were to pay but 7.₶ 10 and the sols per livre. The letter of M. de Calonnes promised us 'la meme moderation de droits dont jouissent les villes Anseatiques.' This then was professedly the basis on which the arret of Dec. 29 1787. was formed. But unfortunately and undesignedly that happened to vary the expression, thus 'les huiles de baleine &c. des E. U. d'Amerique continueront a n'etre soumis qu'a un droit de 7.₶ 10 par *barrique du poids de 520 livres.*' And the officers of the douane find in this mode of expression a pretext for making us pay the same duties on the weight of the wood in which the oil is contained. This raises the duties in fact to upon 520 ℔. of oil.

When the Arret of Dec. 29. 1787 gave us the right of entrepot in the ports of France for all our productions indefinitely, the merchants of France expressed fears that this might cover a contraband introduction of American codfish. No difficulty was made therefore of withdrawing the right of entrepot from our Codfish. As there was no fear, nor foundation for fear as to any other article, it was not supposed any other would participate of the exclusion. But the draughtsman of the Arret of Feb. 22. 1788. has extended it to all the produce of the American fisheries, so that this privilege is now denied to our Whale oil, and the resource of reexportation is taken from our oil merchants when they find, as at the present moment, that they cannot obtain here a living price for that article. I do not suppose it was the intention of government that the arret of February 22. should exclude from the entrepot anything but Codfish. 1. Because at the Conferences at which I was permitted the honour of attending the merchants asked the exclusion against no other article. 2. Because government has shewn a uniform disposition to encourage the introduction of our whale oil for the consumption of this country. And 3. because as to that which would be for the consumption of other countries, I apprehend they would rather invite than forbid a temporary deposit of it in their ports, for the same reason for which they would wish to see their ports become the entrepot for the exchange of all our productions and for those of the whole earth, could the whole earth be brought to exchange their pr[oductions] in their ports rather than in London, Lisbon, Amsterdam, and other places where those exchanges are now made. While his Majesty's ministers therefore shall be attentive to this subject, I will take the liberty of asking such an explanation of the Arret of Dec. 29. as may prevent this false construction which makes us pay duty on the weight of our casks as if they were oil, and of that of Feb. 22. as may restore to this article the right of entrepot, which I never understood either the government or their merchants wished to take from it, and of which it has real need so long as it is obliged to meet another foreign nation on such unequal ground.

Dft (DLC); endorsed by TJ: "Montmorin. But never sent"; containing numerous deletions and interlineations, most of which involve matters of phraseology and a few of which are noted below. The two items that TJ intended as enclosures for this letter that he composed so carefully but never sent were: (1) The letter from A PERSON IN LONDON, that is, John Brown Cutting's letter to him of 26 June 1788, much of the substance and even phraseology of which TJ incorporated in the present draft. (2) A copy of an Act for the encouragement of the Southern whale fishery, 28 Geo. III. ch. 20; the officially-printed pamphlet copy of this Act that Cutting forwarded to TJ is in DLC: TJ Papers, 46: 7816-23.

For a general comment on the matters to which this unsent letter relates, see notes to documents printed under 10 Apr. 1788; see also TJ to Jay, 23 May, and *Observations on the Whale-Fishery*, 19 Nov. 1788. For the evidences of FALSE CONSTRUCTIONS OF THE LAW, see TJ's correspondence with Thomas Appleton under 17, 26, and 29 July; 24 Aug., and 2 Sep. 1788.

1 As first written this sentence read: "On the first subject I would beg leave to observe that the bounties given by Gr. Brit. enable her merchants fishermen to undersell yours in your own ports, and I have reason to believe that their speculations lately directed into your ports are expressly secured against loss by their government."

2 This word added in margin, which accounts for the faulty punctuation.

3 As first written, these two sentences read: "A great part of the American produce consumed in France goes first to London. These are hints which the wisdom of his majesty's ministers will suppress or improve according to their value. Something seems necessary at this moment to prevent the British from ousting both the French and Americans in the ports of France."

From C. W. F. Dumas

MONSIEUR Lahaie 1er. Août 1788

L'incluse fera voir à votre Excellence la raison qui me presse de faire suivre cette Dépeche à celle que j'eus l'honneur de Lui adresser hier. Il me tarde de recevoir du bon souvenir de V.E. les nouvelles du parfait bien-être de nos Etats et du Sien personnel. De Votre Excellence Le très-humble & très-obéissant serviteur

C W F DUMAS

Ce qui suit dans mon duplicat qui va par le Havre est si bien dans le Supplément No. LXII de Leide sous le derniere Article du 31e. Juillet, ci-joint que je ne puis que le recommander à l'attention de V-E.—L'hotel des Et.Un. devra être illuminé aussi, sous peine de *l'indignation générale*.[1]

RC (DLC); endorsed. FC (Rijksarchief, The Hague, Dumas Papers; photostats in DLC); with postscript not in RC; see note 1. Enclosure: Dumas to Jay, 1 Aug. 1788, stating that the United States should be on guard, if war breaks out between England and France, in respect to navigation and fisheries, impressment of seamen, and western forts; that this hint comes from an important source whose identity he is pledged not to reveal; that he hopes Jay will protect Dumas' honor, interest, and existence against the British party and its adherents in the new Congress; that most of the foreign ministers are away from the Hague on vacation; that he thinks it his duty to point out that, in order not to be deceived by the system of Government and the sentiments now existing in Holland, it must be understood that everything undertaken from 1779 to 1787 is the result of a plot between a cabal at home and the enemies of the republic abroad, or, to speak plainly, of Great Britain; and enclosing a memorial signed by Baron de Helldorf offering to come to America with an assistant and to be employed by Congress in the manufacture and improvement of small arms and artillery, and stating that he had known Baron Steuben while in the Prussian service. (FC of both letter and enclosure in same; at head of text of letter: "Second Postscrit de mon No. 43 [of 18 July] à S. E. Mr. Jay"; at foot of text of enclosure Dumas stated that Helldorf's memorial had been read, sealed, and then handed over to him to be forwarded to Jay for whatever use he deemed proper to make of it; translations of both letter and enclosure are printed in *Dipl. Corr., 1783-89*, III, 623-8).

[1] Postscript not in RC, but supplied from FC. The last article in *Supplément* LXII for 1 Aug. 1788 to which Dumas refers is dated at Leiden, 31 July and announces that, in consequence of the election of the Chamber of Echevins, the city of Leiden will follow the example set by Amsterdam, Rotterdam, and Utrecht by encouraging the citizens to demonstrate "leur joye sur les événemens récens, qui ont eu lieu à l'égard de notre République, tels que la conclusion des Alliances avec les Cours de Londres et de Berlin, la Garantie du Stadhoudérat-Héréditaire mutuelle entre les Provinces &c. par une Illumination générale le 7. du mois prochain, Anniversaire de la naissance de Madame la Princesse d'Orange, 'dont il a plû a Dieu (est-il dit dans la Publication) de se servir comme d'un Instrument excellent pour délivrer la chère Patrie de sa détresse recente &c'."

From John Rutledge, Jr.

Strasbourg, 1 Aug. 1788. Arrived yesterday after pleasant journey along route TJ had proposed, which he found even more delightful than he expected. "At Coblence I paid the Landlord for your Map. He had entirely forgot it, and says you are the best Man in the world for remembering it. As you recommended, I embarked at Coblence to avoid the mountainous Road; I found it slow ascending the Rhine, but was compensated by the romantic and picturesque Scenes. On my passage I visited the Vineyards at [Johanne]sberg. The wines were the most [deliciou]s I ever tasted: but I fear we can never [import] them in America: the keeper of the Cave, if I recollect well, told me the wine would cost four shillings on the Spot. Although much pressed in time Major Geismer prevailed on me to stay three days at Frankfort. He presented me at Court at Philipsbourg, overwhelmed me with Civilities and by his attentions, rendered Frankfort so dear to me that I left it with much regret. . . . He said much of the friendship which you shewed him whilst he was a Prisoner in Virginia and seemed happy in having an Opportunity of being kind to one of your friends."

RC (DLC); 2 p.; endorsed; MS mutilated by breaking of seal, and lost words have been conjecturally supplied.

Shippen, in a letter to his father, stated that they had arrived at Strasbourg in the afternoon of 30 July and would depart early on 1 Aug. for Switzerland (31 July 1788; DLC: Shippen Family Papers). It is curious that Rutledge's letter nowhere mentions Shippen; cf. Shippen's description of the Rhine journey in his letter to TJ, 31 July 1788, wherein, among other variations from the present letter, he stated that it was he who was "not to be dissuaded" by discouraging comments of the natives and that it was Rutledge who "consented to hire a boat."

To John Adams

Dear Sir Paris Aug. 2. 1788.

I have received with a great deal of pleasure the account of your safe arrival and joyful reception at Boston. Mr. Cutting was so kind as to send me a copy of the address of the assembly to you and your answer, which with the other circumstances I have sent to have published in the gazette of Leyden, and in a gazette here. It will serve to shew the people of Europe that those of America are content with their servants, and particularly content with you.

The war with the Turks, Russians, and Austrians goes on. A great victory obtained on the black sea over the Turks as commanded by the Captain Pacha, by the Russians commanded by Admiral Paul Jones will serve to raise the spirits of the two empires. He burnt six ships, among which was the admiral's and vice admiral's, took two, and made between three and four thousand prisoners. The Swedes having hastily armed a fleet of about 16. sail of the line, and marched an army into Finland, the king at the head of it, made us believe they were going to attack the Russians. But when their fleet met with three Russian ships of 100 guns each they saluted and passed them. It is pretty well understood that the expences of this armament are paid by the Turks through the negociations of England. And it would seem as if the king had hired himself to strut only, but not to fight, expecting probably that the former would suffice to divert the Russians from sending their fleet round to the Mediterranean. There are some late symptoms which would indicate that Denmark would still be opposed to Sweden though she should shift herself into the opposite scale. The alliance between England, Holland and Prussia is now settled. In the mean time this country is losing all it's allies one by one, without assuring to herself new ones. Prussia, Holland, Turkey, Sweden are pretty certainly got or getting into the English interest, and the alliance of France with the two empires is not yet secured. I am in hopes her internal affairs will be arranged without blood. None has been shed as yet. The nation presses on sufficiently upon the government to force reformations, without forcing them to draw the sword. If they can keep the opposition always exactly at this point, all will end well. Peace or war, they cannot fail now to have the States general, and I think in the course of the following year. They have already obtained the Provincial assemblies as you know, the king has solemnly confessed he cannot lay a new tax without the consent of the States general, and when these assemble they will try to have themselves moulded into a periodical assembly, to form a declaration of rights, and a civil list for the government. The Baron de Breteuil has lately retired from the ministry and been succeeded by M. de Villedeuil. Monsieur de Malesherbes will probably retire. The Marquis de la Fayette with several others have lately received a fillup for having assembled to sign a memorial to the king which had been sent up from Brittany. They took from the Marquis a particular command which he was to have ex[ercised du]ring the months of August and September this year [in the] South of France. Your friends the Abbés are well and always enquire after you. I shall be happy to hear from you from time to time, to learn state news and state politics, for which I will give you in return those of this quarter of the earth. I hope Mrs. Adams is well; I am sure she is happier in her own country than any other.

Assure her of my constant friendship and accept assurances of the same from Dear Sir Your most obedt. & most humble servt.

TH: JEFFERSON

P.S. Make freely any use of me here which may be convenient either for yourself or Mrs. Adams.

P.S. Aug. 6. Later accounts inform us there have been two actions between the Russians and Turks. The first was of the gallies &c. on both sides. In this P. Jones, being accidentally present, commanded the right wing. The Russians repulsed the Turks. The second action was of the Russian gallies against the Turkish ships of war. The effect was what is stated in the preceding letter. But the command was solely in the prince of Nassau, P. Jones with his fleet of ships of war being absent. Prince Potemkin immediately got under march for Oczakow, to take advantage of the consternation it was thrown into. The Swedes have commenced hostilities against the Russians, and war against them is consequently declared by the empress.

RC (MHi: AMT); endorsed; MS slightly mutilated, and a few obliterated words (in brackets) supplied from PrC (DLC). For an account of Adams' reception as published in the *Gazette de Leide*, see note to TJ to Dumas, 30 July 1788.

To Gaudenzio Clerici

SIR Paris Aug. 2. 1788.

Your letter came to hand too late to allow time for doing what was necessary to be done, and to go by yesterday's post. The present therefore cannot leave this place till the post of the day after tomorrow. Having no means of procuring you a credit on Chalons sur Saone, I have taken a letter from Mr. Grand, banker here to Messrs. Vve. Rameau & fils à Dijon for eight louis, which you will find no difficulty of negociating at Chalons, more especially if you can find the correspondent of the house Vve. Rameau & fils at Chalons.

I am in hopes this will find your health so established as that you can come on and give us the pleasure of seeing you here. I have for you a letter which I was just about forwarding to Milan, but shall now have the pleasure of delivering you in person. I am with great esteem and attachment Sir your most obedt. humble servt.

TH: JEFFERSON

PrC (DLC); at foot of text: "Mr. Gaudenzio Clerici à Chalons sur Saone. poste restante."

From Lucy Ludwell Paradise

My dear Sir August the 2d 1788

As I find, I shall never be able to speak to Your Excellency I thought it best to write to you. Mr. Paradise is an honest Man, and a Man who has had a very good Education, but alas with all that, he never has, since I have been Married given himself the proper time to think upon his affairs as he ought and that is the true reason of my past, and present suffrings. He thinks only of the present Moment, and as for the future, that may take care of it's Self. That my dear Sir you will allow with me, will never do. He is a Man that spends or throws away a great deal of Money without thinking of it, or of the consequences. Had I seen any alteration since our return to Paris, I would have thought that my Sufferings was almost at an End; but that not being the case, I have been obliged to trouble you from time to time. As this will be the last Letter, I hope, I shall have reason to write to your Excellency upon my affairs, you will pardon me taking up your time, and thoughts. *You have it in your power to arrainge my affairs with Mr. Paradise, in such a Manner that I shall* altho' at present deprived of the greatest part of my Income, be at least certain of not being brought to more want, then, I at present suffer. What I want (of the friendship you have for me) is, to speak openly to Mr. Paradise, and tell him, if you was in his situation you would, now, you was agoing to Italy, employ your time in writing something useful for Virginia and you would advise him as his best friend to permit me to receive and take care his money affairs. He has not written a word about my receiving the Dividends to Mr. Anderson which makes me very unhappy. And until he does either write to him to remit to me the whole of the Dividends every Six Months which is £97.10s supposing Count Zenobio not to receive any part of the above sum, or write to Mr. Anderson to remit to me every six months the Sum of £120 arising from the Tobaccoes, and you see he has done it, I shall not be easy. *I beg in the Name of God* that you will tell him, he will forfit your friendship and good opinion of him, if he does not directly write the Letter to Mr. Anderson in the strongest terms and shew it to you. Tell him at the same time, was you him, you would do it directly, as you could not be easy until you had made your Wife happy. Pray, Pray My dear Protector lose not a Moment to see this important business finished. And for which, (as, I know you will succeed, if you take the business up heartily) *God* will bless your family and I and my dearest

Children will have reason to Pray for you and Yours for Ever. I am Your Greatly Obliged Humb. Servt. and Friend

LUCY PARADISE

RC (DLC); endorsed.

To William Stephens Smith

DEAR SIR Paris Aug. 2. 1788.

I congratulate you on two interesting circumstances, your safe arrival in your own country, and your having got rid of me; for I think you will not find there so troublesome a neighbor as I was here. I hope Mrs. Smith has well weathered the voyage, the little one also, and the half a one, for I presume he was begun. You arrive just in time to see the commencement of a new order of things. Our political machine is now pretty well wound up; but are the spirits of our people sufficiently wound down to let it work glibly? I trust it is too soon for that; and that we have many centuries to come yet before my countrymen cease to bear their government hard in hand. This nation is rising from the dust. They have obtained, as you know, provincial assemblies in which there will be a more perfect representation of the people than in our state assemblies; they have obtained from the king a declaration that he cannot impose a new tax without the consent of the states general, and a promise to call the states general. When these meet, they will endeavour to establish a declaration of rights, a periodical national assembly, and a civil list. I am in hopes that even a war will not interrupt this work. Whether, or rather when, this will come upon them, is still incertain. I do not think the present ill-humour between them and England can be cleared up but by a war, and that it is not very distant. England, Holland and Prussia have now settled their alliance. Sweden has shewn dispositions to take side with the Turks, and both, in the event of a general war, would be in the English scale. The contrary one would be formed by France, Spain, and the two empires. It even seems possible that Denmark will attach itself to France instead of England rather than not be opposed to Russia. The symptoms of this as yet however are slight. The victory lately obtained by our Admiral Paul Jones over the Captain Pacha will produce a great effect on the Turkish war. He burnt 6. of his vessels, among which was that of the Captn. Pacha and that also of his viceadmiral, took two, and made between 3 and 4000 prisoners: and this with a much inferior force. It was the effect of a gross error in the Captn. Pacha, instantaneously and dexterously taken advantage of by P. Jones, who hemmed them up in the Swash at the mouth of the Boristhenes, so that their vessels buried themselves in the mud, where they were burnt. The Captn. Pacha escaped in a small vessel. His flag fell into the hands of the Russians. Let me hear from you sometimes, assured I shall always be interested in your success. Present me in the most friendly terms to Mrs. Smith, and accept the best affections of Dear Sir your friend & servt.,

Th: Jefferson

P.S. Aug. 6. Later accounts of the actions between the Russians and Turks inform us that P. Jones commanded the right wing of the little fleet of gallies &c. in the first action which was not at all decisive, but that when the second and decisive action took place, which was still by the gallies &c. the Prince of Nassau alone commanded, P. Jones being absent with the ships of war which he commands.

PrC (DLC).

From Benjamin Vaughan

Dear sir Js. Square, London, Aug. 2, 1788.

I have been honored with your letter of the 23rd. ulto.

Mr. Rumsey has been informed of the result of the inquiries you have been pleased to make on his account, and will I presume, take the necessary measures speedily. By my advice, he has enlarged the description to attend one of his discoveries.

I had no design that Col. Smith should settle for the magnet box; consequently did not mention the thing to him; and as it is a trifle, I hope you will have the goodness to let it rest where it does.

Mr. Nairne says the whalebone hygrometer has its degrees fixed, by water on the one side and unslaked lime on the other. It stands a month and upwards with unslaked lime, in a box. He never saw it vary so much as you state, in his house in London.

I used to keep my fillet of wood *out* of its groove, except when I wanted to measure it; consequently its whole surface was equably acted upon.

From all that I have seen, it will be difficult to find wood, the several pieces of which shall have exactly corresponding sensibilities. Age, depth within the stem, *direction* of the fibres, and other circumstances, will be likely to produce variations. Hence I have always had in view to have the hygrometer, when formed of wood, returned to the country whence it was first sent. This forms a *proof* of the observations; which, as far as relates to the question depending between our part of Europe and the United states of America, are only requisite to determine generally, where the difference lies. The degrees of the more and the less, I fear, must be determined in some future period, when we find ourselves provided with better instruments.

I shall be much obliged for one of your hygrometers, when finished, which is certainly ingenious, and liable to no objection that I foresee, except what depends upon the ingredient used, viz wood.

The fact you mention about the clouds in a certain part of western Europe, in a considerable degree corresponds with what I should have supposed. I have turned over some hundred volumes of accounts, antient and modern, and have fully satisfied myself of the *inland and eastern* climates in middle latitudes in the great continents in the Northern hemisphere agreeing with each other, and differing from Western climates in the same situation. I may some day have the honor to present you with my remarks and extracts; by which you will find that more than one great man has dreamed, or copied the errors of dreamers, in the very face of the authorities on which they all pretended to rest; and in this list I shall include Gibbon, an Englishman, Hume, besides Du Bos, and others. I find it only necessary for one grave man to commit a mistake uncontradicted, to mislead men of learning for ages.

The invention you allude to respecting the air pump, was long ago used by Mr. Nairne, as Mr. Cavendish has confirmed to me; but Mr. Nairne says he laid it aside, finding the great object was not so much to free the receiver from air, as the barrel in which the piston moves. A Mr. Heurter has moved the lower valve in that barrel by a power distinct from the air in the receiver, and it is said with great advantage.

Neither Mr. Cavendish, Mr. Elliot, nor Mr. Nairne are acquainted with an odometer of the kind you mention. We have them fixed to the wheel or carriage, upon other corresponding constructions, and they are said to answer within 1 or even ¼℔ cent of true distances; the cost being from 7 to 10 guineas.

I have much pleasure in thinking that our mutual acquaintance Mr. Romilly will deliver this letter, as his worth, learning and ingenuity, are not often found equalled in this country, or indeed in any other. I have the honor to be with particular esteem, Dear sir, your respectful and faithful humble servt.

BENJ. VAUGHAN

RC (DLC); endorsed.

MR. ROMILLY (Samuel Romilly, 1757-1818) and TJ had met in London; on 15 Apr. 1786 both men dined at Brand Hollis' in company with John Adams, Dr. Richard Price, and others (Adams, *Works*, ed. C. F. Adams, Boston, 1851, III, 396). Romilly arrived in Paris on 9 Aug. 1788, bearing letters of introduction from friends, particularly Lord Lansdowne, and renewing old acquaintances—among "the most remarkable were the Duke de la Rochefoucauld, M. de Malesherbes, M. de Lafayette, the Abbé Morellet, Chamfort, Dupont de Nemours, Condorcet, Mallet du Pan, the Count de Sarsfield, Jefferson the American ambassador," &c. (Sir Samuel Romilly, *Memoirs*, London, 1890, I, 96). Romilly, a disciple of Beccaria, had a life-long interest in the reform of the criminal law. This, together with his standing among English liberals, his Huguenot ancestry, and his intellectual interests, makes it surprising that TJ carried on no correspondence with him.

From John Brown Cutting

SIR London 3d August 1788

I have not yet had the honor to receive that letter of the 24th which you mention in a subsequent one of July 28th. inclosed to Col. Trumbull. I am to thank you for the only satisfactory account of the naval victory on the black sea that has reach'd this Island. It affords me satisfaction to learn that Jones commanded:—tis but a few weeks since the english papers were filled with the most outrageous scurrility against him. He was called a cowardly renagado, rebel pirate, as destitute of naval skill to command as of every characteristic moral or mental that distinguishes a gentleman from the lowest scoundrel in creation. It was likewise mention'd with exultation that every english officer in the navy of the Empress had refused to serve under him and wou'd certainly resign if he were not remov'd; and finally that the Dey of Algiers had offered a reward for the american pirates head. These courteous epithets and desirable circumstances concerning Jones circulated from paper to paper, as every thing that tends to degrade the United States or tarnish the lustre of the fame of their sons is sure to do in England. Why every species of contumely and abuse against the citizens of america is so much relished here it is obvious to discern. Fashion guides the national palate and forms the appetite and the monarch with such adversaries to America as Hawksbury, Dundas and the whole race of Scotch ministers govern and give the political fashion.

There is such a rooted aversion to us grown up in the court that if we cou'd be smitten without the hazard of a general war, or a risk of shaking the present ministry from their places, hostilities wou'd be recommenced against the United States, if it were only to gratify the irascible feelings of the monarch. Happily for both countries perhaps insuperable obstacles at present forbid the renewal of a war the embers of which tho' they are covered are by no means extinguish'd. Yet I am told by very moderate politicians who are not anti-american [in] their theories, that if our new government form a navigation act and attempt to accellerate a commercial treaty with Britain by heavy impositions upon her shipping and manufactures, and at the same time demand an evacuation of the western posts, she will not endure our measures. At such opinions and semi-menaces I smile. Still I own in the present moment of british insolence and royal hatred, a fresh conflict with us may not be very distant.

All the british Islands in the west indias are immediately to be fortified. The board of ordinance are now sending out bricks and requisite materials for this purpose. They are likewise soon to be reinforced with fresh troops. Meanwhile the bustle in every naval department announces busy preparation for blows; but against whom I can only conjecture.

There has lately been a change in the board of Admiralty. Lord Howe has been forced out. His chief defect was the want of parliamentary interest. Mr. Pitt has appointed his brother the Earl of Chatham first Lord of the Admiralty, by which he may dictate to the navy and monopolize a patronage the most extensive and lucrative in the dextrous distribution of which consists the whole art of governing the english nation. Lord Hood is put in with Sir Peter Parker to perform the drudgery, Lords Baynham and Apsly and Arden, are many noble and friendly cyphers which the minister adds to make a board. Lord Hood by this appointment vacated his seat for Westminster. But immediately offered himself again as a candidate under the auspices of the treasury, from whence the expences of his re-election undoubtedly were to be, and have been hitherto discharg'd. Mr. Fox however who has vast personal influence in Westminster, and the prevailing weight also of the Dukes of Bedford, Devonshire and Portland, proposed Lord John Townsend as an antagonist to the ministerial candidate. The contest has been violent. Mr. Fox however calculated the cost of the election and knew the methods of electioneering far better than the ministerial people. He applied his popular and golden rhetoric with such superior skill that he will certainly defeat the minister and seat

Lord John in parliament. Never did I behold such a scene of violence uproar outrage and turpitude as this contested election has exhibited. The cost of the corruptions on both sides will not it is said exceed [o]ne hundred thousand pounds, unless a scrutiny is demanded by the [d]istanced competitor. The scene closes on monday next. The votes [f]or Lord John yesterday exceeded those [f]or Lord Hood, about 800 out [o]f 12,000.

The lesson I have just been taught in Westminster inclines me to beseech of you the application of a few leisure hours to the amelioration of the american modes of bestowing suffrages. So much with us depends upon popular election, that to improve and perfect the system is a work worthy the consideration of our own wisest patriots and legislators.

My late confinement having retarded me three or four weeks, I do not expect to be ready to embark till the last of August. I hope therefore in a few days to transmit you the ratification of Virginia, if not of New York. Meanwhile I have the honor to be with much respect and attachment Your Excellency's obliged And Most Obedt Servt JOHN BROWN CUTTING

P.S. Mr. Jarvis of New York, who will have the honor to present this letter is a modest worthy young man, whom I have promised to mention to you accordingly. Mr. Parker who is confined by illness proffers his best compliments to You.

RC (DLC).

To John Jay

SIR Paris Aug. 3. 1788[1]

My last letters to you were of the 4th. and 23d. of May, with a postscript of the 27th. Since that I have been honoured with yours of Apr. 24. May 16. and June 9.

The most remarkeable internal occurrences since my last are these. The Noblesse of Bretagne, who had received with so much warmth the late innovations in the government, assembled and drew up a memorial to the king and chose 12. members of their body to come and present it. Among these were the Marquis de la Rouerie (Colo. Armand.) The king considering the Noblesse as having no legal right to assemble, declined receiving the memorial. The deputies, to give greater weight to it, called a meeting of the landed proprietors of Bretagne, resident at Paris, and proposed to them to add their signatures. They did so, to the number of about 60. of whom the Marquis de la Fayette was one. The 12. deputies, for having called this meeting were immediately sent to the Bastille, where they now are, and the Parisian signers were deprived of such favors as they held of the court. There were only four of them however who held any thing of that kind. The Marquis de la Fayette was one of these. They had given him a military command to be exercised in the South of France during the months of Aug. and September of the present year. This they took from him; so that he is disgraced in the antient language of the court, but, in truth, honourably marked in the eyes of the nation. The ministers are so sensible of this that they have had separately private conferences with him, to endeavour thro' him to keep things quiet. From the character of the province of Bretagne it was much apprehended for some days that the imprisonment of their deputies would have produced an insurrection. But it took another turn. The Cours intermediaires of the Province, acknowledged to be a legal body, deputed 18. members of their body to the king. To these he gave an audience, and the answer, of which I send you a copy. This is hard enough. Yet I am in hopes the appeal to the sword will be avoided, and great modifications in the government be obtained, without bloodshed. As yet none has been spilt, according to the best evidence I have been able to obtain, notwithstanding what the foreign newspapers have said to the contrary. The convocation of the States general is now become inevitable. Whenever the time shall be announced certainly, it will keep the nation quiet till they meet. According to present probabilities this must be in the course of the next summer. But to what movements their meeting and measures may give occasion cannot be foreseen. Should a foreign war take place, still they must assemble the States-general, because they cannot, but by their aid, obtain money to carry it on. Monsieur de Malesherbe will I believe retire from the king's council. He has been much opposed to the late acts of authority. The Baron de Breteuil has resigned his secretaryship of the domestic department. Certainly not for the same reasons, as he is known to have been of opinion that the king had compromitted too much of his authority. The real reason has probably been an impatience of acting under a principal minister. His successor is M. de Villedeuil, lately Comptroller general. The Ambassadors of Tippoo-Saïb are arrived here. If their mission has any other object than that of pomp and ceremony, it is not yet made known, tho' this court has not avowed that they are in possession of Trincomale, yet the report is believed, and that possession was taken by general Conway in consequence of orders given in the moment that they thought a war certain. The dispute with the States general of the United Netherlands on account of the insult to M. de St. Priest, does not tend as yet towards a settlement. He has obtained leave to go to the waters, and perhaps, from thence he may come to Paris to await events. Sweden has commenced hostilities against Russia by the taking a little fortress by land. This having been their intention, it is wonderful that when their fleet lately met three Russian ships of 100 guns each, they saluted, instead of taking them. The Empress has declared war against them in her turn. It is well understood that Sweden is set on by England and paid by Turkey. The prospect of Russia has much brightened by some late successes. Their fleet of gallies and gunboats, 27. in number having been attacked by 57. Turkish vessels of the same kind commanded by the Captain Pacha, these were repulsed with the loss of three vessels. In this action, which was on the 18th. of June, Admiral Paul Jones commanded the right wing of the Russians, and the prince of Nassau the left. On the 26th. of the same month, the Turkish principal fleet, that is to say their ships of the line, frigates &c. having got themselves near the swash at the mouth of the Boristhenes, the prince of Nassau took advantage of their position, attacked them, while so engaged in the mud that they could not manoeuvre, burnt six, among which was the Admiral's and Viceadmiral's, took two, and made between 3. and 4000 prisoners. The first reports gave this success to Admiral Paul Jones; but it is now rendered rather probable that he was not there, as he commands the vessels of war, which are said not to have been there. It is supposed his presence in the affair of the 18th. was accidental. But if this success has been as compleat as it is represented, the Black sea must be tolerably open to the Russians: in which case we may expect, from what we know of that officer, that he will improve to the greatest advantage the situation of things on that sea. The Captain Pacha's standard was taken in the last action, and himself obliged to make his escape in a small vessel. Prince Potemkin immediately got under march for Oczakow, to take advantage of the consternation into which that place was thrown.

The Spanish squadron, after cruising off the Western isles and cape St. Vincent, is returned into port.

A dispute has arisen between the Papal see and the king of Naples which may in it's progress enable us to estimate what degree of influence that see retains at the present day. The kingdom of Naples, at an early period of it's history, became feudatory to the see of Rome, and in acknolegement thereof has annually paid a hackney to the Pope in Rome, to which place it has been always sent by a splendid embassy. The hackney has been refused by the king this year, and the Pope, giving him three months to return to obedience, threatens, if he does not, to proceed seriously against him.

About three weeks ago a person called on me, and informed me that Silas Deane had taken him in for a sum of 120 guineas, and that, being unable to obtain any other satisfaction, he had laid hands on his account book, and letter book, and had brought them off to Paris, to offer them first to the United States, if they would repay him his money, and, if not, that he should return to London and offer them to the British minister. I desired him to leave them with me four and twenty hours that I might judge whether they were worth our notice. He did so. They were two volumes. One contained all his accounts with the U.S. from his first coming to Europe, to Jan. 10. 1781. Presuming that the Treasury board was in possession of this account till his arrival in Philadelphia Aug. 1778. and that he had never given in the subsequent part, I had that subsequent part copied from the book, and now inclose it, as it may on some occasion or other perhaps, be useful in the Treasury office. The other volume contained all his correspondencies from Mar. 30. to Aug. 23. 1777. I had a list of the letters taken, by their dates and addresses, which will enable you to form a general idea of the collection. On perusal of many of them I thought it desireable that they should not come to the hands of the British minister, and from an expression dropped by the possessor of them, I believe he would have fallen to 50. or 60. guineas. I did not think them important enough however to justify my purchasing them without authority; though, with authority, I should have done it. Indeed I would have given that sum to cut out a single sentence which contained evidence of a fact not proper to be committed to the hands of enemies. I told him I would state his proposition to you and await orders. I gave him back the books, and he returned to London without making any promise that he would await the event of the orders you might think proper to give.

News of the accession of nine states to the new form of federal government has been received here about a week. I have the honour to congratulate you sincerely on this event. Of it's effect at home you are in the best situation to judge. On this side the Atlantic it is considered as a very wise reformation. In consequence of this, speculations are already begun here to purchase up our domestic liquidated debt. Indeed I suspect that orders may have been previously lodged in America to do this as soon as the new constitution was accepted effectually. If it is thought that this debt should be retained at home, there is not a moment to lose; and I know of no means of retaining it but those I suggested to the Treasury board in my letter to them of March 29. The transfer of these debts to Europe will excessively embarrass, and perhaps totally prevent, the borrowing any money in Europe till these shall be paid off. This is a momentous object, and in my opinion should receive instantaneous attention. The gazettes of France to the departure of my letter will accompany it, and those of Leyden to the 22d. of July, at which time their distribution in this country was prohibited. How long the prohibition may continue I cannot tell. As far as I can judge it is the only paper in Europe worth reading. Since the suppression of the packet boats, I have never been able to find a safe conveiance for a letter to you, till the present by Mrs. Barclay. Whenever a confidential person shall be going from hence to London I shall send my letters for you to the care of Mr. Trumbul, who will look out for safe conveiances. This will render the epochs of my writing very irregular. There is a proposition under consideration for establishing packet boats on a more economical plan from Havre to Boston. But it's success is incertain, and still more it's duration. I have the honour to be with sentiments of the most perfect esteem & respect, Sir your most obedient & most humble servant, TH: JEFFERSON

RC (DNA: PCC, No. 87, II). PrC (DLC). Enclosures: (1) "Response du Roi aux Deputés et Commissaires des Etats de Brétagne," declaring that the twelve deputies represented an authorized assembly, not having previously procured permission; that they had themselves convened an irregular assembly in Paris; that the means of meriting the royal clemency was not that of continuing in Brittany through illegal assemblies the cause of his discontent; that these personal punishments, which good order and the maintenance of royal authority required, did not alter the king's affection for the province; that the estates of Brittany would be assembled in October; and that the delegates were required the next day to return to their duty (Tr in French, in Short's hand in DNA: PCC, No. 87, II, accompanied by newspaper clipping of English translation). (2) "Extract from Silas Deane's Account against Congress," 1779-Jan. 1781, totalling (for the period extracted, exclusive of £186, 518 2s. 10d. brought forward) £78,046 6s. 4d. and including such general and vaguely identified items as "sundries (advanced to several officers) [£]20,000," and such details as the item of £16 "for painting coach-Wheels Novr. 1777" (Tr in Short's hand, same; PrC in DLC). This and a translation of enclosure (1) are printed in *Dipl. Corr., 1783-89*, II, 178-80. (3) "List of the letters of Silas Deane contained in his letter-book," totalling 165 entries for the period 30 Mch. 1777—23 Aug. 1777 (Tr in Short's hand, DNA: PCC, No. 87, II; PrC in DLC).

In addition to the foregoing enclosures that TJ secretly caused to be copied for transmittal to Jay, there is in DLC: TJ Papers, 17: 2968-9, another extract in his own hand which takes on significance in the light of TJ's letters to Jay and Madison about his own expenses for an outfit (see under 15 and 25 May 1788). This is in three parts, the first of which is a series of "Extracts from Silas Deane's Daybook" reading as follows:

"1777. May. 27. Dr. Franklin, a month of coach & horses 360tt
Aug. 14. Dr. Fr. & S. Deane, hire of coach & horses. 2448.tt
1778. March. 30 Arthur Lee's expenditures of 22,519tt-5-6 &c.
viz. 1777. June 16. An Atlas or set of draughts of N. America. 120.tt
July 10. a watch, repeater 900.tt
Sep. 9. A chariot, harness &c. 2592tt
26. A bill of lodgings 1500.tt
Oct. 13. pd. his coachman 38.tt
20. 80. bottles Champaigne 203tt-10
24. A bill of linen. 1120-7-9
Nov. 4. A bill of plate 1903tt-13-9
12. A bill of china ware. 1598-11
&c. &c. &c.
S. Deane, vix. 1777.
May 10. a bill of plate 1880tt-12-3
16. a bill of linen 1127-17-9
26. servants wages 66tt
June 6. a bill of the coachmaker 3596.tt
21. hire of coach horses & food of saddle horse 374.tt
Aug. 5. hire & food of horses 361.tt
Sep. 27. do. 600.tt
Oct. 18. six months lodgings 3600.tt
Nov. 18. bill of china ware 1075tt-6
a table 78.tt
a bill of linen 243tt-5-6
July 3. Silas Deane. 6 months lodging 3600.tt
16. Silas Deane credits 2000.tt produce of his coach sold on departure
Silas Deane in his account against Congress charges
1776. July 20. a watch & chain 552tt
1777. July 7. 2 horses 1200tt
1778. Jan. 16. new wheels for coach 169tt-10
25. hire of remise horses 390.tt
Feb. 11. hire of voiture to Dunkirk 215.tt
Apr. 1. hire of furniture 1555.tt-14
'set out from Paris with Capt. Ale Johnson, Nicholson & E. Johnson & my servt. with 2 coaches & a baggage wagon (7 in company)'
One years hire of the house Place Louis XV 7200.tt 'To my salary from Nov. 1776. the time of receiving my commission to June 1778. being one year and 7. months at 11428.tt per annum per resolution of Congress 18,094tt-6-8.' "

The second part of this memorandum is headed: "Silas Deane's 'Journal of cash'" and reads:

"pa. 1.-45.
1st. part begins 1776. Dec. 7. ends 1779. May 19.
2nd part entitled 'Accounts of sundry persons against the Commissioners of the U.S. charged by them to Congress.' pa. 49.-60.
The articles are not dated generally. Those which are, are of 1777. and 1778.
3d. part. entitled 'Congress Dr. to Silas Deane.' Contains his account with Congress from June 1776. to Jany. 10. 1781. It contains the articles of debet only, no credits. Pa. 63-88.
4th. part. entitled 'a continuation of Mr. Grand's account.' Contains 12 pages not numbered. Contains debtor & Credit from 1779. Feb. 11. to 1780. Aug. 16. Makes balance due Grand, 584,074tt-10"

The third part of the memorandum is from Deane's letter book and consists of only one sentence—undoubtedly the SINGLE SENTENCE WHICH CONTAINED EVIDENCE OF A FACT NOT PROPER TO BE COMMITTED TO THE HANDS OF THE ENEMIES. This extract reads: "1777. Apr. 11. Robt. Morris. 'The affair of

John the Painter who came nigh finishing the whole affair at one blow' and his known attachment to America as well as correspondence with Dr. Franklin and my self obliges him to fly and take refuge with me here." It is curious that this evidence should have been so disturbing to TJ, since the English courts had already been sufficiently aware of John the Painter's attachment to the American interest to cause him to be hanged for the incendiary acts he committed in behalf of the United States (see William Bell Clark, "John the Painter," PMHB, LXIII [1939], 1-23). The PERSON who possessed these manuscripts was Foulloy; see TJ to Foulloy, 4 July 1788.

[1] Altered by overwriting from "July 31. 1788."

To James Madison

DEAR SIR — Paris Aug. 4. 1788.

The bearer hereof, Mr. Dobbyns, a native of Ireland, having it in contemplation to dispose of his estate in that country, and to remove with his tenants to America, I have advised him, before he carries the measure into entire execution, to go thither himself, to fix on the part of the country which from climate, soil, and other circumstances would best suit his views, and even to provide a place for the reception of his people on their arrival. His views have at different times, and under different considerations, been attracted by the Chesapeak, the Patowmack, the Ohio, and the Mohocks river. As there is always a possibility that a stranger may fall into the hands of land-jobbers and other sharpers, I take the liberty of asking for him your friendly counsel, and your recommendations of him to good men in whatever quarter he may chuse to visit for the purpose of purchasing, as well as your notice and civilities on every occasion. He comes well recommended to me from a friend in London, and the short acquaintance I have had the honour of having with him here has justified that recommendation. I am with sentiments of the most perfect esteem Dear Sir your affectionate friend and servant, TH: JEFFERSON

RC (DLC: Madison Papers); endorsed; addressed: "The honourable James Madison of the Virginia delegation in Congress. Favored by Mr. Dobbyns." PrC (DLC).

To Parmentier

a Paris ce 4[1] me. Aout 1788.

En vous avertissant, Monsieur, que j'ai deja reçu opposition au paiement du loyers de M. le comte de Langeac jusqu'à la concurrence d'environ vingt mille francs, je consente de recevoir, sous cachet, celle de votre client, le Sieur Bernard Kardt. N'etant pas dans le cas de decider sur l'effet de ces oppositions, je me propose de demander à son excellence Monsieur le comte de Monmorin la permission de deposer les loyers à mesure qu'ils échoient dans tels mains qu'il aura la bonté de m'indiquer, àfin que je pourrois etre debarrassé de toute reclamation. J'ai l'honneur d'etre Monsieur votre tres humble et tres obeissant serviteur,

TH: JEFFERSON

PrC (MHi); at foot of text: "Monsr. Parmentier, procureur au Chatelet. rue Serpente No. 6."

This letter is evidently a reply to Parmentier's (missing) letter of ca. 4 Aug.; Parmentier's response to it of 6 Aug. 1788 is also missing. Both are recorded in SJL Index. See TJ to De Langeac, 12 Oct. 1786.

1 Date partly obliterated; supplied from SJL Index.

To Peter Carr

DEAR PETER Paris Aug. 6. 1788.

The preceding letter was written at it's date, and I supposed you in possession of it when your letters of Dec. 10. 87. and March 18. 88. told me otherwise. Still I supposed it on it's way to you, when a few days ago, having occasion to look among some papers in the drawer where my letters are usually put away till an opportunity of sending them occurs, I found that this letter had slipped among them, so that it had never been forwarded. I am sorry for it on account of the article relative to the Spanish language only. Apply to that with all the assiduity you can. That language and the English, covering nearly the whole face of America, they should be well known to every inhabitant who means to look beyond the limits of his farm. I like well the distribution of your time mentioned in your letter of Mar. 18. and the counsels of Mr. Wythe so kindly extended to you, leave it necessary for me to add nothing of that kind. Be assiduous in learning, take much exercise for your health and practise much virtue. Health, learning and virtue will ensure your happiness; they will give you a quiet conscience, private esteem and public honour. Beyond these we want nothing but physical necessaries, and they are easily obtained. My daughters are well and join me in love to yourself, your Mother, brothers and sisters. I am with very sincere esteem Dear Peter your affectionate friend, TH: JEFFERSON

P.S. Present me affectionately to Mr. Wythe.

RC (ViU); postscript (written in margin) was added after the execution of, and does not appear in, PrC (DLC).

The PRECEDING LETTER to Peter Carr, which was enclosed in the present letter, was that of 10 Aug. 1787. A note to that letter states, erroneously, that it was forwarded in TJ to Peter Carr, 28 May 1788, whereas it now appears that, though such a letter is printed in TJR, II, 325-6, no other text is known and that, with minor variations in phraseology, the text printed by TJR is the text of the present letter. SJL Index has no record of a letter from TJ to Carr of 28 May 1788. In view of these facts, it is clear that TJR erred in thinking there was one and that, in making use of the PrC of the present text, he somehow affixed an erroneous date to it.

To John Brown Cutting

DEAR SIR Paris Aug. 6. 1788.

Truth, holy Truth, obliges me to correct still the intelligence I gave you in my last. Notwithstanding the authenticity with which it seemed to come, there was error respecting the commanders. The 1st. action between the Russians and Turks was of the gallies and flat vessels of both sides. The command of these on the part of the Russians is in the prince of Nassau. But P. Jones having been present in the first action, had the command of the right wing. The Turks were repulsed. The 2d. was the great action, and was of the Russian gallies against the Turkish ships of war. The effects were what my letters mentioned to you. But the Prince of Nassau alone commanded, P. Jones, who commands the vessels of war, being at that time absent with his fleet.—The Swedes have commenced hostilities by land against the Russians, and war is consequently declared against them by the Empress. I am with great & sincere esteem Dr. Sir your most obedt. humble servt,

TH: JEFFERSON

P.S. I have had the intelligence you were so good as to communicate to me respecting the reception of Mr. Adams, inserted in a gazette here, and sent it to that of Leyden also.

RC (MHi: AMT); addressed: "Mr. John Brown Cutting No. 2 North street Rathbone place London"; postmarked "AU 14" and "PAYE PARIS." PrC (DLC).
For TJ's instrumentality in publishing the INTELLIGENCE . . . RESPECTING THE RECEPTION OF MR. ADAMS, see note to TJ to Dumas, 30 July 1788.

From André Limozin

Le Havre, 6 Aug. 1788. Acknowledges TJ's of 25 and 30 July, and will apply for consular appointment at Le Havre. "The bust of Marquis Fayette is still here for want of ships opportunities for Virgina since it came to hand. The Irish beef is much beter cured than that which comes from Hambro, which will not keep long in warm Climates, for want of knowledge how to salt it and how to cure it. They have the most stupid and obstinate method notwithstanding my observations to imploy Lunebourg's Salt, which is white but very weak and the Holstein's Beef being full of Blood the Pickle made with that Salt is soon Spoiled." TJ's articles from Amsterdam left this day "Plombed with acquit a Caution by a Wagon," to be delivered at the douane of Paris and the duty to be paid there; has been informed this date by Holland that Swedish army has begun hostilities in Finland. "Our Government hath it seems sent orders to Bordeaux to purchase all the good Foreign Hemp which was there. Your cask Smoaked Beef is forwarded to you likewise by Wagon along with your articles arrived from Amsterdam."

RC (MHi); 5 p.; endorsed; addressed; postmarked: "HAVRE."

To John Paradise, with Enclosure

DEAR SIR Paris Aug. 6. 1788.

I have sketched a power of attorney for you, which is almost the exact copy of the one I executed in my own case when I left America. Be so good as to make in it what alterations you would chuse. With respect to the money in the funds, you know best to whom you should give the order for paying 130£ of it to the order of Mrs. Paradise, and the remaining £35. to yourself. You should I think furnish Colo. Burwell with a list of your creditors, their habitations and the amount of their demand, and explain to him the motives of your wishing that Dr. Bancroft and Mr. Anderson should still be the persons to receive his remittances in tobacco and money and pay the same to the creditors. To these two gentlemen, and to your steward you will of course give such explanations as may shew them that these arrangements have been taken in full expectation that they will continue to co-operate with Colo. Burwell for your final liberation from debt. It should be mentioned to them as well as to Colo. Burwell for the satisfaction of the creditors, that Norton's debt, that of the state of Virginia, and the cutting and sale of your wood in Virginia are to be applied with all the dispatch possible to the general objects of the power of attorney. When you shall have corrected that instrument I will write it out fairly. I am with great esteem Dr. Sir your friend & servt.,

TH: JEFFERSON

ENCLOSURE

Know all men by these presents that I John Paradise of James city county in the commonwealth of Virginia, but now at Paris in the Kingdom of France, do by these presents constitute and appoint Nathaniel Burwell esq. of Carter's grove in the same county and commonwealth my lawful attorney, for all my property in the said commonwealth, real and personal, in possession and in action, giving to him full power for me and on my behalf to superintend and direct the management of my said property, to sell or otherwise dispose of all parts thereof which I could myself sell or dispose of, to receive and apply as shall be hereinafter directed the proceeds of such sales to purchase and take conveyances for me of property of all kinds, to prosecute and defend all actions and suits in which I may be concerned in my own or any other right, to employ such persons for the transaction of my business as he may think proper to settle with them and all others all matters of account now existing or which may hereafter exist between them and me, giving to whatsoever he shall do in the premises the same force and validity as if done by myself: And I do further declare that the true intent[1] of these presents is that the said Nathaniel Burwell shall out of the profits and proceeds of the said estates in possession and action pay to Edward Bancroft and William Anderson in the city of London and kingdom of England or to such other person or persons as I shall appoint by letter or other writing signed by myself the sum of 240£ sterling annually, in quarterly paiments to be made in the said city of London on the 1st. day of Jan. Apr. July. and Oct. in every year, commencing on the 1st. day of January next, which said sum is for the maintenance and support of my wife and myself, and is to be paid in preference to all other demands whatsoever: and that he shall pay all other the profits and proceeds of my said estates in possession and action as they shall come to his hands for the discharge of my debts contracted before the day of my departure from England in the last year[2] together with lawful interest taking thereon with my creditors such arrangements as he shall think best, and the surplus after the said debts shall be satisfied, to pay or apply as I shall direct from time to time: these presents to remain in full force during the whole time of my absence from the said commonwealth of Virginia unless sooner revoked by deed indented, executed by myself, attested and authenticated according to the forms prescribed by the laws of the said Commonwealth of Virginia for deeds executed in foreign countries, and not otherwise. In Witness whereof I have hereunto subscribed my name and affixed my seal at Paris aforesaid this——day of August 1788.

PrC (DLC). Dft of Enclosure (DLC); with a number of deletions and interlineations, some of which may have been made after consultation with Paradise, but all of which are in TJ's hand, as is Dft.

[1] At this point TJ deleted: "and only limitation."

[2] At first this passage read: ". . . before this date in the kingdom of England" and then was altered to read as above.

From Mary Barclay

SIR St. Germain-en-Laye 7 august 1788

My wishes to meet my friends in America has made me too hastily fix the time of my departure and I begin to fear it will be impossible to leave this next sunday and indeed am inclined to think, that even in case I can, it would be better perhaps to give up the thoughts of going by Bordeaux, which will be attended with much more difficulty and expence than I had any idea of, besides the inconvenience of sending most of my things another way; but before giving up my first plan intirely, should be exceedingly obliged to you if you will be so good as to inform me how long the vessel may probabily be in coming round to Havre as Mr. Barclay has order'd her to do, if she could be there for the last of the month I should not give her the least delay, and suppose it might be time enough to arrive at Philadelphia before the bad weather sets in. Your sentiments on this matter, as soon as you can with convenience, will much oblige me, and help to determine me in what manner to proceed, in which I am greatly at a loss. Pardon my good sir the liberty I take in troubling you so often about my affairs and believe me to be with the highest esteem and respect Your most obedient humble servant M. BARCLAY

RC (MHi). Recorded in SJL as dated 8 Aug. 1788, which was not the date of writing, but the date of receipt.

From C. W. F. Dumas

MONSIEUR Lahaie 7e. Août 1788

En réponse aux 3 honorées vôtres du 30 et 31 du passé, j'ai écrit à Mr. Luzac, pour qu'il expédie sans faute dès demain, selon les ordres de Votre Excellence, et à l'adresse indiquée, de Mr. le Comte Diodati, 2 Exemplaires de sa Gazette et Supplément, à commencer par les feuilles du 25 Juillet et suivantes, que je dois supposer vous manquer, et la suite chaque jour de Poste, jusqu'à la levée de l'Interdit.

J'ai envoyé au même ami l'Article qu'il s'agit d'insérer. Ce sera, quant à l'accession de N. Hampshire et aux bonnes dispositions de la Virginie, une répétition bien agréable de ce que j'avois fait insérer dans son Supplément LXII du 1er. Août, et, quant à Mr. Adams, un régal à tous ceux qui s'intéressent à sa relation officielle et personnelle avec ce pays. Je ne puis vous en promettre autant de la part des Anglois et de leurs Partisans; mais je pense, Monsieur, que vous vous en consolerez hautement; comme moi in petto ici, où les Etats-Unis ne sont pas plus aimés que leur serviteur, à qui les griffes, pierres, massues et canaux, dont on dispose à plaisir, en imposent.

V.E. aura déjà appris le combat naval qui a eu lieu le 17 Juillet entre les Suédois et les Russes. La Victoire que les premiers s'attribuent, quoique moins signalée que celle de Kinburn, lui servira peut-être de contrepoids, surtout s'il est vrai, comme on le débite, qu'une autre Puissance deça la Baltique va fortifier la diversion par 60 m[ille] h[ommes]. Mais dans ce cas la paix avec les Turcs devient probable, et la Guerre ailleurs.—Je pense comme V.E. que cela ne peut guere manquer; et par conséquent j'embrasse avec joie l'espoir que me fait concevoir la Ligne de bonne augure où V.E. m'apprend, que les affaires internes de notre Alliée ont l'air de s'arranger paisiblement; car sa considération et son influence externe en ont grand besoin.

Nous allons allumer les bougies pour illuminer l'anniversaire de Madame la Princesse. La poudre prodiguée depuis l'aube de ce jour eût suffi à notre Paul Jones à prendre Constantinople. J'en ai la tête fêlée. De Votre Excellence le très respectueux très obeissant & humble serviteur, C W F DUMAS

RC (DLC); endorsed. FC (Dumas Letter Book, Rijksarchief, The Hague; photostats in DLC).

From Antoine Terrasson

MONSIEUR amsterdam 7e. aoust 1788.

J'ai eu bien des regrets de partir de Paris sans pouvoir prendre vos ordres pour La Hollande, par Le Desavantage que J'ai eu de passer deux fois à votre hotel sans vous y rencontrer. Quelques mots de votre part pour vos amis en cette ville eussent été d'un grand poids aux Demarches que Je fais pour L'Entreprise du Canal dans la Caroline du Sud à laquelle je ne renonce pas.

Permettés moi d'avoir recours à vous Monsieur pour Les deux cahiers des actes de La Legislature de L'Etat de La Caroline du Sud de 86 et 87 que vous avés eu la complaisance de me preter pendant mon séjour à Paris. Comme ils me sont très essentiels pour mes affaires ici et qu'ils sont introuvables en cette ville vous m'obligerés beaucoup de les remettre à M. Jb. van Staphorst qui voudra bien se charger de me Les faire parvenir. J'aurai Le plus grand soin de vous Les raporter moimême à Paris ou de vous les renvoyer par une occasion sure. Si les actes de la presente année 88 et le complément de la collection des precedents vous etoient parvenus ce seroit un très grand service que vous me rendriés de les y joindre.

J'ai L'honneur D'etre avec un profond respect Monsieur Votre très humble & très obeissant Serviteur A. TERRASSON

RC (MoSHi); endorsed.

It was probably during one of Terrasson's visits to Hôtel de Langeac, but when TJ was present, that Terrasson left with TJ a copy of an agreement between himself and Veuve Leleu & Cie. (Tr in MoSHi, endorsed by TJ). This agreement, dated 9 June 1788, was one that deeply engaged TJ's interest—that of supplying Carolina rice "de belle et bonne Qualité" at different ports of France. The terms of the contract obligated Veuve Leleu & Cie. to advance 16tt or 13s. 4d. sterling per quintal up to 55,000 quintals per year; to accept consignments by Terrasson at his risk; to allow him to draw on them either in France or at London at sixty days, paying 5% interest on advances and allowing 4% to Veuve Leleu & Cie. of the amount of sales; and to carry out the enterprise with the same zeal as if the speculation were their own. The contract, executed in triplicate, was to run for four years and not to be broken by either party, though, on a four months' notice made "en presence de son Excellence Monsieur Jefferson Ministre Plenipotentiaire," &c., it could be altered at the request of Terrasson or of Veuve Leleu & Cie.

From Madame de Tessé, with Enclosure

a chaville ce 7 aoust

Monsieur jefferson aiant eu la bonté de faire connoître à Me. de Tessé que ce moment cy etoit convenable pour demander des plans et des graines de virginie, elle prend la liberté de lui adresser une petite notte de ce quelle désire plus particulièrement et plus abondamment. Elle y ajoute quelque chose pour la caroline dans le cas ou Monsieur jefferson se trouveroit devoir écrire à charles-Town, et souhaiteroit bien qu'il s'adressat aux correspondans de Mr. Short bien preferables a ceux quil employe en ce qu'on Reçoit leurs memoires. La Reine n'aiant point voulu dispenser Me. de Tessé de l'audience des ambassadeurs indiens, elle est aujourd'huy dans une consternation qui ne lui laisse que la force d'assurer Monsieur jefferson de son sincere attachement.

ENCLOSURE

PLANTS DE VIRGINIE

Quercus rubra maxima.
Quercus rubra ramosissima.
Quercus rubra nana.
Quercus Phellos, of all sorts.
Fagus castanea pumila, *dit* chinquepin.

Stewartia Malacodendron. Cet Arbuste d'une grande beauté, ne croit qu'en Virginie et dans le Maryland. Il est très rare, même en Angleterre, et les marchands de Philadelphie n'en mettent qu'une ou deux graines dans leurs assortimens.

GRAINES DE VIRGINIE

Pinus Palustris.
Cupressus Disticha.
Liriodendron Tulipifera.
Diospyros.

PLANTS DE CAROLINE

Populus cordi folia.	*Populus heterophylla Linn.*
Pinus Palustris.	*Pinus Picea Linn.*
Annona glabra.	*Papaw of Virginia*
Andromeda arborea.	
Andromeda plumata. *9*	
Laurus nova. *9*	
Laurus estivalis.	
Callicarpa Americana.	

Syderoxilon. *Not in Virginia and query if in America.*
gardenia *or Fothergilla. This grows in Florida only.*

RC (DLC); the fact that this letter belongs to 1788 is proved by internal evidence (the reference to L'AUDIENCE DES AMBASSADEURS INDIENS) and by an entry in SJL Index. See TJ to Jay, 3 Aug., and to Banister and Moustier, both of 9 Aug. 1788. Enclosure (DLC); in clerk's hand, with some notations added by TJ (indicated here by use of italics) and the word "gardenia" in the final line added by Madame de Tessé.

Two of the items listed by Madame de Tessé were unknown to TJ. For his rearrangement of her list and comment on it, see enclosure in TJ to Banister, 9 Aug. 1788. He did not even list SYDEROXILON and he appears to have deleted GARDENIA in his order to Banister, probably for the reasons here given.

From Nicolas & Jacob van Staphorst

Amsterdam, *7 Aug.*[1] *1788*. Van Damme handed them TJ's favor of 25th July, and they paid to him TJ's draft on them of ƒ148.11. Holland currency, which they charged to his private account. The ship carrying TJ's stoves has long since arrived at Le Havre. "Mr. David Morell has received a Letter from Bordeaux, advising the Convention for Virginia, had postponed deciding upon the New Federal Government until a future day. This News was quite unexpected, as all our late Advices mentioned its Adoption by that State as certain." Will be glad to learn from TJ the "Motives of this postponement. When the Convention will meet again? and What is the general Opinion the Ultimate decision will be?"

RC (DLC); endorsed; in clerk's hand; signed by the firm.

[1] MS is dated "7 April 1788," and underneath this TJ wrote: "Should be 7 August." It was under the latter date that he recorded it in SJL Index.

From De Vernon

ce 7 aout 1788

M. De Vernon, Directeur des fermes, hotel de longueville, ruë St. Thomas du louvre, a l'honneur de renouveller à Monsieur Jeffersonn, l'homage de tous ses devoirs et de sa reconnoissance, et de le prier de vouloir bien lui faire le plaisir de lui marquer s'il a quelques nouvelles de M. Bannister, son Correspondant, qui avoit bien voulu se charger de notre procuration pour poursuivre M. Mark neveu, notre ancien agent en amerique et détempteur de nos fonds.

RC (DLC).

To Mary Barclay

DEAR MADAM Paris Aug. 8. half after ten in the morning

I have this moment received your favour of yesterday, and in answer thereto have the honour to observe to you that if you set out for Havre[1] on Sunday next, you may be at sea the Sunday following, and counting on a voiage of 35. days, which is enough for the season, you will be in the Delaware by the 20th. of September, which is 5. days before the equinox. If the vessel comes to Havre, the time necessary for your letter to go to Bordeaux, for the vessel to put to sea, to come round to Havre, to get to sea again and be out of the British channel, will make you about 3. weeks later in getting clear of the coast of Europe; but will retard you more than that in your arrival in America as you will be out during the whole Equinox, and may be exposed during that to contrary winds. This as to time. With respect to expence, that of the vessel's coming to Havre must greatly overweigh your expences to Bordeaux. Should these exceed the provision Mr. Barclay has made for you, you shall not be retarded for the want of any sum I can furnish you with. Perhaps the matters you cannot finish by Sunday, could be finished for you by some friend at St. Germains. But of all these circumstances you alone can best judge.

I had written thus far when Mr. Swan comes to see me. He sais that the additional time, risk, and expence of the vessel coming from Bordeaux to Havre will be equal nearly to her going from Bordeaux to America: and besides that as, in expectation of going directly from Bordeaux to America, she has probably taken in a cargo, she will be no longer at liberty to come to Havre, as the freighters would never consent to it, their insurance being already made for the direct voiage. They would lose their first insurance money, have a heavier insurance to pay, and their goods would lose a month in the time of their arrival, so that Mr. Swan, judging as a merchant, supposes this measure now impossible; or that if the vessel was to come in defiance of the will of the freighters, it might subject Mr. Barclay to very considerable risks and damages. Of these things, Madam, I know nothing, therefore only repeat them from the information of another much better acquainted with them.

Should you come to Paris on Sunday I shall hope you will do me the favor to call, tho Mr. Short tells me you cannot be here to dinner. I shall myself go to Versailles that day to see the reception of Tippoo-Saïb's ambassadors, but I will be back by 5. or 6. oclock in the evening.

I have the honor to be with sentiments of the most perfect esteem & respect, Dear Madam, your most obedt. humble servt.,

TH: JEFFERSON

PrC (MHi); endorsed. Recorded in SJL Index as dated 7 Aug. 1788.

[1] Thus in MS. TJ clearly meant Bordeaux, for he was endeavoring to persuade Mrs. Barclay to depart from that port, where in the summer of 1787 her husband had been arrested (see Vol. 11: 493-500, 537). See note to Bondfield to TJ, 9 Aug. 1788.

From Cambray

Au Chateau de Villers aux Erables
par Montdidier 8 Aout 1788

Mon Notaire, Monsieur, doit vous adresser un acte double de serment et procuration destiné pour l'Amerique. J'ay l'honneur de Vous prier de vouloir bien y ajouter votre Legalisation. Il a été fait pardevant Notaire. Il a été légalisé par le Lieutenant Général du Bailliage dans lequel je fais ma demeure. Je l'avois envoyé au Prevost des Marchands pour le légaliser, qui a repondu qu'il ne pouvoit legaliser que ce qui est fait dans la Generalité de Paris. Je crois avoir rempli les formalités necessaires.

Je regrette infiniment de n'être pas à Paris pour profiter de cette Circonstance pour Vous rendre mes devoirs et Vous remercier de la lettre obligeante que Vous m'avés fait l'honneur de m'ecrire il y a quelque tems. J'attends avec impatience le moment où je pourray m'en dedommager.

Agrées, je Vous prie, les sentiments de l'inviolable attachement que je Vous ay voué et avec lequel j'ay l'honneur d'être, Monsieur, Votre tres humble et tres obeissant Serviteur

LE CTE. DE CAMBRAY

RC (DLC); endorsed.

From Gaudenzio Clerici

HONORABLE SIR Chalons Sur-Saone the 8th august 1788

I have received the honor of your letter, with the letter of credit on Messrs. Vve. Rameau & fils therein inclosed. The eight Louis have been paid to me this day by Monsr. Desarbre banker here. All the thankfull expressions my mind could suggest me to show You, Honorable Sir, my gratitude for the high favor received, none, I belief, would give your feeling and generous Heart more satisfaction, than to know how effectually they came to prevent the distresses I was menaced of at so unseasonable a time. I considered myself as in a frightfull void, where I should not perhaps have seen a face to inspire me with any degree of confidence to tell him my situation. I was confident however (but in no other occasion but like the present would I have abused of such a knowledge) that you could not, Honorable Sir, fortify yourself against your own sensibility when once an occasion was offered to you to benefit an honest man. Within eight or ten days I promise myself the honor and pleasure to present you personally my respectfull compliments: for altho' I think myself already out of danger of a relapse, till monday or tuesday next I intend to indulge myself here, and then reassume my journey by the diligence. With the greatest respect I have the honor to be Honorable Sir Your very Humble & Most Obedt. Servt.,

GAUDENZIO CLERICI

RC (DLC); endorsed. See Clerici to TJ, 28 July and TJ's reply, 2 Aug. 1788.

From John Brown Cutting

SIR London August 8. 1788.

I have heretofore had the honor to announce to you the accession of South Carolina, Maryland and New Hampshire to the new national System of government for the United States. But neither of those annunciations, not even the assent of the last (which made the *ninth*) State legitimating a fresh union afforded me that degree of satisfaction which I feel in now communicating to you the ratifi-

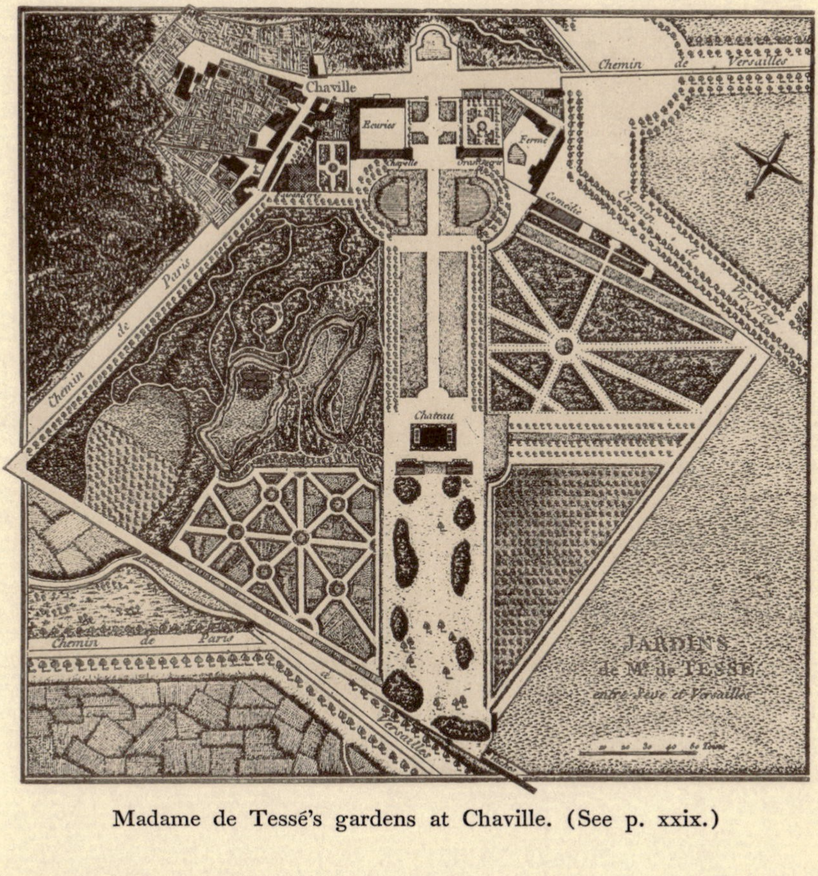

Madame de Tessé's gardens at Chaville. (See p. xxix.)

LOUIS XVI DONNE AUDIENCE AUX
AMBASSADEURS DE TIPPOO-SAÏB.

The reception of the ambassadors of Tipoo Sahib.
(See p. xxx.)

Madame de Bréhan's sketch of New York harbor. (See p. xxxi.)

cation of that important and most essential Commonwealth, Virginia. I very much regret that the result only (and not the details) of your Convention is given me. This however I have just received from Mr. William Anderson a virginian by birth (now a merchant in London) who has unsealed a letter from his brother in Virginia, dated June 26th, who says yesterday being the 25th, the grand question concerning the national government was finally determin'd in favour of adopting by a majority of *eleven*. But notwithstanding the number of the minority they exhibited much moderation after the decision, and promised to conciliate and harmonize their constituents. The vessel which brought the above letter left Virginia the 1st of July and arrived at Glasgow a few days since. There are other letters in town confirming the same fact. Several merchantmen are hourly expected here from Virginia. Therefore I hope to possess all the particulars soon which in that case will be immediately transmitted to you.

Permit me with the most unfeign'd satisfaction to congratulate you upon an event ensuring the establishment of a constitution that with a very few amendments may perpetuate the political freedom and social happiness of a republic which promises to be commensurate with a fourth part of the Globe. With the truest respect and regard I have the honor to be Your Obliged and Most Obedt. Servt.,

John Brown Cutting

RC (DLC); Cutting wrote "(Duplicate)" at head of text. The other copy, if TJ received it, has not been preserved among his papers.

From C. W. F. Dumas

Monsieur — Lahaie 8e. Août 1788 au matin

Je viens de recevoir avis de Mr. L——, que la Commission se fera aujourd'hui conformément à ma Lettre d'hier. Ainsi Votre Excellence doit recevoir de Mr. le Cte. Diodati, en même temps que la présente, ou faire demander chez Lui, les Gazettes et Suppléments du 25, 29 Juillet, 1, 5 et 8 Août, qu'on lui envoye par la Poste de ce jour, et les suites successivement, jusqu'à la Levée de l'Interdit. Espérons qu'elle ne tardera pas, sans quoi je crains que ce brave homme ne se dégoûte tout-à-fait de ce travail; et ce seroit une vraie perte pour toute l'Europe.

Je crois devoir transcrire ici ce qu'on me mande d'Amsterdam en date d'hier.

"Your Conclusion, that the Baltimore ship [On m'avoit appris par Lettre du 26, qu'un Bâtiment de là venoit d'aborder au Texel, et l'on espéroit de pouvoir m'apprendre le lendemain qu'il portoit la nouvelle de l'accession de la Virginie][1] could not bring any Intelligence about the Decision of the Virginia Convention, was very just. And I am sorry to acquaint you, a Vessel arrived at Bordeaux, conveys the News, that the Convention of Virginia had postponed deciding upon the Business until a future day. This is a very unexpected Stroke. However, as we have no further particulars, it will be well not to publish anything on the subject, before we know the Day the Convention was postponed to, and the motives for such a Measure. We must recollect, it is the same step as N. Hampshire pursued. Perhaps they had not yet heard the Accession of the 9th. State, and did not choose to be the concluding one.—Or, it is not improbable, that seeing the Constitution established, they will wait the Meeting of the new Congress, and the passing of the Bill of Right mention'd by Mr. J——n as the term of their coming in. These are but Conjectures. We must wait the Event, which I am as yet very little fearful about."

Après ce que Votre Excellence vient de lire, je ne crois pas avoir besoin de lui dire combien je languis de savoir le positif de tout cela, dès que Votre Excellence le saura elle-même. La derniere conjecture de mon correspondant me paroît profonde et sage; et je l'adopte en attendant.

Grace à Dieu, l'illumination s'est passée sans malheur: mais les orgies ne nous ont pas permi de dormir de toute la nuit. Une multitude de Can[es] ivre *totam incensa per urbem bacchabatur, qualis commotis excita sacris Thyas, ubi audito Stimulant trie terica Baccho Orgia, nocturnusque vocat clamore Cithæron.*

Je suis avec grand respect, De Votre Excellence Le très-humble & très-obéissant serviteur,

C W F Dumas

RC (DLC); endorsed.

[1] Brackets in MS.

From André Limozin

Le Havre, 8 Aug. 1788. Encloses account of expenses of 103[lt]17s.9d. for two shipments forwarded to TJ, and asks that the *acquit à caution* be returned in due form. "It was mentionned yesterday in Sundry Letters arrived from Hambro that the Sweedish army had attacked Wyburg in Finland."

RC (MHi); 2 p. Enclosure (MHi): Account of disbursements by Limozin for commissions, freight, duties, plumbing and cording, &c. of two shipments: the first consisting of five cases of "Meubles venuës d'Amsterdam" by the ship *Le Jeune Bérnard*, Captain Claus Arends, totalling 61[lt] 4s. 3d., and the second being "une futaille Boeuf fumé venu d'Hambourg," by the ship *Le William Elizabeth*, Captain A. Bolek, totalling 42[tt] 13s. 6d. Both statements, in a clerk's hand on a single sheet, were signed by Limozin and dated 7 Aug. 1788; endorsed by TJ: "Limosin. Accts. subsequent to paimt. of Nov. 1.1787."

To John Banister, Jr., with Enclosure

Dear Sir Paris Aug. 9. 1788.

I am to return you many thanks for the trouble you gave yourself in collecting and sending me the plants. A concurrence of unlucky circumstances has in a considerable degree defeated the effect of your goodness. The ship on arriving at Havre in Feb. or Mar. was obliged to go instantly to Dunkirk. My correspondent at Dunkirk immediately wrote to me for orders. I had just set out on a journey to Holland and Germany and did not return till April, and then they had to come here by land, which circumstance with the lateness of the season had destroyed a great part of them. I must trouble you once more for the same lady, who asks me to procure her what is contained in the inclosed list. Be so good as to collect and pack them as soon as the season will admit, and being thus held in readiness they can be put on board the first vessel from Appomattox or James river for Havre addressed to Monsr. Limozin merchant at that place for me, and 'in case of my absence for Madame la Comtesse de Tessé á Paris.' The latter precaution is necessary lest I should be absent.

This country is at present extremely agitated by the disputes between the king and his parliaments. Between these two parties there is a middle patriotic one proceeding with a steady step to recover from both what they can for the nation, and I think they will obtain a pretty good constitution. It is now pretty certain they will call the States general the next year, and probably in the month of May. It is expected that assembly will endeavor to fix some certain limits to the royal authority. The Swedes have commenced hostilities against the Russians, and obtained a small advantage in an engagement on the Baltic. The Russians have had two considerable actions on the Black sea with the Turks. The first was in their favour, the second a complete victory. In the first Admiral Paul Jones commanded the right wing. He was not at the second action. He commands the ships of war on that sea. Both actions were by the Russian gallies commanded by the Prince of Nassau and Paul Jones seems to have been accidentally present in the first. These victories will probably have a great effect. This country wishes to keep out of the war, but I doubt the possibility of it.

I think I have not before acknoleged expressly the receipt of your favors of Sep. 27. 87. and Jan. 31. 88. Pray continue to write me the news of my country, great and small, and do not suffer yourself to fall into the indolence which characterises it's inhabitants. I am with great esteem and attachment Dear Sir your affectionate friend & humble servt., TH: JEFFERSON

P.S. My friendly respects to Mr. and Mrs. Bannister, perhaps I should say to the Mrs. Bannisters.

ENCLOSURE

Aug. 9. 1788.

Plants:
- Quercus rubra maxima. Large red oak
- Quercus rubra ramosissima. Branchy red oak.
- Quercus rubra nana. Dwarf red oak.
  Do we know three kinds of red oak in Virginia? Is the last of the three what we call Ground-oak?
- Quercus Phellos. Willow oak. The several varieties.
- Chinquapin.
- Stewartia Malacodendron. Soft Wood. See Millar's dictionary and Catesby's Carolina Appendix. 13.
- Populus heterophylla. A kind of Poplar described in Catesby Supra. 34 and in Millar's dict. Populus. 5. I believe it is called Black poplar.
- [Clus]ter[1] pine or Black pine. See Millar. Pinus. 14.
- Annona glabra. The common Papaw of Virginia
- Andromeda arborea. Catesby appendix. 17. calls this the Sorrel tree
- Andromeda plumata. I do not know what this is
- Laurus nova.[2] I do not know what this is.
- Laurus estivalis. Summer bay. 2. Catesby 28. Millar. Laurus. 8.
- Callicarpa Americana. 2. Catesby 47.

⟨*Gardenia or Fothergilla*⟩

Cones of:
- Pinus Picea. Blackpine or Pitchpine
- Cupressus Disticha. Cypress
- Liriodendron tulipifera. Common Poplar

Diospyros. Persimmon. Send the seeds. I think they will come best in the fruit.

PrC (DLC). PrC of enclosure (DLC); much faded.

The list enclosed here is TJ's revision and rearrangement of the list of plants sent to him by Madame de Tessé on 7 Aug. 1788, q.v. He omitted one item (*Syderoxilon*) from her list and appears to have deleted another (*Gardenia*), probably for the reasons that he noted on her list. Banister's letter to TJ of JAN. 31. 88 has not been found; it was evidently transmitted with one from his father to TJ of the same date, also missing; both are recorded in SJL Index. MILLAR: Philip Miller, *The Gardeners Dictionary*, which was first published in 1731 and of which TJ possessed a copy of the 8th edn. as early as 1769. This edition included the Linnean nomenclature, which explains TJ's reference to the work in his to Cary, 12 Aug. 1786; in 1785 Chazelles and Holandre brought out a French translation of this 8th edn. TJ obtained a copy of this edition (see Sowerby, Nos. 801-2).

1 This word faded, but supplied from Miller, who referred to it as being commonly called the cluster pine because of the arrangement of the cones.

2 This word faded, but supplied from Madame de Tessé's list.

From John Bondfield

Bordeaux, 9 Aug. 1788. Mrs. Barclay wrote by this day's post that she would set out by 10th or 15th at furthest, and intended to stop at Blaye. "The Diligence dont pass near that post of some miles," and he urges TJ to convey his recommendation that she "stop at a Village or small bourg calld St. André de Cubsac near to which we have a Country Seat, and will give instructions for Carriages to convey her family and Baggage, where after refreshing herself a few Days she may embark. I shall have every thing prepared ready not to detain the Vessel a Day."—Markets for tobacco are "pretty good them by the Missourie will bring from 36 a 38ᵗᵗ a Cargoe of Maryland inferior sold yesterday at 34.ᵗᵗ10."

RC (DLC; endorsed.

Mrs. Barclay's obvious disinclination to pass through Bordeaux (see Mary Barclay to TJ, 7 Aug. 1788) and Bondfield's arranging for her to stop at ST. ANDRE DE CUBSAC, a village about twelve miles from Bordeaux and about the same distance southeast of BLAYE on the Gironde river, indicate clearly that her husband's imprisonment at Bordeaux the preceding summer may have caused her to be apprehensive about staying in that port before boarding the vessel.

To St. John de Crèvecoeur

DEAR SIR Paris Aug. 9. 1788.

While our second revolution is just brought to a happy end with you, yours here is but cleverly under way. For some days I was really melancholy with the apprehensions that arms would be appealed to, and the opposition crushed in it's first efforts. But things seem now to wear a better aspect. While the opposition keeps at it's highest wholsome point, government, unwilling to draw the sword, is not forced to do it. The contest here is exactly what it was in Holland: a contest between the monarchical and aristocratical part of the government for a monopoly of despotism over the people. The aristocracy in Holland, seeing that their common prey was likely to escape out of their clutches,[1] chose rather to retain it's former portion and therefore coalesced with the single head. The people remained victims. Here I think it will take a happier turn. The parliamentary part of the aristocracy is alone firmly united. The Noblesse and clergy, but especially the former are divided partly between the parliamentary and the despotic party, and partly united with the real patriots who are endeavoring to gain for the nation what they can both from the parliamentary and the single despotism. I think I am not mistaken in believing that the king and some of his ministers are well affected to this band: and surely that they will make great cessions to the people rather than small ones to the parliament. They are accordingly yielding daily to the national reclamations, and will probably end in according a well tempered constitution. They promise the states general for the next year and we have reason to believe they will take place in May. How they will be composed, and what they will do, cannot be foreseen. Their convocation however will tranquillize the public mind in a great degree, till their meeting. There are however two intervening difficulties. 1. Justice cannot till then continue completely suspended as it now is. The parliament will not resume their functions but in their entire body. The baillages are afraid to accept of them. What will be done? 2. There are well-founded fears of a bankruptcy before the month of May. In the mean time the war is spreading from nation to nation. Sweden has commenced hostilities against Russia; Denmark is shewing it's teeth against Sweden; Prussia against Denmark, and England too deeply engaged in playing the back-game to avoid coming forward and dragging this country and Spain in with her. But even war will not prevent the assembly of the States general, because it cannot be carried on without them. War however is not the most favorable moment for divesting the monarchy of power. On the contrary it is the moment when the energy of a single hand shews itself in the most seducing form.

Your friend the Countess D'Houdetot has had a long illness at Sanois. She was well enough the other day to come to Paris and was so good as to call on me, as I did also on her, without finding each other. The Dutchess Danville is in the country altogether. Your sons are well. Their master speaks very highly of the genius and application of Aly, and more favorably of the genius than application of the younger. They are both fine lads, and will make you very happy. I am not certain whether more exercise than the rules of the school admit would not be good for Aly. I confered the other day on this subject with M. le Moine, who seems to be of that opinion, and disposed to give him every possible indulgence.

A very considerable portion of this country has been desolated by a hail. I considered the newspaper accounts of hailstones of 10. pounds weight as exaggerations. But in a conversation with the Duke de la Rochefoucaut the other day, he assured me that tho' he could not say he had seen such himself, yet he considered the fact as perfectly established. Great contributions public and private are making for the sufferers. But they will be like the drop of water from the finger of Lazarus. There is no remedy for the present evil, nor way to prevent future ones but to bring the people to such a state of ease as not to be ruined by the loss of a single crop. This hail may be considered as the coup de grace to an expiring victim. In the arts there is nothing new discovered since you left us which is worth communicating. Mr. Payne's iron bridge was exhibited here with great approbation. An idea has been encouraged of executing it in three arches at the King's garden, but it will probably not be done. I am with sentiments of perfect esteem & attachment Dear Sir Your most obedient & most humble servt.,

TH: JEFFERSON

RC (Louis St. John de Crèvecoeur, Montesquieu-sur-Losse, France, 1947); endorsed: "R 20th. Jan." PrC (DLC).

The enormously desolating HAIL, which, with other factors, resulted in a more favorable market in France for American wheat and flour, caused widespread suffering. In his Account Book under date of 4 Aug. 1788 TJ made the following entry: "gave in charity for injury by hail 72.tt"

1 This word interlined in substitution for "hands," deleted.

From Jan Ingenhousz

DEAR SIR Paris Aug. 9th. 1788.

I was at Mr. Pelletier's house, where they told me, that if such a legalisation could be made, it could not be but *au greffe de la ville*, at the town house. I thought it advisable to ask advise to Mrs. Tourton & Ravel how to proceed on that business. They told me such legalisation not being customary and by no means necessary it would be difficult to get it perform'd, and it would be even difficult to get at the *Prevot des marchands* at his office, as there are more important transactions performed at that office, that, if they accepted the Commission, they would certainly not legalise the paper immediately, that they would keep it there, and not return it very likely in 6 or 8 days. They assur'd me, that, as all acts signed by the british minister here are send away without any legalisation of the prevot des marchands, they were very sur such acts would be equaly valid in America. And indeed I should think it inconsistend with common sense, that an inlighted nation should not give as much credid to their own public minister's signature as to a magistrate who does not know personaly the man whose signature he is to legalise. For what certainty has the *prevot de marchands*, that I am the identik man who signed the act, without some witnesses, known to him, should attest that I am the man in question? My power of attorney for England was not signed by a magistrate of Vienna but signed by the Brittish envoyé. If there should be any thing wanting in the power of Atorney, I fancy it would be, that the witnesses have put to their names no quality or their ordinary residence. I send you the power back, on purpose that each of the two witnesses could join to their names at least their abode, if you think it necessary (for instance Mr. N. of London, &c). If not, I begg the favour to join it to the letter adressed to Dr. Franklin and to forward it just as it is, togeather with the printed papers. I am very respectfully Dear sir Your most obedient humble servant, J. INGEN HOUSZ

RC (MoSHi); endorsed by TJ: "Ingenhousz." The enclosed POWER OF ATTORNEY authorizing Samuel Vaughan, Jr., to act for Ingenhousz in the Samuel Wharton land affair (see Van Doren, *Franklin*, p. 394-7) has not been found, and the eminent scientist's somewhat testy animadversions upon TJ's evident refusal to authenticate the document (as he had consistently refused to do on all other occasions) conceal the fact that in this instance, as in that of Paradise, TJ had made an exception by actually drafting the power of attorney, which was forwarded in the LETTER . . . TO DR. FRANKLIN. In that letter Ingenhousz wrote: "I arrived here some Days ago and saw yesterday Mr. Jefferson for the first time; and as he told me he should send a paquet to Philadelphia tomorrow by a lady . . . I proposed him to make up immediately the power of atorney according to the model sent to me by Mr. Vaughan. He did it very willingly and was in every respect very civil and oblidging to me. . . . Your advise and that of Mr. Vaughan to wait with the Congress certificates of the 7000 dollars till the new gouvernment be established is certainly very good and I will follow it, and prefer land for money. Mr. Jefferson approoves also much of it, and the more so as he thinks the new government is already adopted. . . . He thinks the value of paper currency will soon increase and that the states will grant about an aker for every dollar borrow'd" (Ingenhousz to Franklin, 9 Aug. 1788; PPAP). A postscript stated: "The power of atorney is signed by Mr. Jefferson, and two American gentlemen, which will certainly be sufficient."

To James Monroe

DEAR SIR Paris Aug. 9. 1788.

Since my last to you I have to thank you for your favors of July 27. 87. and Apr. 10. 88. and the details they contained, and in return will give you now the leading circumstances of this continent. The war between the two empires and the Turks seemed to be in a languid state when Paul Jones was called into the Russian service with the rank of rear admiral and put at the head of their ships of war on the Black sea, consisting of 5. frigates and 3. ships of the line. The last however are shut up in Cherson. The Prince of Nassau was put over their fleet of gallies and gun boats. The Captain Bacha[1] with 57. gallies and gun boats attacked the prince of Nassau's fleet of 27. P. Jones happened to be present and commanded the right wing. The Turks were repulsed, losing 3. vessels. Eight days after (about the last of June) the Pacha brought up his ships of war to attack the Prince of Nassau, but unskilfully got his fleet up into the swash near the mouth of the Boristhenes, so imbedded in mud that they could not move. The Pr. of Nassau burnt 6. took 2. and made 3. or 4000 prisoners. The Captain Pacha escaped on a small vessel. The Swedes have now entered into the war, and an action has taken place on the Baltic between their fleet and the Russian. We have as yet only the Swedish account which gives to themselves the victory with the loss of one ship on their part and two on that of the Russians. It seems as if the Danes, should they take any part at all, would still be against the Swedes. Should the war become general therefore the arrangement would be France, Spain, the two empires and Denmark, against England, Prussia, Holland, Sweden, and Turkey. This nation is at present under great internal agitation. The authority of the crown on one part and that of the parliaments on the other, are fairly at issue. Good men take part with neither, but have raised an opposition, the object of which is to obtain a fixed and temperate constitution. There was a moment when this opposition was so high as to endanger an appeal to arms, in which case perhaps it would have been crushed. The moderation of government has avoided this, and they are yeilding daily one right after another to the nation. They have given them provincial assemblies which will be very perfect representations of the nation, and stand somewhat in the place of our state assemblies. They have reformed the criminal law, acknoleged the king cannot lay a new tax without the consent of the states general, and they will call the states general the next year. The object of this body when met will be a bill of rights, a civil list, a national assembly meeting at certain epochs, and some other matters of that kind. So that I think it probable this country will within two or three years be in the enjoiment of a tolerably free constitution, and that without it's having cost them a drop of blood. For none has yet been spilt, tho' the English papers have set the whole nation to cutting throats.

I heartily rejoice that 9 states have accepted the new constitution. As yet we do not hear what Virginia, N. Carolina and N. York have done, and we take for granted R. isld. is against it. This constitution forms a basis which is good, but not perfect. I hope the states will annex to it a bill of rights securing those which are essential against the federal government; particularly trial by jury, habeas corpus, freedom of religion, freedom of the press, freedom against monopolies, and no standing armies. I see so general a demand of this that I trust it will be done. There is another article of which I have no hopes of amendment because I do not find it objected to in the states. This is the abandonment of the principle of necessary rotation in the Senate and Presidency. With respect to the last particularly it is as universally condemned in Europe, as it is universally unanimadverted on in America. I have never heard a single person here speak of it without condemnation, because on the supposition that a man being once chosen will be always chosen, he is a king for life, and his importance will produce[2] the same brigues and cabals foreign and domestic which the election of a king of Poland and other elective monarchies have ever produced, so that we must take refuge in the end in hereditary monarchy, the very evil which grinds to atoms the people of Europe.

I sincerely take part with you in your domestic felicity. There is no other in this world worth living for. The loss of it alone can make us know it's full worth. It would indeed be a most pleasing circumstance to me to see you settle in the neighborhood of Monticello, for thither all my views tend, and not a day passes over my head without looking forward to my return. This would be much hastened could I see such a society forming there as yourself, Madison, and Short. Present me affectionately to Mrs. Monroe, and learn the little girl to consider me as a very friendly tho' at present invisible being, and be assured yourself of the sincerity of those sentiments of esteem & attachment with which I am Dear Sir your affectionate friend & servt., TH: JEFFERSON

RC (NN); endorsed. PrC (DLC). [1] Thus in MS.
[2] This word interlined in substitution for "call for," deleted.

From Montmorin

Versailles le 9. Août 1788.

J'ai reçu, Monsieur, la lettre que vous m'avez fait l'honneur de m'écrire le 30 du mois dernier, et par laquelle vous avez bien voulu m'informer que la nouvelle Constitution proposée pour les Etats-Unis, a été établie par neuf Etats. Je me suis fait un devoir de rendre compte de cet événement au Roi. Sa Majesté l'a apris avec d'autant plus de satisfaction qu'elle ne doute pas qu'il ne contribue essentiellement à la considération comme à la prospérité de votre patrie.

J'ai l'honneur d'être très-sincèrement, Monsieur, votre très-humble et très-obéissant serviteur

LE CTE DE MONTMORIN

RC (DLC); in clerk's hand, signed by Montmorin; endorsed. FC (Arch. Aff. Etr., Paris, Corr. Pol., E.-U., XXXIII; Tr in DLC).

To Moustier

DEAR SIR Paris Aug. 9. 1788.

Tho' your numerous and well informed correspondents here must keep you constantly au courant of what passes in Europe, yet I cannot relinquish the privilege of writing to you altogether, merely because I can tell you nothing but what you learn better from other hands. You will have heard of the astonishing revolution in the politics of Sweden, which has lately carried her into the scale favored by England and opposed to France. Hostilities were commenced by the Swedes by the attack of a small Russian post. They pretend the Russians had previously entered on their territory and burnt a village or two, but it is believed that this pretended aggression was by the Swedes themselves in Cossak dress to give a colour[1] for hostilities where none existed before. It is said and believed there has been a naval action on the Baltic wherein the Russians were obliged to retire with the loss of two ships. But the latter have been more fortunate in two actions against the Turks on the Black sea. In the first they but barely repulsed the Turks with the loss of three vessels of the latter. In the second they obtained a complete and decisive victory. I think there is a hope that Denmark will still oppose itself to Sweden. If so, the balance of naval power will still be preserved in some degree. For tho' Sweden may return to France on a future occasion if the latter should not be obliged to enter into the present war, if she does enter into it I apprehend Sweden will ultimately arrange herself with the adverse party. And that she must enter into in the long run I think extremely probable. I sincerely wish this may not be till she shall have arranged her internal affairs. These in my opinion are going on in the fairest way possible to produce good to the body of the nation. The progress already made is great, and the cry for further improvement without being strong enough to induce government to draw the sword and crush the opposition, is strong enough to goad them on towards the establishment of a constitution. I think that among the ministers themselves there are some good patriots who are not entirely displeased at this degree of violence. It is already announced that the states general will be called in 1789. and I have tolerably good information that an arrêt will appear the day after tomorrow announcing them for May 1789. But my letters must go off tomorrow, so that this intelligence cannot be confirmed in them. You will have heard that the Baron de Breteuil is retired and Monsieur de Villedeuil in his place. M. de Malesherbes has endeavored to retire, but as yet he is overpowered by strong intercession. The Marechal de Richelieu died yesterday. The Marechal de Vaux is at the point of death in Dauphiné. The Ambassadors of Tippoo Saïb are to be received tomorrow at Versailles in great pomp. I go to see this jeu d'enfants. I wish Madame de Brehan could be there to paint it. By this time I am afraid she is ready to do justice to my information on the subject of my own country, that the Cultivateur Americain had been too much disposed to see the fair side: that it had two sides as well as all other countries &c. &c. I beg her indulgence for our foibles, and a continuance particularly of her partiality to me. Be so good as to present me very affectionately to her, and to be assured of the sincerity of the esteem & attachment with which I have the honour to be Dear Sir Your most obedt. & most humble servt.,

Th: Jefferson

P.S. I inclose you the bill of lading for your wine, which I hope you have received long ago.

PrC (DLC). Enclosure not found.

1 This word interlined in substitution for "pretence," deleted.

From John Rutledge

⟦[*Charleston*], *9 Aug. 1788.* Recorded in SJL Index. Not found.⟧

To Thomas Barclay

Dear Sir Paris Aug. 10. 1788.

I have duly received your favour announcing the departure of Mrs. Barclay, and assure you that it is with regret that we lose her here. She however will be happier in rejoining you. Far from her having been a troublesome neighbor to me as you suppose, I have been only able to assure her of my dispositions to be useful to her. Once only she has permitted me to accomodate her with the sum of 1200 livres: and she has promised if her money should be likely to fall short, that she will draw on me from Bordeaux. To avoid the trouble of accounts and remittances perhaps it might be more convenient to you, and it is equally so to me, for me to charge to the U.S. one or two of the articles of our private account, of equal amount. By debiting the U.S. with what I furnished you at Bordeaux for example, and a part of the bill to Richards, we may save the necessity of erecting an account. Do in this as suits you best. I have taken the liberty of advising Mrs. Barclay to go to Bordeaux rather than call the vessel to Havre, in hopes she will by this means get into the Delaware before the Aequinox. I am with sentiments of very sincere esteem & attachment Dear Sir your friend & servt.,

Th: Jefferson

PrC (DLC).

From Migneron de Brocqueville

Monseigneur — Bordeaux Le 10 Aoust 1788

La protection Distinguée que vous accordés aux Arts, m'encourage à prier votre Excellence D'accepter un mémoire que j'ai l'honneur de lui envoier cy inclus, qui contient La description d'un Pont et d'un petit hopital que j'ai construit ici en Bois amelioré et ceintré suivant mon nouveau Sistême.

Ces deux premiers essais annoncent de quelle utilité peuvent être mes découvertes pour la construction des grands édifices qui, trop dispendieux en Pierre, est toujours une raison pour etre différée et Souvent pour n'être jamais exécutée.

En priant votre Excellence de vouloir bien en accepter L'hommage j'ose espérer qu'elle accordera son indulgence à ce premier essai, et qu'elle daignera honnorer de Sa protection celui qui est avec un tres profond Respect de votre Excellence Monseigneur Le tres humble et tres obeissant serviteur,

Migneron de Brocqueville
ingénieur

RC (DLC); endorsed. Not recorded in SJL Index. Enclosure: *Description du pont de Brienne, construit à Bordeaux en bois amélioré et ceintré, par Monsieur Migneron de Brocqueville, auteur de la découverte pour l'amélioration et le ceintrage des bois* (n.p., n.d., Sowerby, No. 4200).

From John Brown

DEAR SIR New York August 10th 1788

Your favor of the 28th May came to hand a few days ago for which accept my warmest Acknowledgements.

I am well convinced of the Justness of your remarks respecting the importance of strengthening and maintaining the connection between the District of Kentucky and the Maritime States: During my residence in that Country it was my constant care to cultivate that Idea But I am sorry to inform you that from the present complection of affairs there is reason to apprehend that the Connection will not be of long duration. Congress have rejected their application to be admitted into the Union as an Independent State notwithstanding it was acknowledged to be reasonable, thinking it inexpedient in the present State of the Confederacy and that the admission of a New State might affect the Ballance of power unless Vermont could be brought forward at the same time. This will be considered by the people of that Country as a great disappointment inasmuch as they have been more than three years in bringing forward this application and as they are now refered to the new Government, to be admitted under which in a Constitutional Mode must necessarily be attended with considerable delay. Their vast increase in population (amounting to at least one hundred thousand souls in that District alone) added to the great dangers and difficulty attending a communication with the Seat of Government renders their connection with Virginia so burdensome that there is every reason to expect that immediately on hearing that Congress have refused to receive them they will assume their Independence. Should they take this step I think it very problematical whether or not they will apply for admission into the new Confederacy; especially as they are generally opposed to the new Constitution apprehending much inconvenience and danger from the Judicial System and fearing that the Powers vested in the General Government may enable to carry into effect the proposed Treaty with Spain relative to the Navigation of the Mississippi. Indeed the ill advised attempt to cede the navigation of that River has laid the foundation for the dismemberment of the American Empire by distroying the confidence of the people in the Western Country in the Justice of the Union and by inducing them to dispair of obtaining possession of that Right by means of any other exertions than their own. However as we are informed by the Governour of the Western Territory that there is great reason to apprihend a general Indian War, I hope that Kentucky will see the danger and impropriety of breaking off from the Union at this time and that it may still be in the power of Congress to conciliate their minds and to secure their attachment to the Confederacy.

I inclose you two Gazettes containing the Ratifications of the New Constitution by Virginia and New York. The Convention of N Carolina has been for some time past in Session and we daily expect to hear that she has adopted it. Rhode Island it is expected will shortly see the propriety of acceding as yet there is a majority in that State opposed. Those who were opposed in those states which have ratifyed appear generally to acquiess—Congress has been for some time past engaged in giving it operation. Electors are to be appointed on the first Wedensday in January, to chuse a President on the first Wedensday in February and the New Congress to meet on the first Wedensday in March next but the place where has been the subject of much warmth and is not yet agreed upon—tho I think it probable that it will be at Philadelphia.

I expect to sit out in a few days for the Western Country shall take pleasure in communicating to you the News of that Country by every opportunity. Should you be so good as to honor me with a letter it will find a ready conveyance from New York to me by Post.

Before I conclude this letter I must in Justice to my feelings express my gratitude for the many favors I have received from you; be assured that they have made a lasting impression upon my mind and that it is in a great measure to your friendship and Instruction that I am indebted for my Success in life. Believe me that with the greatest respect I am Sir Yo. mo. Hble. Servt.,

JOHN BROWN

RC (DLC); endorsed. The TWO GAZETTES enclosed were probably the issues of the *New-York Journal and Weekly Register* for 3 July and 7 Aug. 1788, the first of which reported the ratification by Virginia and the second that by New York.

From Edward Carrington

MY DEAR SIR New York Augt. 10. 1788.

Having but a few Minutes notice of this opportunity by Mr. Tillier I can make but little more use of it, than to acknowledge the receipt of your favor of the 27th. of May, and to send you the second Vol. of the Federalist. The first, I hope, you have received before this.—Virginia and New York have both adopted the Constitution, as you will be more particularly informed by Mr. Madison and Mr. Brown, who have written you. North Carolina commenced her session on the 17th. Ult. and is probably the 12th. Adopting State before this day. Rhode Island has taken no regular step in the business as yet—a kind of informal reference of it was made to the people by the Legislature, which terminated something like a rejection. I suppose however that she must soon take measures for adopting. Perhaps no coercive measures would be pursued to compel her, but it is impossible she can continue to treat with contempt a measure which is so generally embraced by the other States.

The good fortune of the Chevalier Jones in the service of the Empress gives me much pleasure. Your hint respecting a similar promotion here, shall be attended if there shall appear, in the Course of the present session of Congress, a prospect of succeeding in an attempt to procure it. I regret however that whilst foreign Nations are contending for eminence in confering distinctions upon this officer, *this*, of which he professes himself a Citizen, should appear, scarcely, to remember the events which founded his Character.

I a few days ago did myself the pleasure to write to Mr. Short by way of Holland. Be pleased to present me to him and assure yourself that it is with much satisfaction that I have the Honor to be Your affectionate Friend & very humble servt.,

ED. CARRINGTON

RC (DLC); endorsed.

To John Jay

SIR — Paris Aug. 10. 1788.

I have waited till the last moment of Mrs. Barclay's departure to write you the occurrences since my letter of the 3d. instant. We have received the Swedish account of an engagement between their fleet and the Russian on the Baltic, wherein they say they took one and burnt another Russian vessel with the loss of one on their side, and that the victory remained with them. They say at the same time that their fleet returned into port and the Russians kept the sea. We must therefore suspend our opinion till we get the Russian version of this engagement. The Swedish manifesto was handed about today at Versailles by the Swedish ambassador, in manuscript. The king complains that Russia has been ever endeavoring to sow divisions in his kingdom in order to reestablish the antient constitution, that he has long borne it thro' a love of peace, but finds it no longer bearable: that still however he will make peace on these conditions 1. that the empress punishes her minister for the note he gave in to the court of Stockholm; 2. that she restore Crimea to the Turks, and 3. that she repay to him all the expences of his armament.—The Russian force in vessels of war on the Black sea are 5. fregates and 3. ships of the line. But those of the line are shut up in port, and cannot come out till Oczakow shall be taken. This fleet is commanded by Paul Jones with the rank of rear-Admiral. The Prince of Nassau commands the gallies and gunboats. It is now ascertained that the States general will assemble the next year, and probably in the month of May. Tippoo Saib's ambassadors had their reception to-day at Versailles, with unusual pomp. The presence was so numerous that little could be caught of what they said to the king, and he answered to them. From what little I could hear, nothing more passed than mutual assurances of good will.—The name of the Marechal de Richlieu is sufficiently remarkeable in history to justify my mentioning his death which happened two days ago. He was aged 92. years. I have the honor to be with sentiments of the most perfect respect and esteem Sir your most obedt. & most humble servt.,

TH: JEFFERSON

RC (DNA: PCC, No. 87, II); addressed: "The honorable John Jay esquire Secretary for foreign affairs to the U.S. of America in Congress." PrC (DLC).

This letter was written on the evening of the 10th: TJ had told Mrs. Barclay that he would return from Versailles around five or six in the afternoon after TIPPOO SAIB'S AMBASSADORS had had their splendid reception (see TJ to Mary Barclay, 8 Aug. 1788).

From James Madison

DEAR SIR New York Augst. 10. 1788.

Mr. Warville[1] has just arrived here, and I sieze an opportunity suddenly brought to my knowledge to thank you for your several favors, and particularly for the pedometer. Answers to the letters must be put off for the next opportunity.

My last went off just as a vote was taken in the Convention of this State which foretold the ratification of the new Government. The later act soon followed and is enclosed. The form of it is remarkable. I enclose also a circular address to the other States on the subject of amendments, from which mischiefs are apprehended.

The great danger in the present crisis is that if another Convention should be soon assembled, it would terminate in discord, or in alterations of the federal system which would throw back *essential* powers into the State Legislatures. The delay of a few years will assuage the jealousies which have been artifically created by designing men and will at the same time point out the faults which really call for amendment. At present the public mind is neither sufficiently cool nor sufficiently informed for so delicate an operation.

The Convention of North Carolina met on the 21st Ult: Not a word has yet been heard from its deliberations. Rhode Island has not resumed the subject since it was referred to and rejected by the people in their several Towns.

Congress have been employed for several weeks on the arrangements of times and place for bringing the new Government into agency. The first have been agreed on though not definitively, and make it pretty certain that the first meeting will be held in the third week in March. The place has been a subject of much discussion: and continues to be uncertain. Philada. as least excentric of any place capable of affording due accomodations and a respectable outset to the Government was the first proposed. The affirmative votes were N. Hampshire, Connecticut, Pena. Maryd. Virga. and N. Carolina. Delaware was present and in favor of that place, but one of its delegates wishing to have a question on Wilmington previous to a final determination, divided that State and negatived the motion. N. York came next in view, to which was opposed first Lancaster which failed and then Baltimore which to the surprise of every body was carried by seven States, S. Carolina which had preferred N. York to the two other more Southern positions, unexpectedly concurring in this. The vote however was soon rescinded, the State of S. Carolina receding from, the Eastern States remonstrating against,[2] and few seriously arguing the eligibility of Baltimore. At present the question lies as it was originally supposed to do between N. York and Philada. and nothing can be more uncertain than the event of it. Rhode Island which alone was disposed to give the casting vote to N. York has refused to give any final vote for arranging and carrying into effect a system to which that State is opposed, and both the Delegates have returned home.

Col. Carrington tells me he has sent you the first volume of the federalist, and adds the 2d. by this conveyance. I believe I never have yet *mentioned*[3] *to you that publication*. It *was undertaken last fall by Jay, Hamilton and myself*. The *proposal came from the two former.* The *execution was thrown by the sickness of Jay mostly on the two others.* Though *carried on in concert the writers are not mutually answerable* for *all the*[4] *ideas of each other*, there being *seldom time for even a perusal* of the *pieces by any but the writer before they were wanted at the press* and *some times hardly by the writer himself.*

I have not a moment for a line to Mazzei. Tell him I have received his books and shall attempt to get them disposed of. I fear his calculations will not be fulfilled by the demand for them here in the French language. His affair with Dorhman stands as it did. Of his affair with Foster Webb I can say nothing. I suspect it will turn out badly. Yrs. affecy., Js. MADISON Jr.

RC (DLC: Madison Papers); endorsed by TJ "Madison Jas." and by Madison "Aug.10.1788."; partly in code. Enclosures: (1) Probably a copy of the *New-York Journal and Weekly Register* for 7 Aug. 1788 containing the ratification of the Constitution by New York (see Elliot, *Debates*, I, 327-31). (2) A copy of the *Circular Letter from the Convention of the State of New York to the Executives of the different States to be laid before their Respective Legislatures* (Evans, No. 21312).

Madison's LAST was that of 24 July, which WENT OFF JUST AS A VOTE WAS TAKEN and to which he added a postscript on the 26th.

1 Late in life Madison added interlineally: "[Brissot]."

2 Here Madison added "against" interlineally, probably late in life.

3 This and subsequent words in italics are written in code and were decoded interlineally by TJ. His decoding has been verified by the Editors, employing Code No. 9. One or two slight errors in encoding have been corrected silently.

4 Madison first wrote "the," then deleted it and interlined the code symbols for "all the."

To John Jay

SIR Paris Aug. 11. 1788.

In my letter of the last night, written in the moment of Mrs. Barclay's departure, I had the honour of mentioning to you that it was now pretty certain that the States general would be assembled in the next year, and probably in the month of May. This morning an Arret is published, announcing that their meeting is fixed at the first day of May next, of which I enclose you a copy by post, in hopes it will get to Bordeaux in time for Mrs. Barclay. This arrêt ought to[1] have a great effect towards tranquillising the nation. There are still however two circumstances which must continue to perplex the administration. The 1st. is the want of money, occasioned not only by the difficulty of filling up the loan of the next year, but by the withholding the ordinary supplies of taxes which is said to have taken place in some instances. This gives apprehension of a bankruptcy under some form or other, and has occasioned the stocks to fall in the most alarming manner. The 2d. circumstance is that justice both civil and criminal continues suspended. The parliament will not resume their functions, but with their whole body, and the greater part of the Baillages decline acting. The present Arret announces a perseverance in this plan.

I am informed from Algiers, of the 5th. of June, that the plague is raging there with great violence, that one of our captives was dead of it and another ill, so that we have there, in all, now only 15. or 16; that the captives are more exposed to it's ravages than others; that the great redemptions by the Spaniards, Portuguese and Neapolitans, and the havock made by the plague had now left not more than 400. slaves in Algiers, so that their redemption was become not only exorbitant but almost inadmissible; that common sailors were held at 400£ sterling, and that our 15. or 16. could probably not be redeemed for less than 25. to 30,000 Dollars. An Algerine cruiser, having 28. captives of Genoa aboard, was lately chased ashoar by two Neapolitan vessels. The crew and captives got safe ashoar, and the latter of course recovered their freedom. The Algerine crew was well treated, and would be sent back by the French. But the government of Algiers demands of France 60,000 sequins, or 27,000£ sterling for the captives escaped, that is, nearly 1000£ each. The greater part of the regency were for an immediate declaration of war against France; but the Dey urged the heavy war the Turks were at present engaged in, that it would be better not to draw another power on them at present, that they would decline renewing the treaty of 100 years which expired two years ago so as to be free to act hereafter, but for the present they ought to accept paiment for the captives as a satisfaction. They accordingly declared to the French consul that they would put him and all his countrymen there into irons unless the 60,000 sequins were paid. The Consul told them his instructions were positively that they should not be paid. In this situation stood matters between that pettyfogging nest of robbers and this great kingdom, which will finish probably by crouching under them, and paying the 60,000 sequins. From the personal characters of the present administration, I should have hoped, under any other situation than the present, they might have ventured to quit the beaten tract of politics hitherto pursued in which the honour of their nation has been calculated at nought, and to join in a league for keeping up a perpetual cruize against these pyrates, which tho' a slow operation, would be a sure one for destroying all their vessels and seamen, and turning the rest of them to agriculture. But a desire of not bringing upon themselves another difficulty will probably induce the ministers to do as their predecessors have done.

Aug. 12. The inclosed paper of this morning gives some particulars of the action between the Russians and Swedes, the Manifesto of the Empress and the declaration of the court of Versailles as to the affair of Trincomalé I have the honour to be with sentiments of perfect esteem & respect, Sir, your most obedient & most humble servt.,

TH: JEFFERSON

RC (DNA: PCC, No. 87, II). PrC (DLC). Enclosures: (1) Printed copy of the Arrêt of 8 Aug. 1788 convoking the Estates General on 1 May 1789, and declaring that the King, "Assurée de recueillir les heureux effets de leur zèle et de leur amour, . . . jouit d'avance, du consolant espoir de voir des jours sereins et tranquilles succéder à des jours d'orage et d'inquiétude; l'ordre renaitre dans toutes les parties; la dette publique être entiérement consolidée; et la France jouir, sans altération, du poids et de la considération que lui assurent son étendue, sa population, ses richesses, et le caractère de ses Habitans" (DNA: PCC, No. 87, II, accompanied by a newspaper clipping of an English translation). (2) Copy of the *Gazette de France* for 12 Aug. 1788 (same). (3) TJ probably enclosed also a copy of the Declaration of Empress Catherine of Russia of 30 June 1788, of which there is an English translation in the form of a newspaper clipping in DNA: PCC, No. 87, II.

No letter to TJ FROM ALGIERS, OF THE 5TH. OF JUNE has been found, though one from Richard O'Bryen of that date is recorded in SJL Index. This was a letter in addition to that from O'Bryen to TJ, 2 June 1788.

1 Preceding two words interlined in substitution for "will," deleted.

To Joseph Bernard

à Paris ce 12me Aout. 1788.

Je vous rends mille graces, Monsieur, pour les observations meteorologiques que vous avez eu la bonté de me faire copier et de m'envoyer, et j'accepte avec empressement l'honneur que vous me proposez de me donner une place dans la liste des souscripteurs pour votre ouvrage sur l'histoire naturelle de votre païs. Il me paroit que vous m'avez fait l'honneur de me dire, quand j'avois celui de vous voir à Marseilles, que vos memoires sur l'olivier et le figuier devoient etre reimprimées à Paris. Oserai-je donc vous demander chez quel Libraire de Paris il faut m'adresser pour trouver ces ouvrages, lesquelles me seront precieux autant pour l'estime que je porte à leur auteur, que pour le sujet qui m'interesse beaucoup. Sachant que vous vous interessez à tout ce qui concerne l'agriculture, le plus interessant de tous les arts, je prends la liberté de vous envoyer quelques graines d'une espece de blé de Turquie dont nous faisons grand cas dans la Virginie. Il faut vous avertir pourtant que nous avons des especes qui donnent des recoltes plus abondantes, mais aucune qui lui est egale pour la beauté et le gout de la farine. Je crois que vous la trouverez digne de l'attention de votre païs. J'ai l'honneur d'etre, avec des sentiments d'estime et d'attachement très sinceres, Monsieur votre tres humble et tres obeissant serviteur

TH: JEFFERSON

PrC (DLC).

To William Carmichael

DEAR SIR

Paris Aug. 12. 1788.

Since my last to you, I have been honoured with your's of the 18th. and 29th. of May and 5th. of June. My latest American intelligence is of the 24th. of June when 9. certainly and probably 10. states had accepted the new constitution, and there was no doubt of the 11th. (North Carolina) because there was no opposition there. In New-York ⅔ of the state was against it, and certainly if they had been called to the decision in any other stage of the business, they would have rejected it. But before they put it to the vote, they would certainly have heard that 11. states had joined in it, and they would find it safer to go with those 11. than put themselves into opposition with Rhode island only. Tho' I am much pleased with this succesful issue of the new constitution, yet I am more so to find that one of it's principal defects (the want of a Declaration of rights) will pretty certainly be remedied. I suppose this, because I see that both people and Conventions in almost every state have concurred in demanding it. Another defect, the perpetual re-eligibility of the same president, will probably not be cured during the life of General Washington. His merit has blinded our countrymen to the dangers of making so important an officer re-eligible. I presume there will not be a vote against him in the U.S. It is more doubtful who will be Vicepresident. The age of Dr. Franklin, and the doubt whether he would accept it, are the only circumstances that admit a question but that he would be the man. After these two characters of first magnitude there are so many which present themselves equally on the second line, that we cannot see which of them will be singled out. J. Adams, Hancock, Jay, Madison, Rutledge will be all voted for.—Congress has acceded to the prayer of Kentucky to become an independant member of the Union. A committee was occupied in settling the plan of receiving them, and their government is to commence on the 1st. day of January next. You are, I dare say, pleased as I am with the promotion of our countryman Paul Jones. He commanded the right wing in the 1st. engagement between the Russian and Turkish gallies. His absence from the 2d. proves his superiority over the Captain Pacha, as he did not chuse to bring his ships into those shoals in which the Pacha ventured and lost those entrusted to him. I consider this officer as the principal Hope of our future efforts on the ocean. You will have heard of the action between the Swedes and Russians on the Baltic. As yet we have only the Swedish version of it. I apprehend this war must catch from nation to nation till it becomes general.—With respect to the internal affairs of this country I hope they will be finally well arranged, and without having cost a drop of blood. Looking on as a bystander no otherwise interested than as entertaining a sincere love for the nation in general, and a wish to see their happiness promoted, keeping myself clear of the particular views and passions of individuals, I applaud extremely the patriotic proceedings of the present ministry. Provincial assemblies established, the states general called, the right of taxing the nation without their consent abandoned, corvées abolished, torture abolished, the criminal code reformed are facts which will do eternal honour to their administration in History. But were I their historian I should not equally applaud their total abandonment of their foreign affairs. A bolder front in the beginning would have prevented the first loss, and consequently all the others. Holland, Prussia, Turkey and Sweden lost without the acquisition of a single new ally, are painful reflections for the Friends of France. They may indeed have in their place the two empires and perhaps Denmark, in which case, physically speaking, they will stand on as good ground as before, but not on as good moral ground. Perhaps, seeing more of the internal working of the machine, they saw more than we do the physical impossibility of having money to carry on a war. Their justification must depend on this, and their atonement in the internal good they are doing to their country. This makes me completely their friend. I am with great esteem & attachment Dear Sir your friend & servant,

TH: JEFFERSON

PrC (DLC).

From Moustier

Monsieur à Newyork le 12. Août 1788

La lettre que vous m'avez fait l'honneur de m'ecrire le 17. de Mai est la premiere et la seule que j'aie reçu en reponse aux miennes depuis mon arrivée ici. La depredation qui se commettoit dans l'administration des paquebots meritoit sans doute d'etre reprimée, mais il etoit facile de les assujettir à un meilleur regime aulieu de prendre le parti de les suprimer. J'espere qu'on sera revenu de cette idée qu'un premier mouvement d'humeur aura fait naitre. J'ai envoyé à la fin de Mars un plan très detaillé sur cet objet, dans lequel j'indiquois les moyens de concilier l'economie avec l'avantage du service. Si vous voulez demander un rendez-vous à M. Le Baron d'Ogny, Intendant General des postes, pour vous entretenir avec lui de l'etablissement des paquebots, je l'ai prevenu qu'il pourroit tirer de vous beaucoup d'eclaircissemens. Je mets le plus grand interêt à contribuer à tout ce qui peut fortifier et augmenter les liens qui peuvent unir nos deux Nations. Il y a beaucoup de besogne à suivre pour y parvenir. Le nombre de personnes qui reunissent les lumieres aux bonnes intentions et qui sont comme vous, Monsieur, de bons patriotes, n'est pas fort considerable dans ce pays-ci.—Je n'ai du moins pas eû le bonheur d'en rencontrer beaucoup. J'aurois bien desiré de pouvoir realiser l'idée de me former une Societé particuliere, où je comptois mettre beaucoup de simplicité, de franchise et d'aisance. J'ai proposé à plusieurs personnes le diné intime, *The family dinner*. Une seule a bien voulu repondre à cette avance, c'est votre ami Mr. Maddisson, que je serois vraiment fort aise de voir plus souvent. Mais il a fait une longue et heureuse absence, depuis son retour je l'ai vû des momens. Vos Senateurs passent un tems infini à des debats sur le sejour futur d'un Corps qu'ils oublient qui ne doit resembler à l'actuel que de nom. On a fait une affaire d'Etat d'une question qui n'en devoit pas faire une et les personalités s'en sont melées. Heureusement que le Congrès actuel expire et que les fautes qu'il a commises peuvent servir de leçons au futur. Ce n'est pas une petite besogne ni celle d'un jour que d'etablir un Gouvernement même en theorie. Cependant on manque encore beaucoup plus de pratique que de theorie dans les E.U. Il est bon d'avoir une certaine confiance dans ses forces, mais la presomption qui en est l'excès peut produire de grands inconveniens. Vous aurez dans votre nouveau Gouvernement une ecole pour former des hommes d'Etat; voilà ce qu'il faut aux Americains. Il y a des lumieres, des connoissances, mais peu d'habitude du Gouvernement surtout en grand. Le Gouvernement de Virginie vient malheureusement de nous en donner un facheux exemple en compromettant son Etat avec le Roi par une conduite dont j'ai eû ordre de demander satisfaction. Les Americains se mettent à cheval sur la loi pour s'autoriser de procédés qui doivent repousser tous les etrangers de chez eux à moins qu'ils ne se fassent citoiens. Le nouveau Gouvernement général ne sauroit trop se presser de remedier au vice de la legislation sur le Commerce et surtout envers les Etrangers. Je presenterai mes demandes, tout dependera des gens à qui j'aurai à faire. Je desire qu'ils soient eclairés et bien intentionés pour leur patrie. Avec du tems et de la patience il faut esperer que nous verrons naître de bonnes mesures tant au dehors qu'au dedans. Le chaos commence à se debrouiller, L'ordre s'etablira par degrés.—Si vous aviez le tems de lire les anciens monumens de notre histoire, les procès verbaux des Etats Generaux, des Assemblées de Notables, les remontrances des Parlemens, les rivalités de maisons de France, d'Angleterre, de Bourgogne, d'Autriche, les ligues, les guerres qui en sont resultés, vous verriez qu'il y a peu de choses nouvelles dans ce qui dit à vos oreilles et se passe sous vos yeux. La nation Françoise est vive, active, inquiete; il lui faut du mouvement de l'occupation. Elle n'a jamais été plus redoutable au dehors qu'à la suite des fermentations interieures. Dans le moment actuel le plus grand mal est de ne pas s'entendre. Le Roi veut le bonheur de la Nation. Le gros de la nation est foncierement plus moderé qu'on ne le croit. Elle sent qu'Elle est faite pour vivre sous un Chef. Quelques ambitieux brouillent les choses; ils veulent se mettre entre le Pere et les enfans. Le Pere et les enfans se rapocheront, les brouillons seront sacrifiés, ils n'auront que ce qu'ils meritent. Les crises sont necessaires aux grands Etats. J'augure bien de celle où se trouve ma patrie. La votre, Monsieur, eprouve celles de l'enfance. Heureusement que personne n'est interessé à la troubler. Pour moi je serai toujours très heureux quand je pourrai contribuer par mes bons offices à lui procurer les secours de son plus ancien et plus naturel Allié et ami. Je ne demande qu'un peu de raison de tems en tems dans les pretentions.

Je compte partir demain pour assister à un Traité de Sauvages avec l'Etat de N.Y. On craint que le grand Traité n'ait pas pû avoir lieu avec les Commissaires du Congrès. Les Sauvages veulent s'oposer aux etablissemens sur le territoire qui forme le Gouvernement de l'Ohio. A mon retour je visiterai les 4. Etats de l'Est. Je suis obligé de differer mon voyage en Virginie jusqu'au printems.

Agreez les nouvelles assurances du très sincere et parfait attachement avec lequel j'ai l'honneur d'etre, Monsieur, Votre très humble et très obeissant Serviteur, LE CTE. DE MOUSTIER

J'attends le Vin de Frontignan. Les occasions entre Bordeaux et N.Y. sont rares.

Ma Soeur est incommodée et malgré celà occupee de ses preparatifs de voyage, ce qui l'empêche de repondre à votre Souvenir. Elle me charge de vous assurer de ses amitiés.

RC (DLC); endorsed.

To John Rutledge, Jr.

DEAR SIR Paris Aug. 12. 1788.

Obliged to make one letter serve for yourself and Mr. Shippen I have the honour to acknolege the receipt of your favor of Aug. 1. and his of July 12. and 31. By news from Virginia of the 12th. of June when their convention had been 11. days in session there was no doubt but that she, soon after that date, would give the 9th. vote in favor of the new constitution. N. Hampshire acceded to it on the 24th. of June. Of North Carolina no doubt is entertained. Congress have agreed to the independence of Kentuckey. An arret was published here yesterday announcing that the convocation of the States general should be for the 1st. of May next, and in the mean time suspending the Cours pleniere, but persevering in the Parliamentary reform. This I think secures the reformation of their constitution without bloodshed. You will already have heard of the commencement of hostilities between Sweden and Russia. This war I think will catch from nation to nation till it becomes general. I imagine you will find it unsafe to proceed from Vienna to Constantinople. I do not think the object will justify any personal risk. Mr. Short is not yet decided as to his route or the time of his beginning it. I am with very great esteem Dear Sir your friend & servt., TH: JEFFERSON

PrC (DLC); at foot of text: "Mr. J. Rutledge junr."

To De Vernon

MONSIEUR à Paris ce 12me. Aout 1788.

La derniere lettre que j'ai reçu de Monsieur Bannister le pere est du 23me. Decembre. Il m'y annonces ses craintes qu'il y aura peu de chose recouvré de Monsieur Marck. Il dit que M. Marck avoit retiré les interets des "Continental loans," et une somme de principal beaucoup plus considerable qui lui avoit eté payé des fonds destinés au remboursement des creanciers etrangers par l'etat de Virginie: que le dividende de cette année sera d'environ 3600.[tt] tournois pour vous, lequel il vous remettra le moment qu'il l'aura reçu, avec les extraits justificatifs des livres de la tresorerie. Je suis faché de vous annoncer en même tems que depuis cette epoque la santé de Monsieur Bannister le pere a eté tellement derangée qu'il a eté obligé de faire une voiage aux isles, ou il attendra son retablissement. Dans ce cas il me paroit que vous ferez bien d'envoyer une autorisation à Monsieur Jean Bannister le fils, semblable à celle que vous avez envoyé au pere, pour que les recouvrements de vos fonds ne souffrent de delai. Vous pouvez conter sur la probité et la bonne volonté du fils autant que du pere. J'ai l'honneur d'etre Monsieur votre tres humble et tres obeissant serviteur,

Th: Jefferson

PrC (MoSHi). Tr (MoSHi); in De Vernon's hand, but misdated 12 Aug. 1786. This Tr, which includes also on verso an extract from Banister to TJ, 6 May 1787 (in French translation), was possibly enclosed in De Vernon to TJ, 25 June 1808, a fact that may explain the errors in date; in addition, it bears on verso the following note concerning TJ's suggestion in the present letter: "En exécution de la lettre dont copie est de L'autre part, le 24 août ⟨*1787*⟩ 1786, Mr. de Vernon à envoyé à Mr. Jefferson La procuration pour M. Banister, fils." According to an entry in SJL Index, De Vernon complied with this suggestion in a (missing) letter of 13 Sep. 1788, but, since that was the date on which TJ forwarded the power of attorney to young Banister, he, too, may have erred.

TJ's reference to Banister's DERNIERE LETTRE as being that of 23 Dec. 1787 is puzzling. The present description of the contents of that letter appears to apply to that from Banister of 6 May 1787, which was written some time after TJ had sent, in his letters of 26 Jan. and 6 May 1786, the papers relating to the case. It is possible that TJ erred in making the entry in SJL Index and that the missing letter from Banister recorded as having been written on 31 Jan. 1788 was actually a letter of 23 Dec. 1787 but received on that date.

To Stephen Cathalan, Sr.

Sir — Paris Aug. 13. 1788.

I have to acknolege the receipt of your two favors of June and July 11. and to thank you for the political intelligence they contained which is always interesting to me. I will ask a continuance of this, and especially that you inform me from time to time of the movements in the ports of Marseilles and Toulon which may seem to indicate peace or war. These are the most certain presages possible, and being conveyed to me from all the ports, they will always enable me to judge of the intentions or expectations of the ministry, and to notify you of the result of the intelligence from all the ports, that you may communicate it to the American commerce.

I have the pleasure to inform you that the new constitution proposed to the United states, has been established by the votes of 9. states. It is happy for us to get this operation over before the war kindled in Europe could affect us, as by rendering us more respectable we shall be more probably permitted by all parties to remain neutral.

I take the liberty of putting under your cover a letter for Mr. Bernard, containing some seeds, and another to Giuseppe Chiappe our consul at Mogador. I thank you for your settlement of the price of the Observations meteorologiques, and I have repaid the 60. livres to Sr. John Lambert in your name.

When the nursery man, whom you have been so good as to employ to prepare the olives and olive plants to be sent to Charleston, shall be executing that commission, I shall be glad if he will at the same time prepare a few plants only[1] of the following kinds

Figs, the best kind for drying, and the best kind for eating fresh.
Raisins. The best kind for drying. A few plants.
Brugnolles. Do.
Cork trees, a few plants.
Pistaches } A few plants.
Capers }

I desire only a few plants of each of these that they may not take too much of the place of the olives which is our great object, and the sole one we have at heart. If you will be so good as to give the Nursery man this order immediately, it will save you the necessity of recurring to my letter when the season comes. I have the honour to be with great and sincere esteem, Sir your most obedient & most humble servt.,

Th: Jefferson

PrC (DLC). Enclosures: (1) TJ to Bernard, 12 Aug. 1788. (2) TJ to Chiappe, following.

An entry in TJ's Account Book for 2 Aug. 1788 and a receipt of the same date (DLC), signed by "Abbema & Cie. successeurs de M. le Chev. Lambert," show when the payment of 60[tt] was made and credited to Cathalan.

[1] The preceding four words are in substitution for "some," deleted, and their repetition elsewhere in the text indicates how strongly TJ felt about the need for concentrating on the "great object."

To Giuseppe Chiappe

à Paris ce 13me. Aout 1788.

J'ai l'honneur, Monsieur, de vous accuser la reception de plusieurs de vos lettres, c'est à dire, du 27me. Decembre, 26me. Fevrier, 6me. Mars, et 24me Mai, et de vous remercier des details que vous avez eu la bonté de m'y donner. L'amitié dont sa majesté l'Empereur (que dieu conserve) daigne d'honorer les etats unis d'Amerique leur est infiniment chere et flatteuse, et j'espere que la commerce qui se fera consequemment entre les deux nations sera d'une utilité reciproque. Il paroit que le moment n'est pas bien eloigné ou l'Europe va etre embrasée d'une guerre generale. Comme les motives de cette guerre n'est nullement interessants à nous, nous esperons d'y garder la neutralité la plus parfaite. Si sa Majesté donc y prend part, ou s'il n'en prend pas, nous resterons toujours egalement ses amis, et nous esperons que notre correspondence avec ses sujets ira toujours de meme. Je vous prie de nous aider de vos bons offices près de lui pour la conservation de ses faveurs dans toutes les occasions, de ne cesser de me donner les informations qui peuvent nous etre interessantes, et d'agreer les assurances des sentiments d'estime et d'attachement avec lesquels j'ai l'honneur d'etre, Monsieur, votre tres humble et tres obeissant serviteur, TH: JEFFERSON

PrC (DLC); at foot of text: "M. Giuseppe Chiappe. Mogador."

From William Carmichael

Madrid, 14 Aug. 1788. After examining his accounts with Congress, he has taken liberty of drawing on Willink & Van Staphorst at Amsterdam for 4614*f.* 3s. 6d. in accordance with TJ's advice of 3 June. "I transmit you the first setts of Exchange in favor of Messrs. Etienne Drouilhet & Cy. who have constantly supplied me with Money for my necessary expences while they have refused credit to others of the Corps diplomatic and even to a Son of Ld. North who lately passed thro this capital." Is informing Willink & Van Staphorst of this, and hopes this is agreeable. [*Postscript*:] After consulting with Messrs. Drouilhet "it appears unnecessary to send the draft . . . as the Advice of its Amount, &ca. will answer your purpose and that of My Friends here."

RC (DLC); 2 p.; endorsed; some calculations in TJ's hand on verso.

From John Brown Cutting

SIR London Aug. 14. 1788

Your letter of the 24th had so tardy a passage to me that I supposed it must have been interscepted, especially as a subsequent one of the 28th came punctually and with speed. To the latter I have already replied. For the political statements and weighty intelligence of the former I am greatly indebted. It is impracticable to learn aught here untinctur'd with english prejudices which are generally fertile of misrepresentation. In making this remark I do not allude to newspapers or any of those fugitive publications which are fabricated for hire, merely, but also to men of some ability and consideration in political situations. I have found means of access to the confidental friend of one of the english administration who I have reason to think communicates freely and with sincerity the creed of his principal, as to foreign affairs. It may perhaps entertain you to learn what is suggested and believed in the higher circles of office here. It is said and credited by the ministerial people that France and not England monopolizes the confidence of the turkish government as she does the commerce of the turkish empire, and that however she may temporize and dissemble, she will sustain them to the utmost against the two Empires, who are too formidable for her to unite with as friends or openly to combat with as foes. Hence she will play a double game with both. It is further asserted that the king of Sweden has been influenced by her and not by England to attack Russia, and that the money enabling him to equip his present armament actually [ca]me from Turkey at the instance of France, whose chief efforts are now bent to defeat the projects of the Emperor and Empress and save the turks. As to taking a part in the war openly either against England or any of her allies it is thought she is totally unable. Mr. Pitt is convinced of this inability and therefore proceeds to form continental connexions and to detach her allies fearless of her efforts and resolute to maintain England in peace by bold preparation and the rugged aspect of war. These are the insinuations of english personages here who likewise indulge a hope that what they call the stupid obstinacy of the french king, whom they suppose weak, or intemperate, headstrong and the reverse of liberal or enlighten'd, will prevent the formation of any constitution for France, and finally end in a seperation of some of the provinces from the monarchy.

I have not yet possessed myself of further details concerning the convention of Virginia, excepting only that the numbers were eighty nine to seventy eight.

Early in Sept. I now expect to sail for Charlestown, as health is quite restor'd again. I believe my passage is secured in the first vessel that shall proceed; if so I shall have the satisfaction to be the bearer of your letters to that City. When I had the honor to obtain a letter or two from You last Autumn to the Governor of South Carolina and to Mr. E. Rutledge, I omitted to enquire if Doctor Ramsay were among the number of your acquaintance. I understand he is an active and industrious member of the legislature:—and as I expect to encounter much difficulty in negotiation with that body, I cou'd wish to have my personal intercourse with such a character smoothed by the weight of such an introduction, as from your repeated kindnesses and condescention, I know you will give me if you can do it with propriety. With much respect and attachment I have the honour to be Your obliged and mo. obedt. Svt.,

John Brown Cutting

RC (DLC).

From C. W. F. Dumas

The Hague, 14 Aug. 1788. Hoping that TJ receives *Gazette de Leide* as ordered, he only encloses a letter to Congress and transmits following from friends in Amsterdam, who have it from Daniel Parker, dated the 8th: "This moment I have received advice, that the State of Virginia adopted the new Constitution on the 25th June. This comes by a Ship arrived this Day, and may be depended on."—"Ce n'est pas ma faute si le dernier article fourni à Mr. Luzac ne parut pas avant hier dans son papier. J'espere de le voir inséré dans celui de Vendredi."

RC (DLC); endorsed. FC (Dumas Letter Book, Rijksarchief, The Hague; photostats in DLC); differing in that Daniel Parker's letter is not quoted but instead there is the following: "(fiat insertio d'après la Lre. de Mr. N. Hubbard, d'hier 12e.)," the phrase "d'hier 12e." being explained by the fact that Dumas altered the date of the above letter from 13 to 14 Aug. Enclosure: Dumas to Jay, 9 Aug. 1788, with postscripts of the 11th, 13th, and 15th, stating that he is sending gazettes by two vessels leaving from Amsterdam; that he cannot emphasize too much the opinion given him that "les Et-Un. prennent toutes les précautions possibles, sans donner de l'ombrage, afin que leurs Pêcheurs et Navigateurs soient sur leurs gardes contre toute surprise," to be put into effect the moment a rupture takes place in Europe; that, aside from the gravity of the source, what gives weight to the warning is (1) the rancor toward the United States on the part of England because former subjects are now become equals, (2) the customary practices of that power in the beginning of its wars with France, and (3) the advantage of procuring sailors for its own use and depriving the United States of them; that the general precaution necessary is that of defending coasts, harbors, and rivers, "bien armés et alertes"; that here the financial affairs of the province are in the greatest embarrassment, a loan of 15,000,000 florins having been opened and, what is without precedent, not subscribed; that various other expedients have been tried in order to stave off total bankruptcy and ruin of commerce; that the illumination on the Princess' anniversary was more splendid than ever before, enough powder having been wasted to enable Constantinople or Belgrade to be taken and the orgies having made sleep impossible; that [*in postscript of 11th*] he encloses a plan for the emission of a loan of five million florins at 4%; that [*in postscript of 13th*] he has just this moment learned of the ratification of the Constitution by Virginia, and he hopes that the prediction made in the attached article in the *Gazette de Leide* will prove similarly valid for the other states; that "Les Russes chantent aussi le Te Deum pour le combat naval du 17 dans la Baltique"; that the gazettes will inform Jay of the probable course that the spreading conflict will take; that he desires to quote from dispatches of 26 July and 1 Aug. 1788 those passages particularly requiring the attention of Congress; that the touchstone for matters relating to the prevailing system in Europe is Cicero's *nihil simplex, nihil in politicis honestum, nihil illustra, nihil forte, nihil liberum*; that, thanks to God, the United States has given "le plus illustre et depuis la création l'unique Exemple de Sagesse et de perfection progressive à tous les Gouvernemens et de félicité vraie à tous les peuples du monde—Ainsi soit-il, et que Dieu les bénisse de plus en plus et avec eux leur honble Congres & V.E."; that [*in postscript of 15th*] Baron de Capellen de Marsh, a refugee in Paris, had been condemned by the Court of Gueldre to be disgraced and to have his head cut off; and that at Overyssel the tomb of Capellen de Pol and the monument erected by the Patriots had been smashed by cannon powder (same; the RC of this letter, along with others from Dumas to Jay between 1 Aug. 1788 and 20 Jan. 1789 are missing, but are listed in *Dipl. Corr., 1783-89*, III, 628-9).

The DERNIER ARTICLE FOURNI A MR. LUZAC was that respecting the reception of John Adams (see note to TJ to Dumas, 30 July 1788). Dumas wrote Adams at this time congratulating him upon his arrival, informing him that he had sent to Luzac the details that he had received "de la bonté de Mr. Jefferson," quoting almost word for word the passage from his letter to Jay about the example set by the United States for all the world, and repeating the words of Cicero (same, dated "Août 1788"). The news of Virginia's ratification, received in London by Parker on 8 Aug., in Amsterdam by Hubbard on 12 Aug., in The Hague by Dumas on 13 Aug., and in Paris by TJ about 17 or 18 Aug., was evidently the first that came to him, Cutting's more direct letter of 8 Aug. having been delayed (see TJ to Cutting, 23 Aug. 1788).

From Benjamin Lincoln

Boston, 14 Aug. 1788. His "amiable young friend Mr. Hays leaves this town in a few days for France where he means to compleat his knowledge in the french language and acquaint himself with the mode of doing business in that nation." He will pay his respects, and TJ's "countenance will essentially serve a youth of real merit."

RC (MHi); endorsed. Recorded in SJL as delivered "(by Mr. Hays)" on 15 Apr. 1789.

From Alexander McCaul

DEAR SIR Glasgow Augt the 14th 1788.

I received your agreable favour of the 12th Ulto only yesterday, and I am very sorry that your expectations from your Estate in Virginia should have so far dissappointed your good intentions of discharging your debt agreable to stipulation. Suffice it to say at present that what remittance you can make this year will be very acceptable and this you will be pleased to do in the manner most convenient to yourself. If it is by bills on London you may remitt directly to me or should it be more convenient to do it in

London make them payable to Robert & Hugh Ingram on my Account. You will no doubt be informed from Virginia that the new constitution was adopted in that state on the 25th of June by a small majority of ten and after a severe contest. I hope ere long to see the Government of that Country in the hands of Men of real property and integrity for sure I am they never can rise to be a great people unless Industry frugality and integrity become their prevailing character. When I first knew that Country I don't beleive there was in general an honester sett of people on the face of the Earth, but wonderfully have they changed of late years, and you will be amazed when I tell you that among the great number of respectable names that owed money to my Partners and myself that not one amongst them have said they would pay their debts except yourself Mr. John Rose and Mr. John Nicholas. It will serve no good purpose for me to complain, but I have been hardly used, my Property confiscated and withheld from me, and instead of its being allowed to go at least to the discharge of Virginia debts these very debts sent to this Country against me to a very considerable amount and which I have been obliged to pay. I would hope this new constitution will be productive of good, establish an effective Government in all the states and make the debtors think seriously of paying. My friend Mr. Lyle whom you know writes thus "had the prohibitory Laws been repealed immediately on the Peace the Planters would have continued the frugal plans they followed during the War, been gradually paying their old debts and have been at this day in better circumstances than they now are in, but instead of this dissipation and extravagance had pervaded all ranks." This very same idea Mr. John Nicholas has of it in a long letter I had from him. I shall be very happy occasionally to hear from you and I am with great regard &c.

Sept. 29. As I have reason to fear my letter of the 14th of August misscarried having wrote to Bourdeaux and Rotterdam by the same Post which I know now did misscarry you have above a copy of that letter to which I have nothing at present to add but that with great regard I am Dr Sir Your mo. hum Servt.,

ALEXR. MCCAUL

Dupl (DLC). As indicated in the postscript of 29 Sep., the original evidently miscarried. Recorded in SJL Index under its earlier date of 14 Aug.

From Thomas Lee Shippen

MY VERY DEAR SIR Berne 14th August 1788

I did not expect to have had the honor of writing to you before I reached Geneva, and it is principally to implore your protection for a parcel of letters which I have finished for America that I have determined to take that liberty. It is a parcel for which I am very anxious to ensure a speedy passage and you will oblige me Sir infinitely by procuring it. If the British Packet should sail sooner than the French I must beg you to send it by that, and if any opportunity present itself before either, to send it by that opportunity, provided it be a good and a safe one. I am extremely sensible of the weight of my obligations to you, and shall never forget them. The letters of recommendation have added much to your former favors, and I am sure I shall have a thousand additional reasons when I deliver to thank you for them. At present I am on the wing for Geneva where I expect to pass a fortnight at least from this time. My address will therefore be poste restante at Geneva. However from that place I shall have the honor of writing to you again and assuring you as I do now with the greatest cordiality and sincerity that I am very much your devoted and affectionate servant, THOS. LEE SHIPPEN

RC (DLC); endorsed. The enclosed parcel of letters has not been identified, but one of them was evidently that of 31 July 1788 to his father, Dr. William Shippen, which TJ enclosed in his to Trumbull, 24 Aug. 1788.

From John Brown Cutting

SIR London Aug. 15th. 1788

Mr. Jarvis has been so long detained beyond the time which he at first proposed as the period when he meant to proceed for Paris, that my letters have accumulated on his hands. This evening however he assures me is the last previous to his departure. I have therefore devoted two or three hours in hunting at the several Coffee houses for recent intelligence from America, and more particularly from Virginia. But with very little success. I can not yet obtain those details concerning the late Conventi[on] of your native Commonwealth, which I believe wou'd be gratifying to one so intimately acquainted with the characters who discuss'd the great question at Richmond. Truth however obliges me to correct my letter of Aug. 8. I find the numbers were only 89 to 79.

The inclosed Newspaper contains all that I know respecting the proceedings of New York, excepting the opinion o[f] a gentleman lately from that City, who says a majority of the Convention will certainly assent to the fœderal constitution. [If] any thing interesting or even amusing from any of the United St[ates] shoud arrive within these ten day you may rely upon an early communication of it.

Your corrective letter of the 6th ulto.—is the m[ost] unpleasant one I have ever had the honor to receive from You. Because *that* previous to it contained not only the [. . .] but details which I so implicitly credited, that I instantly [wrote] the same to Mr. Adams, Col. Smith and one or two other friends.

Still such is my attachment to truth that I th[ank] you sincerely for the ulterior information. The report of [the d]ay here is that France England and Prussia are in councils united for the purposes of preserving peace to the three powers, notwithstandin[g] the present flame in the North. Sir James Harris is here from the Hague. The King returns from Chetenham to Windsor tomorrow. On tuesday a cabinet council assembles—from their decision much is expected to result. If aught transpires that I can catch, I will commit it to paper. In too much haste to be correct, or I fear even intelligible, I have the honor to be, with increased respect and attachment Your obliged & most obedt. Servt.,

John Brown Cutting

RC (DLC); endorsed; MS slightly mutilated, and some words and parts of words supplied conjecturally.

From William Gordon

Dear Sir London Augst. 15. 1788

From the generous encouragement you gave me in your answer to my first letter, I informed your Excellency about April, that I should be greatly obliged to you, could you assist me in a similar way to that by which Dr. Ramsay was benefited. I left it with your judgment to settle the terms, and proposed sending over the printed volumes that the translation might be entered upon. Receiving no answer, I wrote afresh upon the subject about six weeks ago. Neither of the letters being replied to, am apprehensive that either they or their answers have miscarried. I carefully avoided public affairs, lest touching upon them should prove a bar to their progress. A friend of mine, Mr. John Dickinson of Doctors Commons, being upon a tour of pleasure I have intrusted this with him, as I can rely upon his delivering it, and taking all proper care of any letter you may condescend to write. Could you with propriety send me an account where the marquis de la Fayette is, and what is the state of public affairs in France, you would add greatly to the favor. Should you have any package to send by Mr. Dickinson, which you would wish to go by the ship from London to the United States, let it come under cover directed to me, with a request to him to see to the delivery of it, and I doubt not of his bringing it me. With most respectful compliments I remain Your Excellency's most obedient humble servant,

William Gordon

Have printed as far as the 304 page of the fourth and last volume.

RC (DLC); endorsed. Gordon's FIRST LETTER was that of 20 Feb. 1787 and TJ's ANSWER was that of 2 July 1787; Gordon was mistaken in thinking that there was no answer and he erred by thinking he WROTE AFRESH in his letter of 24 Apr. 1788. See TJ's reply of 2 Sep. 1788.

From John Ledyard

Sir — Alexandria in Egypt Aug. 15. 1788.

As I go to Cairo in a few days from whence it will be difficult to write to you I must do it from here tho unprepared: I must also leave my Letter in the hands of the Capt. (who engages to deliver it to Mr. Cathalan at Marseilles) 4 or 5 weeks.—I am in good health and spirits, and the prospects before me respecting my enterprize flattering. This with wishes for your happiness and an eternal remembrance of your goodness to me must form the only part of my Letter of any Consequence except that I also desire to be remembered to the Marquiss la fayette, his lady, Mr. Short and other friends. Deducting the week I staid at Paris and 2 days at Marseilles [I][1] was only 34 days from London to this place: I am sorry to inform you that I regret having visited Mr. Cathalan and of having made use of your name: I shall ever think tho he was exteriorly polite that he rather strove to prevent my embarking at Marseilles than to facilitate it. For by bandying me about among the members of the Chamber of Commerce he had nearly—and very nearly lost me my passage—and in the last Ship from Marseilles for the season. He knew better: he knew that the Chamber of Commerce had no business with me—and besides I only asked him if he could without trouble *address me to the Capt. of a Ship bound to Alexandria.*—nothing more.

Alexandria at large forms a scene wretched and interesting beyond any other that I have seen: poverty, rapine, murder, tumult blind bigotry, cruel persecution, pestilence. A small town built on the ruins of antiquity—as remarkable for its base and miserable Architecture as I suppose the place once was for its good and great works of this kind. A pillar called the pillar of Pompey, and an Obelisk called Cleopatra's are now almost the *only* remains of great Antiquity—they are both and particularly the former noble subjects to see and contemplate and are certainly more captivating from the contrasting desarts and forlorn prospects around them. No man of whatever turn of mind can see the whole without retiring from the scene with a "sic transit gloria Mundi"—but I have not begun yet to view those scenes so affecting in the history of unfortunate Man: and why thus unfortunate?—who can feel the interrogation: who deny the fact: who divine the cause. To be the more confounded I am going to Cairo—from thence perhaps thro scenes embossed with riddles still more mortifying. Untill I arive there I must bid you adieu and have the honor to be with perfect esteem Sr. your much obliged and affectionate hble servt.,

J. LEDYARD

P.S. I send this to the Care of Mr. Cathalan—and if I can will write you again from some quarter.

RC (NHi); endorsed. Tr (Mrs. Jane Ledyard Remington, Cazenovia, N.Y., 1951). For Cathalan's account of his help to Ledyard, see Cathalan to TJ, 17 Nov. 1788.

[1] MS has an ampersand, but the pronoun was clearly intended.

From Schweighauser & Dobrée

SIR — Nantes 15 August 1788

We recieved in course Your Excellency's kind letter of the 20th. Ulto. We knew nothing of the resolve of Congress of the 16th. October 1786. Whatever has been done in America respecting the Alliance since our first application has been witheld from us, and we have never had any answer to our repeated representations. We have shown the resolve and Your Excellency's letter to Mr. Minyer and represented to him that we had little hopes of ever seeing this affair settled unless we adopt the mode you propose. All we have said has been useless and he persists in his opinion.

Vexed to be the only real sufferers in this affair we have applied to an eminent counsellor to be advised by him, but the unhappy disturbances of the province have forced all the lawyers to a resolve not to act till they were arranged, and *he has declined giving us his opinion*. Thus circumstanced we trust that Your Excellency will find some means of rendering us justice and entirely confide on your equity.

As Congress directs that the arms shall be applied to the payment of this affair, we would think it advisable to sell them by public auction before a Notary public in whose hands the amount can be deposited, as the warehouse rent grows heavy and in the neglected state in which they lay become every day of less value. We have the honor to be &c.,

(Signed) SCHWEIGHAUSER & DOBRÉE

Tr (Arch. Aff. Etr., Paris, Corr. Pol., Angleterre, Vol. 566); in Short's hand. Schweighauser & Dobrée were not accurate in saying that what had been done in America had been WITHELD FROM US: TJ informed them on 12 Feb. 1787 that he had received orders from Congress to settle the accounts, and Schweighauser & Dobrée had themselves actually transmitted a copy of those orders to him.

From John Stockdale

SIR — Piccadilly 15th Augt. 88.

I have this Instant received your two Letters by the hands of my good friend Mr. Trumbold and the ballance of your Account up to the present time, as ℔ Account annexed Viz £13.13.6. for which I return you my sincere thanks as well as for your kind remittance of the French Books. From Letters which I have received from different Gentlemen in America I am convinced that the whole of the Impression of your Book would have been sold immediately had they been sent there, but I have my doubts wether I should have been able to have got remittances for them, having not yet received any, or even answers to my Letters, for several Years Past, excepting Dr. Ramsay. But I sincerely hope that the new Constitution will have the desired effect and put them upon a better footing. I am Just inform'd by a friend from Philadelphia that the report of the failure of Mr. Aicken Bookseller was groundless. I am with great respect & esteem Sir Your obliged and yr. very hble. Servt., JOHN STOCKDALE

RC (MHi); endorsed. The ACCOUNT ANNEXED is substantially the same as that stated in TJ's letter to Stockdale of 17 July 1788; the reviews and their appendixes came to 15s. instead of the 13s. 6d. estimated by TJ, thus making the item "By Cash of Mr. Trumbold" £13 13s. 6d. instead of £13 12s. 0d.

From John Trumbull

Dr. Sir London August 15th. 1788

Will you excuse my having so long omitted to write you—the mortification arising from efforts not so successfull as I wishd in my pursuits, have prevented me from attending to anything but the surmounting the difficulties I found. That is in a degree accomplishd and I devote my first moments to you.—Yours of the 17th. 24th. and 28th ulto. are in my hands. The letters enclos'd the 24th. for Mrs. McCaul, Jones and Digges were forwarded instantly. Those for Charlestown there is no better opportunity of sending than by the Ship in which Mr. Cutting proposes to sail, about the end of this month: *if* he goes I shall give them to his care, otherwise I will put them in the Ships Letter bag, where they will be equally secure. I do not find that any time can be sav'd by sending them to New York.

The Letter enclos'd the 28th. for Mr. Bannister was sent by the Louisa, Capt. Dixon, which saild the 5th. inst. for Norfolk in James River.

The Diligence which leaves this tomorrow will bring you Brown's two pictures, your polyplasiasmos, and a picture of Genl. Washington which belongs to Mr. De La Fayette, and which you will be so good to send him. They are all in one case.

Of the Carriage. I have search'd in vain. Perch carriages (which won't do for you) abound, but the crane neck is not so much us'd, tho infinitely more in demand; so that I really don't find any second hand thing for which I should dare give the price which is ask'd.—In the mean time I am offer'd (by a young man who is a principal Journeyman at one of the first Carriagemakers in town, and who wishes to get into business for himself,) to build me as good a Carriage for 105 Guineas as I should get at the Shops for 130—that is He would give it me for a very trifling profit to himself whereas theirs is extravagant:—and He proposes that if when He shall have compleated it I do not like the work or the Fashion, He will not expect me to take it.—I know the Man to be an excellent Workman and honest, and he has some little obligations to me:—If therefore you are pleas'd to give me conditional and plenary powers to go to this price, or to take my chance of searching further for a second hand, I will do for you as I should do for myself.

I have not seen one which I could think of (except the first) for less than £80, and I think that any use almost will make the 25 difference. I wait your answer.

From the Convention at New York we [hear] there is a great probability of their acceding. We expect the Packet every hour when we shall know.

I believe I mention'd *Payne*, *Kings Mews-Gate* as the Classical Bookseller most likely to serve you. I am Yours,

JNO. TRUMBULL

Stockdale is paid.

RC (DLC); endorsed; slightly mutilated and one word supplied conjecturally; addressed; postmarked: "AU 15 88" (within circle) and "D'ANGLETERRE."

From Aleaume

Paris, 16 Aug. 1788. Encloses two letters of procuration that the Count de Cambray hopes TJ will attest "et faire passer en Amerique, ainsy qu'il doit avoir eu l'honneur de vous en prier." These were sent to him to be attested by the Prévôt des Marchands et Echevins of Paris, but this can be done only for documents executed in the city. They are already attested by the royal judge of Montdidier, and so it only remains to affirm that full faith is given this attestation in France and ought to be so given everywhere else.

RC (DLC); endorsed by TJ: "Cambrai, Cte de." Enclosures not found; they were forwarded by TJ to the French consul in Charleston (see TJ to Petry, 21 Aug. 1788; TJ to Cambray, 7 Oct. 1788).

To Angelica Schuyler Church

Paris Aug. 17. 1788.

The urn is well worth acceptance, my dear Madam, on it's own account, for it is a perfect beauty: but it is more flattering to me to accept it on account of the giver. I shall preserve it as sacred as I would the urns of my forefathers, had I all of them from Adam to the present day, and with this difference of estimation that it recalls to my mind a living friend. The memorial of me which you have from Trumbul is of the most worthless part of me. Could he paint my friendship to you, it would be something out of the common line. I should have been happy indeed to have made a third at Down-place with yourself and Mrs. Cosway. Your society would have been amusement enough for me. I never blame heaven so much as for having clogged the etherial spirit of friendship with a body which ties it to time and place. I am with you always in spirit: be you with me sometimes. I have in contemplation to visit America in the Spring, as Madame de Corny has mentioned to you. I have not as yet asked a Congé, because, till the new government is in activity, I know not to whom to address my request. I presume it will not be denied me. The project of carrying with me colonies of animals and plants for my native country, will oblige me to embark at Havre, as being the nearest port. This is but twenty hours distant from London. Can you, my dear madam, sacrifice twenty hours of your life to make my daughters and myself happy? In this event we might make our trips in concert. I allow myself all the months of April, May, and June, to find a good ship. Embarking in either of these months we shall avoid being out during the equinoxes and be sure of fine weather. Think of it then, my friend, and let us begin a negociation on the subject. You shall find in me all the spirit of accomodation with which Yoric began his with the fair Piedmontese. We have a thousand inducements to wish it on our part. On yours perhaps you may find one in the dispositions we shall carry with us to serve and amuse you on the dreary voiage. Madme. de Corny talks of your brother coming to Europe for you. How much easier for him to meet you in Williamsburgh! Besides, I am your brother. Should this proposition be absolutely inadmissible, I will flatter myself with the hope of seeing you at New York, or even at Albany if I am master enough of my time. To see the country will be one motive: but to see you a much stronger, and to become acquainted with your father who must be good, because you are so. The fruit is a specimen of the tree. I had the honour of serving with him in Congress in the year 1775. but probably he does not remember me.

I have just deposited Kitty in good health in the Chaussée d'Antin. I had a consultation with Madame de Corny last night, the result of which was to insist on her being translated from the drawing mistress to the drawing master of the Convent. Write to me sometimes, and permit me to answer your letters. God bless you, my dear madam, your affectionate friend

TH: JEFFERSON

RC (Peter B. Olney, Old Saybrook, Connecticut, 1950). PrC (CSmH).

The MEMORIAL OF ME YOU HAVE . . . FROM TRUMBUL is reproduced in Vol. 10: 466.

From Lucy Ludwell Paradise

Dear Sir Paris August the 17th. 1788

I hope you will pardon my troubling you with my Letters so often, but, Indeed, I do not know the reason, but when, I have the honour, and happiness of conversing with you, I cannot Speak often, what, I would wish to say, therefore it is that I am obliged to have recourse to this method to converse with Your Excellency. I have been turning in my mind what you mentioned to me, for one person to take the whole of the Debt upon themselves, and Indeed, could that person be found, who would do so, I know it to the best method. I was thinking if Count Antonio Barziza my Son in Law would take that upon him, it would be a very good thing for all parties. If your Excellency thinks what, I have said to be right, I should esteem it a favour if you would take the trouble to give me your advice upon it. But suppose he could not do it, does your Excellency know of any Person in England who would? I am certain by your wise, and good Counsels, not only myself will have reason to Bless you, but my dear Daughter and my Grand-Children. Inclosed I have left you the list of all the Debts of Mr. Paradise in England for your perusal. With submission to your Excellency, I think that as Colo. Nath. Burwell is not personally acquainted with the Creditors, the list can be of no use to him. To Dr. Bancroft and Mr. Anderson it is absolutely necessary as they are upon the Spot and know them. What happiness should I enjoy, could I see Mr. Paradise as thoughtful, regular, Active and Industrious as you are. For then I should begin to hope to see him bring back part of the Money he very foolishly spent in England. I do assure you my dear Sir I am not ambitious, what I want, is to see our affairs in a regular train to live a quiet regular Life and doing as much good as I can to those Friends, who when I stood in need of their advice and assistance, served me and my family with all their hearts. The Almighty as been pleased to raise up your Excellency to regulate my affairs so as to bring them into the train I could wish. He has also attached Mr. Paradise to you so, that he absolutely will not ask nor follow any persons advice except yours. This is the work of my God, I see it, and I believe it. Adieu My dear Sir And believe me to be with Gratitude Your Excellencies Humb. Servt. and Friend, Lucy Paradise

P.S. I wish your Excellency would do one thing for me before I go to Italy, which is to get from Mr. Paradise a promise that he will let me in the Spring Summer and Autumn manage his affairs. For to tell you the truth in confidence he is not able hardly at those seasons of the year to write a common Note.

RC (DLC). Enclosure not found.

From Nathaniel Barrett

DEAR SIR New York Aug 18. 1788

An Opportunity offering for france I cannot let it pass with[1] paying my respects to you, and acknowledgeing my Obligations for your polite Attentions.

You will find by the inclos'd Letter to the Marqs. that No. Carolina have rejected the Constitution. The only difficulty apprehended from this is that it may create some uneasiness by the Effect it may have on the Inhabitants of the back parts of Virginia. I wish the Adoption had been unanimous, as there can be no Doubt the Alterations necessary will be made. The Time of meeting is [Fixed upon] the place cannot be agreed—4½ states for Philadelphia, 6½ for New York—R.I. not represented. The members for both very resolute and shewing no present indication to receede. The prospect of a stable Government fills the minds of all people with pleasure except a few who are inimical to the Country. The commercial Affairs of the Country are in a more promising state than for some years. A regular system of duties and firmness in the Execution of Laws of Trade will put the Trade on the most respectable footing. The Exports begin to bear a comparison with the Imports, and in Massachusets are supposed to exceed. There may be some Deception, as I suppose more is run inwards than outwards, but the Increase of exports there is surprizing. As soon as the statement is compleat I will forward you a Copy. I wish the same accuracy was observed in the other states.

I have taken the Liberty of inclosing a Letter to Mr. Parker, of Consequence to him which I beg the favour of you to direct and forward to him as soon as possible.

Also a Letter for Madme. de Vaas which Mr. Short will oblige me by delivering—my compliments to him.

I had the pleasure of finding all your friends here very well, and in high Spirits.

If the misconceptions of some persons here in high Rank from france do not cause prejudices against that Kingdom in the minds of the people here, and their misrepresentations have the same

Effect there, I am sure that the commercial Interests of the 2 Countries will be very much extended in a short Time. But I shall be able to write you more fully on this head soon. I am with the utmost Respect Sir Your obedt & Mo hum Servt,

NAT BARRETT

RC (DLC); endorsed. The enclosed letters to Lafayette, to Daniel Parker, and to Madame de Vaas have not been found.

The MISCONCEPTIONS OF SOME PERSONS HERE IN HIGH RANK were evidently those of Moustier, though presumably Barrett meant to include Madame de Brehan also.

[1] Thus in MS; "without" intended.

From André Limozin

MOST HONORED SIR Havre de Grace 18th August 1788

I had the honor of writing to your Excellency the 8th instant. I hope your articles come from Amsterdam will have reached you without the least Troubles.

I must acquaint your Excellency that our last Harvest of wheat so well in high and low Normandy as well in Brittany a Guyenne have been very short and in general of a bad quality, therefore I believe this Circumstance offers a very fine opportunity to America to import this year wheat and Flour with a great advantage in our Kingdom; for good wheat is sold now as high as 7 Lvers 10s, ℔ Bushell weighing 60 ℔ Paris weight with 4 ℔ C. for good measure. And it is expected that the price will be in short as high as 8 lvers. I believe it would be proper to publish that advice in america. The price of good wheat in Bordeaux is 15 Lvers 10s. ℔ Bushell weighing 140 ℔ Paris's weight. It is unhappy that we have no Ships coming here from America and bound thither back, in order to give that intelligence. I have the honor to be with the highest regard Your Excellency's Most obedient & humble Servant,

ANDRE LIMOZIN

RC (MHi); endorsed; addressed; postmarked "HAVRE."

From Maria Cosway

Down Place August the 19 1788

Many thanks My dear friend for your two letters, had I not reason to scold you? was such a long Silence friendly? and can you wish me not to take notice of it? No, that would be a Mark of too great an indiferance; Next to the pleasure of seing ones friends, is that of hearing from them; I never think so much of the distance we are from them, as the lenght of time we dont hear from them. I am Much flatterd by what you say of My Hours. I am happy you like the Idea, and the Author of that subject has every gratification and recompence by the wish she has inspired you with, of possessing some of her work. I thank you for giving me an opportunity of sending you a little souvenir of a talent that she would wish to possess in a higher degree that the Picture might be More deserving of being hung up in the room you inhabit Most that she may be recald to your remembrance as often as possible. I shall endevor to find a subject suited to your taste, you describe several, and all good, I shall see what I can do from your pinting out your choice. I am at present in the Country therefore it is impossible to begin immediatly an occupation I shall feel most happy when engaged about it, as I have nothing with me to paint with, nor any convineance for it.

Where do you think I am at present? and with whom? How Much we wish for you and think of you and speak of you, it is the amiable Mrs: Church, you know her, that is enough, and you are Capable of feeling the value of this lovely woman.

I have been Made very uneasy with the news that you intend to return soon to America, is it true? and is it possible! Oh then I give up the hopes of ever seing you again; wont' you come to pay us a visit first, it is but a little jurney for so Much pleasure you will procure us, pray lett me intreat you to Make me this promise. But we have hopes of going to Italy soon, I am doing every thing I can, use every argument, to make Mr: Cosway go next year, then My dear friend you should be of the party can you resist this proposition! I leave you to consider of it, and write to Me very soon. Mr: Cosway desires his best Compliments, and Mrs. Church has told me to say many things to you; I reccomand My self to be admitted to half she deserves of affection from you, t'will be a good share but never so much as I have for you—adiu.

Wish me joy for I possess your Picture. Trumbull has procured me the happiness which I shall ever be gratfull for.

RC (ViU); unsigned; endorsed. I POSSESS YOUR PICTURE: Trumbull's portrait of TJ, executed for Maria Cosway, is reproduced in Vol. 10: 466.

From Feger, Gramont & Cie.

Bordeaux, 19 Aug. 1788. Opportunities to recall themselves to TJ being rare, they seize this one eagerly: have just received by the ship *Kitty & Maria* a packet for TJ so voluminous that it would be costly to send by post, and they have taken advantage of an opportunity today to send it to Grand & Cie., whom they have notified also.

RC (MHi); 2 p.; in French; endorsed.

From John Bondfield

SIR Bordeaux 20 August 1788

I receiv'd ℔ last post a Letter under my Cover from you for the Honble. J. Jay, which I have deliverd to Mrs. Barclay.—Mrs. Barclay with her family arrived in good health on Saturday. They are on their passage to America having left this early this morning. One of the papers you deliverd Mrs. Barclay was the Inclosed paquet that she apprehends was put up thro mistake and has given it me to transmit you.

Vessels from America arrive dayly. We have had Eight within few Days, three of Georgia their Cargoes composed of Rice Lumber and Tobacco, some Skins and Bees wax—this last article not being perticuly exprest in the Arret of the 29 Xbre. remains subject to 20 ℔ % ad. Valorum. It is not at this day an Article to merrit perticuler explications but in case of Amendements may be Noticed. The Captains from Georgia report favorably of that State as increasing rapidly.

Government has given orders that before ships from America are admitted to an Entry. To have a Certificate from the American Consul or Agent that their papers are in due form and that the ships are American property. In time I hope to establish such regulations that I may be able to give you an Exact State of our Imports and Exports. I have the Honor to be with due respect Sir Your most Obedient Humble Servant, JOHN BONDFIELD

RC (DLC); endorsed. TJ's letter for Jay was that of 11 Aug. 1788; the enclosed PAQUET has not been identified.

From Francisco Chiappe

Mequinez, 20 Aug. 1788. In his letter of 6 Mch. he promised to obtain a reply to the letter sent by Congress to the Emperor, but on his return to Morocco he found the Emperor on the point of departure on a long campaign against some rebellious provinces. He has been able only now to remind his majesty of the reply, which the latter ordered to be written at once, together with letters to the Beys of Tunis and Tripoli—but not to the Dey of Algiers, who is in disfavor and with whom it is not agreeable to communicate. A recommendation from "del Gran Signore" would be helpful in Algiers. The emperor had ordered him to write the letter to Congress, and all of these letters are being wrapped in kerchiefs in three boxes and sent, in a packet with the present letter, to Mr. Carmichael at Madrid to be forwarded. He has given the secretaries and others employed in this negotiation the usual gratuities. The commandant of the Dutch squadron in the Mediterranean has just departed from the court, where he came as ambassador and was well received; he is to deposit a gift of gold at Tangier, and has been charged to have sent by the states of Holland 1,000 bombs, 10 mortars, and a large table clock. His majesty has ordered Chiappe to write the consuls in Tangier that, since he is at peace with all nations, the captains of vessels need not obey his corsairs' orders to launch their small boats, but may reply from their own vessels when hailed. [*In postscript*:] Encloses translations of the three Arabic letters.

RC (MoSHi); 2 p.; in Italian; endorsed by TJ: "Chiappe Francesco." Enclosures: Italian translations of letters from the Emperor of Morocco (1) to the president of Congress, 17 Aug. 1788, acknowledging receipt of their letter and reaffirming the complete peace between the two nations; and (2) to the Bey of Tripoli, same date, stating that his nation is at peace with America and recommending that Tripoli make peace also, an act which will be of benefit to Tripoli since, when this is done, all munitions that may be sent from Morocco to Tripoli can then be transported in American ships (Tr in MoSHi; in Chiappe's hand, endorsed by TJ). No copy of the letter to the Bey of Tunis was enclosed, but at the bottom of the letter to Tripoli Chiappe stated that that to Tunis was similar. At Tangier early in October Chiappe found that the packet with letters to Carmichael and TJ had not been sent, owing to quarantine of Gibraltar and Spanish ports, and that the caskets and their kerchief wrappers could not be sent. He therefore undid everything and sent only the letters. The original letters in Arabic were forwarded to Jay by Carmichael, and the present letter and its enclosures were sent in Carmichael to TJ, 3 Nov. 1788, wherein Carmichael also enclosed copies of the Emperor's letters, omitting that to Tunis and Chiappe's postscript to that to Tripoli (Tr in DLC; in Carmichael's hand). See also *Dipl. Corr., 1783-89*, III, 370-2.

From Geismar

MON CHER AMI! a Hanau Ce 20. d'Aout 1788

La presence de mon Maitre le Landgrave m'a empeche jusqu'ici de Vous repondre plus tot. Depuis quelques Jours il est retourné à Cassel, c'est ce qui me permet de mieu disposer de mon tems. Msrs. Rutledge et Schippen, les quels Vous m'avés annoncés dans Votre derniere, ont passés içi, deux jeunes Gens qui repondent parfaitement à Votre description et dont l'éducation fait honneur au pais où ils l'ont obtenu; ils n'ont fait qu'une aparition içi, c'est ce qui m'a empêché de leur procurer l'agrément que je desirai;

cependant les ai-je persuadé de revenir prendre un diné à la Cour chés la Landgrave regnante (la Douairiere etoit absente) d'où ils paraissoient sortir assés content de la maniere dont on les avait reçu. Que le peu d'amusement que Ces Messieurs ont eu ne Vous decourage point à m'adresser d'autres de Vos Connaisance et de Vos Compatriottes; c'est en partie leur faute, n'aiant voulu S'areter, et Soiés persuadé, Mon Cher, qu'il suffit que quelqu'un me vienne de Vous pour enflamer toute ma reconnaisance et Souvenir de l'hospitalité dont j'ai jouï près de Vous.

Il vient de passer un jardinier chés moi, nomé Daniel Hoffmann, qui pretend etre mandé par un Mr. Samuel Laub, à Landin en Virginie où il va. Malgres cela il m'a demandé des recomandations pour ce pays, mais je ne suis en Corespondance avec personne dans ce pays. Je lui ai dis que je Vous ecrirais et que si Vous vouliés faire mention de lui dans une de vos lettres par le paquet boat, celui la arrivrait assurement long tems avant lui. Le Comisaire au quel il est adressé demeure à l'ange d'or sur le nouveau marché à Rotterdam. Je le connais etre fort bon Jardinier, aiant soigné et tenu en fort bon ordre le Jardin du Baron de Barlepik, Ministre du Landgrave qui vient d'aller demeurer à Cassel.—Rapellés Vous, mon Cher, que Vous m'aves promis une Description de l'amerique avec des Cartes qui devait sortir bien tot. Je ne Vous en tiens pas quitte, mais Vous prie de me le faire parvenir par une Occasion, et non pas par la Poste sur la quelle les paquets sont d'une Chereté enorme.—En meme tems j'ai une autre faveur a Vous demandé; m'aiant tant dis de l'élegance des Phaetons à 4 et des Cabriolets à deux roues de Paris, je Vous prierais de me faire avoir quelques Estampes de plusieurs de ces formes les plus à la mode, les plus legers et les plus près des Chevaux comme je compte en faire batir un cet hiver ces modeles me seront de grand usage; pour toute Comissions Chés vous, je suis en revenge à Vos ordres. Si je ne vais pas Vous voir à Paris, ce n'est pas faute de bonne Volonte, mais difficulté d'obtenir semestre et manque d'Argent. Si je puis faire tant de surmonter ces deux obstacles, et je ne desespere pas encore tout à fait, je viendrai san delai Vous assurer de bouche de l'amitié sincere avec la quele je Vous suis attaché

Le Major Geismar

RC (DLC); endorsed by TJ: "Geismer."

To Edward Hall, Jr.

Paris. Aug. 20. 1788.

Mr. Jefferson's compliments to Mr. Hall and troubles him with a letter to Mr. Jay, which should not go through the post-office. He begs the favor of Mr. Hall to send it by the best conveiance which shall occur at the sea-ports he is going to, and to be so good as to drop a line to Mr. Jefferson, informing him by what vessel and to what port he sends it. He wishes Mr. Hall a pleasant journey.

PrC (DLC). Enclosure: TJ to Jay, following.

To John Jay

Sir Paris Aug. 20. 1788.

I had the honor to write to you on the 3d. 10th. and 11th. instant with a postscript of the 12th. all of which went by Mrs. Barclay. Since that date we receive an account of a third victory obtained by the Russians over the Turks on the Black sea, in which the Prince of Nassau with his gallies destroyed 2 frigates, 3 smaller vessels, and 6. gallies. The Turkish power on that sea is represented by their enemies as now annihilated. There is reason to believe however that this is not literally true, and that, aided by the supplies furnished by the English, they are making extraordinary efforts to re-establish their marine. The Russian minister here has shewn the official report of Admiral Greigh on the combat of July 17. in which he claims the victory, and urges in proof of it that he kept the field of battle. His report is said to have been written on it. As this paper, together with the report of the Swedish admiral, is printed in the Leyden gazette of the 15th. inst. I inclose it to you. The court of Denmark has declared it will furnish to Russia the aid stipulated in their treaty: and it is not doubted they will go beyond this and become principals in the war. The next probable moves are that the king of Prussia will succour Sweden, and Poland Russia, by land: and a possible consequence is that England may send a squadron into the Baltic to restore the equilibrium in that sea. In my letter of the 11th. I observed to you that this country would have two difficulties to struggle with till the meeting of their States-general, and that one of these was the want of money. This has in fact over-borne all their resources, and the day before yesterday they published an arrêt suspending all reimbursements of capital, and reducing the paiments of the principal mass of demands for interest to 12. sous in the livre, the remaining eight sous to be paid with certificates. I inclose you a newspaper with the arrêt. In this paper you will see the exchange of yesterday;[1] and I have inserted that of the day before to shew you the fall. The consternation is as yet too great to let us judge of the issue. It will probably ripen the public mind to the necessity of a change in their constitution and to the substituting the collected wisdom of the whole[2] in place of a single will, by which they have been hitherto governed. It is a remarkeable proof of the total incompetency of a single head to govern a nation well, when with a revenue of six hundred millions they are led to a declared bankruptcy, and to stop the wheels of government, even in it's most essential movements, for want of money.

I send the present letter by a private conveiance to a sea port, in hopes a conveiance may be found by some merchant vessel. I have the honour to be with sentiments of the most perfect esteem and respect, Sir, your most obedient & most humble servant,

TH: JEFFERSON

RC (DNA: PCC, No. 87, II). PrC (DLC). Enclosures: (1) *Gazette de Leide*, 15 Aug. 1788. (2) The newspaper containing the arrêt of 18 Aug. 1788 has not been identified.

1 This word interlined in substitution for "this morning," deleted.

2 This word interlined in substitution for "nation," deleted.

From John Rutledge, Jr.

DR. AND VERY GOOD SIR Berne [ca. 20] August

On my arrival at this place, two days ago, I had the pleasure to receive yours of the fifteenth[1] of July. It is impossible to desire more than I do to make the journey you propose, and follow the route you have had the goodness to mark out, but the actual state of affairs forbids my thinking of it. Col. Miranda, who has for some days been my traveling companion, is very well acquainted with the route you suggest; if any thing could add to the desire, which your having recommended it has given me to make it, 'twould be the account he has given me of those interesting countries, but he also tells me it is quite impossible to visit Constantinople at this time, and that traveling through the Ottoman Territories, is not only unsafe but absolutely dangerous. Since writing to you I have thought of giving up the danube expidition, and instead of going to Vienna, as I intended, and by the way of Trieste into Italy, to cross the Alps. I cannot propose to myself any advantage which will result from the german tour; the Objects of it would be to know the Country, its politics commerce and manners. The system of their Politics seems intricate. Our commercial connections will never be considerable, and their manners are not to be desired: besides which, not speaking or knowing a word of the german language, it would be necessary to continue a much longer time in the Country than I conceive any advantage from so doing would be adequate to. I flatter myself this alteration of route will meet with your approbation and consent. Added to the reasons which I have stated to influence my making it, there is another, which I think not unworthy of attention. It is, that going from this Country across the Alps I shall be enabled to continue longer in Italy than I otherwise could have done, and the going previously to Germany would oblige me to go rapidly through Italy a country where there must be much for an Inhabitant of the southern States to notice and study. I am entirely of your opinion that the time I shall pass at Lisbon and Madrid will be well employed. To travel through much of Spain and Portugal will require much time and I think whatever one wishes to know of Countries (and Characters in them) may in general be best learnt at their Capitals and in their Environs.

Before this your Excellency will have heard of a second victory obtained by the Prince de Nassau, of the Russians being successful at Oczanow; these things, for a moment, promised that a stop would soon be put to the further effusion of Blood, but the conduct of Sweden has changed the prospect and the present scene announces a long general and bloody war. The Swedes have a considerable fleet at Sea, sixty thousand Prussians are in motion and it is very questionable whether England, fond of meddling in troubled waters, will remain quiet. It gives me great pleasure, my dear Sir, to learn that Virginia was likely to accept the new Constitution; and I hope, before I shall have the happiness of taking you by the hand in Paris, to learn not only that our Government is in motion but that it has been accommodated to the wills of the dissenting States and that all those blessings have been the consequences which the wisdom of those who composed it taught us to hope for. Mr. Short tells me it is pretty certain Genl. Washington will accept the Presidency of our new Government and that Dr. Franklin it is supposed will be nominated as vice president: in making choice of these Gentlemen the good sense of our countrymen will I think, manifest itself exceedingly and I am sure it will acquire great credit to our Government having, in its infancy, placed at its head two such illustrious Characters.

I was much pleased to learn by your letter that Affairs in France were not as bad as believed. I was much chagrin'd to read in the Leyden Gazette that our friend the marquis de la Fayette had experienced the dissatisfaction of his King but hope, from your not having mentioned it (having my information only from the News-Papers) that it is not true. I am very much indebted to you Dr Sir for the introductory letters you have sent me. I entertain the highest sense of your kindness and am with thanks for the many instances of sincere friendship with which you have honored me Your affectionate friend & devoted Servant,

J. Rutledge Junior

In the event of any Letters coming addressed to your excellency's care, I request you will forward them to Geneva Post restante? I shall not leave Geneva before the 15th. of September.

RC (DLC); endorsed.

[1] An error for 13 July 1788.

To James Carmichael

Sir Paris Aug. 21. 1788.

I think myself very unfortunate in having been absent when you did me the honor of calling on me in Paris. Particular occupation prevented my waiting on you immediately but I sent to your lodgings a note to ask yourself and Mr. Collow to do me the honor of dining with me; the messenger was informed however that you had just left Paris. I was the more mortified at this, as, besides the many other circumstances which entitle you both to my respect, yourself had particular right from the civilities you had shewn to me in Havre. I beg of you to be assured that I am incapable of either forgetting them, or of failing to give you a proof of my [sense] of them whenever an occasion shall occur. This one has slipped thro' my hands, but I hope it will not deprive me of the opportunity of seeing you, should your affairs lead you to Paris again at any time. Accept my excuse which I make with truth and regret, and be assured of the sentiments of esteem & attachment with which I have the honor to be Sir your most obedt. & most humble servt.,

Th: Jefferson

PrC (DLC); endorsed. TJ's note to yourself and mr. collow is missing, but see Carmichael to TJ, 25 Nov. 1788.

To André Limozin

Sir Paris Aug. 21. 1788.

Since my last which was of July 30. I have been honoured with yours of Aug. 6. 8. and 18. and the boxes from Amsterdam and cask from Hamburgh are all safely arrived and have been delivered to me without difficulty. The Acquit a caution is now inclosed. My long absence in the spring of the year and close occupation since my return had occasioned a want of attention to the advances you have been so kind as to make for me. On a recapitulation of them as stated in your several letters (since Nov. 1. when I think I last reimbursed you) I find myself indebted to you 254ᵗᵗ-17-9 according to the inclosed note. It is possible moreover that you may have made some advances not stated in your letters, and that some of those so stated may have escaped me. I therefore send you the inclosed recapitulation, begging the favor of you to insert any thing I may have omitted, and when you shall have ascertained the true balance give me leave to pay it to your banker here, or such other person as you please. I must pray of you to send the bust of the Marquis de la Fayette by the first vessel going into James or York river, addressed to the Governor of Virginia.—The Danes certainly enter into the war, and this will probably draw in the King of Prussia. England must come into it also, and France likewise if she can raise herself to strike. But this may not be the present year. I am with great esteem, Sir, your most obedt. humble servt.,

Th: Jefferson

PrC (DLC); endorsed. Enclosures: (1) The acquit a caution has not been found. (2) In MHi there is a statement of account with Limozin covering the shipment of three boxes of books to James Madison of 11 Jan. 1788, a barrel of rice by Jenkins on 1 Feb. 1788, two boxes of seeds sent by packet to James Madison and four barrels of fruit and one box of trees received by the packet on 27 Feb. 1788, five boxes of furniture from Amsterdam and a cask of smoked beef from Hamburgh of 7 Aug. 1788, totalling the amount stated above. On this TJ noted at a later date: "Pd this to Sartorius Nov. 4. 1788. but I ot to have pd 10—7s more for postage. See Limozin's letter Oct. 6. 1788. Carry this sum therefore to next account." Under date of 1 Apr. 1789 TJ also noted on this MS that he had paid Limozin for postage, for expenses of consular papers, for Lafayette's bust, "for a clock for Mr. Moore," and "for a case of vinegar," a total of 63ᵗᵗ 7s. 3d.

From Lucy Ludwell Paradise

My dear Sir August the 21st. 1788

I am, before I begin the Subject of this Letter to beg of Your Excellency to keep Secret what I shall communicate to you. It concerns my Country, It concerns your Exellency to assist many persons, but the assistance is only your advice, and Protection. I am serious when I beg you to keep Secret from every person in the World what I am to beg of you. Before I begin, permit me to open my heart to you which is to Bless you and thank you for the active part you have taken in my unhappy affairs, and to pray of you when we shall be very far seperated from each other that you will never forgit me and my Daughter in protecting our Rights in Virginia. In the last Letter I wrote to Bergamo I tell them that you have acted like my dear deceased Father Mr. Ludwell. I tell them also you have saved my Life. Think my dear Sir what Service I can be of to you as a Woman in Italy. I say a Woman, because you may think I have no abilities and no Industry. I have the latter, when they are to serve you, and my Children, and Friends but to the subject of this Letter. It is then to acquaint your Excellency that by the late Bankrupcy of the French-King there is some friends of mine who say that it is not in their power to live here, and that if it was possible to get to speak to you at your own house they would call upon you. I told the person that, I beleived that would be easy any Morning about 7 O'Clock. My friend said it was to talk to you about going to America. Of course I recommende our State. He said, he had a very large sum of money which he would put into your hands to settle him in a handsome [man]ner in Virginia. He is serious. The Name of this Gentelman is Mr. de Fondate. He told me he should marry there, and settle, or he must Starve here. Will you my dear Sir permit this Gentleman to call upon you to talk with you some Morning Early? If you will, you will be serving him, and many other people. I will not trouble you to write a long Letter a few words will do. Yes he may come will be enough. I shall see him this morning, and, I know your answer will, if favourable, make him happy. I am always a thinking of you, and your great Goodness to me. If it was in my power to act as much as I think I am certain your Excellency would see that I was truly Grateful. Oh how happy should I be if you would let me know what I can serve you in, in Italy, and England. I should be happy to know your thoughts upon my last letter. I am Dear Sir Your Excellencies Grateful Humbl. Servant and Friend,

LUCY PARADISE

P.S. If your Excellency has done with the list of the Debts she shall be obliged to him to inclose it in his answer.

RC (DLC); endorsed by TJ: "Paradise Lucy."

To Jean Baptiste Petry

SIR Paris Aug. 21. 1788.

The count de Cambrai, who resides in the country, having desired his Agent in Paris to put the inclosed papers into my hand with a request that I would forward them to you by any occasion which should occur, I have now the honor to put them under your cover. You will perceive that they are powers of Attorney relative to a claim he has against the state of S. Carolina, to which you have been so good heretofore as to pay attention for him. I obey his commands with the more pleasure, as they give me an occasion of assuring you of the sentiments of esteem & respect with which I have the honor to be Sir your most obedient & most humble servt., TH: JEFFERSON

PrC (DLC).

The Count de Cambray's agent, Aleaume, had not specifically directed TJ to send the letters of procuration to Petry, but TJ had so interpreted his request in the light of earlier advice from Cambray (see Aleaume to TJ, 16 Aug., and TJ to Cambray, 7 Oct. 1788).

From John Brown Cutting

SIR London 22d Aug. 1788.

I have the honor to inclose the latest pennsylvania newspaper which I can procure; likewise a Baltimore paper for the sake of General Washington's letter. I also take the freedom to inclose a letter for Mr. Shippen from his father, not knowing where to direct to him, and imagining that Mr. Short will add to his former goodness the additional kindness to forward it in a direction likely to reach our mutual friend.

There are letters in town from New-York of the 6th of July. Most of those whose written opinions have been communicated to me concur in believing that a majority in the Convention of that State will refuse their assent to the new Constitution, notwithstanding the decision of Virginia has been announced to them. It seems however that they were not in haste to decide ultimately, as the debates thereafter continued. Congress as soon as the ratification of the ninth state reachd them officially took order for the immediate issue of precepts to organize the national government. This is written from Mr. Contee, Delegate for Maryland, to his brother here, dated July. 2d. He adds, "the accession of Virginia it is thought will induce a reluctant vote for ratification on the part of New York."

I hope Mr. Jarvis has ere this delivered you a few lines written at different intervals, from a wish to entertain you with the best fare of a larder politically lean. By the next private opportunity I shall again intrude on your repose. For tho' my passage is taken the vessel will not sail these three weeks. Meanwhile I hope to be indulged with such information concerning the pacific as well as belligerant powers on the continent as shall make me still more deeply your debtor than I feel myself already to be. Especially if any citizen of our country shou'd be coming hither soon.

Mr. Short will please to accept my compliments and good wishes. I hope he will enjoy a classical and of course a pleasurable tour, through Italy. I have the honor to be with the most entire attachment and respect Your obliged and most obed. se[rvt.],

JOHN BROWN CUTTING

RC (DLC); endorsed. Enclosures not identified, but GENERAL WASHINGTON'S LETTER was probably that to Charles Carter, 14 Dec. 1787, which contained this paragraph: "I am not a blind admirer (for I saw the imperfections) of the Constitution to which I have assisted to give birth, but I am fully persuaded it is the best that can be obtained at *this* day and that it or disunion is before us." This letter was copied by Carter for friends and appeared in several newspapers, to Washington's displeasure (Freeman, *Washington*, VI, 130; *Writings*, Fitzpatrick, ed., XXIX, 340).

To Amand Koenig

MONSIEUR — Paris ce 22me. Avril [i.e., Aug.]

Je viens de recevoir de Monsieur Prevost le Platon, l'Aristophane, et le Menandre que vous avez eu la bonté de m'expedier, mais point de note de ce que je dois payer pour ça à Monsieur Prevost. Presumant pourtant que le Platon est de 60.[tt] et l'Aristophane de 36.[tt] comme ceux que j'ai acheté chez vous, et que le Menandre est du prix de 7[tt]-10 comme noté sur votre catalogue, je payerai incessament dans les mains de Monsieur Prevost la somme de 103[tt]-10 pour votre compte. Si je me trompe dans ces prix ayez la bonté de m'en avertir et je ferai la correction necessaire. J'ai l'honneur d'etre Monsieur votre tres humble et tres obeissant serviteur,

TH: JEFFERSON

PrC (DLC); endorsed.

To Lucy Ludwell Paradise

Dear Madam Paris Aug. 22. 1788.

I shall be very happy to see Monsieur de Fondate either this morning or tomorrow morning at any hour before eleven o'clock, after which it might happen that I should be out. He will find me ready to render him every service in my power. To this his merit entitles him, and your request ensures it.

I have the honour to inclose you the list of debts. I think indeed, madam, it would be very desireable could these be all reduced into one hand. I should suppose that Dr. Bancroft or Mr. Anderson could find some person in London who, having money to place on interest, would be glad to place it on so sure a fund as this. If Count Barziza could with convenience take up the accounts of the creditors, pay them off, and stand sole creditor in their place, it would surely be a great consolation to all parties, and I am satisfied that the estate, under so able a manager as Colo. Burwell, would replace his money in 3, 4, or 5 years at the farthest, aided by the debts due to it, and the timber to be sold. Should nothing of this kind take place, I imagine Dr. B. and Mr. A. will apply their first monies to pay off all the small creditors. I observe that about £800. would pay off all the creditors except the six largest. This would reduce them to a more manageable state. I shall always be ready to render every service in my power, being with sincere esteem & attachment, Dr. Madam, your most obedt. humble servant,

Th: Jefferson

PrC (DLC). Enclosure not found.

To Jean Jacques Peuchen

Monsieur à Paris ce 22me. Aout 1788.

J'ai retardé, Monsieur, de vous accuser la reception de votre lettre du 25me. Avril, afin que je pourrois en meme tems vous annoncer l'arrivée des poëles que vous avez eu la bonté de m'expedier. Elles viennent d'arriver chez moi il y a trois jours en bon etat. Permettez donc, Monsieur, que je vous fasse mes remercîments pour vos attentions dans cette occasion-ci, aussi bien que pour les honnetetés dont vous avez eu la bonté de me combler quand j'avois l'honneur de vous voir à Cologne, et agreez l'hommage des sentimens d'estime et d'attachement avec lesquels j'ai l'honneur d'etre, Monsieur, votre très humble et très obeissant serviteur,

Th: Jefferson

PrC (MoSHi); endorsed.

To John Brown Cutting

Dear Sir

Paris Aug. 23. 1788.

I have duly received your favors of the 3d. 8th. 14th. and 15th. inst. and have now the honor of inclosing you a letter of introduction to Doctr. Ramsay.

Since my last Denmark has declared she will aid Russia, and has joined some ships to the Russian fleet. It is expected the K. of Prussia will take side immediately with Sweden, and Poland consequently with Russia. We presume here that in order to restore the equilibrium at sea, England will prefer sending a Dutch squadron into the Baltic rather than one of her own. However in the long run both she and France must enter into the war. Perhaps they may try to put it off to the opening of the next campaign. I think a certainty of this was a great inducement to the ministry here to suspend the portion of public paiments which they have lately suspended. By this operation they secure 203 millions of livres or 8 millions and a half of guineas in the course of this and the ensuing year, which will be sufficient for the campaign of the 1st. year. For what is to follow the States general must provide. The interesting question now is how the States general shall be composed. There are 3. opinions: 1. To place the three estates, Clergy, Noblesse, and Commons, in three different houses. The clergy would probably like this, and some of the nobility. But it has no partisans out of those orders. 2. To put the Clergy and Noblesse into one house, and the Commons into another. The Noblesse will be generally for this. 3. To put the three orders into one house, and make the Commons the majority of that house. This reunites the greatest number of partisans, and I suspect it is well patronised in the ministry, which I am persuaded are proceeding bonâ fide to improve the constitution of their country. As to the opposition which the English expect from the personal character of the king, it proves they do not know what his personal character is. He is the honestest man in his kingdom, and the most regular and oeconomical. He has no foible which will enlist him against the good of his people; and whatever constitution will promote this, he will befriend. But he will not befriend it obstinately. He has given repeated proofs of a readiness to sacrifice his opinion to the wish of the nation. I believe he will consider the opinion of[1] the States general as the best evidence of what will please and profit the nation and will conform to it. All the characters at court may not be of this disposition, and from thence may possibly arise representations capable of leading the king astray. But upon a full view of all circumstances, I have sanguine hopes that such a constitution will be established here as will regenerate the energy of the nation, cover it's friends and make it's enemies tremble. I am, with very great esteem Dear Sir your friend & servt.,

TH: JEFFERSON

P.S. Be so good as to write me by post the moment you hear from N. York or N. Carolina. The accession of Virginia came first to us from London viâ Amsterdam. This information is intended as a rap of the knuckles to you.

RC (MHi: AMT); addressed by TJ to Cutting at "No. 2 North street Rathbone place London"; postmarked "P PAYE [PARIS]" and (in circle) "AU 29." PrC (DLC). Enclosure: TJ to Ramsay, 23 Aug. 1788.

TJ's teasing RAP OF THE KNUCKLES hurt, but was not deserved (see Cutting to TJ, 6 Sep. 1788; Dumas to TJ, 14 Aug. 1788).

1 TJ first wrote "advice of" and then altered the phrase to read as above.

From James Madison

DEAR SIR New York Augst. 23. 1788.

My last went viâ England in the hands of a Swiss gentleman who had married an American lady, and was returning with her to his own country. He proposed to take Paris in his way. By that opportunity I inclosed copies of the proceedings of this State on the subject of the Constitution. North Carolina was then in Convention, and it was generally expected would in some form or other have fallen into the general stream. The event has disappointed us. It appears that a large majority has decided against the Constitution as it stands, and according to the information here received has made the alterations proposed by Virginia the conditions on which alone that State will unite with the others. Whether this be the precise State of the case I cannot say. It seems at least certain that she has either rejected the Constitution, or annexed conditions precedent to her ratification. It cannot be doubted that this bold step is to be ascribed in part to the influence of the minority in Virginia which lies mostly in the Southern part of the

State, and to the management of its leader. It is in part ascribed also by some to assurances transmitted from leading individuals here, that New York would set the example of rejection. The event, whatever may have been its cause, with the tendency of the circular letter from the Convention of N. York, has somewhat changed the aspect of things and has given fresh hopes and exertions to those who opposed the Constitution. The object with them now will be to effect an early Convention composed of men who will essentially mutilate the system, particularly in the article of taxation, without which in my opinion the system cannot answer the purposes for which it was intended. An early Convention is in every view to be dreaded in the present temper of America. A very short period of delay would produce the double advantage of diminishing the heat and increasing the light of all parties. A trial for one year will probably suggest more real amendments than all the antecedent speculations of our most sagacious politicians.

Congress have not yet decided on the arrangements for inaugurating the new Government. The place of its first meeting continues to divide the Northern and Southern members, though with a few exceptions to this general description of the parties. The departure of Rho. Island, and the refusal of N. Carolina in consequence of the late event there to vote in the question, threatens a disagreeable issue to the business, there being now an apparent impossibility of obtaining seven States for any one place. The three[1] Eastern States and N. York, reinforced by S. Carolina, and as yet by N. Jersey, give a plurality of votes in favor of this City. The advocates for a more central position however though less numerous, seemed very determined not to yeild to what they call a shameful partiality to one extremity of the Continent. It will be certainly[2] of far more importance under the proposed than the present system that regard should be had to centrality whether we consider the number of members belonging to the government, the diffusive manner in which they will be appointed, or the increased resort of individuals having business with the Legislative, Executive and Judiciary departments. If the Western Country be taken into view, as it certainly ought, the reasoning is still further corroborated. There is good ground to believe that a very *jealous*[3] *eye will be* kept in that *quarter on in*attention *to it and particularly when* involving a *seeming advantage to the eastern states* which have been *rendered extremely suspicious* and *obnoxious by the Missisipi project*. There is *even good ground to believe that Spain is taking* advantage of *this disgust in Kentuckey* and is *actually* *endeavoring* to *seduce them from the union holding out a darling object which will never be obtained by them as part of the union.* This is a *fact as certain as it is important but which I hint in strict confidence* and with *a request* that no suspicion may be excited of its being *known particularly thro the channel of me.*—I have this moment notice that I must send off my letter instantly, or lose the conveyance. I must consequently defer further communications till another opportunity. In the meantime I am Yrs. affely.,

Js. Madison Jr.

Along with this you will receive a copy of the report you desired from Mr. Thomson, and a copy of the Federalist, a publication mentioned in my last.

RC (DLC: Madison Papers); endorsed by both TJ and Madison.

The accompanying REPORT YOU DESIRED FROM MR. THOMSON had been requested in TJ to Madison, 3 May 1788. In that letter TJ erroneously referred to it as a "Report drawn by Governor Randolph on the navigation of the Missisipi"—probably confusing it with Randolph's report on Virginia's charter claims to western territory (see Vol. 6: 647-55, especially page 653-4)—and stated that Charles Thomson had furnished him a copy of it in 1784 but that he had lent this copy to Benjamin Franklin, who had misplaced it. On 16 May 1784 Thomson had sent to TJ a copy of "the report respecting the Navigation of the Mississippi" (Vol. 7: 261), but this clearly was Madison's own remarkable draft of a letter to Jay, then minister to Spain, setting forth the argument in support of the instructions adopted by Congress on 4 Oct. 1780 enjoining a strict adherence to the claim to a right of navigation of the Mississippi (MS in Madison's hand in DNA: PCC, No. 25; text printed in JCC, XVIII, 935-47; see also Brant, *James Madison the Nationalist*, p. 70-88). With characteristic self-effacement, Madison failed to indicate TJ's error in respect to authorship.

1 This word interlined in substitution for "four," deleted.

2 Madison originally wrote "It is certainly," &c. and then altered the phrase (probably contemporaneously) to read as above.

3 This and subsequent words in italics are written in code and were decoded interlineally by TJ; his decoding has been verified by the Editors, employing Code No. 9.

From John Mason

Sir

Bordeaux 23d. Augt. 1788

Herewith I take the Liberty to cover you a Letter from my Father, Colo. Mason of Virginia, which had promised myself the pleasure of delivering, but a Want of the Language and Engagements in Business have obliged me to defer my Trip to Paris untill some period during the Winter; when I shall do myself the Honour of paying my Respects to you in person.

As perhaps you have had no late Accounts from America, have to inform you, that the new Constitution was ratified in Virginia, after long and warm Debates, on 25th. June by a Majority of 89 a 79. The Question for previous Amendments was negatived by 88 a 80. New Hampshire I presume you know has acceded N. York has not yet determined.

My Father I believe has mentioned to you that my Business in this Country was to join the commercial Establishment made here by Mr. Fenwick in order to negotiate with America. In which Line it will be useful for us to know, and shall be particularly obliged to you for any Information you may be pleased to give us on that head, whether the Tobacco sent here this Year by Mr. Morris is received by the Farmers as Arrearages of his late Contract or on Account of the present annual Requisition of Government.

This and every other Information you may at any Time be so good to give of future Regulations made by this Country regarding American Commerce will be most gratefully acknowledged by Sir your very respectful Obt & Hbl Sert., JOHN MASON

RC (DLC); endorsed. Enclosure: George Mason to TJ, 26 May 1788.

To David Ramsay

DEAR SIR Paris Aug. 23. 1788.

The bearer hereof, Mr. John Brown Cutting, proposing to go to Charleston, I take the liberty of introducing him to your acquaintance and attentions. His merit and talents will justify me in taking this liberty, as they will fully recommend him to your esteem, while I am equally assured he will find in you what will render it reciprocal. He is authorised to ask from your state some arrangements of public justice. In these I know you will aid him as far as shall be right, and farther he will not ask it. I am happy always to find occasions of renewing assurances of the esteem & respect with which I have the honour to be Dear Sir your most obedient & most humble servt., TH: JEFFERSON

PrC (DLC); enclosed in TJ to Cutting, this date.

From John Rutledge

⟦[*Charleston, S.C.*] *23 Aug. 1788.* Recorded in SJL Index, but not found.⟧

From Thomas Appleton

SIR Roüen 24th. August 1788.

I had the honor of receiving your Excellency's letter of July 29th. The absence from Town of the Director of the Customs has prevented my replying till this time. The result of my inquiries is thus. That the Arret in which is Clas'd the SpermaCæti candles, after enumerating the duties upon a great variety of merchandize, there is then article which says that all foreign merchandize of whatever description not herein mention'd shall be subject to a duty 5 ℔Ct. upon its value. In answer to my plea that refin'd SpermaCæti is permitted upon a late Arret, and Cotton always, he replies that altho' Seperately they are incontestably admissable upon a very small duty, and when connected must forever be SpermaCæti and Cotton. Yet being in the form of a candle it must be included in that kind of merchandize which is subject to pay 5 ℔Ct. I have convers'd with some persons of intelligence who agree that it is so decidedly clear that a contestation would ultimately be useless. The director has affix'd the duty of entry upon the Value of 45 Sols ℔ pound and upon going out 20 Sols so that you will observe they are much less than I at first imagin'd. I have the Honor to be Your Excellency's Most Obedient & Most Humble Servant, THOS. APPLETON

RC (DLC); endorsed.

To Edward Bancroft

DEAR SIR Paris Aug. 24. 1788.

Mr. Paradise having been rendered, by the loss of his daughter, incapable of arranging his affairs while in Virginia, he has stopped at this place in order to do this. He will inform you by the present post of the arrangements he has taken. In the first place he has put the Virginia estate under the care of Colo. Nathaniel Burwell, one of the most skilful managers in that country, and of untainted integrity. This estate yeilds from 800. to 1000£ sterling a year, clear, and with the money in the English funds will be about 1000. or 1200£ a year. Of this Mr. Paradise reserves, for his and Mrs. Paradise's subsistence 400£ a year, the residue to be applied to the paiment of his creditors. In aid of this fund he has applied three additional resources: 1st. The sum of £1000. due to him from the state of Virginia. I am not well enough acquainted with the funds of that state to say when this money will be paid. But I know they have made great progress already in the paiment of their state debt, and that they expect to pay the whole in a very short time. Still we must count this article unfixed in point of time. 2dly. A debt of 800.£ sterling due to him from Mr. Norton, and for which judgment is supposed to have been obtained. This therefore will come in during the present year. 3dly. A valuable wood called Chipoaks which has been hitherto preserved in the family untouched and which is of itself more than equal to the paiment of the whole debts. This he has ordered to be cut, till, with the income and credits beforementioned, his whole debts shall be paid off. Mr. Paradise in the mean time proposes to travel oeconomically, staying longest where he can be cheapest. Mrs. Paradise will remain with her daughter at Venice. She is to have 130£ of the 400£ reserved for their subsistence; and on account of the distance of her situation, and a desire that she should not suffer, Mr. Paradise has thought it best that her portion should be paid out of that part of his revenue which is the most punctually paid, that is to say the English funds. To 30£ a year from the same fund his friend Count Soderini is entitled. There will remain a small balance of £35. for himself, to which 240£ is to be added by remittance from Colo. Burwell to Mr. Paradise. The rest of the profits and proceeds of the estate Colo. Burwell is to remit to yourself and Mr. Anderson who, as Mr. Paradise hopes, will still continue the friendly office of receiving and distributing this among his creditors, and of managing every thing for him which is to be done in England. It appears to me that under this arrangement the paiment of his debts must be effected in two or three years, tho' I have persuaded him to make such allowance for accidents as to suppose it will be five years, and to make up his mind for living in this state of exile for that term. He has done so, and I am persuaded he will do any thing for the satisfaction of his creditors: I am so much persuaded of this that I will undertake to engage him always to do whatever further they and you may think necessary. I should think it extremely desireable that the larger creditors should consent to the application of so much of Norton's 800£. as would sweep off all the smaller ones. That sum for instance so applied would pay off the whole of the creditors except the six largest, who would by this means render the affairs much more manageable for them and for you. The arrangements made by Mr. Paradise are by a power of attorney to Colo. Burwell, sealed, and indented, and

requiring expressly such solemnities for it's revocation as guard it[1] not only against the influence of others, but in a great degree against any momentary will of his own. It amounts in fact to a deed of trust which, were he to think of changing any of it's dispositions, would require at least a twelvemonth to comply with the formalities to which the deed binds him. This would give time to his judgment to correct itself. Having been principally consulted by him in this business I thought it proper to give you a full view of his arrangements and to that will only add assurances of the esteem and attachment with which I am Dear Sir your most obedient humble servant,
Th: Jefferson

PrC (DLC).

[1] This word interlined in substitution for "him," deleted.

To John Trumbull

Dear Sir
Paris Aug. 24. 1788.

I have duly received your favor of the 15th. and accede to the proposition of the young workman to make me as good a carriage for £105. as the shops furnish at 130£. I would wish it to be 3 feet 8. inches wide within, a strapontin to unship and ship as may be wanting, the steps to shut within, a box to take in and out, coachman's seat to ship and unship readily, mortise locks, venetian blinds, spring curtains and vallons, a large oval back light of 2 feet diameter lengthwise to let down and up, crane neck. I would wish a mantle painted in front, flanks &c, without either arms or cypher. The carriage to be hung half way between the old fashion and the new, that is to say lower than the new, and somewhat high for the old fashion. It is intended for America, where you know our roads do not admit a high carriage with safety. I shall carry it there with me next spring, and shall probably leave it there for the use of my daughters, so that on my return in the fall or winter I shall want another, and will employ the same hand if his work appears to deserve it. In your letter of Feb. 26. you told me a carriage could be finished in 5. weeks from the time it is ordered. We shall lose the benefit of Mr. Parker's bringing it now, but probably another occasion will occur by him or some other. When it shall be nearly ready, if you will let me know how much will be wanting to make up the price, I will remit it without delay. The taste in the painting, and finishing I leave to you, and leave to yourself to order the new, or send me a second hand one as you think best, if in the mean time you should have seen one to your mind. I shall have occasion for two pair brass harness.

I am sorry to be told you have had difficulties to surmount in your pursuit. If heaven be just, it will smooth all these for you. I know not how to justify myself in my own eyes or in those of the world for engrossing one moment of your time with my frivolous commissions. I endeavor to quiet my conscience by supposing it necessary for you to take exercise sometimes, and that you can do my little jobs en passant. Shippen is very anxious that his father receive the inclosed letter safely and speedily. I suppose it concerns his travelling affairs. If Mrs. Church be in London tell her Kitty is well; I am just come in from a tour I have made with the girls to Bagatelle &c. Kneel to Mrs. Cosway for me, and lay my soul in her lap. I expect daily to receive the project of a treaty from Mrs. Church. God bless her, you, and all such good people. Adieu! Your's affectionately, TH: JEFFERSON

PrC (DLC). Enclosure: Shippen's letter of 31 July 1788 to his father, Dr. William Shippen.

From Madame d'Houdetot

Eaubonne Le 26. aoust 1788.

Recevés, Monsieur, mon Compliment bien sincere sur L'Evennement qui decide votre Constitution Et sur L'Esperance qui suit que vous serés Les peuples Les plus heureux Et Les mieux gouvernés Du Globe. C'est une Consolation pour ceux meme qui sont loin D'un pareil Bonheur. Une Lettre D'amerique Viens de M'aprendre Cette heureuse nouvelle Et La joye que L'adhésion de la Virginie a causé a Newyorck. Comme Citoyene de Votre paÿs j'ay Droit de prendre part a Cette joye, Et Comme particulierement attachée a Votre Bonheur Et a Vos succès, j'En ay Encore Bien Davantage. Le Respectable Docteur n'a plus qu'à dire son *nunc Dimittis* Et termine par Le plus heureux Des Evennemens sa longue Et Illustre Carriere. C'est le Sceau De L'Esprit De Sagesse, De Raison, D'humanité Et de Lumieres qui Caracterise Les principales têtes de Vos nouveaux Etats Et si tout n'Est pas parfait Dans Le plan Reçu, La Sagesse qui a fait sentir La necessité D'En avoir un, fournira Des Lumieres pour perfectionner Celuy qu'on Viens D'adopter. Si je Revenais au Monde, je ne Connaist que Deux paÿs ou je voulusse a present Recommencer ma Vie, *Vous Et La Suisse*. Il y a Bien Longtems que je n'ay Eû

Le plaisir de Vous voir, mais Rien ne peut alterer Le Desir que j'En Conserve Et Les Sentimens D'attachement Et D'Estime que Vous m'avés inspirés. Je suis à Eaubonne jusqu'à la fin du mois; je passe De La a Sannois qui n'En Est que Deux pas, Et j'y Resterés jusqu'a La My Septembre que je ferés Encore une course De quelques jours pour venir me fixer a Sannois jusqu'a La St. Martin, Ensuite a Eaubonne jusqu'au premier Decembre. Je Vous Confie Cette Marche Dans L'Esperance que Vous pourrés Dans Cet intervale, soit a Eaubonne, soit a Sannois, me Donner quelques momens. Le Maitre D'Eaubonne En serait tres flatté Et Vous Scavés, Monsieur, Le prix que j'attache au plaisir de Vous Voir. Voulés vous Bien faire passer Cette Lettre a Mr. franklin. Je ne scay plus Comment Ecrire Depuis La supression Des paquets Bots,

La Ctesse d'houdetot

Vos Etats ont Ressemblé jusqu'a present a Des Membres Eparts qu'on Viens De Rassembler pour En faire une Belle Statüe. Je souhaite qu'elle Devienne un jour Celle De L'Apollon Du Belvedere.

RC (DLC); endorsed.

COMME CITOYENE DE VOTRE PAYS: In 1785, through the instrumentality of St. John de Crèvecoeur, the city of New Haven, Connecticut, had bestowed honorary citizenship upon a group of his compatriots, including the Countess d'Houdetot, the Duke de la Rochefoucault, the Duke de Liancourt, Condorcet, Saint-Lambert, Target, and Lacretelle (H. C. Rice, *Le Cultivateur Américain*, 1933, p. 33).

From C. W. F. Dumas

Monsieur — Lahaie 28e. Août 1788

J'ai appris avec grand plaisir, que la Gazette de Leide a été rétablie en France. Ayez la bonté, Monsieur, de m'apprendre, si Votre Excellence et Mr. Diodati avez recommencé à recevoir vos Exemplaires du Bureau et de la maniere ordinaire, afin que je puisse mander à Mr. Luzac de discontinuer l'expédition qu'il vous en fait par la poste, et lui offrir en même temps le paiement de ce qu'il en a expédié depuis la suspension, selon ma commission, en conséquence des ordres de Votre Excellence. Je doute qu'il veuille rien accepter, mais l'honnêteté exige que je le lui offre. J'espere que l'abolition des Paquebots reguliers du Havre n'empechera pas Votre Excellence d'avoir des occasion fréquentes pour l'expédition de ses Dépeches pour le Congrès. Je continuerai donc d'adresser les miennes à Votre Excellence, comme je fais par l'incluse; étant bien aise d'ailleurs que tout ce qui se fait ici, passe aussi sous les yeux de Votre Excellence et la tienne au Courant. Je suis avec grand respect, de Votre Excellence Le très-humble & très-obéissant serviteur

C W F Dumas

RC (DLC); endorsed. FC (Dumas Letter Book, Rijksarchief, The Hague; photostats in DLC). Enclosure (same): Dumas to Jay, 27 Aug. 1788, stating that, since his last of the 8th, the Compagnie des Indes, needing 15,000,000 florins to forestall its total ruin, and the province having unsuccessfully attempted a loan at 2½%, had issued 5,000 bills of exchange of 2,000 florins each, which were accepted by the province, payable in five years at 4%, free of all taxes and charges of any sort; that these bills, bearing such favorable interest and conditions, had been promptly cornered, but the engrossers could only block up one-third of the outlet; that, in order to complete the amount needed, another issue was contemplated, but that, since the first had caused the national 2½% obligations to fall from 85 to 80 and another would depress them at least 10% more, they dared not; that, instead, there would be a forced loan levied on the real and personal property of everyone; that this, together with the conflicting commitments known to all, would enable Jay to judge the state of the country better than any reasons Dumas could advance; that he is enclosing a memorial of F. van Willigen, Bavarian chargé d'affaires at The Hague, asking that this and the contract to which it pertains be transmitted to Congress in order that justice be done to a Palatine subject "par une personne établie à Philadelphie." A note appended to FC in the Dumas Letter Book shows that the Van Willigen enclosure, together with the gazettes, went with the Jay letter by way of Amsterdam, and that the duplicate enclosed to TJ also included a résumé of Dumas' dispatches of 24 July, 1 Aug., and 13 Aug. 1788. The RC of Dumas' dispatch to Jay of 27 Aug. 1788, together with others between 1 Aug. 1788 and 20 Jan. 1789, is described in *Dipl. Corr., 1783-89*, III, 628-9, as missing, but this description also includes (together with an inaccurate account of the funding operations of the Compagnie des Indes) the statement that the Van Willigen memorial involved a "contract between Louis Conrad Kuhn, of Manheim, and the widow Anne Marie Zeller, residing in Philadelphia."

To Coulon

Monsieur à Paris ce 30me. Aout 1788.

J'ai l'honneur de vous accuser la reception de votre lettre du 24me. Courant, par laquelle vous me prevenez que, comme Commissaire aux saisies reelles vous avez eté etabli au regime et gouvernement de l'hotel que j'occupe scis Grille de Chaillot, et saisi reellement sur Monsieur le Comte de Langeac, et devez faire proceder au bail judiciaire de cet hotel, si je ne demande pas la conversion de mon bail conventionnel en judiciaire. Ne trouvant pas qu'il me conviendroit de faire cette demande, j'ai l'honneur de vous le declarer, et j'aurai celui de vous communiquer mon bail conventionel quand il vous plaira de le voir, n'ayant nul doute que mes droits seront protegés par la justice du pays, à laquelle, aussi bien qu'à vous, Monsieur, qui en est le ministre, je m'empresserai de temoigner en toute occasion les hauts egards qui vous sont dus, et la consideration parfaite avec laquelle j'ai l'honneur d'etre Monsieur votre tres humble et tres obeissant serviteur,

Th: Jefferson

PrC (DLC); at foot of text: "Monsr. Coulon Commissaire aux saisies reelles rue des Blancs-Manteaux."

Coulon's letter DU 24ME. COURANT is listed in SJL Index, but has not been found. There is also recorded in SJL Index under 24 Aug. 1788 a letter from TJ to Coulon, but this must have been an erroneous entry for the present letter, which is not recorded. See TJ to De Langeac, 15 Feb. 1789.

From John Brown Cutting

SIR London 30 Aug. 1788

The inclosed paper contains some few articles of intelligence which perhaps may not have reached you by any other channel. When the last vessels quitted New York about the 8th of July, the convention of that State still continued to debate upon the great question of rejecting or adopting the national constitution and it is with concern I perceive that the probabilities against an immediate adoption of the same seem so much to preponderate. On the 4th of July we are told a riot was excited at Albany by Messrs. Lansing, Judge Yates and a Mr. Jeremiah Van Ransaleer, three of those gentlemen of consideration in that district who have uniformly opposed fœderal measures, and two of whom are now of the *State*, as they were also last summer of the *general* convention. The rumour runs thus—that these chieftains[1] on the day abovenamed (while a large number of the fœderalists of Albany were testifying their joy at the return of an anniversary whereon they cou'd at once celebrate the birthday of the empire and the event of the recent ratification of Virginia) ventured at the head of a considerable throng to disturb the festivity of their fellow citizens by appearing on the same ground with intent to disclose how much they disregarded the example of the Convention of Virginia and abhorred the new system of government. To manifest these sentiments most unequivocally they produced on the spot a copy of the doings of the fœderal convention, and also of the late intelligence from Virginia, to which they applied in contumely a parcel of combustibles previously prepared for the purpose and consumed both. This symbol of their hostile sentiments was the signal of an immediate onset: each party attacked the other with sticks and swords: several were badly wounded on both sides; *two* it is said on that of the antifœderalists mortally. The affray ended in conducting Mesr. Yates, Lansing and Van Ransalear to prison, but reports say the City was not tranquilized. I sincerely wish the whole story may prove a misrepresentation of the truth. The inhabitants of the City of New York, of Long, Staten and York

Islands, and of the Counties of East and West Chester, in fine of most of the maritime territory in the state, seem unanimously resolute to adhere to the general government, and talk loudly of beseeching the new Congress for a dismemberment from those Counties in the rear the representatives of which are so extremely strenuous for a seperate sovereignty. Certain it is that in the Convention at present, Governor Clinton's party, as it is called, outnumber their antagonists in the proportion of two to one. It is no less manifest that this gentleman and all those who are personally attached to him have uniformly acted against the general government argued against it and still continue so to do. Whether this proceeds from honest and patriotic motives or results from sinister views they must surely perceive that the solitary opposition of New York will ultimately prove abortive. Wherefore I am inclined to think they may yet acquiesce after having retarded their assent, perhaps by an adjournment or some other device which may enable them to secure for the seperate use of the state, another years amount of their impost.

I find Virginia did not adjourn immediately after the ratification, but continued sitting for the laudable purpose of digesting suitable amendments which, from the ability of the committee appointed to prepare and bring them in, as well as from the circumstance of their possessing the previous suggestions of so many other states on the same subject, will I hope unite the suffrages of congress and satisfy every candid and rational mind in the minorities throughout the Union. The Assembly of your Commonwealth I observe were convened on the 23d of June and made of choice of Mr. Mathews for their Speaker. Probably your intelligence concerning all these minuter particulars is regular, early and exact, but possibly not, and therefore I hint them. It is for the same reason I subjoin the following extract from the Journals of Congress June 2d 1788.

"According to order the house was resolved into a committee of the whole; and after some time the President resumed the chair, and Mr. Otis reported that the committee of the whole had taken into consideration the subject refer'd to them, and agreed thereon to report; That in their opinion it is expedient that the district of Kentuckey be erected into an independant state, and therefore they submit the following resolution.

"That the address and resolutions from the district of Kentuckey with the acts of the Legislature of Virginia therein specified be refer'd to a committee consisting of a member from each state to prepare and report an act for acceding to the Independance of the said district of Kentuckey, and for receiving the same into the union as a member thereof in a mode conformable to the articles of confœderation." "June 3d. Resolved that Congress agree to the said Report."

I understand from good authority that there are between sixty and one hundred thousand inhabitants within the district of Kentuckey.

The magnificent procession of five thousand citizens of Philadelphia on the 4th of July in honor of the day—of a *new* Æra—and of the ten states which had already contributed to establish it was a spectacle so singularly splendid that I am not surprized to see it copied even into english newspapers. Mr. Paine promises to hand you Mr. Hopkinsons pictured description of it.

By Mr. Parker and Mr. Barlow who will proceed for Paris about the close of next week I shall trouble you with a brief supplement to this letter. Meanwhile I have the honor to be, with the most perfect respect and attachment Your obliged & obedt. Servt.,

JOHN BROWN CUTTING

RC (DLC); endorsed. The enclosed paper has not been identified.

TJ must have received about this time HOPKINSONS PICTURED DESCRIPTION OF the great Fourth of July procession in Philadelphia, enclosed in Hopkinson to TJ, 17 July 1788. The fact that MR. PAINE promised to hand it to TJ indicates that he was intending to go to Paris about this time, but there is no evidence that he actually did so (Copeland, *Our Eminent Friend, Edmund Burke*, p. 184), and the promised description was enclosed in Paine to TJ, 9 Sep. 1788.

1 At this point Cutting deleted: "had the indiscretion."

From John Rutledge, Jr.

MY DEAR SIR Geneva August 30th 1788

I have had the honor to receive by this days post, yours of August 12th. My getting it was very accidental. In the hurry of leaving Berne it never occur'd to me telling the post master what was to be done with any letters he might receive for me, and I am indebted to a friend of mine for sending forward yours from Berne where, I imagine, from the length of time which has intervened between its date and receipt, it must have reached long ago. In a letter which I had the pleasure of writing to you from Berne, I there mentioned my having laid aside all thoughts of going to Vienna and that I should go from this Country directly into Italy. I shall not leave Geneva before the fifteenth of September.

I expect to hear from you in the interim and shall be exceedingly pleased to learn that you think the attention of my Route well judged.

Of all the places I have seen in my travels this pleases me the most. The wealthy and contented appearance of these happy people declares this to be the land of liberty. Everything here is gay chearful and happy and everything proclaims the superiority of the republican over every other sort of government. May such a one ever prevail in our Country is my sincere wish. We have many who are enemies to it, but their efforts are not to be feared whilst the good and great unite to defeat them.

The people of this town have for some time past been made very uneasy by the commotions in france. They are greatly concerned in french funds and it is impossible to conceive the joy which the news of Mr. Neckars appointment has occasioned. They seem to think every thing will be immediately arranged in consequence of this change in the ministry. I hope they will not be deceived. God bless you my dear Sir and believe me to be with the purest sentiments of friendship and affection, Your much obliged and devoted Servant J RUTLEDGE JUNIOR

RC (DLC); endorsed.

To Willink & Van Staphorst

GENTLEMEN Paris Aug. 30. 1788.

Mr. Carmichael informs me that he has drawn on you for 4614[tt]-3-6 for salary due to him. I have only to observe on this occasion that in the Estimate which Mr. Adams and myself left with you, the article of 4000[tt] monthly for the diplomatic establishment was meant to include the demands for salary and incidental expences of Mr. Carmichael, Mr. Dumas and myself, and that these demands, including the present draught of Mr. Carmichael, fall considerably short of the estimate; so that I presume you will find it right to honour that draught, as it appears to me to be. I have the honour to be with very great respect Gentlemen your most obedt. humble servt., TH: JEFFERSON

PrC (DLC); at foot of text: "Messrs. Willem & Jan Willinck Nichs. & Jacob Van Staphorst Amsterdam."

From Madame de Brionne

ce Dimanche 31. Août

Mad. La Comtesse de Brionne fait mille complimens à Monsieur de Jefferson, elle est arrivée de la campagne et doit repartir mercredy; dans cet interval, il lui seroit bien essentiel d'avoir l'honneur de voir Monsieur de Jefferson; l'obligeance avec laquelle il a bien voulu lui répondre confirme sa confiance. Elle lui demande donc de vouloir bien lui faire dire quel Jour et à quelle heure, elle pouroit le trouver chez lui.

RC (DLC); endorsed; year not given, but, while TJ was in France, Sunday fell on the 31st of August only in 1788.

Madame de Brionne was a niece of Madame Béthizy de Mézières, whom she assisted at the Abbaye de Panthémont.

From Gaudenzio Clerici

Honble Sir Hotel de fleury rue Ste. Anne. Noon.

It cannot be pride; it cannot be diffidence; nor can it be a false sentiment of shame to acknowledge my poverty already Known to you, that I feel an unsurmountable discouragement in soliciting again by words of mouth your uman assistance in this present Epoca of distress. It is, Honble. Sir, a right apprehension of the danger, in which I expose myself to lose thro' importunity and indiscretion that little credit, which possibly I might have enjoyed before, and which would be my ambition to encrease. Cruel necessity! Did I foresee but difficulties and sufferings in the way, I am confident my Heart would be willingly disposed to undergo any, However great they might be rather than advancing this repeated indiscret step. But I see no end in my Calamities were I to miss the opportunity of soon returning among some well disposed friends I left in that Continent. Six Louis d'or are all the Tresor I can depend upon to carry me over the Atlantic! Add, Honble. Sir, I beg a few guineas more!—It would be the most unpardonable meaness of mind in me was I to think inducing you to it by a promise of restitution. I would However, if in my life I'll be master of the sum you generously advance to save me from distress return it to your Hands that you may dispose it to Charitable and uman objects which in my consideration might have been posponed.—I am very respectfully Your most Huml. Serv.,

Gaudenzio Clerici

P.S. I propose setting off in about two Hours.

RC (DLC); undated, but see following letter in reply to it; on verso TJ wrote: "sent him 78 livres on this letter which with 192 livres sent to Chalons make 270 livres due me."

To Gaudenzio Clerici

SIR Paris Aug. 31. 1788.

Your letter finds me with only three Louis and six livres in the world, nor any means of commanding more for several days to come. My situation here exposes me to expences and advances which keep me constantly distressed for money, so that I assure you there is not a poorer person than myself. I send you all I have, being seventy eight livres and wish it was ten times as much, since no use I make of money gives me so much pleasure as to assist distressed merit. I am with great esteem & good wishes for you, Sir Your most obedient & most humble servant

TH: JEFFERSON

PrC (DLC).

From George Washington

DEAR SIR Mount Vernon Augt. 31st. 1788.

I was very much gratified by the receipt of your letter, dated the 3d. of May.—You have my best thanks for the political information contained in it, as well as for the satisfactory account of the Canal of Languedoc.—It gives me pleasure to be made acquainted with the particulars of that stupendous work, tho' I do not expect to derive any but speculative advantages from it.—When America will be able to embark in projects of such pecuniary extent, I know not; probably not for very many years to come — but it will be a good example and not without its use, if we can carry our present undertakings happily into effect. Of this we have now the fairest prospect.—Notwithstanding the real scarcity of money and the difficulty of collecting it, the labourers employed by the Potomack Company have made very great progress in removing the obstructions at the Shenandoah, Seneca and Great Falls.—Insomuch that, if this summer had not proved unusually rainy and if we could have had a favourable autumn, the Navigation might have been sufficiently opened (though not completed) for Boats to have passed from Fort Cumberland to within nine miles of a shipping port by the first of January next.—There remains now no doubt of the practicability of the plan, or that, upon the ulterior operations being performed, this will become the great avenue into the Western Country — a country which is now settling in an extraordinarily rapid manner, under uncommonly favorable circumstances, and which promises to afford a capacious asylum for the poor and persecuted of the Earth.

I do not pretend to judge how far the flames of War, which are kindled in the North of Europe, may be scattered; or how soon they will be extinguished.—The European politics have taken so strange a turn and the Nations formerly allied have become so curiously severed, that there are fewer sure premises for calculation, than are usually afforded, even on that precarious and doubtful subject.—But it appears probable to me, that peace will either take place this year, or hostility be greatly extended in the course of the next.—The want of a hearty co-operation between the two Imperial Powers against the Porte; or the failure of success from any other cause, may accelerate the first contingency. The irritable state into which several of the other Potentates seem to have been drawn, may open the way to the second.—Hitherto the event of the contest has proved different from the general expectation.—If, in our speculations, we might count upon discipline, system and resource, and certainly these are the articles which generally give decisive advantages in War, I had thought full surely the Turks must, at least, have been driven out of Europe.—Is it not unaccountable that the Russians and Germans combined, are not able to effect so much, as the former did alone in the late War?—But perhaps these things are all for the best and may afford room for pacification.

I am glad our Commodore Paul Jones has got employment, and heartily wish him success.—His new situation may possibly render his talents and services more useful to us at some future day. I was unapprised of the circumstance which you mention, that Congress had once in contemplation to give him promotion.—They will judge now how far it may be expedient.

By what we can learn from the late foreign Gazettes, affairs seem to have come to a crisis in France; and I hope are beginning to meliorate.—Should the contest between the King and the Parliaments result in a well constituted National Assembly, it might ultimately be a happy event for the Kingdom.—But I fear that Kingdom will not recover its reputation and influence with the Dutch for a long time to come.—Combinations appear also to be forming in other quarters.—It is reported by the last European accounts that England has actually entered into a Treaty with Prussia; and that the French Ambassador at the Court of London has asked to be informed of its tenor.—In whatever manner the Nations of Europe shall endeavor to keep up their prowess in war and their balance of power in peace, it will be obviously our policy to cultivate tranquility at home and abroad; and extend our agriculture and commerce as far as possible.

I am much obliged by the information you give respecting the credit of different Nations among the Dutch Money-holders; and fully accord with you with regard to the manner in which our own ought to be used.—I am strongly impressed with the expediency of establishing our National faith beyond imputation, and of having recourse to loans only on critical occasions.—Your proposal for transfering the whole foreign debt to Holland is highly worthy of consideration. I feel mortified that there should have been any just ground for the clamour of the foreign officers who served with us; but, after having received a quarter of their whole debt in specie and their interest in the same for sometime, they have infinitely less reason for complaint than our native officers, of whom the suffering and neglect have only been equalled by their patience and patriotism.—A great proportion of the Officers and soldiers of the American Army have been compelled by indigence to part with their securities for one eighth of the nominal value. Yet their conduct is very different from what you represent that of the French Officers to have been.

The merits and defects of the proposed Constitution have been largely and ably discussed.—For myself, I was ready to have embraced any tolerable compromise that was competent to save us from impending ruin; and I can say, there are scarcely any of the amendments which have been suggested to which I have *much* objection, except that which goes to the prevention of direct taxation—and that, I presume, will be more strenuously advocated and insisted upon hereafter than any other.—I had indulged the expectation, that the New Government would enable those entrusted with its administration to do justice to the public creditors and retrieve the National character.—But if no means are to be employed but requisitions, that expectation was vain and we may as well recur to the old Confœderation.—If the system can be put in operation without touching much the Pockets of the People, perhaps, it may be done; but, in my judgment, infinite circumspection and prudence are yet necessary in the experiment.—It is nearly impossible for any body who has not been on the spot to conceive (from any description) what the delicacy and danger of our situation have been.—Though the peril is not passed entirely; thank God! the prospect is somewhat brightening.—You will probably have heard before the receipt of this letter, that the general government has been adopted by eleven States; and that the actual Congress have been prevented from issuing their ordinance for carrying it into execution, in consequence of a dispute about the place at which the future Congress shall meet. It is probable that Philadelphia or New York will soon be agreed upon.

I will just touch on the bright side of our national state, before I conclude: and we may perhaps rejoice that the People have been ripened by misfortune for the reception of a good government.—They are emerging from the gulf of dissipation and debt into which they had precipitated themselves at the close of the war.—Œconomy and industry are evidently gaining ground.—Not only agriculture; but even manufactures are much more attended to than formerly. Notwithstanding the shackles under which our trade in general labours; commerce to the East Indies is prosecuted with considerable success: salted provisions and other produce (particularly from Massachusetts) have found an advantageous market there. The Voyages are so much shorter and the vessels are navigated at so much less expence, that we hope to rival and supply (at least through the West Indies) some part of Europe, with commodities from thence.—This year the exports from Massachusetts have amounted to a great deal more than their imports.[1] I wish this was the case every where.

On the subject of our Commerce with France, I have received several quæries from the Count de Moustiers. Besides the information he desired relative to articles of importation from and exportation to France, he wished to know my opinion of the advantage or detriment of the Contract between Mr. Morris and the Farm; as also what emoluments we had to give in return for the favors we solicited in our intercourse with the Islands.—As I knew that these topics were also in agitation in France, I gave him the most faithful and satisfactory advice I could: but in such a cautious manner as might not be likely to contradict your assertions or impede your negotiations in Europe.

With sentiments of the highest regard & esteem I have the honor to be Dear Sir Your Most Obed., G: WASHINGTON

RC (DLC); endorsed: "Washington Genl. Aug. 31. 88." FC (DLC: Washington Papers); differs slightly in phraseology.

[1] MS reads "exports"; corrected in FC to "imports."

From Gaudenzio Clerici

[1 Sep. 1788]

I have received — I am so confused in the generous act and generous expressions you make use of that know not how to thank You, or how to reproach myself. May you live happy Honble. Sir.

RC (DLC); written on a scrap of paper, unsigned, undated, and unaddressed; ascribed to Clerici on the basis of handwriting; date supplied conjecturally on the basis of TJ's letter to Clerici of 31 Aug. 1788.

To C. W. F. Dumas

SIR Paris Sep. 1. 1788

In my letters of the 30th. and 31st. of July I took the liberty of asking the favor of you to procure the Leyden gazette to be sent to Count Diodati and myself, from Leyden by post, during the suspension of the ordinary distribution of that paper here. You were so good as to do this, and we have been in a course of receiving those papers regularly by post. But the suspension here being now taken off, our papers are again distributed to us in the ordinary way, which saves the expence of postage. I have now therefore to ask the favor of you to countermand the countinuance of the Leyden gazette by post to Count Diodati and myself. I must trouble you to apply to my friend Mr. Nicholas V. Staphorst to pay for these papers, and suppose he will be so good as to furnish it and debit it to me. Yours of July 31. Aug. 1. 7. 8. 14. have been duly received. I have the happiness to congratulate you on the accession of New York to the new constitution by a majority of five. Letters of the 26th. of July from N. York do not mention it. But a postscript to the French Consul's letter (M. de Crevecoeur) written just as the ship, which brought it, got under sail, announce us the fact, with the particulars of the universal ring of bells and other demonstrations of joy. I have the honour to be with great esteem Sir Your most obedt. humble servt,

TH: JEFFERSON

PrC (DLC).

It was Edward Carrington's letter to Short of THE 26TH. OF JULY FROM N. YORK that failed to mention the ratification by that state (see note to Madison to TJ, 24 July 1788); the letter from Crèvecoeur of that same date that did include the news JUST AS THE SHIP . . . GOT UNDER SAIL must have been one to Short. This news was promptly published in the *Supplément* to the *Gazette de Leide* of 5 Sep. 1788, and may have been supplied by TJ, by

Dumas, or by one of Luzac's correspondents in Amsterdam. The dispatch reads as follows: "Dans le tems que l'Europe éprouve en plus d'un Pays l'excès des maux, qui accompagnent quelquefois la Société Civile; qu'en d'autres la Guerre est allumée; et que presque tous se voyent menacés du même fléau, l'Amérique-Unie est aujourd'hui au comble de ses voeux: Nous venons de recevoir (écrit-on d'Amsterdam, en date du 1 Septembre) l'agréable Nouvelle, que l'Etat de New-York a accepté, sans aucune condition, la nouvelle Constitution Fédérative; et que le Peuple en général en a montré une satisfaction, qui ne sçauroit être que le présage certain de la prospérité de cet heureux Pays. Le Congrès, formé en vertu de la nouvelle Constitution et sous la sanction de cet Acte Fédératif, s'assemblera le 1. Mars prochain, probablement à New-York, vu que cet Etat est aujourd'hui au nombre de ceux qui y ont accédé. Il ne manque donc, (si l'on excepte l'Etat de Rhode-Island, réfractaire déjà depuis longtems) que le seul Etat de la Caroline-Septentrionale, pour avoir une unanimité complette. L'on n'apprend pas encore, qu'il se soit déclaré; mais il y a peu de doute, qu'il ne suive l'exemple de tous les Etats Méridionaux et des Membres les plus considérables de la Confédération.—Des Avis particuliers, en confirmant également l'accession de la Virginie, ajoutent, que la Convention de cet Etat, en acceptant la nouvelle Forme, a mis à son acceptation les Conditions suivantes: 'Que la Constitution, tirant sa source du Peuple des Etats-Unis, pourra être retirée par lui, toutes les fois qu'il en seroit abusé, pour lui faire tort ou pour l'opprimer; que ni le Congrès entier, ni sa Chambre des Représentans, ni le Président, ni aucun autre Officier de la Confédération des Etats-Unis ne pourront anéantir, diminuer restreindre, ni modifier aucun Droit du Public ou des Particuliers, sous quelque dénomination ou prétexte que ce soit; et qu'entre autres Droits essentiels, qui appartiennent aux Citoyens, la Liberté de Conscience et celle de la Presse ne pourront jamais etre supprimées, restreintes, ni modifiées par aucune Autorité de la part de la Confédération des Etats-Unis.' "

To Nicolas van Staphorst

Sir — Paris Sep. 1. 1788.

Mr. Jacob Van Staphorst having before his departure expressed to me your wish that I would communicate to you whatever interesting news might come to us from America, I have the happiness to announce to you the accession of the state of New York to the new Constitution by a majority of five. The postscript to a letter from M. de Crevecoeur the French Consul at New York announces this, the letter itself which was of July 26. as well as others of the same date having been written before the fact was known. The postscript was added just as the ship was getting under way.

I have taken the liberty to ask Mr. Dumas to apply to you for some little bagatelle to pay for the Leyden gazettes for myself and a friend of mine. I have the honour to be with great esteem Sir Your most obedt. humble servt., Th: Jefferson

PrC (DLC).

To Thomas Appleton

Sir — Paris Sep. 2. 1788.

I have duly received your favor of the 24th. Aug. and think with you there should be no contest for the duty on the candles. I shall be ready to answer it to you whenever you please.

I presume you have heard that New York has acceded to the new constitution. I have the honor to be Sir Your most obedt & most humble servt,

Th: Jefferson

PrC (DLC).

To Migneron de Brocqueville

Monsieur — à Paris ce 2me. Septembre 1788

Je viens de recevoir le memoire imprimée que vous m'avez fait l'honneur de m'envoyer, contenante la description d'un Pont et d'un hopital que vous avez construit en bois prés de Bordeaux. La maniere d'ameliorer et de ceintrer le bois, que vous avez imaginé, et la construction generale de ces deux objets, sont les meilleure preuves, Monsieur, de vos talents et de vos connoissances dans votre art, et je souhaite de tout mon coeur que le public s'en profiteroit en vous donnant souvent l'occasion de les developer. Agreez les remercimens et les voeux d'un etranger qui verra toujours avec plaisir la prosperité de votre nation et la votre, et qui a l'honneur d'etre avec beaucoup de consideration, Monsieur, votre tres-humble et tres obeissant serviteur,

Th: Jefferson

PrC (DLC). Recorded in SJL Index as being dated 1 Sep. The MEMOIRE IMPRIMEE is identified in note to Brocqueville to TJ, 10 Aug. 1788.

To William Gordon

Sir — Paris Sep. 2. 1788.

In my letter of July 16. I had the honor to explain to you the reasons why an answer to your favors had been so long delayed. That letter containing details which were not proper to pass thro the post office, it was itself detained till a private conveiance occurred, so that it had not got to your hands when you wrote your favor of Aug. 15. You must have received it however immediately after, and it will have answered the objects of your letter. As soon as you will be so good as to send a copy of your work, as far as printed, I will do my best to dispose of the right of translating it among the booksellers; tho', from the circumstances mentioned in my letter, I should not form any sanguine hopes. The sooner you send it the better, as I shall, after a few days, be very little in Paris, for some months to come. The Diligence comes from London to Paris four times a week and will bring it safely. But they are apt to let things lie long in their magazine in London, if not attended to. I received yesterday only the Marquis de la fayette's picture of Genl. Washington, which had been delivered them a fortnight or three weeks before to be forwarded. I have the honor to be with great respect Sir Your most obedient humble servt,

TH: JEFFERSON

PrC (DLC).

To John Mason

SIR

Paris Sep. 2. 1788.

I have duly received your favor of Aug. 23. as well as the one from your father which was therein inclosed. I am always happy to hear of his good health, and shall with great pleasure comply with his wishes that I should render you such services as may come within my line. I think the position you have taken at Bordeaux must be a good one, and a trade judiciously conducted between that port and the United states may be advantageous. That it should prove so in your hands will be my sincere prayer. On what footing the Farmers general receive the tobaccoes of Mr. Morris I am not able to tell you, as it is their secret, and they are close-mouthed. I shall be happy to see you whenever your views either of business or amusement may lead you to Paris, and am with great attachment Sir Your most obedient & most humble servt.,

TH: JEFFERSON

P.S. Should you be writing soon to your father, I will thank you to present me to him very affectionately.

RC (MiU-C); addressed: "A Monsieur Monsieur Mason negotiant a Bordeaux chez M. Bondfeild negociant à Bordeaux"; endorsed. PrC (DLC).

From Jonathan Nesbitt

SIR!

Philada. Sept. 2d. 1788

Not having the honor of being Personally known to you, I must begin by beging your excuse for the trouble I am about to give you.

It is by the advice of Mr. R. Morris that I now adress you, who this day assured me that I might do so in full Confidence that you would endeavor to obtain what I desire. I will therefore without further preamble proceed to acquaint you with my situation.

During the late war I was pretty extensively concern'd in Business in France and had shipped considerable quantity of Goods, both on Credit and on my own Account to this Country. Peace took place so suddenly, and so unexpectedly, and in consequence thereof, remittances came so slowly from this Country that few American Houses establish'd in France could stand the shock. As I had large quantitys of Tobacco on hand, and was concern'd in several arm'd Ships, I was amongst the greatest sufferers, but was in hopes that what was due me in this Country would fully enable me to pay the Debts I had Contracted in France, and therefore with the Permission of my Creditors, I came out here to endeavor to collect them. Perhaps there never was a person so greatly disappointed as I have been. Several Houses that were esteem'd as solid as any in America, became Bankrupts on being pushed for payment. Others declare they must do the same unless I give them time. Thus circumstanced, I have found it impossible to fulfil any part of the engagements I enter'd into with my Creditors when I left France, and have written to Mr. M. Amoureux of LOrient, who was formerly a Clerk with me, to endeavor to obtain a further delay, but as it is possible he may not succeed, I have been advis'd to return to France to solicit that favor Personally, which I apprehend I cannot do with safety, as some of my Creditors may be inclined to give me trouble, unless I obtain a safe Conduct. Mr. Morris writes by this conveyance to Messrs. Le Couteulx & Co: to apply to the Minister for that purpose. My request to you Sir is that you will assist them in their endeavors. Indeed I should think that an Application from you could not fail of success, particularly as it must evidently appear that I mean to Act for the general good of my Creditors, yet I know how disagreable it must be in your situation to solicit favors. I must again request your excuse for this trouble and am with great respect Sir Your most humble Servt.

JONATN: NESBITT

RC (MoSHi). This letter was enclosed in that of Le Couteulx & Cie. to TJ, 20 Dec. 1788.

From John Trumbull

Dear Sir London September 2d. 1788

I have your letter of the 24th. August and having seen no secondhand Carriage to my mind, have given orders for the new one: which I trust will be both substantial and elegant:—There are three articles however in your description which being extraordinary will add to the price:—the Venetian blinds are not much us'd here, tho they are much better for a hot Climate than the common ones, and they are much more expensive.—The large back light is another article uncommon, and therefore will be an extra charge. The strapontin is a trifle differenc.—The *Vallons* is what I do not understand. I do not find the word in my french dictionary and the Coachmaker knows as little as I do. There is a part of the common finishing of a Carriage known by that name here, but I suspect you to mean festoon Curtains.—You will inform me and also whether you will have *two* trunks for travelling and an imperial.—When you say you shall want *two Setts* of Brass Harness: do you mean a Harness compleat for *four* horses in the same Carriage, or two Harnesses for two Horses, as there is a difference in the length of Traces Reins &c &c.—The Coachmaker objects to your using *brass* Harness with the Chariot He means to send you because the mouldings, Handles of the Doors &c &c are to be plated, and He thinks the Harness should correspond. Of that which you are to use at Paris, I am of his opinion for the brass and Silver will certainly not look well together. You will judge from the prices, which are for a pair of Horses with brass trimmings plain and *good* in every respect, Nine guineas—you may go as low as Seven.—For do. Plated trimmings plain and *good*, Fifteen to sixteen guineas, and may be had as low as Thirteen:—But in case of the cheap ones, you will find the leather is both *bad*, and the plating so thin that with good care it shall show the copper in the *first* year.—For the first price you are sure of the *best* leather, and the plating so thick as to wear with equal care, *three* years at least. If you have a Cypher, or which is most common a Crest engraved on the Harness trimmings, it may be a Guinea difference.

It will be ready in *five* weeks.

The letters which you sent me some time since for Charlestown I have put on board the London Capt. Curling who sails for that place in two days, (being the first since I received the letters). Mr. Cutting talks of going in her or the next ship:—but this is not certain, and letters always go sooner and safer by the Ships bag and the post than by any private hand. Shippen's letter to his Father, goes in the Charlotte, Capt. Gill for Phila. who sails also this week.

By Mr. Barlow who goes tomorrow or next day to Paris I shall send Lackington's newest Catalogue, and *two* tours thro' Italy. (Addison's and a late one). They cost 4/ and 4/6. I thought the new one usefull from its giving some Idea of the money, distances, expences &c &c. If Mr. Short thinks otherwise He will keep Addison and return me the other by Barlow or Parker.

I wish him a pleasant Tour, and am Dear Sir With the greatest Respect Your Obligd Servant, JNO TRUMBULL

RC (DLC); endorsed; addressed; postmarked (within circle): "SE 2 88."

To John Jay

SIR Paris Sep. 3. 1788.

By Mrs. Barclay I had the honour of sending you letters of the 3d. 10th. and 11th. of August: since which I wrote you of the 20th. of the same month by a casual conveiance, as is the present.

In my letter of the 20th. I informed you of the act of public bankruptcy which has taken place here. The effect of this would have been a forced loan of about 180. millions of livres in the course of the present and ensuing year. But it did not yeild a sufficient immediate relief. The treasury became literally monyless, and all purposes depending on this mover came to a stand. The archbishop was hereupon removed, with Monsieur Lambert, the Comptroller general, and Mr. Neckar was called in as Director general of the finance. To soften the Archbishop's dismission, a cardinal's hat is asked for him from Rome, and his nephew promised the succession to the Archbishopric of Sens. The public joy on this change of administration was very great indeed. The people of Paris were amusing themselves with trying and burning the Archbishop in effigy, and rejoicing on the appointment of Mr. Neckar. The commanding officer of the city guards undertook to forbid this, and not being obeyed, he charged the mob with fixed bayonets, killed two or three and wounded many. This stopped their rejoicings for that day: but enraged at being thus obstructed in amusements wherein they had committed no disorder whatever, they collected in great numbers the next day, attacked the guards in various places, burnt 10. or 12 guard-houses, killed two or three of the guards, and had about 6. or 8. of their own number killed. The city was hereupon put under martial law, and after a while the tumult subsided, and peace was restored. The public stocks rose 10. per cent on the day of Mr. Neckar's appointment; he was immediately offered considerable sums of money, and has been able so far to waive the benefit of the act of bankruptcy as to pay in cash all demands except the remboursements des capitaux. For these and for a sure supply of other wants he will depend on the States general, and will hasten their meeting, as is thought. No other change has yet taken place in administration. The minister of war however must certainly follow his brother, and some think, and all wish that Monsr. de Lamoignon, the garde des sceaux, may go out also. The administration of justice is still suspended. The whole kingdom seems tranquil at this moment.

Abroad no event worth noting, has taken place since my last. The court of Denmark has not declared it will do any thing more than furnish the stipulated aid to Russia. The king of Prussia has as yet made no move which may decide whether he will engage in the war, nor has England sent any squadron into the Baltic. As the season for action is considerably passed over, it is become more doubtful whether any other power will enter the lists till the next campaign. This will give time for stopping the further progress of the war, if they really wish to stop it. Two camps of 25,000 men each are forming in this country, on it's Northern limits. The Prince of Condé has the command of one, and the Duke de Broglio of the other.

I trouble you with the inclosed letter[1] from a Henry Watson claiming prizemonies, as having served under Admiral Paul Jones, which I suppose should go to the treasury or war office. I have the honor to be with sentiments of the most perfect esteem & respect, Sir Your most obedient & most humble servant,

TH: JEFFERSON

RC (DNA: PCC, No. 87, II). PrC (DLC). Enclosure not found; see note 1.

1 A note on MS, keyed to this point by an asterisk, reads: "Sent to the Board of Treasury 25th. February 1789."

To John Brown Cutting

DEAR SIR Paris Sep. 4. 1788.

Letters from New York of July 26. mention that the question

on the new Constitution was not then decided. But a postscript to one of them from Monsieur de Crevecoeur the French consul there, sais that just as the ship was getting under way they received news that the Constitution was accepted by a majority of five, that in consequence thereof the bells were then ringing &c. This news arrived here last Sunday, and I might have communicated it to you by next day's post, had I not taken it too much for granted that you know every thing in London sooner than we do here, and more especially in this case as the letters came to us viâ Amsterdam. Finding by yours of Aug. 30. that you did not then know of it I concluded to amend my fault by writing it late rather than never. No other change in the administration has taken place here, than that of the dismission of the Archbishop and M. Lambert, and taking in of Mr. Neckar. The Secretary of war brother to the Archbishop must surely follow his brother. Considerable sums of money are already offered Mr. Neckar, insomuch that he has been able to pay the demands on the treasury in money all, instead of part money and part paper, except the remboursements which must await the states general, who will probably be sooner called. I am with great esteem, Dear Sir, your most obedt. humble servt, TH: JEFFERSON

RC (MHi: AMT); addressed: "Mr. John Brown Cutting No.2. North street Rathbone place London"; postmarked: "P.PAYE PARIS" and (within circle) "SE 8." PrC (DLC).

On Crèvecoeur's POSTSCRIPT, see note to TJ to Dumas, 1 Sep. 1788.

To Lucy Ludwell Paradise

DEAR MADAM Paris Sep. 4. 1788.

I have spoken to Mr. Paradise on the subject you desire, and he assured me he should, before his departure from Paris, give orders for paying into your own hands or to your order your proportion of the four hundred pounds reserved from your income, and that it should be paid out of the dividends as the most punctual dependance for you. I had understood at first that you and he had agreed on a partition of the sum into 130.£ for you and 270.£ for him, and had written this to Doctr. Bancroft: but in my last conversation with Mr. Paradise he said you insisted on the whole of the dividends, and that this was not yet settled between you. As Count Zenobio's interest £30. a year is fixed on this fund, and could not be changed; there remain but £165-10, the difference between which and the £130. is too small to produce any difficulty of arrangement between you. Be assured, madam, that nothing shall be wanting on my part to facilitate that arrangement and to establish before you leave Paris your separate power to draw for your separate part. I have the honour to be with sentiments of the most sincere esteem & respect, Dear Madam, Your most obedient and most humble servant, TH: JEFFERSON

PrC (DLC).

From John Rutledge, Jr.

DR SIR Geneva September 4th 1788

In the month of September or October last, I do not exactly recollect which, I remember seeing at your house the skin of a very large animal which was sent to you from the northern part of America. You told me, I think, Monsr. de Buffon had seen this skin and that the beast was unknown to him and that you supposed it peculiar to America: Mr. de Saussure, who is engaged in perfecting his cabinet already largely filled with rare and curious animals, tells me he had much conversation with Lieutt. Genl. Haldiman, who has lately been here, about the quadripedes of america, that Genl. H. told him whilst he was in Canada an indian trader presented him with the skin of an animal which was unknown to himself and the rest of the officers, that this animal must have been immensely large from the size of its skin, which was remarkably thick and of a close texture, so much so that the wet could not pass through it, that encamping on the snow this skin was always his bed, that his brother officers and neighbours were never able to get anything which was proof against the penetrating snow, whilst he, hug'd in his skin, was always dry. I am disposed to believe the animal he adverts to is of the same species with that of which I saw the skin at your house and I shall be obliged to you if when perfectly at leisure, you will inform me in what part of America this animal was taken, what name the hunters of that part of the country give it, and if I am right in supposing that it was unknown to Monsr. de Buffon? From the imperfect recollection I have of what I saw at your Hôtel I have given Mr. de Saussure an inacurate account which makes him desirous of having a particular one. I ask many pardons, my dear Sir, for the trouble I am giving you? Nothing could authorize my doing it but the persuasion I have of your goodness and that the information I request of you will enable me, in some measure, to requite the great attentions I have received from Monsr. de S. I shall also esteem it very friendly of you if you will inform me whether it is supposed that the race of Animals, of which very large and huge bones have been found on the Ohio, are extinct, or whether, retiring from the approaches of man, they have fled into the savage and unknown Countries? We have nothing new in this country. Every thing is quiet and peaceable and the people are happy which I hope you always will be and am, dr Sir, with the Sincerest Sentiments of regard & esteem Your much obliged friend & Servt. J. RUTLEDGE

Be pleased to direct to me poste restante at Geneva?

RC (DLC); endorsed.

From Willink & Van Staphorst

SIR Amsterdam 4 September 1788

We have now to acquaint Your Excellency that Willm. Carmichael Esqr. Chargé des Affaires of the United States to the Court of Madrid, has valued upon us ƒ4614.3 Banco, in consequence of your Advice to him. He has however neglected following your Desire to send his first Bills to you, so that they now appear without our having any Instructions on the Subject. We have requested the Holders to wait their Acceptance, until We can procure your Approbation, Which please transmit ℔ Return of the Post. However should they refuse, We will for this time, knowing this Gentleman's Salary is included in your Estimate under the Head of Legation Expences, honor them, to prevent any the least Reflexion on the Credit of the United States or the Respectability of their Ministers, In which Quality the Bills are signed.

If We are to continue paying this Salary, We beg Your Excellency to inform us specifically the Amount, and from what Period it is to commence, to avoid a Repetition of the present disagreeable Case. We are respectfully Your Excellency's Most obedient and very humble servants. WILHEM & JAN WILLINK

℔ Procn. of Nichs. & Jacob Van Staphorst

NICHS. HUBBARD

RC (DLC); endorsed; in Hubbard's hand; signed by Willem & Jan Willink and by Hubbard for Jacob & Nicolas Staphorst.

To John Jay

SIR Paris Sep. 5. 1788.

I wrote you on the 3d. instant, and have this day received Mr. Remsen's favor of July 25. written during your absence at Poughkeepsie, and inclosing the ratification of the loan of a million of florins for which Mr. Adams had executed bonds at Amsterdam in March last. The expediency of that loan resulting from an estimate made by Mr. Adams and myself, and that estimate having been laid before Congress, their ratification of the loan induces a presumption that they will appropriate the money to the objects of the estimate. I am in hopes therefore that orders are given by the Treasury board to the Commissioners of the loans at Amsterdam to apply these monies accordingly, and especially to furnish, as soon as they shall have it, what may be necessary for the redemption of our captives at Algiers, which is a pressing call. I am not without anxiety however on this subject, because in a letter of July 22d. received this day from the Treasury board they say nothing on that subject, nor on the arrearages of the foreign officers. They inclose me the order of Congress of the 18th. of July for sending to the Treasury board the books and papers of the Office of foreign accounts. I shall accordingly put them into the hands of a person who goes from Paris tomorrow morning by the way of Havre to America, and shall endeavor to prevail on him to attend them from the place of his landing to New York, that the board may receive them from the hand which receives them from me.

The reestablishment of the parliaments, and revocation of every thing which was done on the 8th. of May is expected to take place in three or four days.

I have the honour to be with sentiments of the most perfect esteem & respect Sir Your most obedient & most humble servt,

TH: JEFFERSON

RC (DNA: PCC, No. 87, II). PrC (DLC).
Remsen's FAVOUR OF JULY 25 is recorded in SJL Index, but has not been found; see note to Jay to TJ, 23 Sep. 1788.

From Frances Osborn

[*Charly*], *5 Sep. 1788.* Unknown to TJ and ashamed for her request, she is in want, lives in a remote, cheap place, and asks him to send "any relief let it be never so small" in care of "Monsieur Pinondel directeur de la poste aux Lettres a Charli, pour remettre à Madame Osborn."

[*In postscript*:] "I am old and shall not be troubleso[me]. I confide you are too much a Gentleman not to keep my secret."

RC (MHi); 2 p.; endorsed.

From John Trumbull

Dr Sir London 5th Septr. 1788

By the Diligence which left this yesterday morning I sent two Books for Mr. Short and Lackington's Catalogue of September for you. They were made up in a parcel address'd to you, and the Directeur du Bureau here assur'd me should be delivered to you immediately upon arrival without the delay of the office.—I hope you will have receiv'd them and before the departure of Mr. Short: of whom I must beg forgiveness for not having comply'd precisely with his orders.—I thought the opportunity by Mr. Parker better than the diligence, but his not going so soon as He intended, and now going by the way of Brussells, oblig'd me at last to do what should have been done Eight days sooner.

I hope you have my last of the 2d, and that the pictures which I sent some time since came safe.

I am Sir With the greatest Respect Your oblig'd Servant

Jno. Trumbull

RC (DLC); endorsed.

To Nathaniel Burwell

Sir Paris Sep. 6. 1788.

The perfect confidence reposed in you by Mr. and Mrs. Paradise has induced them to ask your friendly aid in the following case. When making the arrangements in their affairs which have been communicated to you, they had occasion to shew me the original of their marriage settlement. I observed on it no proofs that it had been recorded in our courts, nor did they suppose it had. They have desired me therefore to send you the inclosed copy, and beg you would satisfy yourself whether it has been recorded in Virginia? If it has not, then to advise with counsel whether any new execution of the same or a similar instrument, made under any and what formalities, could supply the defect of the record, and whether in any event, an amicable suit in Chancery might not be made to establish this instrument? Both are disposed to do whatever may be necessary for this purpose. The incertainty whether I may not be absent from Paris about the time your answer would come, induces me to ask you to address it to Mr. Paradise to the care of Mr. Anderson merchant in London. I am happy that this little commission furnishes me occasion to assure you of the sentiments of esteem & respect with which I have the honor to be, Sir, Your most obedt. & most humble servt.,

TH: JEFFERSON

PrC (DLC); endorsed. The enclosed marriage settlement has not been found; in Thomas Lee Shippen's diary (Shepperson, *John Paradise and Lucy Ludwell*, p. 253-4) there is a diverting account of the use to which this settlement was put in connection with Lucy Paradise's elopement in the spring of 1787 with Count Barziza. See Lucy Paradise to TJ, 29 May 1790.

From John Brown Cutting

SIR London Sept. 6. 1788

I was sensibly mortified on perusal of your letter of the 23d of Aug. to find that I was not the medium through which the earliest information of the late important event in Virginia reached you from England. Especially as the prompt communication of fresh american intelligence has hitherto been the only return I cou'd make for a throng of obligations with which You have so surrounded me that I fear I may never escape from the amicable thraldom. But the truth is I miss'd my aim from too much anxiety to accomplish it. The moment the intelligence from Virginia arrived I penned two letters of the same tenor and date one of which I instantly dispatch'd to Mr. Jarvis in the City (who then expected to proceed some hours before the mail for Paris was made up) intreating him as it was a letter of moment to deliver it the instant he shou'd arrive in Paris. But if he did not set out to send it directly to the general post office without hesitation. Unfortunately for my reputation of punctuality with you, Mr. Jarvis exercised his own discretion in the business and committed my letter to the care of his friend who was then proceeding to Paris, and who I dare say did not deliver the letter much sooner than he himself the duplicate, weeks after its flavour was extinct. I really beg your pardon unfeignedly for the minuteness of this detail, but I cou'd not obtain my own consent silently to sustain the imputation of being unalert in any agency contributive to your satisfaction.

We have yet no certain intelligence either of refusal from New York or ratification from North Carolina. Vessels however are momently expected beside the packet. Quere. If New York withholds her assent, whether while the State is thus ex-fœderal her citizens are eligible to any office in the gift of Congress under the new union. Your solution of this question will settle a debate which has recently agitated a private circle of us here. I hoped to transmit this letter by Messrs. Parker and Barlow who proceed to the continent tomorrow. But this morning I learn they take Brussels in their way, which being a circuitous route to Paris, I prefer quicker conveyance.

Since my last the editor's of the english newspapers have demolish'd Paul Jones by a putrid fever in the black sea, and every cone at Cherburg by a resistless tempest. Besides which they have totally defeated the Russian Fleet in the Baltic, captured five ships of the line for the King of Sweden, and compelling his majesty to attack the main army of the same power in Finland in a strong fortification have secured him a decisive, but bloody victory, on terra firma, with all the heavy artillery and baggage of the recreant foe together with 4000, rank and file, including the commander in chief and other distinguish'd officers. Nor have they been wholly inactive in the black sea on the great naval scale. For having refitted and reinforced the Captain Pacha's discomfited squadron they have caused the vanquished to seek and then overcome the recently victorious, in a stile of gallantry and naval skill that lifts the name of a true bred turk almost to the transcendent level of a true born englishmen. These atchievments accomplish'd, they have turn'd their types against Joseph and the imperial troops. Two thirds of the *latter* they have delivered into the hands of relentless apothecaries, while the *former* has been inveigled to quarrel with the only surgeon in the universe who cou'd afford effectual Succour to a single soldier of germany. The residue of militant convalescents who crawl about the turkish confines under his command stand quaking behind their ramparts equally fearful of death from a dysentery or a sabre.

After such feats of chivalry in the field and deeds of domination on the ocean, I fear an abridged narrative of their arrangements of foreign civil affairs will appear tame and insipid. Otherwise I might detail to you how they excited an insurrection among the senate in Stockholm, as if purposely to manifest their facile dexterity in appeasing it. This was instantly accomplish'd by compelling the russian minister to embark, whose intrigues had kindled a popular flame. I shou'd then slightly sketch the trouble they have undergone in exhausting the exchequer of France to the last livre, disseminating confusion feebleness poverty and disunion throughout the provinces, perpetuating an edict in the nature of a tender act and finally dismissing the late administration on the 25th of August, whose places these worthy gentlemen cannot exactly agree how to fill, even to this hour. I might then close the doings of these typographical sovereigns and legislators of Europe, by subjoining the following names, and then doubting whether any such appointments had taken or wou'd take place. Namely M. Castries, premier, M. Neckar, minister of finance, M. Villedeuil, comptroller general, M. De Moutholon, keeper, M. De la Porte, minister of marine, M. St. Priest, secretary at war, Baron Briteul, secretary of the home department.

But to be serious the newspapers of this country are actually become such vehicles of scandal, folly, absurdity and palpable or improbable falsities, that when perchance they deal in truth or aught that looks like liberality and commonsense they only excite doubts instead of producing conviction. I shou'd therefore thank you for informing me whether any one of all the paragraphs above alluded to have the smallest foundation in fact. I have the honor to be with much respect & esteem Your Most Obedt. Servt.,

JOHN BROWN CUTTING

RC (DLC); endorsed.

To André Limozin

SIR　　　　Paris Sep. 6. 1788.

The Treasury board having desired me to send to them the books and papers of Mr. Barclay's office, I have engaged a Monsieur Vannet to take charge of them from this place. He proposes to embark at Havre on a vessel sailing from thence to Patowmac, and that he may avoid the inconvenience of making any advances on account of these papers, I have undertaken that you will pay their freight to America, and other small disbursements on their account at Havre, which if you will be so good as to add in your answer to my letter of Aug. 21. I will pay the whole together as soon as I receive your answer. As there is a possibility that the ship may be sailed before he arrives at Havre, I have desired him in that event to deliver you the two cases of papers, and must ask of you to send them by the first vessel going to Philadelphia or New York, writing a line at the same time to the Treasury board to apprize them by what vessel they shall be sent. I am with great esteem, Sir Your most obedt. humble servt,

Th: Jefferson

PrC (DLC).

To the Commissioners of the Treasury

Gentlemen Paris Sep. 6. 1788.

Your favor of July 3. came to hand some days ago, and that of July 22. in the afternoon of yesterday. Knowing that a Mr. Vannet was to leave Paris this morning to go to Virginia in a vessel bound from Havre to Patowmac, I have engaged him to receive the papers which are the subject of those letters, to take care of them from hence to Havre, and on the voiage, and when he shall be arrived in Patowmac, instead of going directly to Richmond as he intended, he will proceed with them himself to New York. I shall pay here all expences to their delivery at the ship's side in America, freight included: unless perhaps he may find it necessary to put another covering over them if he should not be able to get them into the cabin. In this case you will have to reimburse him for that. I engage to him that you shall pay him their transportation from the ship's side to New York and his own reasonable expences from the place of his landing to New York and back to the place of landing. As he takes that journey for this object only, it would be reasonable that you give him some gratuity for his time and trouble, and I suppose it would be accepted by him. But I have made no agreement for this. The papers are contained in a large box and a trunk. They were sent here by Mr. Ast during my absence in Holland. When they arrived at the gates of Paris, the officers of the customs opened the trunk to see whether it contained dutiable articles, but finding only books and papers, they concluded the contents of the box to be of the same nature and did not open that. You receive it therefore as it came from the hands of Mr. Ast. A small trunk which came as a third package from Mr. Ast, and which has never been opened, I have put into the great trunk, without displacing, or ever having touched a single paper, except as far as was necessary to make room for that. I shall have the whole corded and plumbed by the custom house here, not only to prevent their being opened at the custom houses on the road, and at the port of exportation, but to prove to you whether they shall have been opened by any body else after going out of my hands. If the stamped leads are entire, and the cords uncut when you receive them, you will be sure they have not been opened. They will be wrapt in oil cloth here to guard them against the damps of the sea, and, as I mentioned before, Mr. Vannet will put them under another covering if he finds it necessary at Havre.

At the same time with your last letter, I received from the Office of Foreign affairs the ratification by Congress of the loan of 1788 for another million of guilders. As the necessity of this loan resulted from the estimate made by Mr. Adams and myself, which estimate was laid before Congress, I suppose their ratification of the loan implies that of the estimate, one article of this was for the redemption of our captives at Algiers. Tho' your letter sais nothing on this subject, I am in hopes you have sent orders to the Commissioners of the loans at Amsterdam to furnish, as soon as they shall have it, what may be necessary for this pressing call. So also for the foreign officers. If the ratification of the loan has been made by Congress with a view to fulfill the objects of the estimate, a general order from you to the Commissioners of the loans at Amsterdam, to pay the monies from time to time according to that estimate, or to such other as you shall furnish them with, might save the trouble of particular orders on every single occasion, and the disappointments arising from the delay or miscarriage, of such orders. But it is for you to decide on this.

I have the honour to be with sentiments of the most perfect respect Gentlemen, Your most obedient & most humble servt,

TH: JEFFERSON

PrC (DLC).

From Nicolas & Jacob van Staphorst

Amsterdam 8 September 1788

We are honored with Your Excellency's ever respected favor of 1 Inst, with the agreeable Intelligence of the Accession of the State of New York to the New Federal Constitution, For which We return You our most sincere and hearty Thanks. This is an Event We deem of great Consequence, as it will stamp such a Weight upon the Meeting of the new Congress, as will render equally contemptible as ineffectual, the solitary Schism of Rhode Island, there being We believe little doubt of the Concurrence of No. Carolina.

Upon Receipt of Your Excellency's Letter to Messr. Willinks

and ourselves, We acquainted the Holder We would immediately accept Mr. Carmichael's drafts.

Mr. Dumas's disposal upon us for your Account will be honored with that Attention, We shall be proud to shew all such as You may indicate. We are most respectfully Your Excellency's Most obdt. very hble. Servts.

℔ Procn. of Nichs. & Jacob van Staphorst
NICHS. HUBBARD

RC (MHi); endorsed by TJ: "Hubard Nichs." Recorded in SJL Index as from Hubbard.

From William Carmichael

DEAR SIR San Ildefonso 9 Septr 1788

I should have sooner thanked you for your favor of the 12th Ulto which I received on the 24th Had I not expected that the Courier who will bring you this would have set out sooner. I have no Official Letters from America, But by a packet from NY This Court has received despatches from Mr. Gardoqui to the 28th of July which announce the acceptation of the Constitution. Mr. Gardoqui writes me on the 26th that N.Y would accede and he appears in high Spirits and the Cte. de F.B. seems much pleased to see our affairs in so good a way. In a conversation which I had with him the last Week he expressed a hope, that we should now soon be able to Conclude a treaty and in a very candid manner gave me his Ideas upon the actual situation of affairs in Europe and the strong desire of his C. M. not only to prevent the flame of war from spreading wider but to Contribute to the Restoration of Peace among the actual Belligerent Powers. On a future occasion I will transmit to you the Notes I made of this Conversation. Last Post brought us the Changes which have taken place at Versailles. It is to be hoped that a plan may be adopted that will preserve the rights of the Nation and every thing essentially necessary to the Dignity of the Crown. The task is difficult and it is therefore not surprizing that there should be great difference of opinions on this important Subject. The Pleasure which I see the Enemies of France take in their dissentions, is an additional Motive to me to desire to see them at an End and to arrive at this, Every good subject ought to yeild to each other on some points to preserve the whole from anarchy within and destruction from without. I Yesterday dined in Company with Several of the Corps diplomatic here. After Dinner Mr. Eden sent the Bulletin from Paris containing a relation of what passed at Versailles on Mr. Neckers recall to the Ministry with a Note to the Prussian Minister, which without consideration the latter read aloud to the Company. The sarcasms and ridicule He threw on the present situation of France cannot be conceived by a man with any share of Prudence. Indeed the Prussian felt too late his own precipitation in reading it to the Company. I beleive Mr. Necker would not be much pleased with the Epithets bestowed upon him, unless he regards the detraction of the Enemies of his Country as a proof of his Merit. I have enquired of M. Lardizaval, if he had found any of the books you mentioned to him. As yet he hath not. He tells me, he will write to you on the Subject. The Plan seen by the Person you mentioned to me, was presented to this Court in 1777 by an Ingineer not employed for that Purpose, but who being on the Spot, made his observations and formed the project of the opening a communication by the River Chagre. It was judged impracticable. Another has been talked of by the Lake Nicaragua as more feasible, there being but 9 or 12 miles at most to cut in order to join the two Oceans and the ground not of a Nature to render the Undertaking difficult according to the Ideas of those with whom I have conversed on this Subject. I shall Spare no pains to satisfy your Curiosity on this or any other subject relative to your philosophical or historical pursuits, which you may point out to me. In this you render me an Essential Service for I shall Inform myself, while I am contributing to your Satisfaction. Altho' the Atmosphere of this court is seldom ruffled by Storm we have lately had a slight one here, which may make some noise abroad, particularly, as the Effects of it may be misrepresented by Party Spirit. For your Information I shall Recite the Effects of the storm and then give a slight sketch of what is supposed to be the origin of it. On the 1st. Inst. The Ct. D Orally received the King's orders to inspect the Coasts of Gallicia and Asturias. He obeyed the order and set out yesterday. The Marquis de Rubi a Lt. General and Governor in Second at Madrid, Counsellor of War &c. at the same time, received orders to go to Berlin as Minister Plenipotentiary. He refused and after having been allowed three days for reflection on persisting in his refusal he was deprived of all his places and sent to the Chateau of Pampelona. Dr. Horacio Borghesi of the great Family of that name at Rome Lt. General here was ordered to prepare to set out for Dresden in the Character of Minister &c. He obeyed, but since the disgrace of the Marquis de Rubi, He has been appointed to Berlin and the Mission to Dresden is not yet given. Ricardos Lt. Gl. also and inspector of Cavalry ordered to Guispocoa to replace the Marquis de Torremanianal Captn General. He also obeyed the Kings orders. Revillagegido another Lt. Gl. is ordered to Valencia to act as Commandant in the Absence of the Captn. General the Duc de Grillon. All these Gentlemen were well known to me.—Now for the Cause—You know I beleive the Ct. D'A——a late Ambassador from hence to France. It was supposed by those who it appears, did not really know his Character, that Consistent with the Reputation he had acquired, He returned to his Country to spend the remainder of a long life in domestic tranquillity. Perhaps this may have been his original Intention but whether unable to exist without the Splendor of Authority or excited by those who Surrounded him, in a very little time his disrelish of the Administration became apparent and his house became the head quarters of the Malecontents. Anonymous satirical papers were circulated with great assiduity in the Capital and from thence spread rapidly thro' the Provinces. To these were added daily reports of the approaching disgrace of the Minister and Particularly of the Premier at whom these attacks were principally levelled. A Decree respecting the title of Excellency and the Etiquette observed to Certain Persons afforded a motive to the Ct. D'A——a to make a representation to the Monarch in favor of the Grandesse but more particularly of the General Officers. The decree was reversed and this so elated opposition, that the Leaders loudly proclaimed their triumph and their Assemblies became more frequent as well as their determination to overthrow the Minister more declared and open, at least such was the occasional language of their partizans. Attempts were made to draw even C——s to the Party, but in vain, of course he became a subject of ridicule and abuse. This was the Situation of Affairs when the orders abovementioned were made public. At the same time C——s assembled the council of Castille and injoined its members to refrain from Cabals which tended to weaken the Peoples Confidence in the King, by circulating injurious reports against the Ministers to whom he entrusted the Administration and indicated that a noncompliance with his Injunctions as their Cheif, would be followed with disagreable consequences to the refractory. Many still apprehend that others will be added to the list abovementioned. I am persuaded from the Ct. de F B——'s well known moderation since he has been Minister that there must have been very urgent reasons for what has been done. I had some idea of what was likely to take place but a few days before it became public. Altho' well acquainted with several of the persons mentioned indeed with them all, I have for several months without affectation avoided being on an Intimate footing, having the highest reason to be satisfied with the Ministers Treatment of me, besides it is my duty to be a Spectator and not an Actor.

Thus Sir you have the relation of Circumstances which makes most Noise here at present. In a future Letter I will add such circumstances as I may have omitted or other particulars which may occur. I have no late intelligence neither from Morrocco or Algiers. The Spanish fleet of evolution is still at sea, but will probably soon return to Port. A defence to Export all Foreign cloth to Sth. America is or will be issued on the representation of the Manufacturers of that Article in Spain. I beg you to have the goodness to mention me to the Ct. de Montmorin and I have the honor to be with the greatest respect & Esteem Yr Excellencys Obliged & Obedt Hble. Servt.,

WM. CARMICHAEL

RC (DLC).

For a note on the PLAN to cut a canal across the Isthmus of Panama and THE PERSON (Chevalier Bourgoing) who mentioned it to TJ, see note to TJ to Carmichael, 3 June 1788. CT. D'A——A and C——S were D'Aranda and Campomanes.

To John Brown Cutting

DEAR SIR Paris Sep. 9. 1788.

Your favor of the 6th. is just come to hand. To answer your quotations from the English papers by reversing every proposition, would be to give you the literal truth, but it would be tedious. To lump it, by saying every tittle is false, would be just, but unsatisfactory. I will take the middle course and give you a summary of political information as far as possessed here on tolerably sure grounds. On the Baltic nothing of note since the first great action. That was pretty equal in loss, but rather favorable to the Russians in appearance because they kept the field while the Swedes retired into port. Since that the Swedes have had a 64. gun ship, the Gustavus Adolphus run ashore and burnt, and the crew captured by the Russians. Their fleet is rather confined within port, I believe we may say blocked up by Admiral Greigh. On land there has been nothing but a petite guerre. The Swedes have failed in every enterprise. There is a considerable discontent in the Swedish senate and nation, because the king, contrary to their constitution has commenced an *offensive* war without consulting the Senate.

On the Black sea nothing has happened since the 1st. victory obtained by the Pr. of Nassau and P. Jones, and the 2d. and 3d. by the Pr. of Nassau. The Captain Pacha has thrown himself into Oczakow, made a sortie, and considerably discomfited the Russians. The particulars not known: but the siege continues. The Emperor's army has suffered much by sickness and desertion, but more by his imbecility. He has certainly let a campaign pass over without doing any thing. Denmark has notified Sweden and the other courts that she will furnish the stipulated aids to Russia. England and Prussia have offered their mediation, and Denmark is endeavoring to counterpoize their interference by getting this court to offer to join in the mediation.—The ministerial revolution here is the Archbishop of Sens, and Mr. Lambert, gone out, and Mr. Neckar come in, in lieu of the last. Nobody will succeed the former, that is to say there will be no premier. Probably Mr. de Brienne minister of war will go out as his brother is out: and it may be doubted whether M. de Lamoignon will not also go. He is garde de sceaux, as you know. There is no present appearance of any other change. A bed of justice will be held within a few days to revoke all that was done in that of the 8th. of May, and to recall the parliaments. The States general will be called in January probably. The two camps of 25,000 men each in the North of France, are now assembling. They are commanded by the Prince of Condé and Duke de Broglio.—This is the sum of affairs as far as can be affirmed with certainty. If any thing remarkeable still turns up before your departure, I will do myself the pleasure of writing it to you. I am with great esteem Dr. Sir Your most obedt. humble servt,

Th: Jefferson

RC (MHi: AMT); addressed: "Mr. John Brown Cutting No. 2 North street Rathbone place London"; postmarked: "P.PAYE PARIS"; "SE 15"; and "5 O'CLOCK M" (the two last within circles).

From John Paul Jones, with Enclosure

On board the Wolodimer, before Oczakoff, 9 Sept. 1788.

Dear Sir

Since I wrote you last from Copenhagen, the 8th of April, I have been very much hurried; but my greatest difficulty has not been want of time, but want of a private opportunity to write to you. Mr. Littlepage is now on the point of leaving the army of the Prince Maréchal de Potemkin, and talks of being at Paris in the month of October. I avail myself, therefore, of the opportunity he offers, to send you enclosed a copy of my last letter from Copenhagen, with a copy of the official letter I received from the Count de Bernstorff, and a copy of the letter I have just received, on the subject of my public business there, from Monsieur Framery, Secretary to the Legation of France at the Court of Denmark, informing me he had received and forwarded to you the answer I expected from the Consul of France, at Bergen in Norway. This last must necessarily make you acquainted with all you wanted to know respecting our claim on the Court of Denmark.

The within letter to the Marquis de la Fayette, was intended for you as well as him, and I send you the copy because I am not sure if he received the original.

The American constitution, I suppose is adopted; but I am still afraid of the danger that may result from entrusting the President with such tempting power as military rank and command must give him. I can in no situation, however remote I am, be easy, while the liberties of America seem to me to be in danger.

I leave to Mr. Littlepage to inform you particularly of the military events that have taken place here, this campaign. I can take no delight in telling over tales of blood. God knows there has been too much of it spilt. Scenes of horror have been acted under my eyes in which, however, I have the happiness to say, I had no part.

I pray you to inform me, if you possibly can, what is become of Mrs. T———. I am astonished to have heard nothing from her since I left Paris. I had written to her frequently, before I left Copenhagen. If you cannot hear of, and see her, you will oblige me much by writing a note to Monsieur Dubois, Commissaire du Regiment des Guardes Français, vis à vis la Rue de Vivienne, Rue neuve des petits Champs, desiring to speak with him. He will wait on you immediately. You must know, that besides my own purse, which was very considerable, I was good-natured, or, if you please, foolish enough to borrow for her, four thousand four hundred livres. Now Mr. Dubois knows that transaction, and as she received the money entire from me for the reimbursement, I wish to know if she has acquitted the debt. When that affair is cleared up, I shall be better able to judge of the rest. I am, with perfect esteem, dear Sir, &c. J. P. JONES

MS not found, and probably lost as a result of having been lent by TJ to Sherburne, who printed it in his *John Paul Jones*, p. 309, as bearing date according to both the Julian calendar (29 Aug.) and the Gregorian (9 Sep.). Above text from *Dipl. Corr., 1783-89*, III, 732-3. Recorded in SJL as received 27 Apr. 1789. Enclosures: (1) Jones to TJ, 8 Apr. 1788. (2) Bernstorff to

Jones, 4 Apr. 1788 (see enclosure 4, Jones to TJ, 8 Apr. 1788). (3) Framery to Jones, 3 May 1788, informing him that he has sent the packet Jones expected from Dechezaulx, French consul at Bergen, that it had been received and, as requested, forwarded to TJ, whom he was eager to serve and to whom he offers services in every thing that could interest or please him in this country; that he had asked TJ to pay postage for packet, which was voluminous, to his banker in Paris; that news of Jones' arrival in St. Petersburg is awaited with interest, especially because of rumor that he had been lost in a storm in Gulf of Finland, but, as the story of this misfortune changes every day, he is persuaded it exists only in the mouths of evil disposed persons; that the Baron de la Houze does not credit the rumor, sends his compliments, and expects Jones' promised letter; that affairs in Denmark are tranquil, though the twelve ships of the line and eight frigates fitted out by Gustavus III of Sweden raise questions among those who know the state of his finances —whether it is England or Turkey that furnishes him the means of fitting out such a force; what his intentions are, since the armament is too large for a mere naval parade and too small for any enterprise whatever; where he will procure sailors, &c.; that [*in postscript, underlined*] Bernstorff has informed De la Houze that he was about to send full powers to Baron de Blome, to treat definitely with TJ on the matter that was agitated during Jones' stay in Copenhagen (Tr in French in DLC: John Paul Jones Papers, attested by Jones under date of 29 Aug. 1788, O.S.). (4) Jones to Lafayette, 15/26 June 1788. All of the foregoing are printed in *Dipl. Corr., 1783-89*, III, 719-28, the last being given here because Jones intended it also as a letter to TJ. See Framery to TJ, 29 Apr. 1788; TJ to Bernstorff, 19 June 1788; and TJ to Blome, 27 June 1788.

For a note on MRS. T———, see note to Jones to TJ, 4 Sep. 1787. See also, Jones to TJ, 26 and 31 Jan. 1789; TJ to Jones, 23 Mch. 1789; Littlepage to TJ, 12 Feb. 1789. These later letters make it clear why the present letter was so long delayed, and they also explain that the "Extract" of 29 Aug.-9 Sep. actually belongs to this abbreviated text.

ENCLOSURE

John Paul Jones to Lafayette

On board the Imperial ship Wolodimer at anchor in the Liman before Ochacoff June 15/26 1788.

MY DEAR GENERAL AND DEAR FRIEND

The kind Letter you did me the Honor to write me the 20th April was delivered to me at St. Elisabeth, on my way here from St. Petersburg. It was very flattering for me to receive such a letter from a Man whom I so much love and respect as I do, and have long done the Marquis de la Fayette. You will yourself do justice to my Sensibility for all your good Offices and good intentions, so I need only say I shall always be ambitious to merit the flattering Compliment with which you honor me by subscribing yourself my "Sincere Friend."

I must tell you that Mr. Elliot (the same who filched Dr. Lee's Papers at Berlin) was furious when he found my Business at Copenhagen; and that I was received with great distinction at Court and in all the best Societies in Denmark. Every time I was invited to sup with the King, Elliot made an apology; he shut himself up for more than a Month, and then left town. This occasioned much Laughter; and as he had shunned Society from the time of my arrival, People said he had gone of in a fright!—I hope Mr. Jefferson is satisfyed with the train in which I left the Danish Business. It would have been impossible for me to have pushed it any further, as I had not full powers to conclude it finally.

I went through Sweeden to St. Petersburg. The advanced season did not permit my return to Paris, the distance would have been too long through Germany, and Elliot had influenced the English to put difficulties in the way of my Passage by the Baltic. I found the Gulf de Botenea barred with Ice, and after making several fruitless attempts to Cross it in a small open boat (about 30 feet long) I compelled the Sweedish Peasants to steer as I directed them for the Gulf of Finland. After about 4 or 500 Miles of Navigation I landed at Reval, and having paid the Peasants to their Satisfaction, I gave them a good Pilot, with some Provision, to reconduct them to their Home. My Voyage was loo[ked] upon as a kind of Miracle, being what never had been attempted before, unless in large Vessels.

The Empress received me with a distinction the most flattering that perhaps any Stranger can boast of, on entering into the Russian Service. Her Majesty conferred on me immediately the Grade of Rear Admiral. I was detaind against my will a fortnight; and continually feasted at Court and in the first Society. This was a Cruel grief to the English, and I own that their Vexation, which I believe was General in and about St. Petersburg, gave me no pain.

I presented the Empress with a Copy of the new American Constitution. Her Majesty spoke to me often about the United States, and is persuaded that *the American Revolution cannot fail to bring about others, and to influence every other Government.*[1] I mentioned the Armed Neutrality, so honorably Patronized by Her Majesty, and I am persuaded that no difficulty will be made about admitting the United-States into that Illustrious Association, so soon as America shall have built some Ships of War.—I spoke of it to the Danish Minister of Foreign Affairs, who seemed pleased with the Idea.—

The United States have some Commerce with Russia, which perhaps we may be able to encrease. I should think Whale Oil, dry'd fish, Spermaceti and Rice may be articles to suit the Russia Market; If the Mediterranean was not Shut to the American Flag, many articles might be supplied to the Russian Fleet, now destined for the Archipelago. I certainly wish to be useful to a Country I have so long served. I love the People and their cause, and shall always rejoice when I can be useful to promote their Happiness. I am glad that the new Constitution will be, as you tell me, adopted by more than Nine States. I hope however they will alter some parts of it; and particularly that they will divest the President of all Military Rank and command; for though General Washington might be safely trusted with such tempting power as the Chief Command of the Fleet and Army, yet, depend on it, in some other Hands it could not fail to Overset the libertys of America. The President should be only the first Civil Magistrate, let him command the Military *with the Pen*; but deprive him of the power to draw his Sword and lead them, under some plausible pretext, or under any Circumstances whatever, to cut the throats of a part of his fellow Citizens, and to make him the Tyrant of the rest. These are not my Apprehensions alone; for I have mentioned them to many Men of sense and learning since I saw you, and I have found them all of the same Sentiment.

What are you about my Dear General? Are you so absorbed in Politics, as to be insensible to Glory? That is impossible. Quit then your divine Calypso, come here, and pay your court once more to Bellona, who, you are sure, will receive you as her favorite. You would be charmed with the Prince de Potemkin. He is a most amiable Man, and none can be more Noble Minded.

For the Empress, Fame has never yet done her Justice. I am sure no Stranger who has not known that Illustrious Character ever conceived how much her Majesty is made to reign over a great Empire, to make her People Happy, and to attach grateful and susceptible Minds.

Is not the present a happy moment for France to declare for Russia? Would it not be a means to retrieve her Dignity and to reestablish the affairs of Holland? What would England find to oppose to such an Alliance? Denmark is with Russia, and Sweeden ought surely to be with France. An Alliance with Russia might be very advantageous, and can never be dangerous to France. In these circumstances the Isles of Candia and Cyprus appear among the Objects which ought to attract her Attention. Perhaps they might be Obtaind and the affairs of Holland re-established without the Expense of a War; for it is a question if England and Russia would venture to make Opposition. One sure Advantage would result to France. I mean the breaking of her destructive Treaty of Commerce with England. Since the time of the Assembly of Notables, I have always thought that the Ministry ought to have seen the expediency of a War with England; To break the Treaty of Commerce, and prevent the ruin of French Manufactories; To obtain Loans from Holland, and to render that Republic for ever dependent on French Protection; and, above all, to Unite the Nation, and prevent the broils that have since ensued; by exciting a brave patriotic People, to support their National Dignity.

My motives are pure; and I am Influenced only by the affection I feel for the two Countries you Love. Your known Patriotism, assures me that if you can make my Ideas Useful, you will not fail to do it.

My kind respects await Madame La Marquisse, and I hope her interesting Family is well. It would afford me great happiness to see or hear from you—and if you cannot favor us with a Visit, I beg the favor of any News that may be interesting. I am my Dear General, Your Affectionate & Obliged Friend and most Humble Servant,

J PAUL JONES

P.S. Mr. Little Page has arrived at the Army of the Prince de Potemkin, and I expect to see him here in a few days. The Captaine Pacha has been beaten last Week. This is a good beginning, and I hope we shall soon have greater success. The Count de Dumas was in the affair. To speak in our Republican way, he is a Gallant Fellow, I marked him well. He has my Esteem, and his fair Mistress owes him Twenty *sweet* Kisses for his first Effort. He keeps her Picture always at his Heart.

RC (DLC: John Paul Jones Papers); in a clerk's hand, signed by Jones; at foot of text: "Monsieur le Marquis de la Fayette Major General et Chevalier du plusieurs Ordres a son Hôtel a Paris."

1 It is not certain whether Jones or someone else at a later date (such as Sherburne, who obtained this MS from TJ and who, while generally careful of the text, occasionally made alterations in spelling, punctuation, &c.), underscored this and other passages in this letter.

From John Paul Jones, with Enclosure

on Board the Wolodimer before Oczacoff
29 August-9 Septr. 1788

Some of my Friends in America did me the honor to ask for my Bust. I inclose the Names of eight Gentlemen, to each of whom I promis'd to send one. You will oblige me much, by desiring Mr. Houdan to have them prepared and pack'd up two and two; and if Mr. Short, to whom I present my Respects, will take the trouble to forward them by good Opportunities via Havre de Grace, writing, at the same time, a few Words to each of the Gentlemen, I shall esteem it a particular Favor.

Before I left Copenhagen, I wrote to Mr. Amoureux, Merchant at L'Orient, to dispose of some Articles of mine in his hands, and remit you the Amount. I hope he has done it, and that his remittance may be sufficient to pay Mr. Houdan and the expence of striking the Medal with which I am honored by the United-States. But, lest this should not turn out as I expect, I have directed Doctor Bancroft to pay any Draft of yours on him, for my Account as far as four or five thousand Livres. I shall want four Gold Medals as soon as the Dies are finished. I must present one to the United-States, another to the King of France, and I cannot do less than offer one to the Empress. As you will keep the Dies for me, it is my intention to have some more Gold Medals struck; therefore I beg you, in the mean time not to permit the striking of a single Silver or Copper Medal.

I pray you to present me in the most respectful terms to Monsieur de Simolin. However my Situation in Russia may terminate, I shall ever esteem myself under great Obligation to him. I pray you to present my affectionate Respects to the Count d'Estaing and tell him I am infinitily flattered by the obliging things he has had the Goodness to say of me in my absence. I admire him for his Magnanimity and it vexes me every time I reflect how little his bravery and Patriotism have been rewarded by Government. He is the only Officer who served through the Last war without Promotion or honors. It is his honor, to be belov'd by his Nation and to have deserv'd it.

I send inclosed an Extract of my Journal on my Expedition from France to Holland in the Year 1779, for the Information of the Accademy of Incriptions and Belles Lettres. I trust at the same time more to your Judgement than to theirs. There is a Medalist who executed three Medals for me in Wax. One of them is the Battle between the Bon-homme-Richard and the Serapis. The Position of the two Ships is not much amiss, but the accessory figures are much too near the principal Objects; and he has placed them to windward instead of being, as they really were, to Leeward of the Bon-Homme-Richard and Serapis. I do not at this moment recollect the[1] Medallist's Name; but he lives on the 3d or 4th Stage at a Marble Cutters, almost opposite, but a Little higher than your former House, Cul de Sac Rue Taitebout and may be easily found. It would be of use to see the medal he has made, although it is by no means to be Copyed. I owe him a small Sum, perhaps 200 Livres. I wish to know how much, that I may take an arrangement for paying. I have not comprehended in the Extract of my Journal the extreme Difficulties I met with in Holland, nor my Departure from the Texel in the Alliance, when I was forc'd out by the Vice Admiral Rhynst in the Face of the Ennemy's Fleet. The Critical Situation I was in in Holland needs no Explanation, and I shall not say how much the honor of the American Flag depended on my Conduct, or how much it affected all the Billigerent Powe[r]s. I shall only say, it was a principal Cause of the Resentment of England against Holland, and of the War that ensued. It is for you and the Academy to determin, whether that Part of my Service ought to be the Subject of one Side of the Medal?

Before Oczacoff Septr. 16/26[2] 1788.

Mr. Little Page has postponed his Departure. I expected him to remain with me till the End of the Campaign, but he now sets out so suddenly, that I cannot send by him the Extract of my Journal in 1779. I will send it in a Week or two to my Friend the Count de Segur at St. Petersbourg and he will forward it to you with his Ministerial Dispatches. Your Letters with which you honor me may also be forwarded to him. I persuade myself that Count de Montmorin will do it with Pleasure. I trouble you with two inclosed Letters and am with perfect Esteem Dear Sir, your most affectionate and Obliged Servant.

Tr (DLC: John Paul Jones Papers); at head of text: "Extract"; in a clerk's hand, with one marginal note by TJ. As is made clear in Jones to TJ, 20/31 Jan. 1789, in which this extract was enclosed, it actually formed a part of the text of the preceding letter of 29 Aug./9 Sep. 1788. Littlepage did not set out SUDDENLY, after all, for the letter in which the present extract was enclosed reached TJ, as the entries in SJL show, on 28 Feb. 1789, while the letter of 29 Aug./9 Sep. 1788 did not arrive for another two months, a delay explained by Littlepage in his to TJ, 12 Feb. 1789. The two letters that were enclosed, in addition to the one to Short, have not been identified.

The MEDALIST who executed a medal of THE BATTLE BETWEEN THE BONHOMME RICHARD AND THE SERAPIS, with a profile of Jones, was one Renaud; both sides of the medal are reproduced in *Mêmoires de Paul Jones*, Paris, 1798 (frontispiece); a note concerning the engraver and the SMALL SUM Jones owed him is to be found at p. xvii-xix.

1 At this point TJ inserted an asterisk and, in the margin, the name "Reynaud."

2 Thus in Tr, an error for 15/26 Sep. 1788.

ENCLOSURE

John Paul Jones to William Short

on board the Wolodimer before Oczakow 15/26 Septr. 1788.

List of Gentlemen to whom Busts are to be sent.

2.	General St. Clair Mr. Ross	of Philadelphia
2.	Mr. John Jay Genl. Irvine	New York
2	Mr. Secy. Thomson Colonel Wadsworth	New York
2	Mr. J. Maddison Colo. Carrington	Virginia

Admiral Paul—Jones presents his respectful Compliments to Mr. Short, and begs the favor of him to forward the eight Busts mention'd in the above List, by the most direct Opportunities from La Havre de Grace to America. Mr. Jefferson is wrote to on this Subject; and Mr. Houdan, who prepares the Busts, will also have them carefully pack'd up in four Boxes. The Admiral prays Mr. Short to be so obliging as to write a line or two to each of the Gentlemen for whom the Busts are destined.

Tr. (DLC: John Paul Jones Papers); in Jones' hand; in middle of page, below list of names: "Copy."

From Thomas Paine

London Broad Street Buildings No. 13
Sepr. 9th. 1788

DEAR SIR

That I am a bad correspondent is so general a complaint against me, that I must expect the same accusation from you—But hear me first.—When there is no matter to write upon a letter is not worth the trouble of receiving and reading, and while any thing, which is to be the subject of a letter, is in suspence, it is difficult to write, and perhaps best to let it alone—"*least said is soonest mended*," and nothing said requires no mending.

The Model has the good fortune of preserving in England the reputation which it received from the Academy of Sciences. It is a favourite hobby horse with all who have seen it; and every one who have talked with me on the subject advised me to endeavour to obtain a Patent, as it is only by that means that I can secure to myself the direction and management.—For this purpose I went, (in company with Mr. Whiteside) to the office which is an appendage to Lord Sydney's—told them who I was and made an affidavit that the construction was my own Invention—this was the only step I took in the business. Last Wednesday I received a Patent for England, the next day a Patent for Scotland and I am to have one for Ireland.

As I had already the opinion of the Scientific Judges both in France and England on the Model, it was also necessary that I should have that of the practical Iron Men who must finally be the executors of the work.

There are several capital Iron works in this Country, the principal of which are those in Shropshire, Yorkshire and Scotland.—It was my intention to have communicated with Mr. Wilkinson who is one of the proprietors of the Shropshire Iron Works and concerned in those in France, but his departure for Sweden before I had possession of the patents prevented me.

The Iron Works in Yorkshire belonging to the Walkers near to Sheffield are the most eminent in England in point of establishment and property. The proprietors are reputed to be worth two hundred thousand pounds and consequently capable of giving energy to any great undertaken. A friend of theirs who had seen the Model wrote to them on the Subject, and two of them came to London last Fryday to see it and talk with me on the business.

Their opinion is very decided that it can be executed either in Wrought or Cast Iron and I am to go down to their Works next week to erect an experiment Arch. This is the point I am now got to; and until now I had nothing to inform you of.—If I succeed in creating the Arch all reasoning and opinion will be at an end, and as this will soon be known, I shall not return to France till that time, and until then I wish every thing to remain, respecting any Bridge over the Seine, in the State I left matters in when I came from France. With respect to the Patents in England it is my intention to dispose of them as soon as I have established the certainty of the construction.

Besides the ill success of Black friars Bridge, two Bridges built successively on the same spot, the last by Mr. Smeaton, at Hexham over the Tyne in Northumberland have fallen down occasioned by quicksands under the bed of the river.—If therefore Arches can be extended in the proportion the Model promises, the construction in certain situations, without regard to cheapness or dearness will be valuable in all Countries.

I enclose you a Philadelphia Paper 10 of July having the account of the Procession of the 4th of that month. An Arrival from Philadelphia which left it the 26th. July brings nothing new.—The Convention of New-York was still sitting; but we have accounts, tho' I know not how they came, that the Convention of N. York acceeded on the 29th of July. I since hear that this account is brought by the Columbine in 29 days from N. York, arrived at Falmouth, with wheat to Lisbon.[1]

As to English News or Politics, here is little more than what the public Papers contain.—The assembling the States General and the reappointment of Mr. Neckar make considerable impression here. They overawe a great deal of the English habitual rashness and checks that triumph of presumption which they indulge themselves in with respect to what they called the deranged and almost ruinous condition of the finances of France. They acknowlege unreservedly that the natural resources of france are greater than those of England but they plume themselves on the superiority of the Means necessary to bring national resources forth. But the two circumstances, above mentioned, serve very much to lower this exultation.

Some time ago I spent a Week at Mr. Burkes and the Duke of Portland's in Buckenhamshire. You will recollect that the duke was the Minister during the time of the Coalition. He is now in the opposition, and I find the opposition as much warped in some respects as to Continental Politics as the Ministry.

What the extent of the Treaty with Prussia is, Mr. B—— says that he and all the opposition are totally unacquainted with, and they speak of it not as a very wise measure, but rather tending to involve England in unnecessary continental disputes. The preference of the opposition is to a connection with Russia if it could have been obtained.

Sir George Staunton tells me that the interference with respect to Holland last year met with considerable opposition from part of the Cabinet. Mr. Pitt was against it at first, but it was a favourite measure with the King, and that the opposition at that Crisis contrived to have it known to him that they were disposed to support his measures. This, together with the notification of the 16th. of Sepr. gave Mr. Pitt cause and pretence for changing his ground.

The Marquis of Landsdown is unconnected either with the Ministry or the opposition. His politics is distinct from both. This plan is a sort of Armed Neutrality which has many Advocates. In Conversation with me he reprobated the Conduct of the Ministry towards France last year as operating to "*cut the throat of Confidence*" (this was his expression) between France and England at a time when there was a fair opportunity of improving it.

The Enmity of this Country against Russia is as bitter as it ever was against America, and is carried to every Pitch of abuse and vulgarity. What I hear in Conversations exceed what may be seen in the News-papers. They are sour and mortified at every success she acquires and voraciously believe and rejoice in the most improbable accounts and rumours to the contrary. You may mention this to Mr. Simolin in any terms you please for you cannot exceed the fact.

There are those who amuse themselves here in the hopes of managing Spain. The Notification which the Marquis del Campo made last year to the British Cabinet is, perhaps, the only secret that is kept in this Country. Mr. B—— tells me that the opposition knows nothing of it.

They all very freely admit that if the Combined fleets had had thirty or forty thousand land forces when they came up the Channel last War, there was nothing in England to oppose their landing, and that such a measure would have been fatal to their resources, by, at least, a temporary destruction of national Credit. This is the point in which this Country is most impressible. Wars, carried on at a distance, they care but little about, and seem always disposed to enter into them. It is bringing the matter home to them that makes them fear and feel, for their weakest part is at home. This I take to be the reason of the attention they are paying to Spain, for while France and Spain make a Common Cause, and *Start* together, they may easily overawe this Country.

I intended sending this letter by Mr. Parker but he goes by the way of Holland and as I do not chuse to send it by the English Post, I shall desire Mr. Bartholemy to forward it to you.

Remember me with much Affection to the Marquis de la Fayette. This letter will serve for two letters. Whether I am in London or the Country any letter to me at Mr. Whiteside Merchant No. 13 Broad Street Buildings will come safe. My Compliments to

Mr. Short. I am Dear Sir with great Esteem your Obliged Friend & Ob. Hble Servant, THOMAS PAINE

Sepr. 15th.

This letter was intended to go by the last dispatches of Mr. Bartholemey but was too late. I have since seen a New-york paper of the 8th. of August, in which there is a circular letter from the Convention of New-york signed by the President (Governor Clinton) to the several Legislatures which states, that altho' they had acceeded to the foedral Constitution, from principles of regard to the Union, it was, in the opinion of a Majority of them, exceptionable in many points; and recommending that another Convention be hereafter assembled, agreeable to the provision made in the Constitution, for the purpose of reforming altering &c. Nothing particular, as to defect, is pointed at in the Circular letter, the expressions are general, and they disclaim all local Ideas.

A Motion was made in Congress that the New Congress meet at Baltimore which was carried 7 States to 6. The question was reconsidered the next day, and carried 7 to 6 for New York, in this state it stood when the Vessel sailed.

It was said some time ago in the English Newspapers, that five officers of the Sweedish Army had withdrawn and refused to serve, because the King had undertaken an *Offensive* War, without consulting and having the concurrence of the Senate, agreeable to an Article in their form of government; but a Gentleman who is intimate at Baron Nolkins the Sweedish Minister's tells me that a *third* of the officers have made that objection, which has disabled the progress of the Sweedish Army in Finland.

Whether I shall set off a catenarian Arch or an Arch of a Circle I have not yet determined, but I mean to set off both and take my choice. There is one objection against a Catenarian Arch, which is, that the Iron tubes being all cast in one form will not exactly fit every part of it.

An Arch of a Circle may be sett off to any extent by calculating the Ordinates, at equal distances on the diameter. In this case, the Radius will always be the Hypothenuse, the portion of the diameter be the Base, and the Ordinate the perpendicular or the Ordinate may be found by Trigonometry in which the Base, Hypothenuse and right angle will be always given.

I think the Arch will appear rather handsomer if the direction of the Blocks and Bolts, were always in the direction of the Radius as I first proposed but which I changed in the drawing and placed as perpendiculars to the Cord[2] instead of the Curve to remedy the inconvenience of the deverging of the Bolts as you mentioned.

In a very large Arch of 4 or 600 feet Cord, this deverging will be considerable, about 3 or 4 tenths of an Inch on every two feet—but this difficulty may be effectually remedied, and the direction of the radius preserved by making the Bar in two halves, with half a hole in each; they will then be put on sideways and may be united by clamps. This method will exceedingly facilitate the raising or putting the Arch together, and shorten the time of the Work on the River very considerably. I am not fond of hazarding opinions, neither is it proper or prudent to do it, but I think that after every thing is prepared, a Bridge over such a River as the Seine, might be put up in three months time—or less, as all the Arches would be began on at once, and the work would admit of as many hands being employed at the same time as you please.

I have not heard anything of Mr: Littlepage since I left Paris. If you have I shall be glad to know it. As he dined sometimes at Mr. Neckar's he undertook to describe the Bridge to him. Mr. Neckar very readily conceived it. If you have an opportunity of seeing Mr. Neckar, and see it convenient to renew the subject, you mention that I am going forward with an Experiment Arch.

Mr. Le Couteulx desired me to examine the construction of the Albion or Steem Mills erected by Bolton and Watts. I have not yet written to him because I had nothing certain to write about. I have talked with Mr. Rumsey who is here, upon this matter, and who appears to me to be master of that subject and who has procured a Model of the Mill which is worked originally from the Steem, but it will be necessary to know what proposals Mr. Le Couteulx will make to any person who will undertake to construct his spare Steem Engines, of which he has one always in each Building, into a Mill, and conduct the operation. In this case Mr. Rumsey appears to me the very person Mr. Le Couteulx wants. The enclosed letter to Mr. Le Couteulx is on this subject.

There has been some proposals passed on each side between Bolton and Rumsey in which I think the former has taken advantage of the unsuspicious openess of the latter.

I have again enquired about the map, and find it is engraving at the place you mentioned. It will be 8 feet by 6 and the price about 2 Guineas but they cannot tell me the time it will be finished. I informed you of the Air pump in my letter to you by Mr. Quesney. When you see Mr. Le Roy please to present my Compliments. I hope I shall now reallize the opinion of the Academy on the Model, in which case I shall give the Academy the proper information.

We have no certain accounts here of the arrangement of the new Ministry. The papers mention Count St. Priest for foreign Affairs. When you see him please to present my Compliments.

The New York Packet is arrived this Morning. She sailed the eighth of Augs. and brings nothing new. The Majority in the Convention of N. York was but three.

The question for the meeting of Congress at Philadelphia was put and lost. Please to present my Compliment to M. & Madame de Corney.

RC (DLC); endorsed. Enclosures: (1) Paine may have been mistaken in the date of the Philadelphia paper containing an account of the PROCESSION OF THE 4TH of July: Hopkinson's comprehensive description of that notable occasion appeared in the *Pennsylvania Packet* and the *Pennsylvania Gazette* for 9 July, and one of these was enclosed in Hopkinson to TJ, 17 July 1788. (2) The letter to Mr. Le Couteulx has not been found.

The MODEL OF THE MILL of Boulton and Watt may have been similar to that illustrated above (Vol. 10: xxviii, 387). For a note on THE MAP by Cruz Cano, see note to TJ to Smith, [10] Aug. 1786, and also TJ to Madison, 28 June 1791; TJ to Thomas Pinckney, 24 June 1792; Sowerby, No. 3857. On the significance of the WEEK AT MR. BURKES, and its effect on the relation between Burke, Paine, and TJ, see Thomas W. Copeland, *Our Eminent Friend, Edmund Burke*, p. 146-89; see also, Paine to TJ, 15 Jan. 1789; TJ to Paine, 11 July 1789.

[1] This sentence is interlined and was probably added by Paine when he wrote his postscript of the 15th.

[2] Thus in MS.

To John Rutledge, Jr.

DEAR SIR Paris Sep. 9. 1788.

I have duly received your favors of Aug. 30. and Sep. 4. The animal whose skin you saw here is called the Moose. Monsr. de Buffon had well known it by name; but he has supposed it to be the same as the Renne-deer of Lapland in his history. Being satisfied myself that it was a different animal, I asked the favor of Genl. Sullivan to have one killed for me and to send me the skin and skeleton. This is what you saw. It is found only Eastward of the Hudson's river. M. de Buffon describes the Renne to be about 3. feet high, and truly the Moose you saw here was 7. feet high, and there are of them 10. feet high. The experiment was expensive to me, having cost me hunting, curing, and transporting, 60 guineas.—The animal whose enormous bones are found on the Ohio, is supposed by M. de Buffon, and M. Daubenton to have been an Elephant. Dr. Hunter demonstrated it not to have been an elephant. Similar bones are found in Siberia, where it is called the Mammoth. The Indians of America say it still exists very far North in our continent. I suppose there is no such thing at Geneva as a copy of my Notes on Virginia, or you might see the subject treated there somewhat at length, as also some short notice of the Moose. I am glad to hear you have been so happy as to become acquainted with M. de Saussure. He is certainly one of the best philosophers of the present age. Cautious in not letting his assent run before his evidence, he possesses the wisdom which so few possess of preferring ignorance to error. The contrary disposition in those who call themselves philosophers in this country classes them in fact with the writers of romance.—You have heard that Virginia has acceded to the new Constitution. New York has done the same by a majority of five. No news from N. Carolina. Congress were proceeding early in July to put the new government into motion. Probably it will be December or January before the new legislature is assembled. Were I to trouble Mr. Shippen with a letter, I could only repeat the same things over again. Be so good as to say this to him, to deliver him the inclosed letter with my friendly compliments, and to accept yourself assurances of the esteem with which I am Dear Sir Your most obedt. humble servt,

TH: JEFFERSON

RC (Goodspeed's Bookshop, Boston, Mass., 1946). PrC (DLC). The enclosed letter has not been identified.

From John Rutledge

⟦[*Charleston, S.C.*] *9 Sep. 1788.* Recorded in SJL Index, but not found.⟧

From John Ledyard

SIR — Grand Cairo. Septr. 10th. 1788.

I wrote you a short letter from Alexandria and addressed it under cover to Mr. Cathalan and sent it to Marseilles by the same vessel I came in from thence to Egypt where I arrived the 5th. of August. I begin this letter without knowing when I shall close it or when I shall send it—and indeed whether I ever shall send it: but I will have it ready in case an opportunity should offer. Having been in Cairo only 4 days I have not yet any thing curious or particularly interesting to begin with: indeed you will not expect much of that kind from me: my business is in another quarter and the information I seek totaly new: any information from here whatever would not be so was I possessed of it. At all events I shall never be wholly without a subject when it is to you I write: I shall never think my letter a bad one when it contains the declarations of the esteem I have for you: of my gratitude, and of my affection for you, and this notwithstanding you thought hard of me for being employed by an english association which hurt me very much while I was at paris. You know your own heart and if my suspicions are groundless forgive them since they proceeded from the jealousy I have, not to loose the little regard you have in times past been pleased to honour me with. You are not obliged to esteem me, but I am obliged to esteem you, or to take leave of my senses and confront the opinions of the greatest and best characters I know of: if I cannot therefore address myself to you as a Man that you regard, I must write to you as one that regards you for your own sake, and for the sake of my country which has set me the example.

I made the journey from Alexandria by water and entered the western branch of the mouths of the River Nile into the River. I was 5 days coming on the river to Cairo: but this passage is generally made in 4, sometimes in 3, days.

You have heard and read much of this River, and so had I: but when I saw it I could not conceive it to be the same—it is a mere mud puddle compared with the accounts we have of it. What eyes do travellers see with—are they fools, or rogues. For heavens sake hear the plain truth about it: first with respect to its size: plain comparisons in such cases are good: do you know the river Connecticutt—of all the rivers I have seen it most resembles it in size: and being only a little wider may on that account better compare with the river Thames. This is the mighty the sovereign of rivers—the vast nile, that has been metaphored into one of the wonders of the world—let me be carefull how I read—and above all how I read Antient history!

You have read and heard too of its inundations: it is a lye: the banks of this river were never entirely overflowed much more the meadows round it. If the thousands of large and small canals from it and the thousands of men and machines employed to communicate by artificial means the water of the nile to its meadows is the inundation meant it is true—any other is false. It is not an inundating river. I came up the River the 20th. of Augt. and about the 30th. of August the water is at its height i e the freshet: when I left the river its banks were 4 5 and 6 feet above water and here in town I am told that they expect the nile to be 1 or 2 feet higher only—at the most. This is a proof if I wanted one that the banks of the nile are never overflowed. I have made a subject of it and transmited my observations to London: there I have said much at large about it: in a letter I cannot do it.

I saw three of the pyramids as I passed up the River but they were 4 or 5 leagues off. If I see them nearer before I close my letter and observe any thing about them that I think will be new to you, will insert it. It is warm weather here at present, and but for the north winds that cool themselves in their passage over the Mediterranean sea and blow upon us we should be sadly situated: as it is I think I have felt it hotter at Philadelphia in the same month.

The City of Cairo is about half as large as Paris—and by the aggregate of my informations contains 700,000 inhabitants: you will therefore anticipate the fact of its narrow streets and will conceive it necessary also that the houses are high: in this number are included 100,000 of the Coptics or antient egyptians—and these are Christians: there are also many other christian sects here from Damascus, Jerusalem, Aleppo and all parts of Syria.

With regard to my Voyage, I can only tell you for any certainty that I shall be able to pass as far as the western boundaries of what is called Turkish Nubia, and at a Town called Sennar. You will find this town on any chart. It is on a branch of the nile: I expect to get there with some surety—but afterwards all is dark before me: my design and wishes are to pass in that parrelel across the Continent. I will write you from Sennar if I can. You know of the disturbances in this unhappy and forlorn country, and the nature of them. The Beys revolted from the Bashaw have possession of upper i e southern Egypt and are now encamped with an army pitifull enough about 3 miles southward of Cairo: they say—Bashaw Come out from your City and fight us—and the Bashaw says Come out of your entrenchments and fight me. You know that this revolt is a stroke in Russian politicks. Cairo is a wretched hole, and a nest of vagabonds. Nothing merits more the whole force of Burlesque than both the poetic and prosaic legends of this country. Sweet are the songs of Egypt on paper. Who is not ravished with gums, balms, dates, figgs, pomegrannates with the circassia and sycamores without knowing that amidst these ones eyes ears mouth nose is filled with dust eternal hot fainting winds, lice bugs musquetoes spiders flies—pox, itch leprosy, fevers, and almost universal blindness.

I am in perfect health and most ardently wish you yours. Make my compliments to all my friends and particularly to the Marquis la fayette should [he] be with you.

Adieu for the present and believe me to be with all possible esteem & regard Sr. Your sincere friend & most humble & Obedient Servant, J LEDYARD

RC (NHi); endorsed. Tr (Mrs. Jane Ledyard Remington, Cazenovia, New York, 1951); minor textual variations between this and RC. See TJ to Short, 28 Feb. 1789.

To John Trumbull

DEAR SIR Sep. 10. 1788.

Your favors of the 2d. and 6th. inst. are duly received. You conjectured rightly that by 'vallons' I meant festoon curtains. The term is well understood by the upholsterers. The Venetian blind and large backlight to let up and down are essential in a hot climate. I would desire no Imperial, and only one trunk, and that to go behind. Brass harness for four horses. These are for country use, and best for that. I have plated harness for the city use. I would wish the brass harness to be plain, and substantially good. Neither cypher nor crest on them. The pictures are received in good condition, and Mr. Short's books also. I am really pained at your having so much trouble with this, 'sed dabit deus his quoque finem.' I write all the news to Mr. Cutting who will tell it to you. Say every thing soft and affectionate for me to Mrs. Cosway and Mrs. Church. They are a countervail to you for the want of a sun. Adieu. Your's affectionately, TH: JEFFERSON

PrC (DLC).

From C. W. F. Dumas

The Hague, 11 Sep. 1788. As directed in TJ's of the 1st, he has countermanded the sending of the *Gazette de Leide* by post and has asked the cost, which he will take care of and inform TJ. "Un singulier Message qu'on vient de me faire" will require another dispatch for Congress, which he will try to have ready for tomorrow's post.

RC (DLC). FC (Dumas Letter Book, Rijksarchief, The Hague; photostats in DLC).

To Montmorin

Sir Paris Sep. 11. 1788

In the course of the last war the house of Schweighauser & Dobrée of Nantes, and Puchelberg of L'Orient presented to Dr. Franklin a demand against the United States of America. He being acquainted with the circumstances of the demand, and knowing it to be unfounded, refused to pay it. They thereupon procured a seizure by judiciary authority of certain arms and other military stores which we had purchased in this country and had deposited for embarcation at Nantes: and these stores have remained in that position ever since. Congress have lately instructed me to put an end to this matter. Unwilling to trouble your Excellency whenever it can be avoided, I proposed to the parties to have the question decided by arbitrators to be chosen by us jointly. They have refused it as you will see by their answers to my letters, copies of both which I have the honour to inclose you. I presume it to be well settled in practice that the property of one sovereign is not permitted to be seized within the dominions of another; and that this practice is founded not only in mutual respect but in mutual utility. To what the contrary practice would lead is evident in the present case wherein military stores have been stopped in the course of a war in which our greatest difficulties proceeded from the want of military stores; in their letter too they make a merit of not having seized one of our ships of war, and certainly the principle which admits the seizure of arms would admit that of a whole fleet and would often furnish an enemy the easiest means of defeating an expedition. The parties obliging me then to have recourse to Your Excellency on this occasion, I am under the necessity of asking an order from you for the immediate delivery of the stores and other property of the United States at Nantes detained by the house of Schweighauser & Dobrée and that of Puchelberg, or by either of them, under pretence of a judicial seizure.

I have the honour to be with sentiments of the most perfect respect & esteem, Your Excellency's most obedient & most humble servant, Th: Jefferson

RC (Arch. Aff. Etr., Paris, Corr. Pol., Angleterre, Vol. 566); in Short's hand, signed by TJ. PrC of Tr (DLC); in TJ's hand; at foot of text: "Copy." Enclosures: TJ to Schweighauser & Dobrée, 27 June and 20 July 1788; Schweighauser & Dobrée to TJ, 15 July and 15 Aug. 1788, qq.v.

From Lucy Ludwell Paradise

Paris Sept. the 11th. 1788.

I have the honour to thank your Excellency for your Answer, and to assure you of my Gratitude to your family the first Moment I have it in my power. You may suppose Mr. Paradise has, from his Conversation written to England. He has not, and at his house when alone with me, he appears not to seem inclined to write; and if he does not write before he leaves Paris he will not do it after. I should be happy to have the Bills Dr. Bancroft mentions in his Letter paid off directly as it would bring the debts something less, and the next Aprils Dividends would be time enough for me to begin with. Honesty is my Walking Stick, and I would sooner be poor, and Honest, then Rich and the least dishonest. I wish Mr. Paradise was as ready to serve me as You are, I should be easy and happy in my mind. Mr. Paradise ought to write and tell Mr. Anderson every thing before he leaves Paris. I will not trouble Your Excellency any further, But remain with all Gratitude Your Excellencies Most Grateful Humb. Servt. and Sincere Friend,

LUCY PARADISE

RC (DLC); endorsed. Not recorded in SJL Index.

To Lucy Ludwell Paradise

DEAR MADAM

Paris Sep. 11. 1788.

Being much engaged, it was not possible for me to answer your favor of to-day in the moment of receiving it. Mr. Paradise has agreed to give you an order for the whole dividend, except Count Zenobio's part. As to this, he does not seem to have a right to dispose of it, because Count Zenobio lent on an engagement to receive his interest from that fund, and though he has not called for it, he has a right to do so when he pleases, and to impeach the honor of Mr. Paradise should he have diverted that part of the dividend to any other purpose. Dr. Bancroft's application for the same money paiable in the fall seems not admissible. Your support must be attended to in the first instance, and this money, which is the surest, should be sacredly kept for your use. Next to this, Mr. Paradise's support must be ensured. I think therefore he should desire Mr. Anderson to send him the first hundred guineas he receives from America, to Bergamo, to answer his purposes to the first day of January when the regular provision is to commence.

This being done the demands for Abbot and Mrs. Stevenson might come in next on the American remittances. I should hope that Mr. Anderson, seeing that all the American remittances were to come to his hands, would not hesitate to advance immediately 100. guineas to Mr. Paradise by a bill on Milan or Venice, which might arrive at Bergamo nearly as soon as Mr. Paradise would.

I beg you, my dear Madam, not to add to the circumstances of your uneasiness, that of not leaving tokens of remembrance to my daughters. Their acquaintance with you will be a sufficient ground of friendly remembrance. I should be sorry were they to need a motive of any other kind. I have been not a little afflicted that my situation here has not permitted me to relieve yours more substantially. I have the honour to be with very great respect Dr. Madam Your most obedient & most humble servt.,

TH: JEFFERSON

PrC (DLC).

From Willink & Van Staphorst

Amsterdam, 11 Sep. 1788. Acknowledge TJ's letters of 30 Aug. and 1 Sep.; they have taken notice of Carmichael's draft on them for *f*4,613 3s. and TJ's two orders for Grand & Cie. for *f*2,312 10s. and *f*277 10s; and will pay at maturity and charge to the United States.

RC (DLC); 2 p.; endorsed; in hand of Nicholas Hubbard, signed by the two firms.

From Etienne Clavière

MONSIEUR L'AMBASSADEUR　　Paris le 12. 7br. 1788

Le porteur de la presente est Monsieur Dupont Beaufrere de Monsieur Brissot de Warville. Il se propose de passer en Amérique plutot que plutard; et voudroit n'être pas dans la nécessité de s'embarquer en Angleterre. Il merite à tous égards l'interest que vous voudrez bien prendre à lui. La Guerre l'a obligé d'abandonner des établissemens qu'il avoit fait en Crimée et qu'il pourra remplacer plus avantageusement et plus paisiblement dans quelque contrée des Etats unis. Il seroit difficile de leur procurer un citoyen plus recommandable.

J'ay l'honneur d'etre avec beaucoup de considération Monsieur l'Ambassadeur Votre très humble & très obeissant serviteur,

E. CLAVIERE

RC (MoSHi); endorsed.

From C. W. F. Dumas

MONSIEUR Lahaie 12e. 7br. 1788

Je m'étois proposé l'honneur d'écrire aujourd'hui à Votre Excellence, selon ma Lettre d'hier, sur un Message singulier que je reçus hier. Toute réflexion faite, il vaut mieux différer cela jusqu'à la semaine prochaine, afin de mettre le tout en son entier sous les yeux du Congrès et de Votre Excellence, m'étant engagé d'ici à Lundi matin à répondre au dit Message, et à un autre reçu ce matin après ma réponse provisionelle à celui d'hier. Je suis avec grand respect De Votre Exce. Le très-humble & très-obéissant serviteur C W F DUMAS

RC (DLC); endorsed. FC (Dumas Letter Book, Rijksarchief, The Hague; photostats in DLC).

MONSIEUR DUPONT BEAUFRERE DE MONSIEUR BRISSOT DE WARVILLE was François Dupont, who went to America not long after this letter was written. Letters from Dupont relating his experiences in America, beginning with one from Philadelphia, 15 Mch. 1789, are published in C. Perroud, *J.-P. Brissot, Correspondance et Papiers*, Paris, 1912, p. 217 ff.

From Lucy Ludwell Paradise

Paris Sept. the 12th. 1788

Your Excellencies humanity to my Cries to have things arrainged so as to have some supply not to be obliged to beg money of My Children has so indeared you and your family to me that I shall think of it, forever and ever. When your Letter came, Mr. P was not awake, therefore he desired me after he awoke to read it to him. I did, I said nothing to him, but your goodness melted me.—I hope he will do what you have written but I assure you he does not seem very ready. The very first Moment I can shew my Gratitude to your family I will do it to the utmost in my power. To Dear Dr. Bancroft I am greatly indebted, and I shall shew him I am not ungrateful. The Debts must first however be all paid honestly. I am resolved the next October Dividend shall be given to Dr. Bancroft for to pay those debts he has mentioned. Next April I will be happy to have the Dividends to begin for me to receive.

I am with Great Respect and Gratitude your Excellencies Most Humb. Servt. and very Sincere Friend, LUCY PARADIS

Will your Excellency have the goodness to tell Mr. Short that he will make us very very happy to go with us, and therefore, I shall be greatly obliged, if he will send his Trunk to me on Monday morning.

RC (DLC); endorsed.

To John Banister, Jr.

DEAR SIR Paris Sep. 13. 1788.

Monsieur de Vernon, who has an important claim against a Monsr. Mark of Petersburgh, having desired me to recommend some person to seek after it for him, I took the liberty of recommending your father, and he was kind enough to undertake it, and took some steps in it. Knowing that he is now gone to the West Indies, I have advised Mr. de Vernon to send a new power of attorney authorising your father and yourself, or either of you in the absence of the other, to do whatever may be necessary for him. The purpose of the present is to ask the favor of you to finish this business for him, and to remit in good bills of exchange whatever can be recovered for him. I am with great esteem Dear Sir Your friend & servt, TH: JEFFERSON

P.S. I inclose the Power of attorney and Monsr. de Vernon's letter to me.

PrC (DLC). Enclosures (missing): De Vernon wrote TJ on 13 Sep. 1788, according to an entry in SJL Index, and presumably enclosed the POWER OF ATTORNEY that TJ had suggested in his letter of 12 Aug. 1788 and that he forwarded to Banister in the present letter. See Duncan Rose to TJ, 26 Feb. 1789; TJ to Giles, 13 Dec. 1789.

From Lucy Ludwell Paradise

Paris Saturday Sept. the 13th. 1788

As I am now put in full possession of the dividends by Your Excellencies great humanity and exertions, I am to acquaint you that I shall send an Order directly to Mr. Anderson to pay the October Dividend to Dr. Bancroft for to inable him to pay those debts he has mentioned in his Letter to me. I acquainted your Excellency in a Letter, I wrote to you the other day, that Mr. Paradise would not have, after all his Expences were paid here, no more than £50. That not being sufficient to carry Us to Bergamo, I must trouble your friendship for me once more by desireing you will put me in a method to get some person to advance to me on Monday next the sum of £82.10s, that being the amount of the April Dividend due to me. The arraingment I shall make with it, is thus. I shall add £30 to Mr. Paradises £50, and I shall take £20 with us for fear of wanting money, and the £32.10s I shall leave in your Bankers hands. For to remain there until, I shall call for it. If you can oblige me with the above amount, I beg you will take the £2.10s by way of Interest until you shall receive the full sum Next April. Of this transaction I wish Mr. Anderson not to be acquainted with as, I have my particular reasons for it.

I am Your Excellencies Most truly Grateful and Much Obliged Humbl. Servant and Constant Friend, LUCY PARADISE

P.S. I do not mean that Mr. Anderson should not pay you the April Dividend, For I shall write expressly to him to send it to Your Excellency. But what I want is, that it should not be the means of stoping him from sending the £100 mentioned in your Letter.

I beg you will send me three word written that I may know what to do and that I may also write directly to Dr. Bancroft and Mr. Anderson upon the subject.

RC (DLC); endorsed.

To Lucy Ludwell Paradise

DEAR MADAM Paris Sep. 13. 1788.

I am truly mortified that it is not in my power to do exactly the thing which would be most convenient to you. My banker never advances money for any body, at least he tells me so, and my situation here never permitted me to have a shilling before hand. But the proposition which I had intended to make to Mr. Paradise will I hope answer your purpose. When you arrive at Lyons you will have accomplished somewhat more than half your journey. You will know then by the expences of this first half, what will be necessary for the remaining half of the journey from Lyons to Bergamo. You will see what money you have on hand at Lyons, and of course how much will be wanting to put you out of all danger of not having enough to carry you through your journey to Bergamo. I had intended to desire Mr. Short to procure this sum for you at Lyons, by a draught on me, which Mr. Paradise would replace at his leisure. In this way you will be secure of making your journey without risk of want, the money Mr. Anderson is to send on will supply what you may have occasion for at Bergamo and Venice, and your April dividend remain untouched till you call for it.

I repeat it, Madam, that I sincerely wish I possessed the sum you desire, that I might accomodate you exactly in the form you desire. But as I neither have it, nor the means of commanding it, I hope what I now propose will substantially answer your present purposes, and leave your future resources more unembarrassed.

May I hope that yourself and Mr. Paradise will do me the favor to dine with me tomorrow?

I have the honor to be with great esteem and respect, Madam, Your most obedient & most humble servt.,

TH: JEFFERSON

PrC (DLC).

To Vanet

á Paris ce 13me. Septembre 1788.

Monsieur Jefferson prie Monsieur Vannet de vouloir bien se charger de la lettre ci-incluse, et, quand il sera arrivé á Richmond, de la faire passer à Monsieur Bannister á Petersbourg. Il y a la dedans une procuration qui est trés interessante à la personne qui l'adresse á Monsieur Bannister. Il a l'honneur de souhaiter la bonne voiage á Monsieur Vannet.

PrC (DLC). Not recorded in SJL Index. Enclosure: TJ to Banister, 13 Sep. 1788, together with its enclosures.

Vanet had been engaged by TJ to deliver to the Commissioners of the Treasury the box and trunk of papers of Thomas Barclay as Commissioner of Public Accounts. According to an entry in SJL Index, TJ wrote Vanet on 1 Sep. 1788, but the letter has not been found. If, as seems likely, this letter pertained to the delivery of the papers, it is curious that, in a matter in which TJ went to some lengths to insure that the papers remained intact (see TJ to Commissioners, 6 Sep. 1788), no text has survived. Vanet evidently replied to TJ's letter on 10 Sep. 1788, according to another entry in SJL Index, but this letter also is missing.

From Blan

Che philidorts bijoutier rue MaCon N 18 faubou St. Germin a Paris Le 14 7bre 1788.

MONSIEUR

Jei ut lhoneur de me presenter à votre hotel Le 21 du moi dergné pour avoir selui de vous entretenir, Monsieur, dun objet qui et fait pour interreser les eta uni. En juillet 85. jave ut lhoneur de vous presenter des Essé d'un plan de travail quia reuni par un nouvel essé le sufrage des Conneseur, et quil poure meriter le votre lorsque vous En Conetre le produits. Pour Cet Efaits je vous prie, Monsieur, de Mhonnorer dune reponce, et mindiquer leure et le jour que vous pourie macorder une audience a votre hotel.

Jei lhoneur detre avey respec Monsieur Votre treunble Etre obeisen servite[ur] BLAN

RC (DLC); endorsed: "Blan." Blan's proposals submitted to TJ in July 1785 and renewed in Aug. 1788 were probably stated in person; no written text is known, nor is there record of any other letter from him to TJ or from TJ to him.

To Francis dal Verme

SIR Paris Sep. 15. 1788.

I had the honour of addressing letters to you lately by two of my countrymen, Mr. Shippen and Mr. Rutledge who meant to pass through Milan in a visit to Italy. The bearer hereof Mr. Short, tho leaving Paris later with the same view, will meet with those gentlemen at Geneva, and will have the honour of presenting himself to you at the same time. He is from the same state with myself, connected with me there, came to me on my coming here, and has lived with me ever since. These circumstances with his great merit and abilities entitle him to expect that I will use what little interest I may have to obtain for him the honour of presenting himself to you, and will render his acquaintance not unacceptable to you. I will ask for him some indication of the things worth his seeing during the short time he will be at Milan, and to facilitate his access to them. He is so perfectly acquainted with American transactions that instead of detailing them to you, I will refer you to him, only inclosing you a copy of our new constitution, and repeating, as I shall always do with pleasure, assurances of those sentiments of esteem & respect with which I have the honor to be, Sir, Your most obedient & most humble servt,

TH: JEFFERSON

PrC (DLC). The particular printing of the Constitution that TJ enclosed has not been identified; see note to Washington to TJ, 18 Sep. 1787.

From La Rouerie

hôtel des asturie rue du Sepulchre

SIR fg. St. Germain 15th 7bre. 88.

From your conversation with Major Schaffner and myself last spring, I had no doubt But congress would by this time have pay'd us the three year's interest which are due to us By North America. In considering the nature of the debt and the character and wealth of the debtor, we had no reason to fear a delay so very near a Bankruptcy. I confess to you, Sir, that I can not understand the motives of such conduct, and that our right to more attention and justice in giving us every day the hope of Being Better treated, has altogether with your promise, made me Countract engagements which must Be satisfyd now.

I request you, Sir, to give orders to Mr. Grand to pay us immediatly the three's years interest which are due; or to declare us that there is no sort of dependency on the debt of america towards us. If you chuse the last; you will do in that, what we ought to have done ourselves had our attachement for america Been calculated on her testimony of gratitude and Justice—I have the honour to be with respect Sir your most obedt. hble. ste.,

ARMAND MS. DE LA ROUERIE

P.S. I am here only for four days and I request you to give me a positive answer.

RC (ViWC); endorsed: "Rouerie Marq. de la."

From Edward Bancroft

DEAR SIR Charlotte Street (London) Septr. 16 1788.

I feel it incumbent on me first to express my grateful Sense of your Kindness to Mr. Dobbyn, and next to acknowledge your Favour of the 24th. ulto. which Mr. Trumbul obligingly conveyed to me without loss of time.

I have considered the arrangements which you have taken the trouble of stating to me and which Mr. Paradise (by the aid of your Council I presume) has taken for Liquidating his affairs and I think they are the best that could have been devised in the present situation; and that in this respect you have added very Considerably to the many other acts of Friendship and Kindness which he always very gratefully acknowledges to have received from you.

I have not yet received any Letter from Mr. Paradise on the subject to which yours relates; I presume however that it may have been intended that I should make use of it on some future occasion for the tranquility and satisfaction of his Creditors; but I will not venture to act upon this presumption, without further information from either you or him.

I think with you, that it will be best to discharge the small Debts first; and to this, I beleive several at least of the larger Creditors, perhaps all of them will readily Consent, and indeed if they were discharged Mr. Paradise might live here without any trouble from the others, so far as I can judge; but unless his doing so should be highly necessary to his enjoyment of Life which I can not suppose, I think his continuing abroad will be most adviseable, as he may obtain the Conveniences of Life much Cheaper, and will be much less exposed to temptations, incompatible with his plan of Œconomy, abroad, than in England.

I have not seen Mr. Anderson since the receipt of your Letter. Indeed I have both delayed acknowledging it, and calling on him, because I was in dailey expectation of a Letter from Mr. Paradise himself, according to your intimation. I begin now to despair of this, and therefore shall call on Mr. Anderson in a day or two and write to Mr. Paradise by the next Post.

I remember when I had formerly the honor of dining in Company with you and Mr. de Mallesherbes, at the Chevr. de La Luzerne's Country House at Vincennes, that you mentioned the Case of a Gentleman in Virginia, who had benevolently liberated all his Negroe Slaves and endeavoured to employ them on Wages to Cultivate his Plantation; but after a tryal of some time it was found that Slavery had rendered them incapable of Self Government, or at least that no regard for futurity could operate on their minds with sufficient Force to engage them to any thing like constant industry or even so much of it as would provide them with food and Cloathing and that the most sensible of them desired to return to their former state. As this Experiment seemed to me very important in its application to the Question now agitating here of the Liberation of Negroes in the West indies, or at least of the present Generation, who have been long habituated to Slavery, I mentioned it to some friends of mine, who are warmly and benevolently active in the Society instituted here for abolishing negro Slavery, and as they thought it highly deserving of attention and at the same time were desireous of a more ixact and Circumstantial Statement of all the Facts than I could recollect they requested me to sollicit you, at your leisure, to have the Goodness to furnish such a Statement with such observations as you might think proper to add thereto. I delayed transmitting this request to you, because I fully expected before this time to have had the pleasure of seeing you in Paris, but as Circumstances may perhaps still detain me here a month or six weeks longer, and as the winter approaches, when this Business will be again revived, I have thought it necessary no longer to delay the Communication, and my sollicitation that you will gratify these Gentlemen, if there be no particular objection to, or impropriety in, your doing it, as I have supposed there would not be. At all events no name need be mentioned farther than you think proper.

We have no particular news here that I know of worth your Notice. My best wishes ever attend you, and I shall be always happy in any opportunity of demonstrating the sincere attachment and profound respect with which I have the honor to be Dear Sir Your most faithful & most Devoted Humble servant,

EDWD. BANCROFT

RC (DLC); endorsed. Recorded in SJL as written on 21 Sep. 1788, which was probably the date of receipt.

From John Brown Cutting

SIR London Sepr. 16. 1788

Your respective favours of Sepr. 4th and 9th are before me. For both but especially for the last accept my sincere thanks. Truth and certainty are always most grateful to the human mind. Your mode of conveying them and the important objects concerning which you enlighten me, render what is naturally pleasant particularly interesting and grateful. As my passage to South Carolina must be regulated by the intelligence I obtain concerning the probability of a speedy, or more retarded commencement of the operations of the general government, as well of the assembling of the legislature, of the particular state to which I am about to resort, I think you may depend upon the fidelity of my correspondence for some weeks yet to come. Especially if the *new Congress* do not meet until March; and more especially if the circular letter from the Convention of New York shou'd prevail upon two thirds of the states, and among these Carolina, to suspend the functions of *that body* until another general convention can be convoked to consider and decide upon amendments. Or even if the following alteration of the general constitution shou'd by any mean[s] take place as insisted upon by New York, namely "That the judicial power of the United States, in cases in which a state may be a party, does not extend to authorise *any suit by any* person against *a state*"; I fear my proposed negotiation with the state of South Carolina wou'd be baffled, or rather so evidently promise to be abortive as not to be worth attempting.

The August Packet tho' momently expected is not yet arriv'd here from New York. By the next post I hope to announce to you the accession of North Carolina which I look to receive by the packet, since it seems she was to sail three days later than the date of any of the papers I inclose. Among these papers you will observe a transcript of the conventional letter from New York, and certain other articles, which I have with some industry collected and committed to writing for your entertainment. The sources whence I derived most of those extracts were not to be purchased nor even purloyn'd. To Mr. Parker who will be in Paris when this arrives, I have also inclosed an additional newspaper or two, which he will communicate. Those transcripts and these newspapers taken collectively contain the most recent information of american affairs that can be furnish'd from England. Even if you have 'em already, or fresher intelligence, the bulk of my dispatch will at least evince the energy of my zeal to amuse you.   Mr. Barlow will thank you for a perusal of the letter dated *Muskingum*, as he is personally, poetically, and patriotically, interested in the prosperity of that district. As a supplementary satisfaction both to you Sir and to him, I can inform you that the destruction of New Orleans accidentally by fire has open'd a friendly intercourse between the inhabitants of the Spanish and american territories; pro tempore (ex necessitate rei) a brisk and augmenting commerce is now carrying on to the mutual benefit of the respective parties. Tobacco, Lumber and Grain, with other agricultural articles have been plentifully supplied by our people who in return have been kindly received and handsomely paid in Mexican dollars. How natural such a commerce is and how impracticable to be fetter'd by the *one* government or *the other* a few years must demonstrate. I never look over your map of that country without wondering at the short sighted sagacity of our neighbours in attempting to restrain and prohibit a stream of commerce which will take its own course and shape its own channel naturally, and therefore, irresistably. Never do I consider the character of the people who inhabit it without rational delight. A hardy laborious race of independent, civiliz'd freemen, equally distant from the ferocious desine of conquest and the enervation of luxurious refinement, endued with a keen sense of the rights of man, possessing them in their utmost social extent, and neither like the ancient romans or the modern britons disdain to deny any one of them to a single human creature. No nation bordering upon territory of the United States has aught to fear from us excepting only that the mildness of our laws and the wisdom of our political institutions, if too strongly contrasted by harsh edicts and weak regulations, might tempt the subjects of any arbitrary potentates in our vicinity voluntarily to commute themselves into free citizens and thus become attached to the first empire that mankind have ever erected on the solid foundation of truth, reason or common sense.

Why the people from whom we so lately seperated shou'd continue to cherish enmity against the United States I cannot discern. Yet that this is the case is too manifest to need any illustration whatever. Nor is the sentiment limited to *him* or to his peculiar dependents, who might be expected to feel a double portion of *personal* as well as *political* mortification. On the contrary it seems to extend to almost every rank, order and party in the kingdom, or at least to a majority of them. Newspapers, altho' much of the stuff they contain is nugatory and fallacious, especially in England, where the corruption of the best things is sure to commute them into the very worst, yet they are still tolerable indicia of the opinion of political parties that support their editors. I have therefore inclosed the morning Herald the most distinguish'd opposition paper in the country, on account of a fabrication said to be from Virginia, which demonstrates the enmity that I suppose pervades all parties here, so far as a party newspaper can demonstrate it. For it seems that however english parties differ in other points, in this one of dislike to us and our national prosperity they all cordially unite. I have the honor to be with great consideration and attachment, Your Most Obliged & Obed. Servt.,

John Brown Cutting

P.S. Your letters for South Carolina were forwarded by Col. Trumbull, in the London Packet Capt. Cushing.

RC (DLC). Enclosure: An eight-page MS in Cutting's hand consisting of transcripts or extracts of the following: (1) "Extract of a letter from Poughkeepsie dated July 11th 1788," stating that when the convention met, Lansing proposed three classes of amendments to the Constitution, explanatory, conditional, and recommendatory; that the bill of rights was in the first class; that the conditional category included the following (i) that there should be no standing army in time of peace unless Congress by a two-thirds vote decreed otherwise, (ii) that there should be no direct taxes nor excises levied on American manufactures, (iii) that the militia should not be ordered out of the state except on the previous consent of the executive, and then for no longer than six weeks without the approval of the legislature, and (iv) that there should be no interference in elections, unless a state neglected or refused to provide for them; that Lansing, in reading the amendments, observed they had been changed not only in form but in substance as well; that the first of these, Melancthon Smith's, was debated several days and had the effect of doubling the house of representatives in the first instance and increasing it at the rate of one member for every 20,000 population until it reached a maximum of 300; that, after reading the amendments, Lansing proposed an adjournment and the appointment of a conference committee to reach a "quick and friendly decision," and the Convention thereupon appointed a committee of fourteen consisting of an equal number of supporters and opponents of the Constitution, and then adjourned; that when the committee met, Jay proposed that nothing could be effected until the word "conditional" was erased; that this caused an hour's debate, but, the anti-federalists refusing to give up the point, the committee dissolved without accomplishing anything; that in this committee Melancthon Smith and William Jones, both anti-federalists, proved to be moderates, but all others were "quite violent." (2) "Extract of another letter of the same date," stating that that morning Jay had brought forward the great question by a resolution to adopt the Constitution; that "he spoke forcibly and commanded great attention"; that "the Chancellor [Robert R. Livingston] also spoke with his usual energy and brilliancy" and "Our worthy Chief Justice [Richard Morris] was also on his legs," while Smith, Lansing, and Geo. Clinton spoke against the resolution and in support of a conditional adoption, which the federalists considered as a rejection under another name and protested against. (3) "Extract of a letter from one of the Delegates from the County and City of New York in the Convention at Poughkeepsie: dated July 23d 1788," stating that he had not written before because his mind was too much agitated and there was nothing pleasing to say; that things have changed, and that a motion had that morning been carried in committee "for striking out the conditional part of the proposed ratification, and merely inserting our confidence in the forbearance of Congress to exert certain powers until the propos'd amendments shou'd receive a consideration," which motion was carried 31 to 29; that the whole Southern district (except Tredwell), "four of the Dutchess County members and Mr. Williams from Washington voted in the affirmative, the Governor, Judge Yates, and Mr. Lansing" being in the minority; and that he now begins to believe all will go well, or at least that "we shall obtain the substance of what we are aiming at." (4) "Circular Letter from the Convention of . . . New York, to the Executives of the different States," stating that "We the members of the Convention of this state have deliberately and maturely considered the Constitution proposed for the United States"; that "Several articles in it appear so exceptionable to a majority of us, that nothing but the fullest confidence of obtaining a revision of them by a general convention, and an invincible reluctance to seperate from our sister states, cou'd have prevail'd upon a sufficient number to ratify it, without stipulating for previous amendments"; that they had noted amendments had been proposed and anxiously desired by several of the states, as well as by New York, and they thought it of "great importance, that effectual measures be immediately taken, for calling a Convention, to meet at a period not far remote; for we are convinced, that the apprehensions and discontents, which these articles occasion, cannot be removed or allayed, unless an act to provide for it be amongst the first that shall be passed by the new Congress"; that, since it is necessary that two-thirds of the states apply for such an act, they "earnestly exhort and request" the legislatures of the several states to take the earliest opportunity of making it, which they expect the legislature of New York to do; that it "cannot be necessary to observe, that no government, however constructed, can operate well unless it possesses the confidence and good will of the great body of the people; and as we desire nothing more than that the amendments proposed by this or other states be submitted to the consideration and decision of a general convention, we flatter ourselves, that motives of mutual affection and conciliation will conspire with the obvious dictates of sound policy to induce even such of the states, as may be content with every article of the Constitution to gratify the reasonable desires of that numerous class of American citizens, who are anxious to obtain amendments of some of them"; that amendments advanced by New York do not arise from local views but apply equally to all states of the union; that "Our attachment to our sister states, and the confidence we repose in them, cannot be more forcibly demonstrated" than by approval of a government which "many of us think very imperfect; and that they request the governor to lay this communication before the legislature, "being persuaded that your regard for our national harmony and good government will induce you to promote a measure which we are unanimous in thinking very conducive to these interesting objects," signed by George Clinton "*By the unanimous order of the Convention.*" (5) Extract from a letter dated "New York Aug. 9 1788," stating that, on the preceding Monday when the question was "under consideration for filling up the blank in the ordinance for organizing the new government, where the Congress shou'd meet, it was carried for 'Baltimore'—seven to six"; that on Tuesday a motion to reconsider was lost; that on Wednesday a motion to strike out "Baltimore" and substitute "New York" was carried by the votes of New Hampshire, Massachusetts, Rhode Island, Connecticut, New York, New Jersey, and South Carolina; that Pennsylvania, Delaware, Maryland, Virginia, and North Carolina voted in the negative and Georgia was divided. (6) Extract from a letter dated "Newport Rhode Island July 31st 1788," reading: "The unconditional ratification of the fœderal constitution by New York, hath blasted the last hopes of the anti-fœderal Junto in this state as they find themselves reduced to this mortifying alternative—'Adopt the Constitution, and you may yet retain your sovereignty; but if you reject it, your territory shall be partition'd among your neighbors.'—Upon receiving the interesting intelligence of the ratification of the new Constitution by New York, great demonstrations of Joy were manifested by our citizens. The bells echoed the joyful tidings, and the colours displayed the triumph over anarchy. No town on the Continent coud be more unanimous in their sentiments—none more unfeign'd in their gratulations, as none had experienced in so great a degree the scourge of fraud and licentiousness." (7) Copy of the proclamation issued by President Benjamin Franklin and the Executive Council of Pennsylvania, 9 July 1788, stating that, whereas several evil-disposed persons had conspired to oppose the execution of the laws in Luzerne county by seizing, carrying off, and holding as prisoner Timothy Pickering, an officer of the government, they offered a reward of $300 each for the apprehension of John Jenkins and John Hyde and $100 each for the arrest of their followers; to this Cutting added the following note: "NB. Col. Pickering is *retaken* and *safe*—several killed or wounded on each side." (8) "Extract of a letter from a Gentleman at Muskingkum (Ohio Country), June 11th, 1788," reading: "On our arrival here we found that the eight acre lots were laid out on the bottom adjoining the Ohio and Muskingum Rivers, which caused some of them to be twelve miles distant from this City; therefore to expedite the settlement, and that it may be as compact as possible at first, we caused 1000 lots of three acres each to be laid out upon the high lands adjoining the City, and finish'd drawing for them yesterday (a majority of the agents being present). This we found to be absolutely necessary that the people who have come, and are coming on, might have some employ until the meeting in July, at which time some farther conclusions will be had. The eight acre lots appear to be equal as to soil, all as good as land can be. I find this place to be most beautifully situated; better land cannot be wished. I believe it will soon not only be the glory of America, but the envy of the World. The rivers are gentle and easy to be ascended by boats suitable for the purpose. They abound in excellent fish. The climate is moderate and healthy. The City is laid out on the most beautifully elevated spot of earth I ever saw; in full view of the two pleasantest rivers in the world. Boats are continually passing up and down the water to and from Kentucky and New Orleans. The Indians are friendly and the treaty is to be in July. Rights have been sold here at four hundred dollars a right in cash since I came, but now are not to be had so low. I have heard ten dollars per acre offered for land here, and the money to be paid down. The ancient ruins cause much speculation; a particular description of these and many other things here I shall be able to give you at my return; which will be as soon as the treaty is over." (9) Copy of the resolution of Congress of 5 July 1788 ratifying the loan of 1,000,000 guilders made by Adams on 13 Mch. 1788 and directing that Jay send three copies to TJ by separate conveyances; and a copy of the resolution of the same date appropriating $20,000 in addition to the $14,000 already appropriated for the expenses of the Indian treaties, for extinguishing the claims of Indians to lands already ceded and for extending a purchase beyond the limits fixed by previous treaties.

The lyrical description of the Muskingum lands, offsetting in part the disturbing news of the Clintonian antifederalists of New York and their somewhat unctiously-phrased but thinly-veiled appeal to others of similar views elsewhere (especially the faction led by Henry in Virginia), must have appealed to TJ as well as to Joel BARLOW, though the latter's interest was more personal than patriotic or poetic, for he was in Europe as representative of the Ohio Company "which sold in the West many acres to unhappy Frenchmen" (DAB).

From C. W. F. Dumas

MONSIEUR Lahaie 16e. 7br. 1788.

La Lecture que Votre Excellence fera de la Dépeche ci-jointe pour le Congrès, ne me laisse rien à ajouter, sinon le desir de savoir, lorsque V. E. voudra bien m'en accuser la réception, son sentiment personnel du tout, dont je fais le plus grand cas, suite naturelle du vrai et sincere respect avec lequel je suis De Votre Excellence Le très-humble & très-obéissant servitr,

C W F DUMAS

RC (DLC). FC (Dumas Letter Book, Rijksarchief, The Hague; photostats in DLC). Enclosure: (1) Dumas to Jay of 4 Sep. 1788, stating that the forced loan has met with difficulties; that it is astonishing to see the bitterness toward a certain great power exhibited by the English faction, and the lack of concern shown toward these accumulated affronts is still more so; that certain observations of Cicero (*non spes, sed dolor est major*, &c.) apply to the good citizens of the country; that the gazettes are filled with continual bulletins of the armies of the belligerents, and he is thankful that there is more encouraging news from America; that a professor of law at Leiden had been dismissed because he could not bring himself to take a certain new oath; that the tomb of Capellen de Pol had been blown up; that the prince and princess were received at Amsterdam with respect by officials and small crowds, but many did not appear on the streets; that between one and two o'clock they went to the bourse, where only the bankers Hope and Muilman were present, "et une foule de Juifs et de gens du commun des deux sexes," while all the other merchants waited in the cafés for this court to leave, only reassembling at the bourse for business at two-thirty, perhaps the latest ever; that the princess wished to see the Comédie Française, but this proved to be difficult because the performance was not strictly speaking a public affair but arranged by private subscription of individuals, most of them of the Patriotic party and including even the cast; that the difficulty was avoided by the giving of a command performance, 800 tickets being printed and the banker Hope buying fifty at £3 and distributing them free, but only 250 were sold and not more than twenty women were present; that the anniversary of the restoration of the stadtholder will be celebrated at The Hague on the 18th when the prince and princess will attend "un grand Concert de 50 à 60 Musiciens, où l'on donnera entre autres un *Te Deum*," for which between three and four thousand tickets have been sold—a fact that will offset "un peu de la glace d'Amst[erdam]"; that the forced loan has not as yet succeeded, &c. (FC in Dumas Letter Book, Rijksarchief, The Hague; photostats in DLC). (2) Dumas to Jay, 16 Sep. 1788, enclosing four documents and informing him that, if any response is made to him, he will report it, other wise "leur silence me servira de réponse"; that meanwhile he can only guess what draws this upon him, knowing only that, especially since 1782, "je suis noté auprès de certaine Puissance, qui peut tout ici présentement; et qu'après avoir fait insulter l'Ambassadeur d'une Puissance rivale, et l'Envoyé d'une autre grande Puissance," it is not surprising that he should be harassed on the most frivolous pretexts; that "Il se peut aussi, qu'à l'occasion de l'Envoi prochain dit-on de Mr. V. B[erckel]l le fils, on veuille savoir au juste ma relation avec les Et. Unis, soit pour le qualifier conséquemment, ou, ce qui ne me surprendroit nullement, pour lui enjoindre, par complaisance pour la susdite Puissance, de se donner des mouvemens directs ou indirects en Amérique afin d'obtenir mon rappel ou éloignement"; that time will reveal these hidden objects; that the populace continues its orgies; that the forced loan has succeeded; that among those perpetually banished is Jacob van Staphorst, brother of Nicolas; that [*in postscript*] these messages may have only the object of further distressing him in respect to the forced sale of his house; that he must therefore renew his request for a letter of credence. Dumas added another postscript to this dispatch on 20 Sep., enclosing another note from him to Fagel which he wrote on the 19th, having had no reply to his of the 14th; this and the other four enclosures he had shown to "Deux Diplomatiques de mes amis" who had found his procedure "comme absolument en regle" and that of the others shocking (same). The enclosures have not been found, but they were clearly an exchange of correspondence between Fagel, secretary of the Estates General, and Dumas concerning the latter's status. These two letters to Jay are listed in *Dipl. Corr., 1783-89*, III, 628, as being among the Dumas dispatches between 1 Aug. 1788 and 20 Jan. 1789 that are missing. One of the five enclosures was Dumas' letter to Fagel acknowledging receipt of a document signed by Fagel (itself being another of the enclosures) asking in the name of the Estates General that Dumas state, in writing, by what warrant he serves as agent of the United States, and informing him that, the next morning, he would begin to examine his papers and to draw from them those that were pertinent to the inquiry, the originals of which he would always be ready to display to Fagel and to accompany them with a statement tending to satisfy the Estates General (Dumas to Fagel, 11 Sep. 1788, in the evening; FC in Dumas Letter Book, Rijksarchief, The Hague; photostats in DLC).

To La Rouerie

SIR Paris Sep. 16. 1788.

On receiving the first letters which you did me the honor to write to me on the arrears due to you from the United states, I informed you that I had nothing to do in the money department, that the subject of your letters belonged altogether to the Treasury board, and to Mr. Grand their banker here, to the former of whom I forwarded your letters. As I felt an anxiety however that the foreign officers should be paid, I took the liberty of pressing the Treasury board from time to time to exert themselves for that effect; and I availed myself of an opportunity, which occurred last spring, of setting on foot measures which, with their approbation, might furnish the means of effecting this paiment. So far my information to you went, and I added a supposition that the Treasury board would probably give orders on the subject in the course of the month of July. But I made you no promise: it would have been strange if I had. Nor does my office, nor any thing I have ever said or done, subject me to the demand of immediate paiment, which you are pleased to make on me, nor call on me for any declarations or answers positive or negative.

Finding that my interference, which was friendly only, and

avowed to be inofficial, has given occasion to your letter of yesterday in a stile which I did not expect, and to which I can have no motive for further exposing myself, I must take the liberty of desiring that the correspondence between us on this subject may cease.

I presume that the certificate given you points out the person, here or elsewhere, to whom your applications are to be made, and that he will inform you when he receives orders on your subject. I am Sir Your humble servant, TH: JEFFERSON

PrC (DLC). See note to La Rouerie to TJ, 15 Sep. 1788. The present letter affords a good standard by which to gauge TJ's use of the complimentary close: "I am Sir Your humble servant" was as cold as TJ meant it to be, and contrasts strongly with his usual felicitous closing.

From John Paradise

[*Paris, 16 Sep. 1788.* Recorded in SJL Index, but not found.]

To John Rutledge, Jr.

DEAR SIR Paris Sep. 16. 1788.

I received yesterday from your father two bills of exchange for your use, the one for 50. £. the other 100. £. sterling. They were drawn on Mannings & Vaughan of London, paiable at 60. days sight. As I shall be much absent from Paris for three months to come, and I knew that Boyd & Ker possessed your confidence and merited it, I carried the bills to them. They will negotiate them and receive the money, and you will be so good as to take arrangements with them for the time and manner of remitting it to you.

As Mr. Short sets out to-day to join you, he will give you all the news. We have nothing from America later than the accession of N. York to the new constitution. Perhaps the inclosed letter from your father may tell you whether N. Carolina has acceded.

The Garde des sceaux went out of office the day before yesterday. My compliments to Mr. Shippen and am with great esteem Dr. Sir Your friend & servt., TH: JEFFERSON

RC (NcD); addressed: "A Monsieur Monsieur Rutledge á Geneve, Poste restante." PrC (DLC).

From Thomas Russell-Greaves

SIR Nismes September 17th. 1788.

After a journey of three weeks taking Dijon and Avignon in my way I have arrived at Nismes and have been here a fortnight. I was delighted with the Country I travelled through; finding every spot of Ground cultivated in the highest perfection, even the highest and most craggy hills, which Nature seemed to have intended to be useless, by the Industry of the Husbandman are harrowed and covered with the Luxeries of the Earth. And I have alone one complaint to make; while the Country is abounding with all the necessaries of Life, it appears to me astonishing that the policy of France so wise in most other things; should suffer such herds of beggars to croud the roads and fill the Cities, many of them without a second shirt and some with none; indeed it is a sight we are not used to in America and to me a most melancholy spectacle. It appears to me that these droves of poor People might be employed in some kind of work; which would be more honorary and less burdensome to the Nation. I should suppose the labour of their hands would always earn their bread particularly in a Country where living for the Poor is so cheap. I recev'd your billet a few mornings before I left Paris where you desire me to write you sometime. I am very sensible of the honor, and shall always be happy in improving my pen so agreably. I thank you for the very kind and friendly attention paid me while at Paris, as well as for the Letters you procured for me here, which have caused my time to pass away in the most agreable manner. I am treated with the greatest hospitality, and find Nismes very pleasant. The air I believe will be favorable to my cough, at present it is much the same. The Marquis is so well known in this City his Letters insures hospitality. Indeed, I feel greatly indebted to him for them, and possess the highest Esteem and veneration for a Man who in every instance, has shewn the greatest attachment to my Country. I enclose several letters which I beg the favor of you to forward with yours to America. One for Colonel Swan not knowing his address I must request you to have the trouble to see that he has it and you will greatly oblige one who has the Honor to subscribe himself with much esteem and respect Your most obedt. hble Servt., THOMAS RUSSELL GREAVES

RC (DLC); addressed; endorsed by TJ: "Russell-Greaves Thos." Neither the enclosures nor TJ's BILLET has been found, and the latter is not recorded in SJL Index.

There seems to be some confusion

about the name of this son of the eccentric and wealthy Boston merchant, Thomas Russell. The son was christened Thomas Graves Russell, evidently deriving his middle name from an ancestor, Thomas Graves (1608-1653), who was created a rear admiral by Oliver Cromwell (genealogical records in The Boston Athenaeum, cited in a communication from Walter M. Whitehill, 27 Apr. 1955). TJ's use of the hyphen, though none occurs in the signature, suggests the proper form. Russell-Greaves died in Bristol, England, on 9 Feb. 1790, aged 23.

From Vanet

MONSIEUR [Le Havre] 18. 7bre 1788

J'ai resus Votre paquet de lettre que je ne manqueray pas de remettre à sa destination suivant vos Ordres. Le Vaisseau est encore retardé jus-au Vaingt Sinqs du present mois. Si votre Exelence en a ancore d'autres, J'aure ancore le temps de les recevoir avant mon départ, et tout autre chose qui pouroit vous estre agreable.

J'ai l'honneur d'etre Monsieur de Votre Exelence le tres respectueux Serviteur VANET

RC (DLC); endorsed.

From La Rouerie

SIR Paris 19 7ber 1788

Business of importance prevented me to answer sooner your letter of the 16th. and indeed it gives me pain to answer it at all, But I am forced to it By its contents part of which seem to me to be dropt reither inadvertently from your pen than from your heart or politicks, to which I am long ago accustomed to pay all the Justice and prise they do deserve.

You say, Sir, that you have nothing to do in the money's department and that it is to Mr. grand that we must make application for the arrears due to us By Congress; indeed you know that application has often time Been made to him as the Banker of Congress, But we could never Consider him under any other character.

Surely if we were to Consider our notes from the united States of north america as a security of funds placed By their representatives on Mr. grand with his Consent and our own, we would have no right to apply to Congress or to their envoy in france, even in case of a total Bankruptcy on the part of Mr. grand, But we would fall on him and take the Benefit of the law against him.

We would have a right to the same conduct, if the funds remaining in the hand of Congress, they had made with our Consent and that of Mr. grand, a contract with him to pay us the interest of thoses funds.

But neither of thoses Cases is our—Congress owe us money, the debt is a debt of honour and Justice; they pass a contract with us which is a security from them to us for the debt and the ponctual payment of the interest. The part in thoses contract, which concern Mr. grand, is nothing else But Bills of exchange drawn on him By Congress for Certain sums which are to be pay'd to us every first day of January, we present thoses Bills when they are due, Mr. Grand refuse to pay them; how shall we and the whole world call this, without doubt a plain protest of the Bills drawn By Congress: to whom must we direct our complaints of having been deceived; for a bill of exchange which is to be protested is a deceit, leat it be drawn By private men or governments, the diferences is only in the concequences, But the same words Belong to the same things and even the most academical education cannot save a man to Confess the truth of the assertion. Then we must direct our complaints not to a Board of treasury who *never answer* and never pay, is first unpolite and afterwards unjust, not directly to Congress who is much too far to receive them and do Justice the 2d. day of January when we are not payed the first, but to those who represent that honorable body in france, while there are any, and it will Be impossible, unless you have positive orders from Congress not to midle in the engagement they have contracted with us, to persuad our nation and any other, that it is not on you that we must call on the occasion; if you have such an order, Sir, it will Be necessary and candid to render it publick, then the correspondence may cease with you and take an other course; But if you have not such order, the correspondence must Continue untill we are payed.—There are two ways of corresponding, Sir, one which patience dictated By my respect for the representatives of north america, my love for that country, politeness towards you personnaly and regard for your station, had prescribed to me; when that one cease, there remain another of a more publick nature which indeed is as much against my inclination as against any in the world, But which must however Be made use of as the last resource.—You are master of the choice, But certainly, Sir, our right to reclamation, complaint and payment, is to well supported By the conduct of the officers of Congress and by the disagreable and tiresome situation it put us under, for us to be silent. Permit me Sir to assure you that while you shall be Considered in france as an envoy from the honorable the Congress, I shall apply to you, and I shall be allways happy to do it with that confidence and regard which your character inspire.

I will pass tomorrow at Mr. grand, and give you an account of the reception I shall meet with. I have the honour to be Sir your most obedient servant, ARMAND DE LA ROUERIE

RC (ViWC); endorsed.

To Pierre Louis Lacretelle

⟦*Paris, 20 Sep. 1788.* Recorded in SJL Index. Not found.⟧

To William Short

DEAR SIR Paris Sep. 20. 1788.

The evening of your departure came a letter by the way of London and N. York, addressed to you, and probably from Virginia. I think you wished your American letters to remain here; I shall therefore keep it. The passport now inclosed came the day after your departure; so also did a mass of American letters for me, as low down as August 10. I shall give you their substance.—The Convention of Virginia annexed to their ratification of the new Constitution a copy of the state Declaration of rights, not by way of Condition, but to announce their attachment to them. They added also propositions for special alterations of the constitution. Among these was one for rendering the President incapable of serving more than 8. years in any term of 16. New York has followed the example of Virginia, expressing the substance of her bill of rights (i.e. Virginia's) and proposing amendments; these last differ much from those of Virginia. But they concur as to the President, only proposing that he shall be incapable of being elected more than twice. But I own I should like better than either of these, what Luther Martin tells us was repeatedly voted and adhered to by the federal convention, and only altered about 12. days before their rising when some members had gone off, to wit, that he should be elected for 7. years and incapable for ever after. But New York has taken another step which gives uneasiness. She has written a circular letter to all the legislatures, asking their concurrence in an immediate Convention for making amendments. No news yet from N. Carolina. Electors are to be chosen the 1st. Wednesday in January, the President to be elected the 1st. Wednesday in February, the new legislature to meet the 3d. week in March. The place is not yet decided on. Philadelphia was first proposed and had 6½ votes. The half vote was Delaware, one of whose members wanted to take a vote on Wilmington. Then Baltimore was proposed and carried, and afterwards rescinded, so that the matter stood open as ever on the 10th. of August: but it was allowed the dispute lay only between N. York and Philadelphia, and rather thought in favor of the last. The R. island delegates had retired from Congress. Dr. Franklin was dangerously ill of the gout and stone on the 21st. of July. My letters of Aug. 10. not mentioning him, I hope he was recovered. Warville &c. were arrived. Congress had referred the decision as to the independance of Kentucké to the new government. Brown ascribes this to the jealousy of the Northern states, who want Vermont to be received at the same time in order to preserve a balance of interests in Congress. He was just setting out for Kentucké, disgusted, yet disposed to persuade to an acquiescence, tho' doubting they would immediately separate from the Union. The principal obstacle to this, he thought, would be the Indian war.—The following is a quotation from a letter from Virginia dated July 12. 'P———n, tho' much impaired in health, and in every respect in the decline of life, shewed as much zeal to carry the new constitution, as if he had been a young man: perhaps more than he discovered in the commencement of the late revolution in his opposition to Great Britain. W———e acted as chairman to the committee of the whole and of course took but little part in the debate: but was for the adoption relying on subsequent amendments. B———r said nothing, but was for it. The G———r exhibited a curious spectacle to view, having refused to sign the paper, every body supposed him against it. But he afterwards had written a letter; and having taken a part which might be called rather vehement, than active, he was constantly labouring to shew that his present conduct was consistent with that letter, and that letter with his refusal to sign. M—d—n took the principal share in the debate for it: in which, together with the aid I have already mentioned, he was somewhat assisted by I—nn—s, Lee, M———l, C———n and G. N———s. M—s—n, H———y and Gr———n were the principal supporters of the opposition. The discussion, as might be expected where the parties were so nearly on a balance, was conducted generally with great order, propriety and respect of either party to the other.'

The assembly of Virginia, hurried to their harvests, would not enter into a discussion of the District bill, but suspended it to the next session. E. Winston is appointed a judge, vice Gab. Jones resigned. R. Goode and Andrew Moore counsellors, vice, B. Starke dead, and Jos. Egglestone resigned.—It is said Wilson, of Philadelphia, is talked of to succeed Mr. A. in London. Qu?

The dispute about Virgil's tomb and the laurel seems to be at length settled by the testimony of two travellers, given separately and without a communication with each other. These both say, that attempting to pluck off a branch of the Laurel, it followed their hand, being in fact nothing more than a plant or bough recently cut and stuck in the ground for the occasion. The Cicerone acknowleged the roguery, and said they practiced it with almost every traveller, to get money. You will of course tug well at the laurel which shall be shewn you, to see if this be the true solution. The President Dupaty is dead. Monsr. de Barentin, premier president de la cour des aides, is appointed garde des sceaux. The stocks are rather lower than when you left this. Present me in the most friendly terms to Messrs. Shippen and Rutledge. I rely on your communicating to them the news, and therefore on their pardoning me for not repeating it in separate letters to them. You can satisfy them how necessary this economy of my time and labour is. This goes to Geneva, poste restante. I shall not write again till you tell me where to write to. Accept very sincere assurances of the affection with which I am Dear Sir your friend & servt,

TH: JEFFERSON

RC (ViW); endorsed in part: "Recd. at Geneva. Oct. 8." PrC (DLC). The enclosed passport has not been found.

The QUOTATION FROM A LETTER FROM VIRGINIA was taken from that of Monroe to TJ, 12 July 1788; most of the passage was put in code by Monroe; TJ altered the phraseology and punctuation slightly.

William Tatham to William Short

Ship America at Sea, 20 Sep. 1788. Sends this letter by a "Monsr. La'ritz," a French officer from Hispaniola who is on his way from Charleston to Dover and whom he wishes to introduce; sends also the "proceedings of Carolina in Convention on the Grand Fœdral Question. I am allso to return my sincere thanks to Mr. Jefferson and Yourself. I stand indebted for Freindship not heretofore fully acknowledged to him for his unremitted attention on every occasion since my first introduction, particularly his last Testimonial jointly with Mr. Munro and Mr. Hardy, from which I have allready receiv'd considerable advantages in the Southern States and shall now have an oppertunity of applying it to the purpose intended in England." Is also indebted to Short and Beverley Randolph in his "business before the Executive" when he last saw Short in Richmond. "The adjacency of the next Room furnishd my information unavoidably. The idea of my betraying the Secrets of a Government Cituated as Virginia was, had I been base enough for the Attempt, and the ridiculous supposition (which I heard out of Doors) of my furnishing the Enemy with an impression of the States Seal, which they cou'd have taken from any Comission that fell in their hands, was really absurd. The truth is the Haughty disposition of Governor Harrison, whose favors I cou'd not cringe for, wou'd have justified to every Man of feeling or sentiment, the resignation of so humiliating an Office as misfortune induced me to accept under his Administration. I allude to his personall Pride, I mean not to arraign his Official deportment. You can now be inform'd by a Gentleman with you (who spent that Winter in Philadelphia) how far my fidelity as a Citizen was to be doubted. It will not be unpleasing to you both, that the Fruits of Your endeavours are not wholely blasted and it is some consolation to myself, to triumph over private Animosities on a visit to my Native Land if not crowned with the Laurells of America at least with marks of Attention from North Carolina thro' four years practice at the Bar, a Seat in her House of Commons, and the Lieut. Collonelcy of my County. I confess I had much rather have receiv'd such Marks of prosperity from that State in whose Service I have cheifly spent the prime of my Youth and vigour of my constitution but it is still the same. It is the Cause of America and Mankind, to whose services my Time is (I wish I cou'd add 'usefull endeavours are') devoted. With the inclosed extract, I must beg You to recapitulate my obligations to Mr. Jefferson." Is forced to break off because the cliffs of his native land are in view. "I therefore omitt a considerable scrawl on politicks that I had sketch'd of it in the rough and a long Letter intended for his Excellencies Leisure Hours, to amuse him with my observations among the Spaniards and in the Western Country, plann'd as much as in my power for his information as far as I have had a view of the Rise, progress, changes, declension &c. of the State of Franklin, some Indian affairs, observations on the present State and Future prospects of the Western Country thro the Channells of democracy, Aristocracy, and Anarchy. Some of these I have by me, with a Survey of the upper Parts of Georgia. If any of them will be of Service to Mr. Jefferson, he will do me an honor by commanding my Services." Intends to return to his farm near Fayetteville, N.C., in the month of April; meanwhile he will be at Wennington Hall, near Lancaster, his "Family Seat on my Mothers Side"; would be happy to welcome Mr. Jefferson or Mr. Short there.

RC (MoSHi); 4 p.; addressed: "Honl. Mr. Short"; endorsed, in TJ's hand: "Tatham Wm."

To Angelica Schuyler Church

DEAR MADAM Paris. Sep. 21. 1788.

Mr. Short's departure for Italy gives me the pleasure of executing your commission for the duplicate volume of the Antiquités d'Herculaneum. The exchange is made and the right volume will be given to a Mr. Romilly of London who sets out for Paris[1] within two or three days, and will send it to your house on his arrival. Should any thing put this out of his head, I am unable to give you his address: but it can be had at Mr. Benjamin Vaughan's Jeffery's square. However his attention to the charge he has undertaken will I hope save you the trouble of searching his address.

Kitty writes to you to-day, and I have persuaded her to write in French. Madame de Corny and myself are absolutely determined you shall not have her without coming for her. We have interest enough at Panthemont for this, and there is no habeas corpus law in this country, consequently no judge for you to apply to. We have no other means of obtaining a visit from you, nor of convincing you by experience that travelling is good for your health and necessary for your amusement. I do not know whether Madame de Corny has been able to write to you since her overset in the carriage. This happened on Monday by the breaking of the axle of the forewheel. I saw her about an hour after it happened. As M. de Corny had fallen on her, it was presumed she was hurt, and she was put to bed, treated by the Surgeons very methodically, and is now well according to the rules of the art. I am in hopes that by this or the next post she will be permitted to tell you all this herself. The question was, when I saw her, whether all the Voitures Angloises should be proscribed and sold: Monsieur for it; Madame against it. Nous verrons. Our treaty, my dear madam, comes on slowly. As yet your preliminaries are not proposed. Be assured they shall be received with all the favorable dispositions possible. I am preparing an article for Kitty's continuing here, and going hence with you to America.—You see by the papers, and I suppose by your letters also, how much your native state has been agitated by the question on the new Constitution. But that need not agitate you. The tender breasts of ladies were not formed for political convulsion; and the French ladies miscalculate much their own happiness when they wander from the true field of their influence into that of politicks. Present my friendly compliments to Mr.

Church, and accept yourself assurances of the sincere attachment & respect of Dear Madam your most obedient friend & servant,

TH: JEFFERSON

RC (Peter B. Olney, Old Saybrook, Conn., 1951); addressed: "Mrs. Church Sackville street Piccadilly London"; postmarked: "P.PAYE PARIS" and (within circle) "SE 25."

[1] Thus in MS.

From James Madison

DEAR SIR New York Sepr. 21. 1788

Being informed of a circuitous opportunity to France I make use of it to forward the inclosures. By one of them you will find that Congress have been at length brought into the true policy which is demanded by the situation of the Western Country. An additional resolution on the *secret*[1] *journal* puts an *end to all negotiation with Spain*, referring the subject of a *treaty after this* assertion *of right to the Missisipi to the new government*. The communication in my last will have shewn you the *crisis of things* in that *quarter; a crisis* however not particularly *known to Congress* and will be a *key to* some of the *Kentucky toasts in the Virga. gazette*.

The Circular letter from the New York Convention has rekindled an ardor among the opponents of the federal Constitution for an *immediate*[2] revision of it by another General Convention. You will find in one of the papers inclosed the result of the consultations in Pensylvania on that subject. Mr. Henry and his friends in Virginia enter with great zeal into the scheme. Governour Randolph also espouses it; but with a wish to prevent if possible danger to the article which extends the power of the Government to internal as well as external taxation. It is observable that the views of the Pennsylva. meeting do not rhyme very well with those of the Southern advocates for a Convention; the objects most eagerly pursued by the latter being unnoticed in the Harrisburg proceedings. The effect of the Circular letter on other States is less known. I conclude that it will be the same every where among those who opposed the Constitution, or contended for a conditional ratification of it. Whether an early Convention will be the result of this united effort is more than can at this moment be foretold. The measure will certainly be industriously opposed in some parts of the Union, not only by those who wish for no alterations, but by others who would prefer the other mode provided in the Constitution, as most expedient at present for introducing those supplemental safeguards to liberty against which no objections can be raised; and who would moreover approve of a Convention for amending the frame of the Government itself, as soon as time shall have somewhat corrected the feverish state of the public mind and trial have pointed its attention to the true defects of the system.

You will find also by one of the papers enclosed that the arrangements have been compleated for bringing the new Government into action. The dispute concerning the place of its meeting was the principal cause of delay, the Eastern States with N. Jersey and S. Carolina being attached to N. York, and the others strenuous for a more central position. Philadelphia, Wilmington, Lancaster and Baltimore were successively tendered without effect by the latter, before they finally yielded to the superiority of members in favor of this City. I am afraid the decision will give a great handle to the Southern Antifederalists who have inculcated a jealousy of this end of the Continent. It is to be regretted also as entailing this pernicious question on the new Congress who will have enough to do in adjusting the other delicate matters submitted to them. Another consideration of great weight with me is that the temporary residence here will probably end in a permanent one at Trenton, or at the farthest on the Susquehannah. A removal in the first instance beyond the Delaware would have removed the alternative to the Susquehannah and the Potowmac. The best chance of the latter depends on a delay of the permanent establishment for a few years, untill the Western and South Western population comes more into view. This delay can not take place if so excentric a place as N. York is to be the intermediate seat of business.

To the other papers is added a little pamphlet on the Mohegan language. The observations deserve the more attention as they are made by a man of known learning and character, and may aid reserches into the primitive structure of language as well as those on foot for comparing the American tribes with those on the Eastern Frontier of the other Continent.

In consequence of your letter to Mr. Jay on the subject of "outfit" &c. I had a conference with him, and he agreed to suggest the matter to Congress. This was done and his letter referred back to be reported on. The idea between us was that the reference should be *to a committee but*[3] *his letter* coming *in at a moment* when *I happened to be out* it was as in *course referred to his department.*

His *answer suggested* that as *he might be thought eventually concerned* in *the question* it was most *proper for the consideration of a committee.* I had *discovered that he was not struck* with the *peculiarities of your case even when insinuated to him.* How far the *committee will be so* is more *than I can yet say.* In general I have no doubt that both *it and Congress are well disposed.* But it is probable that the idea of a *precedent*[4] *will beget much caution* and what *is worse there is little probability of* again having a *quorum of states for the business.*

I learn from Virginia that our Crops both of Corn and Tobacco, (except in the lower Country where a storm has been hurtful) are likely to be very good. The latter has suffered in some degree from superfluous rains, but the former has been proportionally benefitted. Accept my most fervent wishes for your happiness. Yrs affecty., Js. Madison Jr.

RC (DLC: Madison Papers) partly in code and decoded interlineally by TJ, two minor, obvious errors in coding were corrected by TJ; endorsed. Enclosures: (1) Tr (DLC: Madison Papers) of the first two of three resolutions of Congress, 16 Sep. 1788, on the navigation of the Mississippi. (2) The enclosed newspapers have not been identified. (3) Jonathan Edwards, *Observations on the language of the Muhhekaneew Indians, in which the extent of that language in North-America is shewn; its genius is grammatically traced; some of its peculiarities, and some instances of analogy between that and the Hebrew are pointed out. Communicated to the Connecticut Society of Arts and Sciences, and published at the request of the Society*, New Haven, Josiah Meigs, 1788 (Sabin No. 21971). This pamphlet must have been of great interest to TJ, who was, himself, a pioneer in linguistic research. An excellent treatment of this subject is found in Clark Wissler, "The American Indian and the American Philosophical Society," Am. Phil. Society, *Proceedings*, LXXXVI (1942), 189-204. Wissler says the following about Edwards' pamphlet: "He was on the threshold of a great discovery but did not know it."

Madison was free to send TJ a transcript of the first two resolutions concerning THE WESTERN COUNTRY because they were intended for publication to remove apprehensions produced by a report that "Congress are disposed to treat with Spain for the surrender of their claim to the navigation of the river Mississippi"; the first stated "that the said report not being founded in fact, the Delegates be at liberty to communicate all such circumstances as may be necessary to contradict the same and to remove misconceptions"; the second "Resolved that the free navigation of the river Mississippi is a clear and essential right of the United States, and that the same ought to be considered and supported as such." Since the ADDITIONAL RESOLUTION was under restrictions of secrecy, Madison summarized its contents in code; as adopted it read: "*Resolved* That no further progress be made in the negotiations with Spain by the Secretary for foreign affairs, but that the subject to which they relate be referred to the federal government which is to assemble in March next" (JCC, XXXIV, 534-5). THE KENTUCKY TOASTS (printed in Burnett, VIII, No. 934, Note 4, from the *Virginia Independent Chronicle* of 3 Sep. 1788), were made at a banquet on 4 July. The 4th toast was to the "Navigation of the Mississippi, at any price but that of liberty"; the 5th to "Harmony with Spain and a reciprocity of good offices"; the 11th, "May the Atlantic be just, the Western States be free, and both be happy"; and the 14th to the "Commonwealth of Kentucke, the Fourteenth luminary in the American constellation, may she reflect upon the original States the wisdom she has borrowed from them."

[1] This and subsequent words in italics are written in code and were decoded interlineally by TJ; his decoding has been verified by the Editors, employing Code No. 9.

[2] This word interlined and underscored; Madison deleted "early."

[3] This word not decoded by TJ.

[4] Madison wrote the code symbol for "president," but TJ corrected this to "precedent."

From Colborn Barrell

London, *22 Sep. 1788.* Enclosure has lain on his hands many months because Joseph Barrell, Jr., to whom it was addressed, was unexpectedly detained at Lisbon; his brother, Joseph Barrell of Boston, has lately told him to "break his Sons Enclosure and forward two small tokens of his respect to the Marquiss de la Fayette and your self."

RC (MHi); 2 p.; endorsed. Recorded in SJL as received 2 Feb. 1789. Enclosures: (1) Barrell to TJ, 24 Nov. 1787, with its accompanying medal. (2) A similar letter to Lafayette, also with medal (not found).

From Richard O'Bryen

⟦*22 Sep. 1788.* Recorded in SJL Index. Not found.⟧

From Thomas Lee Shippen

MY VERY DEAR SIR — Geneva 22d. Septr. 1788.

A combination of unexpected circumstances but principally the delay of Mr. Short, has detained us here until this day. Altho' my dissappointment in not setting off for Italy on the 15th. has given me some uneasiness as it will occasion my stay in that Country to be so much the shorter yet there are many counterbalancing circumstances which reconcile me to the event. Among them I place the occasion I desire from it of writing to you. I should have endeavored to find one much sooner, had I not hoped to have had the honor to receive a letter from you, which I might have answered at the same time that I communicated my present designs. But as your last letter to Mr. Rutledge, puts an end to my hopes on this subject, I take the liberty of addressing to you now these few lines.

Mr. Short has probably communicated to you already my abandonment of the plan which I had the honor of submitting to you when I left Paris, as that which was to regulate my future travels: and he must have told you at the same time that a letter I received from my father at Berne, had been the occasion of it. As soon as I received it, I began to consider how I could employ to the greatest advantage the short time which my father seemed to wish me to confine myself to in my Continental plans; and the extreme hospitality of the good people of this place, the advantage of a good Spanish master, and the hope of crossing the Alps in company with Mr. Short, have decided me to pass 4 or 5 weeks at Geneva. From this place I shall proceed probably as far as Milan and then make the best of my way to London. In what manner I am to gain that place, I am at present altogether uninformed, that is to say, I have not yet been able to learn in what way I can do it with the greatest expedition. Your universal knowledge of European routes must make you perfectly competent to the task of advising me, may I beg you Sir to have the goodness to favor me with your advice? My address will be poste restante at Turin until I have the honor of writing to you again. And may I beg you too Sir to let me know how any letters sent to you during your absence from Paris will be able to find you. There is one more favor which I am almost ashamed to ask, because I fear it will be very difficult if not impossible for you to grant it. Among twenty most agreable families where I have been domesticated since my residence here, that of Mr. Syndic Cayla has been one to which I have owed the greatest obligations. The Syndic is good enough to interest himself in our affairs, and the character I gave him of your excellent book which treats of them made him desirous to become its possessor. I could not do less than promise him to endeavor to procure it for him, and I know of no possible way to do it, unless you would have the kindness to send it to his address at Geneva. Unless you should happen to meet with somebody coming to this place who would take charge of it, or unless Mr. Tronchin (Minister from Geneva to the Court of France) would undertake the commission, I do not know how it could be done, all I know, is that you would add very much to the many favors you have already bestowed, by granting this. If you should be able to do it, I must beg you to send it in French as the Syndic does not read English.

I have omitted until now, and I am very much ashamed of it, acknowledging how much I owe to your excellent friend the Baron de Geismar, and to you Sir for having procured for me his acquaintance. It would have been impossible for a man to receive a long absent and much beloved brother with more cordiality or friendship than I experienced from that gentleman. He introduced me to the Court of Hesse Cassel as his friend; shewed me every thing that was to be seen in or near Hainault, and behaved in every respect with the greatest possible attention and amiability.

It was not among the least of his recommendations to me, that he loved and respected you as he often assured me he did without bounds. There was not in short, a thing which he did, or a word which he said which did not prove him worthy of that friendship which you have honored him with and a valuable acquaintance. His sentiments do alike honor to his head and his heart, and his conduct seems to have always been in unison with them. How he has been able in a military life and under a despotic government to preserve his principles so pure, so free and so liberal, is alike surprizing and honorable to his character. But you know much better than I do his merits. Excuse me for having given this little vent to my gratitude and admiration à son egard.

My father desires me in his last letter to assure you of his gratitude for your kindness to me, and his inviolable attachment which has been of long duration. He speaks to me of the immense preparations they were making for the celebration of the 4th of July in Philada. and tells me that the expence of them was computed at £1500, a circumstance which gives me a mixed sensation of pleasure and pain, pain to think of the extravagance of the times which could call for such an expenditure, pleasure to know that my fellow citizens were ab[le] to afford it. However the former preponderat[es.] The [more] I see of the extravagance and its effects in oth[er] Count[ries, the] warmer advocate I become of œcono[my] in [my o]wn. I have the honor to be with every sentiment of respect considera[tion] and regard, my very dear Sir your most obliged and devoted servant, Th: Lee Shippen

RC (DLC); MS mutilated by the breaking of the seal, affecting a few words at end of text; addressed; endorsed; postmarked: "GENEVE."

From John Brown Cutting

Sir London Sepr 23d 1788

I am but this moment returned from an excursion into the Country which has occupied me almost ever since I wrote You on tuesday last. I hope You did not think the parcel too large which I then forwarded. The New York packet brought nothing so interesting or so recent.

I now inclose You *two* Philadelphia *Newspapers* which I have just received from a gentleman who was a respectable member of the general Convention which framed the constitution lately ratified by eleven of the states. He says they will inform me "of an unfortunate dispute between the supreme judicial court and Mr. Oswald the Printer. The Court have ventured to put in practice the doctrine of attachment. The *manner* in which the chief Justice does business heightens the offensiveness of the measure. Petitions are signing, one to Council to pardon Oswald, another to the legislature to remove the Judges (which by the bye they can not do.) In fine there is a ferment excited here, nor do I forsee when it will subside or how it may terminate."

Mr. Parker will read you a single sentence concerning the right disposition entertain'd by our neighbours on the Missisippi, or rather by the government of their nation. You may rely upon the authenticity of the paragraph.

By the next post I wish I may have occasion to be more prolix. Meanwhile I am with much consideration and attachment Your Most Obedt Sert, JOHN BROWN CUTTING

RC (DLC); endorsed. The enclosed newspapers have not been identified.

From John Jay

DR. SIR Office for foreign Affairs 23d. September 1788

My last to you was dated the 9th. June, since which I have been honored with yours of the 4th. 23d. and 30th. May last, which with the Papers that accompanied them were communicated to Congress.

Two Copies of the Ratification of Mr. Adams last Contract have been transmitted to you, under Cover to Messrs. Willinks and Van Staphorsts, by Vessels bound to Amsterdam. A Triplicate will be enclosed with this, together with the following Papers, Vizt. The Requisition of Congress for the present Year, passed the 20th. of last Month; a Copy of an Act of the 13th. Instant, enabling you to provide for the Subsistence of the american Captives at Algiers, and approving of your supplementary Instruction to Mr. Lamb on that Head; a Copy of an Act of the same Date for putting the Constitution into Operation, and also the printed Journals necessary to compleat your Set, and a Parcel of the latest Newspapers.

These Dispatches will go from Boston in a Vessel bound from thence to France. How far this Conveyance may be a safe one I am not well informed. I nevertheless think it best to postpone Details for the present, as well as the private Letter which you have Reason to expect from me on the Subject you also hinted to Mr. Madison with whom I have conferred respecting it. There is a

Reluctance in some to adopt the Idea it suggests, and I apprehend that others will prefer Delay to a Decision upon it. With very sincere Esteem and Regard I have the Honor to be &ca:

JOHN JAY

FC (DNA: PCC, No. 121). Dft (NK-Iselin). Enclosures: (1) Tripl of resolution of Congress of 2 July 1788 ratifying the contract for the loan of one million guilders negotiated by John Adams on 13 Mch. 1788. The TWO COPIES transmitted by vessels bound for Amsterdam were probably enclosed in the (missing) letter from Henry Remsen to TJ of 25 July 1788 (see note to TJ to Jay, 5 Sep. 1788). A copy of a translation of the contract, with a clause of the ratification, in the hand of Henry Remsen, dated 4 July 1788, signed by Cyrus Griffin and Charles Thomson, with seal attached, is in DNA: PCC, Miscellany. (2) Resolutions on the requisition for 1788 (JCC, XXXIV, 433-42; 634, No. 611). (3) Resolutions of Congress of 13 Sep. 1788: "That out of the fund appropriated for the redemption of the American captives at Algiers or any other monies belonging to the United States in Europe, the Minister plenipotentiary of the United States at the Court of Versailles be and he is hereby authorised to make such provision for the maintenance and Comfortable subsistence of the American Captives at Algiers and to give such orders touching the same as shall to him appear right and proper. That Congress approve the instructions heretofore given to Mr. Lamb by Mr. Jefferson their Minister at the Court of France for supplying the said Captives"; "That the first Wednesday in Jany. next be the day for appointing Electors in the several states, which before the said day shall have ratified the said constitution; that the first Wednesday in feby. next be the day for the electors to assemble in their respective states and vote for a president; and that the first Wednesday in March next be the time and the present seat of Congress the place for commencing proceedings under the said constitution" (same, p. 523, 524-5, 635, No. 613).

On the SUPPLEMENTARY INSTRUCTION TO MR. LAMB see Vol. 8: 616-7.

From John Rutledge, Jr.

Geneva, 23 Sep. 1788. Acknowledges TJ's letters of 9 and 16 Sep. and expresses his deep gratitude for "the many instances of friendship" shown him; will leave Geneva in a few days; waits only for William Short's arrival, which is expected in a few days according to a letter received from him this morning.

RC (DLC); 2 p.; endorsed.

From Vitré

Rue du Temple No. 113.
Vis à vis la rue portefoin
Tuesday Eveng. 23d. 7ber. 88.

SIR

Last Sunday when I did myself the honor of writing you the scrawl I left at your Suisse's; I inquired whether I might hope to see you the next morning betwixt 8 and 9, and notwithstanding I was told it was very uncertain, being in a country house aux

Termes, I should have still waited on you, had it not been for the very bad weather.

As my departure will hardly take place earlier than to morrow, or Thursday week, I shall have more time than I at first imagined to take your commands, and all I at present have to hope is, that I shall have the good luck of meeting you at home.

Besides the letters of recommendation you may be so kind as to favor me with for the inland towns, I'll be infinitely obliged to you to procure me the means of being known to whatever American houses you may have at Rouen, Havre, St. Malo, Brest, Nantes, l'Orient, Bordeau[x,] Marseilles &c. as I have proposals to make for some objects of the manufactories of this kingdom which I believe would turn out reciprocally advantageous. I have the honor of remaining with the most respectfull sentiments Sir Your Excellency's Most obedient & most humble Servante,

DE VITRÉ

RC (DLC); endorsed. Vitré's SCRAWL . . . LEFT AT YOUR SUISSE's has not been found and is not recorded in SJL Index.

To John Brown Cutting

Sep. 24. 1788.

Th: Jefferson begs the favor of Mr. Cutting to contrive the inclosed packet to the Treasury board. It contains the keys of some trunks of papers which are gone by another conveiance. Many compliments and assurances of esteem. [*In postscript*:] Mr. C's favor of the 16th. is received.

PrC (DLC). Enclosure: TJ to the Commissioners of the Treasury, 24 Sep. 1788.

To John Jay

SIR Paris Sep. 24. 1788.

Understanding that the vessel is not yet sailed from Havre which is to carry my letters of the 3d. and 5th. instant, I am in hopes you will receive the present with them.

The Russian accounts of their victories on the Black sea must have been greatly exaggerated. According to these the Captain Pacha's fleet was annihilated. Yet themselves have lately brought him on the stage again with 15. ships of the line, in order to obtain another victory over him. I believe the truth to be that he has suffered some checks, of what magnitude it is impossible to say where one side alone is heard, and that he is still master of that sea. He has relieved Oczakow, which still holds out; Choczim also is still untaken, and the Emperor's situation is apprehended to be bad. He spun his army into a long cord to cover several hundred miles of frontier, which put it in the power of the Turks to attack with their whole force wherever they pleased. Laudon, now called to head the Imperial army is endeavoring to collect it. But in the mean time the campaign is drawing to a close, and has been worse than fruitless. The resistance of Russia to Sweden has been successful in every point, by sea and land. This, with the interference of Denmark, and the discontent of the Swedish nation, at the breach of their constitution by the king's undertaking an offensive war without the consent of the Senate, has obliged him to withdraw his attacks by land, and to express a willingness for peace. One third of his officers have refused to serve. England and Prussia have offered their mediation between Sweden and Russia, in such equivocal terms, as to leave themselves at liberty to say it was an offer, or was not, just as it shall suit them. Denmark is asking the counter-offer of mediation from this court. If England and Prussia make a peace effectually in the North (which it is absolutely in their power to do) it will be a proof they do not intend to enter into the war. If they do not impose a peace, I should suspect they mean to engage themselves, as one can hardly suppose they would let the war go on in it's present form, wherein Sweden must be crushed between Russia and Denmark.

The Garde des sceaux, M. de Lamoignon, was dismissed the 14th. inst. and M. de Barentin is appointed in his room. The deputies of Brittany are released from the Bastile, and M. d'Epermesnil and M. Sabatier recalled from their confinement. The parliament is not yet reinstated, but it is confidently said it will be this week. The stocks continue low, and the treasury had a hard struggle to keep the government in motion. It is believed the meeting of the states general will be as early as January, perhaps December. I have received a duplicate of the ratification of the loan of 1788. by Congress, and a duplicate of a letter of July 22. from the Treasury board on another subject, but none on that of the captives or Foreign officers. I suppose some cause of delay must have intervened between the ratification of Congress and the consequent orders of the treasury board. I have the honour to be with sentiments of the most perfect esteem and respect, Sir, Your most obedient & most humble servant,

TH: JEFFERSON

RC (DNA: PCC, No. 87, II). PrC (DLC).

To William Short

DEAR SIR Paris Sep. 24. 1788.

I entirely forgot when you were here that I could get you a good letter for Geneva from M. Tronchin. I now inclose you one. The Garde des sceaux M. de Lamoignon, is replaced by Monsr. Barentin. The stocks continue low. The Britany deputies are released; so are M. d'Epremesnil and the Abbé Sabatier. It is expected the parliament will be recalled to it's functions, unconditionally, this week. This is all the domestic news since my last. Compliments to your companions. I am with sentiments of sincere esteem & attachment Dear Sir your affectionate friend & servt.,

TH: JEFFERSON

RC (ViW); endorsed: "recd. Geneva. Oct. 8." PrC (DLC). Enclosure not found.

From William Short

DEAR SIR Au Chateau de L'Aye Sep. 24. 1788

I came here yesterday evening from Villefranche where I parted with my travelling companions. It is now early in the morning and M. de L'Aye being engaged in writing by the post of to day, I have only as yet seen the inside of the Chateau. With it as well as my reception both by the master and mistress I am perfectly content. I hope I shall continue to be as well pleased with what is to follow and that I shall be able to pick up here information that may be useful to me one day or other in my own country.—You will perhaps wish to know something of our journey thus far relative to Mr. and Mrs. Paradise. Every thing went exceedingly well as far as Villefranche for which Paradise considered himself indebted to the fear his wife had of shewing herself openly before a person in correspondence with you, and perhaps there was something in it; but on the whole her conduct was much more moderate than I had any reason to expect. Indeed our journey went on so smoothly that it was scarcely possible to be in an ill humour.

There was a manifest disposition in Madame to quarrel with the postilions as well as the tavernkeepers but as she had given up those departments to me before leaving Paris I insisted on her not interfering and succeeded pretty well, owing probably and as Paradise thought, certainly, to the desire she has to preserve your good opinion.—We with difficulty passed the Pont neuf on account of the mob assembled there, and who stopped several carriages and endeavoured to exact of us money to purchase *fusees*. We got only as far as Villeneuf that night, because Mrs. Paradise insisted on staying there. We breakfasted the next morning at Fontainebleau, visited the Chateau and Park and slept that night at Fossard. The next night at Auxerre, the next at Vitteaux, and the day after we dined and slept at Dijon. I called for Irish potatoes, which they gave us. They were excellent, but I have seen much better beyond the blue ridge. We were at the same hotel with you. Paradise and myself walked over the principal streets and ramparts. It is certainly much the cleanest town I have ever seen in France. The next morning we went to Beaune. I wished to spend that day there. The first thing I did was to go to Parent's. Unfortunately he was gone some distance from home. A heavy rain was falling, but still his wife insisted on sending for him. On our return to the tavern we found Mrs. Paradise in a fever to be gone. We dined and finding that Parent did not arrive and that her fever increased we ordered the posthorses, after being assured by two Benedictins, who were at the tavern and who had come there to superintend the making their wine, that even if Parent should arrive he would not be able to shew us what we wished to see, as the vintage was finished, and there were no considerable cellars in Beaune. These Benedictins themselves were setting off for Chalons because the business of wine making was finished. After the posthorses were put to and we in the carriage Parent arrived. He assured us the contrary and said he should have been able to have shewn us several cellars where the wine was still making. It was now too late and we were obliged to go on. I saw with a great deal of pleasure Volnais, Meursaut and Montraché. I paid with sincerity my tribute of gratitude to the two last for the many glasses of fine wine they have given me, by gazing at them as we passed and by never quitting them with my eyes as long as we remained within sight of them.—They made us pay at the tavern at Beaune three livres for a bottle of Volnais. I did not however think it equal to a wine we had at Auxerre for the same price and which I think was made in the neighbourhood. It was of the year 84, and that at Beaune much newer. I learned with pleasure from Parent that this year would be still better for wine than that of 84. He begged me to assure you of his zeal for your service and the fidelity with which he would continue to furnish you. I ate of the grape of which the Volnais is made. I was struck with its resemblance to some of our wild grapes in Virginia and particularly some that grow in Surry on my fathers estate. The shape of the bunch, the size and color, and still more the taste of the grape, so absolutely the same, that I think it would be impossible to distinguish one from the other. The vine at my fathers grew on an oak tree which stood in an old field quite separate from any other, so that the sun acted on it with its full force. I could wish much to see a fair experiment made on the grapes of that tree. I recollect my father made one year by way of experiment some wine, of what grapes however I know not. The wine was very sweet and very agreeable to my taste, but not at all resembling the Volnais.—We slept that night at Chalons, and the next at Villefranche. We stopped in the evening at the pavillon of M. de l'Aye, where we learned he was at Lyons. Our intention was to go and stop at Villefranche, from whence I was to write to him my arrival there. Luckily we met him as we entered Villefranche on his return from Lyons. He invited the company to his house which was declined. We took leave to meet the next morning. He was obliged to come and dine at Villefranche the next day with the Chancellor of the Duke of Orleans who arrived there. He came to the tavern where we were and it was agreed he should call on me after dinner to bring me to his house in his carriage. Mr. and Mrs. Paradise sat off about 11 o'clock. Before their departure we settled all accounts. Their expences were twenty eight guineas, mine five. They had therefore remaining on hand twenty two only so that it was determined by both of them to receive the whole of the amount of the letter of credit which was accordingly indorsed to them. The postillions who sat out with them from Villefranche returned there before I left it, and told me they had gone on well and safely the first post. I should not have entered into all these details about myself and my companions with any other than yourself Sir because few would have the goodness to excuse it; but as I know you will I do not make an apology.

I have not time to tell you how certainly and with how much pleasure I experience that I can quit Paris without regret, notwithstanding what you think to the contrary. I am told that my letter must be finished in the instant as it is the last moment of the post. When I say I do not regret Paris I hope you will remember that I mean Paris without any person from America in it.—Be so good Sir as present my most respectful compliments to the amiable and agreeable part of your family at Panthemont and yet I can hardly flatter myself that they will be recieved by the two little prudes. Adieu my dear Sir. Should you think of it let Pio know I will write him as I promised, that I intended it to day, but am prevented by the departure of the post. Believe me with the greatest sincerity Yr. friend & servant, W. SHORT

RC (DLC); addressed and endorsed.

To the Commissioners of the Treasury

GENTLEMEN Paris Sep. 24. 1788.

I wrote you on the 6th. inst. by a Mr. Vanet to whose care were committed the Consular papers. The vessel was bound to Alexandria, and himself to Richmond; but he promised to go express with the papers to New York and to deliver them to you himself. I thought it better to send the keys by a different conveiance. You will therefore receive them inclosed in this letter which goes by the way of London. I received a few days ago your duplicate of July 22. on the subject of the Consular papers, and a duplicate from the Office for foreign affairs, of the ratification of the loan of 1788. by Congress. But as yet I hear nothing on the subject of the captives and foreign officers. I have the honour to be with the highest esteem Gentlemen your most obedt. & most humble servt.,

TH: JEFFERSON

PrC (DLC). Enclosed in TJ to Cutting, this date.

From Joseph Willard

SIR Cambridge September 24. 1788.

I embrace the favorable opportunity which offers by Mr. Duquesne, a Lieutenant of a Man of War in his most Christian Majesty's Squadron, which is just upon sailing from Boston, to send your Excellency a Diploma for a Doctorate of Laws, which was conferred by Harvard University, in this place, more than a year ago, and which various circumstances have prevented my conveying before. Mr. Duquesne says he will do himself the honor of presenting it with his own hand.

The Governors of the University were happy, Sir, in the opportunity of distinguishing a Gentleman of whom they have the highest esteem on account of his literary and political character and personal worth, and they hope the honor intended by the Degree will not be unacceptable.

As your Excellency, at present, resides in a quarter of the world where the Sciences flourish, I should esteem it a favor, if you would inform me, what works of most merit have appeared, within these two or three years, in Europe, and particularly in France. The most distinguished publications, in that kingdom, that I have met with, within that period, are M. Bailly's History of Astronomy, and Pingrè's History and Theory of comets. M. De La Lande's Astronomy I have long had, in my own Library, in three volumes; which I highly esteem. Several years ago he published a fourth volume, and promised a fifth: I could wish to know whether the fifth is yet published.

Should your Excellency have time to write and honor me with any curious communications, I should esteem it a peculiar favor. I have the honor of being, with sentiments of the highest esteem & respect, Sir, your Excellency's most humble and obedient servant,

Joseph Willard

RC (MH); endorsed; at foot of text in TJ's hand: "Dr. Joseph Willard President of the University at Cambridge Massachus." Recorded in SJL as received 13 Feb. 1789. Enclosure: Diploma of Harvard University, dated 18 July 1787, awarding an honorary degree of Doctor of Laws to "THOMAS JEFFERSON armiger, scientiis multis variisque ornatus, in Republicae suae natalis historia naturali atque antiquitatibus versatissimus et praecellens, juris legumque peritissimus, patriae suae hominumque, libertatum civilium ac sacrarum Amicus et Defensor; qui politiae cognitione et rerum gerendarum probitate sese tam praeclarum ac aestimatum reddidit, ut a civibus suis ad summos honores domi evectus fuerit, et a Congressu postea Legatus ad aulam Galliae missus" (diploma not found; the above text is taken from a typescript in the Harvard University Archives made "from the original in the Jefferson Papers at the Massachusetts Historical Society").

To Maria Cosway

Paris Sep. 26. 1788.

Your favor of Aug. the 19., my very dear friend, is put into my hands this 26th. day of September 1788. and I answer it in the same instant to shew you there is nothing nearer my heart than to meet all the testimonies of your esteem. It is a strong one that you will occupy yourself for me on such a trifle as a visiting card. But sketch it only with your pencil, my friend, and do not make of it a serious business. This would render me uneasy, because

I did not mean such a trespass on your time. A few strokes of your pencil on a card will be enjoiment enough for me.

I am going to America, and you to Italy. The one or the other of us goes the wrong way, for the way will ever be wrong which leads us farther apart. Mine is a journey of duty and of affection. I must deposit my daughters in the bosom of their friends and country. This done, I shall return to my station. My absence may be as short as five months, and certainly not longer than nine. How long my subsequent stay here may be I cannot tell. It would certainly be the longer had I a single friend here like yourself.—In going to Italy, be sure to cross the Alps at the Col de Tende. It is the best pass, because you need never get out of your carriage. It is practicable in seasons when all the other passes are shut up by snow. The roads leading to and from it are as fine as can possibly be, and you will see the castle of Saorgio. Take a good day for that part of your journey, and when you shall have sketched it in your portefeuille, and copied it more at leisure for yourself, tear out the leaf and send it to me. But why go to Italy? You have seen it, all the world has seen it, and ransacked it thousands of times. Rather join our good friend Mrs. Church in her trip to America. There you will find original scenes, scenes worthy of your pencil, such as the Natural bridge or the Falls of Niagara. Or participate with Trumbull the historical events of that country. These will have the double merit of being new, and of coming from you. I should find excuses for being sometimes of your parties. Think of this, my dear friend, mature the project with Mrs. Church, and let us all embark together at Havre. Adieu ma tres chere et excellente amie. Your's affectionately, TH: J.

PrC (ViU).

From C. W. F. Dumas

The Hague, 26 Sep. 1788. The enclosed letter for Congress, together with that sent in his letter of 16 Sep., will inform TJ of his situation; hopes his conduct will meet with the approbation of Congress and of TJ.

RC (DLC); 2 p.; in French; endorsed. FC (Dumas Letter Book, Rijksarchief, The Hague; photostats in DLC). Enclosure (FC, same): enclosing "deux Pieces" which will show the outcome of the affair set forth in his last dispatch with its enclosures, and stating that he had substituted "à la porte de l'hotel des Etats-Unis le terme de leur *Correspondant* à celui d'*Agent*"; that in spite of all obstacles, he will continue to fulfill, to the best of his ability, his duties to the United States; and that he is not the only representative of a foreign power who has been humiliated. This letter and its enclosures are listed in *Dipl. Corr.*, *1783-89*, III, 628 as being among Dumas' dispatches between 20 Aug. 1788 and 1 Jan. 1789 that are missing, but the enclosure is there described as being "an extract from the Register of the Resolutions of their High Mightinesses of September 23, declaring him to be a private individual."

The resolution affecting Dumas' status no doubt explains the following remark in Washington's letter to Gouverneur Morris in providing him with letters of introduction for his projected trip to Europe: "I could have addressed a line to Mr. Dumas the former agent of the United States at the Hague, but he is too much under a cloud to be of any utility to you" (Washington to Morris, 26 Nov. 1788, *Writings*, ed. Fitzpatrick, XXX, 142).

From William Robertson

London, 26 Sep. 1788. Is a stranger to TJ, but not to his "good and humane character." Has met with misfortune "thro' very heavy losses by the late failures in this country"; his affairs are in the hands of assignees for his creditors; has asked his friends to lend him money or to fit out a ship "with a Cargo for the East in which business I have some experience under American Colours, the former of which they seem inclined to do provided I can procure American papers for a ship of Six hundred Tuns burthen"; he would sail from London, Ostend, or Dunkerque, and return "with a suitable Cargo for the american markett"; would thereafter reside in America, sending his family there before his departure on the voyage. Asks TJ to grant the papers necessary for this plan.

RC (DLC); 4 p.; addressed and endorsed.

From Chastel

[*27 Sep. 1788.* There is the following entry in SJL Index: "Chastel. 88. S. 27."; this is the only letter recorded under this name, and there is no record of a reply. Since TJ customarily entered surnames in full in SJL Index, and since letters to and from Chastellux are explicitly recorded under other entries on the same page, it is very unlikely that this refers to a letter from Chastellux. A further evidence in support of this conclusion is that Chastellux was evidently in ill health at this time; his death was reported in the *Journal de Paris*, 28 Oct. 1788.]

From Vanet

Le Havre, 27 Sep. 1788. Has received the letters TJ sent him on 20 and 24 Sep. The ship on which he intended to embark is still here, but in a condition that destroys the confidence of the passengers and the merchants: she is "absolument pourri"; the captain, fearing condemnation, refuses to make repairs, but proposes to effect them in England. Vanet has decided not to take passage, on the advice of the merchants at Le Havre, especially Limozin who has promised him that another ship will arrive in the next fortnight or three weeks; will take care of any further commissions TJ may have for him in that period.

RC (DLC); 2 p.; in French; endorsed.

There are no entries in SJL Index for letters to Vanet of 20 and 24 Sep. 1788, and no such letters have been found. The first was probably a covering letter for Dumas' dispatch to Jay of 16 Sep. 1788, and the second for that from TJ to Jay of 24 Sep. 1788.

From De Langeac

[*28 Sep. 1788.* Recorded in SJL Index, but not found. See TJ to De Langeac, 10 Oct. 1788, and reply of the same date.]

From Cambray

Chateau de Villers aux Erables, 29 Sep. 1788. Wrote about two months ago to ask TJ to attest letters of procuration and an affidavit required of him by Carolina. These were sent TJ by his notary in Paris, M. Aleaume. Asks that TJ forward the documents so that he can close this matter.

RC (DLC); 2 p.; in French; endorsed. Cambray wrote on 8 Aug. 1788 and TJ, misunderstanding Aleaume's request of 16 Aug. 1788, forwarded the documents to South Carolina (see TJ to Petry, 21 Aug. 1788).

From Lanchon Frères & Cie.

L'Orient, 29 Sep. 1788. Have turned up three sets of exchange from the United States on its Commissioner in Paris, dated 19 and 27 Dec. 1781 and 10 Jan. 1782, amounting to 84 dollars, which had been "laid by until lately"; presented them to Mr. Grand for payment; Grand allowed them to be protested "for want of advice"; this "leaves doubts whether said Bills will be paid in France or Should be sent back to America"; ask whether TJ can give advice for their payment.—Would also like to know whether an American consul will soon be sent to France; the tobacco trade particularly labors under the difficulty of having no representative to whom remonstrances can be made. "The Underlings of the Farm for Instance prevents now Irish Vessels under 50 Tons which is the properst for the Smuggling Trade, from lading Tobacco in this port, although called free, which prejudices much the Interest of America, as well as the Commerce of this Place."

RC (MHi); 2 p.; endorsed.

To Thomas Lee Shippen

Dear Sir Paris Sep. 29. 1788.

Your favor of the 22d. is just received. My occupations obliging me to economize my time and labour, where it can be done, I have, since your departure, addressed either yourself or Mr. Rutledge singly, hoping your goodness would excuse my writing to either for both. In like manner I have lately written to Mr. Short for all three. I now take the liberty of addressing you, for the triumvirate. No news yet from North-Carolina: but in such a case no news is good news, as an unfavorable decision of the 12th. state would have flown like an electrical shock through America and Europe. A letter from Govr. Rutledge of Aug. 10. says nothing of N. Carolina: this silence is a proof that all was well. That Convention was to meet July 23. and not July 4. as we had been told. A dispute is excited in Philadelphia which is likely to make a noise. Oswald the printer being sued, published something in his own paper relative to the cause. It was construed by the judges a contempt of the court. They made a rule against him to shew cause why he should not be attached. He appeared. The attachment was awarded, and he was called on to answer interrogatories. He refused to answer interrogatories. The court gave him till next morning to consider. He appeared then and still refused. By that time however it would seem as if the court themselves had considered better of it, for their Counsel (I suspect it was W——n) declared it was never the intention of the court to compel him to answer interrogatories, and accordingly without proposing any, or hearing his Counsel they committed him to prison for one month, and fined him ten pounds. Hereupon petitions were signing, one to the Executive to pardon Oswald, the other to the Legislature to punish the judges.—The news of this country, since my letter to Mr. Short, is that the Bretagne deputies are released from the Bastile, and D'Espermenil and Sabatier from their prisons; the etats generaux are to meet in the course of January, the court keeping the day of the month still in reserve: the parliament has returned to it's functions by permission. Their first arreté has been to demand the etats generaux in the form of 1614. Here the cloven hoof begins to appear. While the existence of parliament itself was endangered by the royal authority, they were calling for the etats generaux: now they have obtained a kind of victory, they see danger to themselves from those very etats generaux and determine either to have them in a form which will neither merit nor command the confidence of the nation, or to prepare a ground for combating their authority if it should be well-composed and should propose a reformation of the parliaments. I will immediately, according to the desire you are pleased to express, send a French copy of the Notes on Virginia to the Syndic Cayla. M. Tronchin goes there himself this week.

I am sorry you are obliged to abridge your tour. With respect to your route from Milan, to London, on which you are pleased to consult me, I would certainly prefer Genoa, thence along the coast to Nice (absolutely by land in defiance of all the persuasions you will be exposed to to go by water) thence to Toulon and Marseilles. There it will depend on your time, whether you will go by Nismes, the Canal of Languedoc (in the post boat) Bordeaux, Paris and Calais, or whether you must come directly from Marseilles to Paris and Calais. But even in the latter case, make the small deviation to Nismes, to see the most perfect remains of antiquity which exist on earth.—My absence from Paris becomes more doubtful than it was. I had hoped to go to Champagne to see the vintage. I am not certain now that my business will permit it. In every case, letters sent to me here, will be properly forwarded. Present my affectionate regards to your two travelling companions, and be assured of the esteem and attachment with which I am sincerely dear Sir your affectionate friend & servt., TH: JEFFERSON

PrC (DLC).

It is possible, but unlikely, that the allusion to a LETTER FROM GOVR. RUTLEDGE OF AUG. 10 refers to the (missing) letter from John Rutledge of 9 Aug. 1788, since the latter is recorded in SJL Index and the former is not. As on other occasions, the brothers John and Edward Rutledge probably wrote TJ by the same vessel but on different days; neither letter has been found.

From William Carmichael

Madrid, *30 Sep. 1788.* Introducing the Marquis de Trotti.

RC (DLC); endorsed. Recorded in SJL as received 5 Feb. 1789, "by Marq. Trotti." This letter is erroneously printed in this edition under 30 Sep. 1785, q.v.

From John Brown Cutting

SIR London Tuesday Morning, Sepr. 30 1788 (No. 1)

My two last to you were dated on the tuesday mornings preceding the present. I hope you have at least received that letter which is now a fortnight old. In it I had condensed the most recent articles of american intelligence: a portion of 'em in newspapers but the greatest part in writing. Possibly the worthy gentlemen in the respective post offices of the two nations were longer in amusing themselves with our correspondence than they have heretofore been. Still I trust you will ultimately obtain a letter which was *principally* written for *your* entertainment and but casually for *theirs*. In future however as often as I send through european post offices I intend numbering my letters and shall begin with the present.

North Carolina has refused to ratify the new constitution by a majority of *one hundred* votes—*six* only voting to receive it unconditionally. The report however subjoins that a delegate or delegates are appointed to negociate amendments with the new Congress, and upon condition that these are adopted, she will reunite with her sister states. The account of this unexpected event comes confirmed by different private letters from persons in Pennsylvania, Maryland and New York, two of which have been read to me. One by Mr. Smith dated 23d of Aug: another by Mr. Eddy, a day or two earlier. Neither of them mention any particulars of the debate, or the reasons, private or ostensible which are said to have influenced the Convention—no not even the date of their non-assent. The clearest notice of the affair I obtain from a young Mr. West, son of an episcopal clergyman of that name in Baltimore, who says he was on a visit with his father at Mount Vernon about the 10th of Aug: where he heard Colo. Humphreys express his surprize at the decision of North Carolina, the certainty of which he knew by a private letter from North Carolina; an official account of the proceedings of her Convention not being arrived when Mr. West sailed on the 13th. From this gentleman and a Dr. Shofe who came passengers together, I learn what is above hinted concerning an appointment to negociate amendments &c. &c. Upon the whole evidence I am inclined to believe the fact, altho it does not come quite untinged with obscurity.

You may recollect perhaps some statements of mine in a former letter concerning the internal affairs of North Carolina and likewise the co-ercive management of certain persons at one of the elections for conventional delegates. To these circumstances and to the interference of some able members of the late *minority* in Virginia, rather than to any holy political zeal for the liberties and welfare of their own peculiar country, do I venture to attribute the non-assentive vote of their convention. Perhaps after all no serious detriment and some substantial benefit to the union may result from an event that being totally unlooked for in America to some seems not a little untoward. Certainly eleven states, and among those the three leading ones in point of population, *light* and opulence are sufficient to cement the new union beyond the hazard of imbecility or dissolution. I take it for granted the organization of the fœdral government will not be retarded either by the contumacy of Rhode-Island or this hesitation of North Carolina. Nor will their voluntary absence from the first ensuing Congress deprive us of the first talents in our country. The absence of Virginia or of New York might have been regretted on such an account. But even if all the essential appointments to office were now made ere the two seceding states take their new rank possibly neither america in general nor these states in particular wou'd have just cause to complain. At the same time from the equity and moderation of the eleven fœdral states and their truly republican desire to conciliate every citizen of the late thirteen united states so far as it can be done without trenching upon the wisdom of their fresh league, little doubt need be entertain'd that sensible and satisfactory amendments will be speedily adopted and established. In what mode these amendments shall next be brought forward is now the chief remaining question to be determin'd?

Altho I have not given this subject that maturity of consideration which a sound decision upon it might exact, like other young men and green politicians I find myself inclined to prefer the most expeditious method; I mean the most expeditious in which so important a business can be constitutionally dispatch'd. And this method seems to be pointed out in the three first sentences of the fifth article in the new confœderation. My objection to convoke a new general Convention for the purpose of considering amendments and legitimating them in the fœtus of our constitution, does not solely arise from a wish to expedite a measure so momentous but springs also from an examination of the nature of the two modes. If another general convention is assembled its voice must in fact be ultimate and decisive before any of its new enactions can be put either to the test of *experience* or any genuine criterion of *theoretic* approbation. Besides if it shou'd be composed of the same men or nearly the same, will they not adhere to their former system? If it shou'd be composed of different men, or a majority of it consist of different men, who can tell whether the alterations they might introduce wou'd not be rejected by five state-conventions or state-legislatures; or who can foresee whether if so disposed they might not set every principle of the system of Sepr. 17th afloat and purposely recur again to seperate systems. But suppose they did not do so, still it might happen and probably wou'd, that the *ratifiers* and the *proposers* of new amendments wou'd be *one* and the *same* specific and individual citizens, which seems repugnant to the spirit of our best political opinions. Hence it is that I have said above that the *voice* of a new general convention wou'd *in fact* be *ultimate*; for in whatever mode their doings were ratified the *identical* men might in another capacity ratify their own *identical* doings, thereby rendering a provision *nugatory*, which ought to be a *check*. Whereas if *two thirds* in both houses of the new Congress propose amendments to the constitution, and these are ratified by the *legislatures* of three-fourths of the several states, this check will be duly exercised, and the alterations receive a firmer validity (if one may so speak) from the double suffrages of two thirds of the fœderal and three fourths of the local legislatures. Methinks too it might not misbecome the new Congress early to manifest an anxiety to anticipate the wishes of many respectable citizens among the minorities on the late national question, whose propositions do not militate against the general principles of the fœdral plan, even if fewer than two thirds of the state legislatures shoud aim at alterations therein.

The last letter I had the honor to receive from you is dated Sepr. 9th. Your wonderful punctuality so reprehensive of junior gentlemen, idly, or at least less importantly employed, makes me conceive I must have miss'd the reception of another from you since that date. I do not say this either to extract a fresh letter from your goodness, or to repeat my acknowledgments for the many improving and pleasant ones with which I have lately been honor'd; but merely and simply to insinuate that which I do believe.

Until late in October I have not a prospect of embarking. With very great and growing respect & esteem I have the honor to be Your Most Obedt. Servt., JOHN BROWN CUTTING

RC (DLC); endorsed.

To C. W. F. Dumas

SIR Paris Sep. 30. 1788.

Mine of the 1st. inst. acknoleged your several favors down to the 14th. of Aug. I have now to add those of Aug. 28. Sep. 11. 12. 16. and 26. The dispatches they inclosed for Mr. Jay have been duly forwarded, except the last which shall go in a few days. Notwithstanding the orders you were so kind as to undertake to give in your's of the 11th. inst. and which I am sure you have given, the gazette of Leyden continues to come *by post* to Count Diodati and myself. He complains of this. Doubtless it has been from inadvertence in Mr. Luzac's office, and therefore I will ask you to repeat the countermand.

With respect to your affair, I think you have done exactly what was right. It remains for Congress to supply formalities and to expose themselves no longer to so unfriendly a procedure on the part of an ally.

I have no intelligence from America later than the 12th. of Aug. It was not then known what North Carolina had done: but it was not doubted. The new legislature was to be convened in March. It was proposed to proceed immediately to the necessary measures for making those amendments to the new Constitution which the states had generally desired. New York had written a circular letter to this effect. I have the honor to be with sincere respects to your family & much esteem to yourself Sir your most obedt. humble servt.,

Th: Jefferson

PrC (DLC).

From Le Roy

aux Galeries du Louvre ce 30 Septembre 1788

J'ai L'honneur de vous ecrire Monsieur au Sujet de M. Le Chr. Quesnay et pour vous certifier que connoissant les diverses personnes qui ont signé L'écrit qu'il a donné à M. Rouelle (et qui atteste Les Suffrages unanimes qu'il a obtenus pour La Place de Professeur dans L'académie naissante de Richmond) et en même tems le caractère de leur écriture, Vous pouvez y avoir foi et y donner votre attache en Conséquence. On m'a donné Monsieur des nouvelles allarmantes sur Le Compte de M. Franklin. J'espere cependant qu'avec L'excellente constitution que La nature lui a donnée, il se tirera de cette crise comme des autres. Je suis bien enchanté que M. Quesnay me procure cette Occasion de vous renouveller les assurances des Sentimens distingués avec Lesquels J'ai L'honneur d'être bien Sincèrement Monsieur Votre très humble et très obéïssant Serviteur,

Le Roy
de l Acade. des Scienc.

RC (ViWC); endorsed.

To William Robertson

SIR Paris Sep. 30. 1788.

I am this moment honoured with your favor of the 26th. inst. and in answer thereto have to inform you that the power of granting Sea letters for the East-Indies is lodged by Congress solely in the hands of their Secretary for foreign affairs, Mr. Jay. He is the person therefore to whom it will be necessary for you to apply. I have the honor to be Sir Your very humble servt.,

TH: JEFFERSON

PrC (DLC).

From H. & L. Bergasse, Frères

Marseilles, Sep. 1788. Introduce "Mr. Simon" who proposes to establish a business in America and wishes, therefore, to talk with TJ.

RC (DLC); 2 p.; in French; endorsed by TJ: "Bergasse. Gave M. Simon lre. to T. Barclay." The letter of introduction of Simon to Thomas Barclay is not recorded in SJL Index and has not been found, nor is the present letter recorded in SJL Index.

To Rayneval

SIR Paris Oct. 1. 1788.

I have now the honor of inclosing to you a copy of the letter of Sep. 16.[1] which I had that of writing to his Excellency the Count de Monmorin, with the papers therein referred to, and of solliciting the order I have asked for. The originals were sent at the date before mentioned. Notwithstanding the refusal of the houses of Schweighauser & Dobree and of Puchelberg to settle their claim against the United states by arbitration as I proposed to them, the United States will still be ready to do them justice. But those houses must first retire from the two only propositions they have ever yet made, to wit, either a paiment of their demand without discussion, or a discussion before tribunals of the country. In the mean time I shall hope an acknolegement, with respect to us, of the principle which holds as to other nations, that our public property here cannot be seised by the territorial judge. It is the more interesting to us, as we shall be more and longer exposed than other nations to draw arms and military stores from Europe. Our preference of this country has occasioned us to draw them from hence [alone] since the peace: and the friendship we have constantly experienced from the government will, we doubt not, on this and every other occasion, ensure to us the protection of what we purchase. I have the honor

PrC (DLC); lacks end of complimentary close and signature (see Vol. 9: 217, note 1). Enclosures: Copies of TJ to Montmorin, 11 Sep. 1788, and its enclosures.

[1] An error for 11 Sep.; TJ's letter to Montmorin of 16 Sep. dealt with the subject of the Consular Convention, q.v. under 14 Nov. 1788.

To John Brown Cutting

Dear Sir Paris Octob. 2. 1788.

I am now to acknolege the receipt of your favors of the 16th. and 23d. Ult. and to thank you for the intelligence they conveyed. That respecting the case of the Interrogatories in Pennsylvania ought to make noise. So evident a heresy in the common law ought not to be tolerated on the authority of two or three civilians who happen unfortunately to make authority in the courts of England. I hold it essential in America to forbid that any English decision should ever be cited in a court, which has happened since the accession of Ld. Mansfeild to the bench. Because tho' there have come many good ones from him, yet there is so much sly poison instilled into a great part of them, that it is better to proscribe the whole. Can you inform me what has been done by England on the subject of our wheat and flour? The papers say it is prohibited even in Hanover. How do their whale fisheries turn out this year? I hope a deep wound will be given them in that article soon, and such as will leave us in no danger from their competition.

The Bretany deputies are discharged from prison: so also M. d'Epremesnil and M. Sabatier. The change in the ministry is not yet gone as far as it will go. That in the war office is immediately expected. The parliament has returned to the exercise of it's functions, the edicts of May on their subject being suspended till the meeting of the States general. The parliament has peremptorily demanded their convocation in the form of 1614. This shews evidently what game they are going to play. It is happy that they have so far been able to counterpoise the authority of the king, as to render an appeal to the National assembly necessary for both parties, and to enable that assembly to incline the balance as they shall chuse. But here ends the utility of the parliament, which has pursued the good of the nation just as far as it coincided with their own. This would not be promoted by States general convoked in the form much talked of, to wit ¼ clergy, ¼ noblesse, ½ tiers etat, and all in the same chamber. This composition would be so enlightened and so liberal that this aristocratical excrescence of a parliament would have every thing to fear. They insist therefore on convoking the states in the aristocratical form of 1614. If so convoked, they count on their alliance. If not so convoked, they will deny their legality, and reject all their decisions.—The campaign between Sweden and Russia by land is at an end. It will finish by sea too probably as soon as the Swedes can get their fleet safe into port. Not a tittle from the Black sea. But there is great reason to suspect that the victories there so puffed by Russia were merely small affairs, immensely exaggerated. I am with very great esteem Dear Sir your most obedt. humble servt.,

TH: JEFFERSON

P.S. No news of N. Carolina yet.

RC (MHi: AMT); addressed; postmarked: "P.PAYE PARIS"; "5 O'CLOCK M"; and (within circle): "9 OC." PrC (DLC).

To Thomas Payne

SIR Paris Octob. 2. 1788.

Having occasion for a correspondent in your line in the city of London, I take the liberty of addressing myself to you on the recommendation of my friends Mr. Trumbull and Mr. Paradise. In the execution of my commissions, I would wish you to attend to the following general rules.

When I name a particular edition of a book, send me that edition and no other.

When I do not name the edition, never send a folio or quarto if there exists an 8vo. or smaller edition. I like books of a handy size.

Where a book costs much higher than the common price of books of that size do not send it, tho I write for it, till you shall have advised me of the price.

I disclaim all pompous editions and all typographical luxury; but I like a fine white paper, neat type, and neat binding, gilt and lettered in the modern stile. But while I remain in Europe it will be better to send my books in boards, as I have found that scarcely any method of packing preserves them from rubbing in a land transportation.

Send my books always by the Diligence which plies 3 or 4 times a week between London and Paris. But, consulting their own convenience only, they are apt to keep packages long by them, if not attended to by the person sending them.

My friend Mr. Trumbull will pay the bill for the parcel of which I now inclose you the catalogue. As some of them will perhaps require time to be found, the rest need not wait for them. Hereafter you will be pleased to send my account once a quarter or once in six months while I remain in Europe. When I return to America, my demands shall be accompanied by the ready money. Be so good as to state the Parliamentary debates, and Hattsel's book in a separate account, as these are not for myself. Let the accounts come by post when you send off the books. I am Sir your very humble servt., TH: JEFFERSON

Adams's essays on the microscope. 4to.
Tyson's Oran-outang, or anatomy of a pigmy.
Raleigh's history of England. 2. vols. 12mo.
Pilpay's fables. 12 mo.
Gregory's comparative view. 12mo.
5th. vol. of Watson's chemical essays. 12mo. Evans. (I have the 4 first)
Whitehurst's attempt toward invariable measures. Bent. 1787.
Pownal's hydraulic & nautical observations. Sayer.
Zimmerman's political survey. 8 vol. Dilly.
Prospects on the Rubicon. Debrett.
Barton's observations on Natural history. Dilly.
Families of plants by the Litchfeild society. 2. vols. 8vo.
Mc.kenzie's strictures on Tarleton's history. Faulder.
Concordance to Shakespeare. Robinsons.
Indian vocabulary. 12mo. Stockdale.
Additions to Robertson's history of Scotland. 8vo. Cadell.
Additions to Robertson's history of America. 8vo. Cadell.
Burns's poems.
Builder's price book. 8vo. Taylor. London. No. 56. opposite great Turnstile Holborn. 1781. A later edition if any.
Potter's Aeschylus. 2. vols. 8vo.
Chandler's debates of the Lords and Commons
Hatsell's book on Parliamentary subjects. I do not know the title, but it is the latest edition, containing a digest of his former publications on different parts of Parliamentary learning, with some additions.

Spelman's life of Alfred, Saxon, with Wilbur's translation.
Boethius, Anglo-Saxonicé Aelfridi regis. Oxon. 1698.
Thwait's Saxon heptateuch.
Spelman's Saxon psalms.
Mareshall's Saxon gospels.
Saxon homilies (I think some have been published.)
Lye's Junius's etymologicon by Owen. 2. vols. fol. latest edition.
Thompson's translation of Goeffry of Monmouth.
Lye's sacrorum evangeliorum versio Gothica. 4to.
Knitell's fragments of Ulphilas's translation of the epistle to the Romans. 4to.

What is the price of Anderson's history of commerce?

PrC (MoSHi); at foot of first page: "Mr. Payne, bookseller London."

From William Short

Dear Sir Lyons Oct. 2. 1788

I have this moment arrived here, and the first thing I do is to announce it to you. I left this morning the Chateau de Laye and came by water diligence to this place. It is my first navigation in France and I am much pleased with it. We were from 10. o'clock to five en route of which one hour was spent in dining, the rest in passing through such a variety of pleasing and rich prospect as cannot be out-done. The banks on either side were low enough to give us a view from the deck of the vessel, of the fine meadows which border the Saone. These meadows are bounded by fertile hills on one side and mountains on the other. The Mont d'or, with which you are acquainted, was the part which gave me the most sensible impression, because it recalled to my mind at every instant, and in every direction in which it was presented to us, some part or other of the rich mountains of Albemarle and Amherst. It may not have presented perhaps the same aspect to you as I was told that the side on which the main road passes was much less fertile. It produces the goat cheese so much admired. These poor animals are kept there for the purpose of making this cheese; they are born and die in houses without ever passing the threshold on account of the injury they do the vines. One would suppose, under that circumstance they would make as good cheese any where else, but the amateurs pretend that they distinguish easily that which is made on the Mont d'or. For my part I tasted it several times and think it a very poor kind.

Our diligence stops at the upper end of the town and my lodgings being toward the lower I had an opportunity of seeing a good part of it as I passed along the Quai. I have sent to purchase a plan of the town and intend to-morrow to visit its principal streets, places and other curiosities.—An accident brought Paradise to lodge at the Hotel D'Artois. I had put your paper into my trunk so as not to be able to turn to it at the moment of our separating at Villefranche. He determined to follow Dutens' recommendation. I have done the same that I might learn with greater certainty in what manner Paradise arrived and set off from hence. By your paper I find you lodged at the Palais Royal, which is the next door to this. Intending to stay here two or three days at most, it was indifferent where I lodged. The Landlady here tells me that P. staid from tuesday to thursday, that he set out in good health and in a good way for Turin, having employed a Voiturier to transport him thither. She says she found him *un peu chicaneur*, and what astonishes me still more is that she is perfectly content with Madame.

My last letter was written the day after I arrived at the Chateau de Laye and consequently I could only speak of my first reception there. The kindness and civility of every part of the family continued the same during my whole stay there. I was left perfectly at liberty to pursue my enquiries in every manner I thought proper, sometimes attended by M. de Laye, frequently instructed by Madame and always treated with a degree of kindness, ease and freedom which gave me great pleasure. I must mention to you also Sir what I promised them I would not fail to do, how much they are really attached to you and how much they desire to see you again at their house. They frequently drank and made me drink to your health, and with an air of so much sincerity that I could not help giving full faith to it, and the more so as we were in a plain kind of dining room as different from a *salle à manger* in Paris, as the table of some of our Albemarle friends is from that of a rich financier in Philadelphia. One circumstance which had weight with me will very probably appear to you trivial. It is that whilst we were dining in one end of the room there were women sewing and employed in domestic works in the other. Having seen this no where but in a country where I have been accustomed in my early days to see so much sincerity, I could not help by a kind of association of ideas to consider as pure and sincere every thing which I heard there.—The Prieur yields to none in his attachment to you and seemed to have a pleasure in speaking of you which could not fail to augment my friendship for him.

The objects which occupied my attention whilst at Laye were 1. wine making and 2. the metairie. Eight days spent in constant walking over the estate of M. de Laye, in constant examination and constant enquiry have put me fully in possession of these two subjects as they exist there. Less time would have sufficed but for the difficulties occasioned by a difference of measure, and a want of precision in answers to questions relative to rural matters. They have been accustomed to consider them in the mass only and frequently differ among themselves when questioned on particular parts. This circumstance obliged me often to correct what I had at first marked as certain information.—On the whole I am persuaded we may make wine in Virginia as easily as we make cyder. But I fear we shall find a greater difficulty than I had expected in the article of metairie. Every mĕtayer in the cultivation of grain has a certain number of hands employed by him. It would seem that that kind of husbandry could not be carried on by one person alone, and it will be a long time before our slaves become sufficiently intelligent and provident to direct the work of others, viz. to employ themselves and others under them. This requires in the first place a certain degree of combination more than would be necessary, if each was to work for himself, and in the second a certain fund in money or property to begin with. In the Beaujolois the proprietor furnishes the land, the houses, and cattle of all sorts. Still M. de laye thinks that a *Granger* in order to begin well should be possessed of 3 or 4,000.[tt] I am persuaded however that his estimation is too high—still it must necessarily be something considerable. A granger generally employs under him three or four bouviers and two or three women. He furnishes also in this part of France the instruments of husbandry. I was told by a Provençal whom I saw at Laye that in Provence that is not the case; but there the proportion of the proprietor is ⅔ instead of ½.

A day or two ago I received a letter from Rutledge in answer to one I had written him on my arrival at Villefranche. He tells me that he and Shippen find it impossible to wait longer than a given day and desires I may without fail get to Geneva by that time. The day was passed before I received the letter. He says he shall be much mortified if I fail, as he has waited for me 19. days longer than he had intended to stay at Geneva. I am certainly much more mortified than he can be since he has a compagnon de voyage and I have none. I am destined therefore to pass the Alpes alone. I hope I shall do it without vinegar.

I long very much my dear Sir to hear from you and hope I shall have that pleasure at Geneva. The constant occupation in which both my mind and body have been since leaving Paris has prevented every thing like ennui. Still I feel most sensible how much pleasure it would give me at this moment to see you and your agreeable family.

Oct. 3. I have already seen enough of Lyons to make me repent that I did not purchase at Paris the maps which you recommended to me and which it was my intention to have procured there, I mean that of modern France and ancient Gaul on the same scale. I had hoped it would be [ea]sy to repair this omission here but find it impossible. I shall feel it, as I have done at every stop I make. I wish now also I had endeavoured at Paris to have procured a small thermometer and barometer, such as I think I have seen, which are in a case and easily carried in the pocket. It is my constant change of place and the view of the mountains which has made me desire the one and the other of these articles. It is not probable I shall find them at Geneva as they are not here and after crossing the Alpes I shall have little use for the barometer. The first idea of the barometer occurred to me in going up to that height where you were on the estate of M. de Laye. I wished to form a just idea of its height. Do you recollect an eminence which commands it and on which stands a chapel, called St. Bonnet. It appeared to me that it was about the height of Monticello, but M. de Laye seemed so positive that it was higher than any person's house whatever that I was obliged to agree with him that Monticello was between St. Bonnet and the *croit*, where you were. I will thank you to tell me what your opinion is.—I am now under the direction of a Valet de place and am going to begin my peregrinations with him. We have held a counsel and I find I shall with difficulty confine him to a small number of chosen objects. He seems much more fond of paintings than the remains of Roman antiquities which are in the suburbs and which I am panting after, having as yet seen nothing of the kind. Is not the Rhone a fine noble river? I remember well having read of it as well as the Arar in Caesar's commentaries. Paradise and myself have agreed to read over together when we meet in Italy this excellent author and some of the chosen epistles of Horace. The view of these two rivers, and of a city founded by the Romans makes me impatient to begin the execution of our agreement. He has thoughts of leaving Madame with her daughter and going with me to Rome.—I have only seen two Leyden gazettes since leaving Paris. In neither of them was anything respecting America, so that I am now as to that article where I was when I sat off. Adieu my dear Sir. Give me a place sometimes in your recollections and be assured it will afford a much greater satisfaction than you imagine to Your friend & servant,

W: SHORT

RC (DLC); addressed and endorsed.

THE ALPES . . . WITHOUT VINEGAR: A reference to Hannibal's troops making a passage through the Alps by heating the rocks with a great fire and then pouring vinegar on them to make them crumble (Livy, *History of Rome*, Book XXI, Ch. 37, from translation by George Baker, N.Y., 1847, II, 262-3). THE ARAR: i.e., the Saone (*Harper's Latin Dictionary*).

To John Trumbull

DEAR SIR

Paris Octob. 2. 1788.

I trouble you with the two letters herein inclosed. I hope you note my postages and pay them out of my funds, as the contrary would deprive me necessarily of the convenience of your cover. The letter to Payne is left open for your perusal. You will see that I have referred him to you for paiment of this bill which will be a little over 20. guineas. My reason for this is that as you will have to call on me immediately for the deficiency of my former bill towards paying for the chariot, it will be more convenient to me to add this to that and remit both together. I subjoin below a little note of what I wish to have from Lackington. It would be best to have them sent to Payne's and packed with those he will forward me.—What chance do you think there will be of sending my chariot by a private hand so as to clear it of the expenses of portage and duty? Mr. Short set out for Italy a fortnight ago. When do you intend to visit Paris and America? Adieu. Yours affectionately,

TH: JEFFERSON

1127. D'Acugne's voiages in N. America. 1/3
8368. Fortis's Viaggio in Dalmazia. 10/6
8787. Xenophontis Lacedaemoniorum respublica. 1/6
438. Raleigh's history of the world. 7/6

PrC (DLC). Enclosures: (1) TJ to Maria Cosway, 26 Sep. 1788. (2) TJ to Payne, 2 Oct. 1788.

From M. Amoureux

L'Orient, 3 Oct. 1788. Has postponed replying to TJ's letter of 29 July last because he hoped from day to day to dispose of the small items belonging to John Paul Jones which remained unsold. This trifle has kept him from closing the account and informing TJ of the net result; just as soon as "ces petits objets" can be sold he will make a report and will remit the balance due when the term of credit has expired.—Has learned "avec la plus vive Satisfaction" from American friends that eleven states had adopted the new constitution and that there was still hope that the other two would accede; "Dieu veuille que cela soit ainsi, et que les bons citoyens des Etats unis puissent, sous l'empire de loix sages et bien ordonnées, jouir de cette liberté, qui leur a couté si cher." —Takes sincere satisfaction in Admiral Paul Jones' success in the Black Sea and the fact that the Empress "l'en a recompensé honorablement." Appreciates the information TJ gave him about the franchise at L'Orient; he wrote to TJ about it because he assumed that no change would take place without TJ's knowledge.

RC (DLC); 2 p.; endorsed.

To Willink & Van Staphorst

GENTLEMEN Paris Octob. 3. 1788.

I have the honor to inclose you by Mr. Parker the act of ratification by Congress of the loan of a million of florins for which Mr. Adams executed and deposited bonds with you in March last. You then supposed that if the new constitution should be adopted, these bonds might be disposed of readily and advantageously. That adoption has taken place; and I should be glad to have your present opinion whether we may count on the monies being ready in time for the several demands stated in the estimate of which we left a copy with you, specifying the times at which the different sums would be wanting.

I have the honor to be with great esteem, gentlemen, your most obedient & most humble servt., TH: JEFFERSON

PrC (DLC). Enclosure: Resolution of Congress of 2 July 1788 ratifying "the contract made by John Adams Esqr. minister plenipotentiary in behalf of the United States of America on the thirteenth of March 1788 for the loan of one million Guilders" (JCC, XXXIV, 282-3). See TJ to Jay, 5 Sep. 1788; Jay to TJ, 23 Sep. 1788.

From Burrill Carnes

Nantes, 4 Oct. 1788. Introduces "Mr. Henry Caldwell of Connecticut who passes thro' Paris on his way from London to Tours where he proposes to reside for some time to Learn French." Carnes expects to return to America in the course of a few months; will notify TJ before he goes.

RC (MHi); 2 p.; endorsed.

From John Brown Cutting

SIR London 5th Octr. 1788

Mr. Gardner the bearer hereof is a citizen of Massachusetts (and a mercantile inhabitant of Boston) in whom is no guile. Being a total stranger in France, (as well as unacquainted with the language,) and ever likely so to remain from the simplicity of his habits and the modesty of his disposition, I cou'd not refuse affording this opportunity to him of adding his grateful attestation to mine and to that of more respectable citizens who concur in thinking the countenance of the minister of their country a panacea for difficulties incident to such characters in every foreign region and preferable to all letters that an american might obtain for any other personage in Paris. This opinion is now so generally diffused throughout America, and especially among the people inhabiting the eastern states that were I to refrain putting its truth so often to the test my countrymen wou'd apply elsewhere for letters to you, thus hindering the nicety of such a coyness on my part from contributing aught to your repose. Hence it is that since the departure of Mr. Adams from England I have ventured to wave ceremony on these occasions with you, apparently and seemingly as unconscious of the freedom assumed as you of the trouble given.

The accounts of North Carolina sent in my last letter come confirmed.

By the letter of an intelligent correspondent in Philadelphia I understand Mr. Adams is much mention'd for Vice-President; he having intimated that the office of Chief-Justice wou'd not be acceptable to him. In the most perfect confidence I mention such rumours to you, being with unlimited regard Your respectful and Mo. Obed Sert: JOHN BROWN CUTTING

RC (DLC); endorsed.

From James Swan

[*5 Oct. 1788.* Recorded in SJL Index. Not found. This letter presumably concerned the proposals made by Swan and Samuel Blackden to supply the City of Paris with flour and wheat from America, in view of the threatened scarcity caused by the great hail storm and by crop shortages in the Mediterranean basin. These proposals, dated 22 Sep. 1788, and correspondence concerning them are in Archives Nationales, Paris, H 1444. TJ's friend, M. de Corny, in transmitting the proposals to M. Tarbé, commis des finances, 23 Sep. 1788, remarked that he had known the two Americans during the last war and that they were recommended to him by "le Ministre plénipotentiaire des Etats-Unis"; and in another note to Tarbé four days later, De Corny asked what action was being taken, so that he might transmit the information to TJ, adding: "ils imaginent que les affaires se décident avec la même celerité qu'on les propose." De Corny repeated his request on 5 Oct. 1788, stating that Swan and Blackden "ont hâte de savoir ce que l'administration a décidé, ayant retardé le départ d'un bateau de L'Orient."⟧

From William Tatham

⟦*5 Oct. 1788.* Recorded in SJL Index, but not found. See William Tatham to TJ, under 1 Dec. 1789.⟧

From John Brown Cutting

SIR London 6th October 1788

Truth, lovely truth, obliges me to correct the intelligence transmitted in my two last concerning the purport of the proceedings in North Carolina. It is true that the Convention of that State have *not* ratified the new fœderal constitution. But it is not true either that they have absolutely abstracted the state from the[1] Union or manifested a disposition to remain detached therefrom. Neither is it fact that the middle course they have attempted to hold has been taken by so large a majority against so small a minority, as I had reason to believe when I last wrote you.

The day before yesterday the New York packet arrived in fifteen days from Halifax. Having recently come in from a rural excursion I knew it not when Mr. Gardner's letter was writing at the other end of the town early yesterday morning: I mean the introductory note I gave him to you. And even now I cannot furnish you with any accounts which proceed directly from North Carolina itself. But I believe you may rely upon the authenticity of the following extract, namely "State of North Carolina, In Convention Aug. 2. 1788." "Resolved, That a declaration of rights, asserting and securing from incroachment the great principles of civil and religious liberty, and the unalienable rights of the people, together with amendments to the most ambiguous and exceptionable parts of the said Constitution of Government, ought to be laid before Congress, or the Convention of the States that shall or may be called for the purpose of amending the said Constitution, for their consideration, previous to the ratification of the Constitution aforesaid on the part of the state of North Carolina." Yeas 184. Nays 82. By another account from Virginia, dated Aug. 14th, and which I credit as genuine from its intrinsic probability, it appears that on the opening of the Convention, a motion was made for the question to be put immediately upon the supposition that every member had made up his mind on the subject and therefore an immediate determination wou'd save both expence and debate. This measure it is thought might have been carried, had not one of the principal supporters of the new government in a most animated and excellent speech, proved the extreme indecorum and impropriety of such precepitance in a business so serious and important: whereupon the motion was withdrawn and the Constitution being discussed clause by clause in a Committee of the whole Convention the result was conformable to the principle of the above resolution. It seems to have been taken for granted by this body that Congress wou'd soon call a fresh general Convention to consider of the proposed amendments; and likewise that after deliberating hereon their decision wou'd again be submitted to a new Convention in each state; and that the state of North Carolina not having rejected the Constitution absolutely will not be precluded from calling a Convention again to adopt such an ultimatum shou'd they think proper so to do. Previous to their dissolution, two recommendations to the state legislature pass'd—the *one* to make the most speedy and effectual provision for the redemption of the paper money now in circulation, the *other* to lay an impost for the use of Congress on goods imported into North Carolina, similar to that which shall be laid by the new Congress, on goods imported into the adopting states. These two recommendations are to be transmitted with dispatch both to Congress and to the Executives of the several states.

Through the whole of the discussion of these subjects the Convention manifested every disposition to adhere to the Union and promote the general welfare: But many being previously and positively instructed by their constituents, and themselves perceiving or thinking they perceived objections to the new constitution which their own vote might have a strong tendency to remove, they thought themselves justified in thus postponing the ultimate decision of the important question, until it shou'd be re-considered by the several states, and such amendments made as might be found universally conciliating.

Most of the amendments proposed by the committee were the same that Virginia and other states recommend. Two only being *local* to North Carolina And these two (which are not communicated to me) it is said do not militate with the great principles of the fœderal system.

This supplement to my late letter altho I have sketch'd it in great haste, contains the substance of all that is known here relevant to North Carolina.

I have the honor to be, with great consideration and unaffected regard & attachment Your Most Obedt. Servt.,

John Brown Cutting

P.S. Shou'd Mr. Parker remain in Paris when this scrawl reaches you an early communication of its contents to him will particularly oblige me.

RC (DLC).

1 At this point Cutting deleted "new."

From André Limozin

Le Havre, 6 Oct. 1788. Has postponed answering TJ's letters of 21 Aug. and 6 Sep. in expectation of being able to inform TJ that Barclay's papers and Lafayette's bust, together with sundry other articles sent him by TJ for America, had been shipped; but the English vessel on which Vanet expected to embark was found by the "admiraltys Surveyors" to be "in the most dismall condition" and to need heavy repairs, which the English master refused to comply with, so Mr. Vanet refused to take passage.—An American ship, *The Sally*, Capt. Kennedy, arrived last week from Baltimore and expects to return there at the end of the month; will send the papers and the "Case of Vinegar and parfumery" by her, but will send the bust of Lafayette by a later ship unless TJ disagrees.—Reports on "the very bad Sucess of our last harvest so well in Normandy as in Brittany and Guienne."—TJ will recall mistake Limozin made 26 Feb. last by sending James Madison, "on board the Kings New york Packet No. 3 under Capt. Rollands command," two cases when he should have sent one; wrote Madison on 8 Apr. asking return of that sent by error, "but Mr. Madison never complyd with my beseech, nay even did not honor me with a letter"; encloses copy of that letter and asks TJ's aid.—Has looked over note of his disbursements for TJ and finds it "quite right," but to it must be added 10ᵗᵗ7s. "for Postage of sundry Letters received from Messrs. Wm. Short fulwar Skipwith," making the total 265ᵗᵗ4s.9d.; will send later a note of cost of shipping other articles.

RC (MHi); 6 p.; endorsed. Enclosure (MHi): Copy of Limozin to Madison, 8 Apr. 1788, explaining error in shipping two boxes and asking the return of one of them (see Limozin to TJ, 27 Feb. 1788).

To Cambray

Sir Paris Oct. 7. 1788.

Your favor of the 29th. September is duly received. Monsieur Aleaume had sent me, in the month of August, the letters of procuration to be legalised and sent to America. The expression in his letter was 'que M. le comte de Cambrai espere que vous voulez bien legaliser *et faire passer en Amerique*.' An opportunity occurring just at that time of sending them to Charlestown, I availed myself of it and inclosed them to Mr. Petrie, consul there, whom a former letter of yours had named to me as having asked that instrument of you. I am in hopes that by this time it is safe in his hands, and that in forwarding it without delay I have fulfilled your desire, while I obeyed my own dispositions to serve you, being glad of every occasion to convince of the esteem and attachment with which I have the honour to be, Sir your most obedient & most humble servant, Th: Jefferson

PrC (DLC).

From John Brown Cutting

Sir London 7th of October 1788.

Since my letter yesterday which I prepar'd with rapidity for the mail of today (resolute not again to incur the accusation of inattention or tardiness as heretofore) yours of Octr. 2d is received: and likewise a small parcel which I can safely convey to New York as you request within a few days. I propose directing it to Mr. Osgood that the official superscription may neither alarm the fears nor excite the curiosity of the bearer.

I am not correctly informed upon the subject of prohibiting our wheat. I believe however that in virtue of the powers granted the privy council to make temporary regulations of the Commerce of the United States, a proclamation has been issued directing the Commissioners of the Treasury upon the suggestion that a dangerous insect infects the wheat of that country to take such order thereon as may prevent its introduction here. In consequence of which Sir Joseph Banks and other ingenious persons are appointed to inspect every parcel and upon their report of its safe or dangerous qualities it is either permitted to be or totally prohibited from being sold. I will make farther enquiry and let you know if I have mistated aught herein. The whale fishery this year is boasted of as being prodigiously productive. With bounties so enormous, and impolicy in other nations so glaring how can it be otherwise? The encouragement here is sufficient to cover the merchant even if he were purposely to send out to Nantucket for whalemen the most expert in the Universe. And I doubt not in some instances this has been done. Apropos did I ever send you Mr. Bufoy's speech upon the extension of the fisheries in Scotland. If not I will. In your opinion of the utility that might result from rejecting the decisions of a Murray—if unless this be done we must adopt them *all*, I do most heartily concur. But tho' thus concurring and wishing I fear it never will take place. For many of his determinations are so ingenious, leading and authoritative in commercial cases and ambiguities of meum and tuum that it is much to be apprehended his celebrity in decisions of property will contribute to sanction his heretical opinions concerning civil liberty.

You mention the aristocratical form of convoking the states general as in 1614. Pray in what manner were they then convoked? If I ever knew I have forgotten.

Will you excuse the liberty I take in recommending the inclosed letters for Mesrs. Rutledge and Shippen to your care. I believe they are both still in Geneva; but am not certain.

With the truest respect and esteem I have the honor to be Your obliged and mo. obedt sert, JOHN BROWN CUTTING

RC (DLC); endorsed. The enclosed letters have not been identified.

TJ's reply of 3 Nov. 1788 does not state whether Cutting had already sent him MR. BUFOY'S SPEECH or not, but Cutting's letter of 26 June 1788 refers to it in a way to suggest that it was already in TJ's possession. The speech referred to was that of Henry Beaufoy, *The Substance of the speech . . . to the British Society for extending the fisheries*, &c. *at their General Court, held on Tuesday, March 25, 1788. To which is added a copy of the act for the Society's incorporation* (London, 1788). The copy that Cutting gave to TJ bears this inscription on its title-page: "to His Ex Thomas Jefferson by John Brown Cutting" (see Sowerby, No. 2780). Beaufoy (d.1795) was a whig member of parliament and a Quaker (DNB).

From Pierre de Labat

Cadiz, 7 Oct. 1788. Under the patronage of "Le Commandeur de Bausset," solicits TJ's commissions for the purchase of fine wines from that province; sends price list for the different qualities and vintages; has supplied a number of "Seigneurs, Ambassadeurs et Personnes de distinction des diverses Cours de l'Europe." Since there is no glass-works in all Spain, they have no bottles; ships the wine in small casks. Can also supply fine Havana tobacco, Peruvian bark, cocoa, and vanilla.

RC (MHi); 3 p.; in French; endorsed by TJ: "Wines at Cadiz." The enclosed price list has not been found.

Preliminary indexes will be issued periodically for groups of volumes. An index covering Vols. 1-6 has been published. A comprehensive index of persons, places, subjects, etc., arranged in a single consolidated sequence, will be issued at the conclusion of the series.

See the Foreword to this volume, page vii, announcing a new format for the Table of Contents. It is hoped that the new Contents will prove useful until the preliminary indexes covering several volumes are issued.

The Papers of Thomas Jefferson is composed in Monticello, a type specially designed by the Mergenthaler Linotype Company for this series. Monticello is based on a type design originally developed by Binny & Ronaldson, the first successful typefounding company in America. It is considered historically appropriate here because it was used extensively in American printing during the last thirty years of Jefferson's life, 1796 to 1826; and because Jefferson himself expressed cordial approval of Binny & Ronaldson types.

✧

Composed and printed by Princeton University Press. Illustrations are reproduced in collotype by Meriden Gravure Company, Meriden, Connecticut. Paper for the series is made by W. C. Hamilton & Sons, at Miquon, Pennsylvania; cloth for the series is made by Holliston Mills, Inc., Norwood, Massachusetts. Bound by the J. C. Valentine Company, New York.

DESIGNED BY P. J. CONKWRIGHT